# SATURDAY NIGHT

## A Backstage History of *Saturday Night Live*

Special 50th Anniversary Edition

# DOUG HILL AND JEFF WEINGRAD

# SATURDAY NIGHT

## A Backstage History of
## *Saturday Night Live*

HISTRIA
A&E

# Histria A&E

Las Vegas ◆ Chicago ◆ Palm Beach

Published in the United States of America by
Histria Books
7181 N. Hualapai Way, Ste. 130-86
Las Vegas, NV 89166 U.S.A.
HistriaBooks.com

Histria A&E is an imprint of Histria Books dedicated to outstanding books from the world of arts, entertainment, and sports. Titles published under the imprints of Histria Books are distributed worldwide.

Library of Congress Control Number: 2024943082

ISBN 978-1-59211-530-3 (hardcover)
ISBN 978-1-59211-536-5 (softbound)
ISBN 978-1-59211-547-1 (eBook)

This is the original history of *Saturday Night Live*.
It tells the show's story from its conception in early 1975
through the end of its 10th season in 1985.

# Contents

## PART TWO

## PART THREE

# Foreword

The authors would like to underscore at the outset that this book is about people—highly creative and consciously eccentric people, for the most part—who were operating under extreme pressure. In particular, the effects on the psyche of major stardom, though a part of popular legend, are underestimated. Readers are urged to keep this in mind.

For the sake of the show's writers, we would like to point out that in almost every instance where we've quoted sketches, they are excerpts, not the complete scripts. Readers should note in addition that we have usually used the name *Saturday Night* instead of *Saturday Night Live* because the former is shorter, and because that's what many of the people who worked there called it, unless they just said "*SNL*" or "the show."

# Introduction

Fifty years. That's a long time for any show to be on television, especially a comedy show that's required to come up with 90 minutes of fresh material, week in, week out, for a nine-month season. It's one thing to produce a news show that covers current events, or to do a talk show that starts with a ten-minute monologue and fills the rest of its time chatting with guests, with a couple of breaks for a band and maybe a standup routine thrown in. Those endeavors take skill to do well, no question, but giving birth to a sketch comedy program is an infinitely more complicated, more stressful, more risky enterprise, especially when you consider that all that effort is supposed to add up to something that's truly funny. *Saturday Night Live* is often accused of failing in that department, of course. It's been that way from the beginning, but as those responsible for getting the show on the air will tell you, it's a miracle it gets on at all.

This was never more true than in the show's first season, 1975–1976, when a group of people who for the most part had zero experience in television were trying to figure out how the whole thing worked, while at the same time staving off the resistance of a corporation whose bosses were not only expecting them to fall on their faces, but who were eagerly waiting for them to do so. For that reason, the fact that SNL has lasted fifty years is something of a miracle itself. The question in the beginning was whether it would last fifty weeks.

As the authors of the first history of the show, we're proud of the reporting we did that revealed the personal turmoil that went on behind the SNL scenes, stories that legions of writers, TV and radio personalities and gossip columnists have feasted on for years. For our part, if anything, we're more proud of the against-the-odds, David-versus-Goliath story we told of how a ragged band of rebels from the sixties comedy underground took on a powerful and conservative television network and won.

There's a chapter in the book called "The Show That Was Always a Hit." That was an ironic comment from one of the show's staffers, who knew it wasn't true. In fact, for most of its first season its survival was by no means assured, not only because of its mediocre ratings, but also because of the kind of comedy it was putting on the air, which a lot of people, including a lot of NBC executives, considered indecent. These were the days, after all, of the infamous "generation gap."

The comment that SNL was always a hit referred to the attitude of its creator, Lorne Michaels, who from the beginning was absolutely certain that nothing could stop the show from becoming one. ("Absolutely" was one of Lorne's favorite words in those days.) Never mind the lukewarm ratings reports, or the negative feedback the show was getting from the network, Lorne always managed to find some reason that proved it was only a matter of time before massive success would arrive. That the original cast named itself the Not Ready for Prime Time Players was a double joke. Not only were they making a point of distancing themselves from the Prime Time Players who were a featured act on a competing network variety show (*Saturday Night Live with Howard Cosell*), they were also distancing themselves from everything else on television at the time. True, they were inexperienced, but that was a point of pride, not of humility. They had no doubt they were infinitely better than the miasma that permeated prime time. Some of them may have harbored secret fears that they wouldn't get the chance to prove it, which is why Lorne felt it was necessary to assure them they absolutely would.

Lorne told himself the same story, and he believed it. The plot of the story was simple. He was confident that the generation that grew up on television would respond to a comedy program that told the truth, and he was determined that *Saturday Night* would be that program. He was a member of that generation and he knew it had in large part turned its back on television because of the utter lameness – the basic dishonesty – of the programs it put on the air. John Belushi shared that disdain – like everything John did—to the max. He told Lorne on their first meeting that the only TV set he owned was a beaten-down black-and-white model and it was covered with spit.

Lorne found Belushi's rant over the top, but he was familiar with the sentiment, and the style. One of the fundamental reasons SNL survived those early days was that Lorne was a classic bridge figure: He understood and believed in the comedy rebels he was hiring while at the same time he was able to convince a roomful of network executives that he could deliver a show that would help them fill the gaping hole in their audience profile, the 18-to-34-year-old demographic that advertisers were desperate to reach. Lorne was capable of being slick in his ability to tell people what they wanted to hear, no question, but it was his conviction that carried the day.

The show's ratings were slow to build at first in part because much of its target audience had long since stopped looking for anything worth watching on TV, and they had other things to do at 11:30 on Saturday night. They'd found other sources of entertainment and edification, rock and roll and LSD among them. But when word about *Saturday Night* started to get around, the show was embraced by the TV generation with unprecedented passion. To suddenly be offered a program that accurately expressed their experience and their sensibility was a huge surprise, and an electrifying one. It became a show you *had* to watch, usually with a bunch of friends and a bag of weed at hand. As we note in the book, one reason NBC let SNL slide in the early days was that the kids of network and advertising agency executives were relentlessly begging their fathers to get them tickets to the show. The executives knew well enough how rare that was. One member of the television generation who got the point sooner than most was a little-known comedian who was in Aspen, Colorado, on October 11, 1975, the night *Saturday Night* premiered. He remembers being stunned by what he saw. "Fuck," Steve Martin said to himself, "they did it. They did the show everyone should have been doing."

It's very likely that there are many fans of SNL today who have no idea what the television industry was like in 1975. To say it's vastly different now would be a vast understatement. ABC, CBS and NBC were essentially the only games in town; they absolutely ruled the television world. Cable and satellite TV were both in their infancy and not yet a threat to the networks' sovereignty. The home video era was just getting started. Anyone who talked about streaming at that point was either high or writing science fiction or both.

Dominating TV as thoroughly as the three networks did in 1975 made them by far the most powerful advertising medium in the world. Most of their commercial profits came from the prime-time shows the networks bought from the Hollywood studios, but they also enjoyed huge profits from the shows they produced themselves, such as the *Today* show and the *Tonight* show with Johnny Carson (both on NBC). It's no wonder, then, that the networks grew not just fat but complacent. Not every show they put on clicked, and the battles they waged for ratings were fierce. But the competition between ABC, CBS and NBC was like the competition among the three leading casinos in Las Vegas. One of them always came out on top, but everybody was making a fortune.

We won't retell the story here that we tell in detail in the book; suffice it to say that for a variety of reasons it was a fluke that *Saturday*

*Night* got on the air at all. The network's programmers didn't care about the time period it was in – the advertising profits they made there were negligible. So it was that once Lorne got the job he was able to put *Saturday Night* together relatively free from network interference; no one was paying attention. It didn't take long for that to change. The trouble started when the people he hired went to work in their offices on the 17th floor of 30 Rock and in Studio 8H. What had been a nebulous concept suddenly became unsettling reality. Word spread in the building that an unsavory group of people had appeared in their midst.

Lorne quickly gained a reputation as a pushy know-it-all who was making demands for network resources that were way out of bounds for a late-night experiment that was doomed to fail. From the executives on the upper floors to the security guards in the building's art deco lobby, there was no shortage of people who went out of their way to not go out of their way for *Saturday Night*. This isn't to say Lorne didn't find any allies; he did, and he was good at cultivating them. Overall, though, the show's staff felt as if the 17th floor served as an outpost in hostile territory, which was fine with them, because they knew it was a place they could hang out all night and smoke pot with impunity. It was the network suits who dared not enter.

Tensions also flourished in Studio 8H, the domain of the technicians who handled everything from lighting and cameras to props and cue cards. Many members of the 8H crew had worked there since the 1950s, when Arturo Toscanini and the NBC Symphony Orchestra held court, and they didn't appreciate that their turf was suddenly being invaded by a bunch of arrogant amateurs who had no idea how television production worked but who thought their scripts, which the crews felt were either unproducible or unfit for TV or both, were masterpieces that demanded first-class attention. Another chapter in our book bears the name the 8H pros started using to describe what they felt 8H turned into when the *Saturday Night* people came around: The Children's Television Workshop.

Opinions at the network began to change over the course of the first season as a growing media buzz inaugurated SNL the new kid in town. A significant benchmark was the guest host appearance in April of Ron Nessen, the press secretary for the President of the United States, Gerald Ford, which turned out to be bad for Nessen (for reasons we explain in the book) but good for the show. The true breakthrough came a month later when SNL won four Emmy awards, including the one for best comedy-variety show. That ended any hopes executives at the network had that the show would quietly go away, even though it wasn't until the third season that its ratings qualified it as a genuine hit. After that, SNL gushed money.

It would be easy to say that SNL has gone through a lot of changes in these past fifty years, but in many respects it hasn't, really. The format that took shape over the first four shows of the first season has stayed the same ever since. And with the exception of an interlude when Lorne and the original team left and the show was taken over by two different producers (a period documented in Part Three of our book), Lorne's genius for finding comedy talent has remained wonderfully consistent.

As we said, the show is regularly criticized for not being funny anymore, and often for being a pale imitation of its early glory years, when Chevy Chase, John Belushi, Gilda Radner, Dan Aykroyd, Jane Curtin, Laraine Newman, Garrett Morris and Bill Murray lit up the screen. That perspective is at least partly due to the fact that SNL in the beginning had the unbeatable advantage of getting there first. In form SNL may have been similar to Sid Caesar's *Your Show of Shows* and *The Carol Burnett Show*, but its *attitude* was nothing like theirs. And despite their lack of TV experience, the cast members had spent years honing their comedic skills in improv theaters and comedy clubs around the country. So it was that, despite how they looked to the old guard at NBC, they were experienced pros, and prepared to make a favorable first impression. Hence the title of another chapter in our book, "Enlightened Amateurs," which is what Lorne said he was looking for when he set out to hire his team.

The shock of the new that the show provoked in its first year and the momentum it built for several seasons thereafter have left an indelible impression, but as everybody knows, there's been plenty of brilliant comedy since then. It's amazing to think of the number of great performers who've been a part of SNL's cast these past fifty years. We'll resist the temptation to name names. We're sure to leave somebody out, and everyone has a list of their own. It's been said that everybody's favorite SNL cast is the one that was on when they were in high school.

* * *

We started researching this book in March 1983, soon after we signed our contract with William Morrow, and finished it two years later. Jeff had written about television as a reporter for the *New York Post* and as a freelance columnist at the *SoHo Weekly News*, *Circus* magazine and the *Toronto Globe & Mail*. Doug had worked in the New York bureau of a television trade journal called *Broadcasting* and at *Panorama*, a short-lived monthly published by the editors of *TV Guide*.

From the outset of the project we had a priceless advantage: Lorne Michaels' blessing.

Jeff had done numerous articles about *Saturday Night* from its beginning and had a good relationship with Lorne, and that opened the door. At first, people we called for interviews would put off talking to us until they checked with Lorne, but soon enough word spread through the SNL grapevine that we were okay, and that step was no longer necessary. It's likely that Lorne's approval also helped open doors for us at NBC, although as reporters we were both known quantities there. In any event, the head of NBC's publicity department, Bud Rukeyser, gave us permission to interview whoever we wanted to at the network. We took full advantage of the opportunity, talking to everyone from production assistants to the Chairman of the NBC board. The generosity we received at NBC reflected the fact that the network had justifiably become very proud of a show they had once wished would disappear. Landmarks like SNL don't come along every day, after all, especially when they're as profitable as this one.

Another advantage we had in doing the book was that we were unknowingly helping salve an old SNL wound. Starting with Chevy Chase's breakout during the show's first season, everyone who wasn't a cast member on the SNL team, and some who were cast members, hated that the press invariably gave the stars of the show all the attention, ignoring everyone else. That's standard operating procedure in the entertainment business, of course, but it still grated, especially in the beginning, when the team naively believed that *Saturday Night* was a communal effort among equals. We were writing a biography of THE SHOW. The writers seemed especially pleased to finally be asked about their time at SNL – understandably so, considering their contribution to its success -- which was great for us, given that they were invariably smart, insightful and funny as hell.

Unfortunately, most of the people who'd gotten the lion's share of the attention while the show was on the air – the cast members – turned down our requests for interviews. By the time we came around they'd been away from SNL for three or four years, and it's likely they were still recovering from the incredible pressure they'd been under as big-time celebrities. It's even more likely that, despite the mountains of publicity the Not Ready for Prime Time Players received, they knew there were still plenty of secrets they'd never told.

We did interview, from the original cast, Chevy Chase and Laraine Newman. Chevy talked to us for hours, which demonstrated a rule of thumb in showbiz journalism: The people who feel the most worried about what other people will say about them often go out of their way to make sure their side of the story gets told. That was certainly the case with Chevy, but we heard a lot of contrary opinions. After the book came out he told *Playboy* magazine that he'd like to meet us in a dark alley while armed with a pair of pruning shears.

We spent many hours talking to Al Franken and his partner, Tom Davis, and Al became sort of an ambassador for us, urging Gilda Radner and Dan Aykroyd, among others, to talk. Gilda kept saying she'd do an interview – she told Al she felt a responsibility to do it – but it never worked out. Danny was among the cast members we most wanted to interview, both because we regarded him (and still regard him) as one of the true comic geniuses in SNL history, but also because we'd learned that he played a central role in some great behind-the-scenes stories. After many calls from Al, he finally agreed to an interview.

Danny was in California shooting a movie, so the plan was that he'd talk to us on the phone from his trailer (this was well before Zoom, Skype and FaceTime came on the scene). At the designated hour we placed the call, but the assistant who answered said that Danny was busy; we should call back in an hour. We did. Same answer. We called again. Same answer. Finally our phone rang.

"Hold for Dan Aykroyd, please."

"Gentlemen," he said. He didn't give us a chance to return his greeting. Instead, he immediately let loose a nonstop, two-minute verbal assault, a barrage of staccato invective that sounded to our ears like machine-gun fire. The gist of it was that we had a lot of nerve thinking that we could write a history of a show we were never a part of; who did we think we were? Specific comments we remember included a sneering dismissal of our business card (it simply read "The SNL Book" with our names and phone numbers) and an accusation that we were no better than "pornographers."

Insulted and frustrated, we were waiting for a chance to respond, but we didn't get one.

"That's it, gentlemen. I'm done," Danny said, and hung up.

This story ends on a more positive note. A couple of years later, soon after the book came out, Jeff was on his way to the restroom during an SNL end-of-season party when he ran into Danny coming from the other direction. He introduced himself and braced for another onslaught, but again Danny cut him off.

"I should've cooperated, should've cooperated," he said. "You did a great job."

That was it. Jeff said thanks and they went their separate ways.

Jeff had an earlier chance encounter with another cast member we'd been trying unsuccessfully to reach, Garrett Morris. It happened while we were spending a couple of months doing interviews in Los Angeles. We stayed at the Oakwood Gardens apartments in Toluca Lake, a well-known stopover for B- and C-level showbiz types having extended business in town. Jeff was in the habit of starting his day with a run, followed by a shower in the complex's locker room. It was there one morning that he ran, almost literally, into a naked Garrett.

Simultaneously catching his breath and regaining his composure, Jeff managed to explain that he was one of the reporters who'd been trying to reach him for an interview for a book on SNL.

"I'm not talking to you guys," he immediately answered.

Jeff persisted. "Garrett, if you could give me one minute ..."

"No," he repeated, almost shouting. "I am not talking. That's it."

Just as abruptly he turned and walked away.

Jeff didn't follow, but as he left the locker room a few minutes later he spotted Garrett (by this time wearing a bathing suit) sitting next to two women in the hot tub. Jeff gave it one more try.

"Garrett," he said.

"No!" came the immediate, high-pitched response, this time definitely shouted. "Get away from me."

Jeff did. Obviously, Garrett's strategy for avoiding bad press was the opposite of Chevy's. We knew by then why. We describe in the book what happened to Garrett during his troubled tenure on SNL.

All told we interviewed well over 200 hundred people for the book, many of them several times. We also watched videotapes of every program Lorne produced during his five years at the helm. Lorne graciously provided us access to the tape library at his production company, Broadway Video (again, this was well before virtually everything on television was available one way or another on your TV at home), and let us use a funky office a few floors down in the Brill Building to watch them. Dick Ebersol was producing SNL during those years and he generously gave us backstage access to see the show every Saturday. Eddie Murphy would walk by and to our reminders that he said he'd do an interview would wave us off with a quick "Oh yeah" and move on. The interview never happened. We did have a couple of extended interviews with a 22-year-old pre-*Seinfeld* Julia Louis-Dreyfus, who recounted how frustrated she was with the paltry amount of airtime she was getting on the show, thanks mainly to Dick.

Dick was another one of those people who spent many hours being interviewed for our book, probably for the same reason Chevy did. We would be remiss, however, in failing to note the important roles he played in the show's history. As NBC's new head of late-night programming in 1975, he hired Lorne and fought many network battles alongside him. In 1981 he returned to become SNL's producer, brought in to save the show from extinction after a disastrous partial season produced by Lorne's former talent coordinator, Jean Doumanian. He remained SNL's producer through the 1984–85 season. At first he leaned heavily on the talents of Eddie and Joe Piscopo and, in his final year, hired a trio of name stars (Christopher Guest, Martin Short and Billy Crystal) to fill out the cast. Dick had a personality that tended to put people off and he was far from a comedy genius, but he showed that sometimes raw ambition is what a show needs.

* * *

After we'd finished our research on Lorne's first five years as SNL's producer, we spent several weeks compiling the information we'd gathered and outlining the book. Doug then retreated to a house on the Saint Lawrence River in upstate New York to write the first draft of the book's chapters on that period while Jeff stayed in New York and interviewed people who'd worked on the Doumanian and Ebersol shows. In late 1984, we rented a house on the Jersey Shore (when the beaches were empty and the rents were cheap) where we worked together to polish Doug's drafts while Jeff wrote up the first draft of Part Three. After several more rounds of polishing we turned in the manuscript in March of 1985.

Obviously we hoped the book would become a big best seller, but it didn't, despite receiving nearly unanimous rave reviews. TV critics around the country loved the book. We also got some nice notices from big-time writers, among them Jay Cocks, who collaborated with Martin Scorsese on the screenplays for two Scorsese movies (*Gangs of New York* and *The Age of Innocence*) and Frank Rich, who's gone from being a longtime critic and columnist for the *New York Times* to producing hit TV shows like *Veep* and *Succession*. Howard Stern, on his way to becoming the king of New York radio, couldn't stop talking about the book for at least a month. There were some disappointments, of course. *Rolling Stone*, which had done at least eleven cover stories on SNL cast members, printed not a single word about the book.

The reaction of the most prestigious television critic at the time, Tom Shales of the *Washington Post*, was mostly one of shock that so much nastiness had been going on behind the scenes. Shales had been one of the earliest supporters of SNL, and the enthusiasm he expressed for the show in so important a publication probably helped Lorne hold SNL's enemies within NBC at bay. But this article, which was more of a report about the book's revelations than a review, made it clear that he was much more approving of the ways the show's stars behaved onscreen rather than off.

"You may not have to be crazy to work in television," he wrote, "but after a few weeks, you will be.

> Additional proof of this, as if any were needed, comes in 'Saturday Night: A Backstage History of Saturday Night Live,' a fascinating and lurid new book about the landmark comedy program's 10 tumultuous years on the air.
> A more disagreeable, egomaniacal, selfish and dissipated crowd you wouldn't want to meet than the changing casts and staffs of the show, at least as authors Doug Hill and Jeff Weingrad portray them. It appears they all took turns behaving like swine."

He went on to provide a lengthy list of various stars' misbehaviors, saying almost nothing about the show's battles with NBC.

To his credit, Shales wasn't content to accept what he read at face value. He took the trouble to call Brandon Tartikoff, the head of NBC programming at the time he wrote the piece, to ask if what he'd read in the book was true. Tartikoff said that he'd read the parts of it that covered the years he'd personally experienced at the network (beginning in 1977) and that he'd found it "incredibly accurate." Shales called Lorne, too, who had less complimentary things to say, despite the fact that he claimed he hadn't read the book. Many of the stories it told were second-hand, he said, from frustrated and bitter people. "What surprised me, he added, "was who talked and how loud their voices were."

That surprised us, given that Lorne certainly knew who we talked to, both because the SNL grapevine kept good track of our travels while we were doing our research, and because pretty much everyone we talked to felt incredibly grateful for the time they'd spent at SNL, despite the problems. We don't remember running into a lot of bitterness. Most of all, we find it hard to understand how Lorne could think what we wrote could be considered anything other than a testament to the significance of his achievement. As Jay Cocks put it in his review for *Time*, "[T]his book gives full measure to the size and weight of SNL's substantial legacy."

The most gratifying reviews we received were from SNL insiders who told us that we'd gotten it right. This included Bernie Brillistein, Sandy Wernick and Barry Secunda, who between them managed the majority of the cast members and most of the writers on the first five years of SNL. Marilyn Miller, one of the original writers on the show (and one of the most respected) told us that reading the book was "like you guys had a two-way mirror looking into our lives." We've also heard some very nice compliments from people who joined the show later or who had other careers in comedy, among them Adam Sandler, Judd Apatow, Jim Belushi and Mark McKinney (a cast member on *Kids in the Hall* and a writer on SNL). Jan Hooks remembered devouring the book during the week she was deciding whether to accept Lorne's offer to join the cast, which happened to be the same week she was sitting at her mother's bedside in the hospital. She told Jeff, with a laugh, that she was so engrossed in what she was reading that there were moments when her mother would ask her for something and she'd hold up her hand and say, "Wait a minute, Mom. Just a second."

\* \* \*

The book was published in hard cover by William Morrow in January 1986; a soft-cover version published by Vintage followed a year or so later. Untreed Reads issued an ebook version in 2012. Jeff continued working in television journalism as the editor of the TV and Radio section of the *New York Daily News* and as an entertainment editor at *The Associated Press*. Doug worked as a staff writer for *TV Guide* but quit when Rupert Murdoch bought the magazine. He subsequently wrote about health for Rodale Press and the Robert Wood Johnson Foundation. In roughly 2000 he developed a passion for studying the history and philosophy of technology; his book on those subjects, *Not So Fast: Thinking Twice About Technology*, was published in 2016. He's now working on a book on the thought of sociologist Max Weber.

There are plans for NBC to celebrate SNL's 50-year anniversary with a three-hour live TV special. In prime time. Assuming the cast and others from the original show appear in some fashion, it will be interesting to see how the people who made the first television show for the TV generation have aged. We were so much younger then; we're older than that now.

# PART ONE

Now the war has come, bringing with it a new attitude. Youth has turned to gods we of an earlier day knew not, and it is possible to see already the direction in which those who come after us will move. The younger generation, conscious of strength and tumultuous, have done with knocking at the door; they have burst in and seated themselves in our seats. The air is noisy with their shouts.

—W. Somerset Maugham, *The Moon and Sixpence*

It was an age of miracles, it was an age of art, it was an age of excess, and it was an age of satire.

—F. Scott Fitzgerald, "Echoes of the Jazz Age"

# CHAPTER 1

# Mirrors and Blue Smoke

It wouldn't be the first time Dick Ebersol had pitched the new program called *Saturday Night* without having more than the vaguest idea of what that program would be.

This time his audience was management: executives from most of NBC's 219 local affiliated stations around the country who had gathered at the Century Plaza Hotel in Los Angeles for their May 1975 convention. NBC's affiliate conventions in those days were typically described as "love feasts," more occasions for golf, gourmet dinners, and celebratory toasts of champagne than for arguments about the way the network was handling its business.

True, NBC had trailed CBS in the prime-time ratings for more than twenty years. But the profits in second place were enormous, and in 1975, CBS seemed more within reach than it had for many seasons. Advertising revenues, and profits, were rising to unimagined new heights. Let ABC suffer, as it always had, the humiliation of being a distant third. Television's longstanding status quo was, for those at NBC, very comfortable indeed. There was as yet no inkling that within the year the status quo would be overturned and NBC would find itself, for the first time in its history, in third place.

Dick Ebersol was counting on the affiliates' cheerful mood to discourage any bothersome questions about the new program he was about to describe. Ebersol, who had joined NBC just nine months before as director of weekend late-night programming, cut a somewhat strange figure on the podium. At twenty-seven he was shockingly young for a network executive. He was tall and pug-nosed. His hair hung down to his shoulders in a Prince Valiant cut that framed his head like a helmet.

The lenses of his glasses were so thick they looked like miniature TV sets. Usually he wore bizarre patchwork sports jackets of brightly colored madras more suggestive of the Brothers Ringling than the Brothers Brooks, but, in deference to the affiliates, that day he chose a muted dark suit. At a time when businessmen still worried about radicals running wild in the streets, Ebersol, his long hair evenly trimmed and well washed, his tailored suit neatly pressed, came across as less dangerous than curious, an odd combination of rebellious youth and white-collar convention.

Despite his youth, Ebersol was no newcomer to speaking at network affairs. He had come to NBC after spending seven years as an aide and surrogate son to the legendary Roone Arledge, president of ABC Sports. Ebersol had produced a number of sporting events on weekends for ABC, but his main job had been representing Arledge at the dozens of meetings and conferences each year that Arledge habitually avoided. Ebersol knew enough, then, to come to his first appearance before NBC's affiliates with several jokes written out on index cards to help fill the empty spots—of which there were quite a few—in his speech.

The affiliates had heard a little about *Saturday Night* from a press release NBC had issued a couple of weeks before. The release had been hurried through in anticipation of the affiliates' convention; whatever chance *Saturday Night* had for success would depend on the affiliates agreeing to carry it on their stations. But the network's public relations experts had been unable to mask how little they'd had to go on when they wrote it.

The show was described as "a new concept in late-evening programming—a live, 90-minute comedy-variety series titled *Saturday Night*." It was to originate from studio 8H in NBC's 30 Rockefeller Plaza headquarters in New York beginning October 11. The producer, the release said, would be Lorne Michaels, who had won an Emmy award a year before for his writing on a Lily Tomlin special.

The release went on to list some of Michaels's other credits: producer of a Flip Wilson special, a writer for *Laugh-In*, co-host and producer of *The Hart and Lorne Show* on Canadian television, and a writer for British television's *Monty Python*. All but the last credit were true. Ebersol was quoted as saying that Michaels was "the best young producer in the comedy-variety field" (he was actually two years older than Ebersol), but it's likely that none of the affiliates had ever heard of him. And if they had, they might have reflected that there were very few young producers in the comedy-variety field in 1975, mainly because comedy-variety was then considered a dying form.

That was about as specific as the release had gotten. Further quotations from Ebersol stated that *Saturday Night* would feature "a mixture of new and established talent," but there was no mention of who that talent might be. The show would "introduce new forms of comedy-variety," but there was no explanation of what new forms Ebersol had in mind. The release was filled out with a few paragraphs extolling NBC's long tradition of innovative late-night programming, the grand history of studio 8H, where Arturo Toscanini had held forth in the days when NBC had its own symphony orchestra, and the network's dedication to bringing television production back to New York City. It concluded by promising that "within the next four to six weeks a program format and names of performers who will appear in the show will be announced."

But as Ebersol stood before the affiliates he had little of substance to add. He told them he'd signed Jim Henson, creator of the Muppets, to provide a series of new characters for the show. In 1975, however, Henson was known mainly for his work on public television's kids' show *Sesame Street*, so his agreement to contribute to a late-night comedy show for adults could hardly be considered a coup. More impressive was Ebersol's announcement that comedian Albert Brooks would provide *Saturday Night* with a short film each week. Brooks at the time was one of the hotter young comics in the business, almost a regular on the *Tonight Show*. But since Henson's and Brooks's segments on *Saturday Night* were to total about five minutes apiece, that still left something like 80 percent of the program's content unaccounted for.

Ebersol went into what he called his "dance." He promised that the show would have weekly guest stars "such as" Lily Tomlin, Richard Pryor, and George Carlin (none of them had been signed); a "repertory group of young comedians from the comedy clubs of New York and other cities" (none of them had been auditioned); and regular music acts "such as" the Rolling Stones and Stevie Wonder (none of their agents had been approached). He alluded to such earlier TV comedy breakthroughs as *Laugh-In* and *Your Show of Shows*, tacked on a concluding joke or two, and left the stage.

Ebersol felt the affiliates' reaction to his smoke-and-mirror show had been "mild"—meaning noncommittal. They could afford to be.

The affiliates knew that NBC had put virtually no effort into its late-night time slot on weekends for years, filling it on both Saturdays and Sundays with reruns of Johnny Carson's *Tonight Show*. The affiliates had their choice of airing the reruns either night, but less than half had run them at all, choosing instead to fill the time with their own programs, usually old movies. As a result, Carson's weekend ratings were so negligible that the network's sales department often gave away advertising spots in the show as a free bonus in other deals.

If NBC now wanted to risk a little money producing a new show for that moribund time period, the affiliates figured, why not? Fresh programming was always welcome. Ebersol and everybody else at NBC had also talked about what a "youth" show *Saturday Night* was going to be, and the affiliates didn't need to be told that NBC's ratings in the eighteen-to-thirty-four-year-old age group were dismal, as were those of the other networks. There was, the affiliates knew, a whole blooming, unpredictable but overflowing youth market out there that wasn't, for the most part, watching TV. Millions of consumers were going to waste, and advertisers were aching to get at them.

Ebersol just might be the guy to do something about that—he was obviously of an age to have a clue to what the kids would buy. But *Saturday Night* was NBC's gamble, not the affiliates'. If it bombed, they always had the option of bumping it, returning to their own programming, and being no worse off than they'd been before. Which wasn't bad at all, youth gap or no.

* * *

After Ebersol's presentation the affiliates adjourned to a dining room in the hotel for one more luncheon, to be followed by one more afternoon of golf. Ebersol's meal was interrupted, however, by his boss, Marvin Antonowsky, vice-president of programs on the East Coast, and David Tebet, NBC's vice-president of talent.

"We have to talk to you," Antonowsky whispered, and the three men slipped out to a hallway behind the dais.

"I just got a call from Johnny Carson," Tebet told Ebersol. "He's heard about the show and he wants to know what it's all about. He wants to see you and Lorne as soon as possible."

This message—summons, really—was not a complete surprise. One of the details Ebersol had omitted from his speech to the affiliates was the fact that the impetus for the development of *Saturday Night* had come, indirectly, from the King of Late Night himself. Carson had let it be known within the network that he was unhappy with the weekend reruns of the *Tonight Show*. Five nights a week were enough, Carson believed; on the weekends he wanted his show to have a rest.

Carson had gotten his wish; the weekend reruns of the *Tonight Show* would soon be gone. Nonetheless, it was no secret at the network that Carson was fiercely protective of his late-night turf, and he had more than enough power to defend it effectively. Since Carson seemed to regard almost any new late-night program as a pretender to his throne, it stood to reason he'd want to learn more about *Saturday Night*. Ebersol dutifully called Carson's office. He wasn't sure whether to be pleased or concerned when he was given an appointment for the following afternoon.

The next day Lorne Michaels, dressed as he almost always was in jeans, Hawaiian shirt, and green corduroy jacket, picked up Ebersol at his hotel and they rode in Michaels's red Volkswagen convertible to Burbank. When Carson's secretary announced them over the interoffice phone, they heard Carson say, "Okay, send the kids in." Evidently he'd been told of their youth.

Carson was sitting at his desk, working on his monologue. There were traces of perspiration stains on his denim shirt, and Michaels was impressed that after all these years, even the great Johnny Carson still sweated over his comedy. Carson cordially waved for them to sit down. "So," he said, with a smile, "you guys are only going to be on one night a week, huh?"

Then he came to the point. "Well, guys," he said, "I've heard about your show, and I think we've really got to talk about it. It's got similarities to mine."

Michaels said he didn't think there would be a conflict, and Ebersol, taking care to speak with the utmost deference, quickly agreed. "What we really have is a comedy-variety show," he said, "as opposed to a comedy-talk show."

"Well, we have variety here too," said Carson.

"Our show will be mostly sketches," Ebersol answered. "You mean there's going to be no talk or interviews?" Michaels and Ebersol nodded their heads. "No, none at all."

Carson asked about the guest hosts *Saturday Night* would have. "Our biggest problem is going to be people," he said. He was concerned that Ebersol and Michaels were going to be using some of the stand-up comedians that the *Tonight Show* had spent years nurturing. At that point Carson's producer, Fred deCordova, walked in. The conversation started over from the beginning for his benefit, coming back to the question about the guest hosts. Ebersol and Michaels explained that they were mainly looking for people who hadn't appeared on television before, people who would appeal primarily to college audiences.

"But you're talking names," Carson said. "Lily Tomlin, Richard Pryor, George Carlin, Albert Brooks."

Michaels explained that Albert Brooks would only be doing films for their show, not stand-up routines. Ebersol hastened to assure Carson they would gladly adhere to a policy known in show business as "21 and 8," meaning that any guest appearing on the *Tonight Show* would not be booked to appear on *Saturday Night* for a minimum of twenty-one days before or eight days after they sat on Carson's couch.

"Well, I guess that will work for us," Carson said. "Fred, is there anything else to say to the boys?"

DeCordova wanted to know what sorts of musical acts *Saturday Night* would have. Again Ebersol assured him there would be no conflict, since their show would feature only rock groups.

"Oh, there's no problem there, then," deCordova agreed. "That's not our kind of music."

There were handshakes all around, and as Ebersol and Michaels were on their way out, Carson again smiled and said, "Just one night a week?"

Later that day Ebersol got a call from Dave Tebet at NBC. "They liked you," Tebet told him. "They thought you were fine boys." It would not be long before Johnny Carson would decide this initial assessment had been incorrect.

* * *

Dick Ebersol first met Lorne Michaels six months before the affiliates' convention. Lorne's agent, Sandy Wernick, had heard that a new guy at NBC in New York was putting together a show. He gave Ebersol a call, thinking at first of putting him in touch with another client. But Ebersol said he wanted to produce something out of the ordinary, a show that combined comedy and rock music, appealed to young audiences, and took some chances. Wernick thought immediately of Lorne Michaels, who had been talking of producing just such a show for years. "Dick," Wernick said, "there's only one guy you should meet."

Dick Ebersol and Lorne Michaels, the summer before *Saturday Night* premiered.
*Courtesy of Dick Ebersol/NBC*

Wernick arranged a meeting for Ebersol's next trip to Hollywood, and in late December, Ebersol, Wernick, and Michaels met in Wernick's eighth-floor office at the Ashley-Famous Agency on Sunset Boulevard. Bob Finkel, a longtime variety producer and early champion of Michaels, came along to lend moral support. Ebersol explained that he had been hired by NBC president Herb Schlosser to develop programming for the *Tonight Show* time period on Saturday nights. Ebersol's master plan was to commission forty pilots that could be tried out in late night, and then, if they worked, be moved to prime time. He thought one of them should be a comedy show for young people that was irreverent and out-spoken— which was all Michaels needed to hear.

He started talking, which by all accounts was one of the things Lorne Michaels did best. Wernick used to say Lorne gave the most entertaining presentations he'd ever seen. Among his friends Lorne was known as a man from whom words gushed; sometimes people found it nice just to sit back and listen while Lorne rambled musically on. He spoke at length that afternoon of a show that would have a repertory company of young comedians from improvisational theater groups like Second City, young writers with fresh points of view, parody commercials, short films, and rock music. All the elements, in other words, that would later end up in *Saturday Night*. "I want," he concluded, "to do a show for the generation that grew up on television."

This was not, for Lorne, a new pitch. He was talking about a show he believed should have been on the air in 1968, a show he had, in fact, unsuccessfully proposed to NBC two years before. In Dick Ebersol, Lorne finally found a receptive network ear. Sandy Wernick and Bob Finkel saw Ebersol's eyes light up as he listened to Michaels. Ebersol himself felt an immediate "bonding" between them.

"We spoke the same language," he said. "Nobody else to my knowl-edge in the networks was talking about the television generation, but that was Lorne's rap, and that was my rap."

Lorne in truth was more wary of Ebersol than Ebersol was of him, but he was able to avoid giving that impression when it suited him. Ebersol and Michaels left Wernick's office, drove to a coffee shop, and talked for several hours. When they parted, Michaels had a verbal com-mitment to produce a one-hour comedy-variety pilot for NBC.

CHAPTER 2

# The Revolution Will
# Not Be Televised

I thought I was on my way to Nirvana, but all I got was recurrent flash-
backs of the original Mouseketeers.

        —Jim, the space cadet on the TV series *Taxi*

There's something happening here, but you don't know what it is, do
you, Mr. Jones?

        —Bob Dylan, "Ballad of a Thin Man"

Television and the television generation had drifted so far apart during
the 1960s that they hardly communicated at all, an ironic disaffection
considering that this was the first generation in history to have grown
up taking television for granted as an everyday, ubiquitous fact of life.
Lorne Michaels liked to say that his generation was as familiar with TV
as French kids were with wine. For millions of children born after World
War II, television had marked many of the milestones of their coming
of age, from *The Mickey Mouse Club*, Davy Crockett, Superman, and
Saturday morning cartoons to *Ozzie and* Harriet, *Leave It to* Beaver,
Elvis Presley on the *Ed Sullivan Show*, and the coverage of John F.
Kennedy's assassination in 1963.

    The Beatles appeared on *Ed Sullivan* two and a half months after
Kennedy's murder, and it was after the Beatles that the television generation and television began to diverge, just as the television generation

was diverging from many of the values of its parents, joining in the countercultural extravaganza that would come to be known as the Woodstock Nation. Rock music carried the Woodstock Nation's banner while television represented much of what the bands and their audience stood against. More than a wasteland, TV was the idiot engine of the Establishment, electronic opiate of the consumerist masses, and thus a favorite object of ridicule and contempt. "The revolution will not be televised" was the saying in the streets, testimony to the counterculture's conviction that, with the occasional, almost inadvertent exception of the news, nothing close to the truth ever appeared on network TV.

Television comedy wasn't even attempting to speak to the urban youth of America in the 1960s. The networks' sense of humor was represented by such shows as *Green Acres*, *Gilligan's Island*, *Petticoat Junction*, and *The Beverly Hillbillies*. Some of the performers who'd helped invent TV comedy in the fifties—Red Skelton, Lucille Ball, Jackie Gleason—were still hanging on with weekly series, but all were in the twilight of their TV careers.

The decade's comedic breakthrough was *Rowan & Martin's Laugh-In*, which became a phenomenal hit in 1968. But *Laugh-In* was a revolution of form, not of content: It was the first show consisting largely of rhythmically edited snippets of videotape. *Laugh*-In's humor, on the other hand, was mainly silly, and its politics, despite an illusion of irreverence, were toothless on-screen and conservative behind it. Head writer and later producer Paul Keyes was a friend and speechwriter of Richard Nixon's; hence candidate Nixon's appearance on the show during the 1968 presidential campaign, when he uttered the prophetic line "Sock it to me." For the youth of America, no booking could have been more appropriate: One of the few things that exceeded their contempt for television was their loathing of Richard Nixon.

The only network show to reflect directly and aggressively the subversive attitudes of the sixties was the *Smothers*

Dick and Tom Smothers, the first comedians to reflect the '60s sensibility on network TV. They were canceled for their efforts. *Courtesy of Smothers Brothers*

*Brothers Comedy Hour.* With virtually no expectations of success, CBS threw the Smothers Brothers on the air in February 1967 in the time period opposite NBC's *Bonanza*, which had been one of the highest-rated programs on television for more than six years and *the* highest-rated for the previous three. The network expected a standard variety show, but like most of their peers, the Smothers Brothers, especially Tommy, had been going through some changes, and they had other ideas.

Tommy Smothers at the time was recently divorced and sharing a bachelor pad in Hollywood with Mason Williams, a musician who became the Smotherses' head writer. "We'd watch TV and be appalled," Williams remembers. "There was nothing on for him, me, or anybody we knew to watch. There was a void as far as a certain kind of element. You could sense there was a revolution in the works, but it wasn't being reflected on TV at all, except maybe with Mort Sahl on PBS. Tommy had done [a sitcom for CBS] and had gotten burned on that; it was one of those deals where you go out and people laugh at what you do no matter what, blowing smoke up your ass. He felt betrayed by that whole system.

"Tommy came home one night and said, 'Hey, we got an offer to do a variety show opposite *Bonanza*,' which was known as 'The Kamikaze Hour.' We talked about what the show could be about. The entree was that the network surely thought the Smothers Brothers were going to be some cutesy-pie college boys, like the Brothers Four. They had no idea that Tommy was waking up, curious about what was really going on around him. We had a shoe box in the living room, and whenever we'd get an idea we thought was different we'd throw it in the shoe box. By the fall it was pretty full. When we started we just played their game ... but after about ten shows we started to try to find what was happening on the streets."

Suddenly the Smotherses were doing jokes about politics, sex, religion, and drugs. The Vietnam War and Lyndon Johnson were favorite targets. One sketch that several CBS affiliates in Texas refused to air pictured Johnson moving his ranch to Washington, complete with barbecues and ten-gallon hats. That approach pleased young viewers—miraculously the Smothers Brothers attracted high ratings despite the competition from *Bonanza*—but it made CBS extremely nervous. Topical satire with bite was all but unheard-of on television in 1967, and there were constant, vicious battles over what the Smotherses could and could not say. One memo from CBS's censors said, "It's OK to satirize the President, as long as you do so with respect."

With success the Smotherses grew even bolder, hiring young, inexperienced writers like Steve Martin and Rob Reiner and eventually taking over production of the show themselves. The controversy they provoked increased, as did the resistance from CBS. For Tommy Smothers, the battles became a cause and an obsession. "I was all passion and youth and belief," he said later. "There was no room for softness at that time—you were either a short-hair or a long-hair."

He pored over law books, federal regulations, and the censor's policy guidelines and carried his arguments all the way up the network hierarchy to CBS president Frank Stanton and chairman William Paley. Finding no satisfaction there, he went public and complained bitterly to the press about CBS's harassment. He traveled to Washington and sought the support of Nicholas Johnson, a young, maverick member of the Federal Communications Commission who had become similarly embattled applying his own brand of activism to the regulation of the television industry. The Smotherses became television's symbol of dissent, and the power of their pulpit made them seem, to some, potentially galvanizing forces in that dissent; after the 1968 Democratic convention in Chicago there were rumors they were being investigated by the FBI. Paranoia was fashionable then, and not always unjustified.

CBS canceled the Smothers Brothers in June of 1969, five months after Richard Nixon became President. The reason the network gave was that one of their shows had been turned in after the deadline stipulated in their contract, but Tommy Smothers, Mason Williams, Rob Reiner, and Steve Martin believe to this day the cancellation was politically motivated. "Nixon came in and we were off," Smothers said. "We were thrown off the air because of our viewpoint on Vietnam." They were also thrown off, Smothers adds, "because we had no ally in high places" at CBS. That was a key mistake that Lorne Michaels, six years later, would not repeat.

The lesser-known story is what happened at CBS after the Smothers Brothers were canceled. The network decided it should draft an official statement, a "White Paper," to explain to the public that, despite the Smothers Brothers affair, CBS remained committed to representing the viewpoints of America's youth. Donald West, an executive assistant to CBS president Frank Stanton, argued that rather than just writing a White Paper, CBS ought to put another show of "contemporary relevancy" on the air. West believed a revolution really might be happening in the streets, and he became impassioned with the idea that by giving young people an honest forum to express their views television could help bridge the generation gap. He persuaded Stanton and Michael Dann, CBS's head of programming, to let him give such a series a try. Its working title was *The Real World*; later it became *The Now Project* and finally *Subject to Change*.

Among those who were involved with *Subject to Change* early on was Bernie Sahlins, director of Chicago's comedy repertory troupe, Second City. Sahlins dropped out when West hooked up with a group of video freaks called, appropriately enough, The Videofreex, whom an assistant of West's met at the Woodstock music festival. For several months the Videofreex traveled around the country taping segments that featured a "free" school near San Francisco, Yippie leader Abbie Hoffman, Black Panther Fred Hampton, and other stalwarts of the radical left.

A first screening of *Subject to Change* was arranged for program chief Mike Dann in December of 1969. Don West and the Videofreex had insisted that Dann see the show on their turf, which turned out to be a run-down loft in SoHo. Dann, accompanied by several other CBS program executives, including daytime programming vice-president Fred Silverman, arrived at the loft by limousine. What the executives didn't know as they rode upstairs in the building's rickety elevator was that the Videofreex had staged a coup. Afraid that some of their interviews with radicals might be shown to the FBI, and leery of a hatchet job in CBS's editing rooms, they had refused to turn the tapes of the program over to Don West. CBS would see the raw truth from the streets, undiluted. A sizable contingent of the freaks and their friends filled the screening room, smoking grass, drinking wine, and waiting to see how Dann and his companions liked it.

The raw truth was raw indeed. Shot in the crudest of *cinema write* styles, it included heavy doses of radical proselytizing laced with uncut streams of profanity. As Mike Dann got up to speak afterward, it's likely his principle concern was getting out of the building alive. "I won't know for several days," he said, "what I think of this show. We may have witnessed something that's a little ahead of its time."

Dann, once he escaped, didn't for a moment consider putting *Subject to Change* on the air. Soon thereafter Don West lost his job at CBS. Dann stuck with another program the network had developed to replace the Smothers Brothers. It was a series conceived by a Hollywood packager named Bernie Brillstein, who a few years later would coincidentally begin managing a young writer- producer named Lorne Michaels. Brillstein had presented his idea— a combination of *The Beverly Hillbillies*, *The Andy Griffith Show*, and *Laugh-In*—to two of his producer clients, Frank Peppiatt and John Aylesworth, during a breakfast meeting at the Polo Lounge in the Beverly Hills Hotel. Spotting Mike Dann and his aide Perry Lafferty eating at a table nearby, Peppiatt and Aylesworth walked across the room and pitched the concept to them. By the end of the day they had a commitment from CBS. The series was called *Hee Haw*.

\* \* \*

The Smothers Brothers' cancellation left hip comedy without a signifi-cant outlet on television for the next five years—five years that happened to coincide with a truly remarkable burst of activity in comedy clubs, rep-ertory theaters, humor magazines, and video groups all over the country.

A generation of young comedians came of age and developed their craft in the comedy underground during those years. In some respects they were no different from any other generation of show biz hopefuls banging at the door: They had the dedication of the young to their art, but they were also more ambitious than most of them probably cared to admit. Nonetheless, they were distinguished by their numbers—this was, after all, the largest generation in American history—and by a sense of community and purpose that, as quickly as it might evaporate and as hard as it would subsequently be to remember, united them in a spirit of grand adventure with their peers.

The comedy underground very much reflected that spirit, even though the young comedians often ridiculed the counterculture as ruth-lessly as they did everything else. There was what Lorne Michaels called "a code" to comedy then, a code that included knowing drug ref-erences, casual profanity, a permissive attitude toward sex, a deep dis-dain for show business convention, blistering political satire, and bitter distrust of corporate power. It articulated a sensibility that challenged and mocked most of what the Establishment stood for.

A few stand-up comedians, among them Lily Tomlin, Robert Klein, George Carlin, and Albert Brooks, were able to express toned-down traces of the underground sensibility on TV, thanks mainly to Johnny Carson's *Tonight Show*. In 1971 producer Norman Lear's *All in the Family* opened the network door a crack for situation comedy that dealt directly with serious social and political issues, including the generation gap. But for the most part television still wasn't interested. There were writers and producers who were growing their hair long, smoking joints, and living in trailers in Laurel Canyon, but they worked on such series as *The Partridge Family* and *The Brady Bunch*.

Neither were the underground comedians overwhelmed with pop-ular success among their peers. Rock and roll was the art form of the day; no accident that perhaps the best-known hip comedy group of the sixties, The Firesign Theatre, appeared on record albums, not live. Comedians who opened concerts for rock bands were not infrequently booed offstage.

So the hip comedy scene simmered, mostly beneath the surface. There was a tremendous amount of cross-pollination within it, and the breadth and quality of the talent there, once it did break out, would help define movies as well as television for the next decade and beyond.

In comedy clubs around the country, young comedians like Andy Kaufman, Steve Martin, and Martin Mull were doing strange routines quite unlike the stand-up comedy of the past. Steve Martin, for example, would take his entire audience with him to McDonald's, where he would order several hundred hamburgers, then switch to a single order of fries. In run-down theaters and sometimes in the streets there were dozens of comedy groups performing, some of them improvisational, some of them repertory, many varying combinations of the two. Second City's companies in Chicago and Toronto would in later years become by far the best known of these for graduates like John Belushi, Bill Murray, Brian Doyle-Murray, Dan Aykroyd, Gilda Radner, John Candy, and Joe Flaherty. But there were also The Committee and the San Francisco Mime Troupe in San Francisco, The Proposition in Boston, and The Groundlings, The Credibility Gap, and The Ace Trucking Company in Los Angeles, to name a few, which between them produced performers like Rob Reiner, Jane Curtin, Laraine Newman, Harry Shearer, Michael McKean and David Lander, Fred Willard, and Teri Garr.

Second City, Toronto, 1972, Eugene Levy,
Dan Aykroyd, Gilda Radner, Rosemary Radcliffe, John Candy.
*Courtesy of Second City*

The best-known humor magazine of the period was the *Harvard Lampoon*, which spawned the very successful *National Lampoon* in 1970. The watershed event of sixties underground comedy was probably the intersection of the *Lampoon* with Second City on the Lampoon's syndicated radio series, record albums, and Off- Broadway revues, an intermingling of styles that would later be fundamental to the success of *Saturday Night*. In 1972, John Belushi arrived in New York from Chicago to star with Chevy Chase and Christopher Guest, among others, in the stage production Lemmings, a parody of the Woodstock music festival and the generation that attended it. The collaboration continued the following year with the start of the *National Lampoon Radio Hour*, which featured, at one time or another, Belushi, Chase, Michael O'Donoghue, Bill Murray, and Brian Doyle-Murray. In early 1975 there was another revue, *The National Lampoon Show*, which brought Gilda Radner into the circle.

As active as the *Lampoon* was, however, it was only one of scores of humor magazines that flourished during those years. Most were college-based, including the Stanford *Chaparral*, the MIT *Voodoo*, and the Occidental College *Fang*, which counted as one of its editors Terry Gilliam, the only American member of the English comedy group Monty Python. Other exponents of published satire toiling underground in the late sixties and early seventies included R. Crumb, whose *Zap Comix* were read in communal bathrooms from Berkeley to Boston, and Garry Trudeau, who was drawing a strip called *Doonesbury* for *Bull Tales*, the student paper at Yale.

It's possible that the underground might have bypassed television altogether had it not been for the Sony Corporation's introduction in the late 1960s of portable video cameras and recorders that were affordable by the public at large. That technology spawned a movement known as guerrilla television, which was populated by hundreds of long-hairs carrying Porta-Pak units, nascent auteurs who'd previously had no access to the mechanisms of television production and who set out to invent their own kind of programs. One such guerrilla remembers showing up with his partner at the house of a famous Hollywood writer, hoping to tell him some of their ideas. They were laden with gear, their hair hung well past their shoulders, and they wore fatigue jackets and pants. The memory of the Manson murders was still strong at the time, and the writer's wife, answering the door and seeing the equipment they were carrying, thought it was some kind of machine gun and ran screaming back inside.

One of the most important of the guerrilla groups was TVTV, which began as a convocation of members from several video communes from the East and West Coasts—the Raindance Corporation and the Ant Farm from California and the Videofreex and Global Village from New York. TVTV took comedy off the stage and literally to the streets to improvise in conjunction with real events, among them the 1972 political conventions. Two of TVTV's principals were Michael Shamberg and Allen Rucker, who in college had lived in the same apartment building

with Harold Ramis. Ramis became a member of Chicago's Second
City troupe, and through him Bill Murray, Brian Doyle-Murray, John
Belushi, and other Second City performers appeared in various TVTV
productions. More than a decade later, Michael Shamberg would produce a movie called *The Big Chill*, a bittersweet paean of sorts to the
bygone days of the sixties.

The first direct connection of underground comedy to television was
a group in New York called Channel One. A young man named Ken
Shapiro founded Channel One in 1967 with help from two of his friends
from college, Lane Sarasohn and Chevy Chase. Shapiro's credentials
as a child of television were better than most: He had been a regular on
Milton Berle's *Texaco Star Theater* in the early fifties, playing the brat
who nagged pitchman Sid Stone into saying, "Get outta here, kid—ya
bodda me."

In 1966, Shapiro, then twenty-four, spent $1,200 on the first Sony
video system to come on the mass market. He dropped out of graduate school and, with Chase and Sarasohn, started taping comedy bits
in the attic of his house in Brooklyn, where they all lived more or less
communally. Their first ninety-minute show was shot in black-and-
white and edited with scissors and aluminum tape. They rented a run-
down theater with 150 seats on West Fourth Street in Manhattan's East
Village, installed a closed-circuit TV system with three 23-inch screens,
and opened for business. Their advertising slogan was "ultra high frequently"; their target audience, "heads."

"We concentrate on psychedelic satire," Shapiro said in an interview with the *East Village Other*. "The heads are a gorgeous subculture,
with their own language, their own jokes—and since so little of it can
be broadcast over regular media, drugs and sex and such, it gives us a
whole world of totally new material to work with. We like to think we're
providing heads with their own CBS."

In fact, Channel One was criticized in those revolutionary days for
being more scatological than psychedelic and for being too derivative
of conventional TV. Which was part of the point. Shapiro's debt to the
shtick of Milton Berle was in distinct evidence. More important, Channel
One was the first underground comedy group to base much of its satire
on television itself. There was a kids' show parody featuring Ko-Ko the
Clown, who shooed all the Big People out of the room for "Make Believe
Time," then read excerpts from *Fanny Hill*. A parody commercial for the
Uranus Corporation touted a product called Brown 25, which dripped
repulsively from a stainless steel tube. "At Uranus," the announcer said,
"things come out a little differently." In a parody of ABC's *Wide World
of Sports*, breathless commentators called the play-by-play for the world

championship of sex. A hippie talk-show host pitched Zig Zag cigarette papers, and a straight news anchorman, finding himself still on camera after ending his report, smiled uncomfortably, tried to look busy for a minute or two, and finally ended up crawling out of the studio on all fours.

The hapless anchorman was played, as most of the parts in Channel One were, by Shapiro. Chevy Chase, who would later play a hapless newsman himself, left Channel One after the first show and went on to appear in *Lemmings*. Another fledgling comic, Richard Belzer, replaced him.

Ken Shapiro and Richard Belzer play dope dealers in the 1972 film *The Groove Tube*, an outgrowth of the pioneering underground video comedy revue Channel One. *Courtesy of The Pickman Film Corporation*

By 1970, Shapiro began sending a collection of Channel One's best bits on tour to college campuses around the country under the title *The Groove Tube*. It directly inspired two other groups: Kentucky Fried Theater, which started in the back of a bookstore in Madison, Wisconsin, in 1971, and the *Chicken Little Comedy Hour*, which aired on a Spanish-language UHF channel in San Francisco in 1972. Among *Chicken* Little's guest performers was a dropout from the advertising industry named Don Novello, who appeared as a chain-smoking Vatican priest called Father Guido Sarducci. A year later, *Chicken* Little's founders, Matt Neuman and Stuart Birnbaum, moved to Los Angeles, where they produced a parody of *War of the Worlds* that featured, among others, a young comedy team named Franken and Davis.

In 1972, Ken Shapiro put together $350,000 from various investors, including his father, and transferred *The Groove Tube* to 35mm film. Distributed to theaters independently after every major studio in Hollywood turned it down, *The Groove Tube* grossed something like $30 million and made Ken Shapiro one of the first of the underground comedians to strike it rich. Kentucky Fried Theater, which by then had also moved to Los Angeles, followed suit with an independent movie of its own, *Kentucky Fried Movie*, the second independent feature directed by a brash young filmmaker named John Landis. Later Kentucky Fried Theater's three principals, David and Jerry Zucker and David Abrahams, would achieve mainstream success with the movie *Airplane*; Landis would go on to direct such films as *Animal House*, *An American Werewolf in London*, *The Blues* Brothers, and *Trading Places*.

The Groove Tube helped prove to the movie industry the incredible untapped potential of the youth market, which wasn't going to beach-party movies anymore. Paramount Pictures promptly gave Ken Shapiro an office, a secretary, and a generous salary to develop more films appealing to the unorthodox tastes of the counterculture. One of the first people Shapiro hired was Lorne Michaels, who was just starting to write a film script for Paramount when he met Dick Ebersol.

Television in 1975 still hadn't figured out a way to tap that same youth market, but NBC was about to stumble upon it. Timing is everything in comedy, and the timing was right. The mood of the country was changing. Gerald Ford had pardoned Richard Nixon and declared the long national nightmare of Watergate over. Saigon finally fell in April of that year; urban guerrilla Patty Hearst was captured and repented; Nelson Rockefeller was Vice President. It was a cynical time, a time ripe for satire. And with rock stars fading into post-sixties dissolution, a time ripe for comedians. All they needed was for someone to provide a forum.

# CHAPTER 3

# Herb

Lorne and Ebersol saw each other again in January 1975, spending an evening watching a performance of Kentucky Fried Theater in a ramshackle warehouse near Century City. Lorne's wife, Rosie Shuster, came along too, but Lorne didn't introduce her as his wife, and Ebersol, to his later embarrassment, tried to hustle her.

By this time Ebersol's forty-pilot idea had been toned down at the behest of his superiors in New York. He was working instead on a "wheel" concept of variety shows that would have rotating hosts and air on alternate weeks of the month. But he wasn't having much luck putting those together, either. With the May affiliates convention drawing nearer, NBC president Herb Schlosser began to grow impatient.

Schlosser, forty-eight, had been elevated from head of the television network to president of the National Broadcasting Company the year before. A Phi Beta Kappa graduate of Princeton University and a graduate of Yale Law School, he was an average- looking man who had an air of not being average at all. Charming, urbane, and soft-spoken, he was very much a businessman of the Eastern Establishment. He was known as an ambitious executive skilled in the art of corporate politics who liked to socialize with powerful friends, among them Henry Kissinger. Schlosser sometimes chuckled that it was he who introduced Kissinger to the actress Jill St. John.

At a staff meeting in early February, Schlosser said that he disapproved of Ebersol's "wheel" idea because it wouldn't build any viewer loyalty as a series. He also thought it too similar to a late- night series ABC was experimenting with at the time called *Wide World of Entertainment*. What Schlosser had in mind, he said, was something closer to the tradition of the *Today* and *Tonight* shows, both developed at NBC in the early 1950s by the legendary programming genius Sylvester (Pat) Weaver. Schlosser had already followed in Pat Weaver's footsteps by developing, in 1973, Tom Snyder's *Tomorrow* show, the first network series to air after 1:00, a.m. Now he was looking for something else along the same lines: a program that would open up a new time period and lay claim to it becoming in the process what Schlosser called "a little business" that would keep making money forever. We have *Today*, *Tonight*, and *Tomorrow*, he said. Let's do a show called *Saturday Night*.

For the next week or so, Schlosser and his aides discussed various alternatives for what *Saturday Night* could be. On February 11, Schlosser drafted a memo combining those ideas with his own and with Ebersol's plans for a variety wheel. Although Schlosser later admitted that the show he ended up getting was quite different from the show he'd envisioned, if there was ever a blueprint for *Saturday Night*, this was it.

"I would like a thoroughgoing analysis done on a new program concept called '*Saturday Night*,'" the memo read. "This would be an effort to create a new and exciting program. '*Saturday Night*' should originate from the RCA building in New York City, if possible live, from the same studio where we did the *Tonight Show* or perhaps from 8H." (Aside from the connection to the *Tonight Show*, which originally aired from New York, and to *Today*, which still did, Schlosser was looking to make use of some of the studio space sitting idle, and eating up overhead, within NBC's headquarters. It had also been suggested that broadcasting the show live would encourage affiliates to carry it live, so the station lineup wouldn't be split between Saturday and Sunday, as it had been for the *Tonight Show* reruns.)

The memo continued: "It would be a variety show, but it would have certain characteristics. It should be young and bright. It should have a distinctive look, a distinctive set and a distinctive sound. ... We should attempt to use the show to develop new television personalities. We should seek to get different hosts who might do anywhere from one to eight shows depending on our evaluation of each host. It should be a program where we can develop talent that

NBC President Herb Schlosser, whose call for a new late-night program led to the creation of *Saturday Night*, and whose support helped it survive. © *NBC*

could move into prime time. ... It would be a great place to use people like Rich Little, Joe Namath [both recently signed to NBC contracts] and others. ... The show should not only seek to develop new young talent, but it should get a reputation as a tryout place for talent." (Schlosser didn't mention it on paper, but he was also thinking of developing personalities who could take over the *Tonight Show* should Johnny Carson ever decide he'd rather do something else.) "With proper production and promotion, '*Saturday Night*' can become a major show in television that people will talk about. It can carve out its own audience and increase sets in use [the number of TV sets in use during the time period] if we do a good job on it. I would like to have a meeting this week to discuss the project."

According to many people who worked with Schlosser at the time, memos such as these were dispatched with some regularity from his office, and were not always well received. "Herb," said one executive who worked for him, "was always writing memos saying, 'Why don't we look into this? Why don't we look into that?' That was his style." Other executives add that Schlosser was anxious to make his mark with some program innovation, and *Saturday Night* was but one of many ideas he tried. "Herb was running for president of the world at that point," said Julian Goodman, who as chairman of NBC was Schlosser's boss, "and he was casting about in all different directions for a breakthrough." Also mentioned was the fact that Schlosser was not known as a man with a particular flair for comedy. He had come up through NBC's ranks as a lawyer and a negotiator, and during his tenure as head of programming NBC had maintained its reputation as the network with the least comedy on its schedule. The principal exception was *Laugh-In*, with which Schlosser was immensely proud to have been associated.

Nevertheless, Schlosser's memos, coming as they did from the president's office, tended to get things moving within the company, and various executives were soon calling Dick Ebersol, asking him what he was going to do with this new show called *Saturday Night*. One afternoon a couple of days after the memo made the rounds, Ebersol was sitting in Marvin Antonowsky's office with Antonowsky and Dave Tebet. They asked who Ebersol had in mind to produce the show. Off the top of his head, he threw out two names. One was his friend Don Ohlmeyer, Roone Arledge's other surrogate son at ABC Sports, who'd handled the bulk of the production jobs while Ebersol took care of the business end. The other was the young producer who had so impressed Ebersol in California, Lorne Michaels. Later that day Ebersol called Lorne, explained the new plan for the show, and set an appointment for him to meet Antonowsky and Tebet on their next trip to the Coast.

Two weeks later Lorne arrived home sometime after 2:00 a.m. to find an urgent message from Ebersol: His bosses' schedule had changed; Lorne was to be at the Polo Lounge in the Beverly Hills Hotel at seven-thirty that morning. Seven-thirty wasn't Lorne's favorite time of day; he lived rock-and-roll hours and seldom rose before ten. But he knew the meeting was a necessary nuisance. Antonowsky and Tebet had to meet him to make sure he wasn't, as Ebersol put it, "Genghis Khan with a heroin habit." In 1975 you could never tell.

# CHAPTER 4

# Lorne

Lorne Michaels was very much a child of the television generation, and something of an angry young man of the sixties as well. He was living that February at the Chateau Marmont hotel off Sunset Boulevard in Hollywood, having moved from Toronto permanently two years before. His wife, Rosie Shuster, had stayed behind in Canada for a time before joining him in Los Angeles. Like many couples in the early seventies, they'd had their troubles adjusting to the unsettling beginnings of the women's movement, and Rosie, unhappily for Lorne, had wanted some time on her own.

The Chateau Marmont wasn't the most luxurious hotel in town, but it was probably the hippest—discreet rather than flashy, with just the right touch of faded California elegance and a few glamorous ghosts. A loose amalgamation of sixties survivors passed through the Chateau in those days, some who'd made it in music, movies, or TV, many others more or less on the make, everyone trying to have as good a time as possible in the process.

Lorne was the sort of man women described as "cute"—sweet-faced and slight of build, intensely funny but, beneath the jokes, intensely serious. He was also very smart, and something of a dreamer. The Hawaiian shirts and reindeer-patterned ski sweaters he wore were casual but carefully chosen. His dark hair, which he sometimes let grow well past his shoulders, had a flyaway quality, as if he'd just come out of the wind. There were periodic Zapata moustaches, too. Gilda Radner, who'd known Lorne in Toronto, used to say that when he'd put on a few pounds, he looked a little like David Crosby of Crosby, Stills, and Nash.

Lorne possessed what one of his friends called "a catalytic personality." He had a talent for gathering interesting and disparate friends around him and for offering himself as their center. It was always comfortable dropping by his room at the end of the day. Invariably a few people would be there, talking and smoking joints. Later, everyone would go out to dinner at Mr. Chow's or Tana's, and then it would be back to Lorne's for more smoke and talk far into the night. It had been the same in Canada. It struck Lorne once when he looked around a roomful of his friends in Toronto that the only thing they had in common was that they all knew him. Rosie Shuster used to say that as a child Lorne once spent a year without furniture in his living room and had been overcompensating for it ever since. He loved the idea of the salon.

Among the regulars at the Chateau were actress Margot Kidder, a friend of Lorne and Rosie's from Canada, and John Head, an English filmmaker and critic they'd met in London. Joe Boyd, a record producer whose artists included the English folk groups Fairport Convention and The Incredible String Band, came by a lot, as did Tom Schiller, another filmmaker, who enjoyed a certain cachet by nature of his living as a surrogate son with the novelist Henry Miller in Pacific Palisades. A third filmmaker friend was Gary Weis, who had, among many other adventures, been a cameraman at the Altamont rock festival, smoked a joint with Charles Manson, and produced, with Joe Boyd and John Head, a documentary on Jimi Hendrix.

It was Weis who scored the capsules of powdered psilocybin mushrooms that he, Lorne, and John Head would take at Topanga Beach or out in the desert east of Los Angeles. There were moments during those trips that the three of them would end up rolling on the ground, laughing so hard they thought, as stoned people sometimes do, they might never be able to stop.

What distinguished Lorne from his friends more than anything was his love of television. Lorne not only worked in TV, he watched it, constantly. Barbara Burns, a friend who lived in the Chateau, says the set was always on when she came to his room, tuned to whatever comedy show was on at the time. Lorne was the only person she knew who religiously watched the *Tonight Show*. It was said that when Lorne moved from his room on the second floor of the Chateau to one on the seventh, he had to be picked up and carried upstairs in his chair during a commercial.

He analyzed comedy endlessly, theorizing, with an acid head's attention to the underlying dynamics of it all, about what worked, what didn't, and why.

One of his favorite themes was the expressionistic barrenness of the old *Honeymooners* set; later he would become an advocate of realism, saying that humor derived from the one off-center element in a setting of absolute normality. Herb Sargent, a longtime producer of television comedy who worked with Lorne in Hollywood, remembers Lorne sitting cross-legged on the floor during office bull sessions, listening in silence, soaking things in. Then he'd start talking, and the thoughts would pour out for hours.

Lorne had learned during his brief career in network television that television wasn't particularly interested in what he had to say, and, despite his relative success, that lesson left him with his fair share of bitterness toward the business. One of his mentors in Hollywood was Tom Schiller's father, Bob Schiller, a television comedy writer whose credits included *I Love Lucy*, *The Red Skelton Show*, and *Maude*. Lorne would spend weekends at the Schillers' house at the beach, and Bob Schiller remembers Lorne worrying obsessively about whether he would ever be satisfied working in TV. "Restlessness, restlessness was all I saw," Schiller says.

Part of the problem was that for most of his time in Hollywood Lorne was a nobody, which was not the way it had been in Canada. His given name was Lorne Lipowitz. He grew up in the affluent Toronto suburb of Forest Hill, the son of a successful furrier who died when Lorne was fourteen. Friends who would subsequently have occasion to analyze him say it was his father's death that prompted Lorne's need to become a surrogate father for others, and to find surrogate fathers for himself.

One of the first was Rosie Shuster's father, Frank, who was the straight-man half of the comedy team Wayne and Shuster. Wayne and Shuster were legends in Canada and they performed often in the States on *The Ed Sullivan Show* and other TV variety programs. After his father died, Lorne became a sort of older son in the Shuster family. It was at the urging of Rosie's parents that Lorne changed his name—they didn't think "Lorne Lipowitz" had the ring to it their future son-in-law would need in his show business career, and Rosie's mother also couldn't bear the thought of her daughter becoming Rosalind Lipowitz. Among the alternatives Lorne and Rosie jokingly considered before settling on Lorne Michaels were Lorne Ranger and Lorne Zwelk.

Early on, Lorne showed an affinity for being in charge of things. One of his first part-time jobs was at a Toronto department store named Eaton's. A friend recalls that by default Lorne became assistant manager of the sweater department, and he discovered that he liked it; calling the shots was not only easy for him, but fun. At Forest Hill High School he became a mentor for Rosie Shuster when she was fourteen and he was sixteen, drawing her out of her adolescent shell. "It's hard to be a mentor when you're sixteen," says a friend who knew them both, "but he was. He attracted people who needed an umbrella of confidence and support. He always seemed older than he was, and he always acted like he'd done something before even if he hadn't."

Another quality of Lorne's that people remember was that he was an enthusiast, completely absorbed in and passionate about whatever he was doing. "Wherever he was, it was always Broadway," a friend who knew him remembers. He was no different when the sixties came along. Like millions of his peers, his passions became the Beatles, psychedelic drugs, and the New Vision they proclaimed. "It was always the Beatles, acid, and mushrooms," that same friend says. "Take this button and you'll be smart. … Why live life on the surface?"

* * *

Lorne had been aiming himself toward show business at least as early as fifteen, when at Camp Timberlane in Ontario he and his friend Howard Shore organized, first as campers and later as counselors, productions of *Bye Bye Birdie* and *The Fantastiks*. While attending University College in Toronto, Lorne co-wrote and directed the 1964 *UC Follies*, a mixture of songs and satirical sketches that was one of many early prototypes for *Saturday Night*.

While working on the *Follies*, Lorne met Hart Pomerantz, a former law student who for the next several years would be his comedy partner. They developed a stand-up act, Lorne the straight man, Hart a frenetic character in the Mel Brooks mold. In 1967, Hart and Lorne were hired as writers and performers on a Canadian Broadcasting Corporation radio comedy show called *Five Nights a Week at This Time*. Like Tommy Smothers that year, they were filled with youth and passion and they set out, as Lorne laughingly put it later, to "bring down the government" with their satire. But the CBC was the government's network, there were fights with management, and eventually Hart and Lorne departed.

During this period they were also submitting jokes to Woody Allen in New York, but Allen was working more in movies than stand-up by then and he never used any of Hart and Lorne's material. He did, however, call Lorne once to tell him that a joke he'd written was "brilliant." Soon after that, Lorne and Hart headed for Hollywood, and Lorne often said that the inspiration from Woody's compliment was one of the few things that kept him going for the next several years. (Lorne's joke was that he'd become obsessed with the notion that somewhere in the world there was a person having the exact same thought he was having at exactly the same moment. He decided to call that person, but the line was busy.)

Lorne and Hart's initiation into the ways of American television came as junior writers on an NBC comedy-variety series called *The Beautiful Phyllis Diller Show*. Bob Schiller was one of the writers, Bob Finkel the producer. Everyone was enthusiastic before the show went on, congratulating themselves on how great it was going to be. Rosie Shuster tried in vain to be the voice of reality, telling Lorne the material was awful. She was right: *The Beautiful Phyllis Diller Show* was canceled after nine weeks on the air, a shockingly quick demise in those days.

Hart and Lorne moved on to *Laugh-In*, again as junior writers. Mostly they wrote dialogues for Dan Rowan and Dick Martin, but whatever they submitted immediately disappeared into the comedy Mixmaster that is standard equipment in network TV. Lorne and Hart submitted their jokes to head writer Paul Keyes. If Keyes didn't reject them outright, as he automatically did their jokes about Richard Nixon, he'd pass them on to other, more senior writers. They'd rewrite them and give them back to Keyes, who would rewrite them again before giving them to the performers, who would rewrite them some more. Writers weren't encouraged to come to the studio on taping days, so the first time Hart and Lorne would see their material performed was when they watched the show at their motel in Toluca Lake, near Burbank. Sometimes they recognized little pieces of their ideas.

The whole process was a division of labor and a dilution of personal involvement that Lorne found despicable, and he vowed then it wouldn't be that way if he were the producer.

Lorne got that chance in 1969 when the CBC offered him and Hart their own series. They returned to Canada and produced four specials a year for the next three and a half years. The specials aired under various titles, among them *The Hart and Lorne Terrific* Hour and *Today Makes Me Nervous*, in the same Sunday nighttime slot Wayne and Shuster had occupied for many years. They were very much forerunners of *Saturday Night*. Hart and Lorne, the front men, were backed by a repertory company, musical guests such as Cat Stevens and James Taylor, and guest comedians such as Dan Aykroyd and his partner, Valri Bromfield, who had a radio show together.

Plainly in evidence as well on Hart and Lorne's specials was the influence of England's Monty Python, whose comedy series started running on the CBC in 1970, four years before it appeared on public television in the States. To Lorne, Monty Python was a sign of the New Millennium every bit as earth shattering as the Beatles. Like the Beatles, Python not only had humor and style, they had nerve: They dared to break the rules and got away with it. Python was hip and smart, and they didn't underestimate their audience. They turned traditional comedy inside out, making jokes in the middle of sketches about the sketches themselves, mixing film segments with videotape segments, ending sketches in the middle and moving on to something else, never stopping even as the credits rolled. "It was miraculous to me, a revelation," Lorne said later. "It seemed that once again the winds of change were blowing from England."

England's Monty Python, whose freeform TV comedy was a major influence on Lorne Michaels and on *Saturday Night*.
*Courtesy of PBS*

Hart and Lorne's shows were a minor hit in Canada, especially with the press and young viewers, but the two partners were having troubles between themselves. Lorne wasn't satisfied with being the straight man, and he started devoting more of his energies to producing, taking on other CBC projects in addition to the Hart and Lorne shows. He liked being in control of his work for a change, and he devoted himself to developing the production expertise that would enable him to maintain that control. Hart, those who knew him say, began to resent that, feeling he was being shunted aside into the Wacky Partner role while Lorne was ingratiating himself with the network. He and Lorne started alternating as producers of their specials, and by 1972 they parted company, not on cordial terms.

Lorne could easily have stayed at the CBC, but he fell prey to a well-known Canadian psychological phenomenon, which holds that, as marvelous a place as Canada is to learn your craft, the true test of talent is in the United States. By then, Sandy Wernick was representing him in the States, and Wernick kept calling to say that if Lorne continued to pass up chances for work, there weren't going to be any more chances. Lorne brooded for a while in Toronto and started flying back and forth to Hollywood. It was during one of these trips that Lorne pitched his idea for a comedy show aimed at the television generation to Herb Schlosser's chief programming aide, Larry White.

Lorne, accompanied by Sandy Wernick and Bob Finkel, brought with him to White's office in Burbank some clips from the Hart and Lorne shows and from *Monty Python's Flying Circus*. White and his assistants laughed heartily as they watched, but when the screening ended, White stood up and said, "What are you, crazy? We can't do this stuff."

Stunned, Wernick said, "But you guys loved it!"

"No one will understand what you're doing!" White replied. Lorne struggled through another unsuccessful network project—a short lived series starring the comedy team Burns and Schreiberthat was, in Lorne's view, "mangled" by ABC—before his luck finally changed. In the fall of 1973 a mutual friend introduced him to Lily Tomlin, who was just starting to produce her second prime-time special for CBS.

Tomlin was one of the two performers from *Laugh-In* (Goldie Hawn was the other) whose reputations had continued to grow after the series went off the air. When Lorne met Tomlin she was, along with Richard Pryor, at the top of the hip comedy pantheon, respected for her unusual characters, her commitment to new comedy forms, and her feminist politics. During their first meeting Lorne and Lily talked for almost seven hours, and Lorne was hired as a writer. Their professional relationship nearly ended about ten days later.

Tomlin is known for being a perfectionist. Along with her longtime collaborator and companion, Jane Wagner, she was firmly in control of her specials and not especially flexible about what she wanted to do. Lorne at first failed to appreciate that. Lily was irritated when Lorne didn't show up for work until after noon, and she liked it even less that he then sat around, seemingly for hours, analyzing comedy, distracting the other writers. Worse, his theories of comedy clashed with hers. Tomlin wanted as much detail in her sets as possible, while Lorne was in his *Honeymooners* minimalist period. Lorne also resisted, Tomlin says, Jane Wagner's plan to produce some sketches live, in front of an audience, in order to avoid using the canned laughter the network was demanding. "Live TV is never coming back," Tomlin remembers Lorne saying. "With all the technology it just isn't going to happen."

Lily's and Lorne's personalities also clashed. She found him "pretentious" and felt he was "subtly undermining" her in conversations. Tomlin told her manager, Irene Pinn, that Lorne had to go. Pinn called Lorne into her office to break the news. Over the course of the next several hours, Lorne talked his way out of it. He told Pinn he was used to being "the golden boy" in Canada, and that working for someone else was a hard adjustment to make. But he promised to make it. Pinn and Jane Wagner persuaded Tomlin to give him another try. From then on, Lorne carefully deferred to Tomlin, although he sometimes had to take long walks in the parking lot to keep himself in check.

Lorne and Lily never became close friends, but they gradually developed a healthy working relationship, mainly, Irene Pinn says, because he proved himself so utterly committed to the work. It was rare to find someone whose standards were as high as Lily's, but Lorne's were. He was rewarded by being named co-producer, with Jane Wagner, of Lily's next two specials, both of which aired on ABC.

The writers and performers assembled by Tomlin, Wagner, and Lorne for Lily's specials represented, more than any network show since the Smothers Brothers', a gathering of the underground comedy tribes. Many who worked on them would end up, sooner or later, on *Saturday Night*, including, besides Lorne, Rosie Shuster, Gary Weis, Laraine Newman (from The Groundlings), Herb Sargent (the producer of Lorne's first Lily special), Christopher Guest (of the *Lampoon* shows in New York), and writers Matt Neuman (of the *Chicken Little Comedy Hour*), Barbara Gallagher, and Marilyn Miller. Earl Pomerantz, Hart's brother, also worked on the Tomlin specials, as did Valri Bromfield, who by then had ended her partnership with Dan Aykroyd. Ken Shapiro of *The Groove Tube* came aboard briefly, but quickly left to take his job at Paramount Pictures.

Tomlin's specials were daring—self-consciously so. They seemed to have *experimental* written all over them. There were surrealistic pieces, mood pieces, and political pieces that were several steps beyond what the Smothers Brothers had attempted. Not surprisingly, there were also prolonged battles over that material with both CBS and ABC. CBS program executive Perry Lafferty, who had also battled the Smothers Brothers, waged a spirited campaign to keep Tomlin and her people somewhere near the boundaries of conventional television. At one point he stormed onto the set to stop in mid-taping a sketch in which guest star Richard Pryor played a junkie.

Like Larry White at NBC, Lafferty thought viewers wouldn't understand this strange new humor. Every time he saw Tomlin, he'd wag his finger at her and say, "Remember Podunk!" Lafferty was supported in his resistance by his boss, Fred Silverman, who had replaced Mike Dann as head of CBS programming. Silverman let it be known often during production how displeased he was with the way things were going. Lily was later told Silverman took one look at her second special and called it "a $360,000 jerk-off."

Tomlin's specials were successful enough in the ratings, especially with young urban viewers. But she had been marked as a troublemaker, and, to Lorne's deep disappointment, neither CBS nor ABC continued them as a series. Lily went off to make the movie *Nashville*, and Lorne, once again, was out of work. He signed on to do four specials with comedian Flip Wilson but quit after the first, beaten down once again by battles with the network.

By February of 1975 he'd accepted Ken Shapiro's offer to write a movie script for Paramount, thinking he might leave the television business altogether.

CHAPTER 5

# Breakfast at the Polo Lounge

Lorne didn't know it, but by the time he reported to the Polo Lounge to be scrutinized by Marvin Antonowsky and Dave Tebet, he was Ebersol's sole remaining candidate to be the producer of *Saturday Night*. The executives had already met with Ebersol's other choice, Don Ohlmeyer, and Ohlmeyer had turned the job down, in large part because Antonowsky had spent much of their meeting telling Ohlmeyer he didn't think Herb Schlosser's new show had a chance in hell of succeeding. Lorne would soon discover for himself that *Saturday Night* did not enjoy the enthusiastic support of the programming executives behind it.

Dave Tebet was the eldest of the foursome that morning. His exact age was uncertain because he periodically revised it downward in NBC's executive biographies, but he must have been somewhere in his mid-sixties. At any age, Tebet was one of the great behind-the- scenes figures of television, a power broker who had been pulling network strings for almost as long as there had been network strings to pull.

Tebet had the fireplug physique and gravelly voice of a Mafia enforcer. In the early fifties he'd been a press agent for Max Liebman, the producer of Sid Caesar's classic *Saturday Night* comedy series, *Your*

Dave Tebet, NBC's "Mr. Talent," in charge of keeping Johnny Carson, among other performers, happy. © NBC

56

*Show of Shows.* In 1955, General David Sarnoff, chairman of RCA, installed his son Robert as president of NBC, which the elder Sarnoff had founded as an RCA subsidiary in 1926. To help guide his way in the new world of television, Robert (called Bobbie behind his back by most of those who worked with him) surrounded himself in the executive suite with two unlikely aides: Dave Tebet and a man named Al Rylander. Both were rough- edged operators by the genteel standards previously maintained in NBC's executive suites. "It was," said an executive there at the time, "like a B movie: Bobbie phumphering around up there with these two street guys with him, giving him advice and getting him honorary degrees at universities you'd never heard of."

Tebet used this power base to establish himself as NBC's chief liaison to its stars, a key position in an era when stars made television, not the other way around. When a performer's series was canceled, it was Dave Tebet who called to break the news delicately, ensuring that the star's relationship with the network wasn't damaged irreparably; when a major star was getting out of hand in a Broadway dive, breaking up the place with her lesbian lover and passing out under a table, it was Dave Tebet who arrived to pay off the manager and get the unconscious performer into a taxi; when one of the network's important supporting players fooled around with young girls and a mother was threatening to sue, Dave Tebet kept it out of the papers.

He was an indispensable fixer, handling these affairs with such acuity that over twenty years he became known as NBC's "Mr. Talent." The walls of his office bathroom were literally covered with pictures of himself alongside most of Hollywood's major stars of the fifties, and he enjoyed an empire within NBC that was the envy of almost every executive there, including not a few above him in rank. "He operated," said one, "as a law unto himself." His annual expense account was rumored to be well into six figures and he lived in permanent suites paid for by NBC at the Dorchester Hotel in London, the Hotel Dorset in New York, and the Beverly Hills Hotel in Los Angeles. He was generous to those who helped him; it was said Dave Tebet gave away TV sets (RCA sets, of course) like Rockefeller gave away dimes. His office was a dim, opulent sitting room filled with the finest Chinese art. There was no desk; Tebet's job didn't require one.

By 1975, Tebet's power within NBC was beginning to erode. A new generation of stars was coming along, stars Tebet often hadn't met and didn't understand, and Bobbie Sarnoff was about to resign under pressure from the board of directors of RCA. But Dave Tebet knew nothing if not how to land gracefully on his feet. He had already cultivated a new niche by aligning himself with the only performer at NBC whose power almost exceeded the president's— Johnny Carson. Tebet was becoming something of a personal network executive for Carson, which is undoubtedly how Carson had heard so much about *Saturday Night* before he'd met Ebersol and Michaels.

If Dave Tebet was a character out of television's rough-and-tumble beginnings, then Marvin Antonowsky was almost chillingly a man of its up-and-coming corporate future. Like Ebersol, he'd recently moved to NBC from ABC. (It was Antonowsky, in fact, who'd introduced Ebersol to Herb Schlossser.) Antonowsky had been ABC's vice president in charge of research, and he was one of the first modern research experts to play a powerful role in the selection of network programs. As television's advertising revenues soared in the 1970s, network programmers became less and less inclined to base their decisions on instinct—either their own or that of the creative types who actually produced their shows. Hence the development, by Antonowsky and others, of "concept testing," where the viability of program ideas, performers, even titles was measured, supposedly scientifically, by polling average viewers. Sometimes these viewers were contacted at random by telephone or gathered in "focus groups" with trained interviewers. Sometimes they were seated in screening rooms, watching shows and turning knobs that registered when they were stimulated and when they were bored. The results were fed into a computer, which would spit out thick analysis reports that were used to advise producers about the programs they should make and how they should make them.

Antonowsky himself was as cool as the computers he used in his work. Tall and lanky, with slumped shoulders, he inspected people rather than looked at them, and his handshake was one of the limpest in the business. Soon after he'd joined NBC, Antonowsky had embarked on a campaign to depose the network's current head of programming, Larry White. According to many executives who witnessed it, Antonowsky pursued this campaign with skillful determination, undercutting Herb Schlosser's support of White by, as one observer put it, "pouring poison" in Schlosser's ear about White's every decision. In January, Schlosser had transferred White permanently from New York to Hollywood. Ostensibly this put the head of programs closer to the producers of those programs, but everyone in the network knew it was really Larry White's first step out the door. Within four months of Antonowsky's meeting with Lorne and Ebersol, he would win the job he coveted.

Ebersol and Michaels knew when they arrived at the Polo Lounge that morning that Antonowsky and Tebet had other, more important matters to think about than *Saturday Night*—the time of the meeting alone told them that. For the executives, a new late-night show was hardly a matter of life and death. Its budget would be small and its potential nearly meaningless. Hardly anyone was watching television at that hour, and Antonowsky was of the opinion that this show wasn't going to change that state of affairs. The prime-time ratings were the ratings that counted anyway. If *Saturday Night* failed, well, it was Herb Schlosser's pet project. A bit rash, perhaps, but no serious harm done. Dick Ebersol could take the fall.

Thus, as Ebersol and Lorne ran through their ideas for the show, Antonowsky and Tebet barely heard them. Their eyes kept shifting from their corner table to the entrance of the dining room. Then, as now, the Polo Lounge was one of the wheeling-and-dealing hubs of show business, and every time an important executive from one of the studios walked in, Antonowsky and Tebet jumped to their feet, waving greetings.

"Hello, Stanley!" one or the other would say. "How *are* you? How's the wife? When are we going to get together to talk about that project?"

It happened time and again, and each time Ebersol and Lorne just looked at each other, bemused, picking at the food on their plates and talking quietly about what they were going to say next. After a while they were chatting about what they would do once the meeting ended.

Tebet and Antonowsky, when they were seated, did have a few comments to make about *Saturday Night*. They suggested that impressionist Rich Little, who had recently been signed to an NBC contract, would be a marvelous host for the first show. Tebet also thought the University of Southern California marching band would be a great, offbeat choice as musical guest. They blanched when Lorne said he'd like to book Richard Pryor. Lorne, presenting his ideas with his usual air of confident reasonableness, knew enough not to use words like *underground* or *radical* in describing what he intended to do; he substituted *innovative* and *youthful* instead. He did say he wanted the show to have a spontaneous, casual look. *Saturday Night*'s viewers should get the impression, Lorne said, that the network had gone home and a bunch of kids had slipped into the studio to put on a show.

Fine, fine, Antonowsky and Tebet said. Then they jumped up to greet another executive passing by. Lorne had, in a fashion, been approved.

\* \* \*

Lorne wasn't surprised by Antonowsky's and Tebet's behavior at the meeting—to him it was network business as usual. But for just that reason he found himself, now that the job was his, surprisingly ambivalent about taking it. He had his movie deal with Ken Shapiro at Paramount. He liked the idea for the script he'd be writing, which was based on the true story of a young computer wizard who ripped off the telephone company by ordering truckloads of expensive equipment and then selling it back to Ma Bell.

More than that, though, Lorne was tired of fighting the networks. *Saturday Night* was a year's commitment for who knew what sort of nightmare. It bothered him that NBC, not an outside production company, would own the show. That meant he'd be an employee of the network, not the most sympathetic of bosses. Nor did he trust Dick Ebersol. Yes, Dick was young and his hair was long. But he was also an archetypical Ivy League WASP, Connecticut upper- crust, a sports guy who found himself with a variety show to produce and not many ideas of how to go about it. "He's putting," Lorne thought to himself, "all his eggs in one basket, and I'm the eggs *and* the basket." It was also clear that, despite his hair and his youth, Ebersol was far more ambitious than hip. He was, in fact, vastly, transparently ambitious, and Lorne Michaels was not the only one to notice. Marvin Antonowsky called Ebersol "the WASP Sammy Glick."

Still, Lorne thought *Saturday Night* definitely had the potential to be the show he'd always dreamed of doing. He told Rosie Shuster he liked the idea of late night: It was closer to the edge of the subconscious, more dangerous. Interesting things happened there, breakthroughs sometimes—Jack Paar came to mind. New York, too, was nearer that ragged edge than Hollywood. And going out on the network airwaves live was a big step closer still. Lorne had learned on the Tomlin specials that live production lessened the network's opportunity for meddling. With *Saturday Night* it meant he wouldn't even have to make a pilot. As for Ebersol, perhaps his inexperience and ambition could be turned to advantage. He wouldn't know enough to interfere too much, and he'd have as big a stake in making the show a success as Lorne would.

So Lorne agreed to do *Saturday Night*, although his manager, Bernie Brillstein, held out for certain conditions. Most important of these was that Lorne be guaranteed a paycheck for seventeen shows. Forever afterward this would be interpreted in the press as a commitment by NBC to leave *Saturday Night* on the air for seventeen shows, but that's not the way it works in network television. Any show can be canceled at any time. Lorne simply wanted a guarantee that if *Saturday Night* was canceled he wouldn't have moved to New York only to be stranded there with no money coming in.

NBC's negotiators resisted that condition for a while, then haggled about Lorne's salary. Eventually NBC agreed to pay him $115,000 for his first year on the show, $145,000 the second year, and $175,000 the third. This was not a great sum of money considering the fact that Lorne, if he chose to, could stay in Hollywood and pick up $100,000 for a few months' work producing some specials.

Lorne accepted the deal on April 1, 1975—April Fool's Day— and flew to New York. NBC put him up in the Plaza Hotel and gave him a temporary office on the fourth floor, down the hall from Ebersol, Antonowsky, and Tebet. It turned out to be Larry White's old office, vacated when White moved to the coast. Lorne glanced into the desk drawer his first day there and found a *Racing Form* and a few old Maalox tablets. He sat in White's big leather chair and wondered what he'd got- ten himself into.

\* \* \*

Lorne and Ebersol still had a couple of exercises to go through before the show would be finally approved. The first was setting the production budget. They spent most of the next few days figuring out how many per- formers they'd need, how many writers, how many musicians, how much rehearsal time—a long shopping list of details. They were making things up as they went along. Ebersol had no idea what sort of budget the show should have, and budgets were not one of Lorne's fortes either. They both adopted a policy that the less said to NBC the better: It would be harder for the network to question the show as long as it remained undefined.

Ebersol and Lorne took their plans to Don Carswell, the network's chief financial controller. Carswell and two aides listened to their descrip- tion of the show, and Lorne once again did a masterful job of imitating a man who knew just what he wanted. One of Carswell's aides took notes, and after a few more conversations with Lorne and Ebersol he translated it all into a budget for *Saturday Night* of $180,000 per program. This was about $30,000 more than Ebersol and Lorne had expected. Then, to their dismay, Don Carswell called them back into his office.

Carswell had reviewed the figures and decided the budget would have to be lower: $134,600 per show would be more in line with the advertising revenue *Saturday Night* could be expected to bring in. Carswell was projecting that thirty-second commercials on the show wouldn't sell for more than $8,000 apiece, which translated into another vote of no confidence in *Saturday Night*. "I want you to know that we're going into this thing at a loss," Carswell told Ebersol and Lorne. He pointed out that NBC was risking the $20,000 or so in profits it earned from the Carson reruns each weekend, adding that the network "won't see a dime of profit on this thing for at least a year."

So $134,600 per show it was. This amount, an NBC financial plan- ner would later remark, was roughly comparable to what it would take to produce "a cross between the *Tonight Show* and *Meet the Press*." No matter. It was a budget that would never be met.

The following Thursday, Lorne and Ebersol presented the show to Herb Schlosser and the heads of all the network's major divisions: research, sales, finance, negotiations, affiliate relations, and public relations. Tebet and Antonowsky were also there. The meeting was held in NBC's oak-paneled Art Deco boardroom, where a butler was waiting to serve the executives as they arrived.

Lorne wore his green corduroy jacket and Hawaiian shirt, rejecting a suit and tie on the theory that the executives expected him to represent the audience he was trying to reach. He impressed one of those in the room as "something of a hippie," while someone else thought he looked like "a serious-minded college professor who was very interested in his subject." He ran through another vague description of the show: comedy for young people with a repertory group, a band, musical guests, and guest hosts. He dropped a few names of those he'd worked with in the past, including Lily Tomlin and Richard Pryor, and told a couple of amusing stories about them. Dave Tebet brought up Rich Little and the USC marching band again, and Herb Schlosser suggested Bob Hope.

It occurred to Lorne that perhaps *Saturday Night* was being perceived by the brass as NBC's version of *Up with People*, a relentlessly cheerful touring group of apple-cheeked kids who sang inspirational songs and danced around in crew-necked sweaters. Knowing he risked a backlash if he surprised the network too severely once the show went on the air, he emphasized that he wanted "raw, disposable" comedy, and that the format would have to evolve over time. "I know the ingredients but not the proportions," he said. "We will always be experimenting, on the air, responding to our own mistakes."

Several of the executives present remember that Lorne's presentation was "mysterious" but somehow inspiring. "He seemed to have a clear idea of what he wanted without communicating to us exactly what it was," one of them said. "He conveyed a real sense of excitement about the show." This was precisely the effect Lorne hoped to have. "I was," he remembers, "absolutely convinced of the rightness of what I was doing."

The major resistance in the meeting came from Bill Rubens, vice-president in charge of research. Rubens's department had completed the usual program analysis and was projecting that *Saturday Night* would achieve a rating and share of audience about equal to that of the *Tonight Show* reruns. The demographics—the composition of the audience by age group—might be slightly younger, but that was about it. "This show is a very high risk from a research standpoint," Ebersol remembers Rubens saying, "because I don't believe you can get enough eighteen-to-twenty-fours [eighteen- to twenty-four-year-old viewers] to stay home on *Saturday Night*s to watch this show."

Ebersol argued that *Saturday Night* would attract new viewers to the time period, but Rubens didn't buy it, saying there wouldn't be enough of them to justify the cost of the show. There was some discussion of the point. Don Carswell expressed concern about the budget, and there was discussion of that. Ebersol began to worry that if one more executive weighed in with reservations, a "brush fire" of dissent might sweep the meeting and the show might not be approved.

But Lorne's presentation had convinced Herb Schlosser. It had been Schlosser who laughed loudest at Lorne's jokes that afternoon, and when Lorne had said that he should have the mix of ingredients he wanted by the tenth show, Schlosser had said, "I'll watch show ten." Finally it was Herb Schlosser who overruled the doubters in the room. "I want a live variety show done from 8H," he said, "and these boys are going to give it to me."

## CHAPTER 6

# Enlightened Amateurs

After his meeting with Johnny Carson in May, Lorne decided to take one more trip to the desert.

He and Tom Schiller drove in Lorne's VW out Route 62 toward the Joshua Tree National Monument, Lorne steering with one hand and talking nonstop about the show, Schiller listening and nervously watching the road.

They took two $7-a-night rooms at the Joshua Tree Inn, a modest little twelve-unit, "earthquake-proof" brick and terra-cotta motel huddled on the highway in the middle of nowhere. Joshua Tree was well known among Los Angeles heads as a magical place, a vast moonscape dotted with towering cactus trees and clusters of giant boulders stretching away to the mountains on the horizon. The perfect setting for Lorne to eat some magic mushrooms, clear his head from the events of the last few months, and prepare for his new thrust in New York.

Lorne spent most of his time at Joshua Tree "formatting the format" of the show, thinking about how he would integrate all the different elements he wanted it to have, how to open the show, where the music would fit, how to accommodate the commercial breaks, how to pace it. Tom Schiller, who says he faked eating the mushrooms, marveled at how Lorne could sit by the pool and talk business on the phone with Dick Ebersol back in New York, nodding his head and saying, with authority, "Right, Dick ... right ... um hm."

Schiller had a mystical bent, and he was by nature an observer. Ever since he'd met Lorne he'd found him fascinating. Lorne's astrological sign, Schiller knew, was Scorpio, and Schiller had often thought how perfectly Lorne fit that sign of fire. Lorne's enthusiasm was so intense, so catching, Schiller sometimes felt engulfed by it.

As for himself, Schiller worried about whether or not he should postpone his filmmaking career, his art, to work in television with Lorne. The advice of his mentor, Henry Miller, kept ringing in his ears. "Don't do it, Tom, don't *do* it," Miller had said. "You were made for better things!"

Lorne, of course, was arguing in his usual persuasive manner in favor of it. Wrestling with the decision, Schiller wrote in his journal at Joshua Tree, "I'm being auditioned for this job as Lorne's assistant in New York—the NBC late-night show. All my dreams of power, wealth and TV glory seem to crystallize in images I imagine or am made to imagine: The RCA Building at 30 Rockefeller Plaza looms like neon magnets of the mind. Banks of gleaming Art Deco elevators ready to whisk me to the studio and offices of my choice ... dreams of fluffy seances of flittering talent and excitement open their hearts and purse strings to my imagination."

Later that day, still uncertain, Schiller threw the fortune-telling coins of the *I Ching*, asking, "Is this offer favorable? Will it harm my true direction and work?"

The hexagram he threw was "abundance." Be not sad, it said; blessing and fame draw near.

\* \* \*

Finding office space for the show on NBC's 17th floor was another potent omen from Tom Schiller's point of view.

For the better part of a month, Dan Sullivan, a dapper and amenable facilities executive, led Lorne, Ebersol, Schiller, and Gary Weis on a search in and around 30 Rockefeller Plaza. They'd inspected everything from an elegant but impractical suite in Radio City Music Hall to a torn-out floor filled with twisted girders and trash in the Exxon Building. When they discovered that half an entire floor within NBC's own headquarters was available, Sullivan couldn't believe it. Yes, it would be cramped, Sullivan repeatedly said, but offices overlooking the famous Rockefeller Center ice-skating rink and its magnificent gold statue of Prometheus occupied some of the most valuable real estate in the world.

Schiller was still in a state of shock at coming so quickly from the desert into the heart of the corporate beast in midtown Manhattan. When he looked out the window and saw the glittering statue below, it seemed to him one of those cosmic puns he never believed were entirely coincidental. Ah, Prometheus, he smiled. Bringer of fire.

\* \* \*

This, then, would be Lorne's salon, a gathering place for the best, most original and daring comic minds of the day. They would come, he said, from different cities and different schools of comedy and they would coalesce on 17 into something wonderful and new. During calls late at night to Rosie Shuster back in Los Angeles, he would tell her of his dreams for the show, and there would be talk of Paris in the twenties, even of a renaissance—visions too grand to be taken seriously, she knew, but that was the fantasy.

Lorne set out to find what he called "enlightened amateurs." He wanted nobody working by the timeworn TV comedy rules, no pre-conceptions about what could or couldn't be tried. Like *Monty Python*, *Saturday Night* was going to be something completely different, and to Lorne that ruled out hiring virtually anyone who had ever made a living in television. Director Dave Wilson and chief studio assistant Audrey Peart Dickman were among the very few people Lorne hired who had extensive experience in television, and he made it clear in his interviews with both that he wouldn't tolerate their laying down any old-fashioned rules to his people. Comedy, Lorne often said, is too important to be left to professionals.

In a sense this was economically imposed. NBC hadn't given *Saturday Night* a budget to pay for a show on anywhere near the scale Lorne had in mind unless the people he hired worked cheap. All the members of the repertory company were to be signed to identical five-year contracts, which Gilda Radner quickly dubbed "Mickey Rooney-Judy Garland deals" because they essentially turned the performers into indentured servants to the network. Each was to be paid $750 per show for most of the first year, with gradual increases that brought them up to a grand total of $1,600 per show in the fifth year. With payments at union scale for rerun shows, that meant the cast members in the first season would make between $25,000 and $30,000, an absurdly paltry sum by television standards. Lorne's policy on the cast was "favored nations," meaning they would all be paid the same, and that if one of them even-tually negotiated a better deal, they would all get the same raise. The writers were paid different, but lesser, salaries. The so-called "top of the show" writer's fee in the first year started at $650 a show and jumped to $700 in March. The other salaries ranged downward from there.

Lorne wasn't particularly concerned about the money. He knew the comedy underground was where the truly original talent was, anyway, and the comedy underground was impoverished. Besides a paycheck, however small, Lorne's bait for attracting that talent would be to offer them an honest chance to get their work across to a huge audience they all believed was out there, waiting. Lorne often said that in television creative people were usually given a great deal of money and no freedom. He promised to reverse that ratio. The money would come in time.

The strength of the comedy underground also allowed Lorne the luxury of searching out what he called "disciplined shock troops"—people who could go in and get the job done. He wanted *Saturday Night* to be different and startling, but not for the wrong reasons. The sensibility should be fresh, even raw, but the execution smooth, if not seamless. He didn't want people saying of the show, "They're going to be great when they get it together." Monty Python's Eric Idle had once described Python as "the best comedy fighting team ever assembled," and that's what Lorne said he was after.

Although *Saturday Night* was still an unknown entity, word of the show spread quickly in New York. There was very little television production in town, and Lorne's office was immediately besieged by the city's teeming show business subculture of agents, personal managers, and struggling performers. Lorne was interested in checking out the scene, and over the next few months he had an interview every twenty minutes or so, seeing about five hundred people in all. A table was always available for *Saturday Night* at clubs like Catch a Rising Star, The Improv, and The Bottom Line, and Lorne, Ebersol, and their retinue dropped by often. One evening a special showcase of several aspiring comedians was arranged specifically for them at The Other End. Andy Kaufman, Billy Crystal, Martin Mull, and Richard Belzer were among those who performed. Lorne invited all of them to appear on the show (Mull was the only one who never did), but the key members of his team came through other channels.

One of the first people Lorne contacted in New York, and ultimately one of the most important for the comedy synthesis he hoped to achieve, was Michael O'Donoghue, the Dark Prince of the *National Lampoon*. Like most of those in the television business, Lorne hadn't paid much attention to the *Lampoon* when he was in Hollywood, but Marilyn Miller, who'd worked with Lorne on the Lily specials, had insisted he must get in touch with O'Donoghue. While he was still staying at the Plaza Hotel in April, Lorne called to ask O'Donoghue to drop by his room.

In East Coast comedy circles Michael O'Donoghue, thirty-five, was considered a difficult genius, a reputation he cultivated and enjoyed. His temper tantrums at the *Lampoon* were the stuff of legend, but he also affected a worldy, elegant decadence at once both antique and avant-garde. About six feet tall, and thin, he favored pleated trousers, loose-fitting shirts with billowing sleeves, dark sunglasses, wide-brimmed hats, and long brown cigarettes that he held between thumb and forefinger in the European manner.

It had been O'Donoghue's work that gave the early *Lampoon* much of its outrageous, brutal flavor, and he was a principal architect of one of the new comedy's most distinctive schools, what O'Donoghue called Cut and Slash humor. O'Donoghue saw the world as a Hieronymus Bosch canvas of horrors unimagined, indeed, actively ignored by those he called The Others, meaning the whole of American society. Consequently, a fundamental tenet of his comedic philosophy held that it was impossible to go Too Far. He was fond of quoting William Burroughs's maxim: "Nothing is true: everything is permitted." (Burroughs himself borrowed the quote from Hasan-i-Sahhah, the Persian founder of the Order of Assassins.) One of O'Donoghue's more notorious pieces at the *Lampoon* was the Vietnamese Baby Book, which had pointers for busy Vietnamese moms on the treatment of napalm burns and gunshot wounds. Baby's first word was *medic*. He wrote a cartoon strip in which Lurleen Wallace rose from the grave to poison her husband, Governor George Wallace, by feeding him cancer-riddled rats. O'Donoghue was also an aficionado of mass murderers, whom he considered to be genuine American folk artists.

The bleakness of O'Donoghue's world view was not unshared by an entire generation of disillusioned American youth, but to his admirers it was the measure of O'Donoghue's brilliance that he carried disillusion to new heights—squared it, at least—and laughed. Whereas Lorne Michaels was in many respects a passionate believer, Michael O'Donoghue was a passionate disbeliever. He took it as a point of honor in his comedy to savage everything.

Upon their meeting at the Plaza, Lorne immediately offended O'Donoghue by launching into one of his expositions on the rules of comedy. "How dare he lecture me on comedy?" O'Donoghue said to himself. But O'Donoghue had been intrigued by Lorne's promises of artistic freedom, and he needed the work—the corporate backing for a new humor magazine he was putting together had recently collapsed. So O'Donoghue invited Lorne to have dinner at the Chelsea apartment he shared with his girlfriend, Anne Beatts, whom Lorne was also thinking of hiring as a writer. The purpose of the invitation was partly to talk about the show, but also, Beatts knew, to allow Lorne to glimpse in full the accouterments of the O'Donoghue style.

O'Donoghue and Beatts lived on the parlor floor of an elegant 150-year-old brownstone. It had high ceilings, mahogany woodwork, beveled mirrors, marble fireplaces, and Corinthian columns, and they'd filled it with stuffed birds, hula-girl lamps, leopard-skin pillows, and countless other objects from their vast collection of exotica and kitsch. It was said among their friends that Beatts and O'Donoghue endured their tumultuous affair as long as they did mainly because neither could bear giving up the apartment.

Anne Beatts herself added considerably to the atmosphere. On her forays with O'Donoghue through the shadowy corners of New York's modern cafe society, she played Zelda to his F. Scott Fitzgerald, dressing in thirties backless dresses, veils, seamed nylons, and high heels. Beatts, twenty-eight, had been the *National* Lampoon's only female editor, and her humor, like O'Donoghue's, was dark. Volkswagen successfully sued the *Lampoon* for a parody she wrote of their magazine ads; Beatts's version had a picture of a VW floating upside down on a lake and the headline "If Ted Kennedy drove a Volkswagen, he'd be President today." She was every bit as biting in person; her aggressive sarcasm often seemed calculated to challenge and offend. O'Donoghue liked to say that Beatts burned her bridges before she came to them. She once considered having business cards printed that read "ANNE BEATTS, BALL BUSTER."

When Lorne arrived with Tom Schiller for dinner, Beatts typically went straight to the attack, saying she'd seen the Lily Tomlin specials but hadn't liked them. Too feminist, she said, too self-conscious. She preferred Cher's specials—they were unintentionally funnier, and she liked to see the outrageous gowns Cher wore. Beatts and O'Donoghue made it clear they had no use for television in general. They called it a lava lamp with sound.

Lorne held his own. When Beatts asked why the show was called *Saturday Night*, he said, "So the network can remember when it's on." He seemed to believe what he was saying about creative freedom and risk, and he obviously had ideas. It was clear, too, he had more class than the ordinary medallion-bedecked TV hack from Hollywood. He was, after all, a man in search of a salon, and could therefore appreciate, if not necessarily believe, O'Donoghue's boast that the *Lampoon* dinner parties in their heyday would have left those who sat at the famous Algonquin Round Table speechless, so sharp and fast was the wit displayed.

So O'Donoghue and Beatts joined the show, and through them Lorne gained instant credibility in New York's *Lampoon*-connected comedy underground. One of those impressed by O'Donoghue's presence on *Saturday Night* was John Belushi. At the time, Belushi, twenty-six, was creative director and star of the Lampoon's current Off-Broadway revue, *The National Lampoon Show*. He'd also been a star at Second City in Chicago and, like O'Donoghue, was considered, by his admirers and himself, to be a genius of comedy whose talent justified his frequent lapses of decorum. Lorne, however, immediately offended Belushi by demonstrating that he failed to appreciate that genius. He arrived with his party in a limousine one night to see the *Lampoon* show, then left halfway through the performance. Belushi was outraged: The stupid jerk, he said, had only come to see a performer he already knew, his old friend from Canada, Gilda Radner.

Gilda, twenty-eight, had by then become the first performer Lorne signed. He had seen her in a Toronto production of *Godspell* a few years before, and Lorne knew as soon as he got the deal that he wanted her for *Saturday Night*. But she was in danger of being stolen by the comedian David Steinberg, who had offered her a job on a new syndicated talk show he was starting. Gilda found deciding between the two suitors difficult. She liked Lorne, and his show sounded good, but it wasn't going on the air for another six months, and it was late-night. Steinberg was talking immediate employment, five days a week, at more than double the salary on *Saturday Night*. Lorne had his manager, Bernie Brillstein, call Gilda to help persuade her not to do the Steinberg show. When he did, Brillstein explained that her exposure would be far greater with NBC's full network complement of stations than with Steinberg's piece-meal collection of individual stations in syndication. Still she hesitated.

"Should I wait?" she asked Lorne.

"I don't know," he answered. "I wouldn't say you have to … but, yeah, I think you should."

Before she was officially hired, Gilda had to be approved by Dick Ebersol. She came to NBC to meet him one morning in April accompanied by a scruffy young friend she'd worked with in the Toronto company of Second City. He waited on a stool outside Ebersol's office while Gilda and Ebersol conferred within. He wasn't introduced, but his name was Dan Aykroyd. Danny, just twenty-two, knew Lorne well: Besides being a guest on Hart and Lorne's CBC shows, Danny had sometimes dropped by an improv class Lorne taught at the New School of Art in Toronto. He'd also been a frequent visitor to a big pink house Lorne and Rosie lived in near the university, known by its many residents as Hormone House because of all the unwanted pregnancies conceived there. When Rosie moved out, Danny had helped her move her refrigerator. Although Lorne had talked to Danny about the show, he wasn't as sure about hiring him as he was about Gilda, and it wasn't until several months later that Aykroyd, or Belushi, joined the cast.

*Saturday Night*'s Canadian contingent was rounded out by Rosie Shuster, who was hired as a writer, and Howard Shore, Lorne's old buddy from Forest Hill, who signed on as musical director. (Lorne and Rosie's on-again, off-again marriage was by this time mostly off, and eventually they were divorced.) Later that summer Shore brought in another Canadian, pianist Paul Shaffer, to anchor his band. Lorne resisted hiring

Shaffer at first because of the trouble he was having getting U.S. work permits—green cards—for so many foreigners. NBC's lawyers spent a considerable amount of time and money on that problem as well; one NBC executive would later complain that Lorne had the most expensive green card in history.

*Saturday Night*'s reception on Lorne's home turf in Los Angeles was perhaps the most circumspect of all. In June, Lorne and Ebersol returned to the Coast and held a two-week blitz of interviews at the Chateau Marmont and at the Beverly Hills Hotel, where Ebersol stayed. The waiters at the Beverly Hills pool looked down their noses at the strange characters parading by in torn jeans, T-shirts, and sandals, and Ebersol himself sometimes wondered where on Earth, if it was Earth, they'd come from. Michael O'Donoghue had come along, too, taking the chance to do a little slumming in the video ghettos of Tinseltown. "This will be amusing," he thought. But O'Donoghue looked pasty and out of place by the pool, and during a meeting with Rob Reiner, who by then had become a major star playing "Meathead" on *All in the Family*, O'Donoghue spilled a glass of fresh California orange juice on Reiner's clean white tennis shorts.

Several of those Lorne approached in California declined to be lured across country for a fraction of what they could earn in Hollywood. Marilyn Miller and Matt Neuman from the Lily specials were among those who turned him down, although after watching the first show, Miller, twenty-five, would change her mind. Neuman wouldn't join the show until four years later.

Another writer who rejected Lorne's first offer was Chevy Chase. Chevy, thirty-one, had left New York to make his fortune in Hollywood in 1974. His motel room had been robbed the day he arrived and the portfolio of material he'd written was stolen, but he soon got a job as a writer for the Smothers Brothers, who were making a short-lived attempt at a comeback on NBC. Chevy had met Lorne that March while waiting in line to see *Monty Python and the Holy* Grail at the Los Angeles International Film Exposition. It was a midnight screening, the movie's world premiere, and a large contingent of Python devotees turned out for it. Chevy was "on" that night, as he usually was when he had a captive audience, cracking jokes and taking falls. Lorne was charmed, and after a couple of talks at the Chateau, offered him a job as a writer.

But Chevy was determined to make it as a performer, and when Lorne refused to hire him for the cast he left for the Midwest to act in a summer stock production with Paul Lynde. He was soon back in Hollywood, though; he didn't mesh with Lynde's entourage, and after a week he simultaneously quit and was fired. He called Lorne to see if the writing job was still available, and Lorne said it was. For most of the next week Chevy hung out with Lorne at the Chateau, kibitzing during other interviews and beginning a friendship between them that would grow over the next few months into something akin to brotherhood.

The only performer hired in Los Angeles was Laraine Newman, whom Lorne had met on one of the Lily specials. When Laraine (who, like Danny, was just twenty-two) came to talk to Lorne at the Chateau, she somehow came away with the impression *Saturday Night* was only a summer replacement show, and that it would be a combination of *60 Minutes* and *Monty Python*. That was a mixture, Laraine thought, that would certainly get her to watch. At the time, Ebersol was sick in bed with pneumonia, and to get his approval Laraine had to meet him in his room at the Beverly Hills Hotel. Shortly thereafter she and her boyfriend strapped her possessions atop their Volkswagen and drove to New York, where the Volkswagen, along with everything she owned, was promptly stolen.

The rest of the *Saturday Night* nucleus more or less fell into place back in New York. As the show's set and costume designers, Lorne hired Eugene and Franne Lee, a young team from the legitimate theater who'd just won a Tony award for their adventurous work in a Broadway production of *Candide*. When the Lees met Lorne at the Plaza, they told him they were suspicious of TV—neither had ever set foot in a television studio—and that they didn't want to spend much time away from their home in Providence, Rhode Island, where Eugene was building a boat. Lorne sat barefoot on the bed and made it all seem very casual, telling them *Saturday Night* would be the Off-Broadway of television, a true departure, and that people who were suspicious of TV were exactly the people he wanted. He also promised there would be no time clocks; they could come and go as they pleased. Franne Lee would later laugh at how innocently this baby-faced producer had looked at them and lied.

Herb Sargent was in town writing and producing some comedy specials for Alan King. He wasn't enjoying himself much, and grabbed the chance to join *Saturday Night* despite the blow it dealt his income. When the people at the Writer's Guild learned what Sargent was making on *Saturday Night*, they called him in disbelief that he'd accepted it. He was hired as a senior script consultant, and he was the only member of the writing staff over forty. He was also the only writer who'd had experience in live TV. Sargent's credits, in fact, included many of *Saturday Night*'s most important precursors in live television comedy, beginning in the early fifties with *Broadway Open House*, the grandfather of all late-night television shows, continuing with Steve Allen's *Tonight Show* and the *Colgate Comedy Hour*, and running all the way up through the news satire series *That Was the Week That Was* in the mid-1960s and the

Lily Tomlin special he produced in the early seventies. He'd also been Johnny Carson's first head writer when Carson took over the *Tonight Show* in 1962.

Sargent was a bearlike, silver-haired New York City liberal who had worked for a variety of, as he put it, losing political causes. He was famous for his acerbic wit and taciturn manner; people who'd worked with him often noticed that if more than two people congregated in a room Sargent was in, he tended to slip quietly out the door. Sargent was not the type to throw his weight around, and he would serve as a reassuring, fatherly presence for many of the younger members of the staff, including, some thought, Lorne. Anne Beatts used to say that whenever Sargent was ambling away she felt like running after him, shouting, "Shane, Shane ... Come back, Shane!"

It was a Writer's Guild concession that allowed Lorne to round out his staff with several "apprentice" writers who were paid well below Guild minimum. One of these apprentices sent over by the Guild itself was a playwright, singer, and actor named Garrett Morris. He was hired, but he had almost no experience writing comedy sketches, and after a couple of weeks it became apparent he had no particular talent for it either. Lorne, having seen Garrett's performance in the movie *Cooley High*, quickly decided he should be a member of the cast instead. Other than the receptionist, Garrett, thirty-eight, was the only black on the 17th floor. Many saw him as one of the first examples of Lorne's deeply ingrained aversion to firing anyone, for any reason, although in Garrett's case few on the 17th floor doubted that race had something to do with his being included in the cast.

Another of the apprentice writers hired was Alan Zweibel, a self-described "huge Jew from Long Island" who was working days for $2.75 an hour in a delicatessen in Queens and nights writing one- liners for Borscht Belt comedians. Lorne met Zweibel, twenty-four, at Catch a Rising Star and, figuring that a one-liner specialist would be a good thing to have, asked to see some of his material. Zweibel stayed up all night at his mother's kitchen table, typing out his "book" of more than a thousand jokes. He put at the top what he considered one of his best, a joke about the post office issuing a stamp commemorating prostitution. The stamp cost 15 cents, a quarter if you wanted to lick it.

The final apprentice position was filled by a comedy team, Al Franken and Tom Davis. Franken and Davis, both in their early twenties, were then enjoying a life of near-total failure on the fringes of show business in Los Angeles. They were so broke that during the holidays they played Santa Claus and Winnie-the-Pooh at the local Sears. Marilyn Miller, whom Franken and Davis had met and looked up to as someone who'd made it, sometimes paid Franken to play tennis with her. They'd heard about *Saturday Night* from two writer friends who were up for the show, but they hadn't known their own agent had submitted some of their material. Tom Schiller came across it in the reams of submissions he was reading for Lorne in New York. He liked what he saw—it wasn't especially sophisticated, but it represented what Schiller called "college humor," a style the show could use. Lorne and Herb Sargent agreed, and Schiller was told to call them.

Franken and Davis were outside playing basketball when he did. They booked seats on a plane, gave away their tickets to a Rolling Stones concert that weekend, and reported for work in New York three days later. Between them they split one apprentice salary of $350 a week.

*Photos courtesy of F.T. Eyre*

Herb Sargent

Al Franken

Michael O'Donoghue and Anne Beatts

Rosie Shuster

Tom Davis

Tom Schiller

Marilyn Miller

Alan Zweibel

CHAPTER 7

# On the Submarine

The first *Saturday Night* staff meeting commenced about noon on Monday, July 7, 1975. The champion racehorse Ruffian had been crippled in an accident and destroyed over the holiday weekend just past, and as people straggled into Lorne's office some of the writers traded Ruffian jokes, one venturing a "second bullet theory"; another insisting it was all a cover-up—the horse was alive and well in Brazil; a third proposing a match race between Ruffian and paralyzed baseball star Roy Campanella.

Lorne started the meeting by saying that *Saturday Night* was going to be a comedy-variety show, which meant, he said, that it would have a variety of comedy styles. Looking around the room at the group he'd assembled, it was obvious what he was talking about. It was a strange mixture: Alan Zweibel, the deli clerk from Queens, for one, remembers looking at Michael O'Donoghue and thinking he must have come from a different planet.

Most of those in the meeting found Lorne vague, just as NBC's executives had. He wanted everybody to start thinking about some parody commercials, but exactly what he envisioned for the rest of the show went largely unexplained. Zweibel, who was so nervous he brought a change of clothes to avoid being under- or overdressed, asked if it would be okay to write parodies of other TV shows. "Do anything you want," Lorne said.

Lorne did, however, lay down some ground rules, in the process outlining an attitude toward the show. *Saturday Night* would do sketches, not skits; kids do skits, he said, and so did Carol Burnett. Lorne made it clear that Burnett's style encompassed everything *Saturday Night* should avoid. It lacked subtlety and nuance; it was too broad, too bourgeois, and too smug—especially when the performers broke out laughing in mid-sketch, doubling up at the hilarity of themselves. There will be more integrity and respect for the writing here, he said. From then on many an idea would be derisively dismissed on the 17th floor with the words, "That's Carol Burnett."

Lorne similarly discouraged going for cheap laughs with funny names, a technique he called the Walter Crankcase School of Humor. This seemed directed at Chevy Chase, who was fond of playing a pompous newsman he called Rick Bulova. Finally Lorne made his case for realism in comedy, which he said led to a willing suspension of disbelief by viewers, setting them up for the joke.

Dick Ebersol also gave a little speech, feeling uncomfortable as he did because he'd worn a tie that day. He told the group not to worry about NBC, that they shouldn't let anyone at the network tell them what to do (to which more than one of those listening silently added, "Including you"). On the other hand, he added, neither should *Saturday Night* make needless trouble. He didn't want to have to deal with any "discipline problems" before the show was on the air and established. "Don't abuse the fact that we've got this open field," he said. "There are certain things you don't do."

Some of Ebersol's listeners assumed he was referring specifically to the fact that the odor of marijuana smoke was already noticeable on the 17th floor. The first day they arrived, Franken and Davis had slipped across the street to the steps of Saint Patrick's Cathedral to get high, assuming one did not light a joint within a national television network's headquarters. They soon learned differently, and despite Ebersol's speech did not feel compelled to leave the offices to get high again. From the beginning, grass was a staple of *Saturday Night*, used regularly and openly on 17 as, in Tom Schiller's words, "an inspirational tool." Cocaine was consumed less visibly and in less copious amounts, but it, too, was around.

Dope, however, was only part of an all-encompassing chaos that immediately prevailed on the 17th floor, a gleeful, spontaneous embracing of disorder and abandon in conscious defiance of the straight network world all around. "There seemed to be," Lorne said later, "no decorum in our office."

The staff was lean, almost skeletal, and the amenities provided by the network few: The production assistants had to take anything that needed to be copied downstairs to another floor until NBC finally broke down and provided the show with an ancient Xerox machine of its own. When Lorne chose the furniture for 17, he had disdained the steel-case desks and bookshelves that were standard NBC issue. Instead, he and

Dan Sullivan rummaged around storerooms deep inside 30 Rock looking for older wooden pieces of a style Sullivan called "early courtroom."
With all the blinds and doors open, the 17th floor was a sunny place, and
because there wasn't nearly enough room for everyone to have an office,
there was an unavoidable, almost communal intimacy. Desks were
scattered everywhere and people flowed through in a sort of ongoing,
free- floating comedy convention. Meetings seemed to generate sponta-
neously whenever two people stopped to talk to each other for more than
a minute or two, and there were few distinctions at first about who could
join in. Members of the band and secretaries wandered in and out of the
group discussions in Lorne's office along with everyone else.

A shorthand quickly developed among them, almost their own language. Watching it happen thrilled Herb Sargent, who in all his years in
the business had never seen anything like it. "It's like musicians jamming," he thought. "They can come from all over the country and immediately sit down and play together because the level of their art is in the
same place."

Everyone always seemed to be laughing, and a rushing, manic sense
of hilarity took over. There was a constant, competitive throwing out of
lines, all of them showing what they had, looking for openings, and timing their licks. A giggling group from the show poured into a crowded
NBC elevator one day, and as they rode down Chevy put his arm around
a balding executive standing next to him, turned to the others, and asked,
"Have you met my wife?" Coming back from lunch together they'd pass
an especially ragged bum on the street and, as one, all would chorus,
"There's my agent." Chief production assistant Audrey Dickman walked
into the offices for the first time and introduced herself to Al Franken,
Tom Davis, Alan Zweibel, and Tom Schiller, who were all sitting on
each other's desks.

"Hi, I'm Al," one of them said. "No, *I'm* Al."

"I'm Tom."

"No, *I'm* Tom."

Dickman walked away with her head spinning.

The offices, clean and repainted when *Saturday Night* moved in,
became over the course of the summer a shambles. Cigarette butts were
ground into the carpet; messages and jokes were scribbled on walls;
pencils were jammed into ceilings. NBC's maintenance department had
to send people up regularly to clean gobs of paper towels, socks, underwear, and other miscellaneous debris out of the toilet. One of the male
writers tried to avoid the walk down the hall to the john altogether by
using the sink behind the water cooler, much to Gilda Radner's displeasure, since her desk was right beside the sink.

Lorne himself was relatively tidy, but he made no effort to impose his habits on others. To him the atmosphere of anarchy was necessary to the work they were trying to do. Kathy Minkowsky, who'd left a job as a secretary in Herb Schlosser's office to become Lorne's assistant, once told Lorne how disgusted she was by the mess.

"You're wrong," Lorne answered. "These are creative people. Get rid of that NBC mentality." Lorne did get upset, however, when somebody used his potted lemon tree for an ashtray.

No one was immune from practical jokes. The papers on people's desks were frequently set afire with lighter fluid. Al Franken and Tom Davis, who were officially on a probationary trial with the show, came in one morning to find their office stripped bare of furniture and a note lying by the phone jack reading, "See me, Lorne." The pranksters had crammed Franken and Davis's furniture into Herb Sargent's office, and he was annoyed when he came in to find he could hardly open his door. Chevy Chase once burst into Lorne's office when actress Ellen Burstyn was there to talk about hosting the show. Holding Lorne's watering can between his legs, Chevy re-created the urination scene from her movie *The Exorcist*, staring silently into space while a stream of water hit the carpet. Burstyn decided against hosting *Saturday Night*.

Michael O'Donoghue's office, like Lorne's, was neater than the rest, although by no means conventional—his wall decorations included a picture of mass murderer Richard Speck and a nude pinup of a multiple amputee. His bulletin board was scrupulously organized, with index cards aligned in rows, affixed by silver push pins. Over a period of several weeks, Rosie Shuster sneaked into his office at night and slowly moved every item on it imperceptibly to the right, an eighth of an inch or so at a time. Everything remained in its relative position so that the entire contents of the board gradually oozed into the corner, and eventually around it.

A weird procession of characters came and went. Magicians were invited up often, ostensibly to audition but in fact only to entertain the group. One of them put coins on his eyes and performed a mind-reading act so phony he was laughed out of the office. Actor Sylvester Stallone strolled through dressed in leather from his hat to his boots, but this was before *Rocky* was released and nobody knew who he was. A sweet-looking older woman appeared one day sitting patiently in a corner. She turned out to be Andy Kaufman's mother, waiting to take Andy home after his meeting with Lorne. Even Anne Beatts found Andy Kaufman eccentric. "He twitches!" she said.

As it happened, Dan Aykroyd twitched too. He came to visit Lorne one day dressed in full motorcycle regalia, with leather gloves and heavy black boots, his wallet and keys attached to his jeans with a chain. Michael O'Donoghue was appalled at his appearance, and said so to Lorne. Aykroyd, meanwhile, entertained a couple of the other writers by writhing around the floor for several minutes, curled in a tight ball with his hands behind his back, struggling desperately to free himself from the bonds of some imaginary rope. Then he calmly got up, dusted himself off, and glanced out the window to make sure his Harley, which he'd parked on the street below, hadn't been stolen.

Word of what was going on at *Saturday Night* spread quickly throughout NBC, where in 1975 an air of formality prevailed, as it had for decades. Sure, there were plenty of stories about the wackos in the so-called creative community, but they were out in Hollywood, not sitting in the company's lap in New York. And *Saturday Night*'s shenanigans went well beyond even Hollywood's twisted standards. Dave Tebet, who in thirty-odd years of dealing with talent had seen his share of craziness, called the gang on 17 "a motley crew." Dan Sullivan overheard the buzzing in the NBC commissary and in the halls: "Did you *see* those characters on *Saturday Night*?" NBC executives soon learned to avoid if at all possible a visit to the show's offices, never knowing what they might encounter there. "It was," said an NBC senior vice president, "like visiting a war zone." At least one executive walked into a meeting on 17 and was casually offered the circulating joint. "Want a toke?" he was asked.

The collective suspicions of those at NBC toward *Saturday Night* seemed to manifest themselves at the stanchions of the security guards in the lobby of 30 Rockefeller Plaza, which became a psychic and sometimes physical battleground between the network and the show. The guards were instantly suspicious of anyone who looked and acted as strange as the *Saturday Night* crowd did, while people from the show saw the guards as corporate henchmen, petty authority figures to be abused or ignored. Thus the guards failed somehow to recognize members of the *Saturday Night* staff far longer than they might have, inevitably requiring that they display their passes each time they approached the elevator banks. This was taken by many of those on the show as harassment, and some refused to comply.

One of the principal offenders was Eugene Lee, a brilliant set designer but a man who had little use for words, passes, or, for that matter, a wallet. He'd brush by the guard desk saying, "I've got no pass. I'm going to work." The guards would isolate the car he was in, taking everyone else off and holding it in the lobby, and Lee would stay there until somebody upstairs was called to come and get him. Dan Aykroyd once did the same thing and dared the guards to try to take him out of the elevator. *Saturday Night*'s cast members continued to be stopped downstairs long after the show went on: eventually NBC supplied the guard stations with 8 X 10 glossies of each performer to aid in their identification. Hosts, too, received their share of scrutiny: Paul Simon and Buck Henry were among those the guards refused to let by. Some hosts gave up in frustration and returned to their hotel rooms to call Lorne for help.

Those who resisted security too strenuously generally lost. Michael O'Donoghue once swung at a guard and a legion of security heavies emerged from the bowels of the building to take him away.

He was rescued at the last minute by an NBC executive who worked with the show. Eugene Lee made the mistake of pushing a guard one day, causing him to trip and fall. The guard got up and hit Lee in the face, knocking him cold for a minute or two. He was wearing glasses at the time and blood from his cuts speckled the lobby. A Rockefeller Center nurse was summoned and Lee was taken away in a wheelchair to be stitched up at the nearest hospital. An NBC executive eventually gave Lee a wallet so he'd carry a pass, but he never used it.

Episodes such as these served to reinforce the belief of those on the show that they were a specially selected team of comedy commandos on a mission of truth behind enemy lines. They were united by their eagerness to bite the hand that now fed them, and most shared a conviction that the show couldn't miss—there were too many people out there who had been waiting too long for a program that spoke for them. Since almost everyone on the show was young and single, they were soon spending almost all their time together, enlisting in a crusade called *Saturday Night*.

There were group lunches and late dinners in the Irish pubs and Chinese restaurants around Rockefeller Center. After dinner, people returned to the 17th floor, or maybe to Lorne's place, where the talk would continue well toward dawn. The few who in the early weeks arrived at the offices much before noon discovered them mostly deserted; before long all had shifted to Lorne's nocturnal hours. On Sundays there were group brunches at baroque restaurants like the Russian Tea Room and the Sign of the Dove, the sort of places, Herb Sargent observed, where the food could be indifferent but the ambiance was always great.

It was, to those on the inside, a period of "mutual falling in love," a bonding that went well beyond the usual backstage infatuation. It also spilled over, even those on the inside knew, into arrogance. Tom Schiller saw it as "the bringing together of Lorne Michaels' chosen people … a traveling family circus, like an amoeba, a cell that started to grow. … We lived the show; we breathed the show; we slept with each other about the show. There was no private life. I would compare it exactly to living on a submarine."

\* \* \*

As united a front as *Saturday Night* presented to the outside world, however, as in all families (and all crusades), hierarchies prevailed within. At the top were Chevy Chase and Michael O'Donoghue, who immediately formed, with Lorne, a ruling triumvirate—"Lorne's brain trust," Zweibel called them.

Chevy and O'Donoghue were set apart not only by their age, their salaries (both were paid top of the show as writers), and their professional credentials, but also by the sheer force of their personalities. They made no secret of their condescension toward what they considered the childishly feeble skills of the younger writers. If Chevy heard something he didn't like in a meeting, he'd have no qualms about saying, "Gee, I don't think that's very good at all," and he generally smirked when he said it. He was also a viciously effective put-down artist, the sort who could find the one thing somebody was sensitive about—a pimple on the nose, perhaps—and then kid about it, mercilessly.

Michael O'Donoghue, who used the Rod of Ridicule to critique the younger writers
*Courtesy of F.T. Eyre*

O'Donoghue employed what he called "The Rod of Ridicule," a technique he said derived from the example of certain Zen masters who occasionally broke their staffs over the backs of their devotees, just to keep them alert. Al Franken would ask O'Donoghue what he was doing and O'Donoghue would answer, "Oh, I'm working on something really great. What piece of shit are you working on?" Garrett Morris spent his first couple of weeks on the show writing a long sketch about a black superman called Colored Man. It's said that after O'Donoghue read it, he held the script up for a moment between thumb and forefinger, as if it were maggot-ridden, then dropped it into a wastebasket. "Great, Garrett," he said, smiling. "Real good."

Lorne was especially smitten by Chevy. When Rosie Shuster was still in Los Angeles and Lorne would call, he'd talk about Chevy like a parent whose child had just reached the adorable toddler stage. "Oh, Chevy did the cutest thing today," he'd chuckle. Lorne and Chevy became inseparable. They dressed alike (Chevy quickly picked up Lorne's taste for Hawaiian shirts), commiserated with each other about their troubles with their mates (Chevy's fiancée was in Los Angeles and not happy he was in New York), and shared similar senses of irony and the absurd.

Despite his put-downs, Chevy had what Rosie called "a comic Pied Piper" quality about him then, always trying to win people over, always performing. He'd take one of his pratfalls when he walked into the NBC commissary; in a Japanese restaurant the waiter would deliver hot towels and Chevy would put one on his face and let out a blood-curdling scream. "He had," Shuster said, "a lot to prove, so he was working hard. He worked the room real good." So good, in fact, that over the course of the summer he gradually worked himself into a performing job on the show, winning over first Lorne and then Dick Ebersol with what was in effect a three-month-long audition. After that, Chevy and Lorne also shared a manager, Bernie Brillstein, an intermingling of their personal and business lives that would later complicate matters between them.

O'Donoghue tended to work more on his own and resisted the submersion of his personality in anything so déclassé as a buddy relationship, but his presence and his influence on the comedic sensibility emerging on the 17th floor were too strong to be ignored.

"The pattern in the early days," writer Tom Davis says, "was that Lorne, Chevy, and O'Donoghue would go off to Elaine's and the rest of us would wait to hear what was happening with the show." (Elaine's is the chic Upper East Side restaurant frequented by Woody Allen and other glamorous fixtures of New York's literary and show business aristocracy.)

From the outset, Chevy and O'Donoghue helped set a charged and highly competitive atmosphere on the 17th floor. It was, said one friend who spent a lot of time there, an emotional roller coaster: People tended to be up or down, confident or shattered, from one day to the next. There was a feeling you were always vulnerable to getting zapped if you left yourself open, and you'd better be quick with a comeback. Not everyone was automatically invited to join the traveling family circus, and there were hurt feelings among those left out.

Some adapted better than others. Gilda Radner had a sort of cute and cuddly little-sister persona that helped fend off some of the sharper barbs, leaping on writers' laps and giggling, too irresistible to attack too much. Laraine Newman, on the other hand, felt steamrollered. There were those on 17 who thought she was the funniest of them all during office bull sessions, but she herself didn't believe it. She was terrified of New York and self-conscious about being one of the youngest people there. She considered herself goofy and eager to please—too eager. Soon after she arrived, Lorne asked her to run through some of her characters for the group, and she came away thinking, "They weren't wowed by me—I really felt it. I was so nervous!"

Franken and Davis, along with Zweibel, were probably the lowest on *Saturday Night*'s pecking order in the beginning, and they suffered ceaseless taunting for it. Chevy needled them about their long hair and their writing—they were the ones who always wanted to say *fart* on TV, he'd say. O'Donoghue put them down for their scruffy clothes and their pitiful salaries: "My cats make more than that!" Franken and Davis began to catch on. "I came in with the attitude that you were supposed to support the people around you," Davis recalls, "and the first couple of weeks I just got sand kicked in my face every time. Pretty soon I learned you had to speak up for yourself, because no one else was going to."

For everyone, the primary objective was to impress Lorne. He was the unquestioned leader. Tom Davis called him The Boss; Rosie Shuster gave him a sailor's plaque that read THE CAPTAIN'S WORD *IS LAW*. It hung over the bulletin board in his office, where the show rundowns were charted. Everyone owed his or her job to Lorne, of course, and knew it was Lorne who worked with Dick Ebersol to keep NBC at bay. They never dealt with the network themselves and didn't think too much about it, but they knew somehow that Lorne was protecting them, and his belief that they deserved special treatment permeated the group.

As usual, Lorne projected an aura of utter confidence and conviction, an almost messianic air of total control. *Absolutely* was his favorite word; *exactly* came a close second. People occasionally giggled at Lorne's pretensions, but they were inspired just the same. Tom Schiller remembers Lorne walking into a room one day and saying something like, "I want this show to be representative of people who want to explore their own possibilities as human beings." Whatever it was didn't quite make sense, Schiller says, "but it was his *attitude* that people subscribed to. He was doing it and you couldn't stop him."

*Saturday Night* became the forum in which the full glory of Lorne's gift for speech unfurled. He worked by talking, and this time there was no one to tell him to shut up—he was in charge. Tom Schiller recalls going in to ask Lorne about a new ending for a sketch he was working on. "Lorne would say, 'Well, I like it for three reasons and I don't like it for four reasons.' And suddenly he'd whip off these four reasons, and you'd think to yourself, 'How could he remember four reasons to talk about?' But then you'd think that maybe he was thinking of the next one while he was saying the first one and he made it up. So you would be spellbound at the process, and you would leave sort of befuddled and enthusiastic at the same time, and sort of despondent that you had to rework your piece. That happened over and over again."

Other times Lorne was briefer but still impressive. To one suggestion of Zweibel's he said simply, "Premise overload." Thinking it over later, Zweibel realized that, yes, he's right. Premise overload. Exactly.

Lorne seemed to have no doubt that *Saturday Night* would be a television landmark. He reminded people again and again that when they were older they would see reruns of the show and that they would want it to be the best show ever, something they'd want to take credit for. Franken and Davis were walking with Lorne one day, trying to make small talk, but Lorne kept going on about how they were going to be stars.

Like O'Donoghue and Chevy, Lorne considered the younger writers tabula rasa, initiates to be taught—"little Eliza Doolittles of comedy," as Rosie Shuster put it. But unlike Chevy and O'Donoghue, Lorne kept himself above the battle. He was benevolent more than challenging, the type of leader who was disappointed rather than angry, available for counsel in personal as well as professional matters, a paternalistic or, Anne Beatts thought, maternalistic figure who exerted his authority in an almost tribal fashion. He never wrote memos, preferring that information disseminate organically through the ranks. "People get as much information as they need," he'd say.

Despite Lorne's general policy of making himself available to the writers (something he himself never got in Hollywood), and despite his willingness to roll on at length once his attention had been gained, it was not always easy to see him. Chevy and O'Donoghue would walk right into his office, but the others soon became accustomed to waiting outside for three or four hours, asking Kathy Minkowsky

Lorne Michaels, *Saturday Night's* Fearless Leader.
*Courtesy of F.T. Eyre*

every hour or so how long it would be, listening as she ticked off all the calls he still had to make. He bestowed the joy of recognition sparingly. He was known to withhold a compliment, even an acknowledgment, for weeks and then, at just the right moment, to proclaim his praise extravagantly. Garrett Morris would sometimes chase Lorne down the hall, trying to get him to say hello; Alan Zweibel swore Lorne once didn't look him in the eye for three weeks. Figuring out Lorne consequently became something of an obsession for many on the show. They talked about him for hours, sometimes catching themselves using Lorne's favorite words or phrases, and an acknowledgment from him was enough to keep them motivated for weeks.

Part of Lorne's mystique stemmed from the seemingly effortless way he had come to New York and immediately begun circulating in some of the higher, hipper echelons of New York City chic. He sublet a small but elegant apartment in a building called the Osborne on West Fifty-seventh Street near Carnegie Hall, no small achievement in itself. Tom Schiller, who slept on the couch there his first month or two in New York, remembers late nights when he secretly hoped Paul Simon and Mick Jagger would go the hell home so he could get some rest.

Lorne was introduced to Paul Simon soon after coming to New York by Edie Baskin, a model and photographer friend of Lorne's from Los Angeles who was Simon's current girlfriend. Baskin became *Saturday Night*'s photographer and creator of its color-tinted opening sequences; Paul Simon became Lorne's best friend outside the show. Through Simon and through his own efforts Lorne began developing acquaintances well beyond the ken of the workaday world of television—his circle would eventually include the actress Candice Bergen and the director Mike Nichols, for example—and within *Saturday Night*, invitations to dine with Lorne's society friends became prized symbols of one's standing on the show.

To some of those who had known Lorne in Los Angeles and Canada, there was a certain poignancy to his position in those early days in New York. Many of his old friends now worked for him, and despite his new friendships with Chevy and Paul Simon, he seemed a little lonely, caught between his old and new lives. He had come to New York vowing that he would hang out with the best minds of his generation, and although he seemed to be pulling it off, it was also clear to those who knew him well that Lorne retained a sense of awe and naïveté about the new world he was entering.

The first time Lorne rented a limousine in New York was to visit Simon at his summer home in the Hamptons on Long Island. Lorne was on the phone with Paul, who was telling him he ought to take a limo out, but Lorne wasn't sure how to hire one. "Just pick up the phone and call," Paul said. Lorne did, and with Schiller rode from the Plaza out to Paul's place in Bridgehampton in a metallic-blue stretch limo, listening to music, laughing, and talking about the show. It was an idyllic trip, and at its end was Simon's beautiful home by the beach. They found Paul and Edie on the patio, having a spat about who was going to light the barbecue.

# Chapter 8

# Nola

John Belushi called Paul Simon a folk-singing wimp, which was a lot nicer than the things he had to say about television. Neither of these opinions charmed Lorne Michaels. To everyone who knew John in New York, there was no doubt he belonged on *Saturday Night*. He was, they told Lorne, an absolutely electric performer: unbridled, a force of nature almost—but that had a lot to do with his incredible charisma. Lorne didn't doubt any of this, but he believed from the beginning that John Belushi was trouble.

Their first meeting was anything but auspicious. John came to see Lorne on the 17th floor, wearing his usual T-shirt, jeans, and sneakers, a thick beard covering much of his face. He whirled around Lorne's office loudly proclaiming his contempt for television. "TV sucks!" he yelled several times. He said he'd owned only one TV in his life, a grubby old black-and-white set, and that was covered with spit. He was spouting, Lorne said later, "a batch of rhetoric, rhetoric about guerrilla television and all that stuff, which was not uncommon at that time."

Lorne told John that wasn't where he was coming from. He thought there were a lot of good things on television and mentioned some examples. He was also, he told Belushi, not into revolutionizing the medium. There are certain rules you abide by, he said. What was important was the ideas you put across, not saying *fuck* on the air. Belushi left the office with no commitment and two suggestions from Lorne: Try cutting off the beard and come to the open auditions.

As obstreperous as Belushi had been, he badly wanted to be on the show. He told O'Donoghue, Beatts, Gilda Radner, Paul Shaffer, and others how upset he was that Lorne was stringing him along, and he found the suggestion that he needed to audition "truly degrading," in O'Donoghue's words. Belushi's friend Richard Belzer said that asking John to audition was like saying to Picasso, "Do this drawing and we'll see about the murals." Nonetheless, he arrived at the auditions prepared to blow Lorne Michaels away.

The *Saturday Night* auditions were held on August 12 and 13 in the Nola Sound Studios, down the street from Lorne's apartment on West Fifty-seventh Street. Lorne, Dick Ebersol, the writers, Dave Wilson, Audrey Dickman, and a few others connected with the show sat on folding chairs in a large, windowless room with a piano, mirrors, and a small stage. It was not a dump, but a sad odor of show biz heartbreak hung in the air. It was the sort of place, Dave Wilson thought, that people from Queens would rent to make their piano debut for their relatives. (Rehearsal and writing sessions for Sid Caesar's *Your Show of Shows* in its early days were held at Nola. Besides Caesar, the cast included Imogene Coca, Carl Reiner, and Howard Morris; the writers included, besides Reiner, Mel Brooks, Larry Gelbart, Lucille Kallen, Mel Tolkin, Neil Simon, and Woody Allen.)

A couple of announcements had appeared in the local trade papers, and over the two days almost two hundred performers streamed through—every struggling hustler in New York, it seemed. They bunched up in a hallway downstairs and listened for their names to be called. Appointments were scheduled every ten minutes, but inevitably they ran hours late. It was immediately apparent that most of those who auditioned were entirely inappropriate for the show, though a few were entertaining. There was a roller-skating impressionist everyone enjoyed, and a monstrous singer named Meatloaf who was funny to watch. Every couple of hours Chevy Chase would take a loud fall over the folding chairs, or O'Donoghue would do his imitation of talk-show host Mike Douglas having steel needles thrust into his eyes, just to lighten things up. It was a tedious two days watching a mostly depressing parade.

Some people stood out from the crowd, of course. Jane Curtin, from The Proposition in Cambridge, auditioned with a friend named Judy Cahn. They performed a funny piece Jane, twenty-seven, had written about two

John Belushi, on the 17th floor in 1976.
*Courtesy of F.T. Eyre*

Midwestern housewives preparing for the annual tornado ("Can I borrow your centerpiece for the tornado this year?"). A comedienne named Mimi Kennedy sang a hilarious song called "I Am Dog," a parody of Helen Reddy's "I Am Woman." A lot of people knew Bill Murray when he came in: He'd followed in the footsteps of his brother Brian and of John Belushi as a Second City performer who'd gone on to appear in the Lampoon's shows. He did a slurring, punch-drunk character he called The Honker, and an impression of a sleazy Las Vegas crooner. He impressed those who saw him as very young and very raw.

At one point during a lull on the second day, a strange man burst through the swinging doors leading into the room. He was carrying an umbrella and an attaché case and wearing a derby, and he stood in front of the assembled group and yelled: "I've been waiting out there for three hours and I'm not going to wait anymore and I'm going to miss my plane! That's it, gentlemen, you've had your chance." Then he charged out.

Stunned, Dave Wilson turned to Lorne and said, "What the hell was that?"

"Oh, that was just Danny Aykroyd," Lorne said. "He's probably going to do the show."

Lorne says that in his mind Danny's spot on *Saturday Night* was never in doubt, but he thinks that when Danny saw so many people at the auditions, he misunderstood. Aykroyd, in fact, felt Lorne had been so vague that after the auditions he decided to accept a job with a new company Second City had opened in Pasadena, California. He'd already flown out to the Coast when Lorne called and coaxed him back to New York. Danny and his friend John Belushi didn't like Lorne jacking them around.

Belushi auditioned at Nola the second day. He planned to do one of his favorite characters, the samurai pool hustler, which he'd patterned after the samurai films of Japanese actor Toshiro Mifune. For a pool cue he brought a wooden clothes bar that he'd taken out of his closet at home that morning. His hair was tied up in a topknot. He waited for almost four hours downstairs, and as time passed he grew angrier and angrier, stalking up and down the crowded hallway, waving his clothes-bar pool cue, shouting at the indignity of it all.

"What the fuck am I doing here! I hate television!" he yelled. Occasionally some of this would drift upstairs, and several of those who heard it were intimidated. "Jeez," Tom Schiller remembers thinking, "he'd better be hired or he'll kill somebody."

Finally, after the waiting room was all but empty, somebody said, "Okay, John Belushi."

People braced themselves, ready for anything, but Belushi fooled them. He came out like a lamb, scratching and grunting, rubbing his chin and cocking his prodigious eyebrows as he paced around his imaginary pool table. By the time he was finished the room was crowded with people watching. It was, everyone agreed, an absolutely unexpected and winning performance, a *tour de force*.

\* \* \*

After the auditions ended each day, a large group retired to Lorne's apartment to talk things over. For the most part the debate centered on two choices that had to be made: between Jane Curtin and Mimi Kennedy, and among John Belushi, Dan Aykroyd, and, to a lesser extent, Bill Murray. Several people had fallen in love with Mimi Kennedy's "I Am Dog" parody and lobbied for her, but Dick Ebersol argued for Jane, and won, saying her more conventional "white bread" looks balanced better with the darker, flakier styles of Gilda and Laraine, who'd already been hired.

Almost everyone except Lorne wanted Belushi. Chevy, O'Donoghue, Beatts, and Franken and Davis were among those who urged Lorne to hire him. Lorne was leaning toward Billy and Danny. John's "bad attitude" still worried him, but he had been impressed by the audition and finally relented. After deciding to hire John, Lorne then didn't have enough money in his budget to hire both Billy and Danny. (He hadn't, in fact, had enough money in his budget to hire Chevy Chase as a performer, either. Chevy slipped into the cast with only a writer's contract, and was paid on a per-show basis for his on- air work.)

Ebersol didn't care for Bill Murray; he thought he was too limited. Lorne didn't push it, figuring, he says, that he didn't have enough clout with NBC at that point to force the issue. A week or so after the auditions, Billy showed up at a party at Al Franken's apartment. Franken came up to him and said, "Gee, Bill, I'm real sorry you didn't get it. I thought you were great." That was the first Billy had heard of the news.

\* \* \*

Another reason Lorne hadn't pushed for Bill Murray was that Billy had another job. For there was a second great experiment in variety television underway in New York that summer. Over at ABC, sports impresario Roone Arledge was taking a flyer in entertainment programming with a live show of his own. It, too, was on Saturday, but in prime time. Arledge's centerpiece was none other than Howard Cosell, who like his boss was reaching for new and greater heights outside of sports. The name of his show was *Saturday Night Live With Howard Cosell*, which ruled out the name Lorne and Ebersol had planned to use for their show, *Saturday Night Live*. They went instead with *NBC's Saturday Night*.

The two *Saturday Night*s were very aware of each other over the summer, and a friendly rivalry blossomed between them. Arledge had hired one of Lorne's first choices for director, Don Mischer, and there was some competition for performers as well. Lorne and Ebersol ran into Arledge's co-producers, Alan King and Rupert Hitzig, several times on the New York comedy club circuit, and most of the cast members who joined *Saturday Night* had auditioned earlier for Cosell. John Belushi and Jane Curtin, by coincidence, had read for the Cosell show together (an ironic twist in light of later developments between them). Cosell's people, too, had been apprised by Belushi of his opinions concerning TV, and Belushi was not one of those King and Hitzig pursued. They were thought to be interested in Gilda Radner, however. Eventually they hired three members of the *Lampoon* crowd: Bill Murray, his brother Brian, and Christopher Guest. They comprised what Arledge called The Prime Time Players.

ABC's *Saturday Night* premiered on September 20, three weeks before NBC's. Franken and Davis threw a party in Franken's apartment on Riverside Drive in honor of the occasion. It was a crowded affair, and a spirited one. A large bowl of potent grass sat on the dining room table, so potent it caught Lorne's twenty-year-old cousin, Neil Levy, by surprise. He ended up hiding out in the bathroom, waiting to come down to a lower orbit while a long line of people built up outside the door. Dan Aykroyd finally rescued him and took him outside for a couple of turns around the block, spouting monologues and doing characters as they walked.

By the time the Cosell show came on, a lot of people at the party weren't paying much attention. Those who watched could hardly believe what they were seeing and soon found it hard to hear over the laughter at what Arledge was putting on the screen. Arledge, infatuated as ever by technology, was bringing acts in from around the world via satellite hookup. The big event of the first show was a concert from London by a Scottish rock group, The Bay City Rollers, who were being hyped at the time, without the slightest justification, as the next Beatles. The show was so filled with acts that the resident company of Prime Time Players had very little time to do anything. And of course there was the inimitable Howard Cosell presiding over it all, making Ed Sullivan seem positively graceful by comparison.

To those standing around the set that night at Al Franken's, this was a joke almost too good to be true. Here was prime time incarnate, all the lameness money could buy. The perfect reason a ragged little late-night show with a flyweight budget and an underdog's heart had every chance of showing Roone Arledge and Howard Cosell how retrograde they really were.

A couple of days later they were still laughing about it on the 17th floor. There was a mass meeting in Lorne's office to decide on a name for the repertory players, and people were throwing out suggestions, among them The Group and the *Saturday Night* Repertory Theater Company. Herb Sargent was scribbling some ideas down on scraps of paper and sending them around the room. On one of them was a name inspired by Cosell. If Cosell has the Prime Time Players, thought Sargent, why not call our troupe The Not Ready For Prime Time Players? Everyone immediately liked it. Absolutely, said Lorne.

# CHAPTER 9

# The Children's Television Workshop

From the day he started work on *Saturday Night*, Lorne began earning a reputation for himself at NBC as a troublemaker. He had what one executive who knew him well called "a confrontational style." Another executive who dealt with Lorne frequently called him "a whiner, a complainer, a threatener." A third found him "a tyrant." A fourth described him as "a deceptive little punk," a fifth as "a snot-nosed kid, a boy genius, too clever for his own good."

At the root of his image problem was the fact that Lorne carried into every encounter he had with the network the same air of absolute, unstoppable conviction he showed his staff on 17. Dick Ebersol shepherded Lorne around to meet the heads of various NBC departments over the spring and summer, and with many of these executives Lorne left the impression that, as far as he was concerned, they, along with everybody else at the network, were little more than obstacles standing between him and his grand personal vision of *Saturday Night*. Which was, in fact, pretty much the way Lorne did see them.

There was, for example, his demand that no one over thirty years of age, or much over thirty, be assigned to the show. That was a condition he tried to set for the technical crew, and it had to be explained (by several executives well past thirty) that there weren't enough top-notch people available of that age to staff a studio. Lorne made the same request for the unit managers who would be assigned to oversee *Saturday Night*'s day-to-day budget expenditures. By the time he reached the graphics design department he simply walked in and said, "Give me the youngest person you've got."

Lorne seemed to assume incompetence everywhere he went. He demanded approval over every press release NBC's publicity department put out, and within a few weeks managed to have the first publicity director assigned to the show relieved of her duties. When he met Barbara Hering of the NBC legal department, who would be responsible for seeing that *Saturday Night* didn't libel anyone, he wasn't especially interested in hearing her advice. Instead, he offered to have his own attorney give her a call to go over some of the issues involved. In a meeting with another NBC lawyer, Lorne listened patiently as the lawyer explained what the show could and couldn't do. Then he shrugged and replied, "I've understood everything you've said. But if the show is a failure, nothing you've said really matters. And if the show is a success, then nothing you've said really matters."

The only thing that mattered to Lorne, he told his friends, was that he be able to put on a show he himself would watch, and respect. He used to say there was nothing worse than a show that tried to be hip and wasn't, and he was obsessed with saving himself, this time, that humiliation. *Saturday Night* would be done his way or not at all.

If somebody at the network resisted one of his requests, Lorne would say, "I have to have it." He practiced a policy known in corporate gamesmanship as "shopping for a yes." If one executive turned him down, he'd say, "Well, if you can't approve it, who can? I'll go to them." He tried to find a friend in every department if he could, but usually he simply went to the top. If a camera broke down in the studio, he thought nothing of calling the vice-president of engineering at home to complain. When he learned that NBC Sports had a track meet scheduled in the fall that would result in a late start for *Saturday Night*, he went straight down to the programming department to argue that they should put the track meet on another time. If a lower-echelon employee offended him, he'd call up the head of the department involved and demand that person never work on *Saturday Night* again. If he got advice he didn't want, he ignored it. Dave Tebet kept suggesting different hosts for the show, none of whom was ever called. But when Tebet and Antonowsky balked at Lorne's wanting Richard Pryor as a host, Lorne threatened to resign.

Lorne pulled this off at first mostly on sheer nerve. He'd used the same methods at the CBC in Canada when he'd had to, but that was a much smaller pond than NBC. His previous battles with American networks had been, compared to his daily struggles for *Saturday Night*, relatively indirect. So he wasn't particularly sophisticated about what he was doing, or particularly diplomatic; he just wouldn't take no for an answer. In the process he expended, as Dick Ebersol put it, "a lot of capital" at the network.

Lorne relied heavily on Ebersol to lead him through the labyrinths of NBC. Ebersol knew better than Lorne which executives would be important to the show, which were likely to be resistant, and which might be flexible. Ebersol also knew where the bodies were buried: who was aligned with whom, who had real power and who was just a figurehead, who was on the way up and who was on the way out. And although Ebersol was more attentive than Lorne to covering his flanks, he nonetheless shared Lorne's fundamental belief that *Saturday Night*'s best hope (and his own, if he was going to make a mark with the show) lay in keeping network interference at a minimum. Ebersol consequently fought for *Saturday Night* almost as hard as Lorne did, and expended quite a bit of his own capital in doing so.

Ebersol and Lorne's ultimate card was the knowledge within the company that *Saturday Night* was the pet project of NBC president Herb Schlosser. It was a card they played often. They acted as though Schlosser had given them a mandate (which was the word they used) to produce the show. In times of trouble they frequently invoked Schlosser's name. "I'm going to raise hell with Herb Schlosser about this," Lorne would say, and people generally backed off. This mandate they supposedly had was partly real and partly fiction. Schlosser was indeed committed to *Saturday Night*, but he hadn't necessarily committed to the *Saturday Night* Ebersol and Michaels had in mind. It was only a matter of time before someone called their bluff, and Don Carswell, the head of the network's finance and budget operations, was the one who called it.

Carswell and the people under him felt from the outset that Lorne had double-crossed them. He'd been so reasonable and vague in the initial meetings to set *Saturday Night*'s budget, but after he'd gotten the show approved he essentially tore up the budget and did whatever he wanted. And he was spending a fortune doing it. Every show is assigned a unit manager, whose job it is to ensure that the show stays within budget. The unit managers reported to Carswell through their boss, a man named Steve Weston, by submitting "A and E" reports, which listed actual versus estimated expenses. In almost every case, *Saturday Night*'s "A"s far outstripped its "E"s. Lorne had hired more writers than anyone expected. Lorne had spent more money producing parody commercials than anyone expected.

(He had the unheard-of notion that the parodies had to look exactly like real commercials.) He was planning for dozens of sets, far more than his budget would ever cover. The show had to have new equipment in the control room, more dressing rooms, more wardrobe and makeup rooms, more cabinets and worktables, more props. One of the writers wanted lamps in his office because the fluorescent lights were detrimental to his brain waves. Lorne Michaels wanted it all, and when the overages were pointed out, he clearly couldn't care less.

Steve Weston, the lord of the unit managers, became *Saturday Night*'s nemesis. He was a short, middle-aged man who, according to several people who worked with him, ran his department as a general might run a military campaign; among the knickknacks in his office, in fact, were a riding crop and a collection of toy soldiers. Weston had worked for years to broaden the responsibilities of NBC's unit managers, so that by the time Lorne arrived they were known in the business for having far greater financial control over the network's productions than their counterparts at CBS and ABC. Weston, who'd just earned his vice-presidential stripes at the network, took Lorne's disregard of his edicts as a personal affront.

He also didn't care for the treatment his people were getting from the *Saturday Night* staff. The unit managers were the only outsiders with an office on 17. They were regarded by *Saturday Night* as spies for NBC and treated accordingly. When a unit manager called a meeting to explain the proper expense forms to be used and the proper way to fill them out, he'd been laughed at as if he were some drawling Marine Corps quartermaster: "We have here," one of the writers mimicked him, "a form nine-nine-three-two from the Stationery Requisition Area." During a field trip to shoot commercial parodies at Briarcliff College in upstate New York (Ebersol's half-brother was president of the school and let them use the campus for free), it was discovered that the unit manager had rented a car for the trip from Manhattan. Most of those from the show had ridden up on a rented bus. The next day, the unit manager's car was commandeered and he was forced to ride the bus. To the unit managers it was very clear how *Saturday Night* viewed them. "We were," said one, "the enemy."

Steve Weston objected to that attitude and declared war on *Saturday Night*, challenging every expenditure, raising hell at every overage. He soon learned, however, that Lorne Michaels couldn't be intimidated. He focused his wrath instead on Barbara Gallagher, Lorne's associate producer. Gallagher wasn't really qualified for the job; she was actually a talented comedy writer who had written for such network shows as *Mary Tyler Moore* and *Maude* in addition to one of the Lily Tomlin specials. She was taking a break from writing, and Lorne had talked her, against her better judgment, into becoming his associate producer. Everyone who knew her considered Gallagher a sweet and sensitive woman—it was widely believed in Hollywood that she had been the real-life model for Mary Tyler Moore's character, Mary Richards. Steve Weston, in network parlance, had Gallagher for lunch. He badgered her so mercilessly she burst into tears on at least one occasion and finally, fed up with Weston and the job in general, resigned. For Lorne, who hadn't liked Weston to begin with, that was the last straw. He simply refused to deal with him anymore.

Don Carswell, like Weston, was a tough customer. He was built like a fullback from the Kansas farm country, but he'd graduated *cum laude* from Harvard and gone on to earn his MBA there as well. He'd worked his way up as a budget controller from NBC's scenic shops; by 1975 he'd been the network's vice president of financial planning for eight years. Carswell differed from the stereotype of the corporate "digit head" in one important respect: He had a sense of humor. "Digit head" was what he called himself. On his office wall hung a huge picture of a fierce Scottish warrior brandishing a broadsword; under it was a caption that read "The Spirit of Compromise." Later he put a plaque on his desk reading, "The Answer is No."

In Carswell's alarm over *Saturday Night* there was, even he admitted, some posturing. Producers routinely want the world, he'd say, and it was his job to convince them to accept something less. Still, Lorne Michaels was proving annoyingly hard to convince, and Carswell seriously believed the network could be getting itself in deep trouble with a show that, likely as not, would be off the air in six months or less. The potential for ratings in its time period and the talent involved were both very much unproved. Carswell had therefore been bringing *Saturday Night's* problems to the attention of higher management at every opportunity. "I had the whole company worried about it," he said later. But it wasn't until he saw Lorne's plans for studio 8H that Carswell took his stand.

Lorne was delighted with what Eugene Lee had conceived for 8H. He had redesigned the entire studio. He wanted to turn the layout around so it faced west instead of south. He wanted to rip out the existing bleacher seats and add a large balcony and swivel chairs on the floor. Instead of having one central stage with an auxiliary stage or two around it, TV's standard studio configuration from the time of Milton Berle, Lee's plans called for as many as eight separate staging areas. Each would have to be lit and wired for sound, not to mention shot, separately. New equipment would be needed for that—lots of it.

The staging areas were to be raised off the floor, as in a theater, which meant that the cameras would somehow have to get high enough to shoot them and still be able to move safely through the audience to reach them. The materials he wanted to use included solid oak and real brick, but the atmosphere he wanted to create was that of a seedy nightclub. That was one of the things Lorne liked most about Lee's design. "Instead of looking all shiny and Mylar," he said, "it looked sort of run-down and beat-up, like New York City did."

Lorne, Ebersol, and Lee presented the blueprints and a 4 X 2- foot model of the set to NBC in mid-August. Attending the meeting, along with Carswell, were Jack Kennedy, NBC's vice-president of operations and engineering; Bob Galvin, vice-president of production operations; and several of their underlings. Also in attendance was Lee's assistant, Leo Yoshimura, whose responsibilities included translating for his taciturn boss in any necessary transactions with NBC. Yoshimura's hair hung well past his shoulders and he generally wore coveralls. His recollection of the meeting was of a blur of gray suits.

Typically, Lorne ran down the changes he would require without a quaver in his voice. His attitude was that NBC's facilities were laughingly out of date and that he would be doing them a favor by fixing them up. "I have," he reminded them, "Herb's backing."

Carswell, Kennedy, Galvin, and their people were stunned. For the first time the full scope of Lorne's plans for *Saturday Night* had been put on paper. As Bob Galvin said later, "The magnitude of the thing really hit us."

Their reaction to Lorne's plan was that he was crazy. Studio 8H was perfectly adequate as it was—in fact, it was one of the best studios available. "If it was good enough for Toscanini," one of the unit managers said, "it's good enough for Lorne Michaels." Don Carswell, who was responsible for actually giving the order to start construction, priced the redesign at between $250,000 and $300,000, about three times what Eugene Lee and Leo Yoshimura had projected. Carswell called Lorne and Ebersol to his office and flatly refused to approve it.

Word of Carswell's refusal spread quickly among executives at NBC who were aware of what had been happening with the show. They knew that if Michaels and Ebersol lost this one, things were going to be different with *Saturday Night* from then on. Soon after they left Carswell's office, Ebersol picked up a phone and called Herb Schlosser. He asked the secretary who answered if Herb was in and she said he was. Ebersol and Lorne took Eugene Lee's model of the studio, got on an elevator, and rode to the sixth-floor executive suite. They walked into the foyer outside Schlosser's office, saw Schlosser sitting alone inside at his desk, walked in, and put the model in front of him.

"This is the new set," they said, and they showed him how it would work.

"Great," Schlosser said. "I loved the show-and-tell. But why'd you bring it to me?"

"Because," Ebersol answered, "Carswell won't approve it." "Okay," Schlosser said, "I'll straighten it out, but it'll take a day or two. You have to go through channels sometimes."

"Herb," Ebersol said, "we wouldn't be here if going through channels accomplished anything."

"Okay," Schlosser chuckled. "Okay."

On September 5 a memo was dispatched from Jim Dullaghan, an aide of Don Carswell's, to Dan Sullivan regarding the redesign of studio 8H. "Please be advised," it said, "that management is aware [of the projected cost] and it is to be treated as an explainable overage."

\* \* \*

*Saturday Night*'s victory in the great set battle didn't end the show's fights with the digit heads so much as it bought some time. Before the set was approved, there had been talk of cutting costs by moving the show to Los Angeles or to NBC's studios in Brooklyn— or of stopping the production altogether. Now it was clear *Saturday Night* was going on the air, from 8H, and that it would be something more than a glorified *Meet the Press*. It would have to succeed or fail on the air, and chances were considerably better that it would fail. Then the problems would simply disappear.

All Don Carswell and Steve Weston could do in the meantime was to try to keep the damage to a minimum, a goal they continued to pursue assiduously. The quarter of a million dollars spent on 8H consumed a lot of *Saturday Night*'s capital at NBC, both literal and figurative. Nonetheless it soon became apparent that was just the beginning.

The show's writers and performers emerged from their isolation on the 17th floor in the early fall to go to work in the studio. Their arrival was greeted by the crew in 8H—cameramen, prop men, technical engineers, stagehands, and the like—with all the enthusiasm of decent townspeople witnessing the invasion of a Mongol horde. The crew had heard about Lorne's demands that no one over thirty work on the show, which hadn't made the best of first impressions, since most of the crew members had been working at NBC since the days of Milton Berle's *Texaco Star Theater*, the *Kraft Television Theatre, Your Show of Shows*, and all the other live programs from television's Golden Age. The true outrage, however, came when the crew met the freaks Lorne Michaels *did* choose to work with.

It was a classic generation gap. The crew was characterized by one of *Saturday Night*'s writers as "a bunch of Archie Bunkers" who on the political spectrum fit "somewhere between the Klan and the Mafia."

For their part, the crew members spent much of their time snickering at the *Saturday Night* people in disbelief and disgust, muttering, as they watched the rehearsals, such comments as "This gang just came from Woodstock!" Every day the snack table outside 8H declared the differences between them: The crew had the usual doughnuts and coffee; *Saturday Night* had fresh fruit, vegetables, and nuts.

When the crew saw the material the show was working on, they were even more outraged. There were words, jokes, a whole attitude that to them bordered on the obscene. They couldn't believe that what they were hearing would go on national television. After some sketches were rehearsed, crewmembers turned to one another and said, "Are you kidding me?" Sometimes they actually booed.

Just as appalling was the obvious fact that almost no one on *Saturday Night* had the slightest familiarity with the fundamentals of television production. Scripts came in—long, long scripts—calling for several changes of sets and complicated special effects that could never be achieved. There were either no technical directions on them or voluminous technical directions that made no sense. It became a standard joke among the crew that *Saturday Night*'s writers seemed to regard the chroma-key device, which projects graphics on the screen such as those that appear behind newscasters, as some sort of magic wand. Any time a writer was told that an effect he wanted couldn't be done—flooding the studio for a hurricane scene, for example—he'd shrug and say, "Okay, do it in chroma key."

The cast members, having little or no experience working with cameras, would roam the stage more or less as the muse struck them, as they had when they'd performed in theaters. They disdained cue cards and ignored the instructions of director Dave Wilson and stage manager Joe Dicso. Again and again Wilson's voice came ringing out over the studio's public-address system during rehearsals for the cameras: "I'm looking at the back of your head!"

Eugene Lee's set designs provoked howls of protest from the carpenters in NBC's shop and from the stagehands in 8H. Coming, like the cast, from the theater, Lee ordered things built to last, with steel-reinforced slats instead of the customary plywood, in addition to the real oak and real brick. After long and bitter arguments, the shop built the sets to Lee's specifications—and charged the show a fortune for them. As the stagehands carried them up in the elevators to 8H, they would grumble that all of 30 Rockefeller Center could collapse and Eugene Lee's sets would still be standing.

To the *Saturday Night* staff, the crew's complaints were interpreted as reactionary resistance to change. "We want to do something new and different!" director Dave Wilson remembers the writers saying. "Let's not go with what already exists!" Wilson found himself constantly fighting to hold the line between pipe dream and reality. "Yes, let's experiment a bit," was the gist of his response, "but this is a live show. We have to make sure we backstop ourselves with what I know we need to accommodate a live show." It got to the point that, in writers' meetings, when somebody described an adventurous idea, the group would turn to Wilson and groan collectively, "Okay, Davey, tell us why it can't be done."

The 8H crew members weren't the least impressed with *Saturday Night*'s attempts to break the boundaries of conventional TV—they felt they were the ones who had to bear the burden of the show's ignorance and disorganization. *Saturday Night* became known within 8H as "The Children's Television Workshop." (The Children's Television Workshop is the organization that produces *Sesame Street* for public television.) It didn't help that the kiddies' leader, Lorne Michaels, clearly knew more than his charges did about television, for the crew saw Lorne as the very fount of *Saturday Night*'s arrogance. "He always had an answer, quick and offhanded, not friendly," says stage manager Joe Dicso. "Lorne was full of 'exactlys' and 'ahhs' and 'of courses.' 'Ahh' meant he'd made a mistake. There were no apologies."

Lorne's style was epitomized to the crew by his habit of strolling around the set with a glass of white wine in his hand. The wine had been the cause of a heated row with unit-manager boss Steve Weston. Lorne felt NBC ought to pay for it since it was there to be shared with staff and guests, but Weston refused, citing as his reason an RCA policy prohibiting liquor in the building (a policy that was violated with impunity in the offices of the company's executives). Lorne eventually got his wine, a nice Chablis Grand Cru at about $144 the case, according to the unit manager who approved the invoices. The cost was hidden in the show's prop budget. Members of the crew would watch Lorne walk by, holding his chilled glass properly, by the stem to avoid warming the wine, and say that this must be his way of letting people know who the producer was.

CHAPTER 10

# On the Air

Outright rebellion by the crew may have been avoided because they were confident *Saturday Night* wouldn't last five weeks once it went on the air. Whether it would get on the air in the first place was another question.

The last few days before the premiere show on October 11 constituted a race-to-the-finish of epic proportions. George Carlin, hip stand-up comedian and *Billboard* magazine's Comedy Artist of the Year, was the host. Lorne (who felt a twinge of guilt booking a *Tonight Show* regular after the promises he'd made to Johnny Carson) said in a press release that Carlin was chosen because "he's punctual and he fills out forms well." The real reason, though, was that Lorne hadn't wanted to subject some of the hosts he cared about more, such as Lily Tomlin and Richard Pryor, to the trauma of the first show. He didn't know if he could "protect" them adequately.

Lorne took care to protect the show itself by overbooking it with guests. He wanted to be sure he had plenty of options to fill ninety minutes with if something went wrong. Besides Carlin there were two other stand-ups, Billy Crystal and Valri Bromfield, and two musical guests, Janis Ian and Billy Preston (as close as Lorne could get to his original targets, Carole King and Stevie Wonder).

Despite this insurance, none of the neophytes on the show was at all certain the first Saturday would pass without, as Herb Sargent, the veteran, put it, "some terrible accident or mishap." This was more than the usual first-night jitters: Even the old pros on the crew were coming up to Dave Wilson during the week in a state of near panic, not because they doubted their own abilities to pull it off, but because they doubted the abilities of the people on *Saturday Night*. Outwardly, Lorne projected his usual aura of assurance. "The worst that can happen is that none of us will ever work again!" he'd joke, trying to break the tension. Gilda Radner noticed, however, that Lorne's face was broken out the entire week before the first show.

George Carlin, who had no idea what he'd signed on to when he arrived in New York, was not reassured as the week went on. A practitioner of the monologue, he found himself on a sketch-comedy show with an obviously distraught group of amateurs. Those on the show, in turn, found Carlin difficult and distant, which undoubtedly had something to do with the fact that he was, as Carlin himself later put it, "in another world" on cocaine at the time. From the moment of the first read-through of material on Wednesday, Carlin started expressing more and more doubts about appearing in some of the sketches that had been written for him, preferring instead to stick with the monologues he knew best. Lorne was insisting that whatever monologues he performed at least be new for television, and Carlin assured him they would be. But they weren't, and Lorne knew it.

NBC had its own worries about Carlin's reputation for controversial material. He'd been the focus of a major battle over censorship and free speech in broadcasting after a radio program aired a routine from one of one of his record albums about the seven dirty words you can never say on television. There was serious talk within the network of putting the first *Saturday Night* on a delay of several seconds so that if there were any obscenities they could be cut before going out on the network live. Despite some reports that such a delay was in fact instituted on the first show, NBC gave up on the idea as impractical and the show did air live, as advertised.

Dave Tebet was also concerned that Carlin's appearance would project too ragged an image for the new show. He summoned Lorne and talent coordinator Craig Kellem to his office. Kellem was a bit ragged himself; he was in the habit of writing messages on his arms and he was not in the habit of wearing socks. When he and Lorne sat down in Tebet's office, Tebet, according to Kellem, listed several conditions: "I want Carlin to get his hair cut, and I want him to wear a suit." Pausing, Tebet glanced down at Kellem's feet and added, "And I want him to wear socks!"

Lorne spent much of his time during the week struggling with the studio's sound system, which musical director Howard Shore swore hadn't been upgraded since it was installed in the 1950s. Lorne had been complaining about the sound problems in 8H for weeks. It was vital to him that the studio audience be able to hear everything that was happening, because if they couldn't hear it, they wouldn't laugh, and then the audience at home would think the show was bombing. NBC wasn't buying that theory. As long as the sound came across to viewers at home, Lorne was told, it didn't really matter how loud it was in the studio. Some new equipment had been put in, including a new audio console in the control room. Unfortunately, NBC's engineers were still reading the manual for it as Billy Preston, Janis Ian, and the *Saturday Night* band began their sound checks. It became painfully obvious then that the problems were even worse than Lorne had feared.

Dealing with rock bands was a new and baffling task to the sound technicians in 8H. Toscanini hadn't had electric guitars in his orchestra, and neither had Milton Berle. Now there were as many as fifty microphones all over the studio instead of four or five over a single stage, and they had to be balanced between sound sources ranging from a screaming Marshall amp to a blaring horn section to the soft oohs and aahs of the backup singers. Overwhelmed, the technicians simply turned the volume on everything down, reducing the mix to a muddy blur and Howard Shore to a quaking fury.

On Friday night there was a complete run-through of the show. It was, by every account, a disaster, both creatively and technically. Somebody had forgotten to make sure all the seats in the studio were filled, and at the last moment the pages from NBC's Guest Relations staff had been out on Sixth Avenue pulling in any warm bodies they could find. Thus some of those who witnessed *Saturday Night*'s first full rehearsal were derelicts taking the opportunity to spend ninety minutes off the street. They got more than they bargained for: The rehearsal ran two hours overtime. It was not, however, very funny. It was hard to hear everything, and a lot of the material that could be heard wasn't working. Neither was the lighting director, who disappeared on Friday and had to be replaced on Saturday.

When the rehearsal was finally over, Lorne called a mass meeting of everyone connected with the show, from performers to stagehands. They assembled around the center stage, called "home base," where Lorne sat on a stool with a microphone. He ran through his instructions and comments—that cut was too quick; change that line in the script; speak up a little in that scene; work on such-and- such a camera angle. It was a communal idea, the gathering of the troops at dawn, but it infuriated rather than inspired most of those there. People fidgeted and thought of all the other things they had to do while Lorne went on, one person at a time. Ebersol and Dave Wilson subsequently talked Lorne out of continuing this particular event in the weekly production schedule.

Ebersol got up at the end of Lorne's talk and apologized to the group for the problems with the sound system, vowing that before the show went on the next night he would fix it. He wasn't going to do it with NBC's help, however, since every engineering executive of any stature was in Boston for the network's coverage of the Red Sox-Cincinnati World Series. Ebersol started calling around town, desperately trying to find some equipment. At 2:00 a.m. he reached an outfit called Hollywood Sound, which was in the process of taking down one of its rock concert systems in Madison Square Garden. Ebersol persuaded them to truck their equipment to NBC, where they worked all night setting it up for the show the next day.

The sound technicians had to work around the stagehands, who with Eugene Lee and Leo Yoshimura were frantically trying to finish the set. In the end it had come down to a battle over the bricks on the stage at home base. They were 8 X 8-inch facing bricks, not contact paper or painted. Not only did they weigh half a pound apiece, but they were to be laid on the stage diagonally, which meant they had to be cut to fit. The shop, which was in Brooklyn, refused to build them into the set, saying the bricks would break up in the truck on the way to NBC. So the bricks arrived in a crate along with a single carbide saw blade. To Leo Yoshimura, the implied message was clear: "Cut them yourself, asshole."

A half-dozen or so angry stagehands ended up doing the cutting, sitting in a back room off 8H until 6:00 a.m. Saturday, cursing and asking Leo, who stood over them, "Why the fuck are we doing this?"

"Because," Leo told them, "Eugene and I want it done."

* * *

The thousand details to take care of on Saturday comforted Lorne—they helped keep his mind from dwelling on the terror of the broader perspective. He kept joking. "This could be the most humiliating night of our lives, you know," he chuckled at one point. But as airtime neared, his nerves began to show.

Just before the dress rehearsal, he was in the control room watching a technician cue up the closing credits that would roll at the show's end. The credits were important to Lorne. He liked the idea of playing with them a little, keeping the show funny to the absolute end. He'd recently noted the incongruity of people's using, for no discernible reason, *Bud* as a nickname, and it was decided that the credit roll would list a long string of Buds: Lorne "Bud" Michaels, Gilda "Bud" Radner, Dave "Bud" Wilson, and so on. But when Lorne looked at the credits that night he saw a change he hadn't expected. Dick Ebersol had moved to the top of the list the credits for the airline, the limousine service, and the costume supply house that provided services to the show in exchange for promotional announcements. That way, if the show ran long, the "money credits," as they were called, wouldn't be cut.

Lorne didn't like the idea that, after so much hard work, the creative credits would be preceded by a bunch of plugs. Snapping momentarily, he flew into a rage. He found Ebersol in a hallway outside the control room and shoved him up against the wall. "I'm not doing the show!" Lorne yelled. "I'm walking!" But he didn't walk; he stormed off to watch the dress rehearsal.

Lorne's flare-up about the money credits would, in the long run, pale compared to the grief that would result from the last name on the credit roll that night: Dick Ebersol's. Ebersol had come to Lorne a day or two earlier and asked that, just for the first show, he be listed at the end of the credits as *Saturday Night*'s "executive producer for NBC." Ebersol was clearly emulating his mentor Roone Arledge, who was inevitably billed as the executive producer of every sports event broadcast on ABC. Lorne, feeling that Ebersol deserved some recognition for his role in getting the show on the air, and not thinking an executive-producer credit meant that much anyway, agreed. Neither he nor Ebersol would appreciate until later the implications of that decision.

The dress rehearsal was another disaster, and for the first time Lorne faced what would become a *Saturday Night* ritual: totally restructuring the show between dress and air. As Lorne was on his way to meet with his staff, Craig Kellem heard him say, to no one in particular, "NBC better have a movie ready, just in case." Kellem couldn't tell if Lorne was joking or not.

During the hour between dress and air, George Carlin told Lorne he'd decided once and for all he wouldn't perform in the show's centerpiece sketch. It was an elaborate costume piece, written by Michael O'Donoghue, in which Alexander the Great returns to his high school reunion, having conquered the known world. No matter; his classmates still consider him a jerk. The sketch was cut. The show was still too long, and Lorne told Billy Crystal and Valri Bromfield they would have to cut their monologues radically. Bromfield agreed and, terrified, went off to her dressing room to find a way to trim a five-minute routine down to two minutes, Crystal's manager, Buddy Morra, however, vehemently resisted the change, and Lorne ended up in his second confrontation of the evening in the hallway outside 8H. Crystal and his people stormed out in a huff. Instead of making his network television debut, Crystal was soon riding a train home to Long Island, his face pressed against the window, wondering how things could have gone so wrong.

At eleven o'clock, Leo Yoshimura was still finishing the skylight overlooking home base. Dick Ebersol ran up to him every few minutes, asking breathlessly, "Are you gonna get this done? Are you gonna get done?" Leo, some seventy-two hours without sleep at that point, shrugged and said, "I don't know, Dick. If I don't you can fire me."

Between these conversations, Ebersol was arguing with John Belushi, who didn't want to sign his contract.

"Gilda's right," he was saying. "These are Mickey Rooney-Judy Garland things! I ain't signing it."

Ebersol was trying to explain that John had to sign before he could go on the air, but Belushi was having none of it. Finally, Belushi spotted Lorne's manager, Bernie Brillstein, and waved him over. "This guy is telling me this is favored nations," he said, nodding at Ebersol. "The only way I'll sign is if you tell me it's fair. ... And I'll only sign if you represent me."

Brillstein shrugged and said fine. "I get ten percent and I pay my own expenses," he said. John took Ebersol's pen and signed. Crazy John Belushi, Brillstein would later reflect. He conned himself right into a deal with the boss's manager. Crazy like a fox.

Belushi and Michael O'Donoghue took their places for the show's opening sketch, which had become known on the 17th floor as "The Wolverines" sketch. It was a "cold opening," meaning the show started with it instead of the standard announcements and credits. Lorne decided to go with a cold opening because he wanted the show to come across immediately to viewers as something different from the usual, and it would become a *Saturday Night* trademark.

"The Wolverines" sketch was essentially a dramatized version of an old joke that O'Donoghue had given a bizarre twist with some unexpected dialogue. Belushi played an Eastern European immigrant who came for an English lesson with his professor, played by O'Donoghue.

O'DONOGHUE: Let us begin. Repeat after me,
JOHN: (In tight-mouthed concentration, nods.)
O'DONOGHUE: I would like ...
JOHN (In a thick accent): I would like ...
O'DONOGHUE: ... to feed your fingertips ...
JOHN: ... to feed yur fingerteeps ...
O'DONOGHUE: ... to the wolverines.
JOHN: ... to de wolver-eenes.
O'DONOGHUE: Next, I am afraid ...
JOHN: I em afred ...
O'DONOGHUE: ... we are out ...
JOHN: ... we are out ...

O'DONOGHUE: … of badgers.

JOHN: …of badjurs.

O'DONOGHUE: Would you accept …

JOHN: Would you accept …

O'DONOGHUE: … a wolverine …

JOHN: … a wolver-eene …

O'DONOGHUE: … in its place?

JOHN: … een es place.

O'DONOGHUE: Next, "Hey," Ned exclaimed …

JOHN: "Hey," Ned esclaimed …

O'DONOGHUE: "Let's boil …

JOHN: "Let's boil …

O'DONOGHUE: … the wolverines."

JOHN: … "the wolver-eenes."

O'DONOGHUE: Next …

(O'Donoghue suddenly gasps, clutches his chest, and falls off his chair to the floor, obviously stricken with a heart attack. John looks puzzled for a moment, then repeats O'Donoghue's gasp, clutches his chest, and throws himself on the floor.)

John Belushi and Michael O'Donoghue in "The Wolverines" sketch, the first sketch on the first show. © *NBC*

\* \* \*

For weeks Belushi and O'Donoghue had performed "The Wolverines" whenever somebody new dropped by the 17th floor, and as many doubts as the cast and writers had about the first show, everyone felt good about the cold opening. "It let you know," O'Donoghue said, "that this was our humor, not their humor. You knew you weren't watching George Gobel or Garry Moore, or whatever comedy had been."

Now, sitting onstage as John waited offstage to make his entrance, O'Donoghue listened to Joe Dicso count off the final seconds. As he waited he pondered the fact that, when the red light on the camera came on, his visage would be winging its way into somewhere upward of *five million* homes. His heart raced and he had a sinking feeling in the pit of his stomach. "It was like the feeling you get," he said, "when you're right at the top of the roller coaster, that hovering sensation before you zoom to the valley. I've never been so fucking frightened in my life."

The opening went smoothly—as, for the most part, did the rest of the show. At the end of "The Wolverines" sketch, Chevy Chase ventured tentatively onstage wearing a stage manager's headset, peered at the two figures lying prone on the floor, looked up at the camera, and broke into a grin. "Live from New York," he shouted, "it's *Saturday Night!*"

Then, as the opening montage rolled, announcer Don Pardo read off the names of the performers who would appear on the show. The repertory company came at the end of the long list of guests, and Pardo, with more than thirty years of announcing experience behind him, choked. "… and The Not For Ready Prime Time Players!" he said. Carlin entered for his first monologue, wearing a three-piece suit with a T-shirt, a compromise ensemble that neatly, if unintentionally, summed up the inherent contradiction of an outlaw show appearing on network television.

The Not Ready For Prime Time Players had several sketches on the show, but they were all fairly brief and they weren't really standout scenes. As unfamiliar as their faces were, their presence amidst all the guests was indistinct. The exception was Chevy Chase, who had a three-minute solo shot as the anchorman on *Saturday Night*'s parody newscast, Weekend Update. Chevy owned Update from the minute it went on, and he got off some good lines in the opener. He quoted Teamsters' union officials as saying that the missing Jimmy Hoffa "will always be a cornerstone in the organization." He reported Gerald Ford's new campaign slogan: "If he's so dumb, how come he's President?" And he broke for a commercial with the teaser, "Still to come, earthquake claims San Diego, four million die in Turkey, and Arlene visits an art museum."

(The players in the first show included a middle-aged character actor named George Coe, who had worked on some of the *National* Lampoon's productions and who currently had a part in the NBC soap opera *The Doctors*. Coe had been hired to play the parts of any older men that sketches might call for, but Lorne soon decided his young performers were capable of handling those roles. Coe appeared on *Saturday Night* intermittently and continued a very successful career as an actor and commercial spokesman. One of his more memorable roles was as Dustin Hoffman's boss in the movie *Kramer vs. Kramer*.)

A lot of the material featuring the rep company was, as they say in the trade, "out of the trunk"—pieces of business the writers and players had done before, knew well, and felt safe with. Dan Aykroyd, for example, wrote and starred in a sketch he'd done in Lorne's improv class in Toronto years before. It was about two salesmen for a home security company who broke into the house of a suburban couple, terrorized them, and kidnapped their child to prove how vulnerable to attack the family was. "In the event of a radioactive firestorm," Danny demanded at one point, "how secure are your foodstuffs?"

Guest comedian Andy Kaufman probably made a stronger, and stranger, first impression than any of the regular players. Lorne put him on early in the show, a vote of confidence that was not misplaced. Kaufman stood at center stage next to an antique record player and listened to a scratchy recording of the theme song from the old *Mighty Mouse* cartoon series. He waited nervously until the few bars in the song came up where Mighty Mouse himself sings, "Here I come to save the day!" Kaufman lip-synced that line grandly, then stood, waited, and, yes, twitched, till those few bars came around again. The theme from *Mighty Mouse* was probably as familiar a melody to the generation who grew up on Saturday morning cartoons as Kate Smith's "God Bless America" was to their parents. But

Andy Kaufman © *NBC*

no one had seen a comedian like Andy Kaufman on television before, and, as strange as he was, the audience loved him.

The only serious trouble of the evening for NBC derived from George Carlin's final monologue, a routine about people's self-centered conceptions of God. It was irreverent enough to begin with, but Carlin made it more so by ad-libbing some lines. He speculated that perhaps God was only "a semi-supreme being," since "everything he has ever made died." He wondered why people had the plastic Jesus figurines on their dashboards facing toward them instead of watching the road, and concluded that "middle-class American hypocrites" must like to show off for Jesus. Questioning the Lord's divinity was not a customary source of humor on network television, and neither was making fun of people's religious convictions.

As the show ended and the house lights came up, the packed control room burst into applause in weary relief. The show had actually gone on, and off, on schedule, with no breakdowns in between. Then the phone rang. It was Dave Tebet, who had been watching the show in his suite as the Dorset. He wanted to talk to Dick Ebersol. Tebet was enraged about Carlin's monologue. He said he'd already called the NBC switchboard, and, sure enough, it was lighting up with complaints. Worse, one of those who called was a representative of Cardinal Cooke, who as archbishop of New York presided over the city's Catholics from Saint Patrick's Cathedral across the street from NBC. Tebet was also enraged over Ebersol's executive-producer credit. Ebersol hadn't said anything about it to management, and executives taking any sort of on-air credit was a violation of NBC policy. Ebersol, according to Tebet, claimed that the credit was Lorne's idea.

Ebersol left the post-show party about 3:00 a.m., depressed. As he walked by Saint Patrick's, he peeked in the church offices to see if a light might be on. Maybe if Cardinal Cooke was still up, Ebersol could talk to him to explain what happened with the Carlin monologue. The offices were dark. The following Monday Ebersol learned that the call from Cooke's office had probably been a hoax. The archbishop of New York had not stayed up late to watch the premiere of *NBC's Saturday Night*.

Among those who *had* stayed up was Herb Schlosser, who was in Boston for the World Series. Schlosser and his wife had gone out to dinner that night with baseball commissioner Bowie Kuhn and his wife, and afterward they'd hurried back to Schlosser's hotel room to watch the show. Schlosser was a little surprised by the scale of what Ebersol and Michaels had mounted, and a little puzzled by some of the humor. But Bowie Kuhn had laughed, and since Schlosser knew Kuhn to be a conservative man, he considered that a good sign. If the commissioner of America's game could enjoy this unorthodox new comedy, all must be well.

Halfway across the country, in Aspen, Colorado, Steve Martin, by then pursuing his career as a stand-up comedian, had also watched *Saturday Night*'s premiere. He hadn't so much laughed as looked on in wonder. "Fuck," he said to himself, "they did it. They did the show everyone should have been doing."

CHAPTER 11

# The Show That Was Always a Hit

Lorne had been completely sincere when he told Herb Schlosser in April that *Saturday Night* would have to find itself on-air, that he knew what the ingredients were but not the proportions. He found the mix he wanted surprisingly fast—by the fourth show, to be exact. But it was a rough four weeks getting there, and at their end, Lorne resigned.

Lorne's friend Paul Simon hosted the second show, and his reunion with Art Garfunkel, their first appearance together in six years, dominated it entirely. Many of *Saturday Night*'s writers, still recovering from the premiere the week before, were relieved they didn't have to produce more material for what was essentially a music special. Lorne, some thought, designed it that way on purpose to counteract a malaise well known in show business, the second- show blues.

Director Dave Wilson got a breather, too: The biggest production problem of the week was placating the host, who had a nagging fear that his bald spot might appear on camera. During rehearsals Simon kept checking the monitors in the studio to see how he looked, turning his head from the camera as he did, and so seeing exactly what he didn't want to see, the back of his head. Wilson's voice kept coming over the studio speakers, more mechanically as the days dragged on: "Paul … you're looking at the monitor, Paul." Finally Wilson had to ask Lorne to have a talk with his host.

The cast members were less pleased about the Simon show because of the paucity of their roles on it. The Not Ready For Prime Time Players were threatening, some of them thought, to become as insignificant on

NBC's *Saturday Night* as their prime-time counterparts on *Howard Cosell's Saturday Night* Live on ABC. Chevy Chase was still the only standout. For the first time, he staged one of his falls during the show's cold opening, and he again had his solo showcase on Weekend Update. The rep company appeared only briefly in Simon's show, for about thirty seconds, in Bee costumes.

The Bees were *Saturday Night*'s first recurring characters, and one of its first sources of dissension. They were conceived as a device for getting all the cast members onstage at one time, as a group. Before the show went on, Lorne and Franne Lee had discussed using several other animal species to serve the same purpose, including elephants and cockroaches. On the first show there had been a short sketch, written by Rosie Shuster, about a Bee maternity ward. "Congratulations," the nurse informed the proud father. "It's a drone." There was a silliness to The Bees that Lorne liked, and he wanted to keep bringing them back. But the cast members weren't infatuated with them, especially John Belushi, who felt they were beneath his dignity as a comic actor. Their appearance on the Simon show was particularly humiliating. In mid-show they surrounded Simon at home base, but Simon told them the Bees number had been cut, and they all ran off like obedient schoolchildren. They reappeared momentarily at the end of the show, when in the midst of thanking his guests, Simon added, "Oh, I forgot The Bees."

Rob Reiner hosted the third show, which was the first *Saturday Night* to resemble closely the format on which the show would soon settle. It was also a brush with disaster. All week long Reiner and Lorne had argued about what material should be on the show. Albert Brooks, a good friend of Reiner's, had turned in a film that was thirteen minutes long, about three times what it was supposed to be, and Lorne didn't want to use it. Reiner insisted it go on. He also insisted on doing an opening routine in which he played a sleazy Las Vegas nightclub singer, similar to the character that would later become one of Bill Murray's most famous bits. Reiner's version, however, was not very funny, and it seemed interminable—six minutes and twenty-five seconds long. Lorne tried throughout the week to convince Reiner to drop it, but Reiner refused. Lorne didn't have enough confidence yet to overrule a celebrity host's demands, nor did he think it was worth it in this case to force a showdown.

Between dress and air, Reiner blew up anyway, "sniveling and whining," as one of the writers put it, that he would be embarrassed by a terrible show. "Lorne, you've sold me out!" he said. "This is going to be awful! I don't know why I'm here … I quit. … I'm not doing it!"

Reiner did go on, and his Las Vegas parody predictably bombed. He didn't have that much else to do on the show; instead, The Not Ready

For Prime Time Players, for a change, stood out. Jane Curtin moderated a talk show called "Dangerous but Inept," in which Laraine Newman played guest Squeaky Fromme, the failed presidential assassin from the Manson Family. John Belushi and Gilda Radner played another suburban couple and Dan Aykroyd their kindly doctor in a public service spot for the National Pancreas Association ("I'm sorry, Ed, but your pancreas is on the fritz"). Gilda had a segment to herself called "What Gilda Ate," in which she was silly but charming. John Belushi had two star turns, first with his spastic imitation of blues singer Joe Cocker (a showstopper in *Lemmings*), and then, surprisingly enough, as a Bee in the final sketch of the show.

Belushi played a Bee waiter serving Reiner and his wife, Penny Marshall, in a restaurant. Reiner broke character and (sounding a lot like he had backstage before the show) started complaining. "I was told 'no Bees' when I signed on to this," he said. "They're not helping the show—they're ruining the show!"

Fed up, Belushi tried to explain. "I'm sorry if you think we're ruining your show, Mr. Reiner. But, see, you don't understand—we didn't ask to be Bees. You see, you've got Norman Lear and a first- rate writing staff [on *All in the Family*]. But this is all they came up with for us. *Do you think we like this?* No, no, Mr. Reiner, we don't have any choice." The audience broke into applause at that point. John stalked away but quickly returned to resume his rant, angrier than ever. "You see, we're just like you were five years ago, Mr. Hollywood California Number One Show Big Shot! That's right— we're just a bunch of actors looking for a break, that's all! What do you *want* from us! Mr. Rob Reiner, Mr. Star! What did you expect? *The Sting?*"

That speech was the first time *Saturday Night* incorporated its backstage life into its material on-air, a technique that would become a staple of the show. It also marked the show's declaration of independence from the tyranny of its hosts, and it went a long way toward defining *Saturday Night*'s budding stance as an underdog show getting bolder by the minute.

On the fourth show, hosted by Candice Bergen, everything fell into place. Everyone loved Bergen as soon as she walked in. Part of it was her looks. The women on the show watched in bemusement as Lorne, Chevy, John, and Danny ran around "like puppy dogs" all week, vying for her attention. Bergen was also a genuine movie star, the only movie star many of those on *Saturday Night* had ever worked with. She had an aura of glamour and class that reflected well on them. But more than that, *Saturday Night* loved Candice Bergen because Candice Bergen loved *Saturday Night*. She was the first host to come in singing the show's praises, acting as though it was she who was honored to be among them. She had, as well, no pretensions to being a comedienne, and so put herself entirely in the show's hands, another first. It was an irresistible combination.

Bergen would later compare the experience of hosting *Saturday Night* to being kidnapped by the Symbionese Liberation Army—you either converted and became Tanya, she said, or you died. Bergen definitely converted. At one point during the week John came into Lorne's office to explain an idea he had.

He would play the macho film director Sam Peckinpah; Candice would play an actress Peckinpah abuses on the set. To show Bergen how it would work, he grabbed her, slammed her against the wall, pummeled her with his fists, shook her, threw her on the floor, and leaped on top of her, screaming madly all the while. Lorne and O'Donoghue watched as John and Candice disappeared behind Lorne's desk. O'Donoghue resisted the temptation to get up to see what was happening, thinking it would be best to act as if this were merely part of the everyday routine. He sat listening to the sounds of their struggle as Lorne, frozen, looked on in wide-eyed horror. Bergen, the glamorous movie star, laughed through it all.

The good feelings came through on-air. The Not Ready For Prime Time Players were in nearly every moment of the show, equals with Bergen. There were several *Saturday Night* firsts: the first opening with Chevy Chase playing a bumbling Gerald Ford, the first Weekend Update opening with the line "I'm Chevy Chase and you're not." Everyone was especially happy with the "Jaws II" sketch in the middle of the show, in which Chevy, wearing a huge foam-rubber shark's head, persuaded unsuspecting women to open their apartment doors by muttering "Candygram" in a tight little voice. It was one of the show's longer sketches to that point and the first two-set sketch; it involved every member of the cast and the host, and, like "The Wolverines" sketch, it had a distinctive, crazy style all its own.

At the end of the show, the entire cast gathered around Bergen, and to her obvious surprise and delight, each of them handed her a single red rose. It was the first time the rep company had joined the host onstage to bid the audience good night. The format for *Saturday Night* had been established, and would remain essentially the same from then on.

\* \* \*

By the time Bergen stood onstage with her roses, *Saturday Night* had been without a producer for approximately eighty minutes. Lorne had quit soon after Bergen's opening monologue, although he stayed through the show because he didn't want to abandon his host.

The specific impetus for his resignation was a technical gaffe by an engineer at WNBC-TV, the network's flagship affiliate station in New York. *Saturday Night* had run a filmed commercial parody for a fictional establishment called the Ambassador Training Institute. Done in the style of those cheap late-night ads for schools that promise to open the door to a wonderful new career, it offered, for a sufficiently generous political contribution, to place its students in luxurious ambassadorships in exotic lands. Hard to mistake for a real ad, but WNBC's engineer did, and cut away from *Saturday Night*'s feed to the station's own commercial.

There was no way of telling how often local stations in other cities around the country made the same mistake with *Saturday Night*'s commercial parodies—the parodies were intended to look like the real thing, after all. But when it happened in New York, everyone in the 8H control room could see it on the local monitor. When it was pointed out to Lorne, he went into a white fury. "That's it," he said. "I'm gone."

He came running out of the control room looking for Ebersol. He found him at the end of the bleachers in 8H.

"You fucked this show up," he said. "This network stinks. It's your fault, the show is ruined. I quit. I'll finish the show, but then I walk. And I'm not coming back."

Ebersol didn't take the threat too seriously. "Well, he's threatened to walk before," he said to himself, and he avoided Lorne the rest of the night. But the next Monday at two in the afternoon, about the time Lorne usually came in, Ebersol got a call from Bernie Brillstein. "Dick," Brillstein said, "Lorne's not coming back to work."

"Bernie, this is bullshit," Ebersol replied. He couldn't believe Lorne was making such an issue out of a stupid technical mistake. Granted, it shouldn't have happened, and Ebersol was already in the process of drafting a blistering memo to Bob Galvin in engineering, copies of which went to thirteen other executives, implying very strongly that the woman responsible be fired for her "unprofessional and inexcusable" error.

"It may be bullshit," Brillstein told Ebersol, "but Lorne's mad."

What Brillstein didn't tell Ebersol was that the WNBC incident had been only the last problem in a whole series of problems plaguing the show, and Lorne had decided to take a stand. He'd already been on edge the night of the Bergen show because NBC had run a longer-than-usual movie that pushed *Saturday Night*'s starting time back to 11:45. Lorne knew the delay could be fatal to his ratings, and he considered it an insult to him and to Bergen. He was also still outraged by NBC's refusal to give him a lighting director he could work with. He'd said on Saturday that anyone who couldn't make Candice Bergen look good couldn't do anything.

Those and a few dozen other annoyances caused Lorne to feel he was getting, as director Dave Wilson put it, "the fast two-step" from NBC. Lorne knew that unless he could somehow force the network to give him more support, those were just the sort of annoying details that could destroy the show. And he knew there were many at NBC who wouldn't be in the least disappointed if that was just what happened.

The reason Brillstein didn't mention any of this to Ebersol on the phone was that Ebersol himself had become a major annoyance to Lorne. Before the show went on the air, Ebersol's expertise within the network and Lorne's expertise as a comedy producer had complemented each other quite well. But from the moment *Saturday Night* premiered, Lorne felt that Ebersol started to push more and more into his territory, and their relationship had grown increasingly strained.

Ebersol's executive-producer credit on the first show was one of the first signs of his overreaching. According to Dave Tebet and Marvin Antonowsky, Ebersol had been called into Antonowsky's office the Monday after the show to explain how the credit had come about. Ebersol, they say, again told them Lorne had suggested it as a way of thanking him for all he had done for the show. Antonowsky says he immediately got Lorne on the phone. "Mr. Michaels," he said, "what were you thinking of, putting that credit on?"

Lorne responded that Ebersol had asked him to put it on.

Antonowsky hung up and angrily turned to Ebersol.

"How can you lie to us?" he said. "Did you think we wouldn't find out?"

Ebersol, according to Tebet, "hemmed and hawed for a while and then shuffled out of the office."

(Ebersol says this meeting never took place.)

Ebersol might have backed off after that, but he didn't. He kept giving interviews to reporters in which he talked about all the things he'd done with *Saturday Night*, rarely mentioning Lorne's name. It was, one of the writers said, as if Ebersol "was bowing in front of Lorne, upstaging him." One day Lorne was sitting in his office on 17 reading an article in which Ebersol was interviewed. There wasn't a word about Lorne.

"Well," Lorne said to his cousin Neil Levy, "Dick should be here soon."

Sure enough, a few minutes later Ebersol rushed in saying he didn't know how this had happened, he'd been misquoted.

When he left, Lorne turned to Levy and smiled. "I think he was misquoted accurately, don't you?"

It was clear to many of those involved with *Saturday Night* that Ebersol instinctively felt his grasp on the show diminishing as soon as it went on the air. He had been instrumental in the show's birth, and now he was striving—almost desperately, some thought—to maintain control over its future.

The week of Rob Reiner's show, Ebersol had been so disappointed with the scripts that he wanted to discard them all and start from scratch. Then he insisted between dress and air that Lorne tell Reiner he couldn't do his opening monologue as the Las Vegas lounge singer. If Lorne didn't cut it, Ebersol had said, he would. When Ebersol was handed the show rundown just before air and saw that the monologue had not been cut, he angrily confronted Lorne, telling him the monologue would ruin the show. Ebersol didn't understand, Lorne said later, that there are appropriate and inappropriate times to exert pressure.

The following week brought more of the same. Ebersol drafted a memo to Lorne on Thursday suggesting a number of changes he thought should be made in the Candice Bergen show: Some of the pieces were too long; others the audience wouldn't understand; others should be moved to improve the pacing. It was becoming obvious to Lorne that something would have to be done to get Ebersol off his back.

\* \* \*

Unaware that he was one of the principal sources of Lorne's discontent, Ebersol told Bernie Brillstein to talk some sense into his client. Then he went to work to ensure that *Saturday Night* would go on the air the next week, with or without its producer. The host, comedian Robert Klein, was told Lorne was sick in bed with the flu.

Ebersol called the 17th floor and asked some of the writers to come to his office. "I think you're aware that Lorne went berserk over this thing the other night," he told them. "I can't imagine it's a serious thing, but he's decided to treat it as a serious thing. We've got Robert Klein upstairs, a writers' meeting is supposed to start, and you're basically going to have to produce the show until I get this thing straightened out with Lorne."

Then he said everyone could leave except Chevy, O'Donoghue, and Herb Sargent, who Ebersol thought should take control of the show. Anne Beatts refused to go along with that.

"Look," Beatts said, "I think the women should be represented here, and I'm not leaving. I'm sure Lorne would want it that way."

Beatts later admitted that she hadn't been at all sure that's how Lorne would have wanted it, but she said it anyway. Rosie Shuster agreed, saying she wasn't leaving either. Chevy said, "Fine, of course the girls should stay," and they did. After a brief and not especially substantive discussion, they all went back to the 17th floor.

No one on the 17th floor was sure what to think. Chevy and O'Donoghue chaired a meeting of the staff that night. Several of those there suggested everyone on the show resign in support of Lorne. But O'Donoghue, who had already talked to Lorne and offered to tender his own resignation, said that Lorne had expressed the wish that the show go on, saying that maintaining its momentum was the most important thing.

Later, people stopped by Lorne's apartment at the Osborne to see what was happening. To most of them he said, "I'm not coming back," taking care not to undermine his position with NBC by giving anyone the impression he was bluffing. But to a few, Neil Levy among them, he winked and said, "Don't worry."

Lorne was operating at that stage with a certain amount of leverage within NBC, but his resignation was still very much a calculated risk. The network had been suitably impressed with the quality of the show he'd produced, despite the money he'd spent producing it. Getting Candice Bergen to host was considered a particular coup, and after seeing that the format worked so well on that show, Lorne's confidence increased.

Probably his strongest card was a glowing article by Tom Shales, the TV critic for *The Washington Post*, which appeared the morning of the Bergen show. "*NBC's Saturday Night* can boast the freshest satire on commercial TV," Shales wrote, "but it is more than that. It is probably the first network series produced by and for the television generation—those late-war and post-war babies who were the first to have TV as a sitter. They loved it in the '50s, hated it in the '60s and now they are trying to take it over in the '70s ... [It is] a live, lively, raucously disdainful view of a world that television has largely shaped. Or misshaped."

Shales, a Baby Boomer himself, was a widely respected critic and his opinion carried considerable weight. Nonetheless, there remained many, many problems with *Saturday Night*. Almost without exception the press in subsequent years would characterize the show as "an immediate hit." That was not, by most television standards, correct. True, it had immediately improved on the ratings Johnny Carson's reruns had been getting in the time period. But that was hardly a significant achievement, since Carson's weekend ratings had been virtually non-existent. The point was how *Saturday Night* stood up against the competition on other channels—what "share" of the available audience it attracted—and the truth was that when Lorne resigned, *Saturday Night*'s highest shares were 23's for both the Carlin and Reiner shows. Network programs were deemed to be marginally successful in those days with shares of 30. Candice Bergen's show, as Lorne had feared with the late start, dropped to a 16 share. Not only was *Saturday Night* not an immediate hit, it was headed in the wrong direction.

Even more important to NBC was the fact that, while the Carson reruns cost almost nothing to put on and brought in a tidy profit of about $20,000 a weekend, *Saturday Night* was spending about $250,000 a week and losing money hand over fist. NBC's advertising department had issued press releases saying that commercial spots in *Saturday Night* were "sold out" from the beginning. But that was misleading, intentionally so. Every television show is sold out—it isn't often viewers see thirty seconds of blank screen where an unsold commercial was supposed to have been. The real point is how much money commercial time sells for in the advertising marketplace, and there, too, *Saturday Night*'s success was less than immediate.

NBC's initial asking price for commercial spots in the show was $10,000, which was cheap to begin with, but advertisers weren't buying. The sales department was forced to offer package deals wherein advertisers who bought three *Saturday Night* spots for the regular price got one spot free. That brought the true per-spot cost down to $7,500 for thirty seconds, an absurdly low price for a network program (and about what financial chief Don Carswell had estimated when he set the show's budget). Even then, the sales department had to scramble to fill the show.

One indication of how desperate *Saturday Night* was for advertisers in the beginning was its decision to go along with what Lorne and most of the others on the show considered a compromise of their integrity: having The Not Ready For Prime Time Players pitch Polaroid cameras live, on air. Candice Bergen at the time was a spokeswoman for Polaroid, and Polaroid's advertising agency had been taken with Chevy Chase. So the two of them, dressed as Bees, played around with an SX-70 on her show for sixty seconds. Lorne had insisted that all the cast members get in on the action—they could all use the extra money, which was about the same as their weekly paycheck—and each of the players did a live ad over the next several weeks. Polaroid's agency grew dissatisfied with the spots and dropped them after that; there wasn't enough time to show a picture developing on-air, and it was hard at times for viewers to tell if they were really commercials. Polaroid did, however, stay in the show as an advertiser, so the live ads served their purpose. As Robert Conrad, the NBC executive then in charge of selling advertising on *Saturday Night*, put it: "We used them as a gimmick to sell a show nobody wanted."

Neither had the press response been uniformly positive. John J. O'Connor, the TV critic for *The New York Times*, had issued a review of the first two shows and (after admitting that "an unusually good dinner on Long Island" had caused him to miss a half hour of the premiere) delivered a thumbs-down verdict. "It's not enough," O'Connor said, "for the new *Saturday Night* concept to be transmitted live. Even an offbeat showcase needs quality, an ingredient conspicuously absent from the dreadfully uneven comedy efforts of the new series." O'Connor was one of the few critics in the country whose clout equaled, if not outweighed, Tom Shales's. Dick Ebersol, who had assumed O'Connor would react more positively, since he was known to loathe more conventional TV fare, felt the review was "a nail in the heart."

On the 17th floor there wasn't the least bit of concern about O'Connor's pan, or, for that matter, about the show's poor ratings and weak sales. The Monday after the first show, Lorne had said matter of factly, "Well, I guess we're a hit," and, despite any evidence to the contrary, no one on *Saturday Night* ever doubted he was right. Lorne posted O'Connor's review and other bad reviews on the bulletin board on 17 so people on the show could laugh at them with contempt. "We weren't waiting for John J. O'Connor to decide the show was a hit," said talent coordinator Craig Kellem. "The attitude was that O'Connor made a mistake."

Since ratings were a mystery to almost everyone on the show, Lorne would explain them. Lorne was no expert at reading ratings either, but he interpreted them so that even if they looked disappointing, he always had a reason why they were great.

"Are you kidding?" he'd say. "Do you know what our lead-in was this week? I'm thrilled! Kathy, bring in a bottle of wine!"

On the 17th floor, *Saturday Night* was what Craig Kellem called "the show that was always a hit … a manifest destiny hit." It was inevitable that, sooner or later, the rest of the world would catch on.

* * *

None of this meant Lorne would be successful in getting what he wanted from NBC with his walkout, of course, since the rest of the world hadn't yet caught on. But timing, as in comedy, is everything in network power politics, and Lorne had both instinct and luck with him when he resigned.

The Monday after the Candice Bergen show, when Lorne was still sitting in his apartment at the Osborne, the first demographic breakdown of *Saturday Night*'s viewers was delivered to NBC by the A. C. Nielsen Company. With the show's mediocre overall ratings, this was an especially key report. *Saturday Night* could still justify its existence if it managed to attract the youthful audience for which it was designed. And it did, spectacularly.

The analysis prepared by the NBC sales department said that more than 75 percent of *Saturday Night*'s viewers were between the ages of eighteen and forty-nine, a higher percentage of viewers in that age group than for any other show on television, including those in prime time.

In other words, while *Saturday Night*'s audience was still relatively small, it was amazingly pure, a fact that NBC's salesmen could use with great effectiveness in selling the show to advertisers who were specifically trying to reach young adults. Jim Hicks, one of NBC's salesmen peddling *Saturday Night* on Madison Avenue, heaved a deep sigh of relief when he saw that demographic report. He'd been promising that *Saturday Night* would deliver the youth market, and here was the proof. "That report got me off the hook with quite a few clients," he said.

The report did not open the advertising floodgates to *Saturday Night*. The show's sales remained weak, mainly because its overall ratings remained poor through the first season, averaging only a 21 share. But the demographics proved that at least the show had potential. The sales rationale was there.

Dick Ebersol was ecstatic. On Tuesday he sent the sales department's analysis to the 17th floor with a cover memo that read, "I have a lot of trouble understanding television numbers [a comment probably intended to ingratiate himself with the *Saturday Night* staff by playing hip, since Ebersol knew numbers extremely well] but the attached report is so fantastically incredible that one does not have to read numbers to understand it. What it all means is that Lorne and all of you have produced a show which has the most attractive audience on television today."

The news of *Saturday Night*'s demographics circulated quickly within NBC's top management, and undoubtedly was taken into account there when the decisions of the next few days were made. But Lorne hadn't known about the demographics report when he resigned, and he hadn't resigned counting on it—he would say later he was too naive about ratings then to think about exploiting them. Lorne's talents lay elsewhere. As Dick Ebersol put it, ruefully: "I was very sophisticated about business and not very sophisticated about people. Lorne was not very sophisticated about business and very sophisticated about people. And in the final analysis being sophisticated about people will win, every time."

Lorne, in short, was politically astute enough not to rely solely on Dick Ebersol for support within NBC. He hadn't known much about the NBC hierarchy when he came to New York, but he was a fast learner, and he was more adept than Ebersol at making the right friends. He quickly developed his own allies, gradually reducing his dependence on Ebersol as he did.

Herb Schlosser was chief among those allies. Schlosser and Lorne, both fond of cultivating an air of sophistication and powerful friends, shared similar temperaments, and they liked each other. Lorne's assistant, Kathy Minkowsky, who had worked for them both, says that Lorne and Schlosser did not develop a father-son relationship, as Lorne might have hoped. As president of the company, Schlosser maintained a certain distance. But Lorne visited Herb regularly, and he was closer to Schlosser than most producers ever got.

For day-to-day support, Lorne turned to Mike Weinblatt, the executive vice president of the network and a key behind-the-scenes power at NBC. A quiet, balding man in his mid-forties, Weinblatt also projected a diplomatic demeanor; he was low-key, even nondescript, but he had a sardonic smile and the reputation of being a consummate network politician. Weinblatt's closest network protégé at the time, Aaron Cohen, watched "a tremendous admiration society" develop between Lorne and Weinblatt. Weinblatt was ordinarily a punctual man, and when Lorne came to see him, which was often, Weinblatt would allocate thirty minutes for the meeting. Two and a half hours later, Lorne would leave Weinblatt's office, and the next day in the studio Lorne would be telling unit managers and engineering executives all the things Weinblatt had promised him. Lorne and Weinblatt became so close they talked on the phone every Sunday night; Bernie Brillstein called Weinblatt "Uncle Mike."

It was to Mike Weinblatt that Lorne and Brillstein turned when Lorne walked out. Brillstein called Weinblatt and told him Lorne wanted more support from the network, and that something had to be done about Ebersol's meddling. Herb Schlosser was also called. It's likely that those calls accentuated a growing feeling in NBC management that Ebersol had become too closely involved with his new show, that he was losing the perspective an executive needed to keep a production in line. In any case, within a week Ebersol was removed from direct responsibility for *Saturday Night*, although by admirably diplomatic means.

Lorne returned to work on Tuesday. Four days later, exactly a week after the Bergen show, Herb Schlosser turned to Marvin Antonowsky during an affiliates' conference in Florida and said, "Marvin, do you have an announcement to make?"

Indeed, Marvin did. Dick Ebersol, who had done such a good job launching *Saturday Night*, had been promoted to vice president, late-night programs. He was, at twenty-eight, the youngest vice-president in NBC history, overseeing not only *Saturday Night* but also the rock concert show *The Midnight Special*, Tom Snyder's *Tomorrow* show, and all late-night specials. (Dave Tebet made sure the *Tonight Show* was not included in Ebersol's new domain.) Ebersol was still nominally Lorne's boss, and he continued to be involved with the show, but he had been elevated above direct, day-to-day responsibility for it. That job fell to Mike Weinblatt's aide, Aaron Cohen, who was named vice-president of programs on the East Coast.

To Dick Ebersol, being named head of the late-night division was a promotion richly deserved, a conviction that grew daily as *Saturday Night* evolved over the next several months into a cult phenomenon. He would brag often about being the company's youngest V.P. ever. But privately, he'd found the promotion "breathtakingly abrupt," and he understood, if most of the world did not, how his power over his favorite child had been taken away. He was bitter about it for years.

Aaron Cohen had spent his entire network career in sales and he made no pretense of expertise in programming. Immediately upon assuming his new position, Cohen met with Don Carswell, who told him *Saturday Night* had to be brought under control. The budget overruns, Carswell said, were averaging more than $100,000 per show, and the network was looking at a loss of millions. Carswell showed Cohen *Saturday Night*'s A&E reports with all the overages circled, and Cohen was shocked at what he saw. Then he went up to 17 to meet Lorne Michaels.

Lorne welcomed Cohen and introduced him to some of the people on the show. They went into Lorne's office to talk, and Cohen started telling Lorne that *Saturday Night*'s excessive spending would have to be curbed. Lorne cut him off.

"Fuck NBC!" he said. "It's a miracle anything gets on the air because of NBC! And you're saying it's *my* fault?"

Lorne went on to enumerate a long list of reasons why, as Cohen remembers it, "everything at NBC was designed to prevent him from doing the show the way he conceived it."

Cohen left Lorne's office, a trifle unsteadily, promising to see what he could do.

CHAPTER 12

# Television of the Subconscious

ALL CAST MEMBERS MUST WEAR UNDERWEAR ON
SATURDAY. THIS MEANS YOU!
   —Notice posted outside studio 8H by costume designer Franne Lee

The Candice Bergen show had done as much for the confidence of the
whole *Saturday Night* team as it had for Lorne, but with all the distrac-
tions, the Robert Klein show the following week was something of a
step backward, not truly bad, but dull. It wasn't until Lily Tomlin and
Richard Pryor hosted the next two shows that *Saturday Night*'s writers
and performers became convinced they were good enough to hold their
own with the best in the business.

Tomlin's show was by far the more orderly of the two. As was her
habit, Tomlin was reserved and careful about what material she would
and wouldn't do, and Lorne escorted her around during the week like
visiting royalty. The women on the show in particular were thrilled to be
working with Tomlin and tried hard to write material for her. But at that
point the women were still struggling for a voice in the show, and a lot
of what they wrote didn't make it on.

The major exception was a sketch by Rosie Shuster and Anne
Beatts in which a group of women took instruction on how to ogle
and harass construction workers in the same way construction workers
ogle and harass women. A hard-hat in shorts and a tank top paraded
back and forth in front of the class while the teacher, played by Tomlin,

suggested suitable jeers, among them "Hey, studmuffins, wanna make bouncy bouncy?" The problem had been getting one of the men to play the hard-hat. Belushi, who didn't like Tomlin and wasn't comfortable going onstage in such a revealing outfit anyway, flatly refused the part. After much cajoling, Dan Aykroyd finally agreed to do it, but onstage he felt naked and vulnerable (just the way women on the street feel, Rosie Shuster noted) and his discomfort showed. Michael O'Donoghue didn't care much for Tomlin, either. After dress rehearsal, when a piece he'd written hadn't gone over well, he affixed her with what she called the Evil Eye, staring at her so piercingly she broke out laughing.

O'Donoghue also had his problems with Richard Pryor. In the early seventies Pryor had developed a reputation as a dangerous genius, an explosive embodiment of Black Rage, and at the time he hosted *Saturday Night* he retained an atmosphere of paranoia and violence around him—some on the show noticed that members of his entourage were carrying guns when he arrived in New York. It hadn't been easy getting him there. During the summer, Lorne, Craig Kellem, and John Head had flown to Miami, where Pryor was performing in concert, to talk him into doing the show. Pryor agreed only after making a number of demands. He would bring with him a black writer named Paul Mooney; a black actor named Thalmus Rasulala; a black musical guest, Gil Scott-Heron; and his white former wife, Shelley Pryor, who had a bizarre stand-up act Pryor insisted be included on the show. Lorne remained delicate and acquiescent throughout the meeting and cheerfully agreed to Pryor's conditions, but on the plane back to New York he wondered if he'd given away too much. "He'd better be funny," he said.

Like Lorne, most of the *Saturday Night* staff was awed by Pryor's talent and deferential toward him in the extreme, although some, especially Garrett Morris, were offended that he thought it necessary to bring his own people with him. Pryor himself was by turns funny and charming, then suspicious and intimidating, and he was as sensitive about material he found racist as Lily Tomlin was about material she found sexist. Michael O'Donoghue dropped by Pryor's hotel room at one point during the week and, in the course of the visit, told Pryor a joke he'd written for Weekend Update. A man should not be judged by the color of his skin, the joke went, but by the size of his nostrils. As Pryor began to protest, O'Donoghue made the mistake of interrupting him in mid-sentence. Pryor picked up a cognac bottle and threatened to bash O'Donoghue's head in. He laughed as he did it, but O'Donoghue took him seriously enough to stay away from the show the rest of the week.

NBC, too, was intimidated by Pryor, terrified he would utter on- air some of the profanity for which he was infamous. Lorne, who had waged a major fight to get Pryor approved as a host in the first place, argued through most of the week with executives who wanted a five-second delay used so that any ad-libbed obscenities could be bleeped. Finally one of the censors came to Lorne and said he could use the delay or not as he chose, but he would suffer the consequences if Pryor misbehaved. Lorne, going against all his own arguments, decided to play it safe and agreed to the delay. He thought Pryor could be trusted, but he wasn't willing to bet the show's future on it. He suspected that if Pryor learned of the delay he'd probably walk out, so it was arranged in the strictest secrecy. All the clocks in the studio were set back five seconds, and the few who were aware of the change were told not to breathe a word out loud for fear Pryor or one of his people would discover it.

NBC was also nervous about Pryor's fans, who were assumed to be as dangerous as he was, and armed security guards appeared in the studio on Saturday. Still there was trouble. Pryor had demanded that more than fifty seats for the show be held for his personal use, which meant that seating was even scarcer than usual. A large contingent of Pryor's friends and fans milled around outside the studio as the show was about to go on. It was becoming an ugly scene, but NBC's pages, mindful of fire regulations, adamantly refused to allow any standing in 8H. Finally someone opened a side door for a moment and dozens of gate crashers thundered in.

They saw one of the best shows in *Saturday Night*'s history. Pryor's monologue, about white dudes who take acid and go see *The Exorcist*, was a masterpiece. That was followed by John Belushi's first Samurai sketch, "Samurai Hotel." Pryor and Belushi played samurai bellboys arguing over which of them would carry a guest's bags upstairs. Pryor ended the argument by cutting the hotel's check- in counter in half with his sword, causing Belushi's samurai to respond, "I can dig where you're coming from," the only line he would ever say in English. Gilda Radner's character, the sweet little old lady Emily Litella, delivered her first editorial on Weekend Update, deploring the "busting" of school children. When anchorman Chevy Chase informed her the issue was actually *busing* school children, her "Oh. ... Never mind" brought down the house.

The peak of the show may have been a sketch in which Chevy played a job interviewer giving Pryor a word association test. They began with the usual neutral words like *dog* and *tree*, but soon started slipping into more volatile territory.

"White," Chevy said.

"Black," Pryor answered.

"Bean." "Pod."

"Negro." "Whitie."

"Tarbaby." "What'd you say?"

"Tarbaby." "Ofay."

"Colored." "Redneck!"
"Junglebunny." *"Peckerwood!"*
"Burrhead." "Cracker!"
"Spearchucker." *"White trash!"*
"Junglebunny!" "Honkey!"
*"Spade!" "Honkey honkey!"*
*"Nigger!"* "*Dead* honkey."

The tension generated by Pryor and Chevy during this sketch could be felt distinctly in the audience, and there was a nervous edge to the laughter not usually associated with TV comedy.

Pryor used the word *ass* twice on the show, but the censor manning the delay device let both go by. (They were edited out of the taped version that was broadcast in the western time zones later that night.) Pryor's show was the first and last *Saturday Night* that did not air live.

* * *

After their triumph with Pryor, *Saturday Night*'s performers and writers were never again so deferential with a guest host. Once and for all they had erased any lingering doubts in their own minds, and they never looked back. They were now locked in a rhythm they would maintain, more or less, for the next five years, and as the show hit its stride, it became more and more difficult for the majority of hosts to keep up: The sheer lunacy of *Saturday Night*'s production process overwhelmed them. The production process also shocked every executive who dealt with it at NBC and appalled the crews in studio 8H and the Brooklyn scenery shop. For all the attention that would soon be paid to what *Saturday Night* put on the air, *how* it got on the air was every bit as radical.

Those at NBC who had been in television since the medium was born, who had worked with Milton Berle and Sid Caesar and all the other founding fathers, say they had never seen anything like it. Certainly the show had many elements in common with its predecessors in live television entertainment—indeed, *Saturday Night* resurrected styles many of its viewers were too young to remember. And certainly for pure, unselfconscious spontaneity it couldn't approach the likes of Caesar and Berle and Ernie Kovacs, Steve Allen, Dave Garroway, Arthur Godfrey, and Jack Paar, to name a few of those who invented television when there were fewer rules to break. *Saturday Night*'s distinction was that it tried to re- create their sense of reckless adventure twenty-five years and a lot of rules later, on a modern and gargantuan scale. When it came to mounting a regular, weekly program (the usual production cycle was three consecutive shows and then a week off), *Saturday Night* was the most complicated, ambitious, and chaotic ever attempted in the history of television.

Once a weary member of the crew in 8H came up to Lorne and gave him a folder. It was an old program, a playbill from Sid Caesar's *Your Show of Shows*, *Saturday Night*'s most direct antecedent in live television comedy. The program, listing the sketches for the show and the performers in them, was distributed to the audience as they walked into the Center Theatre on Forty-ninth Street for the broadcast performance. It was printed on Fridays for a Saturday evening show, meaning the configuration of the show had been set in place almost forty-eight hours in advance. "Why don't you try doing this, Lorne?" the crew member said, and both he and Lorne laughed. No program was ever distributed to the studio audience for *Saturday Night* because not once in the five years Lorne produced it did the show stay the same between the end of the dress rehearsal on Saturday and the air show an hour or so later.

*Saturday Night* was chaotic by design. From Lorne on down, the tenets of the show's production philosophy were that inspiration, accident, and passion were of greater value than discipline, habit, and control. *Saturday Night* was the first program of its kind to commit itself consciously to the subconscious, to emulate as much as it could the spirit of artistic abandon embodied and endorsed by the gods of twentieth-century hip. Baudelaire, William Blake, D. H. Lawrence, William Burroughs, Henry Miller, Jack Kerouac, Lenny Bruce, Ken Kesey, the Beatles, and Hunter S. Thompson were as much the fathers of *Saturday Night* as Kovacs, Carson, Benny, and Berle. Dan Aykroyd called it Gonzo Television. They were video guerrillas, he'd say. Every show was an assault mission.

\* \* \*

The slowest day of the week was Monday. Everyone showed up at 5:30 or so for the writers' meeting in Lorne's office. The host would be introduced to the group and the writers would toss up for consideration whatever ideas they were working on, if any. People often pretended they had some great things in mind even if they didn't, since the meeting served the function of assuring the host that, yes, there was a good chance there'd be sixty-six minutes of material—the amount of actual program time without commercials—written by *Saturday Night*. It was a sure bet there wasn't much written by Monday.

Pitches in the writers' meetings ranged from full-blown sketch ideas to oblique one-sentence summaries. Chevy Chase was one of the most animated pitchers: He'd fall all over the room and the people in it acting out a bit he wanted to do. Dan Aykroyd sometimes gave full-scale manic performances in which he'd play several parts in several different voices, leaping up on chairs and desks, doing the entire sketch and then storming out of the room. Marilyn Miller, on the other hand, usually offered only the barest outlines of an idea. "Well, Lorne," she'd say, "I'm working on a piece where Danny is a Hammond organ salesman in a shopping mall with the organ going around on a turntable."

Other writers would chime in with suggestions, offers to work on a piece, derisive comments, or gratuitous remarks. Lorne would sit back, at ease (Michael Palin, a member of Monty Python who hosted *Saturday Night* several times, described Lorne as "the very definition of laid back"), throwing out comments and jokes of his own. One writer suspected that these meetings served as "the last refuge of Lorne's performing ambitions," since he usually delivered an almost Carsonesque stream of wry comeback lines as he kept the proceedings moving along.

"I don't have anything this week, Lorne," Anne Beatts said once, "but I noticed that if you fold a grapefruit juice label like this, it looks just like a little mouth."

"Information is always acceptable in lieu of ideas," Lorne said.

When the writers' meeting broke up, various pairings would generally go out to dinner, during which ideas would frequently be fleshed out on place mats, napkins, menus, matchbooks, or checks. By midnight a majority of the writers were back on 17, where they'd often work through most of the night. The serious all-nighter, however, was Tuesday, because pieces had to be in some reasonable shape for the readthrough on Wednesday afternoon, when all the scripts for that week's show would first be read by the performers and the host. All night, people would drift in and out of one another's offices, sometimes sitting down and brainstorming for ten minutes, adding a line or two to a piece and moving on, other times staying in one office battering away at an idea till daybreak, when one writer would be stretched out on the floor asleep and two more would still be working.

The unspoken rule was that the more time spent on 17 the more material one was likely to get on the show. The writers were there virtually nonstop from Monday night till Wednesday morning and sometimes for sixteen-hour days the rest of the week. Of the cast members who weren't writers, Gilda Radner was probably the most dedicated. She hung around constantly, handing out Linzer tortes and improvising ideas that often turned into sketches. If she went home to sleep she kept her telephone next to her in bed, always ready to come back to work on a piece. She once showed up on 17 in her pajamas at 2:00 a.m., claiming she'd actually been dressed when the writer called but that she'd changed into more appropriate attire to come to the office.

The production assistants—two of them in the first year—came in before ten o'clock Wednesday morning to find a stack of scripts jammed under the head p.a.'s door. Everything had to be typed and copied by three o'clock to be ready for the read-through. Most of the scripts were handwritten on yellow legal pads with pages ripped apart and stapled back together, no page numbers, lots of inserts, and lots of misspellings. If a script was especially hard to read, the writer stood looking over the p.a.'s shoulder as it was typed. The production assistants soon learned to discourage this habit if at all possible, because inevitably the writer would start changing the script on the spot. Worse yet were scripts written by two or more people, because they would all end up standing behind the p.a., editing, rewriting, and arguing over lines. Other times the writers had to be called and awakened at home for help in deciphering what they'd written, although as time went on the production assistants learned to let them get an extra hour's sleep if at all possible.

The Wednesday read-through was the crucial test for a script. If the reception was good, it was launched into the production chain: Sets were ordered; blocking time was scheduled; costumes, sound effects, and props people went to work on it. The read-throughs were held in various rooms within NBC and were attended by key members of the production staff as well as by Lorne, the host, the writers, and performers. If a sketch died in read-through, its chances of making the show were significantly reduced, although Lorne was known not to be totally swayed one way or the other by the vagaries of a read-through performance.

After the read-through, about five, Lorne, Dave Wilson, Audrey Dickman, Eugene Lee, often Herb Sargent, and sometimes Chevy Chase retired to Lorne's office to lay out the show. Then the writers were called in and told what was in and what was out, what should be cut down and what should be expanded, what needed to have another cast member written into it and what cast member already had too much to do that week.

Dave Wilson, meanwhile, would be conferring with Eugene Lee and Leo Yoshimura, figuring out what sets had to be built, which should be built first, where they would work best in the studio, and how the show should be configured to accommodate costume and set changes. Lorne would come in periodically to explain the inevitable missing sketch— the great idea someone just thought of that wasn't written yet but would definitely be ready by Saturday.

That was another quality Lorne had that the writers and performers appreciated, if Davey, Eugene, and other members of the production staff did not: He was always ready to rip up the show at any point during the week to make room for a new idea he really liked. The first Samurai sketch, for example, was written two days before the Richard Pryor show.

On the 17th floor: A meeting in Lorne's office, 1976. Lorne (behind desk), Alan Zweibel, John Belushi and Michael O'Donoghue.
*Courtesy of F.T. Eyre*

Eugene and Leo worked all night Wednesday designing the sets. They might need as few as three new sets or as many as nine. By eight o'clock Thursday morning Leo was at the shop in Brooklyn with their drawings (which, like the scripts, were often sketched on napkins or tattered scraps of paper), arguing with the head carpenter over how much the construction was going to cost. The first sets would leave Brooklyn for NBC about four o'clock Thursday afternoon. When they arrived they were carried to the elevators and taken upstairs, piece by piece. Sometimes the pieces wouldn't fit in the elevator and Leo would have to take a saw down to the loading dock, cut the set apart, take it upstairs, and reassemble it in the studio.

As the sets were being built, Franne Lee was choosing costumes at the Brooks Van Horne warehouse on Seventeenth Street; her assistant Karen Roston was riding cabs around the city looking for other clothing they needed; Leo Yoshimura and prop master Trip Ullrich were scouring furniture stores and hole-in-the-wall shops for set dressings; various production assistants were tracking down the obscure pieces of film, odd photographs, or impossible-to-find sound effects called for in the scripts. Realism by then had become almost a religion to Lorne, and as a result the detail he wanted in sets, costumes, and props was painstaking, and expensive. The unit managers on the show often tried to talk Lorne into cutting corners on these expenditures, but he almost always refused. Once a unit manager confronted him with an invoice from Saks Fifth Avenue for a cashmere sweater, wanting to know why he had to spend all that money for real cashmere. Lorne quoted the great Broadway impresario Florenz Ziegfeld, who Lorne said always put real silk next to the skin of his Ziegfeld girls because it made them feel good. Another unit manager once asked him why he spent $65 on a skirt for Gilda Radner that would be visible on camera for only a few seconds.

"Who's gonna know the difference?" the unit manager demanded.

"Gilda will know," Lorne replied.

While the production wheels churned through Friday and into Saturday, the writers continued to confer with Lorne, still honing their pieces. Rewritten scripts kept coming in marked "Revised Thursday," "Revised Friday," "Second Revise Friday," "Revised Friday night," and so on. Every change had to be immediately inserted into the master script and distributed to the entire production team. The production assistants learned which restaurants the different writers and performers frequented so they could be found if there were questions or changes in the studio schedule as the sketches were blocked.

Blocking sessions were on Thursday and Friday afternoons in 8H. First there was "dry" blocking, when the cast members would quickly run through a piece to get a general feel of how it worked onstage, then camera blocking, when Dave Wilson painstakingly choreographed the actors' every move to match it with whatever shot he decided to use. Camera blocking was a long, tedious process that the cast abhorred; Dan Aykroyd would complain that they were forced to become robots, mechanically following Davey Wilson's endless commands. It consumed time that might otherwise have gone to rehearsal, which was one of the most frequent complaints of both the writers and the performers on the show.

Even as the cast went through their paces with Davey, the writers were standing nearby with Lorne, taking notes that would turn into more changes in the script, and subsequently in the blocking. Thus, camera blocking often stretched until 11:00 p.m. or later. For the same reason, the cast members soon got over their aversion to cue cards, since there was no use memorizing lines that would all be different by Saturday.

On Friday after the dinner break the cast would be fitted for their costumes. It wasn't always easy getting them to cooperate. The men in particular were known for being slovenly dressers outside the show; Belushi and Aykroyd sometimes stopped by wardrobe during the week to pick up some clean clothes. Belushi was the most reluctant to try things on. He was in the habit of deciding half an hour before air that he didn't like what he was wearing. "Remember that jacket I wore in that other sketch?" he'd say to Karen Roston. "I'll wear that." If Dan Aykroyd found something he liked, he'd magically be able to make himself fit into it. He became especially fond of the black polyester suit he wore when he played Richard Nixon and looked for ways to work the suit into a sketch. He was also a stickler for detail. He had a reference book of badges from which he'd copy designs for any uniforms he wore on the show, and munitions manuals that he'd consult to specify the exact make and caliber of any guns he needed. Danny was such an aficionado of weaponry that when a fully functional M-16 rifle being used as a prop one week disappeared from the set, people assumed Danny had taken it. They did not, however, mention this to the agents from the Federal Bureau of Alcohol, Tobacco & Firearms who came to investigate the theft.

Friday was a long night for a lot of people. The wardrobe ladies stayed until 3:00 or 4:00 a.m. altering and pressing costumes; sometimes they were back in 8H a few hours later to finish their work. Sets were still being finished in the Brooklyn shop, trucked to NBC, and assembled in the studio. As the hours ticked by, the union crews shifted into the overtime category called, for obvious reasons, golden time.

The writers were still rewriting sketches they'd been rewriting all week and just starting work on the three parts of the show that were almost always put off till the last minute: the cold opening, the host's monologue, and Weekend Update. The cold opening and the monologue often as not were merely the victims of procrastination during the week, but Update was intentionally left flexible to make it as topical as possible. The idea was to approximate a real news operation, and the writers took great pride in getting jokes on Update about an event that had just happened.

Alan Zweibel was sitting in a restaurant with Lorne late one Friday night just after a news item appeared that the equine star of the television series *Mr. Ed* had died.

"Can we get a horse?" he asked Lorne.

"You're not thinking of interviewing Mrs. Ed, are you?" "Yep," Zweibel answered.

Lorne told him to go ahead, and Zweibel called the property master at home at 4:00 a.m. By Saturday afternoon a horse was contentedly munching hay backstage.

The production assistants tried to avoid being assigned to Update if at all possible because inevitably new material was being written all day Saturday. Much of that material required finding new photographs, graphics, or sound effects; all of it had to be typed, copied (on green paper to indicate a change), and distributed to the forty or so members of the production team as soon as it came in.

About noon Saturday the production assistants handed out the latest, but by no means final, version of the script for the entire show. The first full run-through of everything except Update was scheduled for one o'clock but usually didn't get rolling until two. Costumes were worn (theoretically, at least) but not makeup. Lorne and Davey Wilson started with the most difficult sketches because they almost never had time for them all. That meant that many sketches—often as many as half—were never performed in costume until dress rehearsal that night.

The run-through always ended at 5:30, when the inviolable one-hour dinner break required by the unions began. The writers and performers ate in the ninth-floor green room; letting anyone out of the studio at that point could be disastrous. The production assistants used the time to make sure the cast members had all the latest changes in their scripts. Dinner was an important cooling-out period during which some wits were gathered and many desserts consumed in preparation for the seven-hour blitz to come.

After the meal break Weekend Update was rehearsed for the first time. The cast members, when they weren't on the Update set, prepared for dress, going over script changes as they sat in the makeup room or in their dressing rooms. Some were more diligent about keeping track of the changes than others. Gilda Radner carefully marked off her parts in each new script with a yellow felt pen. Dan Aykroyd, usually refreshed by a nap during the dinner break, seemed to have an almost photographic memory. He'd flip through the pages of the scripts, mechanically ticking off the changes as he read: "Got it. Good cut. Got it." John Belushi and later Bill Murray relied more on cue cards; Belushi often retired after the dinner break to his dressing room for a massage.

The NBC pages ushered the dress rehearsal audience into the studio around 8:00 p.m. and dress began about 8:30. Lorne positioned himself next to his monitor to the left of center-stage. During rehearsal he watched the screen more than he did the stage so he could see how the show would look on-air. As their sketches were rehearsed, each of the writers came down from the green room and stood beside Lorne, listening as he gave them notes on what should be changed. These were usually minor word changes or fixes that had to be coordinated with props or costumes. Lorne's attention to detail often astounded the writers. One of Rosie Shuster's sketches opened with a man giving a woman a bouquet of flowers. "Make it candy," Lorne told her, "because she'd have to put the flowers in water and we don't want to take the time to do that. If you don't, it sets up an anxiety in the audience's mind—'Why aren't the flowers in water?'"

At the same time, Lorne was judging how well the sketches worked overall and gauging the reaction of the audience. He liked to give himself some room to maneuver by having more material in dress than he could possibly use in the show. Audrey Dickman kept track of the timings with a stopwatch, and before dress she'd say to Lorne, "We're twenty minutes over," a millennium in television time.

"No, we're not," Lorne would answer, "because I'm going to cut this and this and this." This was another policy of Lorne's that drove the unit managers to distraction, since sketches that were cut were often abandoned forever, along with their sets.

Often as not the show came out of dress twenty-five minutes long, so the writers knew their sketches were always vulnerable. It was considered a bad sign if Lorne didn't give them notes in dress, because that usually meant he'd decided to cut their piece and he wasn't worrying about it anymore. It was, of course, also a bad sign if the audience didn't laugh. But here again, Lorne went with his own instincts, knowing there were too many variables even in dress to depend solely on the audience's reaction there.

One of the most important of those variables was the quality of the performances. The cast members held back a bit in dress, often quite a bit, to keep something in reserve for air. It took a while for some of them to learn that technique. Dan Aykroyd had an especially hard time pacing himself in the beginning, often giving his best performance in the Monday writers' meeting and gradually watering it down as the week progressed. Laraine Newman tended to give so- so readings throughout the week and then suddenly to come alive on air, fully defining her characters for the first time. John Belushi would be so loose in dress that it was hard to tell if he had the slightest idea what he was doing, or if he cared, but when the cameras went on for real, he was almost always electric. If a Samurai sketch called for Belushi to slice a loaf of bread or a piece of fruit in half with his sword, he'd usually miss all week long, including in dress, and then split it like a surgeon on-air.

Dress usually ended about 10:20, but sometimes ran as late as 10:50. All that had transpired through the week was but preamble to the insanity that ensued between dress and air at 11:30.

* * *

There were two meetings, both in Lorne's ninth-floor office overlooking the studio. In the first, Lorne met with the writers and the heads of all the production teams; in the second, with the cast members and the host. In cases of extreme time pressure, the two meetings were compressed into one.

The atmosphere in these meetings was one of controlled hysteria, the main idea being to take care of necessary business without succumbing to the tension. Lorne kept his comments short and to the point—"Lose a minute from that" was a frequent request. There might be some argument from a writer or a cast member about a change they didn't like, but Lorne could usually cut them off quickly. Everyone knew there wasn't time now for debate. Lorne joked a bit when he could and seldom raised his voice, but on occasion he'd be insistent. "Goddamn it," he'd say, "make this work!"

As a rule he wanted changes in virtually every sketch, at least one or two sketches cut entirely, and the show's running order completely restructured. Each change had its impact on everything else in the show, and as Lorne went down his list, people would be shouting out whether they could handle them.

Audrey Dickman continuously recounted the timings as production assistants ran in and out, taking notes, typing them up, and distributing them to the rest of the production team.

Although Lorne generally had a good idea of what could or couldn't be done, it was always a moment of truth when he'd turn to someone in the room and say, "Can you do it?" People often amazed themselves when they said yes; then they had to scramble to deliver. Karen Roston once raced downtown to Brooks Van Horne at 10:30 looking for a coat Belushi could wear to play Babe Ruth in a sketch added at the last minute. Brooks's owner had been called to send someone to open the building, but once inside they couldn't find the light switch and ended up rummaging through the racks with a flashlight till they found what they needed.

When the first meeting ended, the production people dispersed to confer with their staffs while the writers who still had rewrites to do hurried to a typing room off 8H. The production assistants had to make sure all the changes got to the control room, to the performers, and to cue cards. The man in charge of cue cards was Al Siegal, a gentle, pear-shaped soul in his fifties. As air time neared he would be besieged by frantic production assistants and writers, sometimes five of them at once, all shouting and waving scraps of paper in front of his face. Often he was still scribbling out new cue cards as stage manager Joe Dicso counted down the final seconds before the show, and often he would be handed more changes during commercial breaks after the show began. Sometimes the performers didn't get all the changes before they went on, and in the control room people would be holding their breath as a sketch came up, knowing the actors would be reading lines they'd never seen.

As the show went on, Lorne again took his place by his monitor, pausing to scan the audience to make sure there weren't too many people in camera range wearing suits and ties. He didn't want viewers at home to see *Saturday Night* as a party for businessmen, and sometimes he'd ask NBC's pages to move people who were too conservatively attired.

During the show he'd stare at his monitor and silently mouth the words of every sketch as it played. Backstage, the performers rushed in and out of the wardrobe and makeup rooms. Often they'd go onstage wearing three different costumes in layers; other times their costumes would be cut down the back and attached with strips of Velcro so they could be ripped off in a second. One problem with the quick changes was that at times some of the men didn't wear underwear. During the show they'd often have to change in the crowded hallway outside 8H, and they'd end up stumbling around behind the wardrobe racks trying to preserve a modicum of modesty. Franne Lee finally posted a notice insisting that all cast members must wear underwear on *Saturday Night*s. She kept an extra box of Jockey shorts around in case somebody forgot.

Periodically during the show Lorne walked into the control room to check timings with Audrey Dickman. If there was time to fill, a short film or parody commercial could usually be added to absorb a few minutes. More often the show ran long, since sketches had a habit of expanding on-air. That meant something had to be cut, and in this case any short films and commercial parodies scheduled in the show were expendable. But occasionally more radical measures were required. Some sketches were cut in half backstage as the show was on the air. Once when Steve Martin was the host, he and Gilda Radner ran out of time in the middle of a sketch. When the show came back from the commercial that interrupted them, Martin shrugged and said they'd have to finish the sketch the next time he hosted. They never did.

The miracle of *Saturday Night* was that things didn't go wrong on-air more often than they did. Catastrophe struck many times in dress rehearsal. Writer Don Novello, who joined the show in the third year, broke his hip during rehearsal of an ice hockey sketch; a week later, on crutches, he made his first appearance as Father Guido Sarducci. Dan Aykroyd was once bitten by a snake in dress rehearsal, and Laraine Newman nearly drowned. She played an accused witch in a sketch with Steve Martin called "Theodoric of York, Medieval Judge." Theodoric decreed that Laraine's character be submerged in the Trough of Justice—if she sank, she was innocent; if she floated, she was guilty. She was innocent. The trough was filled with real water but equipped with a hidden wall. Newman, her hands tied loosely behind her, had to work her way under the wall to be pulled from the trough by stagehands off camera. She almost didn't make it, and by the time the stagehands finally got her out, she'd inhaled a dangerous amount of water. Still, she repeated the stunt an hour later on-air.

Chevy Chase suffered a painful accident on-air during one of his famous falls. Playing Gerald Ford, he tumbled over a podium, which was supposed to have been padded but wasn't. He missed two shows, and the cover story was put out that he'd aggravated an old back injury. In truth, his testicles had borne the brunt of the blow. Buck Henry, in one of his Samurai sketches with John Belushi, stood too close as Belushi wielded his samurai sword and ended up with a nasty gash on his forehead. Stunned, Henry's first instinct when it happened was to turn away from the camera, a move he later regretted. What he should have done, he said, was to walk directly at the camera to show that this indeed was live television, where anything, including bloodshed, can happen.

Animals, as usual, proved to be unpredictable on air. During Zweibel's "Mrs. Ed" interview, the horse playing Mrs. Ed suddenly grew anxious, tugging at its halter and dancing around so that most of the time its rear end faced the camera. During an opening monologue, host Michael Palin put several cats down his trousers, where they were supposed to eat the seafood salad he'd dumped there. All had gone well in dress rehearsal, but the cats apparently sensed the tension of the air show and, clawing to escape, defecated in Palin's pants. He had no time to clean up before his next sketch, in which he played a Catholic priest in a confession booth. Dan Aykroyd entered the booth, and as Palin slid back the window he could see Aykroyd's nose twitch in disgust. It was one of the few times Danny muffed his lines on-air.

There were also the inevitable mechanical difficulties. When consumer advocate Ralph Nader hosted, he fretted all week about a joke that called for an air bag, such as those he was then lobbying to have required in automobiles, to inflate inside his shirt. "What if it doesn't inflate?" he kept asking. Sure enough, it worked in dress, but on-air it produced only a pathetic wheeze, leaving Nader standing with a silly grin on his face.

The real terror, seldom talked about, was that a member of the studio audience would yell, run on camera, or perhaps even pull a gun. One over-enthusiastic fan was intercepted as he rushed the stage during a musical act, and once or twice someone heckled the host during the monologue. But never in the history of *Saturday Night* was there a serious disruption of that kind, a remarkable fact considering the type of fans the show sometimes attracted and how easy it would have been to do it.

In fact, not a few on *Saturday Night* complained that the show was *too* controlled. Director Dave Wilson was a principal focus of these complaints. His detractors felt he was more concerned with having a neat and tidy show that wouldn't embarrass him with his cronies in the business than in taking risks that might be genuinely thrilling if they worked. His defenders, including Lorne, would say that *Saturday Night* was like a huge jet plane and Davey was the pilot who had to land it every week. But Don Novello echoed the sentiments of many when he said, "Yeah, Davey was a pilot all right, but he was no test pilot. Strictly TWA."

Lorne, too, took his knocks for being overly concerned with control. His philosophy that he didn't want the show to be different for the wrong reasons was too inflexible in the eyes of those who would have liked *Saturday Night* to look more ragged and experimental. Chevy Chase was the only one who got away with ad- libbing with any regularity on the show, usually on Update, when it was relatively safe. Tom Schiller was among those who felt Chevy's looseness had a lot to do with his appeal, and one of those who regretted that *Saturday Night* did not more often use the opportunity of being live to, as he put it, "take the moment to comment on the moment."

But Lorne had already taken his moments before the show went on. His high was snatching it back from the brink.

# CHAPTER 13

# Teamwork
# (Show Notes One)

The furnace of the production schedule welded the *Saturday Night* team even more tightly together than it had been before. Nonessential activities were quickly weeded out. Weekly improv sessions for the cast ended, as did the group post-mortems of the previous Saturday's show in Lorne's office each Monday. Friends and relatives slipped further by the wayside; personal calls on the 17th floor were often limited to a chilly "I can't talk to you. I'm writing. Goodbye."

For the first few weeks most of the writers tended to work by themselves, and much of the material continued to be "out of the trunk." But soon collaborations began, new characters and new ideas emerged, and the synthesis of comedy styles Lorne had dreamed about became a reality.

The collaboration that clicked first and counted most was that between Chevy and Lorne. Together they, and to a lesser extent O'Donoghue, shaped, edited, and polished the work of the less experienced writers, and it was their writing that dominated the show, especially in the first half of the season. It was always Chevy and Lorne who would come into the office exulting about the great new sketch they'd been up all night writing. They spent the show's first Christmas break sitting around the 17th floor coming up with enough material to fill much of the next two shows, material that would eventually win *Saturday Night* an Emmy.

Lorne had such confidence in Chevy that sometimes on Mondays, when he asked Chevy what he had for the show that week, Chevy would say, "Trust me," and Lorne would put a card up on the bulletin board that read "Chevy will be funny." As a writer, Chevy had an inspired silliness that produced some of *Saturday Night*'s best-known jokes that first season, among them News for the Hard of Hearing, in which Garrett Morris repeated the headline story of the day shouting at the top of his lungs, and the non sequitur Update opening, "I'm Chevy Chase and you're not," which quickly became Chevy's signature line. He came up with it one day on the spur of the moment after watching a local anchorman who always opened his newscast with the portentous phrase, "I'm Roger Grimsby; here now the news."

On-air, it was no surprise that Chevy stood out from the rest of the rep company as much as he did. As the anchor of Weekend Update he had a showcase that gave him a tremendous head start. He appeared by himself in a simple suit and tie instead of a costume and, thanks to Lorne's aversion to the Walter Crankcase school of humor, using his own, very memorable name. He also had a natural instinct for the camera, an intuitive ability to look it directly in the eye, and he played it like a master. Even if a joke wasn't working, he had a way of looking knowingly at viewers with an eyebrow raised that was totally disarming.

That style gave him a foolproof safety net, and it derived in large part from his utter confidence in himself. Chevy never seemed to have a moment of doubt when he read the news that he was going to be funny. That is comfortable to watch. He had, in addition, the natural advantage of being good-looking, but not in a chilling, fashion-model way. His handsomeness was cocky but still reassuringly all-American, like Johnny Carson's. That, too, is comfortable to watch.

Chevy also appeared as Chevy in his other standout bit, playing Gerald Ford. There was no makeup, no attempt at mimicking Ford's voice or mannerisms, only the play on Ford's clumsiness. And no one, not even the President, took a fall better than Chevy Chase. And just as it would have been difficult to invent a better presidential caricature for the times than Gerald Ford, there couldn't have been a better time than the silly seventies for a revival of the out-and-out physical humor—slapstick—that was Chevy's performing stock in trade. Chevy's comedic gurus weren't of the Lenny Bruce school of reflective, intellectual comedy, nor the softer-edged performers like Bob and Ray, nor the classic stylists like Jack Benny, nor the character comedians like Lily Tomlin, all heroes of others on *Saturday Night*. Chevy idolized Ernie Kovacs, the genius of "device" TV comedy; probably Kovacs's most famous bit, the Nairobi Trio, involved three men in monkey suits hitting each other on the head. Chevy was also, like John Belushi, an admirer of Milton Berle. As with Berle, you didn't have to think too much to appreciate Chevy Chase: he'd do anything to make you laugh, including drool all over himself—which is just what he did in a public service announcement parody for the National Droolers Association.

Chevy himself feels that what he, and the show, did best was to parody television. But beneath the parody of television there was something else: the persona of the anti-comic, which along with the parody of television distinguished seventies humor more than anything else. The anti-comics were satirists who commented on the stupidity of their times by embodying it. Their characters were unrelentingly idiotic. Unlike Jackie Gleason's Ralph Kramden or Lucille Ball's Lucy Ricardo or even Carroll O'Connor's Archie Bunker, they never had a redeeming, humanizing moment of realization or regret. The comic release they provided came not from pointing up the human foibles we all share, but from the more cynical exercise of pointing an accusing finger at the banality of others. Chevy was one of the first true anti-comics to gain national exposure; Steve Martin and Bill Murray were other practitioners of the form.

Lorne's humor was of a more conceptual style. One of his fortes was the sketches, many of them cold openings, that "broke reality"—those that spilled off the stage, and supposedly out of character, to the hallways outside 8H, to the studio control room, to the lobby of 30 Rockefeller Plaza, or to Lorne's office.

An early example of that technique was the "Killer Bees" sketch on the Elliott Gould show in January, written by Lorne and Chevy. It started as a fairly typical sketch, by *Saturday Night*'s standards, when a band of killer bees from south of the border (Gould, Belushi, Aykroyd, Garrett Morris, Neil Levy, and Tom Schiller) invaded the home of a suburban couple (Chevy and Gilda), demanding "Your pollen or your wife, señor."

The sketch rolled along for several minutes until, in the midst of a poignant confessional speech by Gould, the camera started slipping off to one side and then down to the floor. Belushi and the other bees tried to pull Gould within camera range, then gave up in disgust and called out to Lorne. Lorne, as himself, walked onstage, got down on his hands and knees to peer into the camera, then assured them he'd take care of the problem. Another camera followed Lorne as he walked, shaking his head and pounding his fist, into the studio control room, where he found director Davey Wilson swigging scotch and waving his arms, completely drunk. Lorne could be seen slapping Wilson around and taking over the controls while Belushi was heard explaining to Gould what had happened:

Let me tell you one thing about Lorne Michaels. Lorne Michaels has the biggest heart in show business. He hired that director when nobody else would hire him. Twenty- two years ago, Dave Wilson was the best young director in television. He was direct-ing *I Married Joan*. Then, one day, the pressure got to him and he started hitting the bottle. He went on a bender, and didn't pull out of it till Lorne found him six months ago and gave him this job, and a new sense of himself.

Since then, he's been on the wagon, at least until tonight. Okay, so Lorne took a chance and gave an old-timer a new start, and maybe the pressure got to him again, and he cracked. That's not Lorne's fault. He knows we've got a show to do, and if he has to fire him, he will, because he's that kind of producer. But let me tell you one thing, Elliott ... I wouldn't be in Lorne Michaels's shoes for all the money in the world, because right now, he's probably in there firing his own father.

Lorne performed more himself in the first season than he would thereafter (he was never entirely comfortable on camera, and it showed), always appearing, as in the "Killer Bees" sketch, as The Producer. This, too, was a way of breaking reality, and a way of defining *Saturday Night* as the show that didn't stick to conventional pretenses. Probably the appearance that received the most attention was his appeal in April 1976 to the Beatles to reunite on the *Saturday Night* stage. Lorne sat at his desk and addressed the camera directly:

Hi. I'm Lorne Michaels, the producer of *Saturday Night*. Right now we're being seen by approximately twenty- two million viewers, but please allow me, if I may, to address myself to just four very special people—John, Paul, George, and Ringo—the Beatles. Lately, there have been a lot of rumors to the effect that the four of you might be getting back together. That would be great. In my book, the Beatles are the best thing that ever happened to music. It goes even deeper than that. You're not just a musical group. You're a part of us. We grew up with you.

It's for this reason that I am inviting you to come on our show. Now, we've heard and read a lot about personality and legal conflicts that might prevent you guys from reuniting. That's something which is none of my business. That's a personal problem. You guys will have to handle that. But it's also been said that no one has yet to come up with enough money to satisfy you. Well, if it's money you want, there's no problem here.

The National Broadcasting Company has authorized me to offer you this check to be on our show. (Holds up check.) A certified check for three thousand dollars. Here it is right here. Dave— can we get a close-up on this? Which camera? Oh, this one. (Camera moves in to show check.) Here it is. A check made out to you, the Beatles, for three thousand dollars. All you have to do is sing three Beatles songs. (Sings.) "She loves you/yeah, yeah, yeah." That's one thousand dollars right there. You know the words. It'll be easy.

Like I said, this is made out to the Beatles—you divide it up any way you want. If you want to give Ringo less, it's up to you. I'd rather not get involved. I'm sincere about this. If this helps you to reach a decision to reunite, it's well worth the investment. You have agents. You know where I can be reached. Just think about it, okay? (Holds up check again.) Thank you.

A few weeks later Lorne appeared again to "sweeten the pot"— to $3,200. Lorne actually did have hopes his offer might succeed.

He'd heard that some of the Beatles were in New York, and he allowed himself to dream that maybe they'd respond in the spirit of the joke. He knew he would never forgive himself if they came to 30 Rock and then were unable to get by NBC's security, so he assigned Neil Levy in the strictest secrecy to brief the page staff to disperse themselves around the entrances of the building, just in case the Beatles showed up. Several times as the show went on Lorne pulled Levy aside to ask, "Anything yet?" but there never was. John Lennon confirmed in an interview with *Playboy* magazine just before his death that Lorne's dream had very nearly come true. "Paul and I were together watching that show," Lennon said. "He was visiting us [John and Yoko Ono] at our place in the Dakota. We were watching it and almost went down to the studio just as a gag. We nearly got into a cab, but we were actually too tired. ... [We] went, 'Ha ha, wouldn't it be funny if we went down?' But we didn't."

Another stylistic twist Lorne favored became known on *Saturday Night* as "dropping the cow." The idea, inspired by Monty Python, was that sketches did not have to follow the traditional beginning/middle/end structure that had always been fundamental to sketch comedy. The point, Lorne felt, was to tell the joke. After the joke was told, it wasn't necessary to worry about inventing an ending as a way of getting out of the sketch: just drop the cow and go on to something else. *Saturday Night* ended bits by literally dropping a cow—a life-size, stuffed canvas cow that crashed onstage from the rafters—several times, the first of them being a merciful termination of host Dick Cavett's opening monologue in January. This abandonment of the classic beginning/middle/end structure was a major reason why many comedy professionals of earlier generations believed *Saturday Night* simply didn't know what it was doing.

The most frequent complaint about *Saturday Night* from older comedians, among many others, centered on the show's seeming obsession with death humor, an obsession attributable primarily to Michael O'Donoghue. O'Donoghue's death jokes were so prominent on *Saturday Night* for a while that even on the 17th floor some thought it was too much, and there were attempts to tone it down. But black humor remained a staple of the show, and was another element that distinguished *Saturday Night* from what had come before on television.

One of O'Donoghue's most outrageous pieces the first season was "The Claudine Longet Invitational" ski tournament. He put it together a few weeks after Ms. Longet, estranged wife of singer Andy Williams, killed her lover, ski champion Spider Sabich, supposedly by accident. Chevy and Jane Curtin played sportscasters covering the competition. A succession of skiers was shown on videotapes taking dramatic falls. Each fall was preceded by the sound of a gunshot and followed by a cheerful comment from Chevy or Jane along the lines of: "Well, Jessica, he seems to have been accidentally shot by Claudine Longet!"

An O'Donoghue joke on Weekend Update that similarly offended a lot of people was his line about the real-life shooting death of the comedian who played Professor Backwards, a regular on early TV variety shows whose gimmick was to turn words and sentences around. O'Donoghue wrote that "according to reports, neighbors ignored the professor's cries of 'pleh, pleh.'"

O'Donoghue was in the habit of withdrawing into his office, sometimes for weeks on end, to pound away on his Smith-Corona, giving laborious birth to some comedic masterpiece. He was not prolific, as Chevy was, but the occasional masterpiece did emerge. The first of these was his "Citizen Kane" sketch on the tenth show of the season. The premise was that "Rosebud" was not, in fact, Charles Foster Kane's dying word. A reporter pursues the mystery and learns that what Kane really said was "roast beef." Further investigation reveals that his full thought had been "roast beef on rye with mustard."

It was a very silly joke, but it was, O'Donoghue would point out, a silly joke about a very sophisticated movie. Who on television had ever parodied *Citizen Kane*? The real achievement of the "Citizen Kane" sketch was its technical complexity. It was in black-and-white (an effect Dave Wilson argued against because he feared viewers would think there was a problem with their reception), used several sets and several special effects. In rehearsal the sketch was a disaster, but it worked perfectly on-air and there was applause in the control room when it ended.

O'Donoghue's crowning achievement came at the end of May with his "Star Trek" parody, which is unanimously considered by those on *Saturday Night* to be one of the best sketches ever on the show. The action unfolds on the control deck of the Starship *Enterprise*, which is being pursued by an unidentified alien ship. It turns out to be a 1968 maroon Chrysler limousine carrying an NBC program executive named Herb Goodman (a combination of NBC president Herb Schlosser and chairman Julian Goodman), played by host Elliott Gould. Goodman boards the *Enterprise* and confronts Captain Kirk, played by John:

GOULD: Everyone please, can I have your attention? I have an announcement to make. (Sound effects stop. Blinking lights on control panel fade.) Due to the low Nielsens, we at NBC have decided to cancel Star Trek.

JOHN (to crew): Fire at my command.

GOULD: On your way out, stop by the cashier's office and pick up your checks.

JOHN: Set phasers on "stun." Fire. (Nothing happens.)

DANNY (playing chief medical officer McCoy): They're not firing, Jim.

JOHN: Try "kill."

DANNY: Nope, still nothing.

GOULD (referring to phaser guns): You'll make sure the property department gets those things back, won't you, fellows?

CHEVY (playing Spock): Most peculiar, Captain. I can only conclude that they possess some sort of weapons deactivator, in which case, I shall merely render him unconscious with my famous Vulcan nerve pinch.

GOULD: Of course, if it was up to me you could keep them—as souvenirs, give 'em to your kids, whatever. But, you see, they're planning to market a complete line of Trekkie merchandise, and I have to send these to Taiwan to be copied. (Spock tries to knock Goodman out with a nerve pinch. It has no effect. He tries a second time and Goodman thinks he's admiring his suit.)

GOULD: Isn't that fabric something? You just can't buy material like this in the States. No way! But I was lucky enough to find this great little tailor who flies in from London four times a year. (Spock turns to walk away.) Oh, Nimoy, we'll need these ears back, too, I'm afraid. (Pulls off tips of Spock's ears and pockets them.)

DANNY (to Gould): For God's sake, man, we're on a five-year mission to explore space, the final frontier, and dammit, we've only been out three years!

GOULD: Sorry, but it's those Nielsens. If it was up to me, of course ...

JOHN: What are these "Nielsens" that the alien keeps mentioning, Mr. Spock?

CHEVY: If I remember my history correctly, Captain, Nielsens were a primitive system of estimating television viewers once used in the mid-twentieth century. (Most of the crew walk off, defeated, but Spock and Kirk refuse to accept the cancellation.)

JOHN: No, it can't end like this. I won't let it! This is my ship! I give the orders here! I give the commands! (Five or six stagehands enter and start taking the set apart.) I am responsible for the lives of 430 crewmen, and I am not going to let them down! There's got to be a way out!

CHEVY: You're becoming quite emotional, Captain. Needless to say, my trained Vulcan mind finds such open displays of emotion distasteful. Emotion, you see, interferes with logic, and it is only by dealing with problems in a logical, scientific fashion that we can arrive at valid solutions. Now, with regard to the alien takeover of the Enterprise, I would suggest that we seek some new alternative, based upon exact computer analysis, of course, and taking into consideration elements of ... (suddenly breaks down sobbing) ... Oh, God! I don't believe it! We're canceled! How could they do this? Everybody I know loves the show! I have a contract! What about my contract? I want my ears back!

(Goodman and his assistant lead Spock off, leaving Kirk alone on the bridge.)

JOHN: So it's just me, is it? Well, I've been in tougher spots. Surrender? No way, I'd rather go down with the ship. ... Captain's log, final entry. We have tried to explore strange new worlds, to seek out new civilizations, to boldly go where no man has gone before. And except for one television network, we have found intelligent life everywhere in the galaxy ...

John had found playing James Kirk unusually difficult— physically, John and William Shatner, the actor who played Kirk in the series, were distinctly dissimilar—but he kept insisting to O'Donoghue he could pull it off. His performances were terrible all week, but when it came to the air show he succeeded beautifully, and it was one of the acting roles of which John was most proud.

\* \* \*

The broader synthesis on *Saturday Night* that first season derived from spontaneous configurations among the other writers and performers, who didn't influence the show as distinctly as Lorne, Chevy, and O'Donoghue did, but who all added something of their own.

John Belushi's Samurai sketches, conceived by Tom Schiller and written for the most part by Alan Zweibel, were examples. Lorne had put Schiller's desk next to Zweibel's on 17, and a more unlikely pairing would be hard to imagine. Zweibel the jokesmith was a sports fanatic, while Schiller the artiste didn't even know who Hank Aaron was.

The "Star Trek" sketch, one of O'Donoghue's masterpieces.
Host Elliott Gould plays the network exec who informs Captain Kirk and the crew
that their mission has been canceled. © *NBC*

Ever since Belushi's audition at Nola, Schiller had been trying to think of a way to get John's Samurai character into the show. One day he was walking down the street with Chevy and, free-associating as he often did, suddenly said, "Samurai Hotelier." "That's it!" Chevy said, and they went back to the office, where Lorne, Chevy, Schiller, and Zweibel worked up the first Samurai sketch for Richard Pryor's show. Lorne changed it to "Samurai Hotel" because he thought *hotelier* might confuse some viewers. Belushi loved the sketch and it was an immediate hit on-air. Then Schiller wrote up a long list of other ordinary professions the Samurai might pursue, among them "Samurai Deli." Lorne asked Zweibel to write that one up, since Zweibel had experience in that field. From then on, Zweibel took the Samurai formula and plugged it into all sorts of everyday locales, from "Samurai Tailor" to "Samurai Divorce Court" to "Samurai Psychiatrist."

John Belushi's Samurai Warrior (with his usual foil, Buck Henry).
© *NBC*

One of the show's most fruitful early partnerships was that between Zweibel and Gilda Radner. It began a month into the season when Gilda came to Zweibel and asked him to help her write a sketch about "why I love being a fireman." They went out to dinner at Downey's Steak Pub to talk it over. It was one of those dinners where pretenses are dropped and confessions of terror and bewilderment are made. It lasted several hours and set a work pattern of going to restaurants, ordering half the dishes on the menu, and picking over them all as they talked and wrote, running up hundreds of dollars on Gilda's American Express card as they did.

Their first big hit was Emily Litella, a character of Gilda's based on the nanny of her childhood, Aunt Dibby. Emily originally appeared in a talk-show sketch written by Gilda and Tom Davis, in which she promoted a book she'd written about "itsy bitsy teeny weeny" things. (Hence the name Litella.) Two shows later, Rosie Shuster wrote Emily's first Update appearance for the Richard Pryor show. Looking for a way to get out of the bit with Chevy, Gilda came up with "never mind." As he had with Belushi's Samurai, Zweibel picked up Gilda's Emily and ran with it. She would subsequently editorialize on Soviet jewelry, canker cures, endangered feces, making Puerto Rico a steak, and a host of other topics. Gilda and Zweibel would later repeat the same pattern with another of the show's most popular characters, Roseanne Roseannadanna.

Weekend Update anchors Chevy Chase and Jane Curtin with editorial commentator Emily Litella. © *NBC*

Marilyn Miller, like O'Donoghue, was a writer who worked mostly by herself and who had a style uniquely her own. She wrote what were immediately recognized by everyone on the show as "Marilyn pieces." More one-act plays than comedy sketches sometimes, Marilyn pieces were warm character studies with few hard laughs. Miller's break-through came with her "Slumber Party" sketch on the Madeline Kahn show in May. Based on her own memories, it depicted four prepubescent girls (Kahn, Laraine, Gilda, and Jane) in their sleeping bags talking about sex:

MADELINE (confidentially): ... so then, the man gets bare naked in bed with you and you both go to sleep, which is why they call it sleeping together. Then you both wake up and the man says, "Why don't you slip into something more comfortable?"—no, wait a second, I think that comes before—anyway, it's not important— and then the man says ... (A light comes on at the top of the staircase.)

MOTHER'S VOICE: Gilda, it's five a.m. When does the noise stop?

GILDA: We're going to sleep now, Mom.

MOTHER'S VOICE: What are you talking about at this hour?

GILDA: School!

MOTHER'S VOICE: Well, save it for the morning. (Door slams, light goes out.)

JANE: And then the man ... ?

MADELINE: ... Anyway, then the man ... (She whispers inaudibly, and the other girls make loud, retching sounds) ... and then you scream and then he screams and then it's over.

LARAINE: That's *disgusting!*

GILDA: You lie, Madeline.

MADELINE: Cross my heart and hope to die. My brother told me about it in my driveway ...

Although the "Slumber Party" sketch didn't equal some of Miller's work to come, it had a familiarity that struck home with many viewers, and for years it was used as a point of discussion in social science seminars and child-rearing classes all over the country.

Al Franken and Tom Davis, to their relief, also broke through on the Madeline Kahn show. For most of the first season they'd submitted so much material and gotten so little on the air that their apprenticeships as writers were considered tenuous by some on the show. They bought some time with a long parody of *The Untouchables* in December, but it wasn't until they wrote a sketch called "The Final Days" that they established themselves.

"The Final Days" was based on the just-published book of the same name by Watergate reporters Bob Woodward and Carl Bernstein, their follow-up to *All the President's Men*. The temptation to gloat about the book's sensational revelations of Nixon's decline was irresistible for Franken and Davis, who'd been hammering away at the ex-President for years in their comedy. Surprisingly, though, after hours wracking their brains they still failed to come up with a sketch. Finally, exhausted at three o'clock on a Wednesday morning on the 17th floor, trying to keep going and looking for inspiration, they took some LSD. As the sun came up they were both stalking around their office with hunched shoulders and waggling jowls, two demented Richard Nixons trading lines and laughing hysterically.

The basic outlines of the sketch were written that night, although in the course of the week it would go through some changes. Lorne, feeling it needed a setup, wrote a different beginning which he planned to deliver himself, again addressing viewers directly.

"Hi. I'm Lorne Michaels," his introduction read. "As producer of this show, I make weighty decisions every day. But this week, I had to make the toughest decision of my career: whether or not to ridicule Richard Nixon one more time." Lorne's speech went on to say that it would be "too easy" to "make light of a man who hasn't slept with his wife for fourteen years," and that "jokes about Alexander Haig's belief that Nixon and Bebe Rebozo were having a homosexual affair have no place on network television." In the end he confessed he'd been overruled by the network: "NBC insisted that there are certain political events our show cannot ignore, and, frankly, my hands are tied. We don't like doing this, ladies and gentlemen, but *Saturday Night* proudly presents ..."

That opening was discarded on Friday when Anne Beatts suggested that the piece be restructured as a diary recollection by Pat Nixon, to be played by host Madeline Kahn. Garrett Morris, at Lorne's request, was written in as Sammy Davis, Jr. On-air, Dan Aykroyd did his impression of Richard Nixon for the first time; John, his first Henry Kissinger. The sketch opened with Pat Nixon, obviously tipsy, recalling the final days of the Nixon White House. Nixon was then seen talking to a portrait of Abraham Lincoln. "Well, Abe, you were lucky. They *shot* you." David and Julie Eisenhower, played by Chevy and Gilda, entered and suggested that the President get some rest, and Nixon, in an aside, remarked, "Ugh, he does look like Howdy Doody!"

Asked if he planned to resign, Nixon declared himself an optimist and relayed an anecdote. "Remember that Army hospital I visited in Vietnam? There was a young enlisted man from Des Moines, Iowa. He had been hit in the eye with a surface-to-air missile. And he only had four pints of blood left in his body, and, as you know, a man normally has eight pints of blood in his body. Now, the pessimists in this country would say that that boy was half empty, while I like to think he was half full!"

"That's right, Mr. President," David replied. "You know I was talking to two reporters from *The Washington Post* this morning, and they said they thought you were half crazy, but I told them I like to think of you as half sane."

Later, again alone, Nixon looked at a portrait of John F. Kennedy and said, "You! Kennedy. You looked so good all the time. They're gonna find out about you, too, The President having sex with women within these very walls. That never happened when Dick Nixon was in the White House. Never! Never! Never!"

Despite Lorne's discarded introduction, *Saturday Night* had not to that point really had an opportunity to savage the counterculture's old nemesis, Richard Nixon, and "The Final Days" sketch no doubt provided an opportunity for millions of Nixon-haters to savor gleefully, one more time, his spectacular downfall.

* * *

The one person most universally admired on *Saturday Night* as both a writer and a performer was Dan Aykroyd. Danny got a bit of a slow start on the show, in part because he was distracted by a movie he was commuting to in Canada, in part because he was inexperienced in television. He was also amazingly young. But he was so intense that sparks seemed to be coming out of his head, and once he caught on he couldn't be stopped. His talent was so original that Lorne, Chevy, and O'Donoghue looked upon him as a sort of Orson Welles of comedy.

Danny would become best-known for his impressions of Richard Nixon, Tom Snyder, and Jimmy Carter, but as much an edge as he brought those characters, it was when he wasn't tied to a recognizable personality that he truly soared. His pinnacle the first season, everyone on the show agreed, was the "Bass-O-Matic" sketch on the show hosted by Gerald Ford's press secretary, Ron Nessen, in April. What made the "Bass-O-Matic," along with all of Danny's other commercial parodies, work so well was the sheer lunatic power of his performance, which amplified the sleazy essence of late-night television pitchmen to dizzy new heights.

Danny, wearing a garish sports jacket and tie, stood at a table on which were a dead fish and an electric blender:

DANNY: How many times has this happened to you? You have a bass (holds up fish). You're trying to find an exciting new way to prepare it for dinner. You could scale the bass, remove the bass's tail, head, and bones, and serve the fish as you would any other fish dinner. But why bother now that you can use Rovco's amazing new kitchen tool, the Super Bass-O-Matic 76?

Yes, fish-eaters, the days of troublesome scaling, cutting, and gutting are over, because Super Bass-O-Matic 76 is the tool that lets you use the *whole* bass with no fish waste, without scaling, cutting, or gutting.

Here's how it works: Catch a bass, remove the hook, and drop the bass, that's the *whole* bass, into the Super Bass-O-Matic 76. (Drops bass into blender. Covers top.) Now, adjust the control dial so that that bass is blended just the way you like it. (Turns blender on, reducing fish to pulp.) Yes, it's just that simple.

LARAINE (drinking glassful of bass): Wow! That's terrific bass!

DANNY: We've got fish here, fast and easy and ready to pour! Bass-O-Matic 76 comes with ten interchangeable rotors, a nine-month guarantee, and a booklet, "One Thousand and One Ways to Harness Bass." Super Bass- O-Matic 76 works great on sunfish, perch, sole, and other small aquatic creatures. Super Bass-O-Matic 76: It's clean, simple, and after five or ten fish it gets to be quite a rush. Super Bass-O-Matic 76—you'll never have to scale, cut, or gut again.

How this came across on air to the many viewers who, because Ron Nessen was the host, were watching the show for the first time that night is anybody's guess, but to those on the 17th floor the "Bass-O-Matic" was so exhilaratingly strange that many remember sitting and listening, open-mouthed, when Danny presented it at the Monday writers' meeting. Nobody felt jealous of it because they couldn't imagine writing anything remotely like it.

\* \* \*

As their confidence grew, Lorne and everybody else on the 17th floor soon realized that they, not the hosts or special guests or special features, were going to be the stars of *Saturday Night*. Pictures of The Not Ready For Prime Time Players appeared in the opening credits for the first time in March, acknowledging that they were now to be the focus of the show. With the fountain of material being generated internally there was less need, or desire, for the contributions of outsiders. The inner circle tightened, and the format was refined accordingly. The Muppets and Albert Brooks were the first to go.

Jim Henson, creator of the Muppets, had designed a new set of puppets for the show, lizardlike creatures with names like Scred that were the prototypes for the characters of his 1982 movie *The Dark* Crystal. *Saturday Night*'s writers were responsible for coming up with dialogue for Henson's segments, and it was a collaboration doomed to fail. By Henson's standards, Scred and his friends were, as Henson put it later, "weird and strange and very peculiar." But Henson also didn't want to "color" the Muppets' image by becoming too hard-edged, and by *Saturday Night*'s standards the characters he created were sickeningly sweet. The sensibilities clashed. Henson and his people were far more sympathetic with the sunnier side of the sixties counterculture than *Saturday Night* was, and they were put off by what Henson called "the whole angry, negative, decadent humor" of the *Lampoon* school.

Writing for the Muppets was considered the most loathsome assignment on the 17th floor. Many weeks Lorne would have to shepherd everyone into his office, where, grumbling, they tried to come up with something for the Muppets. Before long *Saturday Night* started poking fun at the Muppets on-air, putting Scred in a Bee costume and having him say, "I'm Scred and you're not." In the spring, Henson and Lorne by mutual agreement failed to renew the Muppets' contract, and Henson went off to England to produce *The Muppet Show*, which would become one of the most successful syndicated shows in television history.

Albert Brooks departed with more bitterness than Henson did. The problem wasn't the quality of the films Brooks was making— they were meticulously stylish pieces admired by everyone on the 17th floor. Brooks starred in most of them, and he, too, combined an obnoxious, anti-comic persona with off-center satirical scripts. In one film he traveled to a computer research laboratory near Phoenix, Arizona, that had prepared, after extensive tests of Brooks' humor, an 822-page report on the strengths and weaknesses of his act. "I'm willing and able," Brooks told his viewers, "to change in any direction you choose."

As funny as Brooks' films were, the three thousand miles between Brooks in Los Angeles and *Saturday Night* in New York soon began to tell. It seemed to Brooks he was resented for not being "at the manic center of the show," and gradually he began to feel "disinherited" from *Saturday Night*. His films, instead of being welcomed, were greeted, Brooks sensed, like "this virus, this foreign thing that arrived in the pouch each week, an intruder."

Brooks' suspicions were not without basis in fact. From *Saturday Night*'s point of view, he was a niggling perfectionist who went over-budget on his films (Brooks denies this) and who demanded constant attention. His biggest sin, though, was consuming too much time in the show. His relationship with *Saturday Night* was forever soured when he delivered the thirteen- minute film that Rob Reiner had insisted go on the air. The film, which followed Brooks on a Plimptonesque attempt at open-heart surgery, was so long that a commercial break had to be inserted in the middle of it. All told it took viewers away from the live show for almost twenty minutes, an unforgivable usurpation of time to *Saturday Night*'s writers and performers.

After nine shows, Brooks, too, agreed with Lorne not to extend his contract. Years later Lorne would still complain to mutual friends how

Albert had so foolishly blown his opportunity on *Saturday Night*, and years later Albert would complain how shabbily he'd been treated.

Lorne's friend Gary Weis replaced Brooks as *Saturday Night*'s official filmmaker and soon began making his own mark on-air with a distinctly different style. He shot streetwise documentaries and eccentric mood films, some of them unfathomably obscure, others minor masterpieces. Among his best was a film that followed host Buck Henry on a quest to find the funniest person in Irvington, New York, and one in which a little old lady demonstrated some of the more popular items in her jokes-and-novelties store. Weis worked out of New York, but he also worked mostly on his own, and before long he, too, began to feel isolated from the others on the 17th floor.

The one outsider besides the hosts and musical guests who continued to be a regular on the show was Andy Kaufman. Kaufman never fit in with the *Saturday Night* group either, and never tried to. But Lorne needed the flexibility of a stand-up segment he could insert in the show here and there, and Kaufman was far less troublesome than Brooks and the Muppets had been. He came, quietly did his routines, and left. He also happened to be a brilliant comedian, and his humor, like Dan Aykroyd's, was unique, so people on the show didn't feel they were competing with it. In one of his more notorious bits, he stood onstage and read a long excerpt from *The Great Gatsby*, refusing to stop even when the audience began hooting for him to leave.

CHAPTER 14

# When Do We Tape?

"Usually it takes me two or three takes just to warm up, but tonight I predict we'll get it on the first take." "We always get it on the first take. We have to … This is live television."
"Live? Live? What does *live* mean?"
"That means that the exact moment you're cavorting and leaping around that stage over there, twenty million people are seeing it."
"Wait a minute. Wait a minute! … You mean it all goes into the camera lens and then just spills out into people's houses?! Why did nobody have the goodness to explain this to me before?!"

—The moment in the movie *My Favorite Year* when a swashbuckling screen idol played by Peter O'Toole discovers that his appearance on a fifties TV comedy show will be broadcast live.

It was 11:28, two minutes before air, and the host, actor Gary Busey, had disappeared. Stage manager Joe Dicso yelled, "I can't find him! I can't find Busey!" and a half dozen people ran from dressing room to dressing room looking for him. One of them ran by Jane Curtin, who was waiting to take her place in the opening sketch, and frantically asked if she'd seen Busey. She smiled. "I think he said something about going out for a pizza."

Busey at the time—the spring of 1979—was up for an Oscar for his starring role in *The Buddy Holly Story*. He was hot, and living the rock-and-roll life with a vengeance. All week long he'd been partying hard and

160

showing up late. Lorne had assigned talent coordinator Barbara Burns to keep an eye on him, but it hadn't been easy. On Wednesday she'd had to get the key to his hotel room so she could roust him out of bed, and on Friday she'd had to dispatch a security guard to search for him.

Busey was a willing victim of a little trick John Belushi sometimes played on vulnerable hosts. He'd take them out on the town for several nights in a row, and by Saturday the host would be completely wiped out, nursing a three-day hangover and trying to hold on. Belushi, meanwhile, would take a steam bath, get a massage, goof around in dress rehearsal, then snap into shape for air.

On Saturday, Busey wandered in at four o'clock, two hours late. Julia Fraser, a production assistant, came to his dressing room to tell him they were ready to start the run-through, but he ignored her. "I need steak and eggs," he said. "Order them." At least they knew where he was.

That night they were still looking for him as the countdown to air reached one minute. One of the talent coordinators finally found him fueling up in the dressing room of musical guest Paul Butterfield. She screamed at him to get to the studio, and as the countdown reached thirty seconds he came running down the stairs, almost colliding with Joe Dicso. Dicso grabbed him and dragged him toward the set.

"Where the hell have you been?" Dicso shouted. "I went to get a Coke," Busey answered.

* * *

Busey was not the most troublesome host in *Saturday Night*'s history, though he'd make the top ten. Every week the intermeshing of *Saturday Night* and its hosts courted disaster, and met it frequently. In the first five years of the show alone, nearly eighty stars from show business, politics, and sports allowed themselves to be shanghaied by *Saturday Night*. Some, like Candice Bergen, went along peaceably. Many others, like Gary Busey, did not.

Lorne and Ebersol had at first contemplated finding a permanent host for the show, or at least a rotating group of three or four regular hosts. Albert Brooks was asked to be one of these and turned it down; George Carlin had agreed to host several shows, but after he hosted the first the deal was quietly dropped. Through most of the first season the main problem was getting hosts: $2,200 for a week's work on an unknown late-night TV show was not a job that had actors and agents beating down the door. After the first season that changed, and the problem became fending candidates off.

Lorne took sole responsibility for choosing the hosts and musical guests, and, typically, the selection process was what one of the show's talent coordinators called "unbelievably arbitrary." Lorne often got around to making up his mind so late that *TV* Guide's sacred listings deadline passed with no one chosen. Music guests were selected with an utter disregard for the record charts or releases, and it wasn't unusual for an act to be booked just a week ahead of time. Lorne sometimes listened to the recommendations of people on the show, especially to bandleader Howard Shore's advice on music, but he religiously ignored suggestions from NBC. Many times NBC's executives had never heard of the people Lorne put on. Some still shake their heads that *Saturday Night* gave Kinky Friedman and the Texas Jewboys their national television debut.

Lorne had his own criteria, and they were either deliberately off-key, as with Kinky Friedman, or impossibly high. One of his strictest rules (relaxed in later seasons) was that he didn't want people who usually did TV. Traditional stand-up comics were out: David Brenner, Bert Convy, Norm Crosby, and Jackie Mason were just a few of those who let their availability be known but never received a call. Neil Levy, who was the show's assistant talent coordinator for a time, once made a verbal offer to the agent who handled Carroll O'Connor, TV's Archie Bunker, without first clearing it with Lorne. Realizing as soon as he hung up the phone that he'd made a mistake, Levy walked into Lorne's office during a meeting and said, as casually as he could, "Hey Lorne, sorry to bother you, but what about Carroll O'Connor.'"

"No, TV," was the immediate response, and Levy had to extricate himself from the deal.

As popular as *Saturday Night* became, Lorne never succeeded in getting many of the superstars he pursued. Woody Allen, Dolly Parton, Donald Sutherland, Michael Caine, Richard Nixon, and Muhammad Ali were among those who turned him down cold, while Mia Farrow, Diane Keaton, and Diana Ross all backed out after their bookings were announced. Jack Nicholson and Warren Beatty came to *Saturday Night*'s parties after a while, but they wouldn't host the show. John Travolta also started hanging around and at one point agreed to host. In the end he backed out, though, and the talent coordinators always believed his advisers had convinced him that appearing on the show would hurt his chances for an Oscar nomination for *Saturday Night Fever*.

One of the worst freeze-outs came from Andy Warhol, who happened to walk into a restaurant in Greenwich Village where Lorne and a number of others from the show were eating. Lorne approached him and introduced himself, intending to ask him to host. Warhol stared at him blankly, never moving a muscle or uttering a sound, until finally Lorne retreated, cringing, to his table.

Once the hosts arrived, it usually took until about Wednesday for them to figure out what they'd let themselves in for. Film stars were often completely baffled by the whole production process. Despite warnings that the scripts would inevitably change, for the first few days of the week many of them would be memorizing their lines, just as they always did in the movies. Then it began to dawn on them that memorizing lines wasn't going to work, at which point they'd often panic. Cicely Tyson was one who resisted using cue cards until late Friday night, and when she changed her mind, the cue card people had to work hours overtime to get all of her parts written out before show time.

It was generally one of the film stars or their agents who would ask at some point during the week, sometimes on Saturday: "When do we tape?" It would have to be explained that there was no tape, that this was a live show that would be shot in one continuous take on *Saturday Night*. Even for those who were used to working in TV, the start of *Saturday Night*'s week was more casual and the acceleration from there more rapid than anything they'd done before. You could see them looking around, Neil Levy said, scratching their heads and thinking, "Gee, I did the Bob Hope special last year and it wasn't like this."

Candice Bergen's submit-or-die analogy was precisely accurate in describing *Saturday Night*'s attitude toward its hosts. With few exceptions, there was one way to get along on *Saturday Night*, and that was to go along. "We knew what we were doing," said Robin Shlien, one of the show's longtime production assistants. "It was a system that worked and the hosts had to trust that. If they were above it and wouldn't bend, they got nailed."

It did take a certain courage to turn oneself over to the *Saturday Night* team. When Buck Henry walked into his first Monday writers' meeting, he was charmed that Lorne would let all the secretaries sit in. Then he found out the secretaries were the writers. In lieu of courage, foolhardiness sometimes sufficed. "If you got somebody who was an adult and who took their lives seriously," says Robin Shlien, "it usually didn't work." Gary Busey proved, on the other hand, that it was also possible to take the job not seriously enough.

Hosts who didn't fit in were snubbed, often viciously. Madeline Kahn, who admits she was frightened of live TV, kept to herself and took what she describes as a "clinical" approach to her work. Neither habit endeared her to the show, and she felt like "the new girl in town" knowing she wasn't being accepted by the in group at the local high school. "It was not," she recalls, "a pleasant experience."

Almost all the hosts were "kept out of the family business," as Neil Levy put it, and often they were consigned to babysitters to keep them out of Lorne's hair. Raquel Welch was one of these. The men on the show were excited about working with Welch at first. Whenever there was a woman host, the running joke was for the men to ask the wardrobe and costume people what she looked like without her clothes on. There was more than the usual curiosity about Welch, but the men were told she had had every part of her body redone, from chest to tummy to tush, and, true or not, the spell was broken.

Welch spent much of the week turning down the breast jokes the writers were churning out for her. Franken and Davis wrote a sketch called "The Planet of the Enormous Hooters," where Raquel would be an outcast because of her tiny bosom. Franne Lee got so far as actually designing huge fake breasts for the piece before it was cut. O'Donoghue wrote a parody of the famous radio narrative of the Hindenburg disaster in which Raquel's breasts would be turned by special effects into twin zeppelins bursting into flame. All week Chevy Chase pushed the idea that whenever Raquel was onstage, the camera should slowly slip down from her face to her chest, as if the cameraman couldn't resist focusing on it. Chevy planned to keep the joke a secret from Raquel, but Lorne vetoed the whole idea.

Finally Raquel was turned over to keyboard man Paul Shaffer for safekeeping, and the two of them sat in a room with a piano and ran through her nightclub act, ostensibly to choose a song for the show.

"Which one should I use, Paul?" she'd ask.

"Gee, I don't know, Raquel," Shaffer answered. "They're all *fabulous.*"

Another host who was ostracized was Ruth Gordon, the octogenarian star of one of Lorne's favorite movies, *Harold and Maude.* She rejected idea after idea, including one by Franken and Davis in which she was to fall over dead halfway into the sketch. The atmosphere on the show that week grew so hostile that as soon as the camera went off after the air show, Gordon walked directly offstage and out of the building.

Surprisingly, for a show that was made by rock-and-roll fans for rock-and-roll fans, rock stars were some of the hosts *Saturday Night* enjoyed least. When Kris Kristofferson hosted, all week long he started drinking wine at noon and shifted to tequila around sunset. At dress rehearsal on Saturday he was so drunk it was questionable he could go on. The cast members started figuring out which of them could play his parts while coffee was being poured down Kristofferson's throat in the dressing room. Kristofferson in the end did make it, barely, through the night.

Rock star Frank Zappa was roundly despised by *Saturday Night* for overindulgence of a different sort: ego. When he arrived he immediately started giving orders. Al Franken remembers Zappa saying things like:

"Here's some ideas. I want to have pumpkins hanging on a Christmas tree, pumpkins that eat people's faces. Pull that together by Saturday." On the show he committed the cardinal sin of mugging to the camera in the middle of sketches. During the closing goodnights, the cast members stood as far away from Zappa as they could get and still be on the same stage.

A few hosts managed to get away with being difficult simply because they were so respected. Broderick Crawford, the venerable star of the old TV series *Highway Patrol*, had a habit of slipping away to bars for a nip. Neil Levy, among others, was assigned to keep an eye on him, but Crawford, as frail as he was at the time, kept eluding him and disappearing. Crawford happened to be hosting the week of Saint Patrick's Day, and on the Day of the Green itself he went out with Gary Weis to shoot a film walking around the old New York neighborhoods Crawford used to know. The day turned into a liquid tour of Crawford's favorite bars, and when he returned to NBC late that afternoon to tape some promotional announcements for the show, he set a record for the number of takes ever accorded a promo session. On *Saturday Night* Crawford again could not be found; he was tracked down between dress and air to a nearby saloon named Hurley's. Despite all this, Crawford's craggy style was revered by everyone on the show, and he was treated with loving care throughout the week.

The hosts who usually worked best on *Saturday Night* were those, like Buck Henry or Elliott Gould, who were so unflappable they would go along with just about anything. Henry, besides being a performer and writer for *That Was the Week That Was*, had co- written the screenplay for *The Graduate* and co-created the TV series *Get Smart* with Mel Brooks. He appeared on *Saturday Night* so often he was sometimes thought of, both inside and outside the show, as its eighth cast member. Whenever he hosted, he'd fly in from Los Angeles a few days early and sit around the 17th floor reading *The New York Times*, and people were always comforted seeing him there. So comforted, in fact, that by Friday night there'd often be very little of substance written for Henry, which didn't seem to faze him in the least. It became a *Saturday Night* tradition that Henry hosted the final show of the season because by then everybody was so burned out they wanted the easiest possible host to work with, and because Henry usually had no compunctions against doing any leftover sketches that hosts earlier in the season had refused to touch.

The other favorite, although the chemistry was different, was Steve Martin. Martin, after several appearances on the *Tonight Show*, was one of the hotter young comedians in 1975, and people were saying he'd be perfect for *Saturday Night*. But Lorne was so leery of booking another stand-up comedian that he went around the office asking people their advice on Martin, something he hardly ever did with other hosts. When Martin finally did host, in the second season, he, too, felt like an outsider, but it was an attitude he understood from his experience as a writer on the Smothers Brothers show, where the guests were often despised because of what they did to the material.

Like Buck Henry, Martin didn't socialize very much with the *Saturday Night* team, or get stoned with them, but he worked with such diligence, good will, and good humor that he won them over. He was always available to sit in a room and work on something with any of the writers or performers, even if what they were working on wasn't especially good, and his comedic persona—the jerk, in a variety of guises— meshed perfectly with the *Saturday Night* sensibility.

* * *

On the 17th floor most people's choice for worst host ever would be divided between Louise Lasser and Milton Berle, the new queen and former king of TV comedy.

Louise Lasser hosted the next-to-last show of the first season. At the time, her late-night syndicated series *Mary Hartman, Mary Hartman* (produced by Norman Lear) had achieved a cult success equal to that achieved by *Saturday Night* over the course of its first season, while Lasser herself, like Chevy Chase, had become an enormously popular cult figure. Her booking on *Saturday Night* was therefore a huge media event. When Chevy and Louise went together to film a piece at the 1976 Democratic convention, taking place that week at Madison Square Garden, their presence caused such a mob scene outside the hall they could hardly get in.

Unfortunately, Lasser was not holding up well under the pressure of her sudden fame. She'd been arrested for possession of cocaine in Los Angeles not long before she came to New York for the show. When she arrived she was self-obsessed to the point of "solipsism" (Chevy's description); many on the show believed she was nearing a nervous breakdown. She rambled on incoherently in meetings, crawled around the hallways on her hands and knees, refused to do pieces that had been written for her, and insisted on doing her own strange ideas. She demanded that two films be shot, one in which she had a conversation with a dog, the other in which she sat in a diner and babbled a meaningless monologue. Michael O'Donoghue, who finally walked off the show that week in disgust, described Lasser's state of mind as "clinically berserk." "She was a nice woman going through a few problems," he said, "but I wanted to force her to eat her goddamn pigtails at gunpoint."

On *Saturday Night*, twenty minutes before the show began, Lasser decided she wasn't going on and shut herself in her dressing room. Most people on the show were by then happy to hear it. The cast members, as they would for Kris Kristofferson a week later, started dividing up her parts. Chevy planned to play some of her roles wearing a Mary Hartman wig. Bill Murray, who was not yet a member of the cast, happened to be in the studio that night, and he prepared himself to take Chevy's parts in those sketches.

Lorne, so angry he was swearing he'd kick her teeth in, was negotiating with Lasser through production assistants, who were running back and forth between his ninth-floor office and her dressing room on the eighth floor. Because of all the publicity surrounding the show, Lorne was not as sanguine about Lasser's failing to appear as the others were, and he used the threat of scandal with her manager: "If she doesn't go on," he said, "America will want to know why."

Lasser did go on, although it probably would have been a better show if she hadn't. She appeared alongside a cast member only once, in a takeoff on Ingmar Bergman's films in which she and Chevy stared soundlessly into each other's eyes. Equally soundless was the audience's reaction to her films. (The film she shot with Chevy at the Democratic convention wasn't used.) The worst came last, during Lasser's closing monologue. She sat onstage, cross-legged, and launched into a sadly self-indulgent ramble about herself. It began with her musing that she was putting her shoes on in front of twenty-two million people. One line that made sense referred to the wages of stardom and her recent bust in Los Angeles. "They made me rich, famous, and a known criminal," she said.

Milton Berle, who hosted in the fourth season, was terminally afflicted with a disorder known as Comedian's Disease. Hosts from television's old guard often proved hard to work with because they were used to doing things their own way. When Desi Arnaz hosted he blew up during a blocking session and started shouting at stage manager Joe Dicso and the *Saturday Night* band in his famous Cuban accent: "What are you people trying to do, you know! I invented these things, you know! Who the hell you think you're talking to!"

That outburst, however, was an exception, and for most of the week Arnaz was fine. The same could not be said of Uncle Miltie.

Berle has a reputation in the business for being demanding (those who worked with him in the fifties remember how he would bring rehearsals to a dead stop with a blast of the whistle he wore around his neck), but no one was prepared for what he did to *Saturday Night*. "He came in," said one of the writers, "with the attitude 'I am TV.' Not 'I *used* to be TV,' but 'I *am* TV.'"

Evidence of that attitude came in the writers' meeting on Monday when Berle prefaced his explanation of an idea he wanted to do with the comment "Now this might be over your heads. ..." All week he called everyone he talked to "Booby." He constantly waved his cigar around and mugged furiously. In read-through on Wednesday, whenever he had a line, he'd stop and say, "Hey, Lorne, watch this," and as he made his one-hundredth funny face the staff buried their faces in their scripts. Bill Murray got so fed up that when Berle spoke out of turn during blocking, Billy loudly corrected him in a singsong voice reeking with disgust: "That's not your line, Mr. Berle."

Berle's chief defender during the week was John Belushi, no mean mugger himself. Belushi worshipped Berle and repeatedly berated the writers for letting his idol down. "What a great man he is," Belushi said, "and you guys are writing shit for this great man!"

The writers were not impressed. One of them will never forget visiting Berle in his dressing room a few minutes before dress rehearsal. The great man was methodically spraying his bald spot with something resembling brown paint from an aerosol can.

On-air, Berle insisted on doing whatever he wanted to do, turning the show into Lorne's worst Las Vegas nightmare. His monologue was the sort of show biz shtick *Saturday Night* usually ridiculed. It included a joke about forty-four Puerto Ricans being injured in a crash. "The bed broke" was the punch line. Hosting *Saturday Night*, he said, was his biggest thrill since winning Truman Capote on *The Dating Game*. He bemoaned the fact that he only had five minutes for his opening routine, saying he usually bowed for twenty.

As with Louise Lasser, the worst came last. Berle sat on a stool at center stage alongside his piano player, Buddy Freed, and crooned an exquisitely corny version of "September Song." After a few bars he'd pause, and as Freed quietly tickled the ivories in the background, he philosophized on life. "These are precious days, ladies and gentlemen," he said. He also plugged his autobiography. When he finally finished, one of Berle's cronies in the audience jumped to his feet, clapping, starting a not-so-spontaneous standing ovation for the man known as Mr. Television.

Lorne, standing by his monitor, was so mortified during Berle's "September Song" that he started downing more than his usual glass or two of white wine. His face grew steadily grayer just the same. As Berle basked in his ovation, Lorne walked into the control room and muttered to director Dave Wilson, "That was the worst show, ever."

There may be some poetic justice in the fact that Milton Berle will stand in perpetuity alongside Louise Lasser in the ranks of *Saturday Night* hosts whose shows Lorne never allowed to be seen in reruns.

CHAPTER 15

# You Can't Give Noogies
# to the Virgin Mary

I've watched your program prior to this and I've found your program
to be unsettling and insulting and sadistic. I (my family too) will take
no more of your abuse. You've gone too far. ... I (my family and
friends too) will tell others in our community of your Satanistic show.
You must all be demons.

—Letter from a viewer

There is a seat in the 8H control room overlooking director Dave Wilson's
right shoulder that is reserved for the conscience of the network. During
every show, this is where the "editor" from NBC's Broadcast Standards
department sits. The Standards editor, more commonly known as "the
censor," enforces the network's policies and guidelines for acceptable, broadcastable material, which are spelled out in the official NBC
Broadcast Standards for Television handbook. Standards must pass on
every script for every network show before it goes out on the air, and
Standards' word is law. Theoretically.

In practice, there is as much absolute, unbendable policy in the
enforcement of network television standards as there is in law enforcement. Personalities, politics, and money all have their impact on the
interpretation of what is permissible and what is not. More than any
other show in the history of television, *Saturday Night* redefined those
boundaries.

The first Standards editor assigned to *Saturday Night* was Jay Ottley. He was a fortunate choice: He understood the humor, seemed to enjoy it, and quickly became an ally of the show. Ottley was no fool in passing without question material that might cost him his job, but he was usually willing to discuss sketches or lines he thought went too far and, on occasion, to suggest how his bosses might be persuaded to let something by.

The right of appeal is built into the Standards process, and *Saturday Night* routinely took appeals to Ottley's boss, Standards vice president Herminio Traviesas. Traviesas—known to everyone at the network as "Travie"—was a soft-spoken gentleman of Spanish descent in his early sixties. He lived in the affluent Westchester suburb of Larchmont, where he was an elder in his local church. He was a devoted family man and a champion of The Family Hour, a brief, unsuccessful attempt at self-regulation by the three networks, begun in the fall of 1975, which banished programming deemed unsuitable for children to 9:00 p.m. or later. A former advertising executive, Travie's first assignment as a network censor had been *Laugh-In*. He was proud to have been associated with that "breakthrough" show, but at heart he was a conservative man. As the networks' official guardians of morality, vice presidents of Standards tend to be conservative men.

From the moment he saw the material *Saturday Night* was submitting, Travie was appalled. He didn't understand the humor and he didn't like its point of view, which struck him as immoral. For the first six or seven weeks of the show, he rejected much of what he read. But Lorne and Dick Ebersol had a higher court of appeal, vice president of Corporate Affairs Robert Kasmire. Kasmire was Travie's boss, a resident of Greenwich Village and separated from his wife, and his outlook was somewhat more cosmopolitan than Travie's.

Lorne and Ebersol had paid Kasmire a courtesy call months before the show went on, cultivating him, and when Traviesas started vetoing scripts, they went to Kasmire. Many times he was tracked down in restaurants on Saturday evenings to resolve a debate over some last-minute joke the show wanted to put on. Kasmire, too, was put off by some of *Saturday Night*'s humor—"We were always saying, 'God, it's kind of far out,'" he remembers—but he let more of it by than Travie did nonetheless.

Travie spent the weekends of *Saturday Night*'s first two shows "almost sick with concern" that he had made a terrible mistake in acquiescing to some of the show's material. Then something surprising happened: nothing. There were some complaints, to be sure, such as for George Carlin's God monologue, but no substantial outpourings of protest, no pickets outside the building. Traviesas was stunned. Apparently what offended him did not offend the viewers of *Saturday Night*. This was an important revelation, for despite all the speeches made about the networks' moral commitment, despite the Broadcast Standards for Television handbook, the censor's most important function is to prevent people from getting angry at the network. For that reason Standards is most concerned with the subjects that most frequently cause people to write letters or make phone calls. The two most dangerous areas are religion and cruelty to animals.

Traviesas spoke about the public's surprising silence on *Saturday Night* to Marilyn Preston, a TV columnist for the *Chicago Tribune*, in December of 1975. "Don't think the show doesn't worry me," he said. "I must admit, though, some of the things they've done that I thought would absolutely bring hundreds of angry calls didn't get a single complaint. I suppose we have to realize we have a younger, more sophisticated audience out there." Travie sent a copy of this column to Ebersol along with a note that said: "A guy who makes statements like these can't be all bad." He also added a postscript: "Marilyn [Preston] wrote me a friendly note which ended with—'and keep your bleeping hands off *Saturday Night*.'"

The support of columnists like Preston and the failure of the public to rise up in protest caused a new set of standards to evolve for *Saturday Night*. The guiding principle was that because the show was in late night, more latitude was acceptable. Second, it was a program that was building an audience—albeit a small audience at that point—by being irreverent. Ergo, its viewers expected and wanted a certain amount of irreverence from the show. Third, some of the jokes on *Saturday Night* were sophisticated in such a way that if you were going to be offended by them, you probably were not going to understand them, and therefore you wouldn't be offended. When Chevy Chase opened Weekend Update talking on the phone with a girlfriend, for example, saying, "You know that truck that passed us—I'm sure they could see your head. ... It did *not* look like you were napping," it's doubtful straitlaced viewers realized he was talking about oral sex on wheels.

With those amended guidelines in effect, *Saturday Night* had its foot firmly planted in permissibility's door, and as the show's popularity grew, the opening was pushed ever wider.

*Saturday Night* got away with as much as it did mainly because Lorne Michaels was one of the most effective censor fighters the censors had ever encountered. He exploited every opening and every weakness in the Standards system he could find, resisting Standards' rulings with such skill and stubbornness that he almost seemed to consider it a sacred cause—which in a way he did.

One of the weapons he used to full advantage was the fact that *Saturday Night* was live. Because it was live, the network couldn't wait until the show was turned in on tape or film and then simply edit out what it didn't like. Thus *Saturday Night* had a runaway- freight-train quality about it that strengthened Lorne's hand the longer a final decision was postponed. If a censor objected to a sketch on Thursday, Lorne would immediately start the appeals process up the executive line, maybe giving in on a joke or two as the debate went on; the important thing was to keep the disputed piece in production. Often he'd say, "Let's see how it plays in dress." By then, sets would have been built, costumes designed, the sketch scheduled into the show's rundown, and the clock nearing 11:30. If the censors still said no, Lorne would typically resort to one of several last-ditch appeals, including "That sketch is the centerpiece of the show—if it's cut, I'll have nothing to put on the air," or "Why did you let me spend the money and blow my budget if you're not going to let me put it on?" *Saturday Night*'s habit of coming up with new material on Friday nights or Saturday mornings sometimes telescoped this process into a frantic twenty-four hours or less.

Seeing how a sketch played in dress did sometimes change the censors' minds by showing them that what seemed inflammatory on paper could be less so in performance. Traviesas at first refused to go along with Lorne's requests to come to 8H to watch a disputed piece, but later he relented and decided Lorne had been right—it did make a difference how things were played. One sketch Travie came to the studio to see had Chevy Chase and Jane Curtin copulating in bed while the Supreme Court stood looking on to make sure they didn't perform any prohibited sexual acts. When he read the script, Travie thought Chevy and Jane were essentially going to be having sex on camera, but in the studio he saw that all they were doing was rolling around under the sheets, completely hidden from view, and he let it by.

One of Traviesas's biggest mistakes came from *not* seeing how a piece played in performance. The sketch in question was O'Donoghue's "Claudine Longet Invitational" ski tournament, which aired when she was facing trial for manslaughter. Traviesas, to O'Donoghue's complete surprise, let it pass on the basis of a reading over the phone, not realizing that it came across much tougher visually than it did in the script. NBC's legal representative on the show also let it pass after consulting with an outside law firm. Almost as soon as it aired, Longet's estranged husband, Andy Williams, was on the phone with NBC's lawyers in Los Angeles, threatening to sue. To placate Williams, Don Pardo read an apology in a subsequent show. "It is desirable to correct any misunderstanding," Pardo said, "that a suggestion was made that, in fact, a crime had been committed. ...

This is a statement of apology if the material was misinterpreted." Not a very sincere apology, but it served to keep the show out of court.

Demonstrating a sketch for the censors could also be effective by getting them to laugh. Censors supposedly have their sense of humor removed when they're hired, and supposedly they are not to let something offensive on the air simply because it also happens to be funny. In practice neither proposition is true. Michael O'Donoghue once wrote a line that had Don Pardo announcing that Weekend Update was sponsored by Pussy Whip, the first dessert topping for cats. O'Donoghue read it for Traviesas, who laughed out loud and let it by. For the same reason even the censors say that talented performers can get away with a lot more than untalented performers. Chevy Chase in particular was known for making potentially offensive material seem acceptable by nature of his innocent delivery and his prep school looks.

If the censors wouldn't give in on a sketch, Lorne kept arguing. As always he was a persuasive talker, so his appeals up the executive line were usually conducted on a fairly high intellectual plane, but in the end many of his victories came from simply wearing Standards down. Late on many, many Saturday evenings he would be on the phone in two-, three-, or four-way conversations with the Standards editor, the Standards editor's boss, the boss of the Standards editor's boss, a programming executive like Aaron Cohen, a business affairs executive like Mike Weinblatt, and anyone else who might conceivably help carry his cause. These executives could be scattered in offices, homes, restaurants, and hotel rooms from New York and its suburbs to Hollywood— being out of town or out to dinner did not exempt them from Lorne's calls. Eventually most of the executives in NBC's hierarchy with even the remotest connection to *Saturday Night* learned to leave telephone numbers where they could be reached on the day and evening of the show, and all of them have unpleasant memories of dinner parties they missed while they sat in their host's bedroom, arguing on the phone with Lorne Michaels about a sketch.

Failing one argument, Lorne tried another, or he'd get off the phone to confer with his writers about a possible change and then call back, ready to start the debate again. He had what seemed to be an encyclopedic knowledge of television history and often cited precedents, both real and imagined. "Carson used that word on the fourteenth of October," he'd say. "Look it up." Lorne also cited higher authorities. If Standards was resisting a sketch that involved religion, he sometimes quoted scripture or offered to get a priest or rabbi or minister on the phone to discuss the theological implications. NBC had its own religious authorities to consult, but Lorne did too.

An unlikely participant in many of these conversations was NBC's executive vice president and general counsel, a tall, balding, sober-miened man named Corydon B. Dunham. Dunham took over responsibility for Standards from Bob Kasmire in November of 1976, and so became the final court of appeal in many of *Saturday Night*'s fiercest Standards battles. Dunham was accustomed to debating an issue with Lorne on the phone for as long as eight to nine hours over the course of a week, beginning on Wednesday and continuing into *Saturday Night*, an extraordinary investment of time for one of the highest executives in the company. Often when Lorne called, Dunham was at his home near Stamford, Connecticut, where he had a long extension cord on his phone so that in nice weather he could walk in his garden while Lorne argued on. Dunham says he put up with Lorne's persistence because it was important Lorne be able to "exhaust the review process," but it's also apparent that, as a lawyer, Dunham enjoyed the give and take. "Lorne," Dunham says, "didn't make small points."

Another distinctive element of *Saturday Night*'s relationship with Standards was Lorne's policy of encouraging his writers to deal directly with the censors, one of the few exceptions to the shield he kept between his staff and the network. This was highly unusual as far as the censors were concerned: On other programs they dealt exclusively with the producer, never with the writers. Often they wished they didn't have to on *Saturday Night*.

Franken and Davis—or F&D, as everyone called them—were the writers who were most active in dealing with the censors, and who most frequently provoked controversy with what they wrote. They had a knack for coming at issues from an off-center point of view that viewers often mistook as an endorsement of the very point that was being satirized. They created a parody of TV cop shows called "Ex-Police" (sometimes they called it "X-Police") in which Dan Aykroyd and Bill Murray played rogue cops who had been thrown off the force for excessive violence. They still patrolled the community, however, killing anyone whose values strayed even slightly from the farthest reaches of the far right. In one episode they barged into an apartment shared by two women and, assuming they were lesbians, battered one and murdered the other. "Another homosexuality-related death," they said as they walked out. The sketch provoked dozens of outraged letters from gay groups and others who wanted to know what was so funny about killing homosexuals.

A similar idea F&D had that never made it on the air was a David Susskind talk show featuring four guests who wanted to assassinate Ted Kennedy. Dan Aykroyd was to play a twisted character who lived over a muffler shop. "He'll know me when he sees me," was one of his lines. Garrett Morris was a man who had been dishonorably discharged from the Army and wanted to kill not only Kennedy but also the head of the Joint Chiefs of Staff; Gilda Radner had seen Kennedy on TV and thought he was the Devil.

F&D were invited to Herminio Traviesas's office to discuss the sketch.

"I don't believe you guys wrote this," Travie told them. "Usually when I see the things you write they're at least funny, but I don't see what's funny about this."

F&D thought the piece was hilarious and explained its point: "It's about how much insanity there is, about how stupid and out of control it all is."

At length Travie began to concede the humor, but he still refused to let it on. "Suppose we air it and Kennedy gets shot next week?" he said. "If anything could ever get NBC closed down, that would be it. And this might increase the chance of that happening."

It was F&D's turn to concede the point, and they left the office.

Even when their pieces were silly rather than pointed, F&D's humor caused anguish. They wrote a sketch called "Stunt Baby" in which an infant stand-in (actually a doll) was thrown repeatedly against walls and furniture in a child-beating scene for a movie. That provoked one viewer to write, "I once had a sister, but now I don't— my father beat her to death. I didn't find your show the *least bit* funny." That didn't keep F&D from following "Stunt Baby" with "Stunt Puppy." They were going to write a third episode called "Stunt Grandmother" but never got around to it.

Another time F&D did a stand-up routine in which Franken was dying of a brain tumor and wanted to tell one last joke. He made a valiant effort but kept blacking out at the punch line. Once again a painful letter arrived in the mail. "One of the friends I was watching the show with happens to have a malignant brain tumor," the letter said. "Despite all the efforts of medicine his days are numbered. My friend was deeply shaken by this skit and I was speechless ... Dying is tough anytime, especially when you haven't reached 21 yet. Something like this can ruin a person's entire mental attitude, which is a major factor in determining how much longer the patient can expect to live."

Probably the most controversial sketch *Saturday Night* ever aired was another of Franken and Davis's, called "First, He Cries." It was a takeoff of NBC News correspondent Betty Rollin's best-selling book about her struggle with breast cancer, *First, You Cry*. F&D's version supposedly portrayed the tragedy of mastectomy from the male's point of view. Bill Murray played a sniveling husband who couldn't bear to be with his "deformed" wife after her surgery; Gilda Radner played the victimized wife, and host Bea Arthur the understanding doctor.

The point, of course, was the selfishness and insensitivity of the man, but Lorne knew as soon as he saw the sketch it would be trouble. Even within *Saturday Night* there was major resistance; people muttered during the week that "Al Franken has really gone over the edge this time." Bill Murray was mortified. "Do you know what it's like," he asked one of the writers, "to go out there and play something that's going to make people *hate* you?"

Bill Clotworthy, the Standards editor on the show at the time, immediately took "First, He Cries" to Traviesas. Travie decided it addressed a legitimate issue and approved it despite the fact that his own sister was then dying of cancer. Bea Arthur found the sketch funny and had no reservations about it, even though her sister had had a mastectomy; Traviesas was aware of that and it was a factor in his approval. Both Arthur and Traviesas would later have second thoughts about their decisions.

"First, He Cries" provoked the expected avalanche of negative phone calls (160 of them in New York alone that night and 75 more the next day) and letters (more than 300). Bea Arthur received an outraged call late that night from a viewer who tracked her down to her hotel room. One viewer who wrote in to voice her support of "First, He Cries" was Betty Rollin herself. "I just wanted you to know I wasn't the slightest bit offended," her letter said, "and if I were offended I don't think it should matter at all. You have a right to satirize anything and the more unlikely the subject the better. I thought the premise of the sketch was terrific."

With Rollin's permission, Franken quoted excerpts from her note in a letter of explanation he wrote to offended viewers. He also mentioned that his own mother had undergone a mastectomy.

Sometimes when there seemed to be no alternative, *Saturday Night* simply ignored Standards and did what it wanted to do, or didn't ask in the first place. This was a dangerous technique that lost the show considerable good will with the censors. An example was a sketch in which Laraine Newman was to say the words *pissed off.* Standards vetoed the line early in the week, but Lorne told Laraine: "Don't say it in dress, but say it on-air." Laraine did, and the following Monday she had to make an impassioned apology to Traviesas to prevent him from permanently putting the show on tape delay. She didn't mention in her *mea culpa* that she'd received her instructions from Lorne.

Dan Aykroyd once played a refrigerator repairman whose pants, like the pants of countless repairmen in real life, very obviously revealed a goodly portion of his posterior whenever he bent over. The censor ordered Aykroyd to cover up, thereby obviating to a large degree the point of the sketch. In the meeting between dress and air, Danny told

Lorne: "Nope, I'm gonna do it," and that night male cleavage took center stage on national television.

*Saturday Night*'s guest hosts and musicians were also guilty of the occasional intentional lapse. Burt Reynolds, in a commercial parody promoting a sexy photo collection called "The Burt Book," ignored a Standards prohibition against telling ladies to "get your rocks off" by buying a copy. On another show, rock musician Elvis Costello stopped after singing a few bars of his scheduled number and launched into a different song that nobody, including the censor, had heard him play in rehearsals. Unsure of what words Costello might be about to sing, the censor in the control room started shouting "Cut him off! Cut him off!" Bob Liftin, the show's sound consultant, gambled that the new song would be safe and left the sound on, although he stood poised over the volume controls, ready to cut Costello's microphone if he was wrong. (The song Costello played was "Radio, Radio," which, although not obscene, was an attack on the radio establishment, of which NBC was a part.)

There was always the opportunity to add embellishments on-air that weren't written in the script or performed in dress rehearsal. Buck Henry once played a lonely Charles Lindbergh who whiled away the hours on his solo transatlantic flight reading a girlie magazine. Dan Aykroyd, in a voice-over narration, paused meaningfully in mid-sentence when he read that, because of gale- force winds, Lindbergh had been "jerked off ... course." In the control room the outraged censor jumped to his feet yelling, "I've been screwed!"

A little deception sometimes helped ward off assaults from outside NBC as well. Herb Schmertz, the outspoken public relations chief for Mobil Oil, felt all businessmen had been slurred in a speech consumer advocate Ralph Nader once delivered on Weekend Update. "Today marks the 4,621st day that Exxon has held America hostage," Nader said. He also had jibes for the automobile industry, the tire industry, the pharmaceutical industry, the chemical industry, cereal manufacturers, and meatpackers. "You don't want to eat hot dogs unless you're into fat and rodent excrement," he said. Schmertz demanded equal time to respond, but NBC's legal department told him that collective-bargaining rules required that all material on the show be written by the show's writers, as Nader's commentary had been. Schmertz wisely declined an offer to read a rebuttal written by *Saturday Night*. What neither Schmertz nor NBC's lawyers knew was that Nader had in fact written most of his commentary himself with the help of his associate Mark Green.

For all the natural tension that existed between *Saturday Night* and Standards, their relationship remained reasonably cordial until a woman named Jane Crowley was assigned as the show's Standards editor in

April of the first year. Many who worked on *Saturday Night* believe Crowley was brought in because the network perceived Jay Ottley as being too friendly to the show, but the official reason was that Ottley was tired of working weekends and was due for the normal rotation. In any event, the mixture of Jane Crowley with *Saturday Night* was a disaster from the moment she arrived.

Crowley was almost a caricature of what a censor should be: A bosomy, matronly woman, she wore suits with pleated skirts that hung several inches below the knee, bright-red lipstick and nail polish, and a gold necklace that she twisted nervously in her fingers as she talked. She was a devout Catholic, so devout that, according to an NBC executive who worked with her, she once protested the selection of news anchorman Chet Huntley as the luncheon speaker for a religious club she belonged to because Huntley had been divorced.

Crowley's frame of reference was so different from that of *Saturday Night* that for much of the time she spent on the show the main problem was one of basic communication. She often didn't understand the jokes, and sometimes let things by that she probably wouldn't have if she'd understood them. Crowley never questioned, for example, an Update opening that announced, "Brought to you by Hershey Highway: the candy that's turned America's taste around for fifty years." She didn't know, apparently, that the joke was about anal sex.

Taunting Crowley quickly became a favorite pastime of the writers. O'Donoghue would lace his scripts with words he knew would never get by just so he could sit in the control room and watch Crowley turning several shades of red as she scanned them. It's said there were times she nearly leaped over the console to throttle him. Al Franken and Tom Davis would double-team her. First they'd write some outrageous line and then say, "Let's go see what she'll do!" When she rejected it, they'd start offering even more outrageous alternatives. The goal of this game was to cause Crowley to throw up her hands and run out of the room.

Sometimes Crowley scored a point or two of her own. Writer Tom Schiller was once assigned to try to fool her into letting the phrase *golden shower* on the air. He gave her a long, completely fictitious explanation of the term, saying it described a Big Sur ritual in which hippie sun worshippers assumed yoga postures to greet "the golden shower" of the day. Unbeknownst to Schiller, Crowley already knew the real meaning (a reference to sexual practices involving urination), and after patiently listening to Schiller's explanation she smiled and shook her head. "I don't think so, Tom," she said.

Jane Crowley did not last very long as the censor on *Saturday Night*. She covered the few shows remaining in the first season and returned as the show's Standards editor in the fall of 1976. By December, NBC had shifted her to a different assignment, and she would return to *Saturday Night* only occasionally thereafter. If Lorne had had his way, Crowley undoubtedly would have been reassigned much sooner than that, but Standards wasn't going to let the producer start choosing his censors, at least not that openly. During Crowley's time on the show, however, *Saturday Night*'s popularity had grown steadily, and Lorne's power grew with it. Eventually he got what he wanted.

"Lorne always had a list of requests," said an NBC executive involved in the decision. "One was to not have Jane Crowley [on the show]. In the interests of harmony, that was acceded to."

\* \* \*

Broadcast Standards was not the only guardian of social and moral responsibility on duty in studio 8H every *Saturday Night*. The show's advertisers were represented there as well, as a matter of self- defense. Standards' policy is that advertisers are to have no voice in what a show puts on. But advertisers can withdraw their spots from a show if they think they might be embarrassed by it, and being embarrassed by *Saturday Night* was a constant threat for almost every advertiser on the show, not only because of the show's outrageousness overall, but also because *Saturday Night* regularly took pains to attack its own sponsors.

An advertising executive could literally lose his job in a hundred different ways buying time on *Saturday Night*. Say the client is a Japanese car company and its spot follows one of John Belushi's Samurai sketches on the air. The president of the company happens to be in town from Tokyo, sees the show, and is not amused to be associated with such a portrayal of Japanese culture. Perhaps the client is Kodak, which happens to be introducing a new Instamatic camera. Their spot comes on immediately after a sketch featuring one of *Saturday Night*'s more controversial recurring characters, the child-molesting Uncle Roy. In the sketch, Uncle Roy snaps raunchy instant photos of the two little girls he's babysitting, who are perched in their nighties on top of the glass coffee table, playing a game of Uncle Roy's invention called "Glass-Bottom Boat." Not exactly the wholesome image Kodak had in mind. Maybe the client is the U.S. Army. Their spot follows a pitch for the New Army in a sketch in which the recruiter is John Belushi, who is lounging behind a desk that is covered with marijuana, listening to rock and roll on headphones, Or maybe it's the Ford Motor Company, which finds it's the sponsor of a show that has Ralph Nader introducing a cigarette lighter in the shape of a Ford Pinto. The flame strikes in the rear.

All those incidents either happened or almost happened to sponsors on *Saturday Night*. Those that didn't were prevented by representatives of the ad agencies who were in studio 8H every *Saturday Night* to monitor the show for any material even potentially offensive to their clients. These ad reps, as they're called, are regularly employed by the agencies to screen all programs in which their sponsors' commercials air. But almost always, even with Johnny Carson's *Tonight Show*, they have the luxury of seeing the program on tape before it goes out on the network. With *Saturday Night* the reps had no choice but to attend the dress rehearsals. If they spotted something that might concern their clients, they had the option of asking NBC to move their commercial to a different place in the show, away from the offending sketch, or of taking the client's ad out of the show altogether.

The reps often used their own judgment on obviously offensive material, but they were also armed with a list of guidelines from each client that defined material with which they did not want to be associated. Prohibitions ranged from the specific, such as any mention of the client's name or product, to the general, such as the Department of Defense's policy that it not have commercials in programs that criticized, in any way, any agency, official, or policy of the United States government.

With *Saturday Night*, even after dress rehearsal there might be a rewrite that would cause a sponsor trouble. Or the rundown of the show could be changed, putting the commercial next to a different, troublesome sketch. It took a crisis for the ad reps to fully appreciate that danger. During the dress rehearsal for the show of February 18, 1978, there was a sketch called "Great Moments of War." It was a parody of the old World War II movies in which GIs on guard for German spies trying to slip through the lines ask such all-American questions as "What's the capital of Illinois?" and "What's a Texas Leaguer?" The sketch took the premise to the absurd so that by its end, when even the GIs couldn't name the current manager of the Cleveland Indians, they all arrested each other.

A young man named DeWitt Mallary was the rep on duty that night for the U.S. Army's ad agency. He left studio 8H after dress rehearsal. The show rundown changed after dress, and a commercial touting the Army ended up running immediately after the "Great Moments of War" sketch. It was hard to tell if the Army spot was a commercial or a continuation of the joke. In either case, it looked funny.

The following week there was a meeting of the sponsors and their reps with the NBC sales department, in which it was agreed that henceforth all commercials for *Saturday Night* would be put on tape cassettes, instead of on one long tape reel, so that they could be shifted around more readily in the show. NBC also agreed to have its own advertising representative at the dress rehearsal each week to help the agencies' reps make any necessary changes in the commercial running order. And the reps, DeWitt Mallary among them, learned to stay in 8H until the show went on the air.

*Saturday Night*'s first commercial break usually came about ten minutes into the show, so the ad reps had until then to reformat the commercial lineup. They often used every minute of that time. Between dress and air they'd be frantically keeping track of the changes and calling their clients (another set of executives whose *Saturday Night*s were spent near telephones) if they had any doubts. Nine shows out of ten, sponsors either shifted their spots within the show or withdrew from the show entirely. Still, many sponsors got burned. NBC finance chief Don Carswell says that more advertisers withdrew permanently from *Saturday Night* than from any other program, ever.

* * *

*Saturday Night*'s greatest Standards battle ever unfolded the week of December 22, 1979. The sketch at issue was called the "Nerds Nativity." It featured Nerds Lisa Loopner and Todd DiLaMuca, played by Gilda Radner and Bill Murray, two of the show's most popular characters. It was written, as almost all the Nerds sketches were, by Anne Beatts and Rosie Shuster. Lorne wanted something Christmassy for the show, so they had the Nerds performing in a high school nativity pageant. An innocent enough idea on the surface, but Standards didn't see it that way.

As soon as the Standards editor, Bill Clotworthy, read the piece on Wednesday, he raised a red flag with his boss, Ralph Daniels. Daniels had recently taken over Herminio Traviesas' job when Travie, semiretired, moved into a corporate policy position. Clotworthy himself had only been a censor for a few weeks. *Saturday Night* was his first assigned show.

Clotworthy and Daniels didn't care for a joke in the sketch that had Todd describing Lisa as one of the few girls in school who was "physically correct" for the part of the Virgin Mary; nor were they amused when one of the wise men gestured at Joseph's mule (played by Alan Zweibel) and said, "Get your ass out of here." But more than that, they were bothered by the whole concept: It seemed to them to be satirizing one of Christianity's most sacred events, the birth of Christ. Not a good idea, they thought, especially three days before Christmas. Daniels flatly rejected the piece. "The nativity is central to an entire religion," he told Lorne. "You cannot spoof the nativity."

Lorne argued that what was being spoofed was not the nativity but high school nativity pageants, where the wise men wore bathrobes, the star of Bethlehem was made of tinfoil, and the holy family had paper plates pinned to their heads for halos. "I went to that school!" he said. He kept the piece in production, suggesting, as he often had in the past, that Standards ought at least to see how it came across in dress rehearsal.

Daniels wasn't negotiating. He'd watched Travie deal with *Saturday Night* for several years and was of the opinion that Michaels & Co. had been getting away with far more than they should have. The show by then was a huge success at a time when NBC had very few successes. It seemed to Daniels that everybody at NBC had the attitude that, as he put it, "these guys can do pretty much what they want." He decided it wasn't going to be that way under his Standards department, and the "Nerds Nativity" sketch was where he drew the line. Daniels refused even to discuss it.

Lorne, by then used to winning his fights with Standards, was every bit as adamant. The sketch, with some of the racier lines removed, played in dress rehearsal on Saturday. Afterward Lorne told Bill Clotworthy and Josh Kane, an NBC program executive who was brought in to help mediate, "The sketch is staying in the show. You can do what you want."

That didn't leave NBC with many pleasant alternatives. They could take the whole show off the air and put on a rerun. They could run a videotaped sketch from an earlier show over the Nerds sketch when it went on. Or, Josh Kane later joked, they could bring armed guards into the studio and have them stand in front of the set. Any of these choices would result, they knew, in the very public resignation of the producer. At that point, Kane said, "the race was on."

Between dress and air, Clotworthy and Lorne were on the phone in Lorne's ninth-floor office with Cory Dunham and Ralph Daniels. Lorne tried to enlist the aid of Mike Weinblatt, who was at the show, but Weinblatt deferred to Daniels's judgment. Daniels was talking from a phone booth in a restaurant, and he wasn't happy to be talking at all. There was a lot of shouting, but Daniels was softening his position enough to begin to discuss some of the lines that would have to be cut if they were to let the sketch on.

As they talked, Josh Kane was rushing to NBC's videotape archives with a unit manager to look for a sketch of similar length to run over the "Nerds Nativity" if it came to that. They found a suitable sketch and gave it to the engineer in central control, telling him to stand by.

Meanwhile the advertising reps covering the show had seen the "Nerds Nativity" sketch in dress. Most of them didn't want their clients' spots anywhere near it. Uncertain of whether it would be on the air show, several of the reps decided that discretion was the better part of valor and told NBC's ad rep, Sue Schwartz, they wanted out of the show. Schwartz, realizing the company was about to lose an unprecedented 40 percent or more of its revenue for the night, decided to break all the rules and started looking for a program executive to plead that the sketch not be put on. She couldn't find anyone, so she called her boss, Robert Conrad, at home. Conrad's solution was simple: He instructed Schwartz to tell the agencies NBC refused to take them out of the show. Some of the ad reps found that hard to believe.

"I'm telling you we're not paying for the unit," one of them yelled at Schwartz, "and I've gone on record as demanding to be out of the show!" The calls and the shouting between the reps, Conrad, Schwartz, and various agency executives continued as the show went on the air.

Anne Beatts was in the ladies' room at 11:28 when somebody pounded on the door, shouting at her to get to Lorne's office. As she arrived, Lorne raced out saying, "Bill Clotworthy's in there—go talk to him." Beatts, who had been uncertain all week what would happen with the sketch, was bewildered: She thought the "Nerds Nativity" was supposed to be the second sketch in the show, which meant it should be going on within minutes. She didn't know Lorne had moved it back to just after midnight to gain some time. Rosie Shuster came in, and she could see the show in progress on the monitor in Lorne's office as she and Beatts argued with Daniels on the phone.

"You can't say the word *ass*," Daniels told them. "We've used that word before," Beatts protested.

"Not in front of Mary and Joseph, you haven't," Daniels replied. Daniels also wanted a piece of business cut in which Bill Murray's Todd rubbed his knuckles affectionately across the head of Gilda Radner's Lisa in a "noogie attack." Todd gave Lisa noogies in every Nerds sketch, and it always got a laugh, but Daniels wouldn't hear of it in a nativity scene.

"You can't give noogies to the Virgin Mary!" he shouted at Beatts.

"But she's not the Virgin Mary!" Beatts shouted back. "She's Gilda Radner playing Lisa Loopner playing the Virgin Mary with a paper plate on her head!"

Beatts, Shuster, and three production assistants, Julia Fraser, Jeannine Kerwin, and Robin Shlien, ran the changes to cue cards and the control room just as the sketch was to go on the air. They only had time to tell the actors, "Just read the cards. It's all different."

The actors had some choice words in response to that, especially Bill Murray, who yelled at Beatts later: "Don't you ever do that to me again!"

The sketch played fairly well on air, considering, but no one was really happy with it. Too many lines had been lost and too many egos bruised. Todd did, however, give Lisa her noogies that night.

"The Nerds Nativity": *Saturday Night* and the censors were still fighting over this sketch minutes before it went on the air.
Host Ted Knight plays the high school principal. © *NBC*

The following Monday, Ralph Daniels wrote a memo to Cory Dunham saying Standards would no longer cover *Saturday Night*. If Standards made a ruling and Lorne Michaels ignored it, Daniels said, then what was the point? The memo's underlying message was clear: Either Dunham brought Michaels into line, or Daniels would quit.

Dunham called a meeting in his office that Wednesday. Attending were Lorne, Daniels, Clotworthy, Josh Kane, and Mike Weinblatt. Daniels repeated his conviction that Lorne's "steamroller" approach had to stop. "A producer cannot say 'This stays in because I say it stays,'" Daniels said. "That's why we have a Standards department. If the producer is not willing to be flexible, and if it's his determination that something goes on, then I'm removing my people."

Lorne repeated his defense of the sketch, but his tone was concilia-tory. As Josh Kane saw it, Lorne could afford to be conciliatory at that point. At the end of the meeting everyone shook hands and agreed to try to work together more smoothly. Cory Dunham reflected later that an appropriate balance seemed to have been struck: Sometimes the pro-ducer wanted to resign because of Standards, and sometimes Standards wanted to resign because of the producer.

As Daniels staged his protest, Robert Conrad in Sales was soothing the ruffled feathers of the agencies who had been forced to stay in the show. In the NBC mail room, stacks of letters were pouring in from viewers who wanted to know how *Saturday Night* could make fun of the baby Jesus.

# CHAPTER 16

# ... With a Little Help from My Friends

> Narcotic addiction shall be presented only as a destructive habit. The use of illegal drugs or the abuse of legal drugs shall not be encouraged or shown as socially acceptable.
>
> —NBC Broadcast Standards for Television handbook

For all the controversy *Saturday Night* occasionally generated, the consensus at NBC was that the standards of acceptability on television had been relaxed on the show with notable success. The republic did not fall, and, judging from the ratings *Saturday Night* eventually produced, far more people did indeed find the show's irreverence refreshing rather than threatening. The major qualification to that consensus concerned *Saturday Night*'s drug humor, which to this day is a subject of sensitivity and some shame at the network.

There's no question the show violated NBC's Standards guidelines on the presentation of drug use, not constantly, but often. The first joke ever told on *Saturday Night* was a drug joke of George Carlin's: "Football's kinda nice," he said. "They moved the hash marks in. ... The guys found 'em and smoked 'em anyway." Any regular viewing of the program from then on left the clear impression that everyone on *Saturday Night*—as well as a majority of its viewers—frequently enjoyed illegal drugs, mostly marijuana. To name just a few examples:

- On the tenth show of the first season, Chevy Chase announced that a dangerous strain of "Killer Dope" was making its way around the country, and that Weekend Update was offering to test samples of viewers' marijuana to ensure its safety. "Simply place a small amount of the suspected cannabis in a plain brown wrapper," Chevy said, "and send it immediately to [a card appeared on the screen]: Chevy Chase, 827 W. 81st St., New York, New York."

- At NBC's insistence, Chevy had given an address that did not exist (it would have been somewhere in the middle of the Hudson River), but a number of viewers sent their samples to the 17th floor anyway. NBC did not know that the marijuana joint displayed on camera during this segment was, in fact, real marijuana.

- Dan Aykroyd made a similar offer on Update to test viewers' grass when the U.S. government was spraying marijuana fields in Mexico with paraquat. "In no way does this mean we at Weekend Update advocate the smoking of marijuana," he said. "It's just that a survey showed ninety-seven percent of our viewers smoke it daily. It is for that minority that we are doing this test."

- On the same Update, Aykroyd was seen buying an ounce of marijuana from Garrett Morris. Danny complained that he'd been ripped off ("It's light, man") and later in the newscast read a bulletin that Garrett had been found murdered "in what appears to be a drug-related incident."

- Host Eric Idle, a member of Monty Python, once embarked on a search of the hallways outside the studio, trying to find out why no one had written an opening monologue for him. He walked into the writers' room and found himself standing in what looked like an opium den, filled with prostrate figures barely visible through a thick haze of smoke, puffing on hookahs. On another show hosted by Idle, Laraine Newman appeared in a public service spot for the American Dope Growers Union, urging viewers to "buy American" and singing "Look for the Union Label" with a group of pot farmers.

- When actor Charles Grodin was the host, his image as a square was a running joke on the show. John Belushi complained at one point: "He doesn't smoke dope. He's not one of us."

John Belushi was by far the most frequent focus of *Saturday Night*'s drug humor. His first drug bit appeared on the fifth show when he played Ludwig van Beethoven sitting at a piano, trying to compose. He was unable to come up with anything other than lame melodies like "Tie a

Yellow Ribbon 'Round the Old Oak Tree" until he was given his snuff box. After taking a sniff he broke into "My Girl" by the Temptations. The bit was repeated later in the show, when after taking his snuff he put on sunglasses and played a swinging version of Ray Charles's "What'd I Say."

Cocaine at the time was not nearly so well known as it would become in the next few years, and even some of *Saturday Night*'s writers did not realize the implication that Belushi as Beethoven was snorting coke. But from there the jokes about Belushi's taste for drugs became more overt, and gradually he developed an ongoing persona as the drugged-out waif of comedy. For example:

- Candice Bergen once announced an "adopt John Belushi for Christmas" appeal in which it was noted that he liked roast goose stuffed with drugs.
- In a public-service announcement parody with host Fran Tarkenton, John, wearing a Cub Scout uniform, sat staring into space while Tarkenton sadly told viewers Belushi had been "a promising young actor until his mind was destroyed by drugs."
- In a cold opening, John claimed he was too sick to go on the air, but when his doctor threatened to cut off his drug supply, he immediately sat up and introduced the show.
- Soon after returning from the set of Jack Nicholson's movie *Goin' South*, in Durango, Mexico, John was shown on Weekend Update presenting a scholarship to a young Mexican to finance the boy's education— in exchange for a large quantity of marijuana.
- In an Update commentary John talked about "how far we've come" toward the decriminalization of marijuana, mentioned that in Amsterdam people can smoke hash in the streets, and concluded by shouting, "I want hard drugs!" In a similar commentary a few weeks later he talked about exchanging joints for Christmas with a friend.
- Jane Curtin remarked in another cold opening how relaxed John had become "thanks to a little success and a lot of heroin."
- In its third season *Saturday Night* had an "Anyone Can Host" contest that was won by an eighty-year-old grandmother named Miskel Spillman. In the show's opening, John confessed he'd slipped Spillman a joint. Buck Henry was appalled: "Your joints overwhelm even an experienced drug user like myself!" he told Belushi. Laraine Newman asked if the joint he gave Spillman

had any of the rhino tranquilizer in it. No, John said, "just some Michoacan [a potent strain of grass from the Michoacan area of Mexico] and some hash oil."

The familiar use of such drug terms as Michoacan went to the heart of *Saturday Night*'s attitude toward drugs and to the essence of its sub-version of NBC's anti-drug policies. The simple fact was that for the writers and performers on *Saturday Night*, drugs were a part of their humor because drugs were a part of their lives. *Saturday Night*'s view-ers appreciated those jokes because drugs were a part of their lives too. If *Saturday Night* was, as Dick Ebersol often described it, "the post-Watergate victory party for the Woodstock generation," then drugs were as much a shared experience of that generation as growing up with sub-urbs, assassinations, and television itself.

*Saturday Night* employed the same knowing style to address the dangers of the drug culture as well. On several shows Dan Aykroyd and Laraine Newman played two characters named Jason and Sunshine who epitomized mindless drug freaks. John Belushi appeared with them in one sketch as Windowpane Watson, a man who, after taking LSD every day for ten years, was no longer in the slightest touch with reality. (Windowpane is a potent kind of LSD.)

Dan Aykroyd once portrayed President Jimmy Carter talking down a young acid-tripper who called him during a radio phone-in program. "All right, Peter, now just listen, everything's going to be fine," the President said. "You're very high right now; you'll probably be that way for about five more hours. Try taking some Vitamin B complex, Vitamin C complex. If you have a beer, go ahead and drink it. Just remember, you're a living organism on this planet and you're very safe. You've just taken a heavy drug. Relax, stay inside, and listen to some music. Okay? Do you have any Allman Brothers?"

There was, in light of what would happen to his friend John Belushi, a sadly prophetic quality to a bulletin Aykroyd read on Weekend Update one week: "This just in from the National Drug Abuse Association," he said. "Cocaine and heroin do not mix. If you must snort, don't shoot."

The image of a bunch of heads on *Saturday Night* putting together a show for the heads out there in TV land was definitely a large part of the show's appeal. *Saturday Night* became, in many respects, a passing of the communal joint around a circle that spanned, through television, the entire country. Even Herminio Traviesas implicitly acknowledged that *Saturday Night* was the doper's program. The drug jokes bothered him, he said, "but I didn't think we were changing viewers' habits."

NBC did try to curtail *Saturday Night*'s drug humor. Bob Kasmire, among others, says that only about one of every three drug jokes the show submitted got on the air. But in the end the network's reservations were overridden by an even greater fear: that Lorne Michaels and his team might resign and the revenues from the show might cease.

"We really were concerned [about *Saturday Night*'s presentation of drug use]," said Julian Goodman, who until he retired in 1979 was the chairman of NBC. "They always managed to slip something in that gave you the impression it was okay."

Asked if NBC couldn't have simply insisted that no more drug jokes be "slipped in" on *Saturday Night*, Goodman answered, "You could say it, but you could not say it and keep the show."

* * *

There is also no question that *Saturday Night*'s own copious drug use within NBC was tolerated for the same reason. Officially, no one at NBC was aware that marijuana and, in later years, cocaine were consumed regularly by many on the show. Unofficially, more than a dozen NBC executives confirm it was common knowledge in the company, and that for the most part it was conveniently ignored.

It would have been hard not to have known it. The odor of grass was commonplace not only on the 17th floor but also in the hallways and offices around studio 8H. The dressing room on the ninth floor for the *Saturday Night* band was widely referred to, by NBC's Guest Relations staff as well as those on the show, as "the Departure Lounge." The Guest Relations staff also knew that an individual who attended the show almost every week as a guest was, in fact, one of *Saturday Night*'s drug connections.

Although *Saturday Night* did not make a habit of flaunting its consumption of drugs, NBC executives did periodically witness drugs being used by people on the show—again, mostly marijuana, although some saw cocaine use as well. One unit manager's personal policy was indicative of the attitude of the company as a whole: If an illegal substance appeared in his presence, he literally turned his back.

Several times the show's stars talked in interviews about their use of drugs. Laraine Newman once discussed her preference for pot over cocaine (a preference that would later change) with *High Times* magazine, and other more widely read publications quoted her remarks. Chevy Chase once greeted a reporter for the *New York* Post by offering to share with her his Thai stick marijuana joint. The last quote in the article was, "Anybody wanna toke?"

How did those in NBC's press department feel when they read interviews such as these? Says M. S. (Bud) Rukeyser, Jr., NBC's executive vice president of corporate communications, "It's a bitch."

It is not meant to suggest here that NBC *should* have done anything about the show's use of drugs (or even could have if it chose to), only to point out that the network was, in fact, aware of it and did very little. Bud Rukeyser and others say NBC took pains on several occasions to advise Lorne in memos about the network's policies regarding drug use on the premises. There were moments of panic on the 17th floor every so often that a bust might be in the offing, and stashes were disposed of or promptly consumed. Later, when the popularity of the show was at its peak, Lorne would take added precautions to prevent any surprise visits by the police or federal agents.

But there never was a bust at *Saturday Night,* and it's apparent that NBC's warning memos were aimed mainly at making sure the network was covered in case of a scandal. Julian Goodman says NBC's Legal Department was asked at one point to research what legal liabilities the network had in order to ensure it was not "in jeopardy" because of *Saturday Night*'s consumption of drugs in the building. Legal chief Cory Dunham says that to his knowledge NBC never summoned any authorities in relation to the use of narcotics by the show. The general attitude within NBC was that the personal drug habits of those on *Saturday Night* were not a responsibility of the company, and that as long as no one there was selling drugs, it was best not getting into the business of drug enforcement. As one executive put it: "We weren't running a social services department."

A senior NBC program executive summed up the feelings of many at the network when he told of attending the show and of seeing the people there "full of life, very nervous, or full of drugs. Probably all three were true. My only thoughts were, Jesus, we have a hit. The best demographics in the history of commercial TV."

CHAPTER 17

# The White House

I think humor was very important in those grim days following
President Nixon's resignation.
                    —Bob Orben, joke writer for President Gerald Ford


Good evening, ladies and gentlemen. Thank you ... Tonight we'd like
to stick our necks out a little on national television to call for a violent
overthrow of the United States government ... [Applause] ... Thank
you ... Thank you very much.
                    —Franken and Davis on *Saturday Night*


Al Franken sensed a contradiction in candidate Ronald Reagan's position on marijuana.

Franken, during a week off in February of the first season, had gone to
New Hampshire to visit his brother, a professional news photographer who
was covering the 1976 presidential primary campaign. Thinking he might
get some material he could use for the show, Franken spent a day or two
riding on the press bus, following the candidates as they stumped the state.

In a question-and-answer session at a junior high school gym one
morning, Ronald Reagan had said he was opposed to a law requiring
motorcycle drivers to wear helmets because such a law would restrict
personal freedom. At another stop, Reagan said he opposed legalizing
marijuana because marijuana had been proven to cause brain damage.
That night, at yet another forum in a hockey arena at Dartmouth College,
Franken left the press section, maneuvered his way into the crowd of
voters, and stood up to ask the candidate a question.

President Gerald R. Ford Talking with Chevy Chase, Saturday Night Live
Producer Lorne Michaels, John Belushi, Dan Aykroyd, and Others at the 32nd
Annual Radio and Television Correspondents Association Dinner

"Uh, yeah," Franken said. "Earlier today, you said you were against mandatory motorcycle helmets because that was a limit to personal freedom. Yet you are against decriminalization of marijuana because marijuana causes brain damage. Can't not wearing a motorcycle helmet cause brain damage a lot quicker than marijuana by, for example, the head splitting open so that actual material from the road enters the brain?"

Reagan mumbled something Franken couldn't quite follow about being able to tell if the pilot of an airplane had been drinking but not if he'd been smoking marijuana, and quickly went on to the next question. When the event was over, Reagan's press secretary, Lyn Nofziger, angrily confronted Franken and threw him off the press bus. "You can't be a reporter and a member of the public both," Nofziger said. "Now get off the bus." Had Nofziger known what Franken and his friends on *Saturday Night* were about to do to Gerald Ford, he might not have been so hasty.

At a campaign stop on the same trip, Franken met Ford's press secretary, Ron Nessen. Nessen, a former NBC News correspondent, had discovered *Saturday Night* by accident a few weeks before. He was sitting at home spinning his TV dial when he happened on one of Chevy Chase's bits as Gerald Ford. Buck Henry was playing Nessen. The sketch had Nessen explaining to Ford that a new strategy to counter Ford's image for clumsiness had been devised. The plan was called "Operation Stumblebum." The idea was that every time Ford stumbled, so would all the aides around him, so that Ford's gaffes would appear to be just the everyday mishaps that occur to anyone. By the end of the sketch, Chevy, Henry, and two secret service agents (John and Garrett) were wandering around the stage like drunken blind men, ripping their clothes, banging themselves on the head, and falling on the floor.

Nessen was amused in spite of himself. The sketch had accurately reflected the fact that Nessen, among others in the White House, considered the media's portrayal of Ford as a bumbler one of the most serious public relations liabilities of his administration. Nessen had spent a significant amount of time and energy trying to overcome that image. Yet here was Chevy Chase taking Ford's buffoonery almost as far as it could go in the opposite direction.

Nessen asked an aide to get him a cassette of the show, and he watched *Saturday Night* religiously from then on. When Nessen ran into Al Franken in New Hampshire a few weeks later, he told Franken how much he liked the show. Franken, thinking how perfect it would be to have the real press secretary play opposite Chevy Chase's Gerald Ford, broached the idea of Nessen appearing on the show. To Franken's surprise, Nessen said, "Oh, I'd *love* to be on it."

Franken said he'd talk to Lorne. After a few phone conversations with Lorne, Nessen agreed to host the show of April 17.

In accepting the invitation Nessen had a very specific political objective in mind: He hoped to mitigate the stumblebum issue by proving that the administration, too, considered it a joke, and that this administration, unlike any since John F. Kennedy's, had a sense of humor. "You lose by getting all huffy and complaining or demanding they stop it," he said later. "You win by showing you can laugh at yourself and take part in the thing."

Lorne understood Nessen's motivation, and it caused him some reservations about having Nessen on the show. Lorne had never liked the way Bob Hope would make jokes about the President one day and play golf with him the next. It led, he was sure, to pulling punches. He wouldn't have it that way with Nessen. When he talked to Nessen on the phone, he told him that the show wouldn't change the way it did things in deference to Nessen's position. Nessen, for his part, told *The Washington Post* the day his booking was announced: "When we first talked about this I told them I can't do anything truly embarrassing or in bad taste to the White House. And they agreed there'd be nothing like that on the show." Already the lines were drawn.

Nessen spent the next several weeks with his finger to the wind in the White House, feeling out the reaction. Although he says there were very few objections to the idea, there were enough doubts to cause him to waver. The event that convinced him he should go through with it was Chevy Chase's appearance alongside Ford at a Washington banquet that March.

The occasion was the annual dinner of the Radio and Television Correspondents Association. Gerald Ford was the guest of honor; the idea of Chevy providing the entertainment, Dave Tebet's. Ford not only didn't object, he bought Nessen's philosophy of playing along with the joke. The President, with the help of his assistant for communications, Don Penny (a television veteran who had played roles on the series *That Girl* and *The Wackiest Ship in the Army*), began rehearsing a comedy bit of his own.

The day before the dinner, Chevy, his fiancée, his brother, Lorne, John, and Danny took the shuttle to Washington. John and Danny were along to play Secret Service agents. That afternoon, Nessen gave them a tour of the White House. Belushi worried that he would have trouble getting in the gate, having as usual no identification on him whatsoever, but he passed right through. Once inside, Danny was so amused by the decor that he started dropping coins for tips into the spotless ashtrays.

Among the movers and shakers filling the ballroom that night, besides most of the Washington press corps, were Senators Eugene McCarthy, John Glenn, Mike Mansfield, and Hubert Humphrey; Federal Reserve chairman Arthur Burns, and FCC chairman Richard Wiley. Herb Schlosser and a contingent of other NBC executives also attended. During dinner, Chevy sat on the podium with Ford. Chevy claims Ford splashed soup on his tux during the meal, and that it took all the self-control he could muster not to burst out laughing.

After dinner Chevy made his entrance about fifty yards from the dais, stumbling and falling the rest of the way. John and Danny met him at the podium, John arriving from backstage just in time. This is how TV critic Tom Shales, in the next day's *Washington Post*, described the performance:

Ford alternately puffed his pipe and laughed on the dais as the comic went through his Gerald Ford routine, frequently nosediving toward the floor and being rescued [by John and Danny]. "Whoop!" Chase would say, dropping out of view. Then, retrieved: "No problem, no problem." Continuing to lampoon Ford's alleged clumsiness, Chase announced, "I have asked the Secret Service to remove the salad fork embedded in my left hand." When he accidentally bopped himself with a gavel, the two "agents" grabbed the gavel and wrestled it to the floor. ... But some of the real Secret Service agents standing by did not appear to be amused.

... From his stumblebum Presidential impersonation, Chase, 32, went into one of his satirical "Weekend Update" newscasts. He reported that ... on one accident- prone morning, the President "tied his shoe to his hair blower, and it inadvertently pardoned Richard Nixon." In the New Hampshire primary, Chase said, "President Ford accidentally kissed a snowball and threw a baby."

Ron Nessen, in a book he later wrote about his tenure as press secretary, picked up the narrative from there:

Then it was the President's turn. He had secretly developed and rehearsed a routine poking fun at himself. As he stood up, Ford pretended to get tangled in the tablecloth, yanking off a coffee cup and some silverware. The President next placed a sheaf of blank pages on the podium, supposedly his script, and proceeded to spill all the papers all over the floor.

Ford's appearance that night was brief, but it included two big laugh lines at Chevy's expense. First he pointed at Chevy and said, "I'm Gerald Ford and you're not," then commented, "Mr. Chevy Chase, you are a very, very funny suburb." (Chevy Chase, Maryland, is a suburb of Washington.)

Ron Nessen felt his boss had gotten the better of the exchange with Chevy: The "if you can't beat 'em, join 'em" strategy had worked. "Ford performed his bits like a pro," Nessen wrote. "The audience roared. The President had topped his imitator." Tom Shales didn't quite see it that way, reporting that "the bigger roars went to Chase himself."

In any case, Chevy's appearance and his backstage rapport with Ford persuaded Nessen to commit himself to hosting *Saturday Night*. "I finally decided," he said later, "that if Ford could do that, hit it off that well with Chevy on a personal basis, it resolved all the remaining doubts I had."

Once he was sure Nessen would host, Lorne proposed that President Ford videotape a few brief segments for the show. Ford agreed, and four days before the show, Lorne, Dick Ebersol, filmmaker Gary Weis, and unit manager Nick O'Gorman arrived at the White House for the taping.

The taping was scheduled for 3:30 p.m. in the Cabinet Room down the hall from the Oval Office. Weis stopped off in an adjacent bathroom to snort some cocaine. The film crew, provided by the NBC News bureau in Washington, set up their equipment and waited. At 3:30 on the dot Ford marched into the room. It was clear to Lorne and Weis that this was but another stop in a blur of engagements the President walked through every day. With a glimmer of recognition in his eyes, Ford shook Lorne's hand and said, "Chevy, how are you?

As Weis attached a microphone to Ford's lapel, Lorne tried to put the President at ease. "Mr. President," he said, "if this works out, who knows where it could lead." The President smiled vaguely.

Ford had three lines to deliver that would be integrated into the show: "Live from New York, it's *Saturday Night*," "Ladies and gentlemen, the press secretary to the President of the United States," and "I'm

Gerald Ford and you're not." Weis had to urge the President gently to put a little more feeling in his readings, and it took several takes to get them down.

When they were through, Ford got up to leave for the next event on his schedule. He forgot, however, to remove the microphone from his lapel. The NBC News crew had used a relatively old-fashioned microphone, one that was attached by a wire directly to the camera. When the President reached the full length of the cord, he was jerked backward, faltering a step while the camera swayed and almost tipped over.

Ford regained his footing, removed the microphone, and left. Nessen implored Lorne, Weis, and Ebersol never to mention the incident to anyone.

\* \* \*

Considering the amount of political humor *Saturday Night* put on the air, the staff of the show was surprisingly apolitical. Chevy Chase, Herb Sargent, and Franken and Davis were the only serious news junkies and the only ones to pay close attention to the minutiae of the political process. Herb Sargent noticed on election days that very few members of the staff ever took the time to vote.

That didn't mean the others on the show ignored politics. As middle-class children who came of age in the sixties they were products of a relatively political age, and they were all, to the degree they weren't utterly disenfranchised, positioned more or less to the left of the political spectrum. Occasionally those sentiments surfaced overtly on the show. Lorne is proudest of the time *Saturday Night* replayed, three days before the 1976 election between Ford and Jimmy Carter, the speech in which Ford announced his pardon of Richard Nixon. The feeling on the 17th floor was that the pardon had been conveniently forgotten by the press and that a reminder was in order.

But *Saturday Night*'s principal political goal, as it has been for satirists throughout history, was to reveal the underlying absurdity of the political game, whoever was in power—playing, as Lorne put it, "the loyal opposition." *Saturday Night* simply took its opposition further than other television shows. Theirs wasn't the all-in-good- fun, deep-down-we're-all-patriots humor of Bob Hope, or the more corrosive but still liberal style of Johnny Carson. *Saturday Night* wore its contempt for the political status quo on its sleeve.

*Saturday Night* wasn't as committed to political humor as, say, Garry Trudeau, creator of the comic strip *Doonesbury* and probably the greatest political satirist of the day. But then Garry Trudeau wasn't on national television, the most powerful political platform ever devised.

Trudeau, in fact, criticized *Saturday Night* for a lack of social conscience. Its "screw-you" humor, he said in a commencement address
at Colby College in 1981, "adroitly mocks society's victims. ... For all
its innovations this kind of satire tells society's nebbishes that they are
right about themselves, that they *are* nobodies, that to be so un-hip as
to be disadvantaged, to be ignorant, to be physically infirm, or black,
or even female is to invite contempt. ... What worries me about Slash
and Burn humor, and the larger society which has spawned it, is that it
reflects a sort of callousness so prevalent in the survivalist ethic. If this
is to become a society intolerant of failure and uncompassionate in the
face of suffering, then we are lost."

Despite its lack of real commitment, with ninety minutes to fill
every week and the opportunity to be topical, *Saturday Night* got in
more than its share of blows against the empire, and television served
to make its reach, if not its impact, significant indeed. Senator Eugene
McCarthy told Lorne at the correspondents' dinner in Washington that
the first topic of conversation on the Senate floor every Monday morning was *Saturday Night*—the senators loved to relate to one another
the jokes the show had made at their colleagues' expense on Weekend
Update. Maverick presidential candidates like Fred Harris and, later,
John Anderson directly approached *Saturday Night* hoping for, and
getting, some mention on the show. It was, therefore, no surprise that
Ron Nessen thought he could use *Saturday Night* to defuse the stumblebum issue, or that *Saturday Night* was determined not to let itself
be used.

* * *

The first prerogative Nessen exercised as an especially important host
was to arrive on the 17th floor on Thursday instead of Monday. That
proved to be to his disadvantage: *Saturday Night* had several days to get
ready for him, and by the time Nessen came aboard, the momentum of
the show made it that much harder for him to control what happened or
to get his bearings. So it was that *Saturday Night* proceeded to fake the
pants off the press secretary of the President of the United States.

Lorne will forever maintain that *Saturday Night* did not intentionally, as he put it, "take the President and shove his press secretary up his
ass." Nessen happened to host the show while NBC was in the midst of
a strike by its technical union. Much of the studio equipment that week
was manned by management personnel, so that the complexity the show
might ordinarily have had was reduced. All week long Lorne was telling
the writers to "simplify, simplify," and by Saturday he was forced to

use sketches that called for as little camera movement as possible. That ruled out, Lorne says, a lot of the more subtle political material that had been written for the show.

But many of the show's writers say there was more to it than that. They say, without equivocation, that *Saturday Night* was out to get Nessen. The attitude, Rosie Shuster said, was: "The President's watching. Let's make him cringe and squirm." The writers knew that Nessen would be on guard for material that was politically dangerous. Thus, they went in a different direction—"feinted left and went right," as one put it—by writing instead some of the raunchiest material ever presented on *Saturday Night*.

Most of that material was in sketches that did not feature Nessen, and Nessen, thrown into the whirlwind schedule after his late arrival, didn't pay attention to them. But even if he had paid attention, he said later, "What could I do? Walk off in a huff on Thursday, two days before the show?" So Nessen didn't object to a comma of what had been written.

NBC was in a similar bind. There was some concern at the network that *Saturday Night* was about to offend people it shouldn't offend. Herminio Traviesas came to the dress rehearsal that night to pass on some of the material himself. He resisted a few bits, but in the end he let almost everything by. It's likely that NBC, with all the attention being focused on Nessen's appearance, was more than usually interested in avoiding any confrontation over censorship that night. There was also a feeling among NBC's brass that Nessen knew what he was doing and that he could take care of himself.

In his opening monologue and in the first sketch with Chevy, Nessen played along with the sort of Gerald Ford jokes he'd expected— explaining that among the things he'd learned as press secretary was how to remove the President's tie from a helicopter blade (while the President was still wearing it), and watching as Chevy stumbled around the Oval Office talking to a stuffed dog, donning a leather football helmet, stapling his ear, and signing his hand. It was then that *Saturday Night* made its move in the other direction.

One of the sketches Nessen wasn't in and hadn't paid attention to during rehearsals was written by Michael O'Donoghue. It was based on the name Smucker's jam, which O'Donoghue renamed Flucker's. The idea—not one of O'Donoghue's more sophisticated—was that obscene-sounding names must sell jam. The cast members stood onstage (without any tricky camera movements) and recited the most offensive names for jams they could think of, including Nose Hair, Death Camp, Mangled Baby Ducks, Dog Vomit, Monkey Pus, and Painful Rectal Itch.

On Weekend Update, Emily Litella, misunderstanding all the talk
about the presidential elections, editorialized on "presidential erec-
tions." Gilda and Alan Zweibel had originally written this piece as it
sounded—as a commentary on presidential penises—but Lorne made
them tone it down by switching the subject to buildings and monuments
dedicated to Presidents. The point came across anyway.

Another sketch written by Zweibel and Gilda was a parody commercial for a douche called Autumn Fizz. Gilda pitched the product with her
boyfriend, played by Chevy, sitting beside her. (Again, no tricky camera
work, and again no Ron Nessen.) The joke was that Autumn Fizz was
the carbonated douche—"the douche with the effervescence of uncola."
It came in several different flavors, including strawberry, lemon, and egg
cream. As if signaling her approval, Gilda burped. The line that even
those on the 17th floor thought too cheap—although the censors let it
by—was Gilda's exhortation, "Don't leave him holding the bag."

Then there was the sketch that brought the Supreme Court into the
bedroom of Chevy and Jane, the one that Herminio Traviesas had come
to the studio to see performed in dress rehearsal. The justices, in their
judicial robes, stood around the bed while the couple made love, watching to see that they didn't do anything kinky. "You'll have to lose those
high heels," one of the justices said to Jane. As the couple writhed under
the covers, one of the justices remarked, "I'm a little nervous about
where that mouth is heading." Another justice declared a moratorium on
the "butterfly flick."

Even the Home Movie—a regular feature in which viewers sent
in short films—and the music were more controversial than usual. The
Home Movie was set in a men's room. One by one, several men walked
in to relieve themselves, each adding a different harmony to a vocal cho-
rale as they stood at the urinals. At the end they all zipped up and walked
out. The musical guest was punk rocker Patti Smith, whose ragged look
alone probably affronted more conservative viewers. Smith sang her
version of "Gloria," which included the line "Jesus died for somebody's
sins/but not mine." By the time Smith came on, it was past midnight, so
she was singing on Easter Sunday.

This was all a lot different from Richard Nixon's appearance on
*Laugh-In*, although Ron Nessen may have been the last to realize how
different. It was obvious to NBC chairman Julian Goodman, for one.
The Nessen show was the first time that the NBC brass had ever attended
*Saturday Night* en masse. They sat in the front row of the balcony, and
although he tried his best not to show it, Goodman was shocked by what
he saw. "You don't become chairman of a major broadcasting company,"
he said later, "without learning to grit your teeth and smile."

After the show, NBC threw a huge party at the Rockefeller Center skating rink. Julian Goodman, who had known Nessen in the days when they were both at NBC News, danced with Nessen's wife, and she, too, seemed to have her doubts about what she had seen. Ron, she told Goodman, sometimes had a tendency to overextend himself. Nessen himself was in a celebratory mood, roundly toasting his performance. He seemed to be having a wonderful time. So were the people from the show, some of whom, despite the presence of the NBC brass, Nessen, and other dignitaries, were smoking pot at the party. They did, however, take the initial precaution of lighting up their joints all at the same time to minimize the possibility of anyone's trying to stop them.

It wasn't until a post-party party at Paul Simon's apartment later that night that Nessen let his true feelings about the show be known. By then he may have gotten the drift that the show made him look bad, and he'd also had quite a bit to drink. Herb Sargent, who was there, says everyone was in a boisterous mood, Nessen no more than others. Michael O'Donoghue, who was also there, saw it differently, describing Nessen's tone as almost belligerent. Both O'Donoghue and Sargent agree that Nessen was arguing he had "co-opted" *Saturday Night*. Nessen's basic message, O'Donoghue said, was: "You thought you'd get me, but I got you."

\* \* \*

Nessen learned otherwise back in Washington. The wire services quoted senior White House aides as saying that President Ford was "not pleased" by the show. The staffers themselves were said to have found it "vulgar" and "tasteless." Some thought it made Ford "look stupid." There were reports that some of those aides wanted Nessen relieved of his job.

Jerald terHorst, Nessen's predecessor as press secretary to Ford, described the show in a newspaper column as "a travesty of good taste ... grossly offensive ... kinky sex ... bawdy crudity ... a gross error of judgment." The President's son Jack—a devoted *Saturday Night* fan, as were the other two Ford children—sent Nessen an angry hand-written note that read: "I thought as Press Sec. you're supposed to make professional decisions that get the Pres. good press! If you get a min. I'd be happy to explain to you that your job is to further the Pres. interest, not yours or your family's!"

Gerald Ford himself, who had watched the show at Camp David, made no public comment, but his wife, Betty, did. She seemed for the most part to be putting the best possible face on the episode, saying she and Ford "thought the White House material was very funny. We both laughed and had a good time." But she admitted they found some of the other jokes "a little distasteful," and she regretted the impression that her husband, by appearing on tape in the show, might be perceived as "endorsing" *Saturday Night*. "When he did it [the taping]," she said, "he didn't know what was going to take place."

Nessen said later that when he asked the President what he thought, Ford answered, "I found some of it funny, and some of it I didn't find funny and some of it I didn't quite understand why it should be a subject of humor." This was slightly more than Nessen told the White House press corps during the daily briefing the Monday after the show, when *Saturday Night* seemed to be the only thing the reporters wanted to talk about. Nessen said then that the President had "basically no reaction."

Nessen tried to laugh off the rest of the reporters' questions that morning, but he was clearly sensitive about what an issue the show had become. One reporter wrote that when he tried again to raise the subject of *Saturday Night* in Nessen's office later, Nessen "rose from his desk and began shouting that discussion of the program was 'not something grown men should be doing. ... This is stupid. ... It's bull. ... Don't serious journalists have anything better to do than this?'"

Several prominent newspaper columnists (all well over thirty years of age) took the show very seriously indeed. Among the most vehement was Anthony LaCamera, the TV columnist for the Boston *Herald American*. "Instead of foiling the tormentors," LaCamera wrote, "it came out like a Presidential endorsement of the usual *Saturday Night* shenanigans. It didn't do anything for the dignity of the Presidency either, and respect for the nation's highest office is something we desperately need in these troubled times. ... Frankly, I don't care what happens to Ron Nessen, who I never met. But I am deeply concerned about NBC and its seeming irresponsibility in the deplorable matter of its *Saturday Night* series. ... This is yellow television."

Harriet Van Horne of the *New York Post* was equally offended. She said the show offered "more smut than satire," citing *Saturday Night* as a prime example of the moral decay of Western Civilization. "We live, of course, in an age of anti-prudery," she wrote. "That's fine, that's mature, tolerant and at the moment, *de rigueur*. ... But has this new candor produced better entertainment, more brilliant performers or a glorious revolution in art? No, it has given us a decade of thoroughly nasty, violent, corrupting movies. It has debased sex, put massage parlors on every Main Street and made the boob tube the lewd tube on *Saturday Night* ... In our mad rush to liberation, we have meekly accepted the motto of the young and foolish: 'Don't make rules.' ... Let us cry 'Enough' to the vulgarity that spits in our faces."

Worst of all to Nessen may have been the comment a reader made to *Washington Post* columnist Bill Gould. If Gerald Ford agreed to let Nessen host *Saturday Night*, the reader said, "I don't see how I can vote for a man who could be so dumb."

Nessen eventually concluded that *Saturday Night* had in fact been out to get him. He was helped to that conclusion when Chevy Chase, who'd gotten along so well with Ford at the correspondents' dinner, started excoriating the President in interviews, calling him "a totally compassionless man" whose eyes were so empty that looking into them "was like looking into the eyes of 50 milligrams of Valium."

Chevy and others on *Saturday Night* firmly believe they helped defeat Ford in the 1976 election by promulgating so effectively his image as a befuddled klutz. Nessen agrees that Ford's stumblebum image helped defeat him, but he doesn't think *Saturday Night* was that significant in furthering it. Nevertheless, Nessen conceded in the end that his appearance on the show hadn't done the President any good, either.

"Looking back," he wrote in his book, "it's obvious that my attempt to smother the ridicule of Ford by joining the laughter on *Saturday Night* was a failure."

CHAPTER 18

# Welcome to Show Business

The notoriety of the Nessen show sanctified *Saturday Night* in the eyes of its fans, capping a groundswell of support that had been building among young people and in much of the press throughout the first season. But even then the show's future within NBC was not necessarily secure.

*Saturday Night*'s following was, for television, a remarkably passionate one. It was one of those rare shows that people purposely stayed home to see and that they talked about the next day, and the day after that. Lines like "I'm Chevy Chase and you're not" and Emily Litella's "Never mind" got laughs in countless conversations in restaurants and offices around the country, becoming national catchphrases just as "Sock it to me" and "Here come de judge" had on *Laugh-In*.

But *Saturday Night*'s appeal to its audience was far more personal than *Laugh-In*'s had been. Millions of young people had instantly recognized that here, finally, was a show that spoke for them. It wasn't only that *Saturday Night* was funny; it wasn't only the style in which it was funny. It was the whole attitude the show conveyed. Its sensibility was light years away from conventional television's, and to a generation that had grown up on television, and grown to loathe it, the impact of seeing what Lorne called "a certain kind of truth-telling" on TV was exhilaratingly powerful. At a time when the unity of the sixties movements was waning but still strong, the show was seized upon with a gleeful sense of surprise and delight.

At NBC, one of the first signs that something out of the ordinary might be happening was the mailbags. For the first few shows, Craig Kellem, who replaced Barbara Gallagher as associate producer, had to send school buses out to nearby colleges to pick up some suitably youth-ful viewers to fill the seats in 8H. By the third show, the demand for tickets started to pick up. In mid-November a torrent of letters poured in from students who were coming home for Christmas; seeing *Saturday Night* seemed to be high on their list of vacation entertainment. Many of them were disappointed. By December every seat for every show through the spring had been taken and NBC's Guest Relations staff had started a waiting list.

Among those homeward-bound college students were the children of some of NBC's top executives, and it was around the family dinner table that many of those executives first heard the good word-of-mouth on *Saturday Night*. From the head of the television division to the head of Programming to the head of Sales, daddies with clout in the network were being badgered by their kids to get them tickets to the show. It was a home-grown popularity poll of some interest; the executives had heard often enough how little their kids cared for anything else on TV.

Herb Schlosser's children were two of *Saturday Night*'s biggest fans, especially his son Eric, who became a regular fixture in 8H on *Saturday Nights*. Dick Ebersol was always glad to see Eric there, because then he knew that even if Herb fell asleep and missed the show, his son would tell him how great it was at breakfast the next morning.

Top executives in the advertising agencies were getting the same Sunday morning reports on *Saturday Night* from their kids, and the same requests for tickets. Jim Hicks in NBC Sales would get a call from a gruff-voiced agency vice president saying he needed two tickets; when Hicks stopped by 8H on Saturday to say hello, instead of the advertising executive he'd find a couple of long-haired, blue-jeaned relatives sitting in the client's seats. NBC's salesmen quickly learned that one of their most potent sales tools was their ability to look a potential client in the eye and say, "What do *your* kids do on *Saturday Night*?"

If *Saturday Night*'s fans couldn't get into 8H to see the show, they tried to get the show to come to them. The writers and performers began receiving offers for speaking engagements on college campuses, and at $1,500 or so a pop, some of the writers would earn more from those appearances in the first season than they earned from their salaries.

Good reviews continued to come in as critics recognized in *Saturday Night* that most rare and welcome of TV phenomena: something dif-ferent. Many critics found the show sloppy and uneven, but that was forgiven; *Saturday Night*'s freshness was enough to redeem it in eyes bloodshot from screening the same tired TV formulae day after day after day. *Saturday Night* became, in the words of *New York* magazine's tele-vision critic, Jeff Greenfield, "the only new show of the season to stir any critical and audience excitement." Even such conservative publications as *The Wall Street Journal* weighed in on *Saturday Night*'s behalf. So did the biggest of them all, *TV Guide*. Michael Arlen, the TV critic for *The New Yorker* magazine, wrote a typically perceptive piece that was headlined "A Crack in the Greasepaint." Noting that television had come to depend almost entirely on "that strange fantasy language of celebrity public relations which has been concocted for the public by mass- entertainment producers and stars in recent years ... the language of kisses blown, of 'God bless you's,' of 'this wonderful human being,' of 'a sensational performer and my very *dear* personal friend,'" Arlen called *Saturday Night* "an attempt, finally, to provide entertainment on television in a recognizable, human, non-celebrity voice—and in a voice, too, that tries to deal with the morass of media-induced show-business culture that increasingly pervades American life."

Perhaps the most satisfying endorsement, however, came from none other than John J. O'Connor of *The New York Times*. O'Connor kept watching the show after his initial pan, and on November 30 wrote a second review that could hardly have been more glowing. "In the beginning," he wrote, "the *Saturday Night* format didn't quite work. ... In more recent weeks, however, at least 75 percent has proved to be sharply and sometimes wickedly on target. ... For however long it lasts, *Saturday Night* is the most creative and encouraging thing to happen in TV comedy since *Your Show of Shows*."

As a fresh new show of promise, *Saturday Night* stood in sharp contrast to the rest of the new programs on NBC. The network, with Marvin Antonowsky at the programming helm, had fielded its most lackluster fall season in years. Within six weeks of the season's start, four new series had been canceled, and in those days such rapid termination was considered shockingly abrupt. One of the shows Antonowsky had axed was *Fay*, a sitcom starring Lee Grant, and shortly thereafter Grant appeared on the *Tonight Show*, where in a fit of anger she branded Marvin Antonowsky "the Mad Programmer."

What Grant, along with most of the television industry, didn't realize was that television was on the threshold of a new era, an era in which the quick, wholesale cancellation of series would become commonplace. The networks' competition for ratings was about to escalate to unprecedented frenzy. The impetus for that change came from ABC. In June 1975, Fred Silverman moved from CBS to take over programming at ABC. After canceling six shows in December—including *Howard Cosell's Saturday Night Live*—the perennial third-place network suddenly started collecting hit ratings with such shows as *The Bionic Woman, Welcome Back Kotter, Laverne & Shirley, Donny and Marie,* and *Rich Man, Poor Man*. In January, ABC won its highest prime-time ratings in a decade while NBC's ratings began moving sharply in the other direction. Within two weeks ABC drew even with NBC. The week after that, ABC broadcast the Winter Olympics from Innsbruck, Austria, and NBC, for the first time in its history, found itself in third place. In March, Marvin Antonowsky was fired. Within a year ABC would overtake CBS. Nothing in the television business would ever be the same.

NBC's prime-time collapse made *Saturday Night* the only new show the network had that it could point to with any pride. When Gene Walsh, the head of NBC's Press and Publicity department, read what fans like Jeff Greenfield and John J. O'Connor had to say about *Saturday Night*, he told his subordinates to milk the show for all the publicity it was worth: *Saturday Night*'s reviews made NBC, and Walsh's department, look good in the face of all the bad press almost every other program on the network was getting. "Hey, we can't buy this kind of shit," Walsh said in one staff meeting, holding up an article about *Saturday Night*. "Jump on it."

The press acclaim and NBC's troubles in prime time were crucial breaks for *Saturday Night*: They helped obscure the very important fact that the show was still not a success in the ratings. It is testimony to the momentous breadth of television's reach that, despite the fervent support of so many fans, *Saturday Night* could still make hardly a dent in the Nielsens. It had always been the same with rock and roll, which was big enough to make huge profits for the record companies but not big enough ever to achieve much success on television.

In television terms *Saturday Night* remained a cult phenomenon. Its biggest audience had come with the 23 share it had in its third week, for the Rob Reiner show. After that, the numbers went down and stayed down, averaging only an 18 share for five long months, a dry spell that to Dick Ebersol stretched out like the Sahara Desert.

Sales did manage to grow a little easier each time a new demographic report came in showing that *Saturday Night* was attracting an audience of eighteen- to thirty-four-year-olds reachable almost no place else on television. NBC's salesmen explained away the low ratings by saying that hundreds of thousands of *Saturday Night* viewers went unmeasured by the Nielsen sample because so many people were watching in dormitories, bars, and barracks, where there are no Nielsen ratings boxes. They backed up that claim with letters from viewers who wrote in to say that every weekend they had parties to watch the show. Those arguments helped, but raw numbers are the name of the game in television, and the price for thirty-second spots increased only slightly over the first season, to about $10,000.

Since neither CBS nor ABC was at the time putting any shows up against *Saturday Night,* leaving that time period to their affiliates to program, neither network felt compelled to make an issue to the press of *Saturday Night*'s low ratings—another crucial break. But the ratings were no secret within NBC, and a significant body of opinion at the network held that *Saturday Night* was turning out to be one of those shows that was a darling of the press and a few fanatical fans, but little more. Getting Gerald Ford was a coup, sure, but the ratings said that not that many people cared.

One of the skeptics was NBC Research chief Bill Rubens, who complained openly that *Saturday Night* wasn't, as he'd predicted all along, delivering enough viewers to justify its budget. Nor did it seem to have much potential for improvement. In December, Rubens's department finished a report on the results of an opinion survey it had conducted on *Saturday Night*'s first few shows. The report found several "areas of concern" with the program. Viewers, the survey said, found *Saturday Night* "terribly disjointed." It left them feeling "bombarded by a constant stream of short segments." Another "disturbing impression" was that viewers expected more spontaneity from a live show than they were getting from *Saturday Night*: "The production should allow for or include the unexpected or ad-lib." There was "a rather large negative response" to the commercial parodies. Weekend Update, according to the survey, "has potential, though not outstanding strength." The report concluded that "viewers found the comedy inconsistent, often too slapstick and sometimes in poor taste (mostly to older adults). It is also obvious that some people are having problems adapting to the show and that much of the humor was simply over their heads."

NBC's researchers would later admit that this report epitomized one of the fundamental problems of opinion surveys in television: They tend to judge programs in terms of what has come before. They are useless, as one research executive put it, "at predicting explosions."

Another of the NBC skeptics was Don Carswell, who continued to fight in vain against *Saturday Night*'s outlandish spending. Every time Carswell ran into Dick Ebersol in the hallway, he'd complain about the budget. Most of the season was gone and *Saturday Night*'s overages were still averaging $100,000 a show. Carswell would always add a comment about the ratings too. "Geez, Dick," he'd say, "I don't know. Those numbers aren't very impressive." Carswell said roughly the same thing to Paul Klein, the man who in March had taken charge of NBC's programming. In a meeting with Carswell soon after he came in, Klein was shown the budget figures for *Saturday Night.* Carswell strongly suggested, Klein says, that the show be canceled.

*Saturday Night* had more than its share of detractors among NBC's affiliates as well. Standards chief Herminio Traviesas and other executives regularly fielded complaints from station managers around the country who deplored the show's humor. One important affiliate general manager called Travie to say he was taking *Saturday Night* off his station because too many people were confronting him on the steps of his church each Sunday morning, wanting to know how he could justify putting such filth on the air. The affiliate protest was not of an intensity that by itself threatened the show, mainly because the affiliates were far more concerned that season with NBC's problems in prime time. Nonetheless, part of the reason *Saturday Night*'s ratings were so poor was that only 148 of the network's 219 affiliates carried the show in the beginning, a fairly low "clearance" rate for a network program. And some stations that had been carrying it dropped it, so that by March, *Saturday Night*'s station lineup had fallen to 144 stations.

The affiliates' concerns about *Saturday Night* were shared by many within the upper echelons of NBC's executive hierarchy in New York. Bob Howard, who was the president of the NBC television network at the time, remembers NBC board members asking, repeatedly, "Are you sure we're not offending too many people with that show?" Howard and others say that Anthony Conrad, the president and chief operating officer of NBC's parent company, RCA, commented on more than one occasion that he did not want *Saturday Night* to "mess up my damn network." Conrad's reservations stemmed in part from his wife, who hated the show and complained to her husband about it regularly.

(Conrad, who was elevated in June 1976 to chairman of the board and chief executive officer of RCA, resigned his posts three months later when it was revealed he had failed to fill out his personal income tax returns for several years. Al Franken submitted an apology to NBC's viewers to be read on Weekend Update, saying they shouldn't conclude from Conrad's troubles that the network was run by "rich pigs with bloated salaries." Standards didn't let it on.)

NBC chairman Julian Goodman was hearing plenty of complaints about the show at the elegant parties he attended when the guests gathered around the set to watch *Saturday Night*.

"How can you let this stuff on?" his friends would ask. "Because," Goodman answered, "people like you are generally home in bed at this hour."

Nor did *Saturday Night* enjoy any affection from the rank and file at NBC. Most of the middle- and lower-management executives and the studio crews who dealt with the show on a daily basis would have been happy to see it canceled—they were tired of putting up with the arrogant freaks from 17 and all the headaches they caused.

From the delivery docks to the board room, the rumblings in 30 Rock against *Saturday Night* were loud enough to cause Press department chief Gene Walsh to worry that he might lose his one source of good publicity. Walsh told his press representative assigned to the show, Les Slater, to keep pushing for more articles on *Saturday Night*. "Right now," Walsh said, "that's the only thing keeping this show on the air."

Some of these complaints were voiced to Herb Schlosser, but Schlosser remained *Saturday Night*'s staunchest supporter. He attended the show often, and his attendance alone signified within NBC a highly unusual (some thought improper) presidential endorsement. In fact, Schlosser was so closely identified with *Saturday Night* that it got away with as much as it did in part because higher management knew Schlosser would take the fall if his pet project blew up in his face.

Schlosser says no serious talk of canceling the show ever reached his ears, which is not surprising, since it was widely known in the building that the president was inclined to view the eccentricities of the adolescents on *Saturday Night* with the bemused grin of an indulgent father. Schlosser still chuckles about the time in the first season when Lorne came to him to ask that Schlosser make some sign to the *Saturday Night* troops that he was behind them. "They're killing themselves," Lorne said. "How about some gesture?"

So Schlosser invited the cast and some of the writers for lunch in NBC's elegant executive dining room on the sixth floor. He told the chef to serve roast beef, and he was so charmed at how many helpings they shoveled down and at how emaciated they all looked that as they left he asked the butler to wrap up some chocolate chip cookies for them to take along.

With Schlosser's support and that of the press, there was by spring what Julian Goodman called a "grudging" acknowledgment at 30 Rockefeller Plaza that *Saturday Night* was "there." How long it would be "there" was somewhat open to question, and compared to the worries NBC had about prime time, not a pressing question at that. The Emmy awards changed everything.

\* \* \*

The Emmy nominations were announced April 6. *Saturday Night was* nominated for five awards: best comedy-variety program, best writing, best supporting player—Chevy Chase—best direction, and best graphic design. It seemed almost too perfect that the only show up against *Saturday Night* in the comedy-variety category was *The Carol Burnett Show*. Burnett was also competing with *Saturday Night* for the writing and directing awards, and her second bananas, Harvey Korman and Tim Conway, were nominated with Chevy for best supporting player. A showdown was in the offing on Emmy night.

Immediately an argument developed at 30 Rock about how many people from the show NBC was willing to send to Hollywood for the awards ceremonies. Lorne wanted everybody to go, of course, but NBC recoiled at the thought of all the plane tickets and hotel rooms and meals and tuxes and limos so many writers would need. The writers considered this pettiness and ingratitude beyond belief, especially considering what they were being paid every week. One afternoon a few of them were sitting around the 17th floor stewing about it when Tom Schiller decided to bring the matter to the attention of NBC's chief dispenser of official favor, Dave Tebet. Schiller called the Beverly Hills Hotel and had Tebet paged.

"Hi, Dave, Tom," Schiller said. "Listen, Dave, we've got a problem— we've got all these kids from the show up for the Emmy, and, well, let's pay for 'em. Let's get 'em out there for the show. I think it's important."

Tebet, who had no idea whom he was talking to, said he'd see what he could do. NBC finally agreed to pay the writers' round-trip air fare to Los Angeles—coach—and $75 per diem for the two days they would spend there. On Sunday, May 16, the group flew to the Coast.

Flying into Hollywood for the *Saturday Night* crew was a little like landing in an enemy camp. They had never made any secret of the contempt they felt for the place, taking every opportunity in interviews and on the show to snicker at and savage almost everything Hollywood held dear. It was assumed that this nose thumbing had not gone unnoticed there, and so they entered the city feeling like renegades, Young Turks challenging the show business establishment where it lived.

It was a fun feeling, not unlike their days as newcomers at NBC, and everybody felt a little giddy as they hung out by the pool at the Beverly Hills Hotel on Monday, waiting for the ceremonies that night. Michael O'Donoghue and Anne Beatts in particular were reveling in the glamour of the moment. They had taken a bungalow near the pool, and as they held court for visitors and signed for deliveries from room service, everything seemed to be filtered through a sunny, gauzelike mist: the Hollywood high life, on top of the world.

NBC sent several limos to pick them all up that afternoon, and as they rode to Century City they figured out what they would say if they won. It was just as the limos pulled up outside the Shubert Theater that Michael O'Donoghue experienced a profound revelation. The usual crush of fans milled around, waiting to glimpse the celebrities as they arrived. O'Donoghue's limo eased to a halt, flash bulbs went off, and a beauty queen in a low-cut gown opened the limo door. Looking in at

O'Donoghue, she flashed a blinding twenty-four-carat smile and said, in a voice as bubbly as champagne, "Hi! Welcome to the Emmy awards!"

O'Donoghue felt frozen, impaled by the strangeness and beauty of it all. Years later he would look back upon those few seconds as the exact instant he finally and irrevocably sold out. It was then he admitted to himself that he was indeed employed in show business— a practitioner not of literature, not of fine art, but of that most popular of popular entertainments, television. And, by God, he was enjoying every tawdry bit of it.

"I remember thinking to myself," he recalls, "'Why am I fighting this? This is great!' My attitude changed. I embraced television at that moment."

His carefully nurtured disdain for the Emmys, for the blessing of The Others, dissolved, and he found himself wanting desperately to win. "Why lose?" he thought. "Why see *The Carol Burnett Show* take the prize when we were kicking ass?"

It's likely that all the *Saturday Night* outlaws felt the same as they entered the theater. And a fairy tale ending awaited them: They owned the night. Except for the graphic design award, they won everything they were up for. Over and over again the presenters called out "*Saturday Night*," and by the evening's end they had accomplished a near-sweep that declared them, in front of the Hollywood establishment and a prime-time audience of fifty million viewers, the hottest show on television.

Alan King, co-producer of the now-canceled Howard Cosell show, was the presenter for the writing awards, and after he'd read the nominees and opened the envelope, the first words he said were "From New York ..." Sitting in the audience, Alan Zweibel jumped several feet off his chair, and at the pinnacle of his leap he glanced to his right and looked directly into the eyes of Anne Beatts, who seemed suspended alongside him in midair. As the *Saturday Night* writers came to collect their statuettes, there were so many of them it was like some herd trampling toward the stage, and intermingled with the applause the Hollywood regulars could be heard murmuring in their seats about this menagerie from New York.

Director Dave Wilson got his award next. Then it was Chevy's turn. There was a bit of silliness when the nominees were read: Tim Conway started walking to the stage as if he'd already won. Chevy followed suit and so did Harvey Korman, three clowns playing for the crowd. Korman and Conway ended up returning to their seats, and Chevy tripped and took a spectacular fall as he mounted the podium.

"Needless to say, this was totally expected on my part," he said. Everyone laughed. Then it was time to be honestly humble. "I'd just like to say that I sort of got a break on that show because of Lorne Michaels," he said. "There is a cast of Not Ready For Prime Time Players, all of whom are awful good, and it's been great working with them. And I also would like to thank Ernie Kovacs—I swear— and Lorne Michaels. Thank you." Probably few in the audience noticed how Chevy seemed to speak of his presence on the show in the past tense.

The presenter for the best comedy-variety show category was Milton Berle, who had not yet hosted *Saturday Night*. When he opened the envelope and read "*Saturday Night*," Laraine Newman, watching the telecast back in New York, ran out of her apartment and into the street yelling, "We won! We won!"

Lorne thanked Berle for "warming up the studio in New York" twenty-five years before. He thanked the people at NBC, singling out Dick Ebersol, "who was there at the beginning and supported us all along." Lorne got a laugh when he thanked the show's production staff, "a lot of old-timers who worked in live TV and neglected to mention what it was like before we started." He got an even bigger laugh when he thanked the city of New York for "the correct combination of rejection and alienation which keeps the comedy spirit alive." Finally he thanked his family and his manager, Bernie Brillstein, for being there "when I was complaining and yelling about the very people I'm thanking tonight."

The taking of the torch: Lorne poses backstage with Milton Berle after *Saturday Night's* near-sweep at the Emmy Awards, May 1976. © *NBC*

Writers Al Franken, Tom Davis, Michael O'Donoghue, Alan Zweibel, Rosie Shuster
and Anne Beatts at the Emmys. © *NBC*

Backstage, Lorne posed for photographs arm in arm with Berle. Everyone was too wrapped up in the excitement of the moment to think much about what a passing—or taking—of the torch it was, from old television to new. Afterward, everybody went to the Emmy dinner and then a large group returned to O'Donoghue and Beatts's bungalow, where they partied into the night. The Hollywood high life, on top of the world.

\* \* \*

As Lorne was thanking Dick Ebersol in his acceptance speech for being there from the beginning, Ebersol was watching the show on a monitor in an NBC studio control room in Burbank, smiling grimly at each of *Saturday Night*'s awards. He'd thought he might be up on the stage with Lorne that night, but Lorne had seen to it that he wouldn't be.

Lorne had discovered to his horror when the nominations were announced that, by the Emmy rules, the official credits for a nominated program are always taken from the credit roll of the show's first program of the season. Thus, to the Academy of Television Arts and Sciences, Dick Ebersol was the executive producer of *Saturday Night*, despite the fact that his credit had been removed from the show after its premiere.

If *Saturday Night* won the award for best comedy-variety program, Dick Ebersol's would be the first name called.

On Sunday night, the night before the ceremonies, Ebersol was in his room at the Beverly Hills Hotel when he got a call to come to a room just down the hall. When he arrived he found Mike Weinblatt and several other NBC executives there. They informed Ebersol that he must immediately sign a letter to the television academy asking that his name be withdrawn from the official credits for *Saturday Night*. Ebersol was told that the letter would be delivered to the academy's offices by messenger so that by Monday night his name would not be included in the nomination for the award.

It was explained again that his inclusion in the credits had been a violation of NBC policy. When he argued that the policy didn't make sense, he was told that producers coming to him with program ideas in the future would be "intimidated" if he himself was an Emmy winner. That was "bullshit," Ebersol responded, mentioning that Roone Arledge had won plenty of Emmys without hurting ABC Sports. Roone Arledge, the executives said, was a special case.

Still, Ebersol balked at signing the letter. Finally, without mentioning Lorne's name directly, one of the executives let it be known that it was Lorne who wanted Ebersol's name stricken from the award. "Obviously," Ebersol told himself, "Bernie [Brillstein] and Lorne have been working behind the scenes." Ebersol was ordered to sign. Feeling he had no alternative, he did.

The next day Ebersol ran into Lorne in the lobby of the hotel. He didn't ask Lorne directly about the maneuvering that had led to the scene the night before, but he told him that if *Saturday Night* won the award, he'd better say some kind words in his acceptance speech about Dick Ebersol's contribution.

"If you don't talk about me, we'll never be friends again," Ebersol said.

Apparently Ebersol had failed even then to realize that, as far as Lorne was concerned, they hadn't been friends for some time,

\* \* \*

NBC threw no reception for *Saturday Night* upon its triumphant return from Hollywood, but the show's status, both within NBC and within the industry, had fundamentally, unmistakably changed. Their humor had been, as Anne Beatts put it, "certified on national television." There was no ignoring them now.

The show's ratings immediately jumped from a 20 percent share of the audience the week before the Emmy awards to a 28 share the week after, an increase of something like a million viewers in one week, and an increase of more than two million viewers over what the show had been averaging for most of the season. The ratings would remain at that plateau—about ten million viewers per week on average—through the second season. Requests for tickets and V.I.P. guest passes soared, and press coverage grew even more copious and fawning than it had been. Les Slater in Publicity noticed that some columnists who a month or two before had called the show "tasteless" now reversed themselves, jumping on the bandwagon, and Lorne began to worry that too much press adulation too soon might actually hurt the show.

Any talk within NBC of canceling *Saturday Night* immediately ceased and negotiations were begun for the following season. The salaries of all the cast members were jumped from the first year level of their five-year Mickey Rooney-Judy Garland contracts to the fifth year level, $1,600 per show. The writers all got healthy raises; some more than doubled their pay.

Lorne, as one executive put it, "assumed the mantle of boy wonder" at NBC. He renegotiated his contract so that instead of getting $145,000 and then $175,000 for the second and third seasons, he would now be paid $300,000 and $350,000. Two summer shows were added to *Saturday Night*'s current season and the network paid Lorne to produce two prime-time specials, the first of many specials that would be added to his contract over the years.

NBC also began listening more attentively to the thousand and one demands Lorne had been making since he'd arrived. The offices on 17 were expanded for the first time and a prefab shower was added for the benefit of those who worked all night there; new equipment went into the control room in 8H. Most important, the budget for the next season was increased by 50 percent, to $201,750 a show. Aaron Cohen, who remained the NBC executive with direct responsibility for *Saturday Night*, says the new budget represented "a recognition that certain things were going to be done by the show in their style, no matter what the company said, and that the budget had better begin to reflect reality, rather than the dream of some accountant sitting in a back room somewhere."

*Saturday Night* continued to go well over budget—by an average of about $25,000 a show in the second season—but now the overages were approved with less struggle, and they were almost always approved. It fell to Aaron Cohen to handle most of the show's money problems. The pattern was that the unit manager would tell Cohen how much something was going to cost, Cohen would talk to Lorne, and soon thereafter Cohen would call the unit manager back to say, "It's okay, go ahead."

Unit manager boss Steve Weston, knowing when he was beaten, decreed that all *Saturday Night* overages should be circled on the A and E reports and that next to them should be written the words "On approval of Aaron Cohen." The unit managers and others in the company, likewise knowing when they were beaten, began accommodating Lorne whenever they could. "Word spread in middle management," says Arthur White, one of the unit managers, "that it wouldn't pay to take him on. The attitude was: 'I'm not going to win that battle, so why alienate Lorne?'"

(Steve Weston's reign as the lord of the unit managers at NBC would come to an ignominious end three years later when an embezzlement scandal engulfed his department. Unit managers were said to have been lifting substantial sums from the suitcases full of cash they regularly carried with them to production locations around the world. A number of unit managers and Weston himself were fired. Lorne sent a clipping about the scandal to his former associate producer, Barbara Gallagher, with a note that said, "Sometimes the wheel turns slowly, but it turns.")

One symbol of the shift in the balance of power was Lorne's quiet suggestion to Alan Zweibel not long after the Emmys that the network's name be dropped from the show's title in the on-air promotional announcements Zweibel was writing. Now it was no longer *NBC's Saturday Night;* it was simply *Saturday Night.* A year or so later Lorne would send a friendly telegram to Roone Arledge at ABC, asking if he could use the name *Saturday Night* Live now that Arledge and Howard Cosell wouldn't be needing it anymore. Arledge sent a telegram back giving his blessing.

Despite NBC's new courtliness toward *Saturday Night*, the show remained united in its contempt of the network, and in a strange way its newfound success served only to exacerbate the tensions between employees and employer. The writers and performers developed a "where were you when I needed you?" attitude, and a suspicion that, even with all they had done for NBC, the network was still too dumb to appreciate their worth. That suspicion was confirmed to them when NBC took out a full-page ad in the trade paper *Variety* after the Emmys which congratulated the *Saturday Night* "crazies" for their awards. The writers were outraged. "Crazies?" they said to themselves. "So that's what NBC thinks we are. If you write comedy, you're crazy, zany, nuts, wild, but not intelligent. They treat you like something less than you are."

Neither did everyone at NBC automatically become enamored of *Saturday Night*. Some, like Aaron Cohen, clambered aboard the bus and basked in the reflected glory of being involved with one of the hippest happenings in New York. Lorne would joke that Aaron Cohen started wearing tinted aviator glasses after he started working with *Saturday*

*Night*. But *Saturday Night* could bestow that insider status or not, as it chose, and it did so sparingly. As a result many at NBC resented the show more when it was successful than they had when it wasn't. Older executives continued to loathe the show's point of view and the people on it, regardless of awards. The attitude of the NBC brass, says Julian Goodman, went "from skepticism to acceptability" after the Emmys. But, he added, the feeling remained that "this was not a group you'd have at your daughter's wedding."

There were paradoxes to the changes in Lorne's status within *Saturday Night* as well. All along he'd predicted the show would be a smash, that they would all be famous, and now it was coming true. No one ever doubted it would, of course, but still, it was something to beat the odds, and this had all the signs of becoming bigger than any of them had dared imagine. If *Saturday Night* was a show business phenomenon, then most of the writers and performers felt it was Lorne's doing that made it so. It was Lorne who had given them an honest shot when no one else would, Lorne who had been the Fearless Leader and network beater from the beginning, Lorne who had proved to be right about the things that mattered. "Everything had fallen into place just as Lorne said it would," says Alan Zweibel. Lorne's status as Fearless Leader increased accordingly. He was now held by many on the show with a respect approaching awe; there was a love for Lorne and a willingness to sacrifice for him that, Zweibel said, made people ready to follow him anywhere.

But at the same time the seeds of a new dynamic began to germinate on the 17th floor. After the Emmys, Lorne's support, his unshakable conviction in their worth, seemed a little less necessary than it had been. Now that they'd been certified on national television, the whole world knew how good they were. Lorne may have provided the forum, but the thought occurred to some that if Lorne hadn't given them their shot, surely it would have been just a matter of time before somebody else had. To maintain his power, Lorne had somehow to ascend to still-greater heights. Otherwise he would fall.

It was a double-edged dilemma that Lorne sensed acutely. No accident, then, that Lorne had been the one to insist that the writers and performers have their contracts renegotiated for the second season—he was taking care of his people. Nor was it an accident that when NBC agreed, it was Lorne who sat down with Aaron Cohen and figured out the parameters of how much those raises would be, a practice that would continue in all of NBC's subsequent negotiations with the writers and cast. Cohen says that one of the considerations he and Lorne discussed was always what would be "handleable" for Lorne. "It had to be enough to give them the recognition for what they contributed to the show,"

Cohen said, "but not enough to make them stars of a magnitude that they became independent and didn't need Lorne, too." The same observation would be echoed by Rick Traum, the executive who subsequently took over from Cohen as NBC's chief liaison with the show. "Lorne wanted NBC to stay away from his people," Traum said. "He wanted to *be* NBC to them—that's the way he operated. If NBC approached a writer, Lorne would be very pissed. Lorne wanted to be in control ... He didn't want anything to dilute his game plan."

Something else people noticed after the Emmys: Lorne wasn't writing for the show as much as he had before. He continued to edit pieces and to come up with ideas, but seldom did he write sketches of his own. It was as if it had become too risky for him to put himself down on paper for the others to read and evaluate and compare themselves to. A writer remembers that when one of Lorne's last sketches was handed around the office, people looked at it and said to themselves, "Hmm. This is pretty good ... but not *that* good."

The paradox of *Saturday Night*'s being a cult phenomenon on the most massive of mass media would persist for more than a year. Not until its third season would the show regularly achieve TV's passing grade of a 30 percent share of the audience or better. *Saturday Night*'s stars might be hot items with New York's hip elite, but their fame didn't come close to that of, say, Carol Burnett.

Testimony of that came for Gilda Radner and Marilyn Miller one night in the middle of the second season. They had dropped by Lorne's apartment at the Osborne to pick up Lorne's birthday present for Marilyn. Mick Jagger happened to be there, wearing a rakish hat and accompanied by a skinny model named Christine. Gilda and Marilyn were so nervous being in the same room with Mick that they went into the kitchen and pretended to be looking for something in the cupboards.

After a little while they left and caught a cab downstairs. As it drove off they were jumping up and down in the back seat, shouting, "We just met Mick Jagger! We just met Mick Jagger!"

The cab driver, not recognizing Gilda, told them to sit down and quit making so much noise.

"Oh, yeah," Gilda said. "I forgot. Nobody sees me on TV."

CHAPTER 19

# I'm Chevy Chase and You're Not

Fame is a very unnatural human condition. When you stop to realize that Abraham Lincoln was probably never seen by more than 400 people in a single evening, and that I can enter over 40 *million* homes in a single evening due to the power of television, you have to admit the situation is not normal.

—Chevy Chase, in an interview

The only performer on *Saturday Night* whose fame in the first season transcended the show's cult following was Chevy Chase. Chevy was not yet a superstar, by any means, but he was headed in that direction. He was the hottest new face in the country, and the timing of his breakthrough was such that his celebrity was magnified by emotional undercurrents of unusual power.

He took the stage when the press and public alike were anxious for a new diversion, not unlike the Beatles when they landed in New York soon after the assassination of John F. Kennedy in 1963. America after Watergate was ready to

Chevy Chase, whose breakout fame in the first season was a loss of innocence for *Saturday Night*. © *NBC*

proclaim a new clown prince, someone whose very freshness and confidence was a relief and a renewal. In 1975, Chevy Chase was it.

Herb Schlosser was one of the first to notice that Chevy was going to be a major star. In a post-mortem telephone conversation with Dick Ebersol after *Saturday Night*'s first show, he exulted over how good Chevy was. He also learned from Ebersol that Chevy was signed only to a writer's, not a performer's, contract. "Sign him up," Schlosser said.

The rumblings began to be picked up very quickly in the NBC Press department as well. Many of the early reviews singled out Chevy, and in late October, when publicist Les Slater set out to do biographies of the show's cast members, he was told by his boss, Gene Walsh, to do Chevy Chase's first. Choosing his phrasing delicately to avoid offending the other members of the rep company, Slater, two weeks after *Saturday Night* went on, called Chevy "one of the faces more readily identified with the show."

Indeed, there were many who would come to think *Saturday Night* in the first season was the Chevy Chase Show. It was a measure of the scant attention paid to the other cast members that in February, when Les Slater got around to doing a bio of John Belushi, Slater received a note from Gene Walsh that read, "Les … Another excellent feature. Also, it straightens me out, as I thought this guy was Danny Arvayrdk (or however he spells it)."

Certification of Chevy's celebrity came on December 22, 1975, when *New York* magazine, then at the height of its trend-setting powers, put him on its cover. The article dubbed him "the heir apparent to Johnny Carson," a label Chevy didn't so much deny as dismiss. "I'd never be tied down for five years interviewing TV personalities," he said.

Comments such as these did not go unnoticed in Burbank. Although *New* York's article said NBC was planning to put Chevy on the *Tonight Show* as a guest host within six months, it would be a year and a half before Chevy even appeared on Johnny Carson's program, and then only because he was promoting a special for NBC. He never did host it. Nor did any of the other Not Ready For Prime Time Players appear on the *Tonight Show* until Gilda was a guest in 1983, long after she'd left *Saturday Night*. Carson's distaste for NBC's other late-night show (shared by many if not most comedians of his generation) was well known within the network. It surfaced publicly in an August 1976 interview with Tom Shales of *The Washington Post*, when Carson blasted *Saturday Night* for relying on drug jokes and cruelty. He also dismissed the cast as hopeless amateurs who couldn't "ad-lib a fart at a bean-eating contest." *Saturday Night* retaliated the following season with some anti-Carson jokes on Weekend Update. In one, reporting that Carson had announced plans to do the *Tonight Show* live instead of on videotape, anchorwoman Jane Curtin noted that he had been "doing the show dead for the past fifteen years."

Johnny Carson notwithstanding, Chevy's appearance on the cover of *New York* magazine confirmed his status as the most important new kid in town. Seldom had New York's media had a new star so prominently placed in its lap, and suddenly Chevy's face seemed to be in newspapers and magazines everywhere. Outshining the President in April and winning his writing and performing Emmys in May wildly accelerated the onrush of celebrity. By summer, even the stuffy *New York Times* had succumbed to the spell. Chevy wrote a nonsensical piece about the Democratic convention for the Times's op-ed page. The bio box beneath it read, "Chevy Chase is Chevy Chase and you're not. Mr. Chase is also a performer and writer for the television program *Saturday Night*."

* * *

At first, Chevy himself didn't notice the fame that was about to overtake him. He didn't get out much. When he wasn't on the 17th floor or at Lorne's place working he was sleeping in his small studio apartment on East Sixty-first Street. Every few weeks he'd fly out to Los Angeles to visit his fiancée, Jacqueline Carlin, a model and aspiring actress with whom he was passionately in love, and they didn't get out that much either. So Chevy acted surprised the first time publicist Les Slater told him a reporter wanted to do a feature on him. "Talk to me?" he said.

Opportunity for such insouciance soon faded as the evidence of his celebrity became too obvious to ignore. There was a day early in the first season when Chevy arrived on the 17th floor shaking, excited and a little frightened. He'd gotten on a bus on his way to work and suddenly noticed that everyone on it was staring. At him. After a block or two he grew so flustered he got off the bus and fled down the street.

It was a crystallizing moment for Chevy, an instant when he realized that everything was going to change. It was also, according to those who worked with him, one of the few times Chevy Chase ever ran from stardom. More than most people who become famous very fast, Chevy walked into fame with his eyes open, expecting it, taking it as his due, seldom pausing to wonder why it was happening to him. Which is not the same as saying he took fame in stride.

The *New York* magazine cover was the demarcation point. "That cover," Chevy said later, "changed my life." It was shocking because it was so sudden: Chevy says he had no idea the cover was coming before he saw it on the newsstands, and it hadn't really occurred to anyone on the *Saturday Night* team, including Chevy, that one of their members could be picked out and publicized in so prominent a fashion.

From there the proportions and the demands of Chevy's fame only grew. Inevitably he started spending more time in interviews, going out on speaking engagements, and pondering the offers that came in. Just as inevitably, the time he spent working on the show decreased. Lorne told him soon after the *New York* cover appeared that he was "going to be too busy being Chevy Chase" to be as productive as he had been, and Lorne, Chevy agrees, was right.

At first it seemed the outside world had changed more than Chevy had. He was the same ham he'd always been, taking falls as he walked on the street or playing noisy pranks in restaurants. But now people were looking at him differently, muttering things like, "Look at that—he's trying to attract attention to himself." It was, to those who witnessed the process, one of the saddest things about Chevy's stardom.

In many of his interviews, Chevy worried publicly about what was happening to him, fretting that he might become the very thing he'd been parodying—a plastic celebrity. It was apparent he was struggling to maintain the spirit of irreverence that got him there in the first place. In May he told *Vogue* magazine: "I'm a fad. In this business you can come and go in a second. I could be flushed out tomorrow with a big smile and a handshake."

Behind the scenes, however, Chevy began to change, too, and despite the soul-searching interviews, those on the show soon began to feel he was indeed turning into just the sort of obnoxious egocentric he played so convincingly on camera. He was not, in the end, immune; nor was it likely he would be.

According to those who knew him, he liked to ride in convertibles so he could talk to fans who recognized him as he cruised down the street. He made bizarre late-night phone calls to friends, gloating to one, also a performer, that of the two of them he was by far the more famous. Once he bragged to a roomful of people, "I'll go down to the drugstore, pick up the fan magazines, and I'll bet my name is in more of them than any of yours."

He grew gradually more distant from the others on the show. "Within two thirds of the first year," says one of the writers, "it began to seem that Chevy was more worried about his next cold opening than about being part of the team. The more famous he got, the more he pulled into himself. When he was hungry he was more of a team player."

Cocaine had something to do with that. Several of those on the show say Chevy was one of the first to begin using coke heavily, in part because he was the first who could afford to. A personal sense of insecurity—at variance with his public image but not unusual in performers—contributed to his withdrawal as well. "He wasn't," a writer said, "truly confident at all—that was his act."

Even by the aggressive standards on *Saturday Night*, Chevy's ego became a problem. By the end of the season he was ordering other players around on the set, telling them where to stand or how to deliver a line. He talked on and on about which household name he'd been with the night before or about how much money he was making for speaking engagements or other appearances outside the show. It was not the sort of behavior that endeared him to his colleagues, and more and more Chevy became characterized, as one writer put it, as "the asshole around the office."

Chevy's ascension to stardom was an education to the others on the show, a bitter lesson in the mechanics of fame. "We were innocent then," Jane Curtin said in an interview a year later. "We were a repertory company, and we knew that repertory companies do not feature one player. We thought we would all shine. When Chevy became the star, we felt hurt, we felt bad."

They also felt angry. Les Slater would bring a reporter up to the 17th floor for yet another interview with Chevy, and the other players would mutter, "What about me?" or "Is he the only one?" A cover story on Chevy in the magazine *Photoplay* was typical of the press's view that Chevy was the only one worth taking seriously. The story referred to Jane, Laraine, and Gilda as "Chevy's girls," and in mentioning them briefly asked the rhetorical question "Where, oh where would *Saturday Night* be without these beauties?" Chevy's girls were discussing this role the press had assigned them one afternoon on the 17th floor when Marilyn Miller suggested they put their feelings into song. They sang it on the second show of the second season, and it fairly dripped sarcasm in characterizing Chevy as a new teen idol. "Chevy, I love you when you fall down/Every night on my TV," the lyrics went. "But oh, Chevy, when you take that fall/I wish that you were falling, falling for me."

Of all the cast members, Belushi complained the loudest about the attention Chevy was getting. John and Chevy had been rivals since the *Lampoon* days. John never let Chevy forget that it was he, not Chevy, who had gotten the glowing press notices for *Lemmings*, or that it was he, not Chevy, who had won when both of them campaigned to be named creative director of the *Lampoon Radio Hour*. They had a knack for goading each other. The first day Belushi arrived on the 17th floor he walked into Chevy's office and pointed at the picture of Jacqueline Carlin on Chevy's desk. "Oh, you have one of those too?" he said. "You've got the regular one. I've got the one with the donkey dick." Chevy always claimed he was responsible for making Belushi as fit as he was for civilized company by shaving his back and teaching him how to eat with a fork.

Belushi lost his ability to laugh off Chevy's gibes when Chevy became a star before he did on *Saturday Night*. He was appalled at being upstaged by someone whose talent he considered decidedly inferior to his own and humiliated when people would see him on the street and say, "Hey, I love Chevy Chase." It confirmed all John's suspicions about what bullshit television was, and he protested violently that all he was getting were leftover supporting roles. "I go where I'm kicked," Belushi kept saying. "They throw me bones dogs wouldn't chew on."

From the moment Les Slater did Chevy's bio before the others', Lorne did what he could to prevent Chevy's being singled out, but it was like spitting in the ocean. At one point NBC put a poster of the cast members up in the lobby outside 8H. Chevy's picture loomed larger than the rest, and the caption read: Chevy Chase and the Not Ready For Prime Time Players. Lorne was infuriated, and threatened he would have the promotion man responsible for the picture fired.

Lorne was astute enough, however, not to turn his back on a star when he needed one, and when NBC and the public demanded more Chevy Chase, they got more Chevy Chase. Weekend Update alone expanded from three and a half minutes on the first show to almost nine minutes by spring of the first season. Chevy's Fall of the Week openings became such a stock routine that Chevy started writing versions that made fun of what a stock routine they'd become. That, too, provoked its share of grumbling on what was supposed to be a collaborative, risk-taking show. "I think we all got a little tired of the Fall of the Week a lot sooner than America did," Tom Davis says.

Chevy didn't help matters any when in interviews he failed to counter as strongly as he could have the impression that *Saturday Night* was essentially the Chevy Chase Show. In fact, it sometimes seemed to his colleagues he was going out of his way to promote that misconception. He claimed to be solely responsible for the writing on Weekend Update so often that Alan Zweibel, who with Herb Sargent was writing more of Update than anyone but Chevy, finally burst into Lorne's office, waving Chevy's latest clipping in his hands and shouting, "How long are we going to have to put up with this shit?"

Chevy explained away the comments by saying he'd been misquoted, but after a while few people bought it. Jane Curtin once confronted him with some disparaging remarks he'd made in two separate interviews. "You don't get misquoted twice!" she yelled. On a few occasions Chevy felt obliged to correct himself in print. In an interview in the Long Island newspaper *Newsday* in April, for example, he repeatedly stressed how much credit the others on the show deserved. "I do [stress it] all the time when I'm interviewed," he said. "Unfortunately, it never comes out once the interview is written."

\* \* \*

Whether or not he admitted it in interviews, the fact was that Chevy did indeed see *Saturday Night* as his show to a large degree. It wasn't such an unreasonable point of view, considering the contribution he was making to the show itself and to its success in the media. Nor was it easy for him to dismiss all those, both in the press and in private, who were reminding him that he was *Saturday Night*'s centerpiece, that without him it would be nothing. And that maybe he ought to start thinking about finding a showcase more suitable for his superior talents.

Tom Schiller, who was especially close to Chevy that first year, points out an insidious process that occurs when a friend becomes famous. "You alone want to be responsible for their salvation," Schiller says. "You say to them repeatedly, 'Don't do this,' 'Don't do that.' And what you eventually realize is that everybody is saying that—everybody feels they have a part of their career. And as a result they're getting barraged from eighty different angles on what to do next."

An NBC executive with long experience in negotiating with performers, including Chevy, adds that stars are vulnerable not only to the well-meaning advice of friends, but to agents, managers, and other business types who come to them and say, "Hey, you're getting fucked by these guys. I can do better for you." Show business, this executive says, is "rampant" with that.

Thus, as soon as his face appeared on the cover of *New York* magazine, Chevy started receiving career counseling commensurate to the scale of his success, which is to say he was inundated with it. There was, for example, the night Chevy was strolling down Park Avenue with his new friend Warren Beatty. "You should direct," Beatty told him.

The question of what to do next took on a growing urgency as the season progressed because Chevy was still without a performer's contract at NBC. Herb Schlosser had turned the task of signing him over to Dave Tebet soon after the first show, but as of February, Chevy still hadn't been signed. Week by week Chevy's negotiating position grew stronger, NBC's weaker. Chevy was now one of the biggest stars NBC had, and despite the network's denials, reports he was being groomed as the heir apparent to Johnny Carson were true. One executive privy to the network's higher counsels says Herb Schlosser was definitely thinking in those terms, and the same executive quotes Dave Tebet as confiding, in his hoarse whisper, "Chase is the only white gentile comedian around today. Think what that means when Johnny leaves."

So NBC was very anxious to get Chevy Chase under contract, and started offering him the world to sign a deal; nobody wanted to take the blame for letting the next Johnny Carson slip through their fingers. Chevy even wrote a sketch about NBC's entreaties, in which he played a gambler from a foreign country who made up all his own rules in a poker game and kept taking all the money. Nor were the offers only from television. Movies beckoned. The studios in Hollywood were among those bidding for Chevy Chase, and to a generation of performers united in their contempt for TV, movies were infinitely more alluring.

Chevy's manager (and Lorne's), Bernie Brillstein, was advising Chevy to stay with the show another season. Consolidate your success, Bernie told him; capitalize on the foundation you've started. *Saturday Night* was big now, but it was only going to get bigger. Lorne, although he purposely avoided pressuring Chevy, advised the same thing. His theory was that it took three years' exposure to make a superstar on TV. *Saturday Night* was a big hit in the industry, but the public hadn't really caught on yet. He told Chevy he was like a great pitcher for a championship baseball team. If he left, the team would lose a few games, but they'd keep winning. "Think how rare it is to play with a championship team," Lorne said. "You think it's going to happen all the time, especially when you're young, but it doesn't happen that often. ... Play another season, then decide."

Chevy wasn't sure. One problem, he told Lorne, was that his fiancée had given him an ultimatum: Either he return to her in Los Angeles and get married or she'd start seeing other men. Their relationship had been tumultuous all along—friends saw them get into major arguments over such minor matters as what they were going to order in restaurants. Jackie hated the idea of spending another year by herself in Los Angeles while Chevy stayed with the show in New York, where literally thousands of glamorous women would be his for the asking.

Chevy would later say Jackie was the primary impetus for his leaving *Saturday Night*, a bit of reasoning that one of the women on the show described as an example of the "blame the bitch" school of logic. Whatever Jacqueline Carlin's role, it's likely the temptation of other offers carried equal weight at least. Just as important were Chevy's doubts that the show would take him any further than it had already. *Saturday Night* might be a championship team, but Chevy began to think of it as a team at "the top of the minors." He was ready to play in a different league.

Chevy had long talks with Lorne as the first season wore on about where *Saturday Night* would go from there. In those talks he was openly critical of the show and openly skeptical that it would improve. He was tired of the three-week-a-month grind, he didn't know at that point if there'd be any significant change in the show's minuscule budget, and he wasn't confident that the rest of the *Saturday Night* team could maintain standards as high as his own. He thought maybe he'd done everything he was going to be able to do on the show and that he'd only be repeating himself if he came back. He wanted assurances from Lorne that certain things were going to change if he did.

Those talks were the beginning of the end of the friendship between Chevy and Lorne. According to those Lorne confided in at the time, it seemed to him that Chevy was trying to encroach upon his territory as producer, "trying to get behind Lorne's desk," as one friend put it. Lorne felt that Chevy, in the throes of his success, was rankled by the margin of power Lorne still had over him and over the show, and that he wanted to shift that balance of power more in his favor. "Lorne," an intimate says, "was horrified that Chevy was thinking that way. He had made Chevy a star, nurtured him, created the showplace for Chevy's talent, made him look good."

Friends who were closer to Chevy argue that in fact it was Chevy who had made Lorne a star, not the other way around, and that Chevy's contribution to the show was such in the first season that he was "a de facto co-producer." Therefore he had a right, these friends believe, to a voice in determining the creative direction of the show.

In any event, there's no question there was a rupture between them. Lorne said later he had mistakenly put friendship ahead of the show and kept quiet so as not to unduly influence Chevy's decision. Chevy would later say that he interpreted Lorne's silence as a lack of concern about whether he stayed or not. Thus the contract negotiations with NBC that led to Chevy's leaving *Saturday Night* took place under a cloud of hurt feelings, doubt, and suspicion.

According to Chevy, Bernie Brillstein started the negotiations and called him with "great news." NBC, Bernie said, was willing to give Chevy a raise of $22,000 the second season, a thousand more per show. That didn't sound like a lot of money to Chevy. He knew that under Lorne's favored nations policy, anything he got, the other players got. NBC would go only so far on those terms. Chevy also knew that Bernie's first allegiance as a manager and friend was to Lorne. For Chevy the idea of favored nations had begun to seem less than equitable, and he began to suspect that Bernie had a conflict of interest in representing both him and Lorne.

Without saying anything to Bernie, Chevy sought the advice of his brother Ned, who happened to be a lawyer. His brother in turn asked the advice of a lawyer friend of his named Bruce Bodner, who had more experience in contract negotiations. Bodner, too, thought he smelled a conflict of interest and began doing some investigating of his own. He consulted with Art Fuhrer, a chief negotiator at the William Morris talent agency, where Chevy remained a client. It was decided Chevy could do better than the deal Bernie Brillstein had negotiated.

Lorne's old agent, Sandy Wernick, who by then had joined Bernie Brillstein's firm, was in Canada on a business trip when he was called to an emergency meeting with Chevy in New York on May 10, 1976, a week before the Emmy awards ceremony. The meeting was held in the conference room of Bodner's law firm, Weil, Gotshal and Manges, in the General Motors Building on Fifth Avenue, across from the Plaza Hotel. Wernick entered the meeting confident that Chevy was coming back to *Saturday Night* for the second season. That, Wernick says, was the last indication Brillstein's office had gotten from Chevy. Wernick had said as much to both Lorne and NBC's negotiator, Mike Grossman, earlier in the day.

Sitting in the plush conference room, Wernick listened, stunned, as Bruce Bodner and Art Fuhrer explained that they had decided to negotiate a different deal for Chevy. He could, they said, get substantially more money for substantially less time and effort if he signed a contract to do a few prime-time specials instead of returning to *Saturday Night*.

"But you can't do that," Wernick said, several times.

They responded that what they were doing was in their client's best interest. Wernick's view was that they were going for the quick money instead of thinking of Chevy's long-term career. He pointed out too that William Morris's 10 percent commission would be significantly higher on a specials package than on the modest salary increase Brillstein had negotiated for Chevy's second season on *Saturday Night*.

Chevy himself mostly stood by silently while Wernick, Fuhrer, and Bodner had it out. Wernick says it was mentioned several times that Chevy would be the executive producer of his specials and that Chevy indicated how important it was to him that he be able to have creative control of his work.

There wasn't much Wernick could do other than return to NBC and tell Lorne what had happened. Lorne, Wernick and others say, was devastated by the news. Chevy was leaving the show. He had gone behind Lorne's back to pursue a deal that was completely independent of Lorne or anyone else in the *Saturday Night* family. To someone with Lorne's paternal instincts it was an unthinkable breach of loyalty. "Lorne felt," a writer said, "like King Lear: His first daughter had betrayed him."

Bodner and Fuhrer came to terms with NBC's Mike Grossman a few days later. Grossman was at first as shocked as Sandy Wernick had been that Bodner had taken over Chevy's negotiations. "No, no, no, we have a deal!" Grossman protested. Bodner explained that Chevy's plans had changed.

The new deal, which was refined in subsequent negotiating sessions, called for Chevy to be the executive producer and star of two prime-time specials for NBC, with an option, at Chevy's discretion, for a third. The network would pay him $450,000 to produce the first, $500,000 for the second, and $550,000 for the third, plus a bonus for signing of $100,000. Chevy's profit from these specials would depend on how much of that money he spent producing them; what he paid himself was up to him. NBC's offer also specified that Chevy, except for guest appearances, couldn't work at any other network for a period of three years.

Later Chevy called Bernie Brillstein to tell him his services as a manager were no longer required. Chevy offered to pay Bernie his commission on the deal, about $60,000, but Brillstein refused it.

Technically it was still possible Chevy could return to *Saturday Night*. The official story, circulated to many of those on the show as well as to the press, was that Chevy was still debating his decision as the second season began. Lorne and Chevy both insist that was the case. It's undoubtedly true that Chevy could have decided at any time to stay with the show—he could do just about whatever he wanted at that stage—and surely he continued to give it considerable thought as the summer wore on. And despite Lorne's feelings of betrayal, it's apparent he would still have welcomed back his biggest star. But it's also apparent that Chevy intended to quit *Saturday Night* when he agreed to the specials deal. There was a clause in that deal, drafted in May, specifying that he would leave the show in October of the second season. Chevy says the clause was dropped; nonetheless, that's exactly when he did leave.

Chevy says NBC didn't really care if he returned to *Saturday Night* or not—all the network was interested in was getting him into prime time. Those involved with the negotiations for NBC say that, to the contrary, they would have done more to keep Chevy on *Saturday Night* if they could have, but that it was clear Chevy intended to leave the show because of his falling-out with Lorne. NBC wanted Chevy to come back to *Saturday Night* for the first few shows of the season, these executives say, because the network was concerned that the show would fall apart without him, and they wanted him there to help get it rolling for another year. Bruce Bodner confirms that scenario. "It was clear," Bodner said, "that Chevy didn't want to continue on the show." An executive involved with the negotiations for William Morris similarly confirms that Chevy's intention to leave was "absolute" from the outset.

A week after the meeting with Wernick, Chevy won his Emmy awards, which further convinced him it was time to move on. He spent some time in California with Lorne, Belushi, Aykroyd, Zweibel, and others from the show that summer while they were working on a special Lorne was producing featuring the Beach Boys. But except for some conversations with Lorne, he said little or nothing about his plans to anyone on *Saturday Night*.

Many on the 17th floor doubted even as the second season began that Chevy would really go. The official announcement of his departure came in October. There were some on *Saturday Night* who sympathized with his decision and wished him well, but the prevailing opinion was that Chevy had shamelessly betrayed them to cash in on stardom. "Chevy was a scumbag the way he left," one of the writers said. "Deceitful and dishonest about the whole thing. ... Chevy's word meant nothing after a while."

Tom Davis was shocked when he learned Chevy was leaving and went to his office to ask him why.

"Money," Chevy responded. "Lots of money."

* * *

On the first show of the second season Chevy, playing Gerald Ford, injured himself on his fall into the podium. Some believe that the injury, after a million falls, had a psychological component. "Chevy was ready to injure himself," says Rosie Shuster. "He didn't know where he was going."

Nursing his injured testicles, Chevy missed the next two shows. He filled out his contractual obligations to *Saturday Night* three shows later. There was no farewell celebration. Chevy came back in brief cameo appearances for the next few shows, weaning himself, he says, from *Saturday Night* and, by agreement with Lorne, weaning *Saturday Night*'s audience from his presence. On his next- to-last show there was the first of what would become periodic jokes at Chevy's expense. In a futuristic parody of the game show *Jeopardy!*, called "Jeopardy 1999," the moderator asked the panelists to name the comedian whose career fizzled after leaving *Saturday Night*. No one could remember.

Some on the show experienced a twinge of fear that maybe *Saturday Night* would indeed go downhill once Chevy left, but that quickly gave way to a spirit one writer described as "Fuck him, we'll make it even better." Many, including Belushi, were glad to see him go. He was taking up too much air time anyway. Lorne now sat, another writer said, by himself on the *Saturday Night* throne. He drew closer to Paul Simon as his most trusted friend and confidant. Simon was someone Lorne felt he could count on because he had no self-interest in the show. Chevy says Paul Simon never spoke to him after he left.

Chevy married Jacqueline Carlin on December 4, 1976, and took up residence in Hollywood. People who worked and socialized with him that first year after he left *Saturday Night* say he talked constantly about whether he'd made the right decision in quitting the show, always asking about those he'd left behind in New York. "What do they think of me back there?" he wanted to know. He also lost control during this period with booze and cocaine. His coke consumption, witnesses say, often exceeded two grams a day, an amount that caused him to swing at times between megalomania and paranoia, and on occasion left him all but incoherent.

One friend remembers visiting Chevy in Los Angeles that year. He was surrounded in his living room by hangers-on, all of them listening to the rambling piano tapes Chevy had recorded, all nodding their heads as they helped themselves to Chevy's coke.

"Yea, man," they were saying. "Great, Chevy. Great."

Jacqueline Carlin sued Chevy for divorce seventeen months after their wedding. Citing threats of violence from her husband, she asked the court to keep him away from their house. Chevy, she said, had "lost perspective."

# PART TWO

This wheel's on fire
Rollin' down the road
Notify my next of kin
This wheel shall explode
—Bob Dylan, "This Wheel's on Fire"

PART TWO

CHAPTER 20

# The Bully Boys

> In a nation of frightened dullards there is a sorry shortage of outlaws, and those few who make the grade are always welcome … they have that extra "something."
>
> —Hunter S. Thompson, *Hell's Angels*

The only warning anybody on the 17th floor had that the Hell's Angels were coming was a frantic phone call from the security desk downstairs: The Angels just stormed through, the guard said. They were angry and they were looking for *Saturday Night*.

It was a sleepy morning a few days after the Emmy ceremonies and the offices were almost deserted. Michael O'Donoghue, Audrey Dickman, Kathy Minkowsky, Neil Levy, a secretary, and a production assistant or two were the only ones there. None of them had time to react before two Angels came striding through the door and stood, looming, over Kathy Minkowsky's desk. Security was correct: They were obviously unhappy.

The Angel who did the talking was named Big Vinnie. Vinnie stood several inches over six feet and weighed at

John Belushi, a Bully Boy pose in New Orleans. © *NBC*

least three hundred pounds. He wore black jeans, boots, a gold earring, a fur hat, and a snakeskin vest. His huge chest and arms were covered with swastika and skull tattoos. Neil Levy could smell him from several feet away. The only details people remember of the other Angel was that he was nearly as big as Vinnie and that he carried a large hunting knife in his belt.

Vinnie was yelling that he wanted to see whoever was in charge of the operation, that the show had used the Angels' colors and the Angels didn't like it—they were gonna get their fucking colors back or somebody was gonna get fucking hurt.

Kathy Minkowsky cowered, her knees literally knocking together beneath her desk. She finally figured out what Vinnie was ranting about. There had been a sketch on the show the previous Saturday in which a gang of Hell's Angels rampaged through a suburban house singing "Johnny Angel." They'd been wearing the Angels' winged-skull insignia—their "colors"—on their backs. The Angels, Kathy gathered, considered this bad for their image, and they considered the unauthorized use of their colors a violation of some sacred Angels code.

Kathy choked out that she'd get somebody, got up, and ran into Audrey Dickman's office. She slammed the door behind her and locked it. The Angels laughed at her as she ran.

"There are two of the most disgusting men I've ever seen out there!" she gasped.

Audrey's first thought was that they must be some of Belushi's friends. When she heard Kathy's story, they called Michael O'Donoghue's extension. O'Donoghue answered, his voice calm but higher-pitched than usual. "Yes?" he said.

"Are they in there, Michael?" Kathy whispered.

"Yes," O'Donoghue said again, at a slightly higher pitch. Audrey Dickman decided the only thing to do was to go outside and be a witness if somebody got killed.

There are those who claim that when Big Vinnie and his friend appeared in O'Donoghue's doorway, O'Donoghue spilled the tea he was drinking down the front of his shirt. O'Donoghue denies this. Whatever terror he felt, he recovered quickly, walking forward to compliment Vinnie on one of his tattoos. Vinnie laughed, pushed O'Donoghue aside and repeated that he'd come for the Angels' fucking colors.

O'Donoghue did his best to nod sympathetically as Vinnie vented his anger. O'Donoghue claims the tension was broken when Vinnie saw the picture of Richard Speck on his wall. "Hey, I know that guy," Vinnie said. "What's his name? I like that guy."

"That's Richard Speck," O'Donoghue says he answered, "and as a matter of fact, I like him too."

Audrey Dickman by then was standing at the Xerox machine outside O'Donoghue's door, pretending to do some copying.

"Audrey?" O'Donoghue said. "What time does wardrobe open today?"

"About noon," Audrey said.

"These guys would like the Hell's Angels costumes," O'Donoghue said. "I'm sure that can be arranged, Michael," Audrey answered. "Okay," O'Donoghue said. "Let's do that then."

The Angels left peaceably, but still threateningly, with that promise. The rest of the morning was filled with jittery rehashings of their visit for RCA's security guards, various NBC executives, and everyone else on the show as they arrived. A general alert went out in case the Angels decided to return.

When Dan Aykroyd (who had supervised the design of the Angels costumes in the first place) heard the story he was thrilled.

Immediately he insisted that he go along to take the colors back—no way was he going to pass up an opportunity to meet the famous Hell's Angels. Somebody brought the jackets up from wardrobe, and Aykroyd, O'Donoghue, and Neil Levy caught a cab for the Angels' headquarters on the Lower East Side.

Levy says that when the cab driver heard where they were going he refused to take them any closer than several blocks away. As the three of them, on foot, entered the Angels' block on East Third Street, Danny said, "Don't worry. I know how to handle these guys. Just act like you respect them—treat them like they're true men."

A group of Angels standing around a van saw them and started toward them down the street. Vinnie was leading the group, and when they met, once again he launched into a threatening tirade about the colors. Sandy Alexander, the Angels' leader, cut him off.

"We watched the show the other night," Alexander said quietly, "and we didn't like it. We want our colors back."

Danny pulled the jackets out of the bag he was carrying. "We got 'em for ya," he said, and handed them over.

As the Angels took them, Danny kept talking. "You guys are real men," he said. "Real true Americans. We really respect you. You guys are great."

The Angels laughed at that, but they were pleased, and they laughed when they saw that the colors on the jackets Danny had given them were nothing more than blown-up copies on paper, flimsy play-act replicas of the real insignia.

Soon everybody was slapping one another on the back. Danny kept saying what real men the Angels were and the Angels kept saying how much they liked the show. Deciding it was best to withdraw when things were going well, the boys from *Saturday Night* left a few minutes later, smiling and waving and saying the Angels should come to the show whenever they wanted.

*Saturday Night* got along famously with the Hell's Angels after that. Once they did come to the show, en masse, wearing so much armor that as they walked past security they clanked. When the Guest Relations attendant on duty behind the desk tried to stop them, one of the Angels patted him on the head. "That's all right, little fella," he said. They were seated in the back of the studio to keep them out of camera range, and when they sat down they pulled out a bottle of whiskey and passed it around. Danny came up to say hello that night; on other nights the Angels guarded the door at the Blues Bar, a seedy downtown hideaway John and Danny set up for themselves and their friends. The next anybody heard of Big Vinnie he'd been indicted for murder, charged with throwing a woman to her death off the roof of the Angels' headquarters.

* * *

Certainly more than a touch of the Angels' machismo imbued the boys of *Saturday Night*, and accounted in no small part for their success. John Belushi, Dan Aykroyd, and then Bill Murray embraced, consciously and proudly, the romance of the outlaw, the flat-out, no-holds-barred ethic that writer Hunter S. Thompson called "Gonzo."

Their defiance was different from that of Chevy Chase, whose confidence was born of privilege. Tom Shales of *The Washington Post* wrote once that alongside the others on the show, Chevy seemed "like the lone rich kid at the neighborhood birthday party." Belushi, Aykroyd, and Murray were staunchly working-class, their humor and the anger beneath it blunt and hard-edged. Like their personalities.

"They were," Rosie Shuster said, "bad-assed, macho, go-get-em bravado types. They were formidable in that way, and their charisma came from that as well. They weren't the sensitive, crying males— this was not that brand. They were in reaction to that. In the first half of the seventies, feminist and gay rights were coming out, but the New Macho guy started to emerge in the second half of the seventies, and that was very much alive on *Saturday Night*."

Lorne Michaels, who didn't have that Gonzo mentality and who struggled harder and harder as time went on to keep it from overwhelming *Saturday Night*, came to call them "the Bully Boys."

John Belushi embodied Gonzo in its rawest form. It was no accident that he had an intense friendship with the Prince of Gonzo himself, Hunter Thompson—Thompson once said that John was more fun in twenty minutes than most people were in twenty years.

Neither was it a coincidence that Belushi did a superb imitation of Marlon Brando, the original Wild One. Like Brando, John didn't seem to act his emotions onstage so much as exorcise them. Many of his strongest characters—the Samurai Warrior, Rasputin, the demon child Damien—spoke no words at all. Belushi breathed them to life on the power of sheer presence, and, strangely, it is the power of sheer presence that transmits best through the tubes and transistors of television.

Belushi was like that offstage too. Writer Marilyn Miller describes the way he came into a room: "John would go into these paroxysms about life," she said. "He was mad at everybody, or something was wrong. He would talk about anything, like an actor talking. He would come in and be like your brother and breathe real hard; then he'd be like a Shakespearean character, serious. Like a tornado that would spin itself round and round and then be exhausted."

Belushi's friends say he had two distinct personalities: the Teddy Bear and the Creature. The Creature would ask to borrow money and then take every dollar you had out of your wallet (sometimes he didn't ask); the Teddy Bear brought flowers the next day. Many afternoons Belushi came to work and sheepishly made the rounds of people's offices. "Was that you I was with last night?" he'd ask at each stop. "Sorry."

One of the least appealing aspects of Belushi's machismo was his misogyny. He believed, or pretended to believe, that women weren't funny, and he said so all the time. He often urged Lorne to fire all the women writers, and although he undoubtedly would have been surprised if Lorne had taken him up on it, several times he threatened to resign if they weren't.

Anne Beatts and Rosie Shuster (whom Belushi called "the boss's wife") took much of his abuse. There's a long list of parts they wrote, including the Todd part in the original Nerds sketch, that Belushi refused to play, simply because, Beatts and Shuster were sure, they wrote them. Belushi once burst into an office and tore into Beatts about something she'd written, yelling at her so violently that when he left she burst into tears. Those who witnessed it were shocked that the Ball Buster would ever break down, but she said she just couldn't take John's attacks anymore. A few minutes later Belushi came back in and apologized profusely.

There are some who side with Belushi in his disputes with Beatts and Shuster, saying the sketches they were writing, especially early on, simply weren't that good and that he was right to reject them. Marilyn

Miller is one who endorses that theory. Miller found that John would jump at parts that gave him a chance to *act*. "More than anything," Miller says, "he wanted to succeed at that." John worked for days on a sketch Miller wrote for him and Sissy Spacek in which John played a young redneck afraid to admit to himself or his wife that he had a problem with impotence (a "manly powers" problem). All week John kept coming to Miller's office, improvising the character, practicing his accent and a swaybacked swagger, and on air it was clear he was setting out to show he could hold his own with an actress of Spacek's caliber.

Of all the women on the show, Jane Curtin was least willing to laugh off Belushi's chauvinism, his tantrums, and his lack of professionalism. Jane and John became what one habitué of the 17th floor called "arch enemies." Jane was a former debutante from Boston whose husband, Patrick Lynch, was a preppy from the pullover sweater tied around his neck to his penny loafers. Jane was straight, intelligent, and cool, if not cold—qualities that brought out the worst in John. Jane's most common response when John misbehaved was a sneer—she was an artist of the sarcastic putdown, and sneering was something she did extremely well—but sometimes he'd make a sexist remark to her and they'd end up in a shouting match in the hall.

Those who suffered Belushi's abuses and still loved him did so mainly because it was hard to take them personally. There wasn't any real malice behind it, they felt—it was just John. His good side would come out soon enough. It was also very hard to resist the magnetic force of Belushi's personality. It was exciting to be around him, worth whatever price he made you pay.

Tom Davis tells of a day he and John were riding on an NBC elevator together. John, upset about something involving his mother, started crying. Soon Davis found himself crying along with him. By the time they reached the 17th floor, people all around them in the elevator were teary-eyed too. Belushi, Davis says, had an amazing power to pull people into whatever emotional state he was in at the moment.

The Gonzo flame burned every bit as brightly in Belushi's friend and coconspirator Dan Aykroyd, but in more complicated and mysterious ways. Whereas Belushi's private and public characters merged, Aykroyd hid behind his characters onstage, and for that reason he never did become as big a star as Belushi. At Lorne's request Danny played himself as the co-anchor on Weekend Update for the third season, and he couldn't wait to get out of it. When he did he almost never identified himself on camera as Dan Aykroyd again.

Offstage, Danny sometimes hid behind John Belushi. On the street he'd often walk a few feet behind John, and fans would swarm around

Belushi, never seeing Aykroyd standing nearby. Aykroyd was happy to let Belushi take the public heat: John loved it; Danny hated it. Danny had a talent for projecting an aura of anonymity that deflected the glances of passers-by, and as a result he was the only cast member who continued regularly to ride the subways and walk the streets unrecognized at the height of his fame.

He kept a shield around himself that was all but impenetrable. When a production assistant put his address and phone number on a staff list once, he angrily confronted her and forced her to redo it, leaving his whereabouts blank. He alone among the performers never let publicist Les Slater interview him for an official NBC bio. He'd promise to do it but would always beg off, saying he was too busy. He was articulate with the press, but he talked to reporters only a few times in the four years he spent on *Saturday Night*.

Danny had a well-developed contempt for the trappings of money and success. His offstage uniform remained motorcycle jackets and boots, T-shirts and jeans. Steve Martin once invited him to go shopping at Saks. "I'm not into clothes," Danny said. Many Saturdays at the end of the show he'd wave goodnight from the stage already changed, ready to take off on his Harley for Canada or parts unknown.

He called himself a "mercenary" in show business, and it was a business he considered far too ephemeral and phony to trust. "You never know when this show could go off the air," he'd say, snapping his fingers. "It could go like that." Danny always had his bags packed, his friends say, ready to head for the high country, yet he was at the same time a ruthless perfectionist when it came to his own work. After a bad show he'd call himself a "cheap impressionist," and say, "Fuck this. It's worthless shit. I should leave and just forget it."

He talked often about buying and running an auto parts store or a snow removal company, "something," he said in one of his rare interviews, "with an inventory." For a while he had his eye on a truck stop he'd grown fond of on Route 401 outside Toronto. At the end of the third season he said he was going to quit the show and go back to college; he'd once taken some criminology classes in Canada, and he sometimes talked of following in the footsteps of his grandfather, a Canadian Mountie. He was fascinated by the world of cops and small-time thieves. Rosie Shuster's brother used to say that Danny's perfect fantasy would be to rob a bank and then arrest himself for it.

He was more a watcher than a fighter—sometimes on the street he'd wear a pair of thick-framed glasses with no lenses—but he didn't shrink from violence. He often acted as the bouncer at the Blues Bar, a job he took seriously, and he once sported a black eye on the show for a couple of weeks, the result, he vaguely explained, of an altercation outside a club.

Danny's affection for and casual familiarity with what some might consider the seamy underbelly of life gave him an outsider's orientation that accounted in large part for the uniqueness of his genius in front of the camera. Belushi invented his madness from the stuff of legend, but Aykroyd just seemed to be there. Danny had webbed toes, a twist of nature he often pointed to with pride as proof he was a genuine mutant, and many of his friends share the conviction that he always had one ear tuned to frequencies from other planets.

"You look at the floor and see the floor," he said to a friend once. "I look at the floor and see molecules."

Together, John and Danny formed their own alternate energy center within *Saturday Night*, a center that to an unusual degree functioned outside the ken of Lorne Michaels, and often in opposition to him. Danny said in one interview that he and John were "satellites" on the show; their allegiance was less to Lorne's crusade than it was to each other and their work.

The tiny office they shared on 17 was known as The Cave, and it was a shrine to slovenliness, the very epicenter of disorder. "You had to throw meat in before you entered," said one NBC executive. "There were things living in there that were bigger than you." Danny actually moved into The Cave for a period of several months in the second season, which was about when NBC's maintenance staff cleaned it for the last time. Just getting in the door wasn't easy. There were dirty clothes in piles several feet high in the corners, cartons and boxes stacked on the floor, loose pages of scripts littered everywhere, cassettes with the tape streaming out of them in long swirls, scattered collections of armament magazines, industrial manuals, liquor bottles, and motorcycle parts. Beneath it all, somewhere, was a cot. Soiled panties sent in by fans, Polaroid shots of gas station attendants, and other oddities were pinned to the walls, which were scarred with holes, fist-sized and larger, and messages scrawled in Magic Marker. Over one hole was written the inscription "Do not paint this hole." They said they were saving it as a memento.

Rosie Shuster thought of The Cave as John and Danny's "clubhouse," the place where they played pirate. "They didn't have rubber swords," she said, "but they could have."

* * *

Until Bill Murray arrived, the other men on *Saturday Night* didn't approach the randiness of Belushi and Aykroyd, but they were, by and large, no pipsqueaks, either.

In the second season, Franken and Davis got over their initial shyness about crossing the threshold into Lorne's office and learned to barge in whenever they felt like it. Franken in particular developed a reputation for stubborn aggressiveness, and people got used to hearing the hard, nasal sound of his voice raised to express an opinion, any opinion, any time he wanted to express it. When Ricky Nelson hosted the show, he walked into Lorne's office while Franken was there, lying on the floor with his feet up on Lorne's desk.

"Hey, Rick," Franken said cheerfully, "how about an 'Ozzie's Dead' sketch?"

After Franken left, Lorne turned to Nelson and said, "That was Al Franken. You have to understand."

Outwardly, Michael O'Donoghue was more genteel than the Bully Boys, the type of man who needed a long bubble bath at the end of a trying day. Beneath that foppish exterior, however, lay a vicious temper. In the first year, O'Donoghue was incensed to discover he had been cropped out of the photograph accompanying an article on the show in *Mademoiselle* magazine. He dispatched the following letter:

Dear Editors:

I couldn't help but be a bit irked when I noticed that you and [photographer] Duane Michals had cropped my head out of the photograph that appears on page 121 of your March issue. I'd like to come over there and kick every one of you in the cunt if I didn't think it would ruin my shine.

Michael O'Donoghue

*Mademoiselle* contributing editor Amy Gross sent O'Donoghue a sarcastic letter of apology, which concluded that since he had written on NBC stationery, she assumed he was writing in a corporate capacity. Therefore, she said, she'd taken the liberty of sending a copy of O'Donoghue's letter and her reply to NBC president Herb Schlosser. This exchange occurred soon after the Emmy nominations were announced, and O'Donoghue says NBC's only response to him was the delivery to the 17th floor of a box of personal stationery engraved with his name, along with a request he use it for any future missives.

By the third season NBC had replaced at least a half-dozen telephones O'Donoghue had ripped out and thrown across the room, and nearly every member of the technical crew, the building maintenance staff, and all the unit managers had O'Donoghue battle stories to tell.

He went into an especially exquisite rage over a sketch he wrote called "The Attack of the Atomic Lobsters." The idea was to end the show as a mutant herd of giant lobsters devoured studio 8H and everyone in it. It was probably the most elaborate sketch technically the show had ever done, and O'Donoghue thought audio engineer Scotty Schacter had unforgivably botched it. O'Donoghue exploded in the studio after it was over, causing the audience members to cut a wide swath around him as they filed toward the doors. At the climax of his fury he drop-kicked a folding chair so hard it landed almost in the balcony.

Of all the men on the 17th floor, Garrett Morris was the least successful in holding his own against the tanklike aggression of the Bully Boys. Being more than ten years older than most of the others had something to do with it. At first Garrett projected, many on the show say, an aloof, actorish air, coming across as the experienced hipster. No one paid attention. He was also a much more physical person than the middle-class whites on the show—he was always hugging people, and often they drew back from him in discomfort.

On the air Garrett had none of the boldness of Belushi and Aykroyd, nor did he have what O'Donoghue called the ability to easily don and discard the comedic mask—he couldn't shift rapidly from one character to the next. He tended to go back and forth between two or three different accents, no matter what the role, and O'Donoghue would often remark that Garrett seemed to have a bone missing from his neck: His head always tilted to one side when he looked at the camera.

Since Garrett was not a strong enough performer or writer to impose his own sensibilities on *Saturday Night*, *Saturday Night* imposed its sensibilities on him, and they were at best cruel, at worst racist. For all the professed radicalism of the writers on the show, they seemed unable to produce material that dealt with black issues in anything beyond the coarsest terms, if they dealt with them at all. One sketch written for Garrett was a parody commercial for a toothpaste called "Tarbrush," which darkened blacks' supposedly shiny white teeth. After seeing it in rehearsal, Lorne decided it was too much and cut it. Garrett later said in an interview that two black technicians in 8H walked out in protest that it would even have been considered.

In the first couple of seasons, Garrett mainly suffered the indignity of not having much to do on the show. There would be greater indignities to come. Many of the writers argue that they tried to write more material for Garrett but were frustrated by his limitations as a performer. Al Franken expressed the general attitude that Garrett's problems were his own fault more than the writers'. "We relied on him to bring some blackness to the show," he said, "because what's our experience? He had to bring it to us."

\* \* \*

It wasn't until the second season began and Chevy left that the influence of the Bully Boys really began to tell on *Saturday Night*.

The first episodes were Belushi's. John had acted up enough in the first season to confirm Lorne's fears about him, but not until the second season did he begin to lose control. Many believe it was the knowledge that Chevy was going that sparked it: Now John had what he wanted, a clear shot at being the star of the show. He shifted, one friend said, from defense to offense, and in the process started to erect a Bad Boy of Comedy persona for himself that would prove more and more taxing to maintain as time went on.

His initial outburst that season came when Lily Tomlin hosted the first show. Just before dress rehearsal, in a hallway outside 8H within earshot of the audience waiting to get in, John started running Lily down. "She's not funny," he said. "She's the ugliest fucking cunt. … She's terrible." Al Franken and Tom Davis each took one of Belushi's arms and pulled him into a side room; a toot of cocaine calmed him down.

Belushi took an extended plunge into excess three weeks later. NBC News had taken over studio 8H for its coverage of the 1976 Presidential elections. Lorne fought the loss of his studio, unsuccessfully, then announced he would take *Saturday Night* on the road to several college campuses for live shows there. The idea was to bring *Saturday Night* to its fans, but after Dave Wilson, Dick Ebersol, Dan Sullivan, and Eugene Lee scouted out half a dozen schools on the East Coast, the idea was abandoned as unworkable and too expensive. *Saturday Night* ended up, for the fifth, sixth, and seventh shows of the season, in NBC's Studio One at Avenue M and Fourteenth Street in Brooklyn.

Studio One was, in Michael O'Donoghue's words, "a big old evil studio," a massive warehouse of a building built as a movie soundstage for Warner Brothers in the silent picture era. There was still a swimming pool beneath its floor for water ballet sequences. It was disorienting and irritating for everyone on the show to be there—the commute from Manhattan was a hassle, the studio seemed to be in the middle of nowhere, and the support systems they'd come to depend on in 8H were gone. Belushi only added to their troubles.

The limousines probably had as much as anything to do with John's misbehavior those weeks. NBC, for the first time, supplied the cast members with limos so they could get from Manhattan to Brooklyn for rehearsals on time. NBC expected the limos to be taken to and from the studio, period, but Belushi immediately caught on to the fact that the driver would keep driving until John released him. John got a taste of all-night chauffeured club hopping, and he liked it. He was partying hard, so hard that he was too "narcotized," as O'Donoghue put it, to read his lines in some sketches. Laraine Newman remembers being shocked, when she saw John backstage one night, by how burned-out he looked. His skin, she thought to herself, looked green. It was during one of these shows that John cut Buck Henry in their Samurai sketch, and later that night, Chevy, anchoring his last Weekend Update, reported that "a far-gone and drugged-out John Belushi" had hit Henry with a sword.

Despite the limo, or because of it, John showed up late for almost every rehearsal in Brooklyn, and once he failed to show up at all. The limo company was called and it was learned that Belushi had been dropped off at home in Greenwich Village at seven o'clock in the morning. Lorne told the show's unit manager, Nick O'Gorman, to get John's keys from Danny and go to John's place to see, as O'Gorman put it, "whether John was alive or dead." O'Gorman, to his relief, found Belushi eating cold pizza and drinking chocolate milk.

After the first of the Brooklyn shows Dick Ebersol volunteered to help John clean himself up by taking him along to his house in Los Angeles for a little rest and relaxation. It would be best, Ebersol told Lorne, to get John out of New York. Lorne agreed. For the next two weeks, John commuted to Hollywood, getting on a plane Sunday and coming back in time for the show's read-through on Wednesday. He didn't clean up. Ebersol says John was staying out all night, every night, and when Ebersol mentioned on the phone to Lorne the name of one friend John had been spending time with, Lorne cursed, telling Ebersol that friend was one of the heaviest coke dealers in Hollywood.

To Tom Schiller, the pinnacle of this particular breakdown of John's came after the Ruth Gordon show in January 1977. John had just gotten out of the hospital after cracking a cartilage in his knee as he leaped offstage, samurai sword raised over his head, during a college speaking engagement. He'd missed a show, and his feelings had been badly hurt that everyone acted as if he were faking it, trying to get out of working. John had also been hurt that few people from the show came to visit him in the hospital, and that there wasn't as much made on-air of his absence as there had been when Chevy missed performances. "No one even waved," he complained.

John had recently reconciled with his girlfriend, Judy Jacklin, and they'd been married on New Year's Eve. But he continued to ingest massive amounts of cocaine and to be desperately unstable. He said in an interview with *Crawdaddy* magazine several months later that he'd been contemplating suicide. "When in doubt, I floor it, I let my lifestyle play itself out," he said.

The week of Ruth Gordon's show, John was still in a wheelchair, and still on the edge. When a production assistant came to his dressing room before the show, he threw a lamp across the room at her, screaming for her to get out. This was the show that opened with Belushi's doctor supposedly threatening to cut off his drugs.

The post-show party that night was held in studio 8H after the audience was gone and the lights turned off. John was in his wheelchair, and his friend Jack Nicholson was behind it, pushing. Belushi was a man possessed, like a character in a Stephen King novel, and he careened around 8H with Nicholson's wicked grin hovering over his shoulder,

"John was zonko, out of his skull," Schiller remembers, "and they were going behind sets and stages all over the studio, this madman with a cane practically hitting people out of his way. It was frightening, and strange, because the studio was dark and people were walking around not really doing anything. It was almost as if there were spirits and zombies walking around with us, with Belushi at the center of the whole thing."

\* \* \*

More and more as John's success grew and his patience diminished he pitted himself in tests of will against Lorne, usually by showing up late for rehearsals or refusing to play parts he didn't like. He often complained he was treated like some sort of "wild animal" on the show, and he quit *Saturday Night* in arguments with Lorne probably a dozen times. He considered Lorne a snob and called Lorne's circle of admirers on 17 and his society friends "The Dead."

Lorne avoided public confrontation with John. Instead they had long talks in Lorne's office during which John would rant and Lorne would throw his hands up in exasperation. "You're your own free agent," he'd say. "You're acting like an asshole. ... If that's what you want to do ..." Sometimes Lorne tried more punitive measures, such as suspending John from read-through (which John didn't mind) or, on occasion, firing him. Once or twice John thought Lorne really meant it.

Judy Jacklin Belushi and others who were close to John say that this sort of "negative reinforcement" was exactly the wrong tack to take with him, the opposite of what he needed. Nevertheless, John usually got his way. "John would bully Lorne and get whatever he wanted," one of the writers said. "Lorne didn't like John, and would clear his office when John came in. Lorne was upset about giving John concessions—'Why do I cave in to him?' he'd say."

After one of their private meetings, a group of people sitting outside Lorne's office watched as John stormed out, Lorne following a few steps behind.

"John," Lorne called to him, "can't we just *talk* about this?" "No!" John said, still walking. "I'm not coming back."

"There's no reason we can't have something to eat and talk about it," Lorne suggested, still following him.

Again Belushi said "No" and kept walking.

Finally Lorne stopped, watched Belushi walk out, and turned to the group sitting nearby. "You know," he said, "I feel like my own mother following me out of the house."

It was partly in response to John's troubles with Lorne that Dan Aykroyd began to assume the role of John's defender and protector. One of Lorne's assistants heard Danny talking to Lorne after one of John's episodes. "Stay out of it," Lorne told Danny. "Protect yourself."

But Danny didn't stay out of it. Many nights on the 17th floor he could be heard yelling at Belushi to stop the midnight rambles, to dedicate himself to his art and his talent. Danny left a note for John once that began, "John … Read this. … We must formulate premises. We must work and think constantly." To those who heard Danny's pleas they were a touching display of friendship, especially because Danny was going through troubles enough of his own at the time.

Danny was working so hard and was so tightly wound in the first place that his frustrations increasingly erupted into violence. Fists through the walls of his office and dressing room were the least of it. He once came offstage unhappy about the way a sketch had gone and smashed his hand through the glass covering a poster outside the studio, cutting himself fairly deeply in the process. Another time he smashed a glassed-in directory by the elevator on 17 and left a trail of blood on his way to the NBC infirmary on the seventh floor.

He lost control one day when he discovered that his prized bong, a glass marijuana pipe, was missing from his dressing room. He stormed into the studio, shouting that he would kill whoever had the audacity to remove his bong. "I'll take his head off!" he yelled. Then he went back to his dressing room and annihilated it. Surveying the damage later, NBC's maintenance people found the tile ceiling ripped out, the tiles themselves crushed into little pieces, the support beams bent and broken, doors pulled off cabinets, the loudspeaker torn off the wall, a Barcalounger chair destroyed. Maintenance decided to leave it as it was until the end of the season.

The rampage for which Danny was most infamous within NBC occurred early in the third season. NBC's Rick Traum sent him a form letter demanding payment of some $400 in unauthorized expenses incurred during *Saturday Night*'s second trip to the Emmy awards the previous May. Traum, who sent the same memo to several others on the show, considered it a routine dunning notice, but later he would admit it was a mistake sending one to Danny. He especially regretted circling the amount owed in red ink. That, Traum said, was like waving a red flag in Danny's face.

Danny had a thing about money. He was always cursing NBC for taking advantage of them, paying them peanuts while they broke their backs. No one on the show was happy about the situation, but more than any of them, Danny was incensed. "We're Class A humor mechanics," he'd say, spitting it out. So Traum's memo would have troubled Danny enough by itself, but he was also wrestling with other tensions at the time. He'd started a romance with Rosie Shuster, the boss's ex-wife, the woman he'd had a crush on since he was a teenager in Canada. Danny and Lorne's relationship was further complicated by the fact that by then they had the same manager, Bernie Brillstein, and the same accountant, Mark Lipsky. All this was filtered through Danny's growing conviction that Lorne shared some of the blame for exploiting the working classes on *Saturday Night*. Danny took one look at Traum's memo and it all exploded.

In an artistic burst of rage, Danny filled a wall near the elevators on 17 with venomous graffiti. He did so on a weekend when there wasn't a show, and those from NBC's maintenance department who discovered it said the hate-filled mural clearly took several painstaking hours to create. Using spray paints, a variety of felt- tipped and ball-point pens, and some sort of chiseling tool, Danny scrawled evil-sounding satanic incantations, among them "I am Beelzebub, I am the Devil." There were also more conventional threats and profanities, including "I will kill you Rick" and, hacked into the wall in letters four feet high, "Fuck You."

NBC decided that the wisest response to the incident was to do nothing. "Just clean the walls and shut up," one executive said. "It was kept very quiet. There was no discussion, not even with Lorne. The fewer people who knew about it the healthier the situation would be in the long run." NBC's maintenance staff covered the corridor that weekend with brown wrapping paper. A couple of days later the walls were plastered over and repainted.

# CHAPTER 21

# The Girls

It does help when writing humor to have a big hunk of meat between the legs, I find. That may sound sexist, and I say it only in the kindest way, but Mr. Ding Dong, I think, has a lot of comedy genes in there.

—Michael O'Donoghue

I think men feel threatened by women being funny. Men don't like the idea of women making jokes because they think the ultimate woman's joke is, 'How big is it?' So they tend to cross their legs in the presence of funny women.

—Anne Beatts

It took "the girls" of *Saturday Night* about two months to decide they'd better discuss the sexual politics on the show. A note went up on 17 in the fall of the first season inviting all the women to a slumber party at Anne Beatts's apartment. All the women writers and performers showed up, some in their pajamas, bringing lots of potato chips and Tab. The invitation hadn't said so, but everyone knew what the prime subject of conversation would be: how to keep the Bully Boys from eclipsing the women on *Saturday Night*.

Sexism, the women at the slumber party were well aware, wasn't a new problem in comedy by any means. Marilyn Miller, who had the most experience in TV, said that except for Lily Tomlin's shows, every comedy program she'd ever worked on was male-dominated, as much a team sport as football, and she felt it was all but inevitable that it would be that way.

Anne Beatts's experience in underground comedy hadn't been any different. The *National Lampoon* started at an all-male school, she pointed out, and being the only woman editor there had been "like being a black voter in the south: Everyone else had to spell 'cat' and you had to say when the Edict of Nantes was revoked." On the other hand, Beatts knew it could be worse on *Saturday Night*— there were, for instance, no women at all in Monty Python, and women's parts in Python's productions were, often as not, played by men in drag.

Still, despite the denials of the men on the show—who sometimes claimed to be liberated—none of the women questioned that Neo-Macho was in full bloom on *Saturday Night*, or that it threatened to crowd out the women's humor.

The toughest times, everyone agreed, were in the Monday afternoon pitching sessions with the hosts (who were, the women noted, predominately male), when those who talked loudest were those who were most often heard. No one presented an idea as forcefully as Dan Aykroyd or Chevy Chase, and after Chevy left, Al Franken did a credible job of picking up the Gonzo pitching technique. Sound and fury tended to dominate the Wednesday read- throughs as well. Too often the women's fainter voices were lost in the din, and too often the sketches that got the loudest response were the men's hard-edged, go-for-the-belly-laugh sorts of ideas. "The men on the show always wrote sketches where people got dressed up in suits of armor and banged into each other and fell down," Anne Beatts said. "The women just weren't attracted to that kind of humor."

More subtle references in the women's sketches tended to be missed by the men, and therefore dismissed as not funny. The men talked about "hard" and "soft" comedy, Beatts said, as if comedy were erectile tissue. The end result was that a lot of the women writers' sketches weren't making it on the air, and the women performers were getting too many secretary and receptionist parts, written by the men, in which their lines tended to be of the "Mr. Jones will see you now" variety.

How to deal with the chauvinism was something else again. Anne Beatts wanted to confront it directly, in unity, perhaps by forming a "coalition" to take their grievances to Lorne. Marilyn Miller didn't go for that. The show was no different from any corporate environment, she said: You either put up quality work or shut up. Organized movements got you nowhere.

None of the women performers favored the solidarity route either. Gilda, Laraine, and Jane were most sensitive, Rosie Shuster says, to being branded "hairy-legged dyke feminists" because they felt most vulnerable to a backlash. Numerically there were simply more men writers than women, and if they alienated the men, the women performers risked being shut out even more than they were. Jane Curtin in particular didn't feel the sexism on the show was that great a problem, although she would change her mind before long.

Laraine Newman and Gilda Radner, on the 17th floor in 1976.
Tension between solidarity and competition would be an ongoing
struggle for "the girls" of *Saturday Night.*
*Courtesy of F.T. Eyre*

Most of the women felt they had an ally in Lorne. He was looking, they knew, for more gentle comedy on the show; he liked it personally and he thought the show needed it, for the sake of texture, he'd say. The women gave Lorne credit, not only for hiring so many of them in the first place but also for creating an environment where they could at least express their complaints with some hope of success. They knew that on many shows they never would have seen the producer, much less talked to him.

There were times at the end of writers' meetings when Gilda or Marilyn Miller would say, "Hey, are the girls going to be doing anything this week, or what?" Lorne would listen and respond, the women say; as a producer who was also a father figure, he was willing to be democratic in order to protect all of his children. It was, Marilyn Miller said, like daddy saying, "Okay, everybody's going to get to drive the new car. Everyone gets a chance."

Like any man, though, Lorne had his blind spots. Anne Beatts once wrote a sketch in which a man on the night of his thirtieth birthday was having problems with impotence. Lorne told her to make the character ten years older because, he said, "Thirty-year- olds don't have that problem." Beatts laughed to herself that Lorne must have spent more time with thirty-year-old men than she had.

The women also sensed very quickly that Lorne would probably react badly to any sort of unified movement on their part, that he
would see such a campaign as an unacceptable threat to his power. No
one knew this better than Rosie Shuster. Lorne had hired his wife for
*Saturday Night* on one condition: She had to promise not to lead any
"rebellions or riots" against him. The troubles between Lorne and Rosie
in the early days of the feminist movement had left their mark on Lorne,
Shuster says, and she thinks he had nightmares of her leading a wedge of
women into his office someday, all of them shouting slogans and waving
placards that read "Male producer is pig!"

By the same token, the women who were not themselves bullies,
or who didn't learn to be, were at a disadvantage, because as much as
Lorne hated the Bully Boys' confrontational style—he was much more
politic than they, and he recoiled from shouting and threatening—the
fact remained that bullying often worked, as it did for John.

So the slumber party broke up early. Everybody felt they'd gotten
to know each other better, but nobody slept over. The only agreement
reached was that the best recourse was to be so funny they couldn't be
ignored. Beatts and Shuster resolved between themselves to write more
for the women, to try to see that they were covered with material on
every show, but the tacit understanding among the group was that it was
essentially every woman for herself.

* * *

Over time, all the women on *Saturday Night* developed strategies to
defend themselves, but they remained more or less on the defensive
throughout the course of the show. There was an automatic sisterhood of
sorts between the women performers. For three seasons they all shared
a dressing room, and Gilda used to joke that when the show ended, the
three of them would split a gold watch.

Jane Curtin was probably the most direct of the three about going
in and talking to Lorne, calmly and rationally, about the parts or lack of
parts she was getting on the show, although she sometimes confronted
Lorne in anger. One friend described her as a smooth lake that occasionally roiled but quickly settled back down again. She was a member
of a group within the show—assistant costume designer Karen Roston
and associate producer Jean Doumanian were others—that one of the
men called "the Smart Women." The Smart Women would sit in the
ninth-floor green room or, when she got one, in Curtin's dressing room,
sipping tea or wine and commenting wryly on the weirdness surrounding them.

Curtin was so clearly the most responsible, normal cast member that for the first two contract renegotiations the players had with NBC they chose her as the representative for all of them. After discussing objectives with the cast, Curtin sat down with program executive Aaron Cohen (who would already have discussed parameters with Lorne) to present the cast's proposals and take Cohen's offers back to the 17th floor. One observer privy to this process believes another reason Jane was designated the cast's representative was that she was the most suspicious of Lorne's role in the negotiations and therefore would be likely to get them the best possible deal.

Jane took over the Weekend Update anchor slot when Chevy left, and it was a rough transition for her. No one hesitated to remind her that following Chevy Chase was going to be no easy task. Unable to write for herself as Chevy had, she was bitterly upset about some of the material she was given, which for a while relied heavily on sexual innuendo. On one show she responded to all the complaints she'd been getting in the mail from Chevy's female fans. She said she'd mistakenly assumed that responsible journalism, not sex appeal, was what counted, and proceeded to rip open her blouse, crying, "Try these on for size, Connie Chung!"

Despite her embarrassment at that bit, it was one of the times Jane flashed what O'Donoghue called "an icy Tippi Hedren quality" which, together with her considerable abilities as an actress, lent her work more spark than she was generally given credit for. In the third season Jane began to share the Update anchor desk with Dan Aykroyd and later with Bill Murray and an ever-growing list of guest commentators. For much of her time on *Saturday Night*, she felt stifled and underused, stuck in housewife or talk show hostess roles, often the straight woman rather than the lead. As she said to a production assistant once when a rewritten script was brought to her dressing room, "Oh, did my line change?"

A more direct competition developed between Gilda and Laraine, largely because their physical resemblance more often put them in the running for the same roles. They also tended, the other women on the show say, to use more traditional feminine wiles to get their way—in time both of them would not infrequently end up crying in Lorne's office.

Gilda was closer than any of the other performers to Lorne, very much willing to play the part of daddy's little girl. Once she left a note for him saying, "Lorne, I'm happy." She was also in many respects a perfect foil for the Bully Boys. It was often said on the 17th floor that Gilda was best in sketches where Belushi threw her around. In the *Saturday Night* scrapbook, a collection of scripts and memorabilia published early in the third season, there was a note to John signed by Gilda that read,

"In loving memory of John Belushi, who can hit me without hurting me and who can hurt me without hitting me."

One friend who knew Gilda well says she had enough of the high-strung, neurotic actress in her that she sometimes hit herself, hard enough to cause bruises. Another friend says that there was a touch of masochism in Gilda, not unlike those women *apache* dancers who are flung dramatically around by their men under the glow of a street lamp. "Gilda," this friend said, "always kept a certain amount of pain and tur-moil in her life." By the time Bill Murray joined *Saturday Night*, he and Gilda had begun a long and tumultuous affair, one in which she often played the role of victim.

In her work, however, Gilda had a buoyancy about her, a willingness to play that translated into what the men would probably have called guts. She developed slapstick characters like Emily Litella and Rosanne Roseannadanna that were belly-laugh guarantees, and she learned to look directly into the camera without blinking—to love the camera, as actors say. She was far from arrogant, on or offstage, and she didn't face the camera without fear, but the fear didn't come across. A fetching vul-nerability did, and it was that persona that made her a star.

Laraine was more an actress than Gilda was, her characterizations in many cases less broad and more refined. But those aren't the quali-ties that make stars on television, and to a large extent Laraine never developed the stare-down-the-camera nerve that does. She tried to carve out a niche for herself as the sexy woman on *Saturday Night*, and in many roles she was sexy indeed, but in the long run Gilda's image as America's Sweetheart was far more popular. As Jim Downey, a writer who joined the show in the second season, put it, "Sex bombs are never going to compete with people who want to be loved."

Backstage, Laraine's tendency to be withdrawn and tentative grew worse instead of better. She didn't like campaigning for parts, and many times when she was sitting around with the writers, trying to come up with a piece, too soon she'd say, "Oh, this isn't working," and back off without letting it build. Her performing rhythm of not really get-ting a grasp on her characters until the air show also worked against her. Many times on-air she surprised people with a suddenly glowing performance—Lorne would come up to her afterward and say, "How did you do that?"—but her relatively lifeless readings during the week didn't help get her sketches on the air in the first place.

Laraine's biggest mistake, she realized later, was refusing Lorne's requests to repeat characters that might have become her versions of Gilda's Emily Litella or Roseanne Roseannadanna. She hated "hooks," she always said; they reminded her of the curly- haired comedian Marty

Allen, who will forever be known as the guy who says, "Hello dere." That wasn't going to happen to her. And it didn't, but neither did the familiarity repetition brings. Laraine also had the misfortune to fumble a few lines in a couple of early sketches, a cardinal sin on *Saturday Night*. O'Donoghue went into one of his patented apoplectic rages when she tripped on a speech he wrote. She found, as Bill Murray soon would, that the writers stopped trusting her, and her roles grew scarcer still.

Laraine, in fact, would watch in admiration and later try to emulate Bill Murray's response to that problem. "He really took a stand for himself," she said.

He had to.

# CHAPTER 22

# Billy

Bill Murray joined *Saturday Night* on January 15, 1977, five shows after Chevy left. Lorne had kept Billy waiting in the wings to help him avoid as much as possible the onus of being Chevy Chase's replacement, but there was plenty of resistance anyway. NBC didn't care for the choice of Bill Murray at all: After the comforting accessibility of Chevy, Billy looked to Aaron Cohen and others at the network like some Irish Catholic street dog. Which was pretty much what he was.

Billy was such a brawler even Belushi was wary of him. John knew Billy and his brother Brian from Second City in Chicago— Belushi had roomed with Brian when he first came to New York, and John later hired Billy for *The National Lampoon Show*. When Billy arrived in New York, John and Bob Tischler, the producer of the *Lampoon Radio Hour*, on which Billy also worked, felt it necessary to sit down with him to chat about his propensity for rowdy behavior. Cool it, they told him. Some on *Saturday Night* think Lorne didn't push harder to hire Billy for the first season because he knew Billy's reputation and decided he had enough machismo on his hands with John and Danny.

Billy's fashion sense, like John's and Danny's, bordered on the anarchistic. He favored outlandishly baggy pants and wrinkled shirts that

Bill Murray's exquisitely unctuous lounge singer, Nick. © *NBC*

looked as if they'd been picked out of a pile in his closet, which they probably had been. He was a drinker, not a drugger. He could toss down a half-dozen beers before the first-quarter buzzer sounded at a Knicks game, and he sometimes swigged from a fifth of Irish whiskey as he walked around 8H during blocking, a practice NBC tried to discourage.

He had a physical exuberance that always threatened to cross over into violence, even when he was being friendly. Soon after he arrived on the 17th floor he got into the habit of throwing the women down on a couch or the floor and tickling them unmercifully into hysterics. Other times he'd simply pick up a passing woman and bite her on her rear end. Another favorite trick was to stand up in the green room during dinner break and squeeze sandwiches through his fingers.

He had a deeper, mystical side to him as well, what Tom Schiller called "an itinerant monk actor kind of thing." Schiller shared a set of secret code initials with Billy: "T.E.," for Total Enlightenment. But outwardly Bill Murray was anything but sedate. Before a show, people would see him standing in a corner backstage warming up, hopping from one foot to the other, swinging his arms, doing chin- ups. "It was a dangerous energy," says Neil Levy. "You were almost afraid to go over to him for fear he'd attack you."

Billy's assimilation into *Saturday Night* was so bruising that for his first season he all but breathed fire. He once told *Rolling Stone* he was hired initially on a trial basis for three shows; Lorne denies this, saying Billy was simply given the job. In any case, he had a great first show, but after that it got difficult.

He may have known that NBC had tried to talk Lorne out of hiring him, in part because of his pockmarked face. To Aaron Cohen, Billy looked like "the kid in the gang comedies who rode the motorcycle, with the black leather jacket and his hair greased back, the guy you hated looking at." Perhaps it would be better, Cohen told Lorne, to hire someone better-looking, a leading-man type who could "balance out" the other men in the cast. Lorne ignored the suggestions, saying Billy had enough versatility to make up for his supposed lack of looks, and that since Billy was able to write but willing to do so without taking a writer's credit, the network would be saving money. Still, NBC kept reminding Lorne that whatever choice he made didn't have to be permanent, that Billy could always be replaced.

Once hired, Billy had to put up with a flood of vicious letters from fans of Chevy's who assumed Billy was responsible for his departure and who took the trouble to write, telling Billy how much they hated him for it. Billy saw some of the letters before Tom Davis started intercepting them, and Davis says he couldn't believe how ugly they were. "You suck" was a common motif.

Fitting in on the 17th floor was no picnic either. Billy was a familiar face, if not already a friend, to most of the writers and performers on the show, and people felt comfortable with his being there. Nonetheless there was a feeling that he couldn't just come in and immediately assume parity with those who were there before him. John and Gilda and the others had first shot at the spotlight now; Billy would have to wait his turn. Billy understood this, his friends say, but he didn't like it, and, true to form, he reacted virulently. He raged that the writers were giving him nothing but supporting roles—"second-cop parts," he called them—fuming that he would never break out of Chevy's shadow if he didn't get a chance to shine. It didn't help Billy's temper any when he would be walking down the street and somebody would yell out to him, "Hey! How's Belushi?"—just as Chevy's fans used to yell out to John.

Billy shared an office his first season with Jim Downey, the new writer, evidence enough of his low place in *Saturday Night*'s pecking order, since Downey was the only person on the writing and performing team whom Billy technically outranked. Downey couldn't have been less like his roommate. A tall, long haired Harvard grad, he was soft-spoken, introspective, and intellectual. His sketches tended to be spacier and more gentle than those of the other men. One of Downey's recurring formats was a talk show called "What If?", which featured various experts addressing such hypothetical questions from viewers as "What if Eleanor Roosevelt could fly?" and "What if Superman grew up in [Nazi] Germany?" (Downey's "What If?" sketches were surrealistic riffs on an old comedic melody. "What If?" was one of' the games the writers on *Your Show of Shows* used to play to come up with new material.)

Billy and Downey eventually became good friends, but that first season they were anything but. Billy considered Downey an effete Ivy Leaguer whose material was too wordy, and he didn't like the friends Downey brought to the office. Downey, in turn, didn't think Billy was all that bright and didn't especially care for the friends Billy brought to the office either. Downey suffered more quietly than Billy did, however, and he absorbed a lot of Billy's frustration. "He would give me shit, abuse me," Downey said later, "and I would just bow to him. It wasn't screaming matches—he was just pissed off at the writers in general. He was always angry."

The pressure Billy was going through showed up in his performances on-air, causing him to falter in several sketches, which only made the pressure worse and the writers less inclined to feature him. He once said that he'd muffed a line Anne Beatts wrote and she wouldn't look at him for six weeks. One of his worst transgressions came in a talk-show sketch in which he played a victim of "quintlexia," a nonexistent disease that rendered those afflicted incapable of speaking more than five words. The five words Billy was supposed to say were, "That's true, you're absolutely right," but at one point in his tenseness he said, "That's true, you're absolutely right about th ..." and the joke was blown.

Lorne wasn't happy with the way things were going with Billy, and some on the show say Lorne was beginning to think he'd made a mistake hiring him. After one of Billy's onstage blunders, Neil Levy heard Lorne mutter, "That's it—he's gone." Finally Lorne decided to confront the problem directly. He and Billy wrote a piece called "The New Guy," which Billy delivered on the Broderick Crawford show in March. He sat at a desk typing, a little plaque with his name on it facing the audience:

Hello. I'm Bill Murray. You can call me Billy, but around here everybody just calls me "the new guy." I want to thank the producer, Lorne Michaels, for urging me to speak with you directly. You see, I'm a little bit concerned. I don't think I'm making it on the show.

I'm a funny guy, but I haven't been so funny on the show. My friends say, "How come they're giving you all those parts that aren't funny?" Well, it's not the material, it's me. It's not that I'm not funny, it's that I'm not being funny at the right time. Honest. Before, I could be funny whenever I wanted. But now, as a professional, I have to learn to pick my spots, you know. This morning I picked up my laundry, and the guy said to me, "Bill, you know, every time you come in here, you say something funny. But I saw you on the show *Saturday Night*, and you stunk."

Well, that hurts. It totally destroyed my confidence. ... Now what I'm asking for is your support. I've gotten some nice letters from old friends, and people I owe money to, but from you people, I hear nothing. I'm not asking for letters, but—I know this sounds funny: Support. I'm a Catholic. I'm one of nine children. ... I was raised in Wilmette, Illinois, a small mining town north of Chicago. That reminds me of something funny. My father died when I was seventeen. That's not what was funny—he was funny. People always said to me, "Ah, you'll never grow up to be as funny as your dad." And now he's not around, to see me be not as funny as him. My sister, Nancy, is a nun. My mom works to support the family ... But that's all beside the point. It's no concern of yours whether or not they need the money I make.

What I'm talking about is between you and me. If you could see it in your heart to laugh whenever I say something, I don't care what it is, or if you can't laugh, think about my family, and the father that I never really got to know. If I know you're on my side, I'll make you laugh so hard, you'll have to hold your sides to keep from pulling a muscle or tearing a cartilage. It's up to you. Yeah, you. ... Now I don't want letters, I just want to make it as a Not Ready For Prime Time Player. And when that's done, I'll be able to stand here on *Saturday Night* in the middle of Rockefeller Plaza, New York City, New York, 10020, and say, "Dad, I did it," He'd like that.

The idea of the "New Guy" speech, Jim Downey said, was for Billy to "exorcise Chevy's ghost. ... He had to go through this initiation with the audience, to debase himself until the audience accepted him and felt that he atoned for replacing Chevy." Unfortunately, it didn't work: Billy seemed as out of place after the "New Guy" speech as he had before it.

Billy's limbo continued for the rest of the season, and it's possible he might never have broken through if he hadn't taken matters into his own hands. He was standing in his shower at home on the Wednesday morning before the last show of the season, holding one of those microphone-shaped bars of soap, a Christmas gift from John's wife, Judy Jacklin. He got an idea for a sketch, ran to the office, and, with Gilda, wrote it up in time for the read- through, leaving plenty of room for improvisation.

It was called the "Shower Mike" sketch. Billy, playing an average Joe named Richard Herkiman, stepped into a shower with real running water (the audience saw him only from the waist up) and launched into what is clearly his morning routine:

BILLY: All right, okay, another day, another dollar, Richard Herkiman, let's go. Come on, let's go, let's go. Letsgo letsgo letsgo! Haaa! Hoga hoga, haa, heyaheya, ho! Boy, that's cold. Cold! That Mexican family's gotta go! Oh! All the hot water's gone. Okay! (He picks up his shower mike and introduces himself to an imaginary audience.) Ladies and gentlemen, Richard Herkiman!

Hey! Whoo! Thank you, thank you very much. Woo! (He starts singing in his inimitable nightclub style.) "Well, there's something in the way that that girl moves, that attracts me like no other lover. ..." (At this point Gilda, playing his wife, sticks her head in and asks if she can take a quick shower.)

BILLY: Ladies and gentlemen ... "don't wanna leave her now" ... a very special guest ... "You know I be-lieve and how" ... my wife, Mrs. Richard Herkiman, Jane Nash! Come on in, Jane! (Gilda, her arms crossed over her chest, steps into the shower.) Say, Jane, how do you feel about singing a song today, huh?

GILDA: Richard, will you quit fooling around? I'm just taking a shower. (Billy pleads and Gilda starts singing. Then Billy interrupts with a question.)

BILLY: Listen, honey ... a lot of the folks out there wanna know if you really love me—do you, honey?
(Gilda replies that she does and, at her husband's insistence, repeats it a few times. Then Billy turns to address his imaginary audience in a confidential tone.)

BILLY: Well, you know, folks out there, what my wife doesn't know is that I know she's been cheating on me for the last couple of years. ... We've got behind the curtain a surprise guest, the man she's been seeing behind my back for the last two years. (Raising his voice to a shout) Here he is—Richard Cularsky! Come on in, Richard! Good to have you aboard!

(Buck Henry, playing Richard Cularsky, steps fully clothed into the still-running shower. Gilda is shocked to see him there.)

BILLY: Yes, I brought him all the way from his home in the city to be with us here today. Isn't that terrific! ...

Now tell me, you kids, you must spend a lot of time in the shower together when I'm not here, huh?

BUCK: (Getting over his initial discomfort and joining in the spirit) You bet! Nah, it's funny—I'll tell you the truth, a lot of people have the wrong idea about that. It's actually a lot safer to rent a hotel room. You know, there's much less chance of meeting an aunt or an uncle. And you don't have to worry about changing the sheets on the bed!

BILLY: (Laughing) Ouch! I forgot how much is involved in this kind of thing. Woo! (Billy continues in this vein for a while, and as he's running out of time and thanking Gilda and Buck for dropping by, Buck interjects a plug for his and Gilda's next appearance together, the first week in June at the Statler Hotel in Philadelphia.)

The "Shower Mike" sketch was an unqualified hit on-air, and it established Billy's first firm character, the inveterate ham whose repertoire consists of every show biz cliché ever invented. It also established the foundation of the anti-comic persona that would turn him, after another season, into one of the biggest stars on the show. He had found his voice. Soon the writers were coming to him with sketches, and soon he was getting love letters in the mail from fans. Tom Davis doesn't doubt that some of those love letters came from the same people who six months earlier had written in to tell Billy how much they hated his guts.

There was, however, one more act of exorcism to come.

* * *

Chevy Chase returned to *Saturday Night* for the first time as its host in February of the third season. Why Lorne ever asked Chevy back was a mystery to the others on the show. Lorne, they all knew, had been putting Chevy down in office bull sessions ever since Chevy left. People eventually decided that maybe Lorne wanted to bury the hatchet. Surely the fact that Chevy's return came in the middle of a "sweeps" month, when big ratings count most, had something to do with it. Lorne was having trouble getting a host that week anyway.

Chevy himself was apprehensive about coming back. He'd been out of touch since he left, so he wasn't sure what to expect. When he arrived on the 17th floor, he immediately discovered that the atmosphere had been, as he saw it, "poisoned" against him. Whatever support he'd had when he left had been all but evaporated by the stories that circulated about the circumstances of his departure. "Something had happened in the matrix there," Chevy said later, "and people had talked." Chevy didn't doubt that Lorne was one of the "leprechauns" responsible for spreading what Chevy considered to be lies about him, and that John was the other. Bill Murray, who hadn't gotten along that well with Chevy even in the *Lampoon* days, was probably on edge to begin with at the news of Chevy's return, and the stories he was hearing only made it worse.

Chevy's attitude that week seemed to confirm everything that people had been saying about him. He took up where he'd left off, acting the part of the big star coming back to show the kids how it should be done. He kept interrupting people, giving directions, and talking about his decision to leave the show. "I know what you're going to say," he kept repeating. "You all think I made a bad career move."

A rancorous fight developed over who would anchor Weekend Update that week—Chevy or Jane Curtin. Chevy insisted he do it by himself, as he always had, a suggestion Jane understandably found offensive. There was a meeting in Lorne's office to discuss it, and some of those who were there say Chevy must have been out of his mind on cocaine, so egotistical were his arguments. "This isn't really fair to Jane to have both of us on screen at the same time," one writer quotes Chevy as saying. "I'm just going to upstage her. Everyone is waiting for me and I'm just going to destroy her. Jane, let's face it, you can't be on the screen with me at the same time."

Chevy lost that battle. He and Jane did Update together, although there was a bit in which he tried to get rid of her, ending with her telling him he ought to go back to Hollywood. There were other skirmishes as the week went on. A photo session with an Associated Press photographer turned into a disaster. Belushi walked out, cursing. "Chevy comes back and you guys make a big deal of it," he said. The photographer made the mistake of asking for a little more animation from those who were left. Dan Aykroyd stalked out, too, yelling insults as he went. That prompted a letter of protest to NBC from the Associated Press.

Chevy was especially hurt that Lorne acted as if nothing were happening. Lorne, Chevy thought, should have protected him, or at least brought the trouble out into the open. Chevy admits he did more dope that week than he ever had before—"from unhappiness," he says—but he adds that drugs contributed to everybody's tension, not just his. In any event the week was a nightmare.

The friction between Chevy and Billy started sparking before the dress rehearsal on Saturday. Chevy was sitting in Franken and Davis's office when Billy burst in and told Chevy he'd heard what an asshole he'd been while he was on the show. Chevy said later he was shocked—this was the first time anyone had confronted him directly with what they thought, and he knew then why everybody had been treating him so badly. They started shouting and finally Chevy told Billy to get out. There was more tension during dress, while they were rehearsing a sketch together called "Celebrity Crack-Up," and more words exchanged after dress in the hallway outside 8H. It had gotten around that Chevy was having troubles at home with Jackie Carlin, and Billy twisted the knife. "Go fuck your wife," he said. "She needs it."

Chevy came back with a put-down about Billy's face, saying it looked as if Neil Armstrong had landed on it. Their shouts echoed through the eighth and ninth floors.

Billy and Chevy came to the notes meeting between dress and air furious but contained. Five minutes before air, though, it boiled over. Chevy found Billy in John's dressing room and called him out.

"Let's go, sucker," he said. The thought ran through Chevy's mind as he put up his fists that maybe he'd made a mistake, since, as Chevy put it later, Billy was from a tougher side of the tracks than he, and Billy liked to fight.

Billy didn't have to be asked twice, and he came at Chevy swinging. "This is my show now!" he yelled.

Belushi somehow wedged himself between them, and Brian Murray grabbed at Chevy's arms. Gilda and Laraine tried to get out of the way; Tom Schiller did nothing, since he was pinned behind the dressing room door. Both Chevy and Billy were throwing punches, most of which hit John. They were quickly pulled apart and everyone went out, shaken, to get in place for the show.

The acrid air of the fight hung over 8H as the show went on. The studio audience gave Chevy a standing ovation when he entered, but to those backstage he'd clearly been thrown off his stride. Lorne, watching on his monitor and saddened by what had occurred, whispered to no one in particular as he watched, "Chevy doesn't have it tonight."

At the end of the show, as Chevy stood onstage with the rest of the cast members waving goodnight, Billy paced back and forth behind the group with a menacing smile on his face, like a tiger pacing a cage, looking as though he might jump over them all to throttle Chevy as soon as the camera went off. Danny and John slipped back from the front of the stage to stand beside him. The show scored *Saturday Night*'s highest rating ever to that point.

CHAPTER 23

# The B Team
## (Show Notes Two)

Bill Murray's first cast photo as a member of the Not Ready
For Prime Time Players, January 1977. © *NBC*

*Saturday Night* more than made good on its vow to carry on without Chevy Chase. There was an overall broadening of the base of the show's humor after he left: those sometimes referred to on the 17th floor as the B team came on. A more eclectic style emerged, as did some very popular characters.

John and Gilda quickly came into focus as the dominant personalities. John defined "Belushi" as his main character, but also acted brilliantly in parts as diverse as Truman Capote and Humphrey Bogart. Gilda similarly projected herself—in one opening she stood at center stage to say that she didn't have much to do on the show that night, and she wanted to tell her mother not to worry about staying up to watch—while refining such roles as her lisping Barbara Walters takeoff, Baba Wawa, and her archetypical Jewish American Princess, Rhonda Weiss. Emily Litella's popularity soared when, after a protracted battle with Standards, she was able to end her commentaries on Weekend Update by responding to an annoyed Jane Curtin with a cross smile and a ladylike "Bitch."

The full force of Dan Aykroyd's talent flowered in a whole series of characters, among them that of Beldar, paterfamilias of the Coneheads, the extraterrestrial family from "France." The Coneheads made their debut in January of the second season after a long, circuitous gestation period and soon became the characters probably more identified with *Saturday Night* than any other.

The Coneheads, among the most popular characters on *Saturday Night*. © *NBC*

Danny, for reasons only he could fathom, had been musing earlier in the year about something having to do with French pinhead lawyers. He broached the idea in a writers' meeting, but Lorne didn't think it would be wise to make fun of people with deformities. At the same time, Tom Davis and Danny were in the habit of playing around with funny alien voices by hitting themselves in the throat while they talked, and they were both fans of a fifties science-fiction film called *This Island Earth*, in which the aliens had raised foreheads that nobody seemed to notice.

They combined all those elements in a sketch entitled "Blind Dates from Outer Space," about two girls in a car getting picked up by two alien swingers in a flying saucer. But director Davey Wilson said he couldn't get a car into the studio, and Buck Henry, to his everlasting regret, thought it sounded like a bad science-fiction parody and said he'd rather not do it. The idea was dropped until a couple of months later when Davis and Danny took a vacation trip to the South Seas. They were keeping a sharp eye out for flying saucers (something Danny did often, as well as watching for ghosts) and they paid a visit to the giant stone heads on Easter Island. Danny was so impressed that when they got back to New York he kept saying, reverently, "The heads, the heads."

He started making drawings, determined to pursue the idea. At an improv session with the cast, Lorne suggested putting the Coneheads into a traditional family structure, with Jane and Laraine playing Danny's wife and daughter. The first Coneheads sketch fell immediately into place.

Unlike some of *Saturday Night*'s other best-known characters, the Coneheads—Beldar, Prymaat, and Connie—were an instant hit on air. Tom Davis recalls that the first time Danny walked onstage as Beldar and took off the stocking cap he was wearing over his cone, the audience let out a collective gasp. The cones themselves were made of liquid latex that took twenty minutes to put on, which is why the Coneheads generally appeared at the beginning of the show. The latex had to be dissolved with a chemical to get the cones off, a process that could be painful.

The notion of aliens from the planet Remulak trying to fit unobtrusively into American suburban society, serving "shredded swine flesh and fried chicken embryos" for breakfast and exhorting their guests to "consume mass quantities" of beer and potato chips, was a perfect vehicle for expressing the inherent strangeness of civilized human behavior, a strangeness Dan Aykroyd seemed to perceive more acutely than most.

Another of Aykroyd's great characters, E. Buzz Miller, came out of the same trip to the South Seas with Tom Davis. E. Buzz Miller was the real name of an expatriate American they met on an island one hundred miles or so from Tahiti, a man who made his living distributing free magazines for tourists at Polynesian hotels. His publications generally had pictures of topless native women on their covers, disregarding the fact that Catholic missionaries had long since persuaded the women of the islands to wear shirts. Danny turned E. Buzz into a late-night cable TV personality who managed to find prurient interest in anything, from anthropology (like the real E. Buzz, he showed pictures of bare-breasted native women) to biology (he showed films of insects mating) to art (he chortled that the Venus de Milo was so spectacularly built nobody cared if her arms were missing). Laraine Newman soon started appearing with him as his bimbo girlfriend, Christy, possessor of the most vacuous giggle and the tightest leotards on television. It was a testament to E. Buzz Miller's taste that, when gazing upon a print of the Impressionist classic *Le déjeuner sur l'herbe*, he noted, leering as always, "This broad hasn't got a stitch on! ... Bon appetit, boys!"

Dan Aykroyd's cable TV sleaze king, E. Buzz Miller. Laraine Newman plays his bimbo girlfriend, Christie. © *NBC*

Later Danny would introduce Irwin Mainway, who he said was E. Buzz Miller's cousin. Mainway was the penultimate small-time business-man with absolutely no scruples. He always appeared on a talk show with Jane Curtin, who again played the appalled reporter, to respond to her criticisms that his products were hazardous, reprehensible rip-offs of The Public. Mainway invariably took the offensive, seeing nothing whatsoever to apologize about. He was quite proud, for example, of the Mainway line of Halloween products for kids, which included the Johnny Space Commander mask (a plastic bag and a rubber band), an Invisible Pedestrian costume (a set of black clothes), the Johnny Combat

Action costume (complete with real M-1 rifle, very popular in Detroit) and Johnny Human Torch (a bag of oily rags and a lighter).

Danny happened to be a major character in sketches that represented something of a triumph for the softer, more cerebral comedy of Tom Schiller and Marilyn Miller. One of the things Schiller had always found funniest was serious art poorly done, so he decided to create his own bad productions, among them "Bad Opera," "Bad Ballet," and "Bad Conceptual Art." Danny introduced them as Leonard Pinth-Garnell, a tuxedoed master of ceremonies who made Alistair Cooke seem positively plebeian. Schiller's "Bad" series included an opera based on the life of Anton van Leeuwenhoek, the Dutch scientist who refined the earliest microscopes, and a piece of conceptual art consisting mainly of a woman standing on a revolving disk, scratching her feet as if she were a chicken. Though never one of *Saturday Night*'s most popular recurring bits, the Bad series was certainly unusual, and always grandly produced.

Marilyn Miller wasn't especially prolific, and her pieces were usually severely edited because she wrote too long. But the territory she staked out for herself was universally admired within the show. Danny made a point of coming to her office one day to tell her, "I really respect what you're doing; I really like it," implying, Miller says, that he wanted to be included in one of her sketches. The result was called "The Lunch Counter Reunion," undoubtedly one of the best sketches the show ever presented.

In it, a former high-school cheerleader, played by Jane Curtin, ran into the perennial loser, played by Aykroyd, who'd always admired her from afar. The sketch picked up in mid-conversation as they sat beside each other at the luncheonette in Woolworth's, both smoking cigarettes and drinking coffee. Danny's character was clearly excited, Jane's clearly embarrassed.

DANNY:     … every time your underpants showed when you did a cartwheel, I mean, I know they matched your cheerleading skirt and all that, but you must have been embarrassed from time to time. Hah! Maybe you sorta liked it, yeah, you sorta liked it, I guess that's it, you sorta liked it. That's something, ya know—after ten whole years, finding out the captain of the high-school cheerleading team really liked her underpants showing! Heh-heh.

JANE:     They were supposed to show. They matched the outfit. They were supposed to show. Okay?

DANNY:     Well, okay, okay, Patty Rivers!

JANE:     I wish you wouldn't say my name so much.

DANNY: Well, I like saying it. It reminds me I'm talking to you! I, Ralph Bort, "B. O. Bort," talking to you, Patty Rivers! And to think in high school, I was scared of you—you know I was scared of you! But now we're just regular people, just adults, just you and me, here! Huh, huh. You still don't remember me, do ya? Hu-hu-hu-huh. Here's a hint! (Covers mouth as if speaking through a microphone) Testing, one, two, three. Testing, one, two, three.

JANE: I give up.

DANNY: Captain of the audiovisual squad! Seven guys who really gave a damn if the mikes had feedback in the gym and in the auditorium.

JANE: Really.

DANNY: We were the backbone of those pep rallies. You were the underpants! Heh-heh!
(Jane tries at this point to leave, but Danny insists they talk over old times—"We didn't have any old times," Jane replies—and goes on to say that, after a stint in Vietnam, he's now managing the tire department at Sears. He also claims proudly to have been the one who first started using the phrase "would you believe ..." in their high school. He prods her into telling him that she went on to college, got married and then divorced, and he says his mother sent him a newspaper clipping about her divorce while he was in "Nam.")

DANNY: (After noting that they both smoke menthol cigarettes) Isn't that something! Who ever thought we were gonna grow up like this, and I'd be sitting next to you, and you smoking cigarettes, it's amazing, it's just amazing! What kind of car you drive? I got a Chevy Nova, you know. A tachometer, I got rally stripes, baby moon, I got CB radio, tape deck, I got all of that in there. I got factory air conditioning, too, ya know. I wouldn't take it without the air. What kind of car do you drive?

JANE: Toyota.

DANNY: Ahh. You worry about pollution, huh?
(Danny claims that he worries, or at least thinks, about pollution, too. Jane gets up to leave and Danny tries to ask her out.)

DANNY: Isn't this something, though! Both of us are adults, both of us adults, here, equals! It's not like high school. In high school there were all those levels, you know, groups, some people were nothing, ya know, some people were something, right up to the big shots! But in life, it all evens out! We're adults, we both lived, done things, ya know! You've lived, I've lived, ya know, like you were married, divorced, I was in Nam, and here you are smoking cigarettes, ya know, you in high school with your underpants showing, me watching. Things are different, things are really different now! I could even ask you out now couldn't I?

JANE:     (After a pause) No.

Another of Miller's more or less exclusive provinces were the elaborate musical production numbers that every so often appeared on the show. Miller, like most of the women on *Saturday Night*, was on an eternal diet, so it was a blow when the government announced its plans to ban saccharin from the marketplace. She immediately wrote up lyrics for a loving tribute called "Goodbye Saccharin." "They say you gave rats cancer," one verse went, "And I say that can't be true/Because you're just so very sweet/That's something you'd never do." It was sung by Gilda's Rhonda Weiss with the Rhondettes—Jane, Laraine, and a friend of the show who was similarly concerned with her waistline, Linda Ronstadt.

Michael O'Donoghue appeared on air more often in the second season than he had before or would after, developing his performing persona as the evil Mr. Mike. He was most notorious for his impressions of various personalities having long steel needles plunged into their eyes, a bit he'd been doing since his *Lampoon* days. He gradually expanded it on *Saturday Night* until eventually he had the entire Mormon Tabernacle Choir writhing around the stage in agony.

O'Donoghue also developed "Mr. Mike's Least-Loved Bedtime Tales," which were usually revisionist versions of popular children's nursery stories. In one, he retold the story of Brer Rabbit to Uncle Remus (Garrett). In Mr. Mike's version, the Tar Baby was used to fill a pothole, and Brer Bear and Brer Fox took Brer Rabbit up on his suggestion and, instead of throwing him into the briar patch, skinned him alive.

"Oh, dat's jus' terrible, Mr. Mike!" Uncle Remus cried. "An' den what happen?"

"He died and they ate him," Mr. Mike said. "Dey ate Brer Rabbit? Oh, Lawdy!"

"Yeah, and sold his feet for lucky charms. The end."

"'De end?' But, but, Mr. Mike, what am de moral of your fable?" "There's no moral, Uncle Remus, just random acts of meaningless violence."

After a few of these bedtime tales, Lorne began to talk about toning down O'Donoghue's presence on the show. "I'm not sure America is ready yet for Mr. Mike," he said.

About halfway through the second season, *Saturday Night* went on an exhilarating streak of hot shows, a period when the growing strength people were feeling behind the scenes was distinctly in evidence on-air, and a period when the show arguably reached its most consistent creative peak.

One of the best shows of this period starred an improbable host, consumer activist Ralph Nader. The show opened with an exuberant Nader sweeping into the lobby of 30 Rock wearing a flashy cowboy outfit, a scarf around his neck, and a ten-gallon hat on his head. "This is my first experience in show business," he said, "and I'm just gonna cut loose!"

And that's pretty much what he did. He appeared in several sketches that poked fun at his serious, drab image—in one he was caught conducting a product-reliability test on inflatable female "party dolls"—while managing to stick quite a few barbs in the side of the corporate establishment as well. In his opening monologue he started talking about his ongoing investigation of NBC's parent company, RCA, but the picture went out and a notice came on the screen saying that the network was experiencing temporary technical difficulties. During Weekend Update he played the chairman of a giant oil company called Texxon, explaining his company's requirements for the development of solar energy: Texxon should own the sun, there should be a Solar Depletion Allowance since the sun depreciates over time, and Texxon must retain the right to raise prices in the event of a solar eclipse.

The Nader show was also notable for the first appearances of both the Coneheads and Bill Murray. Billy had an especially funny moment playing a hyper movie director working on a dress rehearsal for an execution. (The electric chair was a "Mainway Fry King.") He was having trouble getting the condemned convict (played by Tom Schiller) to emote convincingly.

"You're going to fry!" Billy told him. "Will you let us see what *that feels* like?"

At the end of the sketch, when the switch was pulled, the cue- card man held up a card that read: AAARGHHH!

# CHAPTER 24

# Prime Time

As *Saturday Night* gathered momentum and it became apparent that more stars were emerging from the show, the mantle of Boy Wonder wrapped itself ever more securely around Lorne's shoulders, and NBC started thinking, as networks always do, of other arenas in which he might duplicate his success.

One idea was to turn responsibility for all late-night programming over to him. Lorne liked that idea, and some NBC executives say he was lobbying for it. A stumbling block was Johnny Carson, who, according to those same NBC executives, didn't care for the thought of Lorne's gaining more power over their mutual turf, even though the *Tonight Show* would not have been under Lorne's purview.

NBC had also toyed with the idea of moving *Saturday Night* to prime time. There had been talk of putting the show on at ten o'clock on Friday nights, or of giving Lorne money to develop prime-time programs. It was a long shot, the programmers knew, but, my God, what if the cultish excitement the show was generating in late night somehow caught fire in the big leagues?

Lorne wasn't interested in those offers. He didn't like the idea of being lost in a blur of sitcoms and cop shows, and he didn't think *Saturday Night*'s sensibility would transfer to prime time. The audience there wouldn't appreciate the show's humor, he said, even if the network's censors let its humor on intact, which was doubtful. Lorne told NBC's Aaron Cohen that prime time was a wasteland not worth saving. Lorne changed his mind, though, when he thought of taking *Saturday Night* to Mardi Gras.

Lorne had been to New Orleans before with his friend and aide- de-camp, John Head, who was an aficionado of the city. They were sitting around the office in January, halfway through the second season, and New York was looking straight into the teeth of a cold, snowy, dreary winter. Lorne thought the staff could use a shot of excitement, a change of pace, and *Saturday Night* had a two-week break coming up that conveniently coincided with Mardi Gras. Lorne's eyes lit up. "Let's go get steeped in it!" he said.

Lorne took his brainstorm to Paul Klein, NBC's head of programming. *Saturday Night*, Lorne told Klein, would originate live, in prime time, from Mardi Gras—from right in the bloody heart of it. It was a combination that couldn't miss.

As it happened, Klein had an urgent problem on a Sunday night in the upcoming February sweep period. He'd planned to air a special celebrating Jerry Lewis's Broadway debut in a revival of the musical-comedy revue *Hellzapoppin*. But disaster overtook *Hellzapoppin* during its previews in Boston—Lewis had ended up feuding with his co-star, Lynn Redgrave, and the production folded. When Lorne walked into Klein's office, Klein was staring at a ninety-minute hole in his schedule in the most important ratings month of the year. He bought Lorne's Mardi Gras idea in about five minutes.

Lorne had about a month to set up the show. As soon as director Dave Wilson heard the idea, he, among others, told Lorne he was crazy even to attempt it. Wilson had once done a *Kraft Music Hall* special with Perry Como from the Mardi Gras, and he'd seen drunks urinating off balconies into the crowds below, cars driven up on sidewalks, and people throwing up in streets that were covered with beer cans and broken glass. New Orleans during Mardi Gras, Wilson told Lorne, was a zoo, and a dangerous zoo at that.

Lorne said he wasn't worried. The staff was excited. Some of the cast members took seriously the fact that this would be the show's prime-time debut, but for most that was a decidedly secondary consideration. The main thing was to get out of New York for a couple of midwinter weeks to go party in the French Quarter.

Lorne asked NBC's Dan Sullivan, a production-facilities expert, to be the show's advance man in New Orleans. Sullivan knew that setting up a live ninety-minute show in New Orleans so close to Mardi Gras would be a perilous operation at best. Finding enough hotel space alone would be a monumental task. When he arrived in town he went directly to the office of the mayor, Moon Landrieu, and asked for an immediate audience. "I have," he told the mayor's secretary, "no time to waste."

Moon thought it sounded like a great idea. New Orleans had always felt that its annual festival was underappreciated by the national media. The mayor, Dan Sullivan says, jumped at the opportunity to rectify that lack of coverage, especially since the city had recently completed a beautification project along its waterfront. There was a new Theatre of the Performing Arts within a new complex called the Louis Armstrong Park that Moon wouldn't mind showing off.

So Moon Landrieu welcomed *Saturday Night* with open arms. He placed the city's travel bureau, the police department, and one of his chief personal aides at *Saturday Night*'s disposal. When Lorne arrived, he, too, had an audience with the mayor, and again the mayor offered his assurances that anything the city could do, it would. Moon Landrieu was as confident as Lorne had been that the show could be pulled off. But by then even Lorne was beginning to have his doubts.

One of the things Lorne hadn't adequately taken into account was the degree to which the spirit of Mardi Gras overtakes New Orleans each year. It is in essence a weeklong, citywide bacchanal when a very Southern sense of celebration invades the most sober of souls. Few in New Orleans take anything too seriously during Mardi Gras except Mardi Gras itself. Even police officers have been known to cruise the streets in the middle of Mardi Gras wearing pig masks, blasting Dr. John music over the loudspeakers of their patrol cars. So it was that throughout *Saturday Night*'s preparations, the answer to the show's every request was an immediate "No problem." After that it was anybody's guess whether something would actually be done.

The first people from the show to discover this were the thirty or so members of the production team who arrived early to start setting up. Lorne had decided that the show would have two central locations. One would be the Theatre of Performing Arts, where musical guest Randy Newman would hold forth in concert, the other a reviewing stand in the heart of the French Quarter, from which Jane Curtin and Buck Henry would cover the Bacchus Parade, one of the central events of the festival. Sketches featuring the other players and guest stars Eric Idle, Penny Marshall and Cindy Williams (the stars of *Laverne & Shirley*), and Henry Winkler (the Fonz on *Happy Days* and Bacchus of the Bacchus Parade that year) would originate from half a dozen or so other locations scattered around the French Quarter.

Setting all those locations up for a live network telecast meant stringing lights, building camera stands, moving trailers, finding power supplies, laying miles of cable, and taking care of a thousand other complicated tasks within the winding maze of the French Quarter's streets, which each day grew more clogged with thousands of tourists, students, hucksters, bikers, drag queens, and other assorted merrymakers gearing themselves up for Mardi Gras. It was a little like trying to choreograph a ballet in the middle of Times Square on New Year's Eve.

The cast and writers started arriving the week before the show and immediately set out to have the time of their lives. Dan Sullivan had somehow managed to get rooms in the French Quarter for almost everyone, though some would have to change hotels several times during the week. The rooms, many of them, were the picture of Louisiana elegance: ceilings fourteen feet high, doors nearly that tall, canopied beds with red velvet bedspreads, Louis XIV furniture, ceiling fans, sunken bathtubs, fireplaces, and latticed windows opening on terraces overlooking cobblestone streets.

Unlike the production staff, the writers and performers had plenty of time to sample the delights of New Orleans, and they were welcomed as visiting royalty by much of the city. The New Orleans media pulled out all stops for the show, and all week there were interviews to give and promotional events to attend. One of these was a "sign in" at a shopping mall where the cast members autographed any object presented to them by fans. Among the items passed forward to be signed were a toilet seat, a car door, a pair of panties, and a baby's bottom.

Anything connected to *Saturday Night* became a major attraction, especially the cast members, who were so mobbed the writers had to run interference for them, jabbing people in the ribs to let them through. The scale and fanaticism of the fan worship was a revelation to the people on the show. After being holed up so long on the 17th floor in New York, this was one of the first times they'd been exposed, en masse, to all those people "out there" who'd been watching them for more than a year. It was, to some, more than a little scary; others immersed themselves in it.

There was a constant stream of parties in their honor and wild nights on the town, and some didn't sleep for days at a time. The brewers of Dixie beer sent over a station wagon filled with their product; it was quickly emptied. Friendly locals were also happy to score a gram or two of coke for whoever wanted it. Swarms of Southern belles gathered round, chasing and being chased. The whole extravaganza nearly came to a crashing halt late one night when a car full of people from the show, including Belushi, Aykroyd, Laraine Newman, Anne Beatts, Rosie Shuster, and John Head, were coming back from a reggae club, most of them in various stages of intoxication from substances both legal and illegal, some still carrying contraband. Laughing almost too hard to notice, they found themselves driving the wrong way down a one-way street, staring into the headlights of a couple of police cars coming straight at them. Visions of arrests, headlines, and jail went through the minds of everyone in the car, but the cops just laughed and waved.

*Saturday Night*'s Bully Boys were especially in their element in New Orleans. A sketch was written featuring The Bees as a motorcycle gang specifically so the boys would have an excuse to rent huge Harley-Davidson motorcycles with NBC's money. It was a terrible sketch, but the bikes were great, the perfect vehicles for weaving in and out of the crowds on Bourbon Street at two in the morning. Belushi would sweep into bars filled with bikers, starting instant parties wherever he went, everyone buying him drinks and giving him T-shirts and rides on their choppers. All night long he and Danny careened around the French Quarter.

While the men roamed the streets, the women were left to fend for themselves. Many of them stayed in their rooms and took long baths rather than risk being mauled on streets crawling with drunken men and rabid *Saturday Night* fans. Gilda Radner started wearing a mask when she left her hotel. Gilda also had her hands full comforting Alan Zweibel, who was decompressing after a traumatic breakup with his longtime girlfriend. Zweibel spent the week dosed up on the mood stabilizer lithium, as did Tom Schiller, who was undergoing his own emotional turmoil. Marilyn Miller was a wreck too; she fell ill with a 104° temperature and spent most of her time in her room, which abutted Dick Ebersol's. Ebersol had flown in from Los Angeles to help coordinate the production details, but he spent most of his time in his room, trying to track down his wife on the telephone.

(Ebersol's wife was the beautiful co-host on the NBC game show *Wheel of Fortune*. They'd known each other for only a few weeks before they were married in a bizarre beachfront ceremony in Malibu, California, the previous July. Lorne, Belushi, Chevy, Zweibel, Gary Weis, and Herb Sargent had been among the guests. Ebersol and his bride said their vows while standing barefoot in the surf next to a cross of white carnations. During the ceremony, Louise Lasser, another guest, started mumbling something and the preacher reprimanded her by saying, "The only celebrity at this wedding is Jesus Christ, our Lord." When the bride and groom said "I do," Chevy dashed forward, picked the bride up in his arms and threw her in the ocean. Ebersol and the *Wheel of Fortune* girl separated soon after the New Orleans show and later divorced.)

Not a lot of work got done during the week. To the writers, coming up with sketches seemed like burdensome homework, especially since they had to tailor their pieces to fit the locations Lorne had chosen. Lorne was having a hard time pulling people together, and although on the surface he exuded confidence, as the week went on those who knew him well say they had never seen him more nervous.

There was a daylight run-through of the show Sunday afternoon. The cast members stood for hours waiting to rehearse, surrounded by milling, shouting crowds. Several of the fifteen cameras went out, as did communication between some of the locations and the central control van outside the Theatre of Performing Arts. The police presence was uncomfortably scarce and the actors had to fight their way through the streets to get from one set to another. Lorne's chief production assistant, Audrey Dickman, couldn't begin to get an accurate timing of the sketches, which meant that in a few hours they would be going on with a ninety-minute prime-time special that would essentially have to be structured as it unfolded live on air. Lorne was counting on the Bacchus Parade to save them. If all else fails, he kept saying, we can cut to the parade.

The rowdiness of the crowds built steadily as the sun set and show time neared. Costume designers Franne Lee and Karen Roston had set up dressing areas in Al Hirt's club on Bourbon Street, but so many people were peering in to watch that Roston finally had to spray the windows with Lemon Pledge so the cast could change.

There were no such luxuries at the other locations: The wardrobe trucks simply drove around dumping off piles of costumes at each one. Two thousand revelers poured into the Theatre of Performing Arts like water through a dam when the doors were unlocked, shouting and drinking and dancing in the aisles. The woman in charge of tickets said there might have been some sane people among them, but not many.

At every location huge throngs gathered, waiting for something to happen. Whenever the show's spotlights went on they went wild. Michael O'Donoghue climbed a ladder to take his place on a balcony overlooking Jackson Square, a central intersection in the French Quarter. From there he was to lead the assembled multitudes below in the Antler Dance, a silly step he'd created that he hoped would become a national craze. O'Donoghue discovered on the balcony that he'd become a natural target for those carefree individuals in the crowd who felt like throwing empty beer cans, Jack Daniel's bottles or other debris. His slightest gesture seemed to provoke a new deluge, so when he had to move, he did so in slow motion, and each time he lifted an arm or took a step, he watched, terrified, as a wave of reaction rippled out across the crowd.

* * *

The show was to open with Dan Aykroyd as Jimmy Carter sitting on the statue of Andrew Jackson in the center of Jackson Square. Actually, he was sitting on the rump of Jackson's horse. Ten minutes before air, the remote van at the site lost power, and there were a few panic-stricken moments before it was restored. Sitting in the central control van near the Theatre of Performing Arts with Lorne, Audrey Dickman confessed she was frightened.

"You're frightened?" Lorne said. "I just went outside and threw up."
He wasn't kidding.

At about the same time, somebody called to say that John Belushi
had locked himself in his hotel room, having decided after forty-eight
hours of nonstop partying that, even though he had more to do than
anyone else on the show, his roles weren't adequate for his prime-time
debut. Aaron Cohen was sent to get him. Cohen stood outside John's
room, pleading with him through the door.

"John, you have to do the show!" Cohen cried, shouting to make
himself heard. "Everyone's counting on you!"

"They wrote me out of the show!" Belushi screamed back. "I'm not
coming—I've got nothing to do!"

Finally John relented and opened the door. He and Cohen sprinted
several blocks to his first location. The strongest image several people
have of the show that night is of Belushi roaring through the streets
between locations, standing like a general on the back of a three-wheeled
police scooter, holding onto the roof, the siren wailing, the crowds parting and immediately closing behind him as he passed, as if he were
being swallowed.

After Danny's opening, Lorne cut to Randy Newman in the concert
hall. Newman, accompanied by an orchestra, sang the title track from
his new album, *Louisiana*. Aaron Cohen had done everything he could
to dissuade Lorne from putting Newman on at the top of the show, arguing that Newman was a nonentity to most of America. Though that was
probably true, as it turned out Randy Newman got a lot more air time
that night than even Lorne had planned—four numbers—because the
Theatre of Performing Arts proved to be the only location that could be
counted on to come up on camera when it was supposed to come up,
showing what it was supposed to be showing.

Everything seemed subsumed by chaos. Penny Marshall and Cindy
Williams were supposed to report on a huge drag-queen ball called the
Mystick Krewe of Apollo. Gary Weis, who was directing the segment, had
lost communication with Lorne, and when the camera cut to Penny Marshall,
she was sitting by herself, gazing vacantly around her. Somebody yelled
at Weis, "You're on! You're on!" and he waved frantically at Marshall.
"Now?" she said. Even then Marshall seemed completely undone, staring
at the camera in an apparent state of shock. She later explained to Michael
O'Donoghue that it hadn't been the glittering drag queens that caused her
to lose her composure, but rather what had happened on the way to the ball
from another location. Ill and exhausted from lack of sleep, she'd jumped
on a motorcycle, assuming it was one of those assigned to the show. After
being driven a few blocks through the streets, the driver, who had no

connection whatsoever to *Saturday Night*, asked her where she wanted to go. She had to explain that she was an actress and could he take her to the Apollo Ball. No problem, he said, and drove over crowded sidewalks through much of the French quarter to get there.

Buck Henry and Jane Curtin, meanwhile, were sitting atop their reviewing platform in the middle of the French Quarter, waiting for the Bacchus parade. The exact routing and timing of the parade had been the subject of many hours of discussion between Lorne and the police department during the week, and they had continually assured him that it would arrive at Buck and Jane's location no later than forty-five minutes into the show. But by mid-show there was still no parade, and no indication its arrival was imminent. Every ten minutes or so, usually when something else went wrong, Lorne would cut back to Buck and Jane. Having no parade to cover, they filled time with jokes written by Herb Sargent and Alan Zweibel, who were standing just off-camera, scribbling one-liners. In the control booth people were trying to contact the police, screaming what would become the most repeated question of the night: "Where's the fucking parade!"

The crowd surrounding the reviewing stand, several thousand strong, was growing more unruly by the minute, unhappy at the delay, which many assumed was the fault of *Saturday Night*. They took out much of their frustration on Buck and Jane, who presented convenient targets for cans, coins, beads, bracelets, and other souvenirs. Men were shouting "Take your shirt off!" to Jane, since on the previous show she'd done her blouse-ripping bit on Weekend Update. Buck and Jane sat as calmly as possible and avoided making eye contact with the crowd, because every time they did it seemed to provoke even more abuse. They pretended to be having a civilized conversation. In truth, they feared for their lives.

The police department had promised a contingent of four or five officers to guard the reviewing stand, but only one cop had shown up, and a rather elderly cop at that. As the delay continued, some of the more drunken members of the crowd started forming human pyramids in attempts to scale the platform to get to Buck and Jane. Dan Sullivan and the cop stood on the lower level of the scaffold, which was none too steady in the first place, literally pushing people away with their feet, trying to be as friendly and polite about it as possible. Alan Zweibel kept calling Lorne in the control booth, shouting, "The parade's not here! The parade's not here!" and Lorne was shouting back, "I know it isn't!"

At another location, Mayor Moon Landrieu was shown making a presentation to New Orleans native son Garrett Morris. They stood facing each other as Landrieu was making his speech, and between them, about thirty feet in the background, a member of the crowd could be seen passing by. He noticed the camera, took a quick turn, and started walking directly toward it. He came closer and closer until he was just a few feet away, at which point an arm reached out from off-camera and grabbed him. He abruptly disappeared from view. Moon Landrieu never noticed.

Gilda Radner was not so lucky. She was standing just off Jackson Square, dressed as Emily Litella, talking to a riverboat pilot about "the liverboats" of the Mississippi. As soon as she said "Never mind" and smiled at the camera, Lorne cut to another scene. Suddenly Gilda was attacked, buried beneath a group of three or four drunken revelers who were pawing her in a manner known as a "group grope"—one even stuck his head under her dress. Stage manager Joe Dicso and a policeman waded in swinging, pulling the attackers off. In the control trailer people watched in horror as the scene played out on the monitor in front of them. Many from the show would later wonder how a sweet little old lady like Emily Litella could provoke such sexual frenzy. "That's Mardi Gras" was the best they could come up with.

The parade never did arrive, at least while the show was on the air. There were numerous explanations offered later, among them that there had been a fatal accident along the parade route. Finally, in the closing seconds of the show, Jane Curtin turned to Buck Henry and said, "Shall we tell them, Buck? The parade has not been delayed: The parade never existed!"

"That's right, Jane," Buck said. "Mardi Gras is just a French word meaning 'no parade'!"

There was a cast party afterward at Antoine's, a famous New Orleans restaurant. It was a dispirited affair, though everyone was vastly relieved they had gotten through the ninety minutes without serious injury. Garrett Morris was so upset he was threatening to quit the show: The one sketch in which he was prominently featured had been cut, ruining his homecoming. Lorne gave some post-show interviews to local reporters in which he tried to be cheerful, but at the party he was obviously unhappy about the way things had gone. Dan Sullivan, Leo Yoshimura and most of the other members of the production team were still out in the streets, breaking down sets and packing up equipment. Sullivan saw the parade finally come through, preceded by a phalanx of police officers swinging billy clubs to get the crowd out of the way.

The ratings for the Mardi Gras special were about as bad as they could have been, a 21 share. *Saturday Night* was obliterated by a made-for-TV movie on ABC about a nymphomaniac housewife.

The show's budget was supposed to have been $750,000, but the unit manager came back from New Orleans saying the cost would be at least $100,000 more than that. That estimate proved to be conservative. Bills kept trickling in for the next several months— "forever," it seemed to program chief Paul Klein—and the eventual cost was closer to $1 million. Klein says the NBC hierarchy was so upset over the Mardi Gras debacle it nearly cost him his job.

New Orleans ended any talk of putting Lorne Michaels in charge of NBC's late-night division. It also ended any talk of putting *Saturday Night* into prime time. But the saddest result to many of those on the show was that it ruined any chance of taking *Saturday Night* on the road to even more glamorous locales. Some had been thinking of Paris, others of Barbados.

For Lorne, it was the end of a dream. NBC had recently won rights to broadcast the 1980 Olympic Games from Moscow (games the United States would eventually boycott). Ever since NBC had signed the deal, Lorne had been excited about the idea of doing the show from Red Square, just outside the Kremlin walls. They'd have to go on at seven-thirty in the morning, of course, but he could almost hear the opening: "Live, from Moscow, it's *Saturday Night*!"

# CHAPTER 25

# Black Friday

*Saturday Night* in its third season finally inched over the 30-share ratings threshold on a regular basis, moving for the first time beyond its cult following to true TV stardom. The atmosphere within the show started to turn at about the same time.

Much of it was fatigue, the cumulative effects of three years of too many eighteen-hour days and too many six-day weeks. The toll was etched on people's faces at the end of the monthly three-show run. It became a truism on *Saturday Night* that the last show in the cycle was always the loosest, and sometimes the best, because by then they were running on pure, lunatic adrenaline. More of them kept themselves running on cocaine as well, and the drug's jittery effects had a growing influence on the show.

The production schedule began to lag behind. Few of the writers got anything done on Monday anymore. Intensive writing wouldn't start until after dinner on Tuesday, about 10:00 p.m., and by the Wednesday afternoon read-through a lot of the material was still in ragged, often wretched shape. For the first time there were read- throughs when no one laughed, for the first time people were glancing at each other, wondering how they were going to make a show out of the material they were hearing, and as the week went on bigger holes in the show remained unfilled.

The delays in the writing set up a chain reaction of further delays, and more tension. Sometimes Lorne wouldn't sit down with Dave Wilson, Eugene Lee, Franne Lee, and Leo Yoshimura to format the show and discuss sets and costumes until well after midnight Wednesday. The production staff fumed as they waited outside Lorne's office all day, playing Ping-Pong, getting stoned, drinking coffee, sending out for Chinese food. Eugene Lee kept himself busy designing his boat, but eventually he'd get so angry he'd yell "It's inhuman!" and storm out.

The writers made it worse by getting into the habit of writing longer, more elaborate sketches that were that much harder to produce. Eugene and Franne Lee and their assistants, who felt that in many cases the writers were covering up weak material with fancy window dressing, turned out some of their finest work on those sketches, but they paid a growing physical and psychological price doing so. Lorne often berated the writers about the long sketches. "What the fuck is wrong with you people?" he'd say. "You wrote lots of little things the first and second years, now everything is ten minutes long." They kept coming in anyway. The largest set *Saturday Night* ever built was for a fifteen-minute piece called "The Raging Queen," a parody of old pirate movies in which all the swashbucklers also swished. It required building nothing less than a pirate ship, and the sketch was finished and approved so late in the week that the set didn't arrive in 8H until eleven-thirty Friday night. Assembling it took hours, and as the stagehands put it together, Davey Wilson was blocking the sketch with the cast.

At about this time Lorne's proclivity for postponing any decision as long as possible began to approach epic proportions. There were more delays and more tension as people waited for him to decide if a sketch would be in or out of the show, which host to book, or any of a thousand other details that demanded his attention. It was especially hard for him to tell anybody no, with the result that he kept stringing people along without an answer for weeks. Al Franken was one who would simply go into Lorne's office and force him to make a decision. "Come on, Lorne," he'd say, "you gotta do something about this." But most didn't have Franken's nerve, and so they waited, interminably, for Lorne to make up his mind.

As the person with the most responsibilities on his shoulders and the most decisions to make, the strain and the exhaustion hit Lorne especially hard. During one of the show's breaks, supposedly a week off, Lorne averaged between twenty-five and thirty calls a day. It was in the third season that he made the first of what would become periodic statements to the press that his return for another season was questionable because he was so burned out.

Already, Lorne was involving himself less and less in the details of production. In the first two seasons, he'd supervised almost every sketch, but by the third he was spending much of his time in his office on the ninth floor, often with the curtains drawn. If he looked out and saw something he didn't like, instead of going down to the set to take care of it himself, he'd usually call Audrey Dickman, who would relay his instructions to Dave Wilson, who in turn would relay them to the

cast. Lorne didn't feel he needed to be as closely involved with the production because he was letting the writers take more responsibility for
producing their own pieces. His willingness to let the writers mature in
that way was commendable, the writers thought, but those who watched
production falling further behind every minute, like Eugene and Franne
Lee and Dave Wilson, tended to feel the writers weren't pulling it off.

Lorne was also shying away from the studio more because he was
enjoying dealing with the cast members less. Some of them were developing a propensity to behave like the stars they had become, languishing
in their dressing rooms longer, showing up in the studio later, bitching more about the quality of the writing and the size of their roles.
Belushi was the most frequent offender. Dave Wilson developed the theory that John should be given only one exit in any scene because once
he'd left the stage during blocking he wouldn't come back. Lorne didn't
like playing disciplinarian, and he started leaving it to Davey or Audrey
Dickman to keep the cast in line. It wasn't a task Audrey or Davey particularly cared for. On many Fridays, as the delays dragged on, people in
the studio could look up and see Davey's figure silhouetted on the drawn
curtains of Lorne's office, his arms waving wildly as he ranted about
how impossible the schedule and the stars had become.

* * *

Sitting and listening as people ranted consumed a growing proportion of
Lorne's waking hours in the third season, and more than anything else, the
ranting sapped his spirit, and the spirit of the show. As *Saturday Night*'s
success spiraled ever upward—and there would never be a pause, never a
resting place in that ascension, no matter how tired people became—the
pressure and the competition within grew proportionately. The writers
and performers learned that the key to sharing in the show's success was
exposure—airtime— and they learned that to get it, they had to fight for
it. Much of the all for one, one for all sense of mission of earlier times
gave way to politics and manipulation, and sometimes to open war.

The Wednesday read-throughs began to resemble auditions, so
intense was the competition to get pieces accepted for the show, and thus
they too ran ever longer. Writers learned to cultivate the performers before
read-through started, coaching them on readings and soliciting their support. Those whose pieces flopped in read- through didn't suffer quietly,
and comments such as "Oh, everybody's just in a bad mood today—it's
funny!" became commonplace. Often if a piece was turned down the
writers and performers involved would soon be in Lorne's office, lobbying him to let it on. Knowing when to approach Lorne to appeal a

decision became an art form. One of the women writers claims some of the men watched to see when he was walking to the bathroom, knowing they could corner him there. If he had a magazine in hand, all the better.

If all else failed, there was always pure stubbornness to fall back on. Some of the writers kept submitting the same pieces in read-throughs over and over again, hoping to wear down the resistance. So vehemently did writers argue against changes in their scripts and performers against reductions in their lines that for Lorne editing turned into "bloodletting." Even in the meetings between dress and air, the stoic acceptance of troops going into battle turned more often into what one production assistant called "major sulking" over Lorne's decisions, and sometimes into major arguments as well. Many times Lorne would ask that a piece be trimmed and the writer would simply refuse. Lorne, exasperated, would turn to the others in the room and say, in a tone of disbelief, "I don't have any control anymore. I have no control over this whatsoever."

More and more the makeup of the show was affected by the techniques the writers learned to get their pieces on. The long, grand sketches that caused the production staff such heartaches were effective strategically for several reasons. If Lorne put such a piece in production, it represented a significant commitment of time, studio space, and money, and therefore it was less likely to be cut. The longer sketches were also less likely to be cut because Lorne couldn't afford to lose so much time in the show. Many of these monster pieces were of a genre known on the 17th floor as "garbage pail" sketches, so called because every member of the cast got thrown in somehow, if possible doing one of their favorite characters. That had the advantage of enlisting more cast members in the campaign to get those sketches on the air. The writers knew that the sketches most likely to get on were those featuring the biggest stars on the show, Belushi and Radner. They were, one writer said, "the meat and potatoes." But writing in a part for Laraine or Garrett sometimes worked too, since they were usually light in the show and Lorne wanted to give them more to do. As much as he complained about the length of the sketches people were writing, in fact, many times Lorne would read a shorter sketch and say, "That's good. Now add Laraine and Garrett to it."

The surest route to stardom for writers and performers alike was establishing recurring characters like the Coneheads or Roseanne Roseannadanna, and it was the repetition of those recurring bits that became one of the most divisive issues on the show.

The contradiction between taking risks and being popular was built into *Saturday Night* from the beginning. Lorne had said when he was first interviewing people for the show that establishing popular, repeatable characters was one of his goals. And well it might have been, since the whole history of television comedy, from Lucy to Archie Bunker, argues that the popular, familiar character is fundamental to success. But *Saturday Night* was also founded on the notion that repetition and habit stifle true creativity, true originality. Lorne often said that the show would never become what he called *Laugh-In Junior*—a static collection of safe and predictable bits. Lorne and many of the others on the show, O'Donoghue among them, paid far more than the usual lip service to their commitment to daring: It was a key element of their philosophy, and they really did believe it. In one early interview, Lorne derided network executives who do nothing but repeat what has worked in the past. "Uniformity of product is an enormously important thing when you're a businessman," he said. "For an artist it's anathema. I'm an artist- businessman."

Lorne never entirely sacrificed his commitment to art, not by any means, but it seemed to many on *Saturday Night* that his businessman side won out more often than not. From the second week, the show repeated bits, from Chevy's Weekend Updates and Falls of the Week to The Bees, the Samurai Warrior, and the "Live from New York, it's *Saturday Night!*" opening. Such repetition seemed an acceptable concession to the requirements of hooking in an audience while the show was establishing itself, and certainly all the catchphrases and recurring characters *Saturday Night* came up with in its first season were a major factor in the show's success. But after the show was a success, the repetition only increased, and the accusations both within the show and without that *Saturday Night* was trading in its sense of adventure and pandering to its audience carried more sting, because they were closer to the truth.

Lorne was sensitive to those complaints. At the beginning of the third season, he went so far as to say to the staff and in interviews that there would be no more repetition of such favorites as the Coneheads and Gilda's Baba Wawa. The Coneheads, in fact, had purposely been gotten rid of in their last sketch in the second season by sending them back (via a rocket-propelled Chrysler Building) to their home planet, Remulak. But Lorne backed off from those claims in other interviews a few weeks later, and indeed, both the Coneheads and Baba Wawa did return.

For despite his public statements, internally Lorne as much as anyone was in favor of repetition. Many of the repeats were "ordered up," as O'Donoghue put it, at Lorne's behest. The temptation to repeat familiar bits grew as there were more familiar bits to repeat and as fatigue made it harder to come up with something fresh. They were easier to write, and easier to produce, since they used the same costumes and sets. They were also useful in filling those holes that kept cropping up in the show: Lorne could count on a popular character to deliver, O'Donoghue said, "a guaranteed passing grade."

The most overdone character on *Saturday Night,* and not coincidentally one of the most loved by the public, was undoubtedly Gilda and
Zweibel's Roseanne Roseannadanna. Roseanne appeared on Weekend
Update week after week after week, and her appearances invariably followed the same routine: Mr. Richard Feder of Fort Lee, New Jersey,
wrote in with a long list of questions; Roseanne would begin to address
them and quickly digress into some long, totally unrelated story, inevitably focusing in the end on some grotesquerie—the toenail she found in
her hamburger, or her efforts to get a piece of sparerib out of her teeth.
Within the show, Roseanne became one of the most despised characters
ever, and some writers begged she be put to sleep, shot, or otherwise disposed of. But Lorne kept asking Gilda and Zweibel for more Roseannes.
Gilda was at first hurt by the writers' enmity toward Roseanne (as she
had been hurt earlier by a similar enmity toward Emily Litella), but after
a while she too wanted to give her a rest, and eventually she fought
bitterly against doing more. Writing another Roseanne, Zweibel says,
turned into "a bloodbath" between him and Gilda.

Most overdone, most loved: Gilda's Roseanne Roseannadanna
stuns Update anchor Jane Curtin yet again. © *NBC*

Lorne would respond to those who griped about the repeats that they
were being silly, that viewers liked these characters, and he made no
apologies for giving the viewers what they liked. He once said if you
do something one time it's unique, two times it's a runner, three times
it's an institution. Lorne also argued as the show's ratings grew that the
repeats were new to all the new viewers tuning in. "No one out there,"
he'd say, "is as sick of the Nerds as we are."

Starting to think about the viewers "out there" as different from the people inside the show was one of the early signs of how far *Saturday Night* had begun to stray from its original identification with its audience.

Although many of the writers complained bitterly about the repetition of popular bits, Lorne was far from the only one to fall prey to their allure. "Everybody who was putting down others' repeats," said Rosie Shuster, "had their own favorite doughnut to trot out to be adored." That included the most vocal internal critic, Michael O'Donoghue, who seldom, if ever, passed on an opportunity to appear on the show as the evil Mr. Mike. People caught on very quickly, Shuster and others said, to television's magic formula: "Repetition equals success equals power."

Perhaps inevitably, more success and more power increasingly became the goals on *Saturday Night*, and as they did, factions developed, jealousies festered, and Lorne was cast in the role of mediator. "It got to the point," one of the writers said, "where all week long people were screaming and threatening to quit. It degenerated into emotional blackmail—people had temper tantrums or they pouted or showed up in the studio late and behaved poorly. There were a lot of closed-door private meetings [in Lorne's office] and a lot of backstabbing as time went on. ... There was a lot of ego juggling. I once heard Lorne say, 'You wouldn't believe what goes on in that room, what people are saying about other people. Everybody's trashing everybody else.' Lorne would hear all the shit, and then in the writers' meetings everybody would be good friends, pals, buddies."

* * *

One of the more intense rivalries was that between the former apprentice writers, Alan Zweibel and Franken and Davis. In the first season, Zweibel had been fastest out of the gate with the Samurai sketches and Emily Litella's Weekend Update commentaries. He also contributed a lot of jokes to Update, and by the third season he and Herb Sargent had more or less cornered Update as their private preserve. Franken and Davis, among some of the other writers, came to resent that territorial claim. There was occasional bickering over jokes submitted for Update by other writers that Zweibel and Sargent didn't put on, and Zweibel once sulked for weeks when Franken used some news footage that Zweibel thought might end *Saturday Night*'s ability to borrow such clips from NBC News.

Franken and Davis had had a rough first season, but they came on stronger in the second season, and stronger yet in the third. Gradually they overtook Zweibel in Lorne's favor. Zweibel was hurt at finding himself superseded by Franken and Davis. He was acutely aware of the difficulties of competing against a two-man team; he always felt he had to work twice as hard to keep up with F&D, who were nothing if not prolific. He had also come to depend on Lorne— far too much, he later admitted—for personal as well as professional support.

The strain hit the breaking point near the end of the third season. Zweibel happened to come across a contract he wasn't supposed to see. It was for a deal Lorne had quietly made on the side with Franken and Davis that gave them $5,000 more apiece than the other writers supposedly on their level—Beatts, Shuster, and Zweibel. Zweibel exploded. He complained bitterly to his manager, who happened to be Bernie Brillstein, and to Anne Beatts. Beatts didn't like it, either, and she went into Lorne's office and did some bitter complaining of her own.

"You can't do this!" she said. "If you give one kid a bike for Christmas, you've got to give every kid a bike for Christmas. It has to be favored nations! No one will [go along with it]. I won't, Alan won't, Rosie won't." Lorne, Beatts says, smoothed things over by giving them all the same raise.

Zweibel, nevertheless, was deeply wounded, an injury complicated by a simultaneous rift in his partnership with Gilda Radner. They had begun bickering between themselves, Gilda calling Lorne to complain that Alan was being a baby, Zweibel upset that Gilda was acting like a prima donna. Once she called Zweibel at eleven o'clock at night about a piece Lorne insisted they do together. "Okay," she said, "our producer says we have to do this, so let's be professional and do it." Zweibel responded to the turmoil by collapsing creatively—he compared it to a batter striking out with the bases loaded in the bottom of the ninth—and went into a writing slump that lasted through the show's next season.

Zweibel played a role in another rivalry that blew up in the third season, that between Gilda and Laraine. Although they tried to be friends, Gilda's emergence as the top female star on the show was painful for Laraine. Gilda tried, others on the show say, to be sensitive about it, but there were many times she inadvertently trampled on Laraine's feelings in her exuberance over what was happening to her. For Laraine, the implication was always in the air that Gilda was somehow better, more loved, more talented, more deserving of recognition. There were excruciating moments when those insecurities surfaced: the time during the second season when Lorne came in and announced that Gilda had been nominated for an Emmy, but Laraine hadn't; the time when the *Saturday Night* record album came out with a sticker on the cover that mentioned Gilda as one of "the stars" of the show, but failed to mention Laraine; the times when word got around that Gilda was being pursued for series or movies and Laraine wasn't. But most painful were the week in, week out realizations on *Saturday Night*s, when despite Lorne's efforts to keep everyone's roles equal, it always seemed to turn out that Gilda had more to do than Laraine did.

Laraine didn't keep her disgruntlement a secret from Lorne, and there were many meetings in his office where she complained about her secondary role on the show. But Laraine wasn't by nature a fighter, and more often than not she reacted by sinking into melancholy. By doing so, one of the writers said, she shut herself off from those who might have become her allies, turning her anger not into effective action but against herself. Moping wasn't an especially effective tactic on *Saturday Night*, as Laraine herself knew. Taking her cue from Bill Murray, she decided, in the middle of the third season, to take a stand.

At issue was a sketch called "Mr. Death." It was a sweet idea about Death coming to apologize to a little girl for having recently taken her dog, Tippy. She and Death have a dialogue about the inevitability of dying, and how tired he is of being blamed for it. Alan Zweibel conceived the piece, and as he almost always did, he immediately thought of Gilda for the part of the little girl. Zweibel, Herb Sargent, and Gilda wrote the sketch together in Sargent's office, and in read-through Gilda read the piece with John Belushi.

Dave Wilson suggested that the sketch be held for the English actor Christopher Lee, who would be the host the following week. Everyone agreed that Lee, a veteran of dozens of horror films, would be perfect for the part of Mr. Death.

Laraine had been a horror-film fanatic through much of her childhood, and she adored Christopher Lee. She had, in fact, lobbied Lorne to invite Lee as a host. Laraine thought the "Mr. Death" sketch would be perfect for her, and she began campaigning for the part of the little girl. She talked to Zweibel about it. Zweibel deferred any decision to Lorne, failing to tell Laraine that Gilda had contributed to the writing of the sketch. If he had told her that, Laraine said later, she would have backed off. Instead, she went to Lorne and, in one of those brutal, tearful meetings in his office, threatened to quit if she wasn't given the part. Lorne had a meeting with Gilda, asking her to relinquish the role as a personal favor to him. Gilda, after shedding some tears, agreed, but she was so upset about it that she wouldn't speak to Laraine for a long while after that, and years later, whenever she saw the sketch in reruns, she'd call Zweibel and berate him for letting her down.

So Laraine took her stand and won, and the sketch was a success on air, but it was a victory that probably cost her more goodwill than it was worth. On the way to read-through that week, Dan Aykroyd turned angrily to Laraine and said, "How the fuck can you do that? All of a sudden you worm your way into a part that Gilda wrote?" Danny's reaction was typical of the widespread belief that Laraine had blundered, and that put her even more on the defensive than she had been. Soon she would return to her moping, and never again would she wage such a forceful battle to reverse her fortunes on *Saturday Night*.

In her isolation, Laraine joined Garrett Morris, who went through a similar pattern of fighting and withdrawal. In the third season the writers finally found a formula for Garrett that, they thought, worked: putting him in a dress.

Garrett's first major appearance in drag was as Ella Fitzgerald in the show hosted by Ray Charles early in the third season. A few weeks later he played Tina Turner, a part he had worked long and hard to perfect. His performance on air was probably his most electric ever and a huge success. Garrett was thrilled. Little did he know that it would typecast him as the show's resident drag queen: He would subsequently appear as a maid, a nurse, Diana Ross, and Pearl Bailey, among other female roles.

There was a certain irony to this because Garrett was known on the 17th floor as something of a sexual libertarian and an aficionado of sex magazines like *Penthouse*, *Hustler*, and *Screw*. But after a while his appearances in drag began to seem more sadistic than anything else. It was, said one observer, as if the show actually enjoyed making Garrett "participate in his own degradation."

When Cicely Tyson hosted in the fourth season, Garrett came out dressed as Tyson for her opening monologue. Tyson walked on a few seconds later and asked him what he thought he was doing, and Garrett said that when he heard she was going to be on the show he assumed it was a part for him. "I was hired by this show under terms of the Token Minority Window Dressing Act of 1968," he said, adding that his contract stipulated he play "all parts darker than Tony Orlando."

"Garrett, what is happening to you?" Tyson replied. "Look at what you're doing! When we worked together at the Black Resentment Drama Workshop in the 1960s, I expected something really very big from you. The range you showed, your talent, your voice ... Where's your integrity? What happened to it? You have talent and you're just throwing it away ... Don't you know you have a responsibility as a black actor to perfect your craft? And you are here on this stage, in front of all these people on television, acting like a clown. What are you doing it for? Money?"

"Well, it doesn't look bad on my resume, ya know," Garrett answered. "And I get to keep the dresses."

That script accurately reflected the embarrassment and resentment many in the black community felt over Garrett's subjugation on *Saturday*

*Night.* When Cicely Tyson first came to the 17th floor, in fact, she was so appalled at some of the material she was given that she refused to have anything to do with it. It was common knowledge on the show that when Garrett went home he took a lot of abuse from "his people" for not doing the same. An article on him in the black magazine *Essence* noted that his willingness to perform in stereotyped roles probably accounted for the fact that "he has been virtually ignored by the black press."

Garrett told *Essence* he was puzzled by that lack of attention. But he also acknowledged that he had long been fighting behind the scenes for better parts. "Nobody knows the struggle I've seen," he said.

One friend thinks Garrett may have started giving up the battle when Bill Murray broke through as a star. Once the new guy surpassed him, Garrett could no longer tell himself his problems finding a niche on the show were just the result of a bad first season. It became apparent the situation probably wasn't going to improve. Thus from the third season on, Garrett adopted what one writer called "a diffident attitude" toward it all. Like Laraine, he started spending more time in his office or in his dressing room, and like her, he started taking more and more comfort in cocaine.

\* \* \*

Lorne had predicted even before the show went on that the family spirit on *Saturday Night* would break down with success, but predictable though that breakdown may have been, he wasn't cynical enough not to regret it. He talked often about how nice it had been in the beginning. "Eden," he called it then, when "all the oars were pulling in the same direction," when the performers weren't refusing to do parts, the writers would do what he asked, and people weren't blackmailing him in his office.

At the same time, all the intramural squabbling didn't really constitute a direct threat to him. In a way, by coming to him as mediator, the combatants were affirming Lorne's power as producer. The complaining almost always took place in one-on-one sessions in Lorne's office with the door closed, or sometimes during all-night talks at his apartment. There was, one of the writers observed, an element of divide and conquer to Lorne's handling of the feuds. Therefore the incident that disturbed Lorne most, the incident that in his mind fundamentally changed the atmosphere of the show, was a dispute that came to be known on the 17th floor as Black Friday. Black Friday was the first group rebellion, and it was directed against Lorne.

It started on a Thursday night in November of the third season when Dan Aykroyd came across some budget figures on Lorne's desk. Danny, who as usual had been working harder than everyone else, and who remained resentful of what he was being paid for it, didn't like what he saw. It looked to Danny as if NBC had budgeted more money for writers than the writers were getting. Either Lorne was saving NBC some money by not hiring as many writers as he could, or he was paying himself as a writer far more than the others were getting, or he was spending some of the money budgeted for writers elsewhere on the show, or perhaps a combination of all three.

Danny decided to do his own accounting. Suddenly he was appearing in the other writers' offices, demanding of each: "How much do you make?"

When he got the answer he wrote it down and headed for the next office. After he totaled up the numbers, he liked what he saw even less. There was a discrepancy, according to one of the writers, of about $10,000 per show. Danny immediately started agitating for the writers to confront Lorne.

The first colleague Danny enlisted in his protest was Marilyn Miller. Having worked for years in Hollywood, she was familiar with the duplicitous intricacies of creative show-biz accounting, and like Danny she was angry about the number of hours she was spending on the 17th floor. Lorne was gone that night—he was out celebrating his thirty-third birthday—and all the writers gathered in his office to talk it over.

Some, like Jim Downey, begged off taking part in any confrontation. ("Oh come on, you pussy," Danny sneered at him.) Others, like Franken and Davis, weren't as vocal as Miller and Aykroyd, but they agreed something should be done. It was decided that they'd all bring their grievances to Lorne the next morning. Danny wanted everyone to "testify" to how overworked and underpaid they were, and he had a list of demands. Most of all, he wanted more writers hired. He felt a handful of writers, including himself and Franken and Davis, were producing the bulk of the work, and he was tired of being overburdened. He wanted every dime NBC was paying for writing distributed to those doing it, and he wanted to know how Lorne could justify taking a writer's salary when he was hardly writing anymore. He also wanted an accounting of the royalties brought in by *Saturday Night*'s record album, which had been released the year before.

Some of the writers went home that night assuming the whole thing would blow over, but the next day Danny told everyone to gather in the greenroom outside Lorne's ninth-floor office. Far from cooling down over night, Danny seemed to have wound himself even tighter, and soon after the group was assembled he launched into a tirade. It was, witnesses say, a magnificent tirade in the inimitable Aykroyd style, rattled off with the destructive precision of a machine gun. As they listened,

the other writers were drawn into his zeal like the torch-carrying village mobs in Frankenstein movies, and for that moment there was true
mutiny in the air.

Danny kept going, and as he did he talked faster, his voice got louder
and his face turned redder, until finally, at the apex of his rage, he turned
and with all his force smashed his boot into the wall of Lorne's office,
kicking a hole almost all the way through the sheetrock. Lorne's assistant,
Kathy Minkowsky, was sitting on Lorne's couch when the indentation
made by Danny's foot appeared in the wall next to her head. The "gigantic
crash" by her ear so startled her that she leaped off the couch onto the floor.

Lorne came out into the greenroom and quietly looked around the
group. "What's up?" he asked.

Danny strode up to Lorne and launched into another tirade, pointing
his finger in Lorne's face. "You're fucking spending all your time in that
office and going out to dinner with Candice Bergen and all that stuff
and the fucking show is going to hell and we have five writers who are
writing the show and eighteen people on the credits—we have to have
some new blood!" he said, continuing in that vein for what seemed like
a couple of minutes.

Lorne stood listening without saying anything, occasionally nodding his head. When Danny finished, Lorne turned on his heel, went
back into his office, and loudly slammed the door.

That more or less took the wind out of the rebellion. The group quietly dispersed. Some of them tiptoed into Lorne's office a few minutes
later to apologize. "I'm not angry, I'm disappointed," was about all he
would say.

Lorne, however, was considerably more vocal in a phone conversation he had that night with Barry Secunda, the manager of O'Donoghue,
Anne Beatts, and Franken and Davis. "I will not be bullied by a group
walkout," Lorne said. "They can go fuck themselves. I'll get rid of
everybody. I won't put up with a group thing. I'll deal with everyone as
individuals, as I always have."

Supposedly Lorne told Secunda this in confidence, but Secunda was
familiar enough with Lorne's style to know his remarks were intended
for group dissemination.

After Black Friday, Lorne for the first time began locking his office
door behind him when he left for the day. When he was in his office,
he spent more time than ever by himself, on the phone with the door
closed. Some on the show believe his withdrawal was an aggressive
move, designed to respond to the rebellion by maintaining what one
of the writers called "an edge of anxiety" over the staff. But there's no
doubt that Black Friday was also a painful blow for him. "He was,"

another writer said, "depressed, angry, bitter, enraged, and hurt." Later, when he talked about Black Friday, Lorne told his friends it marked the "loss of innocence" for *Saturday Night*.

It was also after Black Friday that Lorne started talking about quitting the show. Many saw those threats as negotiating ploys— whenever he made them his contract tended to be up for renewal— and they were indeed that. But Lorne's friends say the rebellion also caused him to have sincere doubts about whether it was worth the agony any longer, and it's likely he hoped to convey those doubts to his staff.

Although he didn't mention the mutiny, he seemed to be reacting to it in an interview he gave to *Viva* magazine a few days later. "When it's going real good, I want to do it forever," he said, "because these are the people I love and this is what I do and I think it's special. But when it takes every ounce of my strength to get it on and there's nothing but resistance and nobody seems to give a fuck, then I want out. Because you can only give up your life for something greater than you. So far, it's been worth it."

Years later he still carried the same attitude of fatherly disappointment and weary anger. "With success and fame and the attention that brings," he said, "people are just forced to think about themselves, because the whole world seems to be thinking about them. It just dissipates. And after a while you can't hold it together. I think I was remarkable in being able to hold it together as long as I did. Because it was poised for explosion from day one."

\* \* \*

Despite Lorne's insistence that he wouldn't be bullied, the Black Friday rebellion did achieve at least one of its goals. Within a few weeks, two new writers were hired, Don Novello and Brian Doyle- Murray.

Novello had previously made a small name for himself as Father Guido Sarducci, the character he'd created on the *Chicken Little Comedy Hour* back in 1972, and had played briefly on network TV on the Smothers Brothers' comeback attempt in 1975. He was also the author of a 1977 book entitled *The Lazlo Letters*, a collection of correspondence between a fictional personality he invented, Lazlo Toth, and various public figures, including Richard Nixon. At one point Toth demanded, and with considerable persistence finally got, a $10 refund from Nixon's secretary for money he'd sent in for a tour of San Clemente. A quarter was included for "interest."

Novello quickly became one of *Saturday Night*'s more productive writers and, as Father Sarducci, one of its more popular performers;

Brian Doyle-Murray did not. Despite the two additions, however, the sum of the writers on the show stayed the same.

Before the third season ended, Marilyn Miller resigned. Ostensibly she had decided to go to Florida to write a novel, but in fact she'd become the first casualty of the pressures of the show. She was nearing a nervous breakdown, and she had no doubt she would have gone over the edge had she stayed.

The third season was also the last for Michael O'Donoghue. More than most, O'Donoghue had chafed at Lorne's control over the show. He tired of having to get Lorne's approval on everything he wrote; he wanted to bring in a piece and have it produced, no questions asked. He figured he'd earned that right. Nor was he pleased that Lorne was going out of his way to mute the impact of his Cut and Slash humor.

As O'Donoghue was held back, he watched, appalled, as the younger and, to him, lesser writers like Franken and Davis continued to emerge. He saw them, Rosie Shuster said, as "the potato eaters, the lumpenproletariat rising up and taking over. And here was Baudelaire, shoved to one side ... He was the great auteur overlooked in a scramble of egos ... not getting the reverence and attention that was due him."

The fuse on O'Donoghue's famous temper grew shorter as his influence on the show diminished. His rage was now directed mainly at Lorne. O'Donoghue discovered that Lorne was most fragile early in the day, and he took delight in "blind-siding" him with screaming tantrums as soon as Lorne came into the office. Eventually, Lorne simply ignored these outbursts, which, Neil Levy pointed out, was for O'Donoghue probably the worst thing Lorne could do. O'Donoghue had also finally broken up with Anne Beatts. Theirs was not a delicate parting, which only added to the ferocity of O'Donoghue's emotional displays. So it's likely O'Donoghue was more or less looking for an excuse to leave, and soon enough Lorne provided it.

O'Donoghue by then had stopped writing his long sketches, devoting himself primarily to

Writer Don Novello appeared as Father Guido Sarducci. © *NBC*

smaller bits he felt he could get on with less harassment. Among these were some mock NBC program announcements that opened several shows, including "*The Waltons Eat Their Young* won't be seen tonight so that we may bring you the following live presentation." One day Lorne came to him and said he'd asked Rosie Shuster to write a similar opening. O'Donoghue launched into a vehement protest over this invasion of his niche, but Lorne wouldn't back off. Finally O'Donoghue walked out, this time never to return. "Fuck you," he said to Lorne, "and fuck your show."

No one was surprised when, within weeks of leaving, O'Donoghue began giving interviews in which he sniped at the potato eaters he'd left behind. In one he talked about "the inevitable decay" setting in on *Saturday Night*. "The more creative and imaginative people always move on to other projects," he said. "I wanted to bail out of the plane before it crashed into the mud."

O'Donoghue didn't sever his relationship with Lorne. On the contrary, Lorne financed his next project, a special for NBC called *Mondo Video*. O'Donoghue was sure *Mondo Video* would be the next step beyond *Saturday Night*, an experiment in Cut and Slash humor in its least diluted form. It turned out to be too undiluted for NBC, and the network refused to put it on the air. There was a long and bitter series of fights over that: O'Donoghue would claim Lorne failed to back him up with NBC; others would say O'Donoghue simply repeated his usual self-destruct cycle. Eventually Lorne would take a loss on *Mondo Video* of between $125,000 (O'Donoghue's figure) and $250,000 (Lorne's).

Though O'Donoghue had wallowed joyfully in the pleasures of popular culture during his time on *Saturday Night*, in the end he never fully relinquished his pretensions to art. By leaving when he did, he saved himself the humiliation of working on a successful program. O'Donoghue's attitude, his manager Barry Secunda said, was that if America liked *Saturday Night*, how good could it be?

He got out just in time, then, because the real lumpenproletariat of America was about to discover that it liked *Saturday Night* very much indeed.

# CHAPTER 26

# Greatest Hits
## (Show Notes Three)

One of Lorne's pet theories had always been that *Saturday Night* was not so much in the business of television as it was in the business of rock and roll. The audience, the sensibility, was the same, he said, the show had simply picked up where rock in the sixties left off.

If *Saturday Night* was a rock band, then it produced some of its greatest hits in the third and fourth seasons. A string of recurring characters and sketches appeared that were like hard-rocking singles with very catchy tunes: Less subtle than some of the earlier work, but more accessible and popular. The show was replete with "hooks": John Belushi's "but noooo" and "Cheeseburger ... Cheeseburger ... No Coke, Pepsi." Roseanne Roseannadanna's "It just goes ta show you, it's always somethin'." Dan Aykroyd's reply to Jane Curtin on Weekend Update's debate feature, Point/Counterpoint, "Jane, you ignorant slut." And, perhaps the most popular of all, the swinging Czech Brothers' "We're two wild and crazy guys!"

There was a broadness that hadn't been so prominent before. The costume people made Roseanne Roseannadanna's wig bigger and frizzier each time she appeared. Gilda even out-Gonzoed Belushi at one point: During a sketch in which she played her sleaze-queen punk-rock singer Candy Slice, she took him totally by surprise on-air by spitting a mouthful of "whiskey" in his face. He smiled perceptibly and raised his famous eyebrows.

Wild and crazy guys: Steve Martin and Dan Aykroyd
as the swinging Czech brothers. © *NBC*

Not a few characters were literally broad. John gave a brutal impersonation of Elizabeth Taylor (which had, as usual, not a little of John
himself in it): obese, supine, engulfing a drumstick and choking on it.
Franken and Davis created an all-American family called The Widettes,
whose mountainous rear ends loomed beneath polyester slacks. Their
diet consisted of potato salad, fudge, Tater Tots, and other starches.

Dan Aykroyd's impersonation of the portly French Chef, Julia Child,
had to be one of the most outrageously funny moments ever on *Saturday
Night*. She stood in her TV kitchen, preparing the usual elaborate dish,
when she cut herself, deeply. "I've cut the dickens out of my finger,"
she twittered in her peculiar soprano. She proceeded to bleed to death
on camera, trying to carry on with her recipe as *buckets* of blood gushed
all over the studio. By the end she was deliriously flashing back to her
childhood, and finally she collapsed over the counter, blood still spurting
everywhere.

On the surface there was nothing low-key about the characters that
made Bill Murray famous, either, but like John and Danny he always
added thrilling little touches of detail to the fundamental power of his
performances. He was the very essence of oily insincerity in his role
as the movie critic and gossip columnist on Weekend Update, pulling
down his lower lip and growling, "Woody … come on … Wooo-dy,"
or rejecting movies in his annual Oscar predictions because he hadn't
gotten around to seeing them.

Billy's Nick the Lounge Singer character was equally unctuous, and equally popular. Billy, Danny, Tom Davis, Paul Shaffer, and Marilyn Miller wrote most of the Nick sketches. Billy and Shaffer, who collaborated on the music, were especially fond of Las Vegas sleaze, which was one of the more enduring sources of satire to come out of sixties humor. Probably a dozen comedians will claim they did Nick before Bill Murray did, but Billy didn't steal the character, he just made it his own. He'd been doing Nick since his Second City days. In the early seventies, he and his brother Brian, Shaffer, and *Lampoon* producer Bob Tischler were part of an informal group called The Sammy Davis Club. Its members would get together each week to watch Davis's syndicated talk show and cackle madly as they did about how absolutely slimy Sammy was.

Nick, like Roseanne Roseannadanna, was another greatest hit whose routine never varied, although the locales he appeared in did: He moved from a ski resort to a honeymoon lodge to a tavern on the highway outside Las Vegas to an airport lounge to a train lounge and eventually to an Army base in the frozen wastes of Greenland, wailing some ridiculously banal pop anthem at every stop.

Some of *Saturday Night*'s most popular bits had to be repeated insistently before they caught on. John Belushi's "but nooooo," for example, got absolutely no reaction the first three or four times he used it. Finally, after he concluded his weather reports on Weekend Update that way a few times, the audience got the point and it became John's trademark. Steve Martin and Dan Aykroyd's swinging Czech Brothers were another example.

Danny had noticed that Martin in his concerts did a voice of an Eastern European. He suggested doing something about two immigrant brothers who, having "run from the tanks" in Czechoslovakia, ended up pursuing the loose American sex they'd heard so much about back home. Danny and Martin asked Marilyn Miller for help, since as a woman she was more familiar with the sorts of come-on lines the brothers were likely to deliver, and she was accomplished at writing dialects. Miller and Danny stayed up much of the night writing the sketch; the "wild and crazy guys" line came from Martin's stage act.

The Czech Brothers (their names were Jorge and Yortuk Festrunk) got no more than a few giggles from the audience the first time they appeared, and both Martin's and Danny's characterizations were not nearly as sharply defined as they would become. By their third appearance the Festrunk brothers were snapping their fingers and almost bending over backward in their geeky version of a soul strut, and roars of recognition greeted them the moment they walked on stage.

Steve Martin was in on the creation of another pair of famous characters, the Nerds. Anne Beatts got the idea for the Nerds when Elvis Costello appeared on the show. "This isn't punk rock," she thought, "this is nerd rock." Beatts and her writing partner, Rosie Shuster, developed a sketch in which three nerds come to a radio station to promote their new record album, *Trying Desperately to Be Liked*. The male parts were originally written for John and Steve Martin, but John backed out and Billy took over, playing Todd to Gilda's Lisa. The sketch was cut from Martin's show, and ended up appearing a few weeks later with Robert Klein playing the third nerd. Jane Curtin also created Mrs. Loopner on that show, although she played Robert Klein's mother, not Gilda's. From the beginning, the audience's reaction was stronger for the Nerds than it had been for the Czech Brothers, though not nearly so passionate as it would become.

A bit of a backstage tug-of-war over the Nerds ensued after that. For their second outing, Franken and Davis wrote a sketch in which Todd and Lisa appeared on a talk show to promote a book they'd written, *Whatever Happened to the Class of '77?* Jane Curtin played not Mrs. Loopner but the moderator of the show they were on, *Looks at Books*. F&D named Billy's character after a student they'd known in high school, Todd LaBounta. Todd's namesake eventually threatened to sue NBC for defamation of character (he called a press conference to announce his intention of doing so) and the name was changed to Todd DiLaMuca. F&D started to do another Nerds sketch when Beatts and Shuster, sensing the characters slipping away from them, jumped in and co-wrote it with them. Having established their claim, Beatts and Shuster kept bringing the Nerds back and, with the performers, kept adding details and nuances— Mrs. Loopner's famous egg salad, recollections of the late Mr. Loopner, who was born without a spine and who invented, but failed to patent, the Slinky. The Nerds became so popular that the word *nerd* was added to some dictionaries.

Beatts and Shuster followed up that success the next season with the lecherous babysitter, Uncle Roy, who was based on an actual babysitter Rosie Shuster once had in Canada. The real-life Uncle Roy never actually molested Shuster, but he did like to tell her about how naughty he'd been when he was young, and the punishments he'd suffered for it. The questions-and-answers always came around to her asking, "And then what would happen?"

"Well," he'd say, "then they'd pull down my pants."

Buck Henry, who was known on the 17th floor to take a scholarly interest in kinky sex, played the perfectly perverse Uncle Roy. Gilda and Laraine were his prepubescent charges. Together they played such games as Buried Treasure (which was hidden in Uncle Roy's pants pockets), Horsey (he gave them bareback rides), Ruffy the Dog (he was spanked by the girls for being bad), and the infamous Glass Bottom Boat.

By the time Uncle Roy appeared, *Saturday Night* was pretty much getting its way with Standards, but the censors always shuddered in revulsion when they saw an Uncle Roy sketch. Buck Henry says Standards would try to talk Lorne into "mitigating the evil" of Uncle Roy by toning down some of his raunchier suggestions, but nonetheless he became more outrageous each time he returned. As creepy as he was, he preceded by several years a breakthrough in public awareness of just how prevalent child molesters are in families. To underscore that point, in the last Uncle Roy sketch, Jane Curtin as the mother returned home and thanked him again for being so great with the girls.

"Roy, you're one in a million," she said.

Uncle Roy smiled modestly, winked at the camera, and said, "Oh, there's more of me than you might suspect."

Standards also had its reservations about Don Novello's Father Guido Sarducci, the gossip columnist and rock critic for the Vatican newspaper *L'Osservatore Romano*. Because Novello had performed Father Guido on television before, in prime time, Standards couldn't very well refuse to let him on, but there was always concern that Guido might slip in an obscenity in Italian or set off some sort of furor among Catholics. Once, Father Guido planned to report he'd uncovered an important religious artifact: the check for the Last Supper. Standards compromised and let him say he'd found the check for the Last Brunch instead. Father Guido had an underlying gentleness missing from some of *Saturday Night*'s other greatest hits, a quality that made him safer than he might have been, and that derived mainly from the gentleness of Novello himself. Still, he appeared so frequently on Weekend Update that even he grew tiresome.

Novello wrote one of *Saturday Night*'s most static, and beloved, repeating bits, the Olympia restaurant sketches. Two days after he started work on the show, Novello went to Belushi and said he wanted to do a piece based on a tavern they both knew in Chicago, The Billy Goat, where there really was the constant call and response, "Cheeseburger … Cheeseburger." With John's enthusiastic support, Novello wrote the idea up on Tuesday night, and the next day it was applauded in read-through. The Olympia required one of the larger and more complicated sets *Saturday Night* had ever done, and it was another sketch that was finished late in the week—Leo Yoshimura ended up getting the real burger grill for the set on Saturday afternoon. The Olympia was a huge hit instantly on-air. The cast of characters—John's blustering owner, Laraine's stern waitress, Danny's toothpick-chewing short-order cook, and Billy's counterman, whose cheerful but vacant nod betrayed the fact that he understood not a word of English—were all superb. Unfortunately, there didn't seem to be much to do with them beyond those broad strokes. They reappeared several times nonetheless.

By contrast, Novello wrote another running sketch that evolved wonderfully over time but wasn't greatest-hits material. The locale was a typical American shopping mall. In the first installment, host Fred Willard played the personification of the small-time entrepreneur pursuing his dream. In his case, the dream was a specialty store called the Scotch Boutique, which sold every size, style, and shape of Scotch tape ever made. In subsequent shows it developed that the mall was dying from lack of customer traffic. One by one the stores went under, but the Scotch boutique thrived by selling their owners the tape they needed to put up their OUT OF BUSINESS signs. The Mall sketches were quiet, almost melancholy, and thoughtful. John, playing Kevin the box boy, and Danny, playing the owner of a men's store, delivered two of their most accomplished, low-keyed acting roles. They prompted nary a cheer from the audience. Lorne kept putting them on anyway.

The same sort of dichotomy existed in those later seasons in the popular reaction to the short films on *Saturday Night*. Tom Schiller gradually assumed the duties of house filmmaker from Gary Weis, who was spending more of his time in Hollywood working on full- length movies. Schiller made meticulously detailed, off-beat films that parodied as much as anything different styles of filmmaking— the grainy textures of early Fellini in one called *La Dolce Gilda*, the stark black-and-whites of Warner Brothers film noir in another called *Java Junkie*. The most-remembered Schiller film, however, will inevitably be *Don't Look Back in Anger*, in which John Belushi as an old man visits the graves of all the other *Saturday Night* stars.

JOHN: (Approaching the graveyard) They all thought I'd be the first to go. I was one of those live-fast die-young real-good-looking-corpse types, you know. But I guess they were wrong. There they are, all of my friends. This is the Not Ready For Prime Time cemetery. Come on up ...

Here's Gilda Radner. She had her own show on Canadian television for years and years, the *Gilda Radner Show*. Well, at least now I can see her on reruns. Cute as a button, God bless her. There's where Laraine is. They say she murdered her deejay husband and moved to the Valley in California and had a pecan farm. She was this big (holding up thumb and forefinger) when she died. Jane Curtin, she married a stockbroker, had two children, moved to upstate New York. She died of complications during cosmetic surgery. This is Garrett Morris. Now Garrett, Garrett left the show, then worked in the black theater for years, then he died of an overdose of heroin. There's Bill Murray. He lived the longest—thirty-eight years. He was happy when he died; he'd just grown his moustache back. Probably still growing. Over here is Chevy Chase. He died right after his first movie with Goldie Hawn. Over here is Danny Aykroyd; I guess he loved his Harley too much. They clocked him at a hundred seventy-five miles an hour before the crash. He was a blur. I had to be called in to identify his body. I recognized him by his webbed toes.

The *Saturday Night* show was the best experience of my life, and now they're all gone. I miss every one of 'em. Why me? Why did I live so long? They're all dead. I'll tell you why. ... 'Cause I'm a dancer! (Belushi then snaps his fingers above his head and spins, Zorba-like, atop the graves.)

As interesting as Schiller's films were, they didn't receive a scintilla of the recognition accorded the work of Walter Williams. Williams was the creator (and namesake) of the little Play-Doh doll, Mr. Bill. In every film, Mr. Bill was dismembered and smashed by the vicious Mr. Sluggo in concert with the evil Mr. Hands. Not exactly the height of adult comedy, but undoubtedly one of *Saturday Night*'s most popular characters ever.

Mr. Bill first came in over the transom as one of the home movies submitted by viewers starting in the first season. Williams, an accounting-school dropout in New Orleans, had created the character in 1974 when he was making Super 8 films in his living room. Mr. Bill was an intentionally crude parody of cheap TV cartoons; the first Mr. Bill film to air on *Saturday Night* was put together in one night and cost less than $20 to make. Mr. Bill appeared again once in the second season and then twice more in the third and was such a hit that in the fourth and fifth seasons Lorne put Williams under full-time contract to keep the Mr. Bills coming. Williams's films gradually grew more detailed, reflecting the fact that he was spending about $1,500 on each one, but the "plot" never changed.

* * *

The fatigue and the fighting going on backstage resulted in a growing unevenness on-air, especially in the fourth season, that didn't lend itself to the long streaks of hot shows of earlier years. But there were many nights when everyone seemed to be on. One of them was the Steve Martin show of April 22 in the third season, which some on the show consider the single best *Saturday Night* ever.

The show opened with Paul Shaffer doing his perfect impersonation of rock promoter Don Kirshner. As usual he thanked a long list of managers and record-company executives; because of their efforts, he said, the new band he was about to introduce was "no longer an authentic blues act, but have managed to become a viable commercial product." They were Jake and Elwood Blues, the Blues Brothers.

John and Danny sing "King Bee" during the show's first season. Three years later they morphed into the Blues Brothers, whose smash success led to John and Danny's departure from *Saturday Night*. © *NBC*

The prototype for the Blues Brothers had actually appeared in the first season, when John and Danny, dressed in Bee costumes, performed the old blues number "King Bee." Somehow they managed to come across as funky in spite of the silly outfits they wore. John was more into heavy metal than the blues at the time, but by the third season he'd become a rabid blues fan and had fallen into the habit of jumping up on stage at clubs and singing a few impromptu tunes with the bands. Judy Jacklin Belushi says Lorne saw John sing one night at the Manhattan rock club Trax and suggested he warm up *Saturday Night*'s studio audience. He worked up a couple of numbers with Danny and the *Saturday Night* band; musical director Howard Shore suggested the name the Blues Brothers. They played for *Saturday Night*'s studio audience a few times as a warm-up act, but the Steve Martin show was their first appearance in front of the cameras.

Saturday Night

Steve Martin followed the Blues Brothers with a funny monologue in which he complained about being typecast as a comedian. Then he called up a volunteer from the audience, Bill Murray, and picked his pockets, keeping up a steady stream of sarcastic patter while he removed Billy's wallet, watch, belt, shirt, shoes, and finally his underwear. The Czech Brothers, by then almost national heroes, came next, and after them a sketch Franken and Davis had written called "Theodoric of York, Medieval Barber."

Martin played a barber surgeon who cheerfully prescribed leeches, hanging by the heels, and other brutal cures to a procession of pitiful peasants, all of whom suffered horrible pain and sometimes death. F&D made a specialty out of grand historical productions such as these, and the punch line in Theodoric became another of *Saturday Night*'s catchphrases. After an outraged mother hysterically accused him of killing her family, Theodoric had a flash of inspiration.

"Wait a minute," he said. "Perhaps she's right. Perhaps I've been wrong to blindly follow the medical traditions and superstitions of the past centuries. Maybe we barbers should test those assumptions analytically, through experimentation and a scientific method! Perhaps this scientific method could be extended to other fields of learning—the natural sciences, art, architecture, navigation! Perhaps I could lead the way to a new age! An age of rebirth! A renaissance! ... *Naahhh.*"

Martin quickly changed into a white suit for a sketch with Gilda called "Dancing in the Dark," which was conceived by Marilyn Miller. The setting was an elegant club. Steve and Gilda spied each other across the room, came together, and, as all other action in the room froze, wordlessly began a torrid and passionate dance, sweeping and twirling and, at times, tripping through the entire studio, an amazing performance by both of them.

After Weekend Update, Martin reappeared in another costume, the robes and headdress of an Egyptian pharaoh. He soberly told the audience he'd been appalled at the circus atmosphere surrounding the current exhibition of artifacts from King Tut's tomb. To express his feelings, he wanted to perform a song he'd written. "Maybe," he said, "we can all learn something."

The camera pulled back to reveal a huge set of an Egyptian tomb, with stiff-armed dancing girls in skimpy togas and the *Saturday Night* band in robes and sandals and headdresses. They broke into a bopping rendition of "King Tut," with Martin singing lead: "Now when I die/ Now don't think I'm a nut/Don't want no fancy funeral/Just one like old King Tut! ... (King Tut!) He coulda won a Grammy/(King Tut!) Buried in his jammies ... (Born in Arizona/Moved to Babylonia) ... Got a condo made of stone-a/King Tut!"

Martin had come to the show that week with the song and casually asked if they might try it, not expecting the huge production that
resulted—Lorne put everything behind it. The high point came when
reed man Lou Marini emerged from a full-sized sarcophagus blowing a
raucous saxophone solo.

The rest of the show kept on hitting. There was a Gary Weis film in
which he brilliantly intercut ballet dancers and street dancers; the Blues
Brothers played another number, with John cartwheeling around the
stage; Laraine played TV psychic Maxine Universe in a sketch called
"Next Week in Review," and Martin belatedly got a chance to play his
Nerd character, competing against Todd and Lisa in a school science fair.

Steve Martin, who himself became *Saturday Night*'s greatest hit as
a host (the ratings usually jumped by a million or more homes when he
appeared), shares the opinion that this may have been the best show ever.
"It was like the peak of *Saturday Night*," he said. "It was the peak of me."

CHAPTER 27

# The Beatles of Comedy

"Are you going to see any of the sights in Washington?"
"I don't think so. It's too hard. I *am* one of the sights."
—Gilda Radner, answering a reporter

In the fourth season there was an exponential explosion in *Saturday Night*'s success. The show's highest rating in the third season had come with the Chevy Chase show, which had a 38 percent share of the available audience, but for most of that season its shares continued to hover near 30. In the fourth season, the show *averaged* a 39 share. *Saturday Night* had finally tapped the full, awesome power of television.

To quantify that explosion in terms of the number of viewers watching *Saturday Night*, in its first season the show was seen by an average of 7.5 million people each week. In its fourth season it was regularly watched by more than 17 million people and often by as many as 19 million. In its fifth season it regularly attracted almost 18 million viewers and sometimes exceeded 20 million. Those Nielsen numbers do not include those watching in college dormitories, bars, and other such public places. Taking that not inconsiderable added audience into account, NBC estimated that *Saturday Night* at its peak was seen each week by 25 million people or more.

*Saturday Night* attracted millions of new viewers to its time period. In the show's first season, TV was being watched, on all channels, in an average of 20.6 million homes between 11:30 p.m. and 1:00 a.m. on *Saturday Night*s. By the fourth season there were 24.6 million homes using television in that time period, and the sets in a vast majority of those 4 million new homes were tuned to *Saturday Night*. By the fifth season the sets-in-use figure jumped to 26.6 million homes. Increasing overall viewing levels on anything even close to that scale is one of the rarest achievements in television, which is why NBC Research chief Bill Rubens had always predicted it would never happen.

The allegiance of many of the show's new fans could be traced to John Belushi's performance as the Gonzo fraternity brother Bluto in the *National Lampoon* movie *Animal House*. *Animal House* was released in the summer between the third and fourth seasons and quickly became the highest-grossing comedy film of all time, taking in more than $200 million at the box office. That success linked *Saturday Night* with the vast teenage movie audience, a merging of markets so powerful it helped start a wave of cross-pollination between television, movies, and, soon, records that would have a major influence on those businesses for many years to come.

Lorne liked to call the millions of fans who caught on to *Saturday Night* after the third season "the undeserved audience." These were fans gained more by virtue of the show's momentum and notoriety than by the strength of the work it was presenting. Evidence of that was the fact that reruns of shows from the first and second seasons were now scoring higher ratings than they had when they aired live—sometimes almost twice as high—because the bulk of the show's new audience had never seen them before. What Tom Schiller called "the phenomenology of the show" had taken over.

A firestorm of celebrity consumed them. A new wave of articles showered on *Saturday Night*, far bigger than that generated by the novelty of the show and by Chevy Chase in the first year. Every week, it seemed, NBC's Press department was shepherding reporters from at least one and sometimes several major papers or magazines around the studio and the 17th floor. Belushi's arching eyebrows graced the cover of *Newsweek*; Gilda grinned out from the cover of *People*; gossip columnists like Liz Smith regularly reported on the cast's social activities. *Rolling Stone* did so many cover stories and other articles on the show that for a while it seemed almost a house organ for *Saturday Night*. So desperate was the *New York Post* to do yet another *Saturday Night* story that it offered its readers a thirty- inch article, with photographs, about the show's cook.

Even before she left the show, Marilyn Miller had gotten used to seeing reporters smiling up at her every time she walked into an office on the 17th floor, but when she and O'Donoghue came back to visit in the fourth year, they'd sit and watch openmouthed, amazed at how much more intense it had become. "How could we know *this* would happen?" Miller kept asking.

At the live shows, the attention *Saturday Night* was receiving was magnified as if through some giant looking glass. Every show now had the aura of a big-time rock concert. Kids sometimes lined up with sleeping bags in NBC's lobby on Friday nights, waiting to get the best seats if they had tickets or a shot at standby tickets if they didn't. But there were rarely standby tickets available, since almost everyone who had a ticket showed up. Kay Spiegel, who was in charge of guest relations for the show in those years, described the scene downstairs on *Saturday Night*s as "what I would imagine the Alamo to have been."

The more popular the show became, the less hip it was, by definition, and there was some predictable backlash from *Saturday Night*'s earliest champions in the press, the public, and the industry. *Saturday Night* won an Emmy award for its writing in the second season, and Gilda Radner won one in the third, but there were no Emmys after that. The assumption on the 17th floor was that, as Tom Davis put it, "the puppy had grown up ... People in Hollywood figured out what the show was all about and decided they didn't like it."

In New York, too, the sheen of novelty had worn off. Sometimes it seemed to the performers and writers that the only comment they heard was how *Saturday Night* had gone downhill—indeed, that it had been going downhill since about the fourth week it was on. The higher the ratings got, the more disdainful the criticism became. Anne Beatts grew fond of saying that you can only be avant-garde so long before you become garde.

Nonetheless, massive success has its own chic in New York (it has, in fact, probably more chic than anything else), and as *Saturday Night*'s popularity grew, so did the power and prestige of its friends. An ever more glittering array of celebrities bestowed the blessing of their presence at the show, and after the show at the parties. The guest list for one show in the fourth season included musicians David Bowie and Boz Scaggs, actors Harold Ramis, John Lithgow, and Margot Kidder, Tom Shales of *The Washington Post,* rock promoter Bill Graham, director Mike Nichols, Atlantic Records chairman Ahmet Ertegun and his wife, Mica, and public relations czar Bobby Zarem. It wasn't unusual for stars like Cliff Robertson or Richard Dreyfuss to call the 17th floor directly, not through their secretaries, asking for tickets. The director Milos Forman would show up with the dancer Mikhail Baryshnikov; Jack Nicholson would come late and sit in the aisles; presidential progeny Chip Carter would arrive with Secret Service agents in tow.

Many of *Saturday Night*'s famous friends brought along their retinues, and on the floor of the studio there were often dozens of guests milling around during the show, watching and getting in the way. When the show ended, many of them would sweep onto the 17th floor, and the exhausted troupe of writers and performers would find themselves surrounded by fashion models on the arms of dashing men-about-town. Once one of these visitors indulged in more stimulants than she could handle and keeled over in the hallway. Dan Aykroyd, standing nearby, shrugged and said, "If you can't handle MiGs, don't fly in MiG alley."

To escape the uptown riffraff, John and Danny would retire to the Blues Bar, near Canal Street in lower Manhattan. It was a dark and grimy little place hidden behind a huge steel door; the Holland Tunnel ran thirty feet below its basement. There was a tiny stage with a few instruments on it for anyone who wanted to play and a jukebox stocked with vintage R&B. It was hipness beyond chic to be invited there after a show: Sometimes Rolling Stone Keith Richards or members of the Allman Brothers or the Grateful Dead would be there, jamming all night or serving beer behind the bar.

It got to the point where the stars of *Saturday Night* were, more often than not, more famous than the stars who were guests on the show. The week the top-selling rock group the Doobie Brothers appeared as the musical guests, they trailed around after the cast members during rehearsals shooting snapshots, so excited were they to be there. The Not Ready For Prime Time Players moniker was finally dropped at the end of the third season. Now they were referred to simply as "the stars." Some in the press were calling them "the Beatles of Comedy."

Even the Beatles themselves, who had been among the show's early fans, gradually became part of its social circle as well. Just before the beginning of the second season, John Belushi had been offered $6,000 to perform his Joe Cocker imitation at a birthday party for Paul McCartney, an offer he happily accepted. The party was at the old Harold Lloyd estate in Beverly Hills; there were huge tents scattered around the lawn, and John and Danny both performed in the main tent for about a thousand people. McCartney's invitation confirmed for John's manager, Bernie Brillstein, for one, that *Saturday Night* was becoming something quite out of the ordinary.

A few months later, George Harrison was a guest on a show hosted by Paul Simon. He appeared in an opening in which Lorne explained that his offer of $3,200 for a Beatles reunion on *Saturday Night* had been for *all* the Beatles, not just one. Later in the show Harrison sang with Simon. It was never mentioned publicly that George's segments had been taped earlier in the week because he had a conflict in his schedule.

Monty Python's Eric Idle was a friend of both the Beatles and *Saturday Night*, and through him Lorne and eventually many of the others on the show began to collect their own personal Beatles anecdotes.

Danny and Rosie Shuster were in London once, staying at Idle's house, and he suggested they go visit George Harrison at George's castle. When they arrived, it turned out that George's father had died that day, but George graciously insisted they stay anyway. Another time Alan Zweibel went to dinner in London with Idle, actress Shelley Duval (Paul Simon's girlfriend at the time), George Harrison, and Ringo Starr. Zweibel was so excited he ran to a phone during dinner to call his girlfriend in the States to say, "Guess who I'm having dinner with?"

* * *

Like the Beatles before them, *Saturday Night* had nerve and got away with it, and now the world was coming to them. The cast members found themselves beset by the sort of attention performers dream of, then learn to their dismay they can never turn off. Bill Murray, like Belushi, reveled in it sometimes. When he was recognized at places like the Playboy Club, as he always was, he'd launch into a few characters, performing for the crowd, causing a stir. But when he wanted peace and quiet, he couldn't get it. One day he went with some friends on a ride in the countryside north of New York. They ended up in New Paltz, a little college town where a year before Billy would have gone unnoticed. As he walked down the street a crowd gathered, following him, gradually growing bigger and bigger till he and his friends finally had to run back to their car, the fans chasing them as they fled. They drove from there to Woodstock, where a woman started following them around, and there was a nasty scene when Billy discovered she was a reporter.

Jane Curtin, who was sometimes frightened when people came up to her, started wearing big floppy hats pulled down low and sunglasses whenever she went out. Gilda Radner, who sometimes got angry when she was approached in public and upset when she wasn't, would be sitting in a restaurant, talking with a friend, and look up to see twenty or so fans looking down at her, their faces pressed against the window, watching her eat. NBC finally supplied the cast members with limos because taxicabs weren't adequate for the quick escapes from public places they now required.

John, Danny, Judy Jacklin, and Rosie Shuster got caught once when they were on vacation together in a little lakeside resort town in Wisconsin. The plan was to have a peaceful weekend together, being, as Shuster put it, "regular people." They were getting ready to go out one night when they discovered a crowd had formed on the steps of their rented cabin. They waited awhile, hoping the crowd would dissipate, but it only grew larger. Finally they had to jump out a back window, dropping a fair distance into the bushes below, scraping themselves up in the process. They dashed to their car and drove off with John and Danny keeping themselves out of sight.

Meeting Gonzo John seemed to provoke some of his fans. A few times people challenged him to fight for no apparent reason, and once, when he was eating in a restaurant in Los Angeles, a fan came up to him, said "John," and smashed a hamburger into his face. Belushi had to be restrained from attacking him. He was more receptive to the fans who handed him cocaine in elevators, in clubs, or anywhere else they happened to meet him, and John's reputation as "America's guest" flowered in all its destructive force.

Belushi's encounters were but an exaggerated version of an accessibility that afflicted all the stars of *Saturday Night*. Part of it was the way the show related more directly than other TV shows to the lives and feelings of its viewers. That, along with its deliberately casual style, seemed to give fans the impression that the performers were more real than other people on TV, more like them.

Many viewers concluded, therefore, that anybody could do what the people on *Saturday Night* were doing, given half a chance, and thus the 17th floor was inundated by letters and calls—at the rate of twenty per day most days— from fans who dreamed of being hired. There were so many tapes, cassettes, and scripts sent in that they had to be stored in plastic garbage bags until NBC got around to sending them back. (The show's staff didn't read submissions in order to avoid the possibility of plagiarism suits.) One fan who wrote regularly became known on 17 as the "Go Fuck a Frog" guy because he always closed his letters with that line. *Saturday Night* touched a deep and responsive chord among legions of eccentrics and would- be eccentrics across the land, all of whom seemed to feel a special, personal connection with their idols on the show.

Another reason the stars of *Saturday Night* seemed so accessible was the intimacy of television itself. After watching fans react to John, Gilda, and the rest, it struck Barry Secunda, the manager of many of the show's writers, that television performers are less intimidating than movie stars because they come into viewers' homes shrunk down, smaller than life size on the home screen, whereas movie stars loom so much larger than life in the theaters. That, Secunda believes, is the reason that everywhere the cast members went, they were not just watched, but surrounded, approached, often touched, as if deep down people felt they might put them in their pockets and take them home to show their friends.

In truth, the cast and writers of *Saturday Night* were becoming less like their fans every day. Accustomed to assuming their tastes corresponded with their audience's, they now found themselves dealing with something else entirely. The new fans were generally younger than they were, the teenage rock-and-roll crowd who'd heard what little they cared to hear about the sixties from their older brothers and sisters. If they raised clenched fists, it was in stadiums for heavy-metal bands; those who managed to get tickets for the show came in tanked up on beers and joints, shouting "BA-LOOSH- EE!" at the top of their lungs. Besides Belushi, their favorite character tended to be Mr. Bill. The studio audience in 8H went wild whenever a Mr. Bill film came on, and many times fans greeted the performers on the street—to their utter consternation—by shouting "Ohhhh nooo, Mr. Bill!"

The onslaught of what Belushi himself sometimes dismissed as "the angel-dust crowd" horrified everyone on the show. "It was embarrassing," Rosie Shuster said. "We were the TV literati, very hip, the darlings of some intellectual culture. Then it sort of degenerated into people who thought the more shrill the better. Fan mail started to be from fourteen-year-olds who couldn't spell."

Sophisticated or not, however, the new fans were still consumers, buyers of cosmetics, candy, hair dryers, movie tickets, motorcycles, and beer. There were tens of millions of them, and they still watched very little else on TV. The great American youth market had discovered *Saturday Night*, and *Saturday Night* began to reap the bounty of what it had sown.

The most direct beneficiary of that bounty was NBC. The modest little late-night show Herb Schlosser had conceived four years earlier became a veritable fountain of cash. Thirty-second commercial spots that had once been hard to get rid of at $7,500 were now selling for between $50,000 and $60,000 apiece—a few last-minute sales brought $70,000. The network had sixteen of those spots to sell on every show, and advertisers were standing in line to get them.

NBC's executives still heard periodic complaints from sponsors and affiliates alike that *Saturday Night* was going too far with its humor, but more often than not those complaints were now followed by requests for more commercial time on the show. The affiliates had twenty spots of their own to sell on *Saturday Night*, and although they sold for considerably less than the network's spots, they were lucrative indeed, and virtually pure profit, since the affiliates bore none of the show's production costs. Not surprisingly, the number of NBC affiliates carrying *Saturday Night* rose from 144 stations in its first year to a nearly full network complement of 215 stations in its fifth.

The combination of *Saturday Night*'s high ratings and youthful demographics made it one of the most desirable buys in all of television. Many weeks there were more men between the ages of eighteen and thirty-four watching *Saturday Night* than any other program, prime time or otherwise. NBC's prime-time programs weren't even close. And since *Saturday Night*'s second and third reruns were now attracting audiences almost as large as the live shows—another all but unprecedented achievement—its sales value literally tripled.

Exactly how much money NBC made from *Saturday Night* is buried somewhere in the labyrinthine depths of the network's account ledgers. The digit heads don't deem a show profitable until they've written off every inflated cent they can for studio time, equipment, sets, and a thousand other costs, much of it paid by NBC to NBC. Chief digit head Don Carswell says NBC lost about $3 million before *Saturday Night* started turning a profit in its fourth season. Others say that for all practical purposes the show probably earned back its development costs and stopped losing money in its second season, and certainly by its third.

In any event, after the ratings floodgates opened in its fourth and fifth seasons, *Saturday Night* was earning *profits* for NBC of between $30 million and $40 million a year. About three quarters of that would have come from network sales, the remainder (generally overlooked when figures such as these are tallied) from sales made by the local stations owned by NBC in New York, Los Angeles, Chicago, Washington, and Cleveland. The motley band of freaks from the underground had turned into one of NBC's, and RCA's, most important profit centers.

Those revenues had predictably salutary effects on the show's relationship with the network. After Lorne's threats to leave at the end of the third season, he signed a new one-year contract with NBC that paid him at least $750,000 for the fourth season. On the side, Lorne was also given a substantial "development fund" to produce two *Best of Saturday Night* compilation specials for NBC to run in prime time. One of the NBC executives involved with that deal says that this "development fund" essentially meant NBC agreed to give Lorne the money to set up his own production company, which he named Broadway Video.

The following year he signed another one-year deal that raised his base pay as the producer of *Saturday Night* to $37,500 per show. That deal also gave him a 50 percent share of any future syndication rights to *Saturday Night* and an equal share of all future video rights. The *Best of Saturday Night* specials were successful, and in the fifth season NBC turned them into a regular prime-time series—edited and produced, naturally, by Lorne. In the fifth season, between *Saturday Night* and the *Best of* series, it's likely Lorne was paid at least $1.5 million in salary alone. At the same time he used NBC's money to begin building Broadway Video from a one-room operation into a first-class production company, the foundation of a small empire.

(Broadway Video was located in the Brill Building on the corner of Forty-ninth and Broadway in midtown Manhattan. In the fifties and early sixties, the Brill Building was the headquarters for many record companies and music publishers, among them Don Kirshner, and it was famous for the songwriters who worked there, among them Carole King and Gerry Goffin, Ellie Greenwich and Jeff Barry, Cynthia Weil and Barry Mann, Jerry Lieber and Mike Stoller, Neil Diamond, and Neil Sedaka.)

In the same negotiations, NBC finally accepted fully Lorne's definition of what was necessary to produce his show. In the third season *Saturday Night*'s budget was $260,000, almost twice what it had been in the beginning. In the fourth season the budget jumped to $406,000 a show. In the fifth season it jumped again, to $553,000. That was the first year *Saturday Night* came in under budget.

Those budgets reflected substantial raises for all the writers and performers. The Mickey Rooney-Judy Garland contracts had long since been torn up and renegotiated. In the fourth season the cast members were making over $5,000 per show and half again as much for reruns. With specials and other perks they earned about $200,000. In the fifth season they were given another raise, to $7,500 per show, and fees of $10,000 per show for the *Best of* series, bringing their gross pay up to almost $500,000 for the year. The senior writers, depending on what development deals Lorne cut them in on and how much on-camera time they got backing up the cast, were making between $200,000 and $300,000 by the fifth season.

All that money paled in the face of the offers that were coming in from outside NBC. Bernie Brillstein, by now representing Lorne, John, Danny, Gilda, Rosie Shuster, and Alan Zweibel, said that after *Animal House* "the Hollywood barracudas came out." At read- throughs and rehearsals there were studio executives and big-time agents dropping by, schmoozing and talking deals. Gary Weis, by then living in Hollywood, says that all the major studios were in rabid pursuit of what was being called "the *Saturday Night* movie"— nobody knew what the plot would be, or cared. The *Saturday Night* imprimatur was all that mattered.

As the likely producer of "the *Saturday Night* movie," Lorne became one of the most sought-after untried movie producers in the history of Hollywood. In the fourth season Bernie Brillstein negotiated a lucrative, three-picture deal for him with Warner Brothers after turning down, Brillstein says, a nine-picture offer from Paramount. By the fifth season all the cast members except Garrett had been signed to movie deals, led by Belushi, who was commuting from one film to the next. ("From Samurai Night Live to Matinee Idol" read the headline on one of *Rolling* Stone's cover stories.) John's fee for a film went from $35,000 for *Animal House* to $350,000 and up. Gilda was also besieged with offers. Gary Weis swears that for one movie he was going to direct, the studio was offering her a flat fee of $1 million for a cameo appearance that would have taken a week's work.

Just as rabid were the entreaties from hundreds of hustlers both large and small proposing schemes to establish even the most tenuous of connections to the show. McDonald's wanted to make Roseanne Roseannadanna glasses, an amusement park wanted to use the Coneheads in a series of commercials, people were clamoring for the rights to sell *Saturday Night* posters, T-shirts, jackets, and jewelry ... the gimmicks went on and on, and the promises of shares in millions of dollars in merchandising profits never ended.

Record companies began to realize that an appearance on the show by one of their artists could result in immediate sales of as many as 300,000 albums, which made *Saturday Night* one of the most potent promotional tools ever devised. Billy Joel, not yet as big a star as he would soon become, landed a guest shot on the show after weeks of pleading by his managers. It turned out to be on the same date as his high-school reunion, which he'd dearly hoped to attend. His representatives called to ask if he could play on *Saturday Night* another time. Lorne said no, and Joel skipped his reunion.

The same commercial boost applied to hosts. At his concerts, Steve Martin saw quite clearly the impact of performing on *Saturday Night*: The size of his audiences doubled within six months, from seven or eight thousand people to fifteen thousand, and now his audiences would shout out lines he'd done on the show. Martin had gotten his first major TV break on the *Tonight Show*, but it hadn't produced anything near that reaction. "*Saturday Night*," Martin says, "was a direct line into consumers of pop." The single he released of "King Tut" quickly sold a million and a half copies.

\* \* \*

Finding themselves now among the hottest properties at NBC, and feeling as they did that the network had always done as little as it possibly could for them in the past, some on *Saturday Night* took the opportunity to turn the screws a little.

Franken and Davis, in their negotiations for the fourth season, held out for a huge salary increase and almost left the show before Lorne intervened and NBC caved in. The following year they demanded a clause be added to their contract that required the network to supply towels for the shower on the 17th floor—too often in the past they'd found themselves, after working all night, unable to clean up because the towels were all gone. The clause stipulated that if NBC for any reason failed to provide those towels, there would be a $100 penalty the first day, a $200 penalty the second day, and so on, the penalty doubling each towelless day thereafter. All the penalty funds were to go toward the purchase of new towels.

Similarly, Anne Beatts, during her contract negotiations for the fourth season, realized that for years she'd been spending nights on the 17th floor sleeping on a vinyl love seat that stuck to her skin. So after she resolved the money part of her deal with NBC negotiator Jim Henry (a man viewed with suspicion by most of the *Saturday Night* team), she said, "Wait a minute. If you want me back I want a bed in my office. A hospital bed."

Jim Henry, nonplussed, moved his hand around in a circle, miming the cranking of a hospital bed. "A *hospital* bed?" he said.

"No," Beatts said, holding out her palm and poking it with her finger to indicate a push-button control device. "A hospital bed." Like F&D, she got what she asked for.

Working conditions improved in other ways. The offices on 17 were expanded and redecorated, as were the dressing rooms and offices on the eighth and ninth floors. NBC would spend almost a million dollars on renovations for *Saturday Night* in the fourth and fifth seasons, all of it to the show's specifications. The dressing rooms were fitted out with sinks, telephones, new furniture, and TV sets. Several shower rooms were installed nearby. *Saturday Night* now occupied almost the entire 17th floor, compared to only about half of it at the start. All the stars and writers had their own offices. Herb Sargent affectionately dubbed the new wing in which the writers toiled The Writer's Block. A kitchenette was added, the prefab shower was replaced with a real shower, and new carpeting, new ceilings, new track lighting, and a new air-conditioning system were installed. Lorne, who in a memo a few years before had practically had to beg budget czar Don Carswell to get a single videocassette machine for the 17th floor, received the ultimate corporate benediction, a bathroom in his office. It came equipped with a refrigerator with an ice-cube maker. He also had his own shower, which at his request had six shower heads, three on one side, three on another. When he wasn't satisfied with the first shower heads NBC provided, they were torn out and new ones put in.

The offices were now so rambling and so slick they looked, Alan Zweibel thought, like the headquarters of a Madison Avenue advertising agency, and so crowded it seemed *Saturday Night* had turned into an industry. The lean staff the show had started with expanded to at least three times its original size. Everything people had previously done by themselves was now done by aides; by the fifth season a favorite line was that "everybody's assistant had a secretary." The days when everyone knew everyone else were gone. Once, a new assistant brought a problem to Lorne, and after she left, he looked over to Kathy Minkowsky and said, "Who's she?"

On *Saturday Night*s there were so many people running around on the floor of the studio that it was decided everyone who worked on the show should wear a *Saturday Night* shirt to identify them. Some of the staff already had one that had been designed a couple of years earlier, and now an order went out for more. It was a beautiful shirt, an uptown adaptation of the traditional work shirt, loose but impeccably cut, simple yet elegant. On the back, *Saturday Night* was embroidered in flowing script with aqua thread. The letter S was a musical clef with silver embroidery inside, and the buttonholes were sewn with different colors, blue on some, gold on others. People had their names on the front over the pocket, and on the shoulders in back their jobs—*Producer*, *Writer*, and so on. When *Hired Hand* appeared on one it started a rash of joke job titles. The shirts didn't really serve their purpose, though, because no one could decide who should and who shouldn't have one, and too many people who were supposed to wear them didn't.

Almost any amenity the show asked for was granted. NBC's Rick Traum gradually assumed the role of *Saturday Night*'s chief fixer in those years, working within or, if necessary, around network regulations to keep the show happy. He compared the job to being "a jailhouse lawyer." When it turned out that the television sets in the stars' dressing rooms could be seen only from one corner of the room, Traum fought the bureaucratic battle to have them reinstalled so they pulled out from the wall on movable trays. Another time Traum had to set up a private telephone account in his own name so that the phones in the stars' dressing rooms—which he'd worked for weeks to get approved—wouldn't be removed during an NBC austerity campaign.

Always there was more wine, flowers, and food delivered to the 17th floor. At the read-throughs, there was a wide variety of fruits, vegetables, nuts, cheeses, breads, and pastries. The best Colombian coffee was delivered in the bean; the show had its own coffee grinder. For Lorne there were cases of Evian water, exotic orchids for his desk, and a better white wine. The unit managers still grumbled about some of the requisitions—paying to feed the fish in Lorne's aquarium was not something they deemed a legitimate business expense—but they also understood that normal corporate policy no longer applied to *Saturday Night*.

Franne Lee, who now spent whatever she thought was necessary on costumes, said that as NBC complied with every request, it was as if the company were whispering in their ears. "Here," the whispers said, "take it, *take* it. Just keep up the good work."

CHAPTER 28

# The White Party

Perhaps the specially designed Plexiglas divider at the entry of *Saturday Night*'s offices on 17 spoke best for the madness that swept over the show in 1978 and 1979. The outline of a man had been cut out of its center. It looked as if someone had charged through it in a panic, the way fleeing villains in cartoons used to do. And the way many members of the show's staff felt like doing as the show reached the pinnacle of its success.

Working on the 17th floor was like working in a funhouse filled with mirrors—always the reporters were there, and always there were more articles about the show, strange reflections of themselves staring back from the pages. Everywhere they went—clubs, theaters, discos—stanchions were immediately lowered and they were ushered to the best tables, heads would turn, and people would murmur "*Saturday Night Live*" as they swept inside. Sometimes, sitting in restaurants on Sundays, the writers would overhear conversations about the show, at not one but several different tables.

The glamour of it all was irresistible, and, in contrast to the early years, for many if not most on the 17th floor the partying was now more fun than doing the show. But inevitably their insularity increased. When they couldn't go out without being mobbed, couldn't go to a party without all conversation stopping when they walked in, the natural recourse was to spend more of their time, if not with equally famous friends, then together. They didn't have to explain to each other what John and Gilda and Billy were really like.

In one interview, Lorne was bemoaning the growing isolation of the cast, the writers, and himself. It was hurting them all, he said, not to be out on the streets more, talking to the grocer or the laundryman, being exposed to the realities of daily life that make good comedy. As he talked, it was a Friday afternoon, and he was sitting in his office on the ninth floor, the curtains drawn, while the show was being blocked in the studio.

Even the show's annual dinner gatherings for the Passover seder, which had been quietly celebrated on the 17th floor beginning in the second season, went Hollywood. They became "The Paul Shaffer Celebrity Seder," complete with specially printed matchbooks bearing that title. It was an ecumenical service for both Jews and gentiles, half religious ceremony, half celebrity roast. Shaffer led it in his sleaziest Las Vegas style. "For the blessing over the wine, I'd like to call on someone who has a new movie coming out," he'd say. "We're all very excited about it."

Much of the time, though, their sense of humor about themselves was lost in the celebrity shuffle. Rather than a family united in a cause, they became what one of the writers called "an elite crowd that excluded a lot of people, a sort of hostile in-crowd." The cast and writers grew ever more temperamental, aloof even to those who worked with them. Cherie Fortis, who was hired in the third year as an assistant to Lorne's assistant, Kathy Minkowsky, was surprised that for a show that considered itself anarchistic, everyone seemed to be very concerned with hierarchy. Many times she was told that she was not to do something because it was somebody else's job to do it, and she found that she was not to speak to the cast members directly—there were those whose job it was to relay messages to them.

Dealing with the cast wasn't an easy job. One production assistant said that in the first two years, "if one of the performers yelled at you, you could yell right back. In the fourth and fifth years, that was no longer tolerated." Another production assistant spent much of her time "on tiptoe" around the cast and writers. "We were afraid of them," she said. "To knock on a door and ask for a script could get you your head bitten off." A third person who spent a lot of time on the 17th floor said, "There was a certain pride taken in not treating people well."

Reporters doing articles on the show began to notice that testiness too, and many mentioned how hostile the stars of *Saturday Night* had become. Jane Curtin developed a passionate distaste for the press. Once she was approached by a reporter who was following the show for several days. "No one said anything to me about an interview," she snapped, and stalked off. For the rest of the week, whenever she saw the reporter she glowered.

In August 1979, *TV Guide* ran a devastating article entitled "*Saturday Night* Moribund." In it, reporter John Mariani told of a nasty encounter with Belushi during rehearsals when Belushi grabbed his tape recorder and almost tore it apart. Later, when Mariani asked Bill Murray for an interview, Murray wanted to know if he was writing about everybody on the show or just about him. Informed it was about everybody, he said, "Then I don't want to be in your article." Mariani wondered in the piece the same thing a lot of reporters were wondering in those days: "why everyone in a show generally liked by the media is so suspicious of the media."

Mariani provided part of the answer himself when he quoted a production assistant: "They become paranoid about people wanting something from them." Another part of the answer was their realization that the media, as they often do, had started looking for ways to tear *Saturday Night* down, now that it had risen to such heights. Some journalists also started to look for evidence of drug use on the show (although at other times it was the journalists themselves who pulled out the first joint or offered the first line of cocaine). One day when a reporter was in the office, Belushi threw a bottle of vitamin E tablets out on the floor, lay down with his mouth open, pills strewn all around him, and started yelling. "You want to know about the drugs we take?" he shouted. "Come here!"

Cocaine, in fact, was a principal cause of the surliness the reporters sensed in *Saturday Night*. The drug itself made many of those who used it hostile. It also made them suspicious of the media, because now they had too much to hide. By the fourth season cocaine had become a staple on *Saturday Night*, an integral part of the working process there. Fears of a bust increased. In the fifth season Lorne actually posted a guard, a huge black man named Alvin, outside the elevators on the 17th floor. Ostensibly Alvin was there to keep away fans and other well-wishers, but few on the show doubted that an important part of his job was to prevent any sudden surprises from visiting law-enforcement officers.

Coke became the drug of choice on *Saturday Night* for several reasons. People had the money to pay for it now, and it was immensely useful in keeping them alive and kicking when fatigue was wearing them down. Cocaine is also the drug of success and ambition, a tonic to those for whom doubt and introspection serve no purpose. No accident that it replaced psychedelics in the Woodstock Generation's stash boxes as flower children turned into young professionals. A key member of the show's production staff found that she had to stop smoking pot when she worked on *Saturday Night*—ironically, since it was the first job she'd ever had where she *could* smoke pot—because it made her too sensitive, too soft in dealing with all the people calling in who wanted something. With cocaine she found she could tell them no very efficiently, very fast, with no emotion whatsoever. "Coke," she said, "takes the heart out of people. It's irrelevant if you're hurting somebody. It's all what you want to get across at the moment and who you want to listen to you."

Not everyone used coke, of course: Jane Curtin didn't, nor did Bill Murray, nor did Gilda Radner. Gilda's drug was food. She developed, those who know her believe, into a bulimic in those years, gorging herself and then vomiting, obsessed to the point of physical danger with staying thin. Once she stood up in a restaurant at the end of a meal with friends and announced that she was going to eat everyone's dessert. She did, but she didn't gain a pound.

Gilda's bulimia was supposedly a closely guarded secret, but it was common knowledge on the 17th floor. One or two journalists who profiled her hinted at the subject but danced gracefully around it in their articles. Even Gilda herself, who sometimes confessed the details of her personal life almost as compulsively as she ate, referred to it obliquely on occasion. She told a reporter for one magazine that she'd thrown up in every toilet in Rockefeller Center.

But there was far more snorting than vomiting going on in the restrooms of 30 Rock. Several of those who worked at *Saturday Night* estimate that by the fourth season a good 65 percent of the nontechnical staff, from Lorne down to production assistants, used cocaine, many of them heavily. Consumption of a gram a day was not unusual, and over time that's enough to change anyone's disposition, radically. Even the more mild-tempered among them became snappish and arrogant after too many late nights and too many toots of what Gilda called "the Devil's dandruff." More and more the chill of cocaine settled over *Saturday Night*, gradually undermining several of those who came most heavily under its spell.

As great an effect as cocaine had, however, it was not the only drug that changed people. The narcotic effects of money and fame were equally influential. There were intoxicating amounts of all three stimulants on the show, and the combination was overwhelming.

To many of those around him, Lorne seemed a different person. He was quite rich now, and comfortably assumed the part. He moved into what one of the writers called his "Giorgio Armani phase," shifting from cottons to silk, jeans to slacks, corduroy jackets to fine tweed blazers, the very picture of hip success. "A fashion magazine look," one of his staff described it. He always rode in a limo, and took his vacations on Saint Barts island in the Caribbean. He moved into a new apartment, on Central Park West, which had eight rooms and a sweeping view of the park. Paul Simon was his neighbor; a door in Lorne's kitchen opened into Paul's laundry room. Lorne also had a house in Amagansett in the Hamptons on Long Island, with tennis court, a pool, and an extensive garden. By then he was living with Susan Forristal, a former model who had been his girlfriend for the past couple of years, and they decorated their city place in what one friend described as "*Architectural Digest* style" and always seemed to have workmen refurbishing the country house.

More than ever Lorne spent time in his office on the phone, talking about movie deals or making social arrangements with his growing complement of rich and powerful friends. "Lorne," said one of the writers, "became preoccupied with his new worldly status." Besides Paul Simon, Mike Nichols, Steve Martin, Buck Henry, and Candice Bergen, his intimates now included Ron Delsener, the biggest rock concert promoter in New York, Francois de Menil, an heir to the vast Schlumberger fortune, and Jann Wenner, publisher of *Rolling Stone* magazine.

Lorne at the height of his power.
*Courtesy of Annie Leibovitz/Contact Press Images*

There were distinct parallels between Wenner and Lorne. *Rolling Stone* had tapped into the power of the youth market before *Saturday Night* had, when rock and roll was the motivating force and the counterculture was at its peak. Wenner channeled that energy into journalism with a brilliance that made *Rolling Stone* a phenomenon of its time. *Rolling* Stone's success changed Wenner—Citizen Wenner, he came to be called—as *Saturday Night*'s success changed Lorne. As rock faded, *Rolling Stone* struggled to find a new identity, moving from San Francisco to New York in the process, and there was no better confirmation of Lorne's theory that *Saturday Night* had picked up rock's banner than the way *Rolling Stone* embraced the show. The social elite that revolved around *Saturday Night* included not a few *Rolling Stone* reporters as well as, on Lorne's level, Wenner himself. Wenner was on Lorne's permanent guest list for the show; a guard once made the mistake of turning Wenner away downstairs, which precipitated a nasty scene later between Lorne and the head of NBC's Guest Relations department.

Lorne, according to some of his older friends on the show, grew imperious during this period, even regal. He was less apt to listen or to laugh. No longer was he the slightly scruffy, ambitious, but still romantic Young Turk he'd been in Los Angeles and Toronto, though even back then he would probably have admired the aura of power and sophistication he came to assume. One friend said Lorne became "a porcelain figure: 'The Phenomenon of Lorne Michaels.' He was like a young god. You wouldn't call him loose; he didn't get down and funky with you. You could do that as much as you wanted, but he would withdraw into his own center, like a king, and sit there. He would create an enormous black hole, an impermeable mirror."

\* \* \*

Most of those who worked for Lorne found his transformation something of a surprise. He'd always kept the details of his own finances to himself (probably because he'd always been paid so much more than anyone else) but now he seemed to have grown fabulously rich almost overnight, which he had. There was not a little disdain on the 17th floor for the airs he was putting on and for the high-toned friends he was cultivating. But at the same time, the changes in Lorne profoundly altered the attitudes the others on the show took toward the accouterments of success. As one of the writers put it, "Lorne got the apartment, the limo, the driver, the place in Amagansett. The effect it had on all of us was: 'Wait a minute. He's doing all that; why shouldn't we be able to do all of that too?'" A key member of the production staff was one of many who shared those sentiments. "Because Lorne accepted it," she said, "we all accepted it."

For many on the show, the turning point in that direction was the White Party, an all-day affair in the Hamptons just before the start of the third season. Lorne and Paul Simon were the hosts, together with O'Donoghue, who'd rented a house nearby to work on a movie script with Chevy. The idea was to have an elegant lawn party, a gathering of sophistication and taste with all the ladies and gentlemen wearing white. Supposedly, Lorne had heard of a similar party Paul McCartney once threw.

The party started at O'Donoghue's, then moved in the evening to Lorne's. More than a hundred guests were there, women in long summer dresses and wide-brimmed hats, men in white poplin jackets and starched linen shirts with no collars. Anne Beatts came in a blood-red gown. A harpist played on the lawn, which seemed to stretch out forever. Rosie Shuster sipped some wine, or something, she wasn't quite sure what, that had been dosed with LSD, and soon the whole scene appeared to her as if in a surreal dream, or a painting by Seurat. People floated by in white; sunshine reflected off silver serving trays. It was like Camelot, she thought to herself, something out of another century, a center of energy that had somehow drifted out from Manhattan and settled magically at this beautiful house near the ocean. They all seemed to be redefining themselves, embarking on a new life-style they had only read about or imagined.

The White Party became an annual affair, but back in New York the magic soon faded. Success engendered not so much gentility as what Alan Zweibel called "an overt jockeying for position." By the start of the fourth season, after *Animal House* had been such a huge success that summer, "everything had changed," Zweibel said. "*Saturday Night* became a breeding ground for stars, and people were looking to where they could cash in." Tom Schiller, who all his life had watched his father worry about getting his fair share of the fruits of his labors writing television comedy, found the changes especially ironic. "The Love Children had agents," he said later. "In the beginning it was like hippies working on a commune. Then people became much more conscious of their own worth and success, of what they were getting paid or not getting paid, and everybody began to pursue money. That happened really fast over the third and fourth years. The hippies turned into financial wizards."

Not exactly wizards, as it turned out. Choosing which direction to take when all directions seemed possible wasn't easy, and many on the show would come to regret the decisions they made in those years. In the meantime, the influx of the profiteers acted as a wedge, driving people apart. To manager Barry Secunda, the expansion of the offices on the 17th floor paralleled the split in the interests of those who worked there. "Everyone was divided off into their separate areas," he said, "into their individual trips."

Gilda, for example, signed a development deal with NBC that provided her with a personal secretary. Bill Murray was offended by that and soon he too had his own secretary. NBC provided Gilda with a refrigerator, and soon the rest of the cast demanded refrigerators too. The writers, figuring that they were the ones who were spending by far the most time on the 17th floor, went out and rented refrigerators for themselves and then got angry when NBC refused to pay for them.

There was also what Lorne called "a lot of dissension" about all the merchandising offers being waved in their faces. Whenever a proposal came in, Lorne, who in his negotiations with NBC had been given the rights to all the tie-ins, sat down with the writers and performers involved and discussed the offer, but he generally discouraged any involvement. His feeling was that merchandising was too distracting and too detrimental to the image of the show. Some of the writers and performers felt differently, and they watched unhappily as their characters were ripped off—sidewalk vendors sold copies of Bee antennae, novelty shops sold Coneheads masks, pirated posters turned up everywhere. Dan Aykroyd at one point got excited about setting up a company to produce Coneheads T-shirts, a project that was turned over to his brother, Peter. But Peter was a novice in the marketing of clothes. He made a lot of mistakes, offending buyers and underestimating necessary profit margins among them, and eventually he and Danny bailed out of the business.

Perhaps the saddest case of all was the strange fate that befell Mr. Bill.

Walter Williams, Mr. Bill's creator, was, contrary to the tone of the films he created, an extremely sweet, mild-mannered man. He was also an innocent in the ways of business. In the fourth season, Williams says he was getting no fewer than fifty calls and dozens of letters a day from people wanting to cash in on Mr. Bill. At first he turned them all down. He didn't want to exploit a character he loved dearly, nor did he have time to manage a sales empire. Finally he did authorize an official Mr. Bill T-shirt, in part because he was told he should do something to establish his legal rights to the character.

In the meantime, he saw every imaginable variety of Mr. Bill product produced without his permission—Mr. Bill dolls, Mr. Bill pins, Mr. Bill posters, Mr. Bill coffee mugs, Mr. Bill umbrellas. Although he hated to see his character cheapened, Williams at first ignored the majority of these products. After a while he did sue a few people, again primarily to protect his copyright. Eventually he was forced to hire a full-time lawyer just to threaten legal action against the pirates.

Just before the beginning of the fifth season, Williams got a call from an old friend he hadn't heard from in years, Vance de Generes. It was de Generes who had been, back in the days when Williams was making films in his living room in New Orleans, the original Mr. Hands. Mr. Hands wanted his name on the Mr. Bill copyright. He also wanted half of all the profits the character produced. If Williams didn't comply, de Generes said, he was going to sue.

Williams refused, and two days later de Generes's lawyers filed suit in the federal court in New Orleans. The two-day hearing generated a lot of publicity. Walter Williams feels he emerged vindicated: Mr. Bill was determined to be Williams's "basic idea and concept" and he was awarded most of the profits derived therefrom. De Generes did get a small share of certain sales that acknowledged his participation in the creation of the original films, but Williams considers those merely "token" merchandising rights. Unfortunately, the judge, after announcing he'd decided on a settlement, couldn't resist hamming it up for the crowd in his courtroom.

He pinned a name tag on his robe that read *Judge Sluggo*. He had a Mr. Bill doll lying on his bench, and he raised his gavel over it threateningly. The court clerk jumped up, obviously by prearrangement, and shouted, "I'll save you, Mr. Bill," blocking the judge's blow. Then the judge reached inside his robes and pulled out a pair of scissors. He cut off Mr. Bill's head and threw it to de Generes. He threw the body to Walter Williams. Picking up the cue, the spectators in the gallery started calling out, "Ohh, noooo, Mr. Bill!" Not waiting to hear the details of the settlement, the reporters dashed off to file their stories, assuming there had been some sort of equal division of Mr. Bill's estate, as there had been of his person. Walter Williams sat in the courtroom, relieved the battle was over. He'd enjoyed the judge's joke, but he would soon be disappointed to see it misinterpreted in the press.

CHAPTER 29

# Battle of the Bands

The phenomenology of *Saturday Night* probably peaked with the first show of the fourth season, when the Rolling Stones came to studio 8H to play some rock and roll.

Asked by a reporter how he'd managed to book the Stones for their first TV appearance in some ten years, Lorne casually let it be known that he'd happened to run into Earl McGrath, the president of Rolling Stones Records, at a Bob Dylan concert in Paris that summer. "We started rapping about it and the whole thing fell into place," he said. As matter-of-fact as he sounded, Lorne was anything but casual about the Stones' appearance on *Saturday Night*. As far as he was concerned, this was a television show that was going down in history.

It was a perfect match: the greatest rock and roll band in the world appearing on the greatest rock and roll TV comedy show in the world. The Stones were riding the crest of another resurgence in their long career, still, with the release of their *Some Girls* album, making strong and controversial music, still carrying on as the most notorious Bad Boys of their time. *Saturday Night* was soaring in the ratings and gaining an ever more notorious reputation for Bad Boy behavior of its own. *Animal House* had been the movie of the summer, and Belushi and Aykroyd just the month before had spent nine triumphant nights opening as the Blues Brothers for Steve Martin at the Universal Amphitheater in Los Angeles. Their first record album, *Briefcase Full of Blues*, was recorded at those shows.

For Lorne, the Stones playing *Saturday Night* was confirmation that *Saturday Night* was now playing on the Stones' level, and that the show had indeed picked up the mantle of rock and roll. This was more than a booking; this was a meeting of the gods. Which is why he threw a fit when he returned from Paris and saw what NBC had done to the dressing rooms.

Lorne had left at the end of the third season assuming that all the renovations NBC had agreed to make in the studio area would be completed for the fourth-season premiere. Now that the Stones were coming, he was more anxious than ever that *Saturday Night* be ready for them: He wanted everything to be perfect. Until Lorne arrived, NBC's facilities people felt everything was in pretty good shape. Lorne soon disabused them of that notion.

Escorted on an inspection tour by Jean Doumanian, his associate producer, Lorne took one look and said, "These are definitely out of the question." Each of the dressing rooms had one wall painted white and the opposite wall painted in wide stripes of garish green, blue, orange, or yellow. The fluorescent fixtures overhead made everything seem to throb. NBC had put in a few pieces of its standard-issue furniture. Lorne described the total effect as "Salvation Army."

Over the next few hours Lorne toured the dressing rooms with half a dozen NBC executives, from his friends in senior management Paul Klein and Mike Weinblatt ("Look at this, Mike!" he kept saying to Weinblatt as he took him around) to those responsible in NBC's maintenance department. There was a closed-door meeting in Lorne's ninth-floor office with engineering and facilities vice- president Frank Flemming and four other maintenance executives. Lorne's shouting could be heard down the hall as he informed them in no uncertain terms that something had better be done to rectify this travesty before the Stones arrived a few days later. The executives were insulted that Lorne had the nerve to talk to them the way he did, and they shrugged and rolled their eyes as he yelled, but they acted nonetheless.

Painters were assigned to redo the dressing rooms immediately. Jack Lyons, NBC's manager of "housekeeping services," went out to rent better furniture. It was the Jewish holiday Rosh Hashanah and the showrooms he knew on the Lower East Side were closed, but late in the day he found one open and managed to get some new pieces delivered. There was need for more, so on Saturday Rick Traum scoured NBC's executive offices. He found a couch in program chief Paul Klein's office, another couch in *Tomorrow* show host Tom Snyder's office, and some miscellaneous chairs here and there. All were borrowed for the weekend.

NBC had worries other than interior decoration when faced with the prospect of Mick Jagger and the Rolling Stones playing, live, on their network. This was a band of known boozers and drug fiends whose leader had climaxed a series of concert appearances riding a forty-foot inflatable phallus. Worse, they were appearing on a show that had itself been known to ruffle the skirts of propriety. *Saturday Night*, NBC knew, could not be counted on to display the good sense of Ed Sullivan, who had insisted when the Stones appeared on his show in 1967 that they change the lyrics of their song "Let's Spend the Night Together" to "Let's spend some time together." All week executives in Standards fretted about the outrages the Stones might commit, shuddering at visions of on-camera drinking, open flies, and obscenities being shouted out on national television. According to Paul Klein, warnings were issued to representatives of the Stones that such behavior would not be tolerated.

NBC was also terrified about the security implications of the Rolling Stones' playing a live concert in a three-hundred-seat studio in the heart of sober, dignified Rockefeller Center. Here the nightmare was that waves of leather-jacketed rock-and-roll animals might storm the security desks. The potential horror was underscored by Lorne's friend, rock promoter Ron Delsener, who had offered his services in helping NBC handle the onslaught he assured them was in the offing. Delsener was brought in to act as a security consultant.

Whether any of NBC's concerns regarding suitable behavior on television ever reached the Stones is unknown, and even if they had, the Stones most likely wouldn't have noticed, so hard were they practicing and partying with *Saturday Night*. On Wednesday and Thursday nights the Stones rehearsed in a studio called Bill's on West Fifty-second Street. A small contingent from the show, including Lorne, Howard Shore, Tom Davis, and Paul Shaffer, came to watch, some of them sitting on boxes at the Stones' feet as they played. Later, Jagger and Richards and some of the other Stones came to Belushi's apartment, playing the blues with John and his wife, Judy, in John's soundproof music room, The Vault.

Tom Davis, who four years earlier had given up his tickets to a Stones concert in Hollywood to come to New York for *Saturday Night*, remembers the rehearsals at Bill's as the rock-and-roll experience of a lifetime. The Stones went flat-out every time they plugged in, holding nothing back, rehearsing late into the night. So hard and passionately did they play that Paul Shaffer, for one, had the clear impression as he watched that they were laying down a challenge to *Saturday Night*, showing these pretenders to the Bad Boy throne what they were up against. Shaffer sensed what he called a "battle of the bands" brewing, because Lorne picked up the gauntlet.

Coming back to 17 after one of the rehearsals, Lorne raved like everyone else about the Stones—how professional they were, how much energy they had. Then he paused and asked, "Are they going to blow us away?" He reminded his troops that nearly fifteen years after the Beatles' first appearance on *The Ed Sullivan Show*, it was a show people still wanted to see, a classic. The same could happen with this show, Lorne said, and none of them were going to enjoy watching it fifteen years from now if the Stones made *Saturday Night* look lame. "We'd better be good," he said.

The Stones didn't show up in 8H until well into the night on Friday, hours beyond their expected five-o'clock arrival. They lived up to their legendary rowdiness, drinking Scotch and vodka and snorting coke openly in the studio, oblivious to the Rockefeller Center security guards on special duty all around them. Ron Delsener wasn't taking any chances. Special security badges had been issued for anyone entering the studio, and Delsener had deployed his own concert-hardened bouncers to check them. When the Stones finally played, Jagger was so drunk he was staggering across the stage, but again they rocked without restraint, playing each of their three numbers three times, setting those who had managed to get in to watch them dancing around the floor.

The Stones were late again for rehearsal on Saturday, and again they ingested a wide variety of intoxicating substances once they arrived. At one point Keith Richards, getting thirsty, called the people who distributed Rebel Yell whiskey and said, "Hello, this is Mick Jagger from the Rolling Stones. We need some Rebel Yell. Would you send us some cases?"

Jagger seemed to be the only one of the Stones really to understand what was going on with the show; during rehearsal he was overheard trying to explain it to drummer Charlie Watts. Jagger rehearsed a sketch with Dan Aykroyd in which Aykroyd, as Tom Snyder, interviewed Jagger on the *Tomorrow* show, and once again those watching sensed an underlying current of competition. In the middle of the sketch Tom Snyder got up to show that he could dance like Jagger, and those watching say Jagger, who remained seated, was clearly uncomfortable at being upstaged.

Keith Richards was supposed to be in two sketches, but after dress rehearsal both his parts were cut. In one he had a line to say, but couldn't remember it; in the other he had an entrance that he missed. There was some question whether he could stand up if he did make it; some doubted he remembered he'd been in a sketch at all. "It's nice," Laraine Newman said of Richards, "to be standing and working with a dead person."

The Rolling Stones come to *Saturday Night*. Jane Curtin, Bill Murray, Keith Richards, Paul Shaffer (as rock promoter Don Kirshner) and John Belushi rehearse a sketch that was cut when Keith couldn't remember what to do. © *NBC*

For their entry to the studio *Saturday Night*, the Stones were led on an incredibly circuitous route that wound its way from Radio City Music Hail across the street through the tunnels beneath Rockefeller Center and up in a private elevator to the eighth floor of 30 Rock. Delsener's and NBC's security forces were augmented by a contingent from the New York City police; the tickets were printed with a special ultraviolet ink to thwart counterfeiters. All week people had been trying frantically to get tickets; one production assistant was offered $500 to sneak someone into the studio. An aide to Henry Kissinger phoned the 17th floor wanting tickets for Kissinger's son. Al Franken took the call to say that they would gladly have complied had it not been for Kissinger's role in the Christmas bombing of North Vietnam in 1972.

The Stones' specifications for the audience they wanted in the studio had been spelled out for the staff and NBC in a memo from associate producer Jean Doumanian: "No sophisticated 'Elaine's,' upper east-siders, no moms and pops, no show-biz folks, just young rock and roll fans." Plenty of celebrities made it in anyway, among them Steven Spielberg, Paul Simon, Richard Dreyfuss, and NBC's new president,

Fred Silverman. Silverman had replaced Herb Schlosser four months earlier, a move that had stunned the television industry and made headlines all over the country. He was attending *Saturday Night* for the first time ever.

Downstairs in the lobby, a couple of counterfeiters were caught, but the expected onslaught of hooligans failed to materialize. Thirty Rock was almost eerily quiet, much more so than usual on a Saturday before a show. NBC's security people would later claim that Delsener's precautions had been "overkill"; Delsener argued he had simply done his job well. At any rate, as show time neared there were a few empty seats in the studio, and NBC's pages actually had to go out to the street and round up people to fill them.

The censor on duty was still nervous, having noticed in dress that Jagger's pants seemed to reveal more of his famous crotch than they should have. He told assistant costume designer Karen Roston that Jagger would have to cover himself more adequately on-air. Roston laughed and said, "If you want to go up to Mick Jagger and tell him he has to wear underwear, be my guest." The censor decided against it, and Jagger went on national television apparently—very apparently— sans briefs.

If there was a battle of the bands that night, *Saturday Night* won it. Jagger did indeed pale next to Danny in the Tom Snyder sketch; Jagger's bravado didn't obscure the fact that this was Danny's arena, and against Aykroyd's energy Jagger couldn't help but seem fey by comparison. The highlight of the show was probably Danny's performance as the Norge refrigerator repairman in the Nerds sketch, when he defied Standards and let his trousers hang halfway off his backside. Bill Murray made a hilarious debut as Jane Curtin's co- anchor on Weekend Update, saying that as an entertainment correspondent he hadn't paid as much attention to the real world as he should have, and that in preparation for his new assignment he'd been boning up on current affairs. He admitted to being shocked to learn that people out there were shooting other people—with real guns. "Ouch," he said.

All the anticipation awaited the Stones, of course, but the Stones blew it. They had rehearsed and partied too hard, committing the amateur's mistake of peaking too soon. By the time they came on, Jagger's voice was a raspy whisper of what it had been all week, and their celebrated stage act seemed listless and uninspired.

Their raunchiest moment came during an instrumental break in one song when Jagger leaned up against guitarist Ron Wood and licked him on the lips. Bernie Brillstein happened to be sitting near Fred Silverman, and at that moment he turned around to see a look of shock and revulsion on Silverman's face. It wouldn't be the last time Fred Silverman would experience those emotions as he watched *Saturday Night*.

\* \* \*

John Belushi's big moment on the Stones show came after the opening credits, when New York Mayor Ed Koch walked on stage to present him with a certificate of appreciation for his performance in *Animal House*. Belushi was supposedly incensed that he hadn't rated a key to the city. "Is this it?" he said, looking at the certificate. Then he launched into a tirade about how *Animal House* had made profits of $60 million ("Does New York have sixty million?") and how he'd only made $900 from it ("No points—zip"). Gradually he worked himself into a frenzy, yelling about coming back to work on a miserable little TV show that paid him a measly $450 a week. "I didn't have to come back here!" he shouted. "I could have stayed in Hollywood. It's so much easier there! But noooooo!" The audience burst into prolonged applause, and Belushi walked off with Mayor Koch, ostensibly to go see *Animal House*.

It was all, again, a joke but not a joke, just like John's speech deriding Rob Reiner as "Mr. Hollywood California Number One Show Big Shot" on *Saturday Night*'s third show. Belushi did indeed return for the fourth season feeling he'd outgrown the show. On top of *Animal House*, the Blues Brothers shows at the Universal Amphitheater were fresh in his mind: the band rocking behind him, thousands of people shouting his name, roaring at his every move, holding up matches at the end of their set. It was the staggering fulfillment of a long-held fantasy of rock-and-roll stardom for John, direct gratification on a scale a thousand times more powerful than he ever got in studio 8H.

Two months after the Stones show, on December 5, 1978, the *Briefcase Full of Blues* album was released. It went straight to the top of the record charts, selling by Christmas more than one million albums, and ultimately more than three million. John, just shy of his thirtieth birthday, was riding the crest of an incredible show-business triple play: the number-one record album, the top-grossing movie, and the hottest show on television. He was transformed, Bernie Brillstein said, from "Belushi" into "BELUSHI." Nothing would ever be the same.

John believed passionately in the Blues Brothers. He invested more than $100,000 of his own money, virtually his entire savings at the time, in the recording of the Amphitheater shows. He often told his friends, "We're the greatest fucking band in the world," and he threw himself into plans for a national concert tour. When Bernie Brillstein called production vice president Sean Daniel at Universal Studios to ask if Universal would be interested in backing a Blues Brothers movie, the answer was instantaneous: "Done," Daniel said, and John and Danny had a multimillion-dollar movie deal. At the same time John and Danny were flying back and forth to Hollywood, shooting the movie *1941* with Steven Spielberg, arriving in New York for the show on Wednesday or Thursday—John sometimes didn't get back until Friday or, one week, Saturday—and leaving again on Sunday.

John had real power now, and he loved it. As Chevy Chase had before him, he began to see *Saturday Night* as a minor-league affair. Early in the fourth season he told both Lorne and Bernie Brillstein he would probably not be returning to the show the following year.

Also like Chevy, John behind the scenes became insufferable, his behavior even worse than it had been before. The amount of cocaine he used, the fame he enjoyed, and the amount of money he made grew apace. His personality changed. He rejected the company of old friends and acted, one of the writers said, like "the Godfather … surprised when someone spoke in his presence without his permission, that sort of thing." He terrorized the production assistants. "John in the fourth year," one of them said, "was doing lots of drugs, and was very exhausted, pushed to the physical limit, crisscrossing the country. He was scary around the office. You never knew when he would turn." Once, he started shouting because some pictures that were supposed to have been hung in his office hadn't been, and in the midst of his tirade he swept his arm across a production assistant's desk, knocking everything on it to the floor. A half hour later he brought her an *Animal House* poster of himself signed "Love, John Belushi."

One of his worst weeks came in February 1979, midway through the fourth season, when actress Kate Jackson hosted the show. John arrived at the studio after three straight days of partying with Keith Richards. Al Franken was with him in his dressing room, going over some lines that Belushi hadn't learned, and John was so wasted that Franken jokingly asked if he remembered seeing the script before. Belushi erupted, and friends had to hold John back while Franken left. Much of the show that night was built around John, but he told Lorne he was too sick to go on. Lorne, furious, called NBC's in- house doctor, who examined John as Lorne stood there glowering.

"His lungs are filled with fluid," the doctor said. "If he goes on tonight, the odds are fifty-fifty that he'll die."

"I'll accept those odds!" Lorne said. Belushi did go on, looking pasty and sweaty the entire show.

Within *Saturday Night* there was some jealousy and some disdain for the Blues Brothers. The general feeling was that this was some sort of crazy fluke, nothing more than a comedy routine that had caught on somehow. People thought it ridiculous that John and Danny were taking it so seriously, more seriously than *Saturday Night*. Lorne felt that way more than most, many on the show believe, because the Blues Brothers existed outside his sphere of influence, and because John didn't give him credit for having provided the platform that launched them in the first place.

So it was that as the fourth season went on another battle of the bands developed, between John's Blues Brothers and Lorne's *Saturday Night*. The Blues Brothers were John's show, a project he controlled, and he was immensely proud he'd pulled it off independent of *Saturday Night*. Lorne seemed to dismiss it. His friends think he found it hard to accept that John and Danny might have other interests that were more important to them than the show. Lorne spent many hours on the phone arranging schedules so that John and Danny could film *1941*, and he promised he'd make room for them to tour with the Blues Brothers, but he didn't acknowledge that anything had really changed with them, never deferred to their new status. Lorne's attitude, Bernie Brillstein said, was to accommodate but also to hold the line firmly. "It was always, 'Okay, okay ... but you've gotta do the show, fellas.'"

John was outraged at that, and his patience with what he called "the Lorne Michaels show" began to run out. The fighting between the two of them grew more vehement. John scored one victory the week of the Kate Jackson show when he forced Lorne to book honky-tonk piano man Delbert McClinton, a favorite of John's, as the musical guest. It was a sweeps period and Lorne, more concerned with ratings than he used to be, wanted a bigger name. But John threatened to quit the show if McClinton didn't go on, and McClinton did.

Three shows later, John was unable to fly back to New York from Hollywood because of an ear infection. Again the attitude was conveyed, by Danny as well as by Lorne, that John was just goofing off. Danny told John he could drive across country if he really wanted to. John was, again, hurt and outraged. During the week he organized a little film to take his place on the show. It was shot at Steven Spielberg's house by John Landis, who would soon direct the Blues Brothers movie, and it showed John floating in the pool surrounded by beautiful girls. "I'd really love to be there," he said.

Lorne didn't use the film. He said there wasn't enough time for it, but he did put on a silly film by occasional contributor Aviva Slesin that had birds dressed up in funny costumes. Judy Jacklin Belushi says that to John, it was as if Lorne was saying, "Fuck you, you're not part of the show." Soon afterward John made up his mind definitely to leave.

There are those who suspect Lorne was probably relieved that John wasn't coming back, although others think Lorne never quite accepted the fact he wasn't. The real question, and the real battle of wills, was whether Danny would go with him.

Danny told Lorne that he would be back, but only as a performer, not a writer. He made that commitment "casually," friends of Danny's say, but Lorne clung to it, convinced Danny would return. Lorne says that he and Danny shook hands on the agreement, and that he based his own decision to come back for another season in part on his understanding that Danny would be there. But John was relentlessly urging Danny to leave. Thus Danny was torn between his loyalty to Lorne and the others on *Saturday Night* and his loyalty to John, so that in truth for most of the fourth season he vacillated.

At times Danny grew frustrated with the show and talked about quitting, as he always had, but now he had movies to flee to instead of truck stops outside Toronto. "I don't need this anymore," he'd say. But a minute later he'd be thinking about the next show, asking the other writers, "Okay, what're we gonna do this week?" When the deal for the Blues Brothers movie came through, Danny started writing the screenplay. Sometimes he'd walk through the hallways on 17 with a script for *Saturday Night* in one hand and the script for the film in the other. The movie script seemed to keep growing like some fungus, filling Danny's office with pages upon pages of yellow legal-pad paper. The pressure of juggling the show and the film began to tell. Other writers would come to Danny's office, asking his help on a sketch as they always had before, but now he'd often brush them off. "Guys," he'd say in his clenched staccato, "I can't do it anymore. I have too much other stuff."

Neither was Danny immune to the overwhelming scale of the Blues Brothers' success, or from the enticements that came in its wake. He was the quieter partner in the projects John was developing, but not a passive partner. After years of feeling he'd been ripped off on *Saturday Night* and a hundred other jobs, Danny began to feel that here was the Main Chance, the opportunity to exploit rather than be exploited. He started talking about building an empire, a "megabucks show-biz empire." For periods of a week or two at a time he'd come into the office playing a new character, the Mogul, wearing three-piece suits and smoking cigars. "We're going to the moon," he said once. "We're going to Mars."

Danny and John at the height of their fame.
*Courtesy of Annie Leibovitz/Contact Press Images*

\* \* \*

As much as the other writers and performers on *Saturday Night*, snickered about the gimmickry of the Blues Brothers, no one snickered at the amount of money they made, or the new level of stardom John and Danny had reached. It was obvious now that *Saturday Night* was a platform for success far beyond what any of them had previously dreamed. The pressures within increased accordingly.

The performer in the best position to capitalize on that potential was Gilda Radner (Bill Murray at that point was still a half-step behind), a fact that did not go unnoticed by Gilda herself. As one friend put it, "Gilda saw what was happening with John and Danny and wanted in on the action." For his own reasons, Lorne did too, and it was natural that he and Gilda form an alliance.

Gilda had always been the cast member who most behaved as Lorne would have wanted her to, always deferring to his judgment, always depending on him to help plan her career. The opposite, in other words, of Belushi. As her fame grew, Gilda leaned on Lorne more, not less. NBC publicity man Les Slater remembers the day he told Gilda that *TV Guide* wanted to do a profile of her. To a public relations man that is tantamount to an offer of sainthood from the church, but Gilda hesitated. "I'll have to talk to Lorne," she said. She turned down an offer of $850,000 to star with Robin Williams in the movie *Popeye*, in part because of Lorne's feeling that it would keep her away too long from *Saturday Night*.

Soon after the Blues Brothers album was released, Lorne and Gilda decided to make a record of their own, a comedy album to be called *Gilda Radner, Live from New York*. It started out as a fairly modest project, something to fill the idle weeks during *Saturday Night*'s Christmas break. Gilda, Paul Shaffer, and a few others from the show wrote up some songs and sketches, and about 250 invited friends crowded into the A&R recording studios on Seventh Avenue and Fifty-second Street for the live taping. Bill Murray acted, off mike, as the master of ceremonies. His romance with Gilda was going strong then, and after the show he lifted her up and carried her off the stage. It was probably their most public display of affection, and several of those there found it touching that Billy was so supportive of Gilda's first solo venture. That would change, as would everything else about the Gilda Live project.

After the taping, the same insane momentum that had overtaken the Blues Brothers overtook Gilda's record, turning it in the space of the next few months into a multimedia extravaganza. First somebody got the idea of turning the album into a show and taking it to Broadway, and then on a national tour. Somebody else said why not make a movie? It was decided to do all three. Presto: another show-business triple play of unprecedented proportions. Such were the dreams in the air *Saturday Night* breathed in 1979.

Several of those involved with the Gilda Live project say there's no question it was intended to rival John and Danny's success with the Blues Brothers. Having both come from the underground comedy scene of the early seventies, and having both risen to prominence at the same pace on *Saturday Night*, there was a natural competition between John and Gilda, and Gilda by now was finally feeling her own power in show business. "She had become," one of the writers said, "the Formidable Female. She was demanding parity of attention with John and Danny. It was dueling egos."

John contributed his share to the rivalry as well. As soon as the idea for Gilda's album had been floated, John told both of its co-producers, Paul Shaffer and Bob Tischler—who were, respectively, the musical director and album producer for the Blues Brothers—not to get involved. "Just wait," Belushi told Shaffer. "We're doing the Blues

Brothers [movie and tour] and we won't be coming back. I want you to be fresh. Just rest. Don't do the Gilda record." John called Tischler to his dressing room one night, and when he arrived, John grabbed him, threw him against the wall, and said, "You're not doing the Gilda album! It's going to be a piece of shit."

Shaffer and Tischler didn't take John's advice. They remained co-producers of Gilda's album; in fact, the first hint of trouble on Gilda Live came when they spent five months working on the album in post-production. Finally, in June, it was deemed ready. By then the Winter Garden Theater, a cavernous hall on Broadway, had been booked for the month of August and preparations were under way for Gilda's opening.

On the afternoon of June 28, Shaffer and Howard Shore flew in to the Hamptons in a chartered plane with the master tape. There was a small gathering at Lorne's place in Amagansett for a premiere listening; it was Gilda's birthday, and the unveiling was supposed to be a present for her. Besides Gilda and Lorne, Anne Beatts and production aides Cherie Fortis and Barbara Burns were there. Susan Forristal served fish salad for lunch while everyone waited for Paul to arrive with the tape.

Shaffer came in looking as if he hadn't slept for three days. They all took their wine into the living room and gathered around the tape recorder. Paul put on the tape. It took no more than a few minutes to realize that they were hearing a disaster. Some didn't hesitate to say so; others lapsed into uneasy silence. To everyone the tape sounded incredibly tinny, stripped of the inherent power of television that injected such electricity into the shows in studio 8H. The tape sounded exactly like what it was: a modest little vaudeville act recorded in a studio, a live show on tape, the worst of both worlds. It was decided, "unanimously and instantaneously," said one of those there, that the album could not be released.

The group dispersed. Gilda went off in tears, a "basket case," a friend said. Lorne took a walk outside, pacing around, raging that everything had gone wrong, that they'd blown a fortune on the record, that he didn't know what he was going to do next. It was quickly decided to charge ahead rather than retreat. Gilda's album would have to be rere-corded during the Broadway show, that was all. Everything would go on almost as planned. That was when Paul Shaffer got caught in the middle of the power struggle between Lorne and John.

It had been Shaffer who with John had organized the stellar group of rhythm and blues all-stars who backed the Blues Brothers at the Amphitheater shows. (The Blues Brothers band consisted of Shaffer on keyboards, Steve Cropper and Matt Murphy on guitars, Donald [Duck] Dunn on bass, Steve Jordan on drums, Lou Marini and Tom Scott on saxophones, Alan Rubin on trumpet, and Tom Malone on trombone.)

He planned to go directly from the premiere listening of Gilda's album at Lorne's house to Chicago, where three days later the Blues Brothers movie was scheduled to start shooting.

After that he would accompany John and Danny on their national tour.

Now Lorne exerted all his powers of persuasion to convince Shaffer he should stay in New York to help rescue Gilda Live. Bernie Brillstein, who was also caught in the middle between Lorne, John, and Gilda, all of them his clients, served as the go-between in the tug-of-war over Shaffer. Later Brillstein would call that June 28 his second worst day in show business.

Brillstein phoned Shaffer that afternoon and told him, "Lorne will do anything not to have you in Chicago next week." Shaffer dreaded choosing between Lorne and John. Each, he knew, passionately wanted to win out over the other. Shaffer didn't take missing out on a major motion picture lightly, and he knew if he defied John it would likely mean the end of his participation in the Blues Brothers. But he had already been upset by John's personality changes on cocaine, and specifically by John's refusal to give him as much credit as Shaffer thought he deserved for the Blues Brothers. John hadn't even introduced Shaffer to the audience during the Amphitheater shows because, Shaffer says, John wanted to be considered the leader of the band. Shaffer also felt guilty about letting Gilda down.

So Shaffer decided to stay in New York. When Bernie Brillstein called John to tell him of Shaffer's decision, John screamed, long and loud. Later John called Lorne in a rage.

"Shaffer's out!" he yelled. "He's not a Blues Brother and he'll never be a Blues Brother!"

* * *

Gilda's Broadway show careened toward its opening at the Winter Garden. Lorne produced it with the same sense of last-minute frenzy that had always managed to work on *Saturday Night*. Theater professionals would ask him how he expected to get everything done in time.

"I do this kind of show for ninety minutes every week," he'd answer.

"Yeah, but that's TV, this is Broadway," they'd answer back, and Lorne, who was also directing the show, would shake his head as if they didn't understand.

Even by Lorne's standards the atmosphere was chaotic. There were problems with the sets, fights among the writers (Michael O'Donoghue at one point returned his *Gilda Live* jacket to Lorne, having first neatly slashed the back with a knife), arguments over publicity pictures and concern over slow advance ticket sales. Lorne told Ron Delsener, who was promoting the show, not to worry about the tickets. "Our audience is stoned," he said. "They're still putting on their shoes. They'll be here."

As sanguine a front as Lorne presented, it was obvious to those who knew him how great the pressure was, and many thought he had finally stretched himself too thin. Gilda, too, was a nervous wreck, so much so that in the middle of her run she fell ill from exhaustion and missed several performances.

Lorne was right about one thing: The ticket sales picked up significantly, and the run of the show was extended for a few weeks into mid-September. But the critical reaction was negative. The consensus was that *Gilda Live* on Broadway was essentially the same as Gilda live on *Saturday Night*. The show was basically no more than a compilation of her popular characters, and many felt it was amateurish and misleading to charge people as much as $18.50 for a ticket (on the high end of Broadway's scale at the time) and then give them the same show they could see on television for free.

The same feeling prevailed back on the 17th floor, where *Gilda Live* was seen as a rip-off of *Saturday Night*. "I don't know anybody on *Saturday Night* who didn't hate Gilda's show," said one person who worked on both. There was also not a little resentment that Lorne was lavishing so much time and attention on Gilda—the teacher's-pet syndrome, one writer called it.

Bill Murray in particular came to resent *Gilda Live*. He spurned former friends who worked on it, telling one whom he ran into on 17, "You don't work here anymore—you're doing Gilda's shit." Not surprisingly, Gilda and Billy's romance had begun to fall apart. Several times they split and then reconciled; one friend described it as "a weaning and withdrawal [from each other], mostly cold turkey, but not totally." Their troubles didn't make the pressures on Gilda any easier to bear.

The *Gilda Live* movie was shot in Boston two weeks before the start of *Saturday Night*'s fifth season. Mike Nichols was the director. The shooting, moved from New York because of union problems, was complicated by the chaos surrounding the simultaneous arrival in town of Pope John Paul II on his first visit to that predominantly Catholic city. The filming caused confusion with the publicity for the touring version of *Gilda Live*, which was to start in Boston a few weeks later in a different theater. Mike Nichols subsequently decided he hadn't gotten all the footage he needed in Boston, so the entire show had to be set up for more shooting at the Brooklyn Academy of Music in December. Gilda spent her weeks off from *Saturday Night* flying off to another city to do another performance of *Gilda Live*. Finally the tour was cut short because everyone was too tired to go on.

\* \* \*

It wasn't until a few weeks before the fifth season started that it was known on the 17th floor that Danny wasn't coming back. For most of the summer, Lorne had thought Danny would return, although others say in retrospect there were clear signals to the contrary that Lorne chose to ignore. One such signal was when Danny failed to attend the party after the last show of the fourth season. He hadn't said anything to Lorne about not coming, and people could see disappointment registering on Lorne's face when he saw Danny wasn't there. "Danny," one friend said, "pulled a powder. Forever."

The Blues Brothers movie started production in Chicago on July 1, Danny's birthday. From the beginning it fell behind schedule, and there was talk in New York of how *Saturday Night* could accommodate Danny's need to be on the set finishing the movie as the fifth season began. That talk ended when Danny finally decided once and for all he was leaving with John.

Lorne learned of Danny's decision in a phone call from Bernie Brillstein. Later, Danny came to Lorne's place in Amagansett, and they talked. "You gave me your word," Lorne says he told him. But Lorne knew it didn't matter what had been said: Danny's mind had changed, and Lorne had to accept it. When the news broke on 17, people wandered around the halls, gathering in quiet groups and muttering, "Uh-oh, it's happened."

Bernie Brillstein says Danny decided, finally, to leave when he read an article in *People* magazine in which Michael O'Donoghue talked about John's riding around in limousines with shoe boxes filled with cocaine. In a rage, Danny called Brillstein from a phone booth at Folsom Prison, where the movie was being shot. "I want nothing to do with those people!" he said, meaning those people on *Saturday Night*.

As disappointed as they were, Danny's friends on the show say it seemed the proper moment for him and John to go. It was plain by then that the *Saturday Night* engine was running out of steam, and it made sense for them to take advantage of the tremendous momentum they had going for themselves. The abruptness of Danny's departure and the fact that he didn't return in even a part- time capacity left little doubt that the battles between Lorne and John had something to do with it. The consensus on 17 was that Danny's loyalty to John simply won out.

"The feeling," said writer Jim Downey, "was definitely that John spirited Danny away from the show."

Even those who thought Danny had made the right move took exception to the manner of his leaving. "The words that come to me," said one of the writers, "are 'slink away.'" Lorne told friends he felt Danny had "betrayed" him.

In their comments to the press, Lorne and Danny were generous toward each other on the surface but cool between the lines. "Lorne," Danny said in a written statement announcing his departure, "is a visionary whose guidance and friendship account for a great deal of my success. He supports his staff and lets each writer carry his or her scene through to airtime. In effect this develops each one's production skills. For the most part this is not the situation in the videotape mills of Hollywood."

"Danny," Lorne said in an interview with *Rolling Stone*, "is a highly honorable man, and I think it pained him to make the decision to leave."

Danny's relationship with Lorne thereafter continued to be, as an associate of Lorne's put it, "estranged."

The Blues Brothers movie went millions of dollars over budget and the ticket sales were disappointing. The soundtrack album sold more than a million and a half copies. Paul Shaffer had what he called "a show-biz reconciliation" with John and went on the Blues Brothers tour.

Gilda's record and movie came out in March 1980. Both flopped, financially and critically, tarnishing Lorne's reputation as a miracle man and Gilda's career.

CHAPTER 30

# You Gotta Serve Somebody

You gotta serve somebody The Devil or the Lord
—Title lyric from a song sung by Bob Dylan on the
second *Saturday Night* of the fifth season

You gotta serve somebody The Devil or the Lorne
—Alternate lyric sung around the 17th floor the
week of Bob Dylan's appearance

Lorne had been too busy to make contingency plans for Danny's and John's departures. Instead of seeking out full-fledged cast members to take their places, he devised a new billing called "featured performer." Paul Shaffer and writers Franken and Davis, Jim Downey, Don Novello, Brian Doyle-Murray, and newly hired Peter Aykroyd were all awarded that designation. Shaffer assumed that his loyalty to Lorne on the Gilda Live project had something to do with his promotion.

To fill out the writing staff, Lorne hired Matt Neuman, a veteran of the *Chicken Little Comedy Hour* and the Lily Tomlin specials and one of those in Hollywood who had declined Lorne's offer to join *Saturday Night* in 1975. Lorne also brought in three young rookies as apprentice writers: Tom Gammill and Max Pross, two self-described "geeky" friends of Jim Downey's just out of Harvard, where they wrote for the *Harvard Lampoon*, and Sarah Paley, a skinny, strikingly handsome friend of John Head's who had written for the newspaper parody *Not the New York Times*.

The sole new cast member hired was Harry Shearer, a doe-eyed writer-comedian from Los Angeles. Shearer had been a founding member of the comedy group The Credibility Gap, an early writer for *Laverne & Shirley* and a principal writer on Norman Lear's spin- off of *Mary Hartman, Fernwood 2-Night*. He ran in a sort of young Hollywood comedy Rat Pack with his friends Rob Reiner, Christopher Guest, and Albert Brooks; he'd co-written Brooks's film *Real Life*. Franken and Davis, who'd known Shearer in Los Angeles, had recommended him to Lorne two years earlier, and Lorne had offered him a writing job. But Shearer had also wanted to perform, and Lorne passed.

Lorne hired Shearer in mid-August after a twenty-minute chat at the Winter Garden Theater during rehearsals for *Gilda Live*. Lorne, Shearer says, told him he would be hired as a full cast member, but that the actual announcement would be delayed until December so viewers wouldn't think he was intended to be a replacement for John and Danny. Lorne, however, failed to mention this to the staff, leaving the impression that Shearer was nothing more than another writer and featured player. That lapse, Shearer believes, resulted from Lorne's not wanting to deal with the bruised egos that would result from an outsider's being brought in above those who'd been there longer. Although Lorne may have kept Shearer's status quiet for those reasons in the beginning, it's likely Shearer's abrasive personality quickly caused him to have second thoughts about having hired Shearer in the first place. In any event, the way was paved for a very stormy relationship between Harry Shearer and *Saturday Night*.

Two weeks before the first show of the fifth season, Lorne decided it would be a good idea for the new team to go away for a couple of days together to get in the spirit for the year ahead. *Saturday Night*'s first preseason pep rally—the first such rally it had ever needed, one writer noted—was scheduled for three days and two nights at a resort called the Mohonk Mountain House in upstate New York.

It was a pleasant if somewhat strange few days. Mohonk turned out to be a creaky old haunted house of a hotel with Gothic turrets looming overhead. Most of the other guests were retired middle- class couples. Almost all the writers, featured performers, and key members of the production staff were there, and they spent the bulk of their time rowing on the lake behind the hotel, horseback riding, playing touch football, wandering around the grounds, and giggling that they felt like a group of senior citizens on holiday, forty years too soon. Lorne welcomed the new members of the team, telling them that *Saturday Night* was a family, that they should feel free to ask anybody anything and to share any of their ideas with anyone else. After dinner the first night Paul Shaffer delivered a welcoming speech proclaiming "the new spirit to be created here at Mohonk," a spirit he summed up in one word: "Yea!" Soon Shaffer was shouting "Yea!" and everybody was shouting back "Yea!" and laughing.

But the spirit of Mohonk was not entirely Yea! The senior cast members were notable by their absence, setting a pattern that would continue throughout the season. The residue of the Gilda Live project also cast something of a pall over the proceedings. Gilda's movie was being filmed in Boston at the same time. Lorne, traveling between the set and the retreat via limousine, as were some of the others, was clearly distracted, and not a few of the troops gathered at Mohonk resented it. Little or nothing was said about getting along without John and Danny, but it was a subject avoided consciously.

Memories of John and Danny seemed to hover over everything Saturday Night did in the fifth season. NBC had to reassure many of its advertisers that the show wouldn't collapse without them. The staff heard so often from friends and fans how much John and Danny were missed that it became a joke: Saturday Night's Christmas card that season was a picture of the remaining cast members with ghostly images of John, Danny, and Chevy superimposed over their shoulders.

But it wasn't always funny trying to put together a show without John and Danny to lean on, and on the 17th floor there was what Harry Shearer called an "unspoken yearning" for them. Not always unspoken, actually. Often enough the writers could be heard saying, "If Danny was here this would be a great thing to do," or "John could really bring this off." In the premiere show of the fifth season, Al Franken played the part of a snotty kid in a big production piece, set in the Roman era, called "The Vandals." Standing backstage waiting for his entrance, he was ruminating about how his part was, in truth, a perfect Belushi part. So lost in this reverie was Franken that he missed his cue and ended up making his entrance several seconds late.

More than just John and Danny, the entire accumulated history of the show hung over Saturday Night in the fifth season. The complaints of the press that the show had burned itself out, that it was resting on past glories, became a nearly unanimous chorus.

Lorne got so tired of hearing it he finally told one reporter that everything was going according to plan. "Saturday Night is going to get worse and worse," he said, "and eventually will never be funny again."

The carping of the press annoyed the staff, too, but they were making similar comments among themselves. It was hard now to think of ideas that didn't resemble something they'd done before. In writers' meetings, suggestions would be immediately compared to an earlier sketch, as if they were merely variations on familiar themes. Franken and Davis once sat in their office at three o'clock on a Wednesday morning going back through history, trying to think of a fresh period to write about.

"Medieval?" one of them said, and the other answered, "Nah, we've done medieval to death."

"Spanish American War?" "Nah ..."

Finally they got down to prehistory and wrote a sketch about cavemen called "The Hominids." It turned out to be quite a funny sketch, but it was also a derivation of their old "Theodoric of York" pattern.

Franken and Davis, who are the first to admit that for much of the fifth season they relied more on "pure craftsmanship" than on authentic inspiration, were by all accounts the most dedicated members of *Saturday Night*'s old guard that year. They worked as long and as hard as they had the first year, probably harder, and they spent a lot of time complaining that the others weren't working hard enough. Anne Beatts called them "self-appointed hallway monitors" because they were always confronting people when they were tardy, wanting to know where they'd been. For her part, Beatts said that in the fifth year she finally learned how to do the show and still go out to lunch.

The cast members showed up so seldom that a meeting was finally called to discuss the fact that the writers had become, as one of them put it, "divorced" from the stars. The stars, meanwhile, resented the fact that many of the writers seemed to be less concerned with writing sketches for the cast members than they were with writing juicy supporting parts for themselves. On the production staff, too, many of those who had been there from the beginning moved through the fifth season languidly. There was a sense that *Saturday Night* was just going through the motions, and grumbling about doing even that. "All you heard was bitching and moaning," says actress Teri Garr, an old friend of the show who hosted in the fifth season. "Everyone was complaining. It was sad."

Among those who complained the most was Harry Shearer. Shearer came into *Saturday Night* with his own ideas of how comedy should be written, performed, and produced. Unfortunately for him, his ideas turned out to be diametrically opposed to the system *Saturday Night* had been using for the previous four years, a system that by then was considered an inviolable, almost sacred routine on the show. "It was," Shearer said later, "a highly complex, highly political hierarchal organization masquerading as a college dorm." Shearer resisted that hierarchy and quickly became an outcast. "I couldn't share the myth," he says. "I wasn't that dumb."

To Shearer, everything about *Saturday Night* was unprofessional. He was shocked that the cast members never studied their lines. In one sketch in which Shearer, Gilda, Billy, Garrett, Jane, and Laraine played teachers seated around a table covered with notebooks, papers, and folders, Shearer found on-air he was the only one who didn't have his script sitting on the table in front of him. They're too lazy, Shearer thought to himself, even to read cue cards. Neither could Shearer adjust to the show's late-night writing habits. When actor Howard Hesseman was hosting, Shearer arranged with him to meet on the 17th floor at 10:00 p.m. to work on a sketch together. Hesseman never showed up. Shearer says he later learned Lorne had told Hesseman that nothing ever got done till 2:00 a.m., which is when Hesseman came in.

Shearer started to gain a reputation as a troublemaker and a prima donna. He refused to make changes in his sketches that Lorne asked him to make. He sneered at Lorne's role as the Fearless Leader and hated the way Lorne worked. He called the Monday writers' meeting a "shell game" to fool the host into thinking something was being done. Nobody disputed that, but nobody but Shearer seemed to mind. Shearer also resisted Lorne's requests that he use his own name on-camera, a comedic style that Shearer abhorred, and that Shearer felt was at the heart of Lorne's true ambition. "He wasn't in the business of producing shows," Shearer says, "but in the business of making stars. His pride was in whom he could take credit for, rather than what was on the screen at any given moment."

Most of all, Shearer felt Lorne had crossed him by giving him much less air time than he thought he'd get, and by not telling the rest of the staff about his cast status. As a result, Shearer says, the others on the show looked upon him as one more pushy writer trying to get himself on the air. Lorne told some of the writers that Shearer was making his life miserable demanding to be named an official cast member. In February, to the dismay of some of the others, he was. Shearer's detractors on *Saturday Night* say he was so competitive he wouldn't even talk to them, and that he was willing to do anything to get more exposure. One of them summed up the general attitude toward Shearer when he said, "Harry is brilliant, funny, and detestable."

Much of Shearer's impatience to be recognized as a cast member derived from his conviction that this would be *Saturday Night*'s last season. It wasn't talked about much, but Shearer was by no means the only one who felt that way. The cast members were making movies, the writers were lining up screenwriting projects, and few at that point could stomach the thought of another season inside the maelstrom. "Everyone," said Alan Zweibel, "was looking beyond the show. [The attitude was] 'Gee, maybe the party is going to end. Is there going to be another party that I'll be invited to? What next?'" Lorne was no exception. He spent more time than ever locked away in his office. Only between dress and air (when he remained a master) did he seem as passionately involved with the show as he had been at the beginning. Sometimes on Saturday he'd look at a sketch as if he hadn't seen it before—"Where the hell did this come from?" he'd say. "Lorne," the exasperated writer would answer, "this has been around all week!" One writer laughed that Lorne not only watched blocking sessions on the monitor in his ninth-floor office, now he watched the monitor out of the corner of one eye. At the same time he was drawing his doodle, a little cube, two squares connected by lines drawn upward, from the bottom square to the top. His ear was usually pressed into the phone.

Besides fatigue and the fact that he'd been distancing himself from the show for more than a year, Lorne by the fifth season seemed to be nursing his wounds, grieving from all the betrayals he felt he'd suffered. One writer said it was as if Lorne were sitting up in his office with ten knives in his back, watching to see who was going to be disloyal next. Lorne had grown "clenched," another friend said. "It was hard for him because he couldn't control what he'd set in motion ... People recognized that they had their own power apart from Lorne, and had begun to flex those muscles. It was a natural development—people couldn't just keep shuffling in front of his desk, going, 'Thank you, thank you,' even if Lorne thought that was the credit he was due ... He was looking at what he had lost, dwelling on the loss of control."

One of the wounds Lorne suffered that season, not the first or the last, was inflicted by his trusted manager and confidant, Bernie Brillstein. In the spring ABC premiered a blatant copy of *Saturday Night* called *Fridays*. It was produced by two of Brillstein's other clients, John Moffitt and Bill Lee. (Moffitt was one of those Lorne had asked to be *Saturday Night*'s director before he hired Dave Wilson in 1975.) A third Brillstein client, comedian Jack Burns, was its script supervisor. Brillstein says Moffitt and Lee conceived *Fridays* and brought it to him. Bernie pitched the idea to ABC himself, presenting it as a Los Angeles version of *Saturday Night*. ABC, undoubtedly not blind to Brillstein's connection to Lorne Michaels, bought it immediately.

Lorne couldn't bring himself to watch Fridays' premiere, asking Matt Neuman to watch it for him. Neuman stuck with it for about half the show before switching it off in disgust. He told Lorne it was "yahoo comedy"—people trying to be funny by yelling loudly—and a classic case of television mitosis, a copy produced on the theory that enough people are so asleep they don't notice the difference. Lorne later told Tom Shales of *The Washington Post* he was "disappointed" that *Fridays* was such a "slavish" imitation of *Saturday Night*.

Lorne and his longtime manager and confidant, Bernie Brillstein, at a party to celebrate *Saturday Night's* 100th show, March 1980. © *NBC*

Bernie defended his participation in *Fridays* by saying it was his duty to represent his clients, but almost everyone on the 17th floor considered him a contemptible opportunist for having anything to do with it. Lorne said very little about *Fridays* to anyone on the show, or to Bernie himself, but to one or two of his closer allies he admitted he was deeply angered and deeply hurt. More than anyone else, Bernie had been Lorne's father figure through all the years of *Saturday Night*. Before *Fridays*, Lorne talked on the phone with Bernie in Los Angeles several times a day. After *Fridays* Lorne maintained their professional relationship, but their calls slacked off for a while. Lorne's friends think he basically blocked *Fridays* out of his mind, "built a Berlin wall around it," one said. There were plenty of other problems to worry about in New York.

* * *

With John and Danny gone, Bill Murray became the unquestioned male star of the show. Not coincidentally he also became the most temperamental star of the show, a transition exacerbated by the fact that Billy came back for *Saturday Night's* fifth season having undergone a most unusual change of personality.

Billy had spent that summer making a movie called *Where the Buffalo Roam*, which, as its subtitle explained, was "based on the twisted legend of Hunter S. Thompson." Billy played Thompson, and he was still absorbed in finishing the film as the fifth season started. In a classic case of the role overtaking the actor, Billy returned that fall to *Saturday Night* so immersed in playing Hunter Thompson he had virtually *become* Hunter Thompson, complete with long black cigarette holder, dark glasses, and nasty habits. "Billy," said one of the writers, echoing several others, "was not Bill Murray, he was Hunter Thompson. You couldn't talk to him without talking to Hunter Thompson." (Hunter Thompson was the model for the outlandish Uncle Duke character in the comic strip *Doonesbury*.)

Billy spent a lot of time hanging out with Thompson while the movie was being produced, and they were a volatile combination. One day at Thompson's Aspen, Colorado, home, after many drinks and after much arguing over who could out-Houdini whom, Thompson tied Billy to a chair and threw him into the swimming pool. Billy nearly drowned before Thompson pulled him out.

When the fifth season started, Thompson sometimes showed up backstage, and his presence made some people on the show as uneasy as the Hell's Angels Thompson had once written about so forcefully. Thompson's public and private personas, like those of his other good friend from *Saturday Night*, John Belushi, had essentially merged, and working with Bill Murray-cum-Hunter Thompson wasn't easy. "Hunter," a writer said, "might be a good person to go skiing with, take a vacation with, do drugs with, that's fine. But he doesn't put up with any shit and he has no interest in helping what's going on … Hunter Thompson is not the person you want on a comedy show."

Early in the season the change in Billy was slightly evident on-air—he looked subdued sometimes, other times bored—but backstage he spewed venom. He was, in the words of various people who had to work with him, "a tyrant," "pissed off the whole time, pissed at the writers, pissed at the producer, pissed at the network, pissed at TV in general, pissed at the state of the world," "uncooperative, bullyish and mean," "surly and bitchy," and "doing all the things that the year before he was calling people [namely Belushi] assholes for doing." He regularly showed up hours late for blocking sessions, regularly threw temper tantrums on the set, regularly complained about the hosts, regularly berated the writers for the quality of the material they were giving him and regularly threatened to quit, sometimes walking out on Friday nights and not showing up until late Saturday afternoon.

Many on the show believe Hunter Thompson egged Billy on by telling him how bad he thought the show was, but it may have just been the sheer cantankerousness of Hunter's persona talking through Billy himself. In one Monday writers' meeting, one of the few he came to that year, Billy, cigarette holder in hand and sunglasses in place, launched into a long, loud, and vicious tirade about what a "piece of shit" the previous week's show had been. Anne Beatts made the mistake of saying something, and he glared at her as if to say, "How dare you interrupt me?" After staring her down he continued his rant.

Behind much of Billy's misbehavior was the fact that John and Danny's leaving affected him most. He felt he'd been left behind and told one friend that had he known early enough to make plans of his own, he might have quit too. Billy got his revenge when he had the opportunity as the cloying movie critic on Weekend Update to review the release of Steven Spielberg's, and John and Danny's, *1941*.

"I never saw *1940* [sic]," he said, "but everyone in the newspapers and the press is panning this movie, so I'm going to jump on the bandwagon here. The stars, in alphabetical order, are Ned Beatty, Carrie Fisher, Christopher Lee. Carrie and Chris have both been on *Saturday Night* Live, and if you ask me they should have never left the show … When Chris and Carrie told me they were leaving *Saturday Night* to do this movie, I said, 'Why?' Steve Spielberg is great with the mechanical shark and the flying saucer, but the guy wouldn't know funny if it bit him in the underwear. They wouldn't listen and now they have this Christmas turkey on their hands. And now my two old friends are going to have the most miserable Christmas of their lives. And we all know that more suicides occur at Christmas than at any other time. But don't let these movies spoil your holidays. Take the kids to see *Meatballs* [Billy's first movie] again. It's a warm story, got a great cast. Perfect for Christmas."

Left to fend for himself, Billy bitterly complained that everybody was depending on him to carry the show on his own. He called himself "the white man," and he hated the fact that he had to play virtually every white man part that was written, whether it was suitable for him or not. There was a lot of truth to that: On many shows it seemed Billy was the centerpiece of every sketch. At the same time, Billy objected to playing parts in group sketches where he was cast on a par with lesser lights like Peter Aykroyd, Harry Shearer, or Franken and Davis. He wanted star pieces, not supporting roles. The writers, used to writing ensemble pieces featuring several stars, found that hard to accommodate now that they had fewer stars to feature. It didn't make their task any easier knowing it was dangerous putting Billy and Gilda together in the same sketch.

Billy and Gilda's tumultuous romance had finally ended in an equally tumultuous breakup. Friends say it was Gilda who finally decided to, as one put it, "wash her hands of what she perceived was not a healthy relationship." After that they entered what one friend called "a serious avoidance mode," and they didn't like working together, or being near each other if they didn't have to be. When the Gilda Live show was playing in Chicago, Billy showed up in the theater and Gilda insisted he be thrown out. It was during *Gilda Live* that she fell in love with G. E. Smith, a respected New York session guitarist (he played regularly with Hall and Oates) who was a member of the band for her shows. Gilda and Smith were married in April.

Like Belushi before him, Billy directed much of his abuse at Lorne. Billy felt, his friends say, that he'd had to make it on the show by himself, fighting for everything he'd accomplished, and therefore he owed no particular allegiance to Lorne now that he was, with Gilda, Lorne's biggest star. He was constantly negotiating, saying he'd do a part he didn't want to do if Lorne let him do another Nick the Lounge Singer sketch, or that he wouldn't go on if Lorne didn't book one of his favorite bands. As one of Lorne's chief aides put it, "Billy had Lorne by the balls, and he yanked." It was just the sort of blackmail Lorne hated most, and Lorne told friends he would never forgive Billy for it.

Billy began shedding his Hunter Thompson persona when his work on the movie was finished. He dropped it completely when the movie came out that spring. *Where the Buffalo Roam* was panned by the critics and a disaster at the box office, and Universal Studios quickly pulled it from distribution. Hunter Thompson hated the film. Billy never talked to anyone on the show about his Hunter Thompson period, and nobody mentioned it to him. As one friend put it, "You don't walk up to someone who's just emerged from a coma and tell them how hard they've been to get along with." But they were glad to have Bill Murray back.

After that Billy became more amenable to work with, although he continued to have his troubles with Lorne. And whatever complaining he'd been doing backstage, after the first few shows of the season, on-air he usually injected life into even the worst roles he was given. As a result he emerged from the fifth season a hugely popular performer. Laraine Newman and Garrett Morris were not so fortunate.

\* \* \*

Unlike Billy, Laraine and Garrett seemed all but certain now to miss the brass ring of superstardom, a prize the show had dangled tantalizingly close. They paid an awful price for falling short.

Laraine, when she wasn't at NBC, spent most of her time the fifth season sitting in her apartment watching TV, lonely and depressed. She was especially morose and unproductive when she didn't have a boy-friend. The friends she did have tended to be what one writer called "no-account rock-and-roll types," people who were not particularly nurtur-ing. When she was at the show, she usually stayed in her dressing room by herself; other than in blocking sessions and during the show itself, most members of the production crew never saw her.

She spent so much time playing solitaire that Gilda had a deck of cards printed up for her with Laraine's picture on them. Many on the show believe she suffered as much from anorexia as Gilda did from buli-mia; her weight dropped at times to eighty pounds. She always seemed to be sick and in pain. Production assistants bringing scripts to her dress-ing room would find her lying on the bed. She'd gesture weakly when they came in, as if she couldn't get up. "Oh, okay," she'd mumble, "put them over there."

Laraine's problems were immensely compounded by drugs. According to several of those who worked with her, she developed what one described as "a hornet's nest of drug problems." Cocaine was a major part of that. By the time Laraine left the show, she was all but shattered. "Laraine," one friend said, "just kept getting thinner and more fragile. It got to be very painful. She was quivering like a little dog. She really let the drugs get to her. She got more and more self-defeating. She was really unhappy. She'd sit and twirl her hair and stare. She isolated herself."

Garrett Morris's condition was, if anything, far worse. Garrett had said in his 1979 interview with *Essence* magazine that after Cicely Tyson's blowup at the writers, his situation on the show had improved. In fact, it would become even more cruel. In the fifth season he was cast as a monkey in a takeoff of *The Wizard of Oz.*

He did stumble into one role that brought him some recognition: the retired baseball player Chico Escuela, whose vocabulary consisted mainly of the words, "Base-a-boll been berry berry good to me." Chico was created by Brian Doyle-Murray and, in a familiar pattern, picked up and turned into a regular on Weekend Update by Alan Zweibel. Although Chico was not exactly a flattering stereotype either, Garrett was ecstatic at finally having a popular character to play. But by then the damage had already been done.

Garrett free-based cocaine, meaning he mixed it with ether and heated it to filter out the impurities, then smoked it in its purest, stron-gest form. From the third season on he free-based so much that by the fifth season there's no question it drove him, for extended periods, quite mad.

Like Laraine, Garrett withdrew, spending most of his time alone, "hiding in his dressing room with his [free-basing] apparatus," one writer said. He was almost always late for blocking, and on *Saturday Nights* it became a standard refrain at eleven o'clock to ask where Garrett was. "He's up on 17" would generally be the answer, and everybody knew what he was doing there.

Many times it was impossible to find him. One day a production assistant happened to see Garrett in a phone booth on the eighth floor of NBC. She was on her way to Lorne's office on the ninth floor, and when she got there she mentioned she'd seen Garrett. Lorne, who had just been on the phone with Garrett, had thought he was out of the city. "Are you kidding me?" Lorne said. "He's here?"

Garrett had apparently been hiding in the phone booth, afraid to come out. He had developed acute symptoms of paranoia, complete with hallucinations. He often claimed that an "invisible hypnotist robot" was controlling his actions. Sometimes he seemed to think it was sitting on his shoulder. He insisted to one of the production assistants that he knew people were bugging his apartment because things that happened there were turning up in scripts for the show. He pulled another production assistant aside one day to tell her he had seen her at his apartment and he knew what she was up to. "You're the one," he said.

Limousine drivers reported that while Garrett was riding to and from the studio he argued with people who weren't there. On the 17th floor people walked by his office carefully because sometimes he threw things out the door. Many of the women staffers were afraid of him. One day he refused to come out of his dressing room because, he said, he was being watched. Several people went in to get him and he pointed to five sandwiches he'd laid out on his desk. "Look," he said, "you've got to believe me. There are five sandwiches. We'll leave and the sandwiches will be gone when I get back."

It was scary for the other performers to be on live TV with Garrett. Although he never completely fell apart during a show, his performances in the fourth and fifth seasons grew progressively more mechanical and hazy, and sometimes it was obvious he could barely read his lines. On occasion he had to be tracked down and literally pushed onstage. The writers grew more and more leery of putting him in sketches, which compounded his agony at being left behind on the show, which in turn led to a deeper retreat into drugs.

Garrett's most public breakdown occurred in late February of the fifth season when Kirk Douglas was hosting the show. Garrett had a part in one of Jim Downey's "What If?" sketches, which postulated how Spartacus's battle with the Romans would have differed if he'd had a Piper Cub airplane. When the sketch was blocked on Friday, once again Garrett was late. He was called over the intercom several times. Suddenly he came storming into the studio, marched to center stage, tore his jacket off, threw it into the seats, and, standing bare-chested, started screaming at the top of his lungs.

"How dare you interrupt me during a sacred moment!" he said. "Don't ever do that again!"

Several of those who witnessed this outburst say it consisted mainly of excruciating ramblings about not being respected as a writer or as a performer, interspersed with warnings that he knew he was being watched by the invisible hypnotist robot. "I know who you are!" he cried. "I know why you're watching me. Get him away from me!" He went on like that for several minutes.

In the control room people looked at each other for a few seconds, bewildered, before Dave Wilson said, "Lose the cameras." Until then anyone within NBC could have been watching, since *Saturday Night*'s rehearsals were piped through the building on the network's closed-circuit TV system. Finally Lorne and some of the writers ran down to the stage to comfort Garrett.

No one else in the studio said anything. A small group, including Kirk Douglas, edged uneasily toward the coffee table, where Douglas managed a grim, half-hearted joke, trying to break the tension. "What scene was he doing?" Douglas said. "That's the best acting I've seen here all week."

As much cocaine as John Belushi used, within *Saturday Night* Garrett's habits were seen as more dangerous, because Belushi seemed so much stronger than Garrett. "Belushi," one of the writers said, "was howling against the elements. Garrett sort of just slipped away in his sleep." In the end, of course, that judgment proved to be incorrect, but at the time most would have expected Garrett to succumb long before John.

What to do about Garrett occupied a good deal of conversation on the 17th floor. That he wasn't taken off the show or forced to get some sort of treatment struck many as utterly irresponsible. The countervailing opinion was that taking him off the show would have only completed his collapse. No one could convince Garrett he needed help; he always insisted he was fine. But obviously he wasn't fine, and many blamed Lorne for not dealing with it. "A lot of people felt Lorne ignored the problem," one of the featured players said. "A lot of people thought, 'Lorne's got to do something about this.' It seemed that week after week Garrett was in bad emotional shape. Nobody knew what to do."

Garrett's problems were also ignored by NBC, and not because no one in the network was aware of them. To the contrary, one NBC executive, a vice president, frequently gave Garrett the money to buy his cocaine. Garrett would come to this executive for advances on his salary. He always said he had some different project in the works that he needed it for, but the executive was well aware of what Garrett was doing with the money. The advances were usually $1,000, but once, when the show was ending for the season and Garrett needed enough to tide him over the summer, he was advanced $10,000. The executive says that Garrett thought of him as a sort of friendly banker, and that as a result he and Garrett always got along extremely well. Eventually the advances were stopped.

# CHAPTER 31

# A Wobbling Kind of Machine
## (Show Notes Four)

Given all the turmoil of the fifth season, it was remarkable that the show got on at all, and no surprise it was what Jim Downey called "a wobbling kind of machine" all year. Bill Murray had been, if indelicate in expressing it, correct in his criticisms to a degree. *Saturday Night* had always been uneven, but now the peaks were less frequent and the valleys deeper than ever before. Some sketches were astonishingly amateurish, with no apparent point and hardly a laugh in them.

A nadir of sorts was reached with a Franken and Davis sketch on the show hosted by Burt Reynolds, who exemplified the fact that by the fifth season *Saturday Night* had its pick of hosts. The setting was a Roman vomitorium. Bill Murray, playing an attendant, handed out feathers to customers and scooped out the troughs with buckets. The sketch was so repugnant that Harry Shearer, for one, never forgave himself for agreeing to appear in it. Burt Reynolds didn't seem to mind, though. He gave a little friendly advice to apprentice writer Max Pross, who had a walk-on in the sketch as one of the vomitorium's customers. "Puke louder, Max," Burt said.

As uneven as the show was that season, however, it also displayed definite signs of staging a comeback. More than it had in years, the show explored new territory. There was a real willingness to take chances and to experiment with different comedic forms. The departure of John and

Danny forced an adaptation, and the show's comedy began to move away from the hard-edged, Bad Boys of Comedy style of earlier years. Not all the experiments succeeded, but with a huge audience watching, it took more courage to try them than to churn out pale imitations of formulae that had worked before. Jim Downey correctly called it "*Saturday Night*'s bravest season."

A sketch that exemplified that attitude of risk was called "The Mystery of Toad Island," which was written mostly by Franken and Davis. A traveler (Buck Henry) stopped in a remote New England inn and discovered to his horror that the island's residents had inbred so long they were turning into toads. In order to make the performers' throats swell up and deflate in toadlike fashion, a condom was attached with industrial glue to each person's neck. Several production assistants hidden off-camera inflated the condoms by puffing desperately through long tubes that ran from the actors' necks under their clothes and down to the floor. As the cast members moved across stage, the tubes had to be detached at the bottom and reconnected by other production assistants closer to their new positions. At the sketch's end the floor was strewn with hyperventilated p.a.'s. It was an immensely complicated effect that didn't completely come off onstage, but it was, as Tom Davis put it, "a noble failure."

Much of the show's best work that season derived from the softer, more whimsical humor of Jim Downey, Matt Neuman, and Don Novello. Neuman wrote one sketch, called "Dave's Variety Store," about a rustic establishment that boasts it has everything, and does, from a poker-chip washer to a crossbow made of chocolate, half a TV, and square basketballs. Neuman also wrote a slice-of-life sketch in which two suburban couples getting together for the first time find, after several awkwardly silent moments, that they share at least one thing in common: a deep, abiding passion for Joey Bishop.

Jim Downey contributed a splendidly absurdist sketch about the current commercial campaign for the soft drink Dr Pepper, which exhorted consumers to "be a Pepper!" In Downey's version, Peppers became a sort of new religious cult. Laraine Newman played the daughter who went through the phone book calling people to urge them to drink Dr Pepper, Brian Murray the concerned but finally sympathetic father who agreed it's important that kids have something to believe in.

Don Novello's Father Guido Sarducci appeared too often on Weekend Update, but Novello also wrote some funny pieces that took Father Guido out of that rut. When Paul McCartney was arrested and jailed in Japan for possession of marijuana, *Saturday Night* did a special report entitled "Day 11: Paul McCartney in Japan." Father Guido had supposedly flown to McCartney's aid, taking along plenty of grass, and was himself arrested just as McCartney was released. His report turned out to be a hilarious plea for help from within a Japanese prison. Later in the season Sarducci filed a live interview with McCartney from London. Forgetting that London was five hours ahead of New York, Sarducci arrived outside McCartney's home to find him still in bed.

Father Guido summoned him by throwing pebbles at his window and singing a medley of Beatles songs through a bullhorn.

*Saturday Night*'s Cut and Slash tradition was carried on that year mainly by Franken and Davis, who, for better or for worse, retained the propensity for college humor they had brought with them to the show. Besides the vomitorium piece, they, along with Jim Downey, distinguished themselves with a sketch called "Dr. Shockley's House of Sperm," in which host Rodney Dangerfield replenished the stock with the aid of a *Playboy* magazine. Al Franken outraged hundreds of viewers when, in a stint as Weekend Update's science editor, he decided to prove how indestructible cockroaches are by impaling, dismembering, burning and otherwise torturing several of them for the camera.

But F&D had their higher moments as well, some, like "Toad Island," noble failures, others more successful. They wrote, again with Jim Downey, a *tour de force* called "The Micro Dentists," a takeoff on the movie *Fantastic Voyage*, in which a team of crack dental surgeons were shrunk to microscopic size to repair a tooth in the mouth of Anwar Sadat.

Alan Zweibel, who staged something of a personal comeback in the fifth season, helped keep the belly-laugh tradition alive, most notably with a sketch on the season's final show called "Lord and Lady Douchebag." There was nothing remotely cerebral about it, but it was very funny in an elbow-in-the-ribs kind of way. The scene was an elegant eighteenth-century ball in a royal court, and the butler (Garrett, of course) announced the arriving guests: Lord and Lady Douchebag, the Earl of Sandwich, the Earl of Worcestershire, and the Duke of Argyle. The Lord and Lady were late, prompting the question, "Where the devil are those Douchebags?" After they arrived the Lord gave an impassioned speech, and the Earl of Sandwich heartily concurred. "Spoken like a true Douchebag!" he said. Lady Douchebag, meanwhile, was asking for vinegar and water dressing on her salad.

Of the cast members, Jane Curtin was the one who truly blossomed in the fifth year, She seemed almost visibly delighted not to have to deal with John any longer, and with Gilda's presence muted because of her exhaustion from *Gilda Live*, Jane seized her opportunity to show more range in one season than in most of the previous seasons put together. The best example was her new character Iris de Flaminio, who appeared in several different sketches, including a takeoff on *The Dating Game*.

Iris was one of those tough-talking, gum-chewing dames who talks like a longshoreman, battered but still undaunted, and Jane captured her perfectly. Jane also performed flawless sendups of Ann Landers, Eleanor Roosevelt, and Rula Lenska, the commercial pitchwoman who pretended to be recognizable but wasn't.

Harry Shearer, despite his troubles backstage, contributed some superb work on-air. He did hilarious impersonations of unlikely people, such as newsmen Frank Reynolds and Jack Perkins and fashion designer Richard Blackwell, but his peak was probably a sketch he wrote for the Bea Arthur show called "The Backers' Audition." In it, two aspiring Broadway composers previewed their musical, entitled *Two Guys*, for a group of potential financial angels. There were several songs, all co-written with Paul Shaffer, revolving around the existential relationship between Charles Manson and one of his victims, hair stylist Jay Sebring.

The young apprentice writers, Sarah Paley, Tom Gammill, and Max Pross, approached the show with a reverence that was the antithesis of Harry Shearer's cynicism, and in the end it was they who demonstrated most clearly how far *Saturday Night* had come, and where it might be going.

When Gammill and Pross, both twenty-two, showed up for their first interview with Lorne, they wore suits and ties, and Lorne remarked several times how young they were. "Well," he said, "I suppose you want to know what John Belushi's really like?" Gammill and Pross knew enough to laugh at that, and Lorne soon hired them, but in fact they were awed to be working at *Saturday Night*. Just a few months before, they'd been living on budgets of five dollars a day, drinking beer in dorm rooms, and, on *Saturday Nights*, watching *Saturday Night*. Suddenly they felt as if they were working with gods. "The people we were spending ninety-nine percent of our time with were people we really looked up to," Gammill said. "It was impressive for two kids—there were so many things to be impressed by."

At first, they were so intimidated by Lorne that they ducked inside a doorway if they saw him coming. When they spoke to the cast members, which they seldom did, they called them "mister" or "miss." Sarah Paley, who was twenty-three, felt the same. She was "terrified" to be there, so much so that at the start she could hardly speak at the writers' meetings.

Gammill, Pross, and Paley were adopted as apprentices by the former apprentices, working almost exclusively with Franken and Davis, Jim Downey, and to a lesser extent Anne Beatts and Rosie Shuster. Although they didn't make especially distinctive marks on the show, as Harry Shearer had, their eagerness to learn made them far more popular than Shearer was. Lorne in particular seemed to adopt a fatherly attitude toward them. "We certainly went in there with a very respectful attitude and made sure to be polite," said Pross. "People who didn't like us thought we were harmless."

But Gammill, Pross, and Paley were not nearly so deferential in their attitudes toward the comedic conventions *Saturday Night* had come to stand for. The Cut and Slash humor that had seemed so daring when *Saturday Night* brought it to network TV didn't seem so daring anymore. In fact, it seemed stale and boring. Gammill and Pross had seen their share of the Cut and Slash style reading submissions at the *Harvard Lampoon*: People were always sending in sketches about nice middle-class families who got machine- gunned at the end. They referred to the genre as the "let's be outrageous" school of comedy, and to them it was an outdated relic of more confrontational times, "this generation's version of mother- in-law jokes."

So *Saturday Night* had come full circle. It had broken the rules, made its own, and now its rules had become almost as constricting as the rules that preceded them. A new generation was knocking at the door, albeit a less noisy one, with ideas, and gods, of its own. The apprentices, who hadn't been born when Milton Berle held sway on NBC, were evidence that a rebirth might have been in progress on *Saturday Night*. Unfortunately, that evolution never got the chance to flower.

# CHAPTER 32

# Freddie

The news that Fred Silverman was leaving ABC to become president of NBC broke on the night of January 19, 1978, in the midst of a snowstorm that blanketed New York. It could hardly have been a more spectacular television story. Silverman was already a legend in the industry, and the only programmer ever to become truly famous outside it. His successes as head of programming at CBS and then at ABC, during the time ABC staged its astounding leap from perennial third-place network to first, had earned him the sobriquet "The Man with the Golden Gut."

ABC's ascension to first place in the ratings stood twenty-five years of television history on its ear and ushered the medium into a new era, the era just beginning when *Saturday Night* premiered in 1975. As much as anyone, Fred Silverman helped launch the hell- bent, ultimately self-destructive competition for ratings that swept the networks in the late 1970s. As much as anyone, he defined the sorts of programs that dom-inated network television then, and continued to dominate it for years thereafter. Fred Silverman was not solely responsible for what network television became in those years, but, more than anyone, he came to represent it.

Silverman's talents lay not so much in producing programs as in the art of scheduling—counterprogramming, stunting, lead-ins and lead-outs. He was also a wizard of program packaging, of spin-offs, star vehicles, and "jiggle" shows—shows that prominently featured women's breasts. He was credited with making hits of *Charlie's Angels*, *Three's Company*, *The Love Boat*, *Donny and Marie*, *The Sonny and Cher Comedy Hour*, and *Tony Orlando and Dawn*, and with spinning off Laverne & Shirley from Happy Days, Maude from *All in the Family*, *Good Times* from *Maude*, and *Rhoda* from *The Mary Tyler Moore Show*.

Fred Silverman was also, in his harried way, a tremendously charismatic personality. Portly and rumpled, he chain-smoked cigarettes and worked with a whirlwind intensity that never let up. He had a passion for television that set him apart from most programmers, who tended to be contemptuous of the programs they aired and condescending toward the viewers who watched them. Silverman adored television. His instincts as a television executive were said to be so good because Fred Silverman *was* the television audience.

Now that RCA Chairman Edgar Griffiths had handed all of NBC over to Silverman (as president of the company Silverman was in charge of the news, sports, and radio divisions as well as programming), his prospects for raising the network out of the ratings cellar became high drama more absorbing than any soap opera. Could Fast Freddie pull off the three-network hat trick? Hundreds of millions of dollars and television history were at stake. It would be either an unprecedented triumph or a downfall of mythic proportions.

To Lorne, Silverman's hiring meant, first of all, Herb Schlosser's firing, and the loss of his most important ally in the company. *Saturday Night*'s survival by then no longer depended on Schlosser's support, of course, and now it was Lorne's turn to offer support to Herb. The day after news of Silverman's hiring broke, Lorne sent Schlosser a note. "Wherever you are," Lorne wrote, "whatever you do, remember I'm only a phone call away." Schlosser landed on his feet in an executive post at RCA, overseeing the company's introduction of the video disc.

Silverman didn't take over at NBC until June. His bosses at ABC refused to let him out of his contract until it expired, forcing him, in TV parlance, to "sit on the beach" for six months. He met with Lorne in August.

Outwardly, Silverman and Lorne were cordial to one another at first, but several people who knew them both say there was, as one described it, "an instant chemical dislike" between them. Lorne, having dealt unhappily with Silverman by proxy on Lily Tomlin's special for CBS in 1973, was unfavorably predisposed toward him. Even before Silverman arrived, Lorne, in an interview with *US* magazine, worried half-facetiously that Silverman might try to turn *Saturday Night* into another *Donny and Marie*, or that he'd spin off the cast members into prime-time sitcoms and variety shows. "The Coneheads," Lorne said, "are a touch away from being the new *Munsters*."

The tension between Lorne and Silverman extended beyond the professional to the personal. They were two very different yet similar types of successful Jewish men. Both were used to doing things their own way and getting what they wanted. Lorne was one of the few people at NBC who didn't feel it necessary to defer to Silverman, and Silverman was the type of executive who felt people were either for him or against him. Lorne also reacted adversely, his friends say, to Silverman's rumpled, driven style, so different from the urbane gentility of Herb Schlosser. "Lorne likes attractive, fun people," one friend said, "and Fred was neither."

Silverman was no more disposed to like Lorne. He certainly had no special affection for Lorne's show. "Fred," says one of his close aides at NBC, "did not understand the dynamic of *Saturday Night*— the attitude of the people who made it and the attitude of its viewers. He prided himself as a great variety-show producer, but he produced the type of variety shows that were always satirized by *Saturday Night*, and he couldn't understand their point of view. He totally didn't understand why *Saturday Night* was a hit: It was so anti everything else on TV, it didn't conform to the rules. It was a totally different attitude than on anything he ever did." Another high-level NBC executive added that within the network "it was common knowledge that [*Saturday Night*] was not a thing Fred viewed with great pride."

Nor would Silverman have been charmed by Lorne's sophisticated airs. Irwin Segelstein, an old friend of Silverman's who was his right-hand man at NBC and his neighbor at home, made no secret of his opinion that Lorne Michaels was a terrible snob, and it's likely Silverman felt the same.

*Saturday Night* was the least of Silverman's problems when he took over NBC, and for that reason it didn't occupy an inordinate amount of his attention. The battle that counted was the one to lift NBC out of third place in the prime-time ratings, where it had been for the past two-and-a-half years. But, just as Lorne had feared, Silverman saw the stars of *Saturday Night* as potentially potent weapons in his prime-time assault. One of Silverman's first moves at NBC had been the scheduling of the two *Best of Saturday Night* prime-time specials; when they succeeded, he just as quickly ordered the regular *Best of Saturday Night* series. The problems started when he set his sights on Gilda Radner, Silverman came to NBC convinced Gilda could become the next Lucille Ball, a comparison he made often. A programming executive who worked with Silverman said Fred was "immediately obsessed" with getting Gilda into a prime-time variety series. Silverman broached the idea to Lorne over Chinese food during their first meeting in Silverman's executive dining room in August. He envisioned a big-budget show that would be patterned after *The Carol Burnett Show* with a touch of Sonny and Cher's razzmatazz. It would air, live, from 9:00 to 10:00 p.m. on Wednesday nights starting in January, midway through *Saturday Night*'s fourth

season. Paul Klein, who was nominally still NBC's head of programming at the time, says that in this and subsequent meetings, Silverman
kept repeating the phrase, "Wednesday night at nine is Gilda Time!"

Lorne and NBC President Fred Silverman smile dutifully for the
camera at the 100th show party. The final rupture between them
would occur a few months later. © NBC

Over the course of the next couple of months, Lorne, Gilda, and Bernie
Brillstein had several meetings with NBC's Mike Weinblatt to structure
a deal for the proposed series. And a rich deal it was. The production
budget was to have been about $475,000 a show, Gilda's salary some-
where in the area of $40,000 to $50,000 a week. Gilda and Lorne would
co-own the series. NBC was offering a commitment of seventeen shows,
thinking by this point that it would go on the air the following fall.

Bernie Brillstein says that initially Gilda wanted to do the series, but
that after "playing it through" in the negotiations, she and Lorne decided
against it. Gilda was too tired, Lorne says, for a show that would have
"added five years to her [TV] sentence." Lorne more than likely felt the
same. They had doubts they could do the new show and *Saturday Night*
at the same time. Joining in an unholy alliance with Freddie Silverman
probably gave them pause as well.

Through the fall, both Silverman and Mike Weinblatt assumed the deal was set. NBC, in fact, was prepared to announce it, but Lorne asked that they hold off until February because he was concerned, according to an internal Press department memo, that such an announcement would "seriously disturb" the other cast members too close to the beginning of the season.

In late October, Silverman called Lorne and Gilda to his office to talk about the series. According to Paul Klein, who was also there, Lorne spent most of the meeting explaining all the reasons why the show couldn't be done—there weren't any decent studio facilities, the schedule would be too complicated, the censors would be a hassle, and so on. Silverman kept insisting all those problems could be taken care of, but it was obvious to Klein that Lorne simply didn't want to do the show. Lorne stresses that the decision was entirely Gilda's, not his, and that he would have gone ahead if she had wanted to do so. But to Paul Klein it seemed Lorne was passing up the series on Gilda's behalf. Gilda, Klein says, sat with her head down in complete silence.

Two weeks later, on Election Day, Silverman called Lorne to his office again. He wanted a final decision. Lorne was stunned. He thought it was clear that the decision not to do the series had already been made. To Fred Silverman the refusal was incomprehensible and infinitely disappointing. The Election Day meeting took place in the midst of the first November sweeps period since Silverman's arrival at NBC. Indications were that NBC's schedule was dying, and although it was too soon for Silverman to take the fall, that sweeps period marked the beginning of the downward spiral of Silverman's reign. Silverman was desperate for prime-time hits, and here, in his own building, was a star he was sure could deliver one. Every day hundreds of people came begging for series commitments, yet Gilda Radner and Lorne Michaels were turning their backs on him.

Silverman completely lost his composure and started shouting at Lorne. Lorne shouted back, and left. Silverman later called Mike Weinblatt and asked him to try to patch things up. Weinblatt met in his office first with Lorne and then with Gilda. Gilda broke down in tears, saying she just couldn't do two shows and she didn't want to break up the *Saturday Night* family. Soon thereafter Lorne and Gilda embarked on Gilda Live.

\* \* \*

After the election day meeting, Fred Silverman ran cold on Lorne Michaels. Silverman told aides Lorne wasn't worth worrying about—he was the sort of producer who only had one show in him, and he'd already produced it.

Paul Klein says Silverman generally now had one of two responses when-ever Lorne's name came up: "Fuck him" or "Who gives a shit?"

Silverman's enmity grew as he became one of *Saturday Night*'s favor-ite targets on-air. On the third show of the fourth season, two shows after Silverman had watched with disgust as Mick Jagger licked Ron Wood's mouth, John Belushi played Freddie Silverman for the first time, turning the president of NBC into a repeating comedic character. The host of the show was Frank Zappa. John as Silverman opened the show in a suit, standing behind a podium. He talked about all the changes he planned for the network, then announced the results of a vast NBC talent hunt. "After extensive audience research," he said, "Trendex, Arbitron, Nielsen, over and over again all point to one man as the man America wants to see: Frank Zappa." Silverman admitted "no one was more surprised than me" at the findings. Nevertheless, he said, the public had spoken, and Frank Zappa had been signed to an exclusive NBC contract. "You'll soon be NBCing him," Silverman said, "and I'm not CBSing you either."

Belushi as Silverman was an irresistible piece of casting, and the unwinding of the Silverman saga an irresistible subject for satire. From then on, *Saturday Night*'s Silverman scripts got longer and tougher, and Belushi's caricature of him sweatier and more frantic (in part because Silverman himself was doing just that, in part because John was, too). Never before had a television show so ravaged the hand that fed it.

*Saturday Night*'s most extended laugh at Silverman's expense came when Kate Jackson hosted on February 24. Jackson was one of the stars of *Charlie's Angels*, the series that most epitomized Silverman's jiggle programming at ABC. At the time, the first NBC schedule to truly bear Silverman's stamp was staggering its way through the February sweeps period, mired more deeply than ever in third place in the ratings. John Belushi was having his own problems; the Kate Jackson show was the one he'd said he was too sick to go on for.

John as Silverman appeared in a series of "runners" throughout the show. In the first, the cold opening, Silverman was meeting in his office with Charlie's Angels (Gilda as Jaclyn Smith, Jane as Cheryl Ladd, and Kate Jackson as herself). Freddie confided that in reality he was still working for ABC as a secret agent; his mission was to sabotage NBC's schedule. He had an assignment for all the Angels: Cheryl Ladd was to go on NBC and sing; Jaclyn Smith was to shoot Johnny Carson. Kate Jackson was to host *Saturday Night* and talk the cast members—"some of NBC's best talent," Silverman said—into leaving the show for their own individual prime-time series, all of them sure to fail. By the end of the show Jackson decided she was ashamed of lying to the nice peo-ple on *Saturday Night*. "They're like people you can admire," she told

Silverman. "They're dedicated to an ideal of artistic freedom." For a change, she said, she'd like to do something new and bold on television. Silverman slapped her, shouting, "Don't you ever say that about prime time again!" Jackson recovered and thanked Silverman for bringing her to her senses. But Silverman, catching the spirit, stopped her. "Kate. Wait a minute. Maybe I'm wrong. Maybe *I'm* the one who lost his head. Something you said got me thinking. You said something about artistic freedom. Perhaps that's important. Perhaps there's a place in commercial television for quality. For intelligently conceived, well-acted, inventive programs, programs that aren't written for the lowest common denominator. And NBC could lead the way! NBC could be the network that puts these programs on the air! ... Nahhh."

Whenever *Saturday Night*'s NBC fixer Rick Traum saw a script featuring Silverman, he made it a point to call Paul Klein to alert him the piece was coming. Klein would listen to Traum read the script, laugh, and say, "What can we do? It's funny." Silverman couldn't diplomatically do anything about it either—*Saturday Night*'s immunity was too well established by then—and, to his credit, he didn't try to do anything about it undiplomatically. But privately, his associates say, he was infuriated by the attacks. His fury increased as NBC's ratings plummeted.

Every executive who worked closely with Silverman when it was all collapsing around him repeatedly emphasizes the emotional frenzy that overtook him during that period. Temper tantrums, in which he'd scream and throw things, were not uncommon. As his desperation grew, more and more the Silverman jokes on *Saturday Night*, together with Lorne and Gilda's refusal to agree to a prime- time series, seemed the traitorous acts of an enemy. "Not only were they unwilling to help get Fred to the Promised Land," says one of his aides, "but they were using his own airwaves to attack him."

On occasion Fred struck back. He told one interviewer in November of the fifth season that *Saturday Night* had just one problem: It wasn't funny anymore. When the reporter relayed that comment to Lorne, Lorne said, "Gee, Fred has my number. He could have called."

It was in this atmosphere, midway through the fifth season, that Lorne's negotiations for a sixth year of *Saturday Night* began.

\* \* \*

As much as Silverman might have loathed *Saturday Night*, he wanted very much to keep it thriving. He had enough trouble with his affiliate stations (some of whom were so displeased with NBC they were defecting to other networks) without having to explain that he'd lost Lorne Michaels, producer of one of the very few NBC programs making the kind of money the affiliates liked to make. Silverman turned responsibility for Lorne's negotiations over to Brandon Tartikoff, the young executive who had taken over as head of programming. Tartikoff understood that ensuring Lorne's continued employment at NBC was a top priority. (*Saturday Night*'s friend in NBC management, Mike Weinblatt, who previously would have handled these negotiations, had by then become another Silverman casualty, one of some eighty senior executives to leave the company during Silverman's tenure there.)

The negotiations started when Lorne was in the depths of his exhaustion from Gilda Live and the other trials of the past year, and so from the beginning he professed more serious doubts than ever about coming back. Since he'd signed his three-picture movie deal with Warner Brothers, even if he stayed with *Saturday Night*, it would likely have to be in some sort of reduced capacity. He also knew that, whatever he decided, most of his cast members would be leaving, which meant rebuilding the show.

In March, after NBC had opened Lorne's contract negotiations, he sat down with Franken and Davis and Jim Downey and asked them what they thought about another season. Downey wasn't sure, but Franken and Davis voted against it. The burnout, trying to get along without John and Danny, and the bad press weren't worth it, they said. A poll on the 17th floor probably would have found a majority, from Lorne down to production assistants, agreeing with them. Lorne's assistant, Cherie Fortis, says that after Christmas of the fifth year, "everyone just said, 'Okay, let's just get through the rest of this.' People were praying Lorne wouldn't come back. We were waiting for it to end."

At the same time, however, Anne Beatts spoke for many when she admitted that if Lorne had returned for another season, she could have been talked into it, too. "I said I wouldn't," Beatts recalled, "but I probably would have."

Lorne did, in fact, want to continue, but only on his own terms. *Saturday Night* was his child, and he wasn't going to walk away from it easily. His basic plan was to take the show off the air for a few months to rest and rebuild. During that time, he said, NBC could still make money from reruns of the show. He would audition new cast members in the fall and structure an entirely new *Saturday Night*, possibly to be hosted by some of the old cast members on a rotating basis. The show would be back on the air by January. He had ideas of doing more sophisticated comedy; he said he was tired of telling jokes to kids.

After restructuring the show, Lorne expected to function more as an executive producer, turning the bulk of the production chores over to various members of his current team. His leading candidates for producers were Franken and Davis. Jim Downey's and Alan Zweibel's names were also mentioned. Dave Wilson and Audrey Dickman would continue to handle the studio operations, and Jean Doumanian the talent. Lorne couldn't conceive, one friend laughed, of any fewer than four or five people taking his place.

In addition, Lorne had a shopping list of improvements to be made in studio 8H, which, despite all the equipment NBC had installed over the past few years, remained relatively primitive. There was also talk of a number of new programs Lorne's production company would produce for NBC. One of these was a half-hour series based on Weekend Update, to be called *Yesterday*. It would be produced by Herb Sargent for the 12:30 to 1:00 a.m. time period between the *Tonight Show* and *Tomorrow*. Lorne told Brandon Tartikoff and his chief negotiator, Irwin Moss, that he didn't want to haggle. NBC should think over his demands and get back to him when they were ready with their best offer. He'd respond within twenty-four hours.

Although Bernie Brillstein had periodic conversations with NBC after that, it wasn't until May 8 that a meeting was set for Silverman and Tartikoff to present Lorne an offer. When Lorne and Bernie arrived at Tartikoff's office at four o'clock, Silverman wasn't there. He'd been up all night setting NBC's prime-time schedule for the following fall, which he'd presented to NBC's affiliate Board of Governors that morning. Tartikoff apologized, saying Fred was ill.

Lorne took Silverman's failure to attend, and his failure to even call to apologize and perhaps reschedule, as confirmation that Fred wasn't treating him with the respect he deserved. Lorne and Bernie had already been galled by NBC's very public courting of Johnny Carson that spring. The press had been filled with accounts of Carson's negotiations for a new contract, and it was common knowledge he was holding out for, and getting, a record-breaking deal. To Lorne it was obvious NBC wasn't going to worry about him until Carson was taken care of. Brillstein says that whenever he and Lorne talked with NBC's negotiators, all they heard were complaints about Carson. "We just came from Johnny's house," was the refrain. "He's really busting our asses." Afterward, Lorne would look at Bernie and ask, "What are we, putzes? Why aren't they treating me like Carson? Why aren't they afraid of losing us?"

By May, Johnny Carson had signed his new contract. In it, NBC gave him the money to start his own production company and the right to approve, in essence, any show that followed his on NBC. That effectively ended Lorne's plans to produce *Yesterday*, or any other new series in late night. Within a year and a half the Tomorrow show would be canceled and *Late Night with David Letterman*, co-owned by Carson Productions and NBC, would occupy the time period following the *Tonight Show*. Carson had triumphed; he was still the King of Late Night.

Lorne was still willing to stay, if NBC treated him well. In the hall-way outside Tartikoff's office before the May 8 meeting, Lorne repeated to Tartikoff that *Saturday Night* would have to have a completely different look the next season—he wasn't going to compete with himself. Tartikoff had already let Lorne know that the plan to take the show off the air for a few months was unacceptable: Advertising for the fall had already been sold, and Fred was in no mood to lose, for any amount of time, one of the few hits he had. Tartikoff had also discussed with Silverman the idea that Lorne would oversee *Saturday Night* as a sort of executive producer. That was an alternative, Tartikoff told Lorne, NBC could live with. The affiliates would be satisfied, Silverman thought, as long as there was "continuity" with the old show.

Lorne came to the May 8 meeting expecting NBC to offer him a well-defined, generous contract. But that isn't what happened. Besides Tartikoff (who'd been up most of the night with Silverman setting the new fall schedule), NBC was represented by Irwin Moss and by its new vice-president of specials and late-night programs, Barbara Gallagher—the same Barbara Gallagher who had briefly been *Saturday Night*'s first associate producer back in 1975. In the interim, Gallagher had become a trusted associate of Fred Silverman's at ABC, and she'd followed him to NBC.

The meeting got off to a rough start when Irwin Moss made a derogatory comment about the *Gilda Live* movie. NBC had bought TV rights to the movie sight unseen for about $2.5 million, and Moss jokingly made it clear he thought Bernie had gotten the better of the deal. "So, you're here to gouge us again?" he laughed. Then Moss asked if Lorne could get his children tickets to an upcoming Rolling Stones concert. The capper, Lorne remembers, came when Moss pulled out Lorne's previous contract with a few notes scribbled on it. "Well, here's last year's contract," Moss said. "What do you want?"

The meeting quickly degenerated into what Lorne later called a "large fight" between Moss and Bernie Brillstein. Bernie, like Lorne, was stunned that NBC hadn't given Lorne's contract more thought. As the depth of NBC's lack of preparation became apparent, Bernie kept throwing his hands up and saying, "I can't believe I'm hearing this! I can't believe this is happening!"

Part of the argument centered on a prime-time series deal. Bernie wanted a commitment for seventeen shows, but Moss offered only six. Bernie pointed out that NBC had given Lorne a commitment for seventeen shows on *Saturday Night*.

"There are producers standing in line for a six-show commitment," Moss said.

"Let them produce *Saturday Night*," Bernie shot back. With that, Bernie says, he and Lorne walked out.

Lorne and Bernie went to dinner at a West Side restaurant named Wally's to talk over what had happened. Then they went back to Lorne's apartment and talked until 4:00 a.m. Both agreed there couldn't have been a better demonstration of NBC's failure to appreciate Lorne's value. Under those circumstances, Lorne didn't want, or need, to work for NBC any longer.

Bernie says Lorne was so exhausted at that stage that all he needed was an excuse to quit. NBC provided it. Lorne himself says, "They would have had to make me feel special [to come back], and they didn't. ... By the time they got to me, it was too late for me." That would prove, in the next year alone, to be at least a $10-million mistake for NBC.

\* \* \*

Brandon Tartikoff had informed Fred Silverman that the meeting with Lorne was a disaster. Silverman called Lorne the next day, Friday, apologizing for not showing up, and urging that they talk that afternoon in Silverman's office. "You can't leave without having a meeting with me," Silverman said.

Bernie Brillstein was already on a plane out of town, so Lorne met Silverman by himself. Silverman was, according to Lorne, very courteous. He said Lorne could stay on as *Saturday Night*'s executive producer and only come in on Saturdays if he wanted to, just so long as he helped with the transition.

Lorne was miffed at the suggestion that *Saturday Night* could be produced so easily, but he didn't make an issue of it.

Silverman also offered to sweeten Lorne's new deal substantially. Brandon Tartikoff says Silverman was talking about a production package of prime-time series, specials, and movies, in addition to *Saturday Night*, that was worth between $4 million and $5 million. Barbara Gallagher said simply, "Fred offered everything—the world."

Lorne, too tired and angry to make a decision, said he'd let them know. This uneasy truce with Fred Silverman would last only one day before it was finally and irrevocably destroyed.

Without John Belushi to play the leading role, Fred Silverman had faded as an object of ridicule on *Saturday Night* in the fifth season. But even as Lorne was meeting with Silverman that Friday, Al Franken was preparing to take Fred on again.

Franken had been appearing as a commentator on Weekend Update for most of the fifth season. His continuing theme was that the "Me

Decade" was over: America had entered the "Al Franken Decade." Why the Al Franken decade? "Because," Franken explained in one segment, "I thought of it first, and I'm here on television." Reasonable enough, but Franken's script for the May 10 show brought things closer to home. It was called "Limo for the Lamo." He started by telling a story of how he'd been standing on the street the other day, trying to get a cab. He had a great idea for the show in mind when his thoughts were interrupted by a fan. By the time he got his cab, he'd forgotten the idea.

> Okay, so I get in the cab and I start thinking, "How did this happen to me, Al Franken?" And I figured it happened because I was trying to get a cab—I should have a limousine. I mean, let's be reasonable. Here I am, Al Franken, one of NBC's few bright spots, and I'm forced to compete for taxis with you ordinary people out on the street. So I start thinking, "Who does NBC give limos to, anyway?" Okay, now there are some cast members here on *Saturday Night* Live who do get limousine service from NBC, and I'm not going to complain about that. These people are my friends, and it would seem a bit petty. But Garrett?

> Okay, anyway, I found out that NBC gives limousines to Tom Snyder and to Gary Coleman. Now, taste aside, these guys do star in their own shows, so I can't really complain about them either. But now get this: You know who gets complete, door-to-door limousine service from NBC? Fred Silverman. Now, here's a guy who is a total, unequivocal failure. The guy's been here two years, and he hasn't done diddly squat, and he gets a limo. Now, here's a list of the top ten rated shows this season in TV. Now there's some A's there, some B's, some C's, some S's [for ABC and CBS shows], you see those? You see any N's? Not one N. Why? 'Cause Silverman is a lamo. But he still gets limousine service. I like to call it "a limo for the lamo."

> Okay, now this is where you come in, and you can help me, Al Franken. I want all of you to write NBC and pressure them to get me a limousine. Just send a letter or a postcard to: Get Al Franken a Limo, care of Fred Silverman, NBC-TV, 30 Rockefeller Plaza, New York, New York, 10020.

When Lorne read the piece, he didn't think it was especially funny, but Franken insisted it was. Lorne rolled his eyes and let it pass. His attitude, Jim Downey says, was "Okay, okay, it's only two minutes."

Barbara Gallagher walked into the 8H control room that Saturday just before dress rehearsal. Somebody handed her Franken's script and said, "Wait'll you see this." Gallagher read it, groaned out loud, and went to find Lorne. "We have to do something about this," she told him. Lorne suggested she talk to Franken.

"Al," she said when she found him, "you've never known me to ask you not to do a piece, or to try to censor something. But this is really going a little over the edge, especially now." She explained that Silverman had just been "nailed to the cross" by the affiliates' Board of Governors. This, she said, was kicking a man who was down. "It's really going to hurt him," Gallagher said.

Franken laughed. He told Gallagher the piece was funny and he didn't believe that Silverman would be hurt by it. Nor did he care. He didn't like her even bringing the matter up, but he did say he'd discuss it with Lorne. Later Gallagher talked to Lorne again, and Lorne, she says, told her not to worry, the piece would be toned down. Instead, after dress rehearsal, Franken punched it up by adding another couple of lines: While viewers were supposed to be getting their pencils and paper to write down the address, Franken waited for them to come back to their sets, filling time by shouting so they could hear him. "If enough of you write," he said, "Silverman will have to give me the limo. Even though I've just decimated him, that's the way things are around here—he's timid, indecisive, and easily pressured. He's weak!"

Gallagher left the building for home as the show went on the air. She decided against calling Silverman to warn him. "He might have gotten crazy and done something he would have regretted," she said.

As Gallagher was leaving 8H, Brandon Tartikoff was just coming in. Tartikoff had planned to see a foreign film that night, but the line in front of the theater had been too long and he'd dropped by 8H instead. He knew nothing of "Limo for the Lamo" as he took his seat. Neither did Fred Silverman, who was sitting down at home to watch *Saturday Night*.

Tartikoff laughed heartily when Franken delivered his speech, as did the rest of the studio audience. Not more than a minute later Silverman called the control room. He wanted to talk to Brandon. A page found Tartikoff in the audience and told him Silverman was on the line. "Tell him I'm not here," Tartikoff said.

The phone in Barbara Gallagher's apartment was ringing as she walked in the door. It was Fred. Had she seen it? Gallagher told him she had, in rehearsal, and that she'd tried to talk them out of it. Silverman's voice, Gallagher said, sounded "unbelievably tired." She expected him to use the word *hurt*, and he did. She also wasn't surprised that he took "Limo for the Lamo" as a personal attack by Lorne. "Why would Lorne *do* this to me?" Gallagher remembers Silverman saying. "After I offered him the world, and after the affiliate meetings. Lorne knew what I was going through. I'm so hurt he would do this to me. I've always been fair to the show—I've never done anything against them. How could he do that to me?" Gallagher adds that over and over again Silverman kept asking, "Why? ... Why? ... Why?"

Gallagher relayed Silverman's displeasure to Lorne that night after the show. The following Monday, she and Lorne conferred on the 17th floor. It was decided that Franken should write Silverman an apology. The tone of the first letter he wrote was so aggressive— those who saw it say its basic message was, "If you can't take a joke, fuck you"—that Lorne said it would be better to send nothing at all. So Franken wrote a second letter, which read:

Dear Mr. Silverman:

I learned after Saturday's show that you were quite disturbed and hurt by my Weekend Update segment, While the purpose of this letter is to try to get you to view the segment in a more humorous light, let me say seriously and sincerely that, as hard as it may be to believe, I did not intend to hurt or offend you with this, admittedly, frontal attack,

I did intend the piece to be "brazen small guy attacks the boss." I guess I'm asking you to step back and think of the Fred Silverman I talked about as "the boss" instead of Fred Silverman, your mother's son, your wife's husband, and your children's father.

I understand that at a recent stockholders' meeting, Mr. Griffiths [Edgar Griffiths, chairman of RCA] defended a recent Update presentation of Ralph Nader's attack on Mobil Oil, by saying something to the effect that *Saturday Night* Live has satirized everyone in the country from the President on down. I do believe that my piece made NBC *and* you look good in so far as even the most pointed criticism was allowed on the air by the network and by you, the boss.

I also understand that you were hurt that Lorne allowed the segment on the air. It's difficult to explain to someone who has not worked within Lorne's system, but he really had little choice in the matter. Lorne's system is based on allowing different comic sensibilities to be expressed within the show's style, craft, and taste criteria. These criteria are established by a consensus of Lorne and trusted members of his staff, of which I am, believe it or not, one. It was the overwhelming consensus of the group that my piece was funny. [Franken stretched it a bit there.] Besides, Lorne lets us satirize everything, except, of course, himself and his family.

Sincerely,
Al Franken

After Lorne convinced Franken to delete a postscript mentioning that Brandon Tartikoff had found "Limo for the Lamo" hysterically funny, the letter was dispatched to Silverman's office. Fred didn't respond. By then he'd already told Tartikoff he wanted nothing else to do with Lorne Michaels.

"He's your boy now," Silverman said.

CHAPTER 33

# Off the Air

After "Limo for the Lamo," Brandon Tartikoff told Lorne that any thought of making Al Franken a producer of *Saturday Night* was definitely out of the question. What was left of Lorne's negotiations continued under a cloud, both sides thoroughly disgruntled.

Two weeks later, Buck Henry hosted the last show of the fifth season. The signals that *Saturday Night* was over—at least as it had been—were unmistakable. Henry opened the show by saying, "Some people think it might be the last *Saturday Night* show ever [groans from the audience], but don't worry, because I'm here to announce that *Saturday Night* Live will be back again next year [huge applause]. *Not* with the same people, of course, but with an entirely new cast of young, fresh, talented people to replace the ones who were let go." The supposed new cast (really such backstage members of the *Saturday Night* team as Matt Neuman, Don Pardo, Walter Williams, and production assistant Robin Shlien) proceeded to file on stage as Henry introduced them. He said they were all on their way to NBC's Comedy Camp for training.

At the end of the show, an especially large group gathered at the home base, embracing one another and waving especially vigorous farewells. "Good night," Buck Henry said, "and goodbye." They all walked out of the studio, the camera and applause following them as they left. The final shot of the show was a close-up of the ON AIR sign in the hallway outside 8H. It flickered once or twice and went off.

On the 17th floor afterward, there were tears mixed with relief. Jane Curtin, who'd worn a white dress for the occasion, looked around the offices one last time and said, with obvious determination, "I will not set foot here again." Laraine Newman joked that she should have brought a gun to eliminate the speaker in her dressing room, from which stage manager Joe Dicso's insistent cast calls had emanated for the past five years. On their desks everyone found a gift from Lorne, a cigarette lighter in the shape of 30 Rock. On the bottom was the inscription "Nice working with you/1975–1980."

Lorne hadn't made such a gesture at the end of other seasons, and that was as close as he got to an announcement that *Saturday Night* was truly over. The message was ambiguous enough that those on the 17th floor who hadn't yet made their own decision left that night not knowing if they still had a job or not. But they'd left at the end of previous seasons with the same uncertainty, and by now they were too tired to think much about it. At the party in the Rockefeller Center skating rink, most of the staff got unusually drunk.

* * *

Silverman and Tartikoff hadn't cared for the last shot of the last show: *Saturday Night* still belonged to NBC, and they wanted no suggestion that it was going off the air.

Lorne met with Tartikoff and Gallagher again on June 2. Once again he postponed a final decision, saying, "Even if I don't come back, I'll do my very best to make sure the show doesn't fall apart." He reiterated the list of those he'd groomed to run the show, but when Tartikoff and Gallagher asked him who he would suggest specifically as producer, he shrugged. Gallagher and Tartikoff interpreted that as an indication that he had no one to offer if they weren't going to follow his advice on Franken and Davis.

The name of associate producer Jean Doumanian, a good friend of Gallagher, came up. Lorne said she couldn't handle the job. Gallagher, angered on behalf of her friend, asked him why. Because, Lorne said, she wasn't a producer, she wasn't part of the "core" team, and nobody on the core team would work for her.

It was after this meeting that Brandon Tartikoff gave up on Lorne Michaels and started looking for a new producer for *Saturday Night*. Lorne's unresponsiveness seemed to leave the matter at an impasse, and Tartikoff felt he couldn't leave the show adrift. Just as important was the fact that, after "Limo for the Lamo" and the last show, trust between Lorne and NBC had all but evaporated. There was clearly a strong suspicion that Lorne, having decided to leave, might prefer that *Saturday Night* not go on without him.

The next day, Tartikoff called a producer in Los Angeles named Allan Katz, whose credits included *Rhoda* and *M\*A\*S\*H*, and asked him if he was interested in taking over *Saturday Night*. Katz thought about it for a day or two and declined, saying it would be too great a change in his life-style. At that point Tartikoff turned for counsel to his vice-president in charge of late night, Barbara Gallagher.

Gallagher recommended her friend Jean Doumanian. Jean, Gallagher argued, had several points in her favor. Despite what Lorne had said, she had been a key member of the *Saturday Night* team. She knew how the show was put together and she knew the people who worked there. As Lorne's associate producer, she could provide the all-important "continuity" Silverman was demanding. Also, since most of the cast members were leaving, it would be a good idea to get someone with an eye for talent. Jean, as the show's longtime talent coordinator, had such an eye. And she had production experience. She'd successfully produced a late-night special for Lorne a year before featuring Bob and Ray, the comedy team idolized by many of those on *Saturday Night*. It was noted that the Bob and Ray special had come in under budget.

Tartikoff agreed to meet with Doumanian on June 4. Those who know Jean Doumanian unanimously agree she is a charming woman who is unusually adept at making a good impression. She impressed Tartikoff. He found her very organized—"button down" is how he described her. She seemed to have very clear ideas of how she would handle the show. Within a day, without a word to Lorne, Tartikoff told Gallagher that Jean had the job.

Tartikoff would later explain that, in the absence of a clear alternative, he relied on Barbara Gallagher's advice in his decision to hire Doumanian. Gallagher had "a history with the show," Tartikoff said, while he was new in his job as head of the Entertainment division at NBC. Tartikoff admits that the chaos that prevailed in NBC's executive suites had something to do with it as well. Like everyone else in Silverman's inner circle, Tartikoff was hanging by his fingernails to the prime-time precipice, trying at the same time to cope with a boss whose own grip seemed to be slipping. Any decision that could be deferred was deferred. Nonetheless, Tartikoff concedes, the decision was his to make.

Tartikoff told Doumanian not to say anything to anyone about her new job for a week. Ostensibly this was to keep word from leaking to the press before the deal was set, but that didn't explain why Lorne wasn't informed. Barbara Gallagher believes Tartikoff wanted to keep the news from Lorne simply because Brandon didn't have the energy just then for one more nasty scene. Others believe Tartikoff feared Lorne might somehow try to stop Jean from being hired, perhaps by talking her out of it. Lorne's own theory is that Tartikoff didn't want to rule out completely

Lorne's return to the show. If he did return, Lorne says, Tartikoff would have then withdrawn his offer to Doumanian.

Lorne was in Houston, Texas, that week to attend the premiere of the movie *Urban Cowboy* and to meet the parents of Susan Forristal, whom he planned to marry. He says he went to Houston still debating whether he would return to *Saturday Night.*

Before Tartikoff offered Doumanian the show, she had accepted a job heading up a new East Coast production operation in the New York office of Paramount Pictures. She felt obligated to inform Paramount she wouldn't be available. So it was that Lorne learned in Houston of Jean's hiring from Paramount chairman Barry Diller. Paramount produced *Urban Cowboy,* and Lorne ran into Diller during the premiere festivities. Diller asked him if it was true Jean Doumanian was going to produce *Saturday Night.* Lorne said he didn't know.

Word quickly got back to Tartikoff and Doumanian that Lorne had heard the news. Both called him in Houston. Lorne told Tartikoff he was shocked, and that NBC was making a big mistake—Jean's hiring would mean "a complete break" from the old *Saturday Night.* Lorne asked if the decision was final. Tartikoff said he wasn't sure; he would find out and call Lorne back. Tartikoff called Barbara Gallagher, who told him the deal with Jean was set. Lorne was disgusted: he felt NBC had "broken faith."

When Jean called Lorne, she was apologetic, explaining that NBC had insisted she say nothing to him. "You know I'd never do anything to hurt you," she said.

Lorne told her he couldn't believe she'd shown more loyalty to NBC—the Network—than to him. "What do you *mean* they told you not to say anything?" he said. "*I* hired you, and you did that to me?" That was the last time Lorne ever talked to Jean Doumanian.

A couple of weeks later, Lorne agreed to a holding deal with NBC that called for him to develop some programs and ensured that he not go to work for another network. Then he went on vacation. NBC issued a press release announcing that Lorne had been signed to "a long-term contract," but in fact it was only for a year.

NBC in its release praised Lorne for leaving "an indelible mark" on late-night television. It also quietly made the point that he was leaving "NBC's" *Saturday Night Live.*

\* \* \*

Lorne and Silverman worked together one last time the following fall. Lorne was to be the executive producer of a live, one-hour version of Weekend Update focusing on the presidential election between Jimmy

Carter and Ronald Reagan. It would air at 10:00 p.m. on Saturday, November 1, three days before the voters went to the polls.

The special turned into a reunion. Almost all the members of the *Saturday Night* team were there, even Danny. They worked out of Broadway Video, and they were reveling in the chance to have a pre-election shot at the politicians.

Most of the show was already written when a last minute, prime-time debate between Reagan and Carter was scheduled for Tuesday, a week before the election. Silverman had planned to air two other specials that night, one featuring Bob Hope, the other the Smothers Brothers. Coverage of the debate displaced those specials, and Silverman began looking for somewhere else on the schedule to put them. Against Brandon Tartikoff's recommendation, while Tartikoff was out of town, Silverman chose Saturday. The Weekend Update special was off.

Lorne was offered the opportunity of doing the special a week later, after the election. That, Michael O'Donoghue said, would be about as thrilling as looking at pictures of naked women after having just had an orgasm. Silverman's offer was declined. There was a strong suspicion that the special had been pulled because it was too hard-hitting, that NBC hadn't wanted to offend the political powers that be. Not unlike the suspicions that surrounded CBS's cancellation of the Smothers Brothers eleven years before.

Lorne came back to Broadway Video after hearing the news, look-ing, one of the writers said, like the daddy who's just been laid off at the mill. Alan Zweibel and a few others got on the phone to spread the news of the cancellation to those who weren't there. Not much was said, but soon people started drifting in to Broadway Video. Most of them brought a bottle of champagne or something else to drink; Bill Murray showed up with a few cases of Freixenet, a sparkling wine from Spain. A long, raucous, emotional party ensued. It was, Zweibel said, the wrap party the show never had. The last bond between NBC and the original *Saturday Night* was broken.

# PART THREE

"You can't fake virginity."
—Lorne Michaels

PART THREE

CHAPTER 34

# The Look of the Eighties

One of the few people who seemed to have no reservations about Jean Doumanian's ability to produce *Saturday Night* was Jean Doumanian herself,

Herb Sargent, one of Jean's better friends on the show, called her as soon as he heard the news. First he congratulated her. Then he said, "You're crazy."

It wasn't only Jean's experience as a producer, or lack of it, that worried Sargent, although that was part of it. But Sargent also knew she had taken on the Olympian, quite possibly insurmountable, task of trying to live up to a legend. To succeed, Jean wouldn't just have to produce a program, she'd have to produce magic, with millions of unforgiving fans watching. Sargent urged her to reconsider. Take the job with Paramount, he said, before it's too late. "Hey," Jean answered. "I've got to give it a shot. It's a challenge."

Jean was also warned by Barbara Gallagher, who had won the *Saturday Night* job for her in the first place. Gallagher told Jean to think hard before accepting the position. "It's going to be hell," Gallagher said. Gallagher, who herself tired of network politics and left NBC a few months later, says she specifically mentioned that Jean was probably going to run into a post–Lorne Michaels backlash. A lot of executives, Gallagher knew, were anxious to regain control of a show that for too long had been operating by its own rules. "I can handle it," Jean told her.

Indeed, Jean apparently never doubted for a moment that she could handle *Saturday Night*. More than a few times in the waning weeks of the fifth season, some of those who worked with her on the 17th floor heard her say that if Lorne wasn't coming back, she was the one who ought to replace him. "No one," she said to a colleague, "can produce this show better than me."

The man whose shoes she was to fill was uncharacteristically frank in expressing his own skepticism to the press. Lorne told Tom Shales of *The Washington Post* that he was disappointed in Jean's hiring because he'd always considered himself a radical and had hoped the show would be handed over to someone with a similar outlook. To the Associated Press, Lorne said the truth was that *Saturday Night* was dead. "I think the network is trying very hard to obscure that fact," he said. In private he told friends Jean wouldn't last half a season.

Jean Doumanian was decidedly not a radical. She was. instead, much more in tune with the other side of Lorne's nature, the polished, prosperous side that came, during his five years on the show, to overlay the heart of the sixties dreamer he'd been when it started.

She was a strikingly attractive woman in her late thirties, with long, dark hair, high cheekbones, and a radiant smile. She dressed impeccably in silk blouses and Giorgio Armani suits and high heels. The colors she chose were almost invariably black or gray. Michael O'Donoghue described Jean's fashion statement as that of a rich Spanish widow. She had her cosmetic needs attended to at Elizabeth Arden, and she bought fresh vegetable and fruit juices at a health bar across the street from Carnegie Hall. She was vehemently antidrug; she used to give *Saturday Night* filmmaker Gary Weis copies of magazine articles on the dangers of cocaine. In the evenings she could usually be found at Elaine's, sitting at the table of her good friend Woody Allen.

Jean met Allen during his comedy club days in Chicago, Jean's hometown, in the mid-sixties. In New York they remained, as Jean once described it, "the best of friends." They talked on the phone almost daily, often at length; during Lorne's era, Jean had regularly taken calls from Allen in the 8H control room during the show. Allen used a pseudonym when he called, but nobody was fooled, and until Jean asked them to stop, the production assistants would shout out, "Jean, Woody's on the phone." There was no chance Allen would agree to appear on *Saturday Night*

Jean Doumanian, who was confident she could produce *Saturday Night*. © NBC

for Jean—he simply didn't do television—but they would continue to talk regularly throughout Jean's tenure as producer.

Jean's stylishness had served her well in her work. She'd been the associate producer in charge of talent on Howard Cosell's *Saturday Night Live*, and had joined *Saturday Night* as its talent coordinator when Cosell's show was canceled. Before that she'd been a talent coordinator for Dick Cavett's late-night show on ABC in the early seventies.

Jean was not well liked by some who'd worked directly with her on Lorne's show; one especially bitter former colleague said she had an "evil manipulative streak" that Lorne never saw. But by all accounts she was good at what she did, adept at dealing with agents and managers in booking hosts and bands, and skillful at handling the guests themselves once they arrived. She knew how to pamper them, seeing to it that a limo was there to pick them up at the airport, that the proper reservations had been made at the hotel, that wine, flowers, and fruit awaited them in their dressing rooms. (Sometimes she'd keep the guests' floral arrangements after they'd gone, and as they accumulated there'd be bunches of dead flowers sitting in her office.) Lorne wanted his guests to be pampered, and Jean's image reflected well on the show. "Jean was never ruffled," one of Lorne's assistants said. "She had a style that Lorne liked, the veneer of making it look easy. She was class."

Whether any of this prepared her to become the pilot of the juggernaut that was *Saturday Night* was another question entirely. Brandon Tartikoff, determined to maintain the continuity Fred Silverman demanded, had clearly been misled by Jean's associate producer title. Television is a business in which titles routinely obscure the nature of the jobs they ostensibly describe, something Tartikoff well knew, had he not been too distracted by NBC's other problems to think about it. In truth, Jean had always been *Saturday Night*'s talent coordinator and little more. Her direct experience with the creative and mechanical aspects of producing the show—of working with the writers, the cast, the director, the set and costume designers, the studio technicians, the network executives, and myriad others involved in actually getting ninety minutes of comedy on the air every week—was negligible.

Even Jean's sole credit as a bona fide producer, on the Bob and Ray special she'd produced for Lorne, *Bob & Ray, Jane, Laraine & Gilda*, was misleading. She'd handled the job competently, but she'd used the superstructure and the talent that was already in place for *Saturday Night*. The format was the same, the writers and cast members were the same, the studio was the same, all the production personnel were the same, even the time period was the same. All Jean really had to do was to fill in the blanks, and Lorne was there as executive producer to help her do it. As one observer on the 17th floor put it, "That's not producing a show, that's booking a show."

Still, there had been problems. Jean had been determined to bring the show in under budget, and she'd succeeded, but her penny- pinching offended some of those who worked for her. Lorne had intervened to loosen the purse strings a little; he had also stepped in between dress rehearsal and air to help Jean reformat the show. There had been, in addition, an unpleasant dispute over Jean's decision to list herself in the writing credits because she'd made a small contribution to one of the sketches. When Al Franken first saw the credit list with her name on it, he thought it was a mistake and marked it out. The list came back later with Jean's name reinserted. Franken went to Jean and said, "Hey, they keep making the same mistake, putting your name in the writing credits."

"That's no mistake," Jean told him, "I'm taking a writer's credit." This had not endeared Jean to Al Franken, and Franken was not the type to forgive and forget.

The news that Jean had been named producer made deciding whether to return for another season extremely easy for most on the show who'd been considering it. Members of the original *Saturday Night* team spent a lot of time talking to each other on the telephone the week the appointment was announced, and they were without exception shocked, and almost without exception angered. To all who worked on the 17th floor, the choice of Jean Doumanian was a measure of NBC's utter failure to understand the dynamics of a show that had been produced in their own building for the past five years. It was also a measure of how successful Lorne had been at keeping the network at a distance all that time.

When people called him, Lorne made no secret of letting them know how disgusted he was, not only with Jean's being hired but with the manner in which she was hired. Going to work for Jean was instantly defined as going to work for an enemy, a violation of family honor. And despite all that had happened in the past few years, that sense of family honor remained intensely strong.

Most of the cast members had long since decided they weren't returning anyway; even Jean's friend Jane Curtin wouldn't have dreamed of another season. The writers, every bit as much the heart of *Saturday Night*, were a different story. Jean began calling the writers as soon as she started work in June. It quickly became apparent that not one of them was coming back, and, after talking to a few, Jean didn't bother calling the rest.

Like Lorne, the writers were so exhausted by then that all they needed was a good excuse to quit. None of them felt in need of a job, and none of them had the slightest confidence Jean could produce a show they'd want to work on. It made letting go of *Saturday Night* the obvious choice. "We'd put in five glorious years," says Tom Davis. "We figured, 'Well, now let's go marching into the movie industry.'" Some of the newer writers who hadn't yet made their reputations, like Tom Gammill, Max Pross, and Sarah Paley, were less ready to let go, and for a time they pondered going to work for Jean. But in the end all opted for loyalty to Lorne. Gammill, Pross, and Paley were soon put to work on a movie script for him.

Jean was surprised and hurt that all the writers as well as not a few of the veteran production assistants refused to work for her. So was NBC. The all-important continuity Fred Silverman had wanted so badly had vanished overnight. Jean now presided over a shell of the show.

Several key members of the production team—the more fami-ly- oriented members, by and large—did decide to stay on, including director Dave Wilson and associate producer (a title she'd shared with Jean) Audrey Dickman. Leo Yoshimura replaced Eugene Lee as the set designer, Karen Roston replaced costume designer Franne Lee, and Neil Levy signed on as talent coordinator. All of them called Lorne before they committed themselves to Jean. Lorne was gracious in giving his blessing, saying of course he understood the need to feed families and pay bills. All of them felt like traitors anyway.

The other exception was Harry Shearer, who felt no loyalty to Lorne whatsoever. Shearer met with Jean soon after she took over. He told her she would find it impossible to build a new writing staff from scratch, and that he would be willing to come back if he could bring in some friends— "people," he said, "who know what they're doing." Jean declined. "I'm not sure we want people who know what they're doing," she said.

This was an early indication of what would become Jean's funda-mental strategy: Do what Lorne did. Lorne had started with enlightened amateurs, so would she. But any thoughts of re-creating the formative process of the first *Saturday Night*, when the territory had been wide open and there were six months of work undercover before anyone at NBC realized what was being hatched, was little more than wishful thinking.

Brandon Tartikoff had been quite specific in telling Jean what kind of show he wanted when he hired her: a "middle ground" between old and new. Tartikoff had said she shouldn't use specific characters from the old show—the Coneheads and the Nerds would have to be retired— and of course the cast would have to be new. But the format, the look, and the approach should stay the same. Tartikoff told Jean he realized innovation was part of the "mandate" of the show. Nonetheless, viewers should be able to recognize that this was *Saturday Night Live*.

\* \* \*

Jean's first order of business was to redecorate Lorne's office. She bought new carpeting with natural fiber, all gray. Across one wall she installed four refrigerator units, about three-and-a-half-feet high, covered with black enamel. There was a huge new desk of black onyx, black and silver chairs, and several Art Deco reproductions. A set of metallic-gray Art Deco lamps hung from the ceiling; the lighting was subdued. All told, this project would take nearly a month and $22,000 to complete.

For someone suddenly making $16,000 a week, as Jean was, this may not have seemed exorbitant. Leo Yoshimura, who spent more afternoons than he cared to that month searching for Jean's refrigerators in Queens, found it an odd use of time and money. Nor was he reassured when, soon after the decorating was completed, Jean called him in to talk about the show's basic, central set. That Jean wanted a new set was understandable. Lorne, much to NBC's dismay, had insisted on a new set almost every season (in the last year he'd had two) and Leo knew that the set was one way Jean could immediately define her own vision of the show. The surprise came when she told him what she had in mind. "I want," she said, "the look of the eighties."

When Leo asked exactly what the look of the eighties might be, Jean couldn't say, other than that she wanted what she called a "downtown" feel. Not being a downtown woman, it was difficult for her to be more specific. Again it was apparent she had something not dissimilar from Lorne's sets in mind. She did have a suggestion about where the look of the eighties could be found: in discos. She arranged for Leo to tour, via NBC limo, the hottest discotheques in New York—Xenon, Studio 54, and Bonds among them. "Hang out there," she said. "You'll find it."

Leo spent several nights on the disco circuit, but he didn't find the look of the eighties. He felt like he was back in camp looking for the nonexistent snark. Finally he gave up and conceived his own design, a lovely takeoff on Grand Central Terminal. While he was building his model, Jean and some of her confidants would come into his office after he left for the day, criticize his work, and leave him notes about it, so he started disassembling the model and hiding the pieces. When the set was finished she never said anything to him about it.

Word of the defections of the writing staff and of Lorne's disapproval of Jean spread quickly throughout the show business subculture, and a circumspect, wait-and-see attitude quickly infused the industry. Talent coordinator Neil Levy thumbed through his Rolodex in vain, trying to find a suitable host for the first show. Literally dozens of celebrities turned him down, some out of caution, others out of loyalty to Lorne. Audrey Dickman, among others, believes there was "an active campaign" to discourage people in the business from working on Jean's show.

That campaign may have reduced the quality of the applicants from which Jean could choose her staff, but it didn't significantly reduce the quantity: Hundreds of submissions poured in every week. She quickly assembled a team of five personal friends or acquaintances, none of them from Lorne's era, who would comprise her inner circle. They included Woody Allen's sister, Letty Aronson; the sister of Bill Murray's girlfriend, a former nun named Mary Pat Kelly; and another former talent coordinator, Michael Zannella. The various titles these people were given were not as important as the fact that Jean felt comfortable with them, and she would rely on them ever more heavily for support. Unfortunately, among them there was precious little of the live-television comedy expertise that Jean herself lacked.

Her core team in place, Jean launched a nationwide talent hunt for the new cast. Like Lorne, her goal was to have three women and four men, one of them black. Even more than Lorne, Jean had no dearth of applicants from which to choose. Becoming a cast member on *Saturday Night* was now defined as an instant ticket to fame and fortune: Legends were launched there. Between June and August she and her aides saw hundreds of performers. Special showcases were arranged for her at comedy clubs in Los Angeles, San Francisco, and Chicago. In New York that summer, it seemed that in every corner of every office on the 17th floor comedians were going through their routines for two or three people on the staff, making their way up the chain of command from the talent coordinators to associate producer Michael Zannella and on to Jean herself.

Jean winnowed down the performers to a set of about twenty. The final auditions were held on August 28 in a studio two floors below 8H. By then most of the writers had been hired. There was a novelist, a screenwriter, a host of a cable TV comedy show, an associate producer of *The Mike Douglas Show*, and several magazine and TV comedy writers, among them Sean Kelly, who had been an early editor of the *National Lampoon* and a guiding force behind *Lemmings*. Jean asked all the writers to be at the auditions to take notes; later some would grumble that their suggestions had been ignored. The performers were taped so that Brandon Tartikoff, who had accompanied Jean on some of her talent auditions, could review them. But at that point, Tartikoff says, he was willing to extend to Jean the "carte blanche" Lorne had enjoyed for so long. The choices were Jean's.

One of those who was a hit that day was a curly-haired stand-up comedian and commercial actor from New Jersey named Joe Piscopo. Although he preferred not to mention it, Piscopo had been a co-star on one of Brandon Tartikoff's stranger failures, a prime-time series called *A Dog's Life*, in which all the actors wore dog costumes. Piscopo played one of the leading dogs. He'd been recommended to Jean by a friend from the comedy-club circuit who'd been hired as a writer, John DeBellis. Jean had seen Piscopo at the Improv and again a few days later in a solo audition on the 17th floor. For his final audition, Piscopo did two characters, a prototypical New York Yankees fan ("L-o-u-u-uu") and an obnoxious but sweet-hearted kid named Paulie Herman, who would come to be known as the "Jersey Guy."

Gilbert Gottfried, another veteran of the comedy clubs, also impressed Jean's staff. He auditioned with a manic stand-up routine that had him bouncing around the set, ranting and raving like a madman, and that had those watching laughing hysterically. There was some question, as hilarious as he'd been, whether Gottfried's frenetic style would come across on television, but in the end the decision was made to give him a chance.

Two women were chosen from the group. Ann Risley was, much like Jean, an attractive, dark-haired, polished woman, less a comedienne than an actress. She was also something of a protégé of Woody Allen's. After seeing her in a workshop production, Allen had convinced her she should move from Madison, Wisconsin, to New York, and he'd given her small parts in his films *Annie Hall, Manhattan*, and *Stardust Memories*. Gail Matthius had impressed Jean with her improv work in Los Angeles, and she'd been especially funny during the auditions with her Valley Girl character, a bubble-headed teenager whose vocabulary consisted of "grotie to the max," "gag me with a spoon," and other, similarly articulate southern California expressions. In subsequent years dozens of comediennes would be doing Valley Girls, but Matthius got there early, and she did it well.

The third female cast member, Denny Dillon, would not be chosen for another few weeks. Dillon was a squat, bubbly comedienne who had been struggling on the fringes of the New York comedy scene for several years. She had, in fact, performed on *Saturday Night*'s third show, when Lorne was still putting on "new talent" segments. She'd played a nun with a male partner who was also in nun's habit, a bit that had generated not a few viewer complaints.

For Charles Rocket, the auditions were mainly a formality. Jean already knew she wanted him, and in fact had already picked him out as the performer most likely to become her first major star. Jean was familiar with Rocket's work from a videotape he'd submitted to Lorne the year before; Lorne had asked John Head to look around for some possible cast members for the new *Saturday Night* he planned to put together. Rocket had actually worked as a news anchorman and reporter at several small TV stations around the country, and he did brazen on-the-street interviews he called "The Rocket Report," which were firmly in the anticomic tradition of obnoxious journalism. Rocket was tall, thin, and good-looking in a predatory way, and Jean immediately saw him as the leading man she was looking for. Brandon Tartikoff, when he saw Rocket's tape, agreed. He sent a note to Jean saying he shared her opinion that Rocket was a combination of Chevy Chase and Bill Murray. Rocket took this as a compliment, but there was an ominous undertone to it which he missed. That was the sort of comparison all Jean's cast members would be subjected to, even before they went on the air, and they would not always be so favorable.

As soon as the cast was chosen, Jean, with the encouragement of NBC, set out to make them over. Karen Roston was asked to help make the women, as Roston put it, "sexier and prettier." Diets were ordered for all. Attempts were made to accentuate Ann Risley's image as an icy version of Mary Tyler Moore. Roston spent a lot of time in fittings with Charles Rocket, trying to find a sort of New Wave look for his wardrobe. Joe Piscopo was sent to Jean's hairdresser for a new haircut. It cost him $100, and he wasn't happy that he had to pay for it out of his own pocket.

The real look of the eighties, meanwhile, was about to slip in through the back door, through the servants' quarters.

\* \* \*

Jean still needed an ethnic, and a special series of auditions was set up to find one. For two days in mid-September some thirty black actors and comedians filed through the writers' wing on the 17th floor to read for Jean and her people. At the end, Jean told her group she was leaning toward hiring a stand-up by the name of Charlie Barnett. But talent coordinator Neil Levy had another black performer he wanted her to see, a kid from Roosevelt, Long Island, named Eddie Murphy.

Murphy, who had been performing in Florida when the black auditions were held, had generally been making a nuisance of himself with Levy for several days. He kept calling, sometimes three times a day, insisting he was great, telling sad stories about how desperate he was for a job, and saying all he wanted was a chance to show what he could do. Levy, used to being badgered, put him off for a while, but eventually he relented and told Murphy to come on up to the office.

Eddie was just nineteen, but he'd been working the comedy clubs on Long Island and around New York since he was fifteen, when he was still in high school. He had a hip, aggressive act that owed a lot to his idol, Richard Pryor. When Eddie came to the office he did a routine for

Levy about three guys on a street corner in Harlem; one of them, the short one, mouthed off enough to provoke the other two into fighting each other. Levy was impressed and immediately went to Jean to tell her she had to see Eddie. Jean told him to take Eddie to Michael Zannella, and, a day or two later, he did.

By that time, his foot in the door, Eddie had performed for anyone on the 17th floor whom he and Levy could get to sit down for a few minutes and watch—Eddie said later that he auditioned six times. Several others, including Audrey Dickman and talent scout Liz Welch, were now in his corner. During one of his auditions a script had been pulled out from the old show's files—the job interview sketch that Chevy Chase and Richard Pryor had performed so brilliantly on Pryor's show in the first season. Eddie needed someone to read it with him, and Joe Piscopo volunteered. Joe and Eddie had met a few times at the comedy clubs, but they knew each other only casually. Eddie, Piscopo says, was electrifying that day, and from then on Eddie and Joe started hanging out together, at first simply as friends, but soon out of self-defense.

According to Neil Levy, Michael Zannella was not overly enthusiastic when he saw Eddie, saying the black cast member had already been chosen. With some prodding, however, it was agreed that Jean should see him. A couple of days later, Eddie came up to Jean's office and again did his act. Jean, according to several of those there, liked him, but was unsure about hiring him. Jean herself says that she immediately recognized Eddie's talent and wanted to hire him in some capacity, but she had misgivings about his youth and his inexperience. So she hesitated while Levy and others persisted—quite vehemently, says Levy. Finally Eddie was hired, at $750 a show, as one of five featured players, another element Jean had borrowed from Lorne.

On Lorne's show the featured players were all, except for Paul Shaffer, writers, but with Jean they were mainly glorified extras. Jean made it a rule early on that she didn't want the writers doing sketches built around the featured players; the full-fledged cast members should be established first, she said. Eddie was on the team, but he would spend some time on the bench.

# Chapter 35

# The Ayatollah Doumanian

From the beginning there were disquieting signs of something amiss on the 17th floor.

Most of the cast members didn't notice. They were sure they had just stepped on the express track to success, convinced they were the rightful heirs apparent to the *Saturday Night* legacy. Charles Rocket in particular walked with the air of one who was about to be revealed to the American public as a star. Joe Piscopo, who was not so certain of their prospects, says that with Rocket it was "immediately: sunglasses."

Rocket later said it never occurred to him that replacing the original show's cast might be a problem. He, Denny Dillon, and Gail Matthius quickly formed a threesome—"the Three Musketeers," Matthius called them—and Rocket remembers thinking, "This will be just great. This is our show now." Ann Risley felt the same. "We're funny," a writer heard her say once. "We'll be able to reach the same heights."

The writers weren't so sure. They, too, had arrived on the 17th floor almost euphoric at being hired. For most of them, going to work for *Saturday Night* was like coming through the mountain pass and gazing on Shangri-la. The fact that Jean had been unable to pay them very much, because, she said, of a tight budget, didn't faze them in the least. But within days an unsettling sense of contagious unease started to set in.

It began to dawn on some of the writers how difficult it was going to be to follow the original show. Others were disappointed by the absence of the family spirit that mythology dictated they would find on the 17th floor. One writer said that when he got there it was like climbing into the neat tree house the older kids had built, but now it seemed empty and too quiet.

The writers were immediately uncomfortable with the cast. The performers had what one writer called "an attitude of presumptive arrogance," an attitude unsupported, the writers felt, by talent. Writer Billy Brown remembers that after the first read-through of sketches the writers came away thinking the cast was "awful, hopeless." Most of the players were stand-up comedians with little or no background in improvisational comedy and no experience at working together. It wasn't going to be easy, the writers believed, coming up with material for them. The cast members were similarly unimpressed by the writers. The breach between them would continue to grow.

Just as quickly, the writers realized their biggest problem was going to be dealing with the boss. Although the show was still some months away, Jean wanted everybody to get right down to work, insisting that regular submissions be deposited on her desk. So the writers wrote, only to find, they all say, that nothing happened once they did. The scripts seemed to collect in piles on Jean's desk; eventually there were filing cabinets full of them. Jean held no bull sessions to throw ideas around, never offered alternative premises or specific editorial suggestions. Every writer had the experience of having a script handed back by Jean with the comment, either written on the front or delivered orally, "Make it funnier." Sometimes she'd add, "It isn't hip enough. Make it hipper."

The writers soon began to conclude as well that Jean did not possess a highly developed sense of humor. Almost every writer has a story about a joke they told or wrote that went right by her. Sean Kelly and writer-filmmaker-featured-player Mitchell Kriegman came up with a script in which a series of hackneyed punch lines would reel off in a list across the screen. The fact that they were the most clichéd one-liners in show business history was the point. As Jean went down the list of one-liners, Kelly recalls, she said one of two things about each: "I've heard that one before," or "I don't get it."

Part of the problem, many of the writers say, was simply temperament. Jean seemed especially unable to appreciate dark, subversive humor. She was much more oriented toward the visual, the decorative, and so tended to judge sketches on how she thought they would look onstage. But many on the show also say Jean didn't understand some of the material because she wasn't very well informed. "Jean was not an intellectual," one of the writers said. "She had no knowledge of politics or history, even show business history." Sometimes in read-throughs, to the amusement of those there, she mispronounced words in scripts—*Ode-ipus* instead of *Oedipus* and *quiche* instead of *kitch* were two examples—and eventually, as the atmosphere on the 17th floor grew more combative, some writers would throw polysyllabic words into their material just to see if Jean would trip on them.

There was a curious division in the way she handled the cast and the writers. Even the performers who ended up not respecting Jean say she treated the cast members well. As she had with *Saturday Night*'s guests in the past, Jean knew how to make the stars comfortable—more comfortable, perhaps, than they should have been. Joe Piscopo remembers a meeting Jean held with the cast shortly before the show premiered. She went around the room and asked each of them if there was anything, anything at all, they needed. Piscopo, who, more than any of the cast members, shared the writers' apprehensions about the way things were going, was about to suggest that she fire everyone and start over. His thoughts were interrupted by Ann Risley.

"Yes," Risley said. "I don't like white wine. Can I have red wine in my dressing room?"

"Oh geez," Piscopo thought. "Are we in trouble."

By contrast, Jean seemed insecure with the writers, and she tried to cover that insecurity, the writers unanimously agree, with a firmness that bordered on authoritarianism. At one point she decreed that every script must have three jokes per page. She insisted that the writers work late, as they had under Lorne, and berated those who didn't. Larry Arnstein and David Hurwitz, a writing team from Hollywood who eight years before had worked on the *Chicken Little Comedy Hour*, had grown accustomed to more conventional hours. Comedy, they felt, didn't have to be written in the middle of the night to be funny. Jean, however, would call them at home at two o'clock in the morning, wanting to know why they weren't in the office.

What writers meetings there were, Jean conducted stiffly; many of the writers felt they had to raise their hands before they spoke, and did. She actively discouraged writers who had not been hired as teams from working together, leading many of them to conclude that she perceived a united writing staff as a threat to her control of the show. Many of the staff firmly believe that Jean, consciously or unconsciously, promoted a divisive atmosphere, particularly between the cast and the writers. "She seemed," one writer said, "to like pitting people against one another." Another writer felt Jean operated on the philosophy that "the best comedy comes out of the barrel of a gun."

The collective malaise among the writers developed gradually, but quickly. Some, like Sean Kelly, were disillusioned "in seconds." The younger writers were deferential at first, then puzzled, but soon their doubts, too, turned to frustration, and eventually to anger. Long before the show went on the air the writers had lost all confidence in Jean. They were, according to one of them, divided into three philosophical groups:

those who wanted to revolt, those who hid their displeasure and tried to work closely with Jean to change things, and those who wanted to stay as far away as possible.

One of the last writers hired was David Sheffield, who left an advertising job in Mississippi to join the show. He arrived on 17 three weeks before the premiere to find "an air of doom hanging over the place." Before he'd unpacked his bags, one of the writers, Pam Norris, told him Jean had no idea of how to run *Saturday Night*. "It's in serious trouble," she said.

Whatever Jean's failings, many on the show, including several members of the cast, several members of Jean's inner circle, and some of the writers themselves, believe the writers were by no means blameless in the dissension that soon enveloped them all. David Sheffield found his colleagues "young and inexperienced" and much too quick to judge Jean. "If they'd done a lot less bitching and pulled together," Sheffield says, "the show would have been far better." Joe Piscopo felt the writers were as infatuated with themselves as the cast members were, with as little justification. The writers, Piscopo said, were "walking around like they were writing masterpieces," when in fact they were turning out junk. Several people add that sexism had not a little to do with the resistance to Jean's authority. The male writers, Karen Roston says, didn't like taking orders from a woman. David Sheffield agrees, saying it was always "that woman" the writers complained about.

But most of those who worked for her shared the conviction that Jean had neither the natural force of personality nor the skills to inspire confidence among the creative members of her staff. Most also agreed she needed a strong lieutenant, probably a head writer, to marshal her creative forces and shepherd their work along. Jean's failure to find such a creative leader was widely considered her greatest failure. Some of her supporters, like Alan Stern, an independent producer who was a member of Jean's inner circle, say that Jean would have gladly hired such a leader if she could have found one. Many others, including one of the head writers she did hire, believe Jean was not secure enough to hand over so much authority to someone else. That "inability to accept her inabilities," as Neil Levy put it, was considered Jean's fatal flaw.

There was no lack of people willing to take over the creative responsibilities. One of the first was writer Peter Tauber, and it was Tauber who, a full two months before Jean's show went on the air, touched off the spark that turned the writers' disgruntlement into open rebellion.

By the time he reached *Saturday Night*, Tauber, thirty-three, had been a novelist (*The Sunshine Soldiers*, *The Last Best Hope*), a reporter for *The New York Times*, and a stand-up comedian. He was writing screenplays in Hollywood when a mutual friend put him in touch with

Jean. Before their first interview, Jean, as she did with several others, kept Tauber waiting for four hours outside her office, another habit she seemed to have picked up from Lorne. When he finally did get in to see her, Tauber told Jean he wanted to be more than just a sketch writer. He was, he said, too experienced to be so restricted. He wanted to be in on the shaping of the show, to help her "reinvent *Saturday Night*, not just redo it." When he was hired, Tauber thought that's what Jean wanted him for, but he soon found himself shut out of the decision-making process, and he grew steadily more disenchanted with Jean. Tauber says he asked Jean early on if she was scared. "No," she replied. Tauber found that hard to believe. Jean, he said to himself, apparently hadn't yet grasped the enormity of the task she faced.

Before long, Tauber became convinced there was "no creative center" to the show and decided to take matters into his own hands. With Sean Kelly, he called a meeting of the writers. Jean wasn't invited. Tauber would later claim he only wanted the writers to "cross-fertilize" ideas, but others say his intentions were not so innocent. Ferris Butler, another writer, remembers Tauber suggesting at this meeting that the writers form a little "soviet," a council independent of Jean. Tauber, Butler says, told those there, "I propose to be, in a sense, a head writer, if you want me to be." Writer Barry Blaustein remembers being pulled into Tauber's office the day he arrived on the 17th floor. "I should be the producer of this show," Blaustein says Tauber told him. "I should be making all the comedy decisions. Jean doesn't know what she's doing."

Jean caught on that Tauber was mobilizing people against her and quickly moved to halt it. She announced there'd be no more writers' meetings held outside her office. Tauber kept pushing. He asked if he could set up an open file of scripts so that everyone could look at what was being written and either collaborate or at least not duplicate what others were doing. Jean, Tauber says, didn't respond.

It was about this time that Tauber had a confrontation with Jean's friend Mary Pat Kelly that he believes once and for all ruined his relationship with Jean. Jean had let it be known she didn't want drugs being used on the premises, in itself a significant change of *Saturday Night* policy. Those who wanted to get high did so discreetly. Mary Pat Kelly was among those who shared Jean's distaste for drugs. One day she smelled the odor of marijuana coming from the office of writers Billy Brown and Mel Green. She went in and strongly suggested the group inside stop smoking. Unpleasant words were exchanged.

When Tauber heard what happened, he went to Kelly's office and told her in no uncertain terms to mind her own business. Kelly, Tauber says, responded by swinging her handbag at him, yelling threats that she would go to Jean.

Tauber says he had virtually forgotten the incident when, the next day, a rather large man approached him outside his office. The man had something around his waist that Tauber at first took for a telephone repairman's equipment belt. As he came closer, however, Tauber realized it was a holster with a pistol in it.

"You Tauber?"

"What can I do for you?" Tauber responded, holding out his hand. He didn't get a hand in response. The man, it turned out, was Mary Pat's friend. He was a professional bodyguard, Tauber says, and his message was clear.

"If you ever talk to Mary Pat Kelly again, I'll kill you," he said.

Tauber was stunned. He tried to explain that he and Mary Pat had had a professional disagreement and would settle it themselves. The man, Tauber says, put a hand on his shoulder and repeated: "If you ever talk to her again, I'll kill you. I'll kill you outside the office, but I'll fucking kill you."

When Mary Pat's friend walked away, Tauber almost ran to Jean's office. This, he told her, had gotten a little out of hand. He and Mary Pat had both been silly, he admitted, but that didn't justify his life being threatened. Jean, Tauber says, told him everyone was wrong.

That's not good enough, Tauber answered, raising his voice. He wanted Jean to call NBC security immediately to remove Mary Pat's friend from the offices. If she didn't, he would. Jean repeated that everyone was being silly. Leaning closer to her desk, Tauber, louder yet, said: "Jean, I think you have the wrong handle on this."

With that, Tauber says, Jean "almost came across the desk" at him. Riveting her eyes on his, she shot back: "If I have the goddamn wrong handle, then you tell me what to do!"

"You don't let your writers be threatened by guys carrying guns!" Tauber shouted. "This is a fucking asshole who doesn't work for NBC who is threatening to kill me!"

"Oh, Dennis," Jean said, "he wouldn't hurt a fly." Apparently she knew Mary Pat's friend better than Tauber did.

Tauber and Jean didn't talk much after this. Finding himself more removed than ever from the position of influence he coveted, Tauber decided to make one last effort to change her mind. He met with Jean on September 23, bringing with him a thirteen-page memo spelling out in detail the problems he saw with the show. He held nothing back.

Tauber wrote that Jean's staff meetings were no more than "a kind of ratification process for decisions already made." Because the writers were "deferential" and "respectful" in her presence, he said, the "robust kind of interchange that we have to have does not really develop." The result was "a competition that is more a jockeying for approval, preening for teacher's favor. ... It pains me to say it, but a system of timidity and lack of candor is emerging at every level, and it is fucking dangerous."

The writers, the memo continued, needed a script supervisor, and meetings where they could exchange ideas. "We have to collaborate amongst ourselves ... No less than ten of us want regular meetings of the writers. Some want daily morning meetings. (If someone doesn't want to attend, no one is forced to.) We want them early and now. Nearly all of us want an open file so we can get and give feedback, help and teach each other, and learn ... Each of us can write til doomsday and you will never see a sketch worthy of SNL—or a New vision of it—until we get at each other and goose each other, pushing our work to higher levels of observation, wildness, risk and invention."

Her staff, he wrote, wasn't helping matters any. "I will say it plain: you are very largely surrounded by sycophants, yes-men, fawning admirers, gushy-lucky kids, flatterers and people who are dependent on you for approval and position. I think, unfortunately, you may be, however inadvertently, encouraging this. I'm not sure strong-mindedness or the courage to differ is being bred. Gratitude and obedience are."

Such an attitude, Tauber cautioned, could prove the death of the show. "I not only fear that we cannot win by timidity, but fear that it is both a certain way to failure—and our present course of choice. We can risk, be honest: and either win or fail honorably. Or we can play safe and be a plastic cloned SNL II: our audience will get angry and hoot us off the screens. We won't have 5-8 weeks to build. They'll cut our throats. They gave the show some time last time because they'd never seen anything like it: whatever it was, however ragged, it was better than television. If we come on imitative and ever-ingratiating, they'll turn us off so fast ... and never come back no matter how good we get."

Jean wasn't interested in Tauber's memo. Before he'd had a chance to say anything, she told him, "It's not working out."

Tauber said he had a memo for her. He threatened to send it to her bosses at NBC if she didn't read it.

"It's not working out," Jean said again. Tauber was fired.

Jean called a staff meeting soon after Tauber's departure to clear the air. She said Tauber had been polarizing the group, creating hysteria, ostensibly out of concern for the show but in fact to further his own ends. However they felt about Jean, most of the staff agreed with that. "Tauber thought he was a cut above everybody else," says one of the

*Saturday Night* veterans who'd stayed on with Jean. "He was on an ego trip. He saw a vacuum and tried to insert himself in it."

Tauber doesn't disagree, but cites necessity rather than ego as the root of his actions. "The problems were manifest," he says. "There *was* a vacuum, and someone had to fill it. The writers were pleading for some kind of leadership."

The Tauber incident would have consequences beyond the firing of an unhappy writer. Tauber did indeed send his memo to Brandon Tartikoff and to Fred Silverman, with cover letters explaining his "grave fears" for the show. *Saturday Night* was, he warned them, "in considerable peril, creatively and organizationally." Tauber's personal motives were self-evident, but these missives didn't make upper management feel any more comfortable about Jean.

Far worse, Tauber's memo, and much of the dissension that provoked it, became public a few weeks later in a lengthy feature article in the New York *Daily News*. The article ran under the headline, *Is The All-New Saturday Night Live Not Even Ready For Air Time?* It was filled with unflattering comments from unnamed staffers about Jean. One of them said she had "a whim of iron." Tauber was quoted briefly by name, calling Jean the "Ayatollah Doumanian." Tauber would later claim he had not planted the story, but it clearly relied heavily on his memo to Jean, if not on information supplied directly by Tauber himself. In any case, the *Daily News* article was fundamental in alerting the media that trouble, and a very sexy story, was brewing at *Saturday Night*. Open season had been declared on Jean Doumanian.

Within the show, the troubles with Tauber succeeded in fatally poisoning the atmosphere; whatever chance of rapprochement there had been between Jean and those with grievances against her had disintegrated. As Jean's friend Letty Aronson remembers it, there was now a certain set of people that Jean and her inner circle called the "They" group. Jean and Aronson, although they didn't use the term, were part of the "Us" group. The writers, of course, saw it the other way around.

Evidence of this was two of the comments overheard on the 17th floor the day the *Daily News* article came out. Cast member Charles Rocket was walking by a writer's office when somebody said, "Did you see that great article? ... We got her now." Writer Ferris Butler walked by Jean's office the same day and heard her talking with a member of her inner circle. "What a fuck," one of them said of Tauber. "I hope he gets cancer."

\* \* \*

That things were only going to get worse became apparent the day after the *Daily News* article appeared, when Jean held her first press conference to introduce the cast. There had been a natural drama to the question of who would replace the most famous ensemble in television, and reporters were anxious to break the story.

By the time the press arrived that morning, however, they were angry that the story had already been broken. Jean's initial plan had been to withhold until the press conference any information on who had been hired. But thinking that the *Daily News*, along with its negative report, was about to name the cast members, she attempted to defuse the article by leaking their identities to *The New York Times*. Thus, by the time of the press conference, every other reporter in the country had been, thanks to Jean, scooped by the *Times*. The *News* article did not identify the cast after all.

The press conference was a disaster. Jean would not allow the cast members to answer any questions. They sat uncomfortably at a table as the reporters protested, vehemently. Jean, refusing to give in, explained that the performers would have plenty to say on-air. Some who worked on the show believe her intention was to promulgate the idea that *Saturday Night*'s new stars, like its old stars, were above interviews. The press was not appeased.

Marvin Kitman, from the Long Island newspaper *Newsday*, wrote a column that was an exaggerated version of the general response. He called the new cast members "squeaky-clean California types, even if some of them are from the East." There wasn't, he wrote, a "snaggle-tooth" among them, not a fat one like John Belushi, nor a funny-looking one like Gilda Radner, nor (despite never having seen them perform) "a multi-talented one who could do it all, like Dan Aykroyd." Nor, he added, was there a black one like Garrett Morris. Eddie Murphy, a featured player, not a member of the cast, hadn't been present at the press conference. Kitman called the new cast "lap dogs" for meekly obeying Jean's order of silence and referred to Jean as "Jean Doberman-pinscher." She was, he said, "conservative, insecure, inexperienced [and] unadventurous ... Ms. Christopher Columbus ... trying to explore the new world by sailing around in her familiar bathtub."

Kitman, along with most of *Saturday Night*'s other fans in the press, was obviously awaiting with relish the opportunity to review the first show.

## CHAPTER 36

# "Get Rid of Her"

Neil Levy's search for the first host had ended with barely a week to spare when Elliott Gould, a frequent host of the old show, readily agreed to appear. Some who knew Gould speculated that he may not have been aware of Lorne and the original team's departures.

The premiere show had been delayed until November 15. It was an election year, NBC News had again taken over studio 8H, and Jean had seen enough of Lorne's problems during the Brooklyn shows in the second season to decide she didn't want the agony of starting her show in an unfamiliar studio. The extra preparation time had not been especially helpful, however. The material in read- throughs was obviously weak, although people were pretending it was funny. Too much time had been wasted on cosmetics: Weeks had gone by trying to find a new format for Weekend Update, and more weeks passed trying to devise a new opening montage. Jean had wanted both to be distinctive from Lorne's show, but in the end both came out looking almost identical to his.

Jean had also launched a seemingly obsessive search for the perfect cold opening for the first show, one that would properly introduce the new cast. Scores of scripts had been written and rejected and, a writer said, "eight thousand man-hours consumed" before Jean finally settled on one that attempted to confront head on the problem of following in the footsteps of the old cast.

The first camera shot of *Saturday Night '80*, as Jean had labeled it, was a close-up of Gail Matthius apparently waking up in bed next to Elliott Gould. She said she was worried the show would start without her. Gould, the old hand, told her to relax. Looking at her, he added that she was "kind of a cross between Jane and Gilda." The camera panned out and revealed Charles Rocket in bed with them. Gould told him (as Charles had been told before) that he was a cross between Chevy and Billy. The camera pulled out wider and Ann Risley came into view; she, Gould said, was a cross between Gilda and Laraine. With that, Joe Piscopo popped out from under the covers, and, feigning wide-eyed innocence, asked Gould about the drug use on the old show. "Cocaine was everywhere," Gould said.

The opening didn't get many laughs, although it conceivably could have been seen as a bold attempt to exorcise the ghosts of *Saturday Night* past—had it not been for the material that followed. In Gould's monologue, he reminisced about old underwear he'd worn and loved, fondling various pairs of drawers. He was just about to unzip his fly for a look at the pair he was wearing when Denny Dillon came on and they started swapping panties for boxer shorts. That was followed by a sketch set in the Oval Office of the White House. The sketch apparently referred to Jimmy Carter's famous comments in *Playboy* magazine about having lusted in his heart after women, an interview that had been published four years earlier.

Rosalynn Carter, played by Ann Risley, was talking with her daughter, Amy, played by Dillon. Amy said she'd just seen Jimmy urinating in the hallway. Joe Piscopo entered as a disheveled-looking Carter, wearing a suit jacket, tie, and pajama bottoms. Rosalynn told him how glad she was that he lost the election, because the presidency had taken the fun out of their lives, clearly implying their sex lives. "Darlin'," she said, "we haven't plowed a furrow or planted a seed in four years."

Carter, ignoring her, started blaming the Jews for his defeat. "Those beanyheads," he said, "didn't vote for me."

Rosalynn, after sending Amy out of the room, brought the talk back to sex. "Now honey, you can release all those lustful thoughts ... let it all out. I've been waiting four years for this."

"I want to be naked," Jimmy replied. Rosalynn, growing excited, answered, "Talk dirty to me, Jimbo."

But Jimmy couldn't seem to speak. Haltingly, he told his wife that the last four years had robbed him of any lustful thoughts. "You see, Jimmy," said Rosalynn, "that's why we had to lose. It was either the election or the erection."

Jimmy smiled and told her the power was returning to his body. Rosalynn lay down on the desk top and started unbuttoning her blouse. Jimmy said he could now do what he'd wanted to do for four years. "Then why don't you just do it, Mr. President?" Rosalynn panted. Jimmy said he would, grabbed a gun from a drawer, and shouted into an intercom for his brother, Billy, to meet him in the Rose Garden. Fade to commercial.

That pitiful attempt at political satire would turn out to be sadly representative of the level of humor on *Saturday Night '80*. Later in the first show there was a sketch in which Gail Matthius pretended to give herself a breast examination while her chest was obscured by a black band superimposed on the screen ("Don't do this like this," she said, "or these will look like that"); and another sketch about a homosexual Army brigade— stationed at Fort Dix. They marched to the cadence call: "I won't go down on anyone, Uncle Sam's the only one." At the end of the show Gould reintroduced the cast and declared, "We're gonna be around forever."

\* \* \*

Whatever relief the staff felt about actually getting through the premiere disappeared when the reviews came in. The reaction of the Associated Press was typical: "The new *Saturday Night Live* is essentially crude, sophomoric and most of all self-consciously 'cool.' It is occasionally funny." *The Washington Star* said the show "strained and groaned" while the humor was "almost completely lost, despite desperate attempts to ring it out of raunch." Newsday's Marvin Kitman, as expected, ravaged the show gleefully, calling it "offensive and raunchy," and worse, not funny. "This new edition is terrible," he wrote. "Call it '*Saturday Night* Dead on Arrival.'"

Jean called a meeting of the writers in her office at noon the following Monday. Some of the cast members, including Charles Rocket, actually believed the first show went fine, but most of the writers weren't kidding themselves. "You realized," Barry Blaustein said, "that the whole world unanimously hated you."

As the writers walked into Jean's office, she looked like she hated them too. She didn't say anything until all the late arrivals filed in. Then she picked up Tom Shales's review in *The Washington* Post and read it aloud, slowly, word for word. Shales had always been *Saturday Night*'s strongest and most prestigious booster, and thus his reaction to the new show was more important than most.

The headline on his review read *From Yuk to Yeccch*. The first sentence was: "Vile from New York—it's *Saturday Night*." The show, Shales said, was a "snide and sordid embarrassment." It imitated the "ribaldry and willingness to prod sacred cows" of the Lorne Michaels years without having the least "compensating satirical edge." It was, he wrote, "just haplessly pointless tastelessness." Shales concluded that despite one or two imaginative moments from the show's filmmakers, "from the six new performers and 13 new writers hired for the show, viewers got virtually no good news."

When she'd finished reading, Jean put the paper down and started going around the room, asking each person, one by one, "What do you think?" People weren't sure how to answer, or even what the question was exactly. Did she mean what did they think of the review, or of the show, or perhaps of the future? None of the three was pleasant to contemplate. It turned out that Jean wanted people to comment on the show itself. That initiated what writer David Sheffield called "a huge cat fight" with a lot of "finger- pointing and backbiting."

Jean listened for a while before reclaiming the floor to give her own highly critical postmortem. They had, she said, a long, long way to go before they could even think about turning out anything nearly as good as the original show. Nobody disputed that. Jean made it clear she thought the writing was primarily at fault. "It's just got to be funnier," she said. Then she put a tape of the show on her videocassette machine to begin a sketch-by-sketch critique. According to writer Billy Brown, as she did she said, "Watch this. And I hope you hate it, because you wrote it."

\* \* \*

Brandon Tartikoff hadn't cared for the first show either, but he wasn't yet ready to panic. There was reason, he thought, for hope. Tartikoff was uneasy, however, with Jean's choice of English actor Malcolm McDowell as her second host. He told her McDowell would get a zero in his "Farmers Market poll." By that Tartikoff meant that if he went to the big produce market of that name in Los Angeles and asked ten people who Malcolm McDowell was, not one of them would be able to tell him. Tartikoff had suggested to Jean that she needed somebody with more recognition value for the second show. "Fine," Jean had said. She booked McDowell anyway.

Tartikoff also mentioned to Jean he'd like to come to the show's read-through that Wednesday. "Hey," Jean replied, "you gave me total control. You're not coming." Tartikoff shrugged and said okay. He understood that Jean was sensitive about network interference— Lorne had never tolerated it either—and even after the bad first show, he respected it. His attitude changed when he saw the Malcolm McDowell show.

Many *Saturday Night* veterans consider the Malcolm McDowell show the single worst show in *Saturday Night*'s history. It wasn't McDowell's fault: The writing was so overwhelmingly bad it would be hard to pick a most awful moment. Certainly one of them was a sketch called "Leather Weather," in which Denny Dillon in dominatrix leather gear barked out a weather report while she abused Charles Rocket, who was spread-eagled in chains on the weather map before her. Another sketch, called "Jack the Stripper," was so long, so meaningless, and so expensive to mount that some on *Saturday Night* single it out as the most disastrous sketch ever on the show. It had something to do with Prince Charles being a royal flasher—exactly what it was about was impossible to decipher. A third sketch tried clumsily to satirize the recent acquittals of some Ku Klux Klan murderers in Greensboro, North Carolina.

"Shoot a Jew or a nigger, chances are you're getting a Commie," was one of the lines.

Brandon Tartikoff watched the McDowell show at his home in Los Angeles. He was, in his words, "appalled" and "crazed" by what he saw. He called Jean on Sunday morning. "This is a disaster," he told her. He said the show was mired in "dark humor" aimed primarily at "shock value." There wasn't, he said, any "joy" in it. He warned Jean that unless she somehow rekindled positive word of mouth, the ratings were going to slip into a downward spiral that she wouldn't be able to reverse. Without delivering any specific ultimatums, Tartikoff made it clear he couldn't allow that to happen—the *Saturday Night* franchise was too important to NBC.

Jean, Tartikoff recalls, was surprised his reaction was so strong. She hadn't thought the McDowell show was all that terrible.

That didn't reassure Tartikoff, and, for the first time, he thought of firing Jean. Later that day he discussed his problems with *Saturday Night* in a conversation with one of his best friends: Dick Ebersol. It had been Ebersol who had hired Brandon Tartikoff at NBC in the fall of 1977, when Ebersol was heading up the network's comedy and variety operations in Los Angeles. Tartikoff had come from ABC, where he'd been a minor programming executive. Ebersol left NBC a year later after having a bitter falling out with Fred Silverman; Tartikoff rose quickly through the ranks to become, at the age of thirty-one, Silverman's head of programming. In the meantime, Ebersol had worked as a producer on NBC's *Midnight Special*, as well as on occasional one-shot projects, including a "trash sports" show called *City vs. Country Showdown*.

Tartikoff told Ebersol on the phone that Sunday that he was beginning to have serious doubts about Jean Doumanian, and in the course of their conversation he asked Ebersol what he thought about perhaps coming back to take over *Saturday Night*. Ebersol didn't think it would work. He told Brandon he'd just bought a new house in Brentwood, in west Los Angeles, and he was happy doing what he was doing, which was making lots of money and enjoying his freedom. More to the point, Ebersol couldn't see Fred Silverman agreeing to hire him. He was sure his own loathing for Silverman was not unrequited. Ebersol also said he wouldn't consider taking the job unless NBC agreed to put the show on hiatus long enough for him to rebuild it. Both Ebersol and Tartikoff knew Silverman wouldn't buy that. So the subject was, for the time being, dropped.

Fred Silverman had been as appalled as Tartikoff was by the Malcolm McDowell show. Not being in the most patient of moods at the time, he immediately started saying Jean should be fired. He would express that opinion ever more frequently in subsequent weeks as *Saturday Night* failed to improve. "The show is terrible," Silverman told Tartikoff again and again. "Get rid of her. We've got to do something."

Silverman was saying the same thing to his senior vice president of programming, Irv Wilson, who was seen within NBC's executive ranks as a contender for Tartikoff's head programming job. Wilson said later that after the Malcolm McDowell show he had gone "on record" with Silverman advocating Jean's dismissal, and he let it be known within the network that he considered Brandon "wishy- washy" for not making a move to replace her. Wilson also criticized Jean openly in an article in the show business bible, *Variety*, saying she "needs help badly." Tartikoff was quoted in the same article as saying he was concerned about the show, but he'd seen signs of improvement, implying Jean should be given some time. But Silverman, Wilson says, agreed there was no time to lose, telling him the same week the *Variety* article appeared, "Find another producer." Wilson started looking for one.

The frenzy that imbued Silverman by this point had reached Shakespearean proportions. NBC was in total disarray, not just in prime time but in almost every daypart on the schedule. Silverman's failures had destroyed the network's bottom line: In 1980, NBC's earnings were $80 million less than they were in 1977, the year before Silverman took over, and its profits were about a third of what ABC and CBS were making. Speculation was rampant now that Silverman would soon lose his job, and Silverman was desperately squandering millions more on grandiose program schemes that, he hoped, would miraculously turn it all around. They didn't. Watching *Saturday Night* fall apart on top of it all, Tartikoff said, "drove Fred nuts."

Not only was the show terribly unfunny, but, being unfunny, it was losing viewers, and therefore losing profits for NBC. Jean's first show had attracted a 34 percent share of the audience. Not at all a bad number, especially considering the lack of available superstars, but still about 5 million fewer viewers than had watched the premiere show the previous year. The Malcolm McDowell show lost *another* 3.4 million viewers. While a few of Jean's shows scored slightly better ratings than the McDowell show, for the most part she would never recoup those losses.

Jean's ratings wouldn't have been so disturbing if NBC had looked upon *Saturday Night* as a new program, which is really what it was. But the network made the greedy mistake of promising advertisers virtually the same ratings the old show had delivered, telling skeptical sponsors that *Saturday Night* was "an institution among young people." When the promised numbers weren't forthcoming, NBC had to give the advertisers free commercials to make up the difference—*make-goods* is the term they use. Before long, the rates the salesmen could command for *Saturday Night* had dropped by more than half, to $25,000 or so for a thirty-second spot. By those standards—the standards that count—Jean Doumanian was costing NBC a fortune.

Tartikoff, although he was steadily growing more pessimistic, still hoped Jean might get a grasp on the job and the show would improve. At the same time, he knew Irv Wilson was actively seeking a replacement for her. Tartikoff had no intention of letting his rival make such an important decision. If it came to that, Tartikoff would choose Jean's successor himself, and the one replacement he felt confident with was Dick Ebersol. In the meantime, he was determined to exercise more control over the show.

Tartikoff and his lieutenants descended on *Saturday Night*. So did Irv Wilson and his lieutenants. "There were," Karen Roston recalls, "blue suits everywhere." Program executives attended read-throughs now, whether Jean liked it or not, and afterward tried to tell her what sketches should be chosen for the show. Executives were also in 8H between dress and air, telling Jean which sketches they thought should be cut and which should stay. Executives told Jean who should and who shouldn't host the show, demanded she do something to lift the level of the acting and of the writing, and summoned her to an ever-growing number of meetings to voice an ever-growing list of suggestions and complaints.

The smell of producer's blood had been sensed elsewhere in 30 Rock as soon as the ratings came in. Jean's production budget at the start had been $520,000 a show, only $33,000 per show less than Lorne's budget in his final year. That was amazingly high considering the fact it did not include the huge salaries that *Saturday Night*'s original writers and performers were getting by the fifth season. Budget czar Don Carswell explained later that the budget hadn't been cut more drastically because, if the show collapsed, no one wanted to take the blame for wielding the knife that killed it. Once Jean's ratings took a dive, that onus was removed.

The unit managers began fighting expenditures again. NBC in Fred Silverman's declining days was more cost conscious than it had been for years—the money Fred was throwing away in prime time had to be covered somewhere—and by January Jean's budget was cut back, she says, by between $50,000 and $100,000 a week. Her actual spending was restricted even more by all the executives now hovering around the show. Irv Wilson, for example, remembers vetoing, for economic reasons, a sketch that would have required building a space capsule worth something like $35,000.

Standards chief Ralph Daniels similarly reasserted himself. The censors at the time were being subjected to considerable heat by the television monitoring campaign of the religious coalition, the Moral Majority. And, in contrast to the post-Watergate beginnings of *Saturday Night*, Ronald Reagan's victory in the 1980 election supported the contention that America now believed in more conservative values. It was also not lost on Daniels that Jean's writers and performers, unlike their predecessors, lacked the talent necessary to bring off sensitive material successfully. So it was that Jean, despite her efforts to fight Standards as fiercely as Lorne had, began to find her appeals up the censor's chain of command unavailing. Even subjects that Lorne's show had successfully addressed on-air—marijuana and the hostage crisis in Iran being two examples—were suddenly prohibited for Jean.

One of Jean's pivotal fights with Standards unfolded during the week of her third show. Actress Ellen Burstyn was the host. At issue were three sketches—one about Planned Parenthood, another about a nun who was not a virgin, the third about a junkie selling potholders door to door to support his drug habit. By Thursday, Standards informed Jean that it didn't approve of any of them. By Saturday morning, Jean was still insisting they would be on the show—the network could ran a movie if they didn't like it. Ralph Daniels called Irv Wilson early Saturday morning and told him he'd better come into the office. "The three sketches won't get in, I promise you that," Daniels told him.

Wilson remembers spending most of that day arguing with Jean in her ninth-floor office. He thought the sketches were all in bad taste, not funny, and boring. Jean, he says, refused to give an inch. Wilson called Fred Silverman in California to discuss the problem. Silverman, after talking with NBC's lawyers, told Wilson that the sketches should not go on. Repeat one of Lorne's old shows if necessary, he said. Wilson by then was so angry with Jean he was virtually shouting to Silverman that she should be fired, that day. Jean finally agreed late that afternoon to tone down two of the sketches, but held fast on the sketch about the nun. With air time drawing near, Wilson pulled Jean aside one more time.

"You do not control this show," he told her. "This is the NBC television network. Standards is in control." Wilson said that if she persisted in her resistance, she'd be in violation of her contract. In other words, agree or be fired. Jean dropped the sketch.

CHAPTER 37

# Eddie

Amidst all the *Sturm und Drang* surrounding the Malcolm McDowell show, Eddie Murphy's network television debut slipped by without the slightest notice. It was just as well, because Eddie himself was humiliated by it.

He appeared in a sketch called "In Search of the Negro Republican," which happened to be the one genuinely witty moment on the McDowell show. Written by David Sheffield, it was a parody of the old Mutual of Omaha nature series, *Wild Kingdom*. Charles Rocket played Marlin Perkins, Joe Piscopo his intrepid assistant, Jim Fowler. Fowler, in hopes of flushing out that rarest of political beasts, the Negro Republican, impersonated a waiter at a cocktail party, casually asking the black guests questions that would reveal their political sympathies. When he discovered a black Republican, a stuffy gentleman in a three-piece suit, he tagged him so that his migration patterns could be followed.

The humiliation for Eddie came not from the substance of the sketch, but from the part he played in it: He was an extra, sitting on a couch, seen only for the briefest moment on-camera, lost in the cocktail-party crowd. He didn't have a line. The Negro Republican in the three-piece suit was played by an actor hired especially for that one show.

Between his hiring and the first show of the season, Eddie had spent much of his time on the 17th floor quietly watching. He was not always "on," as many comedians are; he was, instead, sizing people up. He sat around the office by himself a lot, eating cheeseburgers. Sometimes he did uncannily accurate impersonations of the staff members scurrying by, and sometimes he impressed people in rehearsal sessions, although it was apparent he occasionally had difficulty reading scripts. But, for the most part, Eddie Murphy was ignored. He was only a nineteen-year-old kid, after all, and just a featured player.

Charles Rocket made no effort to disguise his condescension toward Eddie; Jean had decided that at nineteen Eddie was too young to be pushed to center stage, and Rocket agreed. Ann Risley, too, looked down on him. She once made the mistake of asking Eddie to fetch her some juice. Eddie didn't move. From then on he took pleasure in poking fun at Risley. Once when he stung her she shouted at him, "Look. I'm an actress. I've done Shakespeare, I've done Woody Allen." Eddie, again, wasn't moved.

It didn't take Eddie long to decide he was more talented than the cast members, especially after the show went on the air, and it was then that he became more vocal about being relegated to supporting roles. "If they'd only give me a chance," he said more than once, "I'd make it *so* funny."

Eddie was from the beginning firmly convinced he'd be a star; he planned to be a millionaire by the time he was twenty-two. Neil Levy says that early on Eddie started autographing the walls on 17, writing *Eddie Murphy #1*. The size of those signatures grew steadily during Eddie's first year on *Saturday Night*, until eventually they covered most of a wall. A lot of people found Eddie's cockiness irritating, especially in the funereal atmosphere that prevailed on the show. Eddie didn't care. "Huh, they're not funny," he told his close friend from home, Clint Smith. "Too bad."

On 17, Eddie was closest with Joe Piscopo, who shared his disdain for the others and his distress at being part of such a terrible show. "The two of us knew the situation we were in immediately," Piscopo said later. Gilbert Gottfried, too, was sympathetic, but he quickly became so demoralized that he was walking around the office in a daze, staring, not saying much of anything to anyone, a demeanor that gradually subsumed his performances on-air as well.

In subsequent years many people would try to take credit for discovering Eddie Murphy, and for helping him break through on *Saturday Night*. The fact was that the only one who made Eddie Murphy was Eddie Murphy. Jean's dictum that the featured players not be the focus of sketches was adhered to, and the writers weren't so impressed with Eddie's genius that they went out of their way to work him into their scripts. "Anybody who says they supported Eddie," writer Pam Norris says, "is lying."

Playing an extra—a prop, really—in the Negro Republican sketch convinced Eddie that if his status was going to change, he'd have to change it himself. He kept asking Jean when he'd have a chance to show what he could do. Jean, according to one person who heard these conversations, would tell him, "You're a featured player. You're learning. You have to understand that you have to be guided by us." Eddie wasn't satisfied with that. "Look," he told a friend, "I'm tired of sitting on the couch."

Finally Jean told Eddie to think about something for Weekend Update. Eddie was friendly by then with two of the writers, Barry Blaustein and David Sheffield, who had started writing together regularly as a team. Blaustein happened to mention to Eddie a news item about a judge in Cleveland who ruled that high-school basketball teams had to have a quota of at least two white players. The next day, Eddie walked into Blaustein's office and said, "Whatta you think of this?" Then, shifting into character as a student he called Raheem Abdul Muhammed, Eddie rattled off a commentary on the judge's ruling. "Great," both Blaustein and Sheffield said. "Do it."

Jean scheduled Eddie's piece for the next show's Weekend Update, two weeks after the Malcolm McDowell show. Weekend Update had consistently been one of the most disastrous segments on *Saturday Night '80*. Charles Rocket was the anchorman, but despite his personal experience in that role, he came across as stiff and uncomfortable, and the jokes he was given to read were so bad that every week Update was greeted with long, excruciating silences from the audience. The lone exception had been Joe Piscopo, who was doing a frenetic TV sports announcer character who bit off his sentences in staccato bursts: "Hello again everybody. Joe Piscopo. Live. *Saturday Night* Sports. The big story. Still. Roberto Duran. Oranges. Beef broth. Steak. Food. Gas. Fix? Maybe." When Piscopo appeared, there'd be a few moments of laughter, but as soon as the camera switched back to Rocket, the excruciating silences descended again. They made Update truly chilling to watch.

Eddie, standing next to Piscopo as they waited to go on that night, seemed a little nervous, but mostly excited. "Geez," he whispered to Piscopo, "the kids at Roosevelt High aren't going to believe this." On-air, Piscopo as the sports announcer mentioned the Cleveland court ruling on white basketball players and introduced Raheem Abdul Muhammed. The instant the camera focused on Eddie it was apparent that here was a presence to contend with. There was a gleam in his eyes that was riveting, a challenge in the tone of his voice that demanded attention.

Yo, baby. Look, I bin a junior at Cleveland High for seven years now, and let me tell you that this is the most disgusting thing y'all have pulled up to date. I mean, we ain't got much, at least let us have basketball. Is nothing sacred? Any time we get something going good, y'all move in on it. In the sixties we wore platform shoes. Then, y'all wore platform shoes. Then in the early seventies we braided our hair, in the late seventies y'all braided your hair. Now it's 1980, we're all on welfare, and by the end of next year y'all will be on welfare too. I don't see no judge saying that every two bathroom attendants have to be white! All I'm saying is y'all stick to playing hockey and polo and we'll stay in the courts. I mean, if God would have wanted whites to be equal to blacks, everyone would have one of these.

Eddie at that point reached under the Update desk and pulled out a huge "ghetto blaster" portable radio and stared indignantly at the camera.

The audience loved him. There was spontaneous laughter and applause from the beginning of his bit that grew louder until the end. When he pulled out the ghetto blaster, there was a roar, easily the biggest laugh to greet any joke of the season. Even Eddie seemed a little surprised. He swallowed, and glanced at Joe Piscopo sitting beside him. Joe winked. The camera switched back to Charles Rocket, who told another joke. Silence returned.

At the end of the show, as the cast waved goodnight from home base, Eddie planted himself directly in the middle of the group. It was a position he would take regularly from then on.

Eddie appeared in almost every Update after that, and every time he did he was a hit. He started working consistently with Blaustein and Sheffield. Often Eddie would provide the core of an idea and Blaustein and Sheffield would then shape it into a script. Eventually, as their collaboration matured, Eddie would come into their office and Blaustein and Sheffield would simply turn on a tape recorder while Eddie improvised a character. Other times they'd take a rough script to him and record the bits of business he'd throw in as he read it. Then Blaustein and Sheffield would go back to their office, listen to the tape, flesh out the idea, and write it up.

Eddie's presence in sketches also increased rapidly, but it was at the end of the January 10 show, hosted by actor Ray Sharkey, that he unexpectedly got the break that acknowledged he was a star. Earlier in the show he'd done a bit on Weekend Update that was a vicious put-down of Garrett Morris. Eddie, as himself, explained that he didn't want to be drafted into the armed forces. "If I get drafted," he said, "who's going to be 'The Black Guy' on *Saturday Night Live*?" No one but him, he said, could do the impressions of people like Stevie Wonder and Bill Cosby. Then, for the first time on the show, he did his impressions of Stevie Wonder and Bill Cosby, to huge applause. After that he leaned over and confidentially addressed the camera. "You want a tough soldier? You want a guy whose very name scares the hell out of me?" He held up a photo of Garrett. "Here's your man. He may be overage, but he's got a lot of free time." That there was now a different sort of "Black Guy" on *Saturday Night* was obvious.

As the Sharkey show went on, Dave Wilson and Audrey Dickman in the 8H control room began to realize there wasn't going to be enough material to fill it: They were something like five minutes short. Neil Levy, standing in the control room with Jean, had a suggestion: Why not let Eddie go on and do his stand-up act? Levy says Jean resisted the suggestion at first, but as the end of the show neared and the empty time loomed, she agreed, and Levy ran to find Eddie.

Eddie did his routine about the three black guys in Harlem, the same one he'd auditioned with, editing out all the obscenities as he went along. His delivery was a little rough, and the reception in 8H was not as overwhelming as legend would later have it. But he'd admirably saved the day, and it was an unquestionable confirmation of his new status on the show.

Eddie Murphy lets it be known that there is now a different sort of "Black Guy" on *Saturday Night.* © *NBC*

Two weeks later, Jean again sent Eddie out by himself, but this time it was planned in advance. He announced that he was no longer a featured player: He was officially the seventh member of the cast. The audience whooped its approval. Eddie had something else he wanted to say. "Now I know what you're thinking. 'The kid's young; he's nineteen years old, an overnight success. Will he burn out? Will he do the wrong things with the wrong people, abuse himself, ego trip, spend money on things he doesn't need?' I don't think so." With that he whipped out a large mirror, revealing that his hand was weighted down with jewelry, and preened.

Eddie was on his way then. The press recognized his charisma as quickly as the audience had, and the black kid from Long Island was immediately declared the hot new up-and-comer on *Saturday Night.*

Eddie never forgave Jean for not recognizing his talent earlier. "She tried to 'Garrett Morris' me," he once told *TV Guide*, "turn me into the little token nigger." He also felt that even after his talent was obvious, Jean didn't bring him along quickly enough. Some on the show say that the resistance at using Eddie came not so much from Jean as it did from cast members who were jealous that a featured player would be given air time at their expense. Two weeks before his promotion to the cast, Blaustein and Sheffield wrote a cold opening that had Eddie delivering the final, sacred line, "Live from New York, it's *Saturday Night*." Blaustein says some of the cast members didn't think it proper that a featured player be allowed to introduce the show like that. Blaustein went to Jean and said, "Come on, he's funny, he deserves it." Jean agreed, and Eddie delivered the line.

In truth, Eddie's immediate impact, especially in juxtaposition with the rest of the show, was impossible to ignore, and Jean, once she saw that impact, wasted little time in exploiting it. Within three shows of his first spot on Weekend Update, he was appearing as much as any other performer except Rocket and Piscopo, which is to say as much as anyone on the show.

Joe Piscopo had actually emerged before Eddie as Jean's first real star. His appeal was different: Whereas Eddie was the only one on *Saturday Night '80* to rekindle the instant chemical response of pure personality that accounted for the stardom of Chevy Chase, John Belushi, Gilda Radner, and Bill Murray, Piscopo made a name for himself as the new man of a thousand faces. Besides his Jersey Guy and sportscaster characters, his dead-on impersonations of such personalities as Dan Rather, Ted Koppel, Ed McMahon, and, most popular of all, Frank Sinatra (all aided immeasurably by makeup man Kevin Haney), quickly established Piscopo as a distinct comedic talent—a bit more traditional than usual on *Saturday Night*, perhaps, but still exciting to watch.

A few other funny moments cropped up in Jean's shows. The short films, some by well-known Hollywood directors, others by staff members Mitchell Kriegman and Mary Pat Kelly, were often successful. Charles Rocket's "Rocket Reports" were consistently good, and Jean's talent for booking music acts resulted in an impressive string of performers not usually seen on television, among them Blondie, Captain Beefheart, Kid Creole and the Coconuts, James Brown, and a little-known singer named Prince. One show, hosted by Karen Black, was actually funny all the way through.

But the successful moments were not redeeming. Overall, the show continued to rely heavily and clumsily on kinky sex jokes and racial stereotypes, and as the season wore on, the desperation of *Saturday Night '80* grew ever more apparent, both onstage and behind it.

# CHAPTER 38

# Bunker Time

For quite a while Jean refused to believe that things were as bad with the show as so many people said they were. She realized there were problems, but she felt that, given a little time, she could fix them. Letty Aronson remembers that after the Malcolm McDowell show, those in Jean's inner circle thought, "We'd better get our act together, but it was never a question that we couldn't."

Jean remained unruffled. Her daily routine never varied. In the morning she had two large cups of freshly squeezed orange juice from a restaurant on the shopping concourse beneath 30 Rock. If it wasn't freshly squeezed, Jean could tell, and she'd send it back. Between two o'clock and four o'clock in the afternoon she had two cups of a health drink mixed from the fresh carrots, parsley, and celery she kept in large plastic bags in her refrigerators. During meetings her assistant would disappear into the bathroom, Jean's blender would whir noisily, and he would emerge to hand her a concoction that looked, one writer said, "like river sludge." People tried not to watch too obviously as Jean drank it down. Each weeknight she had a glass of hot water mixed with the juice of one or two fresh lemons; each Saturday as the show went on she allowed herself a cold Heineken.

Between November and February, Jean gradually eliminated some of the more divisive elements on the 17th floor. Writers Sean Kelly and Leslie Fuller and featured player and filmmaker Mitchell Kriegman—all members of the "they" group—were fired. This was an instance where Jean diverged from the policies of Lorne Michaels, who never fired anyone. In the meantime, Jean had hired a head writer, Mason Williams, the same Mason Williams who in 1967 had been the head writer for *The*

*Smothers Brothers Comedy Hour*. Williams had just finished two new Smothers Brothers specials for NBC, and it was NBC that recommended him to Jean.

Williams, it turned out, was a throwback to the halcyon days of the sixties, a gentle man who still held firmly to his countercultural beliefs—"the Last Hippie," more than one writer called him. He clashed with Jean instantly.

As Peter Tauber had before him, Williams envisioned re-creating *Saturday Night* by making it new and daring; he was fond of saying that the show had become so established it was "like a head shop at Sears." Like so many others, Williams had been charmed by Jean in their first meeting. But as soon as he went to work, he recognized her lack of creative ability; and, like so many others, her refusal to acknowledge it shocked, then angered him. Williams later said that Jean talked about comedy without the slightest intrinsic feel for it, "like an ad man talks about music," and that she imitated Lorne Michaels so blindly he felt as if he'd moved "into a widow's house."

Also like Tauber, Williams began challenging Jean aggressively, telling her "over and over again," he says, that she didn't know what she was doing and that she should turn the creative work over to him. Just as quickly Williams soon found himself without even a semblance of power on the show. He was disinvited from Jean's post-read-through meetings, when the show's lineup was decided, after he abused her a few times with comments like "Why the fuck are you destroying that piece?" Any suggestions he made were ignored, and his access to Jean dwindled. The writers soon recognized his impotence and stopped coming to him with their sketches. Eventually, Williams found he couldn't get his own sketches typed by the production assistants without a struggle.

For Williams the show became a nightmare. When he first arrived, he'd felt so enthusiastic he decided to lay off smoking grass for a while, thinking he'd keep himself sharp for work. Within three weeks he was lighting his first joint of the day at nine o'clock in the morning. He tried taking his complaints about the way the show was being run to NBC's program executives and succeeded only in further alienating Jean. Williams grew more bitter, as did his attacks on Jean. He wrote a sarcastic memo to Jean and her inner circle called "How to Be Funny," in which he made the point that knowing something about comedy is a prerequisite to putting together a successful comedy show. He got no response. Then he wrote a sketch about her, which circulated among the writers, entitled "The Wicked Witch of the East." It told of a woman who went from being the king's juggler one year to being the queen herself the next.

Mason Williams left *Saturday Night '80* (and his $4,000 a show salary) by Christmas, six weeks after he arrived. He went back to his house in the Oregon woods and threw away his television set. Jean was again the de facto head writer.

\* \* \*

As the inexorable weekly production schedule ground on, Jean's lack of experience began increasingly to tell. It was evident from the start how little she knew. Once Jean rushed up to Leo Yoshimura in the studio and said, "Where's Stage Three?" To Leo that was like asking where the balcony was. He told her, and Jean rushed off. Leo looked over to a stagehand who'd overheard, and they both shook their heads.

As Lorne had, Jean expected the writers to produce their own pieces. But the writers didn't have those skills yet—"We didn't know what the hell we were doing," says David Sheffield—and Jean wasn't able to help them. The people who could help, like Audrey Dickman and Dave Wilson, found themselves shut out of Jean's inner circle. Nonetheless, the more Jean proved herself unable to deal with the crushing weight of the production responsibilities— and, like Lorne, she put off making decisions as long as possible— the more Davey and Audrey found themselves having to assume them. Before long they were cutting and shaping sketches to make them work, with or without Jean's blessing, and unilaterally making whatever production decisions they could to ensure that they had the required sixty-six minutes' worth of producible material by Saturday.

When Jean realized how unfunny the shows were, she responded by ordering more material produced. In theory that gave her more options from which to choose, and improved her chances of having a few good sketches every week. Instead of twenty or twenty-five sketches for read-through, Jean wasn't satisfied until she had thirty- five. Instead of going into dress rehearsal with twenty to twenty-five minutes' worth of extra material, as Lorne had, Jean by February was coming in forty-five minutes heavy each week.

The fatal flaw in that strategy is that it overburdens the production mechanism in a hundred ways, which is just what happened to *Saturday Night '80*. There wasn't enough time to edit and polish all the sketches, or to block them, or to build all the sets, make enough costumes, or prepare the proper makeup. The crew, on overtime far more than it had ever been, started to rebel. Strikes were threatened every time a meal or coffee break was missed or delayed, which was often. Dave Wilson, himself deeply depressed and on the verge of quitting, found himself desperately trying to placate his crew. "You're professionals," he told them. "You've got to do your job. Let's just dig in and do it."

Overproducing also generated that much more disgruntlement among the cast and the writers, who worked harder to deliver more material each week only to see more of it jettisoned after the dress rehearsal. The sketches that did go on were not, as Jean had hoped, noticeably better. The writers contemplated filing a formal grievance against her with the Writers Guild, mainly because of overwork, and there was more talk of presenting Jean with a petition, of striking, or of some other form of mutiny. Charles Rocket, who was convinced the writers were intentionally trying to sabotage the show by turning in bad scripts, was pulled into an office one day by some who were seeking his support in a movement against Jean. "Count me out," he told them.

Jean spent more time than ever in meetings with network executives, who passed along the pressure they were feeling from sponsors, affiliates, and NBC brass higher up the ladder. The ratings continued to decline. Jean's shows were now attracting on average almost seven million viewers less than Lorne's shows had the year before. By February, even ABC's imitation of *Saturday Night*, *Fridays*, passed *Saturday Night '80* in the ratings. (Fridays's ratings had benefited from the publicity surrounding a supposed on-air fistfight between Andy Kaufman and the show's producer.)

The cheap sex jokes on the show had inflamed the Moral Majority, then at the height of its power, and helped sour even more sponsors. In Lorne's last year, the NBC sales department had compiled a sponsor pool of 115 clients who wanted to buy time on *Saturday Night*; Jean's client pool dwindled to 52. "The network was scrambling," one agency executive said, "to keep clients in the show." By March, halfway through the season, NBC's profits from *Saturday Night* were off, at a conservative estimate, by at least $10 million.

The unit managers and the censors became that much more intractable. Even NBC's Research department decided its advice was once again required, and in February started conducting focus-group research on *Saturday Night*. "Average" viewers were brought in to watch tapes of the show and then answer questions about which cast members they liked and didn't like, which sketches they liked and didn't like, and so on. Their responses were passed along to Jean. There wasn't any lack of direct feedback from the public at large either, and almost all of it was passionately negative. In viewer letters, at parties, or on the street, anyone who worked on the show was subject to what seemed to be universal disdain. "Thanks for ruining my favorite show—I hate you," was a comment they heard often.

Jean's failure was such a favorite theme in the press that the story took on all the elements of a public crucifixion. Writer Barry Blaustein remembers an afternoon when he went to visit his old neighborhood in Long Island. He ended up sitting in the bleachers at his high school, watching a baseball game. He fell to talking with a man in his fifties who happened to walk by, and when Blaustein said he was employed as a writer, the man asked him where.

"*Saturday Night Live*," Blaustein said.

"Hey," the man immediately responded, "is that Jean character as bad as they say?"

Jean's basic reaction to the network pressure was to "dig in her heels," as several executives put it—a posture that offended many of those executives. "She'd scream and yell about things," one of them said. Brandon Tartikoff thought that Jean, out of insecurity, became "too rigid"; Irv Wilson recalls that "get off my back" was a refrain he heard from Jean often. NBC's pressure increased, Tartikoff said, in direct proportion to its lack of confidence in Jean. Daily, in other words. At NBC's urging, Jean did bring in Del Close, the longtime artistic director of Chicago's Second City, to coach the cast in improv sessions. Later, also at the network's urging, she hired a new team of head writers, Jeremy Stevens and Tom Moore, two Hollywood veterans whose credits included Norman Lear's *Fernwood 2-Night*. But by then it was too little, too late.

Jean herself felt victimized by NBC. "They expected her," one of her allies said, "to be ridiculously loyal … a puppet." Not a few on the 17th floor add that the suggestions the network was offering were not at all helpful—Audrey Dickman called them "ludicrous"—and that by pressuring Jean as they did the executives helped destroy whatever equilibrium might have been left, or found, within the show. Evidence of the network's double-dealing, some felt, was Irv Wilson's coming to Eddie Murphy after Eddie had broken through and offering him a deal for an NBC sitcom. Had Eddie taken the offer, Jean would have been deprived of one of her few assets. Eddie, fortunately for Jean, wasn't interested. "I'm not doing any fucking sitcom," he told his friend Clint Smith.

By February, Jean was growing desperate. The rumors that she was about to be fired, which had literally started after her first show, were now constant. During one especially tumultuous period in January, she actually asked several members of her staff to help pack her things into boxes. "Well, I guess you won't see me Monday," she told Barry Blaustein. Nothing happened, and it was assumed Jean would be given at least another three-week cycle of shows.

Jean now came back from her meetings with network executives shaken, and pleading. "They're all over me." she'd tell the writers.

"We've got to do something. You've got to help me out." She finally started defending herself in public, reversing her former reluctance to talk to the press. She blamed NBC's programmers and censors for their meddling, some of her former writers for "low-life gossip mongering," and the media for conducting a "stalking campaign" against her. She'd been under so much fire, she told one reporter, that "after doing this show I could probably conquer a small country."

She tried loosening her rigid control of the show, conveying an attitude, one writer said, of "Fuck it, let's go nuts—we've got nothing to lose." But at the same time, her temper frayed, she snapped irritably at anything that moved and assigned blame indiscriminately. At one point she told Dave Wilson that Weekend Update wasn't working because the lighting was too dark.

Jean withdrew into her office, closing the door, surrounded by her inner circle. What several observers called "a classic Watergate mentality" developed on the 17th floor. Audrey Dickman called it "bunker time." Alan Stern, a member of that inner circle, denies that Jean's friends tried to shield her from the reality of the situation. "Something was wrong, desperately," he knew. But Stern also admits that the members of the inner circle didn't want to "dwell on the negatives," and he admits they were as baffled as Jean was about how to address them. "Who knew what had to be done, really?" he said.

Jean was not a dilettante when it came to putting in the same long hours she was demanding of others, and, as disastrous week followed disastrous week, even her carefully maintained cool began to crumble. Writer Ferris Butler says that by midwinter the network had turned Jean into "a zombie." Irv Wilson, one of her tormentors, says he watched her go "from a very attractive woman to a sallow- cheeked concentration-camp victim." Dave Wilson remembers being surprised to see her actually coming to work in the same dress two days in a row.

The internal disintegration was all but complete. Some of the writers were, as Charles Rocket suspected, praying fervently that the show would be canceled so the humiliation would end. When they heard Bill Murray had been scheduled to host the first show in March, some of those writers, Pam Norris among them, begged his brother, writer Brian Doyle-Murray, to call Bill and ask him not to do it. They couldn't bear the thought that Billy might improve the ratings and thus prolong the agony. It had gotten to the point, Pam Norris says, where "people were furious with each other, everybody blaming each other, hating each other. Anger was the word of the day."

Neil Levy and Leo Yoshimura, who spent a lot of time on the phone listening to their former colleagues from Lorne's era gloat at Jean's

debacle, started stumbling into Jean's office late at night, drunk, bois-
terously urging her, for the sake of her health, for the sake of *Saturday
Night*, to quit. "You've got to get out, you've got to get out," they'd
say, laughing but still serious. Levy and Yoshimura both say Jean would
stare out the window or put on makeup as they talked, then brush them
off as if she hadn't been paying attention. According to Levy, she once
looked at them after a long pause and said, "Do you think these stock-
ings match this dress?"

The cast members, too, succumbed to despair. Gilbert Gottfried was
all but catatonic. Joe Piscopo fought constantly with Jean and the writers,
sometimes literally stamping his feet in frustration. Piscopo felt mortified that they were, as he put it, "ruining television history." More and
more, he and Eddie disassociated themselves from the others; Piscopo
saw it as "me and Eddie against the world." Gail Matthius, who'd
always considered herself a cheerleader for the show, realized there was
nothing worth cheering about and stopped trying. Charles Rocket, Jean's
favorite, remained outwardly confident, but he was also bitterly angry
that people were deliberately undercutting her. Among those he blamed
were Piscopo and Murphy, who he thought were more interested in their
own careers than in the good of the show. A few times he tried to lecture
them about it, and once the tension between them nearly caused a fight.

There was a cast meeting in Jean's office. Everyone, Joe says, was
in a typically surly mood, especially Rocket, who was angry that Joe
had brought a guest onto Weekend Update, puppeteer Marc Weiner.
Joe thought Rocket was mad because the puppets got more laughs than
Rocket did, and he said so. A shouting match ensued.

"You're not part of this cast at all!" Charles yelled at Joe and Eddie,
who as usual were sitting off to one side, by themselves.

"You're one-dimensional!" Joe yelled back. He started to add
another insult when Rocket stood up and interrupted him.

"You say that, Joe," he said, menacingly, "and I'll rip your throat
out."

Joe sat stunned for a second, then shook his head. "Guys, it's over,"
he said. "We've got to make some changes."

Jean, watching, looked overwhelmed, Piscopo thought. She seemed
not only upset but confused. It was obvious that she had no idea what
to do.

* * *

It was, ironically, Charles Rocket who would issue the final, mortal blow
to the Jean Doumanian era of *Saturday Night*. Letty Aronson and Alan

Stern of Jean's inner circle both believe that, despite his surface veneer of utter confidence, by February Rocket was beginning to crack. He still acted the part of the star, but there was an "I'm dancing as fast as I can" quality to his bravado that seemed, Aronson and Stern thought, to be spinning out of control.

Both Jean and Rocket himself say these theories are patently false. If anything, Rocket believes, his downfall resulted from being too casual, too comfortable onstage. But he also says he never thought the show was so terrible, and that as far as he could tell the audience was satisfied. He thought Weekend Update in particular was going fine. Letty Aronson uses the term "denial" to describe Rocket's perception of events. Out of self-defense, Charles, she believes, refused to acknowledge what was plainly the truth. In her view, and others', Rocket finally uttered a nationally televised cry for help.

It happened on the February 21 show. The host was Charlene Tilton, one of the lesser lights on *Dallas*. The musical guest that night was Prince. While Prince was singing one of his suggestive numbers, it seemed to those in the control room that, although the words were hard to make out, he might have said "fuckin'"—a violation of the ultimate network television taboo.

In the control room, Neil Levy turned to censor Bill Clotworthy. "Did he say 'fuckin'?" Levy asked.

Clotworthy, knowing when not to go looking for trouble if he didn't have to, shook his head. "Nah," he said. "He said 'friggin'.'"

Charles Rocket was the focus of a running bit that night that parodied the famous "Who Shot J.R.?" episode of *Dallas*. The idea was that all the cast members had some reason for wanting to kill Rocket, and near the end of the show an unidentified assailant shot him. A few minutes later, onstage to wave good night, Rocket was seated in a wheelchair, his head bandaged, the cast and host standing around him. There was a minute or so left till sign-off and those onstage were signaled to fill time. Charlene Tilton turned to ask Charles how he felt.

"Oh man, it's the first time I've been shot in my life," he answered. After a brief pause, looking right into the camera with a smirk on his face, he added, "I'd like to know who the fuck did it."

He stumbled a bit on the word "fuck," but there was no mistaking he'd said it. Charlene Tilton slapped her hand over her mouth, gasping. Several members of the cast giggled, all of them looking around in wide-eyed disbelief. Rocket sat calmly in his wheelchair, smoked a cigarette, and grinned. They seemed like a bunch of schoolkids wondering what the teacher was going to do now.

In the control room there was a moment of dead silence. Censor Bill Clotworthy's head was in his hands. "Nice going, Charlie," he said. Dave Wilson muttered, "I don't believe this," and ordered the credits to be rolled. Someone asked if Charlie really said "fuck." "No," Neil Levy joked, "he said 'friggin'.'" Nobody laughed. After the show went off Dave Wilson stood up quickly, threw his script down on the control console, and stomped out, commenting to no one in particular as he went, "Well, that's the end of live television."

Fred Silverman happened to be at home watching the show. He didn't want to believe what he'd heard. He immediately called Dennis Considine, a programming executive who worked with *Saturday Night*, and said, "Did I, or did I not, just hear Charles Rocket say 'fuck' on the air?" Considine answered, sadly, that he did.

Jean didn't want to believe it either. She rushed to the stage, where she caught Joe Piscopo just as he was walking off.

"Did he say it? Did he say it, Joe?" she asked.

For reasons he still doesn't understand, Piscopo found himself trying to protect Rocket. "No," he told Jean. "It may have sounded like it, but it's okay."

Rocket knew what he'd said, but he couldn't quite believe it either. Somebody told him "Congratulations" as he walked off stage. Rocket, hardly hearing, managed a smile. He barely remembered actually saying the word.

"We had a lot of time [to fill]," he explained later, "so they said, 'Talk to Charlie.'" The next thing he remembered was looking at the monitors and seeing everyone around him reacting. Then it sunk in that he'd done something terribly wrong. "What's going on?" he thought to himself. "What is happening?" At that point, he recalls, "I kind of rolled it back in my mind ... 'I said that?'"

Sitting in his dressing room a few minutes later, Rocket felt guilty not so much for saying the word, but for creating another problem for Jean and the show. Jean came in and asked, "Did you really say that?"

"What? 'Fuck'?" Rocket said.

Jean asked why he'd said it, and he answered that he honestly didn't know. She asked if he'd meant to say it, and he told her he hadn't.

"Okay," Jean said. "That's all I wanted to know." She'd decided she would stand by her star.

NBC, meanwhile, was working itself into an uproar. Censor Bill Clotworthy ran directly to the network's control center to make sure the profanity was cut out of the tape-delayed feed to the West Coast. Rick Gitter, a Standards vice president and one of Clotworthy's bosses, rushed downtown to the *Saturday Night* party at a restaurant named One

Fifth to confront Rocket. Gitter says that Charles looked "totally dazed." He told Gitter he didn't remember saying the word. Nevertheless, he apologized.

Rocket, accompanied by Jean, spent most of the following week apologizing to a long procession of NBC executives. The two of them took the position that Charles had made an honest mistake that wasn't as big a calamity as the executives seemed to think it was. Certainly *Saturday Night*'s audience wasn't going to be shocked by the word, a word, they pointed out, that had been said before on the show. In the fifth season, Paul Shaffer had played a Cockney musician in a sketch set in a medieval castle. The script called for him to use the word "floggin'" over and over again, and he'd slipped once and said "fuckin.'" But it was clearly a mistake, and it hadn't been very intelligible, so no one at NBC was especially upset.

Rocket and Jean did not, in fact, take Charles's "fuck" very seriously. Rocket says that each time they got on an elevator that week to go to another executive's office for one more round of apologies, they'd "snicker" about all the screaming they were about to hear. "Maybe we'll see some blood vessels in some necks," Charles would joke. "Definitely forehead veins and red faces." Rocket says that after the yelling was over, "I'd leave and they'd feel better. But I guess it didn't work out, so they'd call me back the next day and shout at me some more. And I'd say, 'I'm sorry, yessir, yessir,' and I'd slink around and bow my head a lot and then I'd leave, and then have to go again the next day."

However humble he pretended to be, Rocket's real feelings apparently came through. "There were," says Standards chief Ralph Daniels, "problems with his lack of contrition." Rocket was eventually forced to sign an official apology. He doesn't know who it went to, or even what it said; by that time he just took the piece of paper and signed. That was the end of it, he thought.

Jean never wavered in her vow to support Charles. Nancy Geller, one of Irv Wilson's lieutenants, remembers Jean saying in the course of one meeting, "If you're going to fire him, you can fire me."

Which is precisely what Brandon Tartikoff had decided to do.

# CHAPTER 39

# Celebration

The constant rumors throughout the season that Jean was about to be fired were all true. It would have happened earlier if NBC had been able to decide who should replace her.

In late January, about the time when Jean was asking for help packing her things, Brandon Tartikoff again talked with Dick Ebersol about assuming command, this time urging Ebersol to do so. But Ebersol again said that he wouldn't consider the job unless he was allowed to take the show off the air for a month to rebuild. Again the matter was dropped.

Irv Wilson and his aide Nancy Geller had talked by then to a half dozen or so potential producers. Their favorite candidate quickly became Charles Joffe, who was partners with Jack Rollins in one of the most prestigious management firms in show business. Among their clients were Robin Williams, Robert Klein, Billy Crystal, and Jean's friend Woody Allen. After several conversations with Wilson and Geller, Joffe told them he was definitely interested. The idea was that he would co-produce the show with another partner in his firm, Larry Brezner. Joffe said later that he had told Woody Allen of NBC's overture, explaining to him that he only entertained the offer because he knew Jean was "gone anyhow." Allen presumably passed the news along to Jean.

Wilson and Geller announced during a meeting in Fred Silverman's office in mid-February that they were ready to deliver Joffe as *Saturday Night*'s new producer, which they considered a major coup. Tartikoff, hooked into the meeting via speakerphone from Los Angeles, was still determined to make the choice himself, and he let it be known that in his view Dick Ebersol was the only acceptable producer. Silverman shook his head. "No, I don't think Dick's a good idea," he said. The meeting broke up with no decision reached, Jean still in place.

When Charles Rocket said "fuck" on the air, any hope Tartikoff had of riding out Jean's season while gradually wearing down Silverman's resistance to Ebersol vanished. It was now clear that if Tartikoff didn't make a move to replace Jean, *he* might be the one without a job. He would convince Silverman that Dick had to be hired, and that if the show had to go off the air for a while, so be it. Tartikoff called Ebersol again immediately after the Charlene Tilton show, and by the middle of the week they were talking twice a day.

That same week, Charles Joffe had a meeting with Silverman's chief aide, Irwin Segelstein, to discuss *Saturday Night*. Joffe's enthusiasm soon faded when Segelstein told him that the show's cast and writers would have to remain essentially in place—NBC wasn't prepared to pay off so many contracts if they were fired. The next day, Joffe again talked to Segelstein, on the phone, and again Segelstein insisted Joffe would have to work with the existing staff. Joffe decided that under those conditions he didn't want the job. To Irv Wilson, Segelstein's inflexibility was a clear indication that he had thrown his weight behind Brandon Tartikoff, and behind Tartikoff's candidate, Dick Ebersol. Joffe, Wilson says, was "pissed on" by NBC.

Brandon Tartikoff kept working on changing Silverman's mind about Ebersol, and Silverman finally relented. On Thursday, Tartikoff told Ebersol he could have his month off the air to rebuild. Come to New York, he said.

It's likely that Tartikoff would have taken Jean off the air right then if it hadn't been for the fact that the host of the show following Charlene Tilton's was Bill Murray. Billy had agreed to host out of friendship for Jean—she'd helped get him hired for Howard Cosell's *Saturday Night Live* in 1975—and out of family loyalty to Mary Pat Kelly, soon to be his sister-in-law. Tartikoff decided the ratings Billy would attract made it worth waiting one more week.

Ebersol arrived in New York a couple of days before Billy's show. His plans for taking over *Saturday Night* were complicated by the fact that he was still the producer of *The Midnight Special*. NBC had been talking about canceling that show, but no decision had yet been made. Ebersol and his good friend and boss, Burt Sugarman, *The Midnight Special*'s executive producer, had a meeting with Irwin Segelstein, who immediately resolved Ebersol's conflict by telling them *The Midnight Special* was definitely canceled. Sugarman left and Ebersol spoke with Segelstein about taking over *Saturday Night*.

Ebersol listed his demands: complete creative control, a month off the air, and more money than Jean was making. Segelstein told Ebersol, as he had told Joffe, that he couldn't come in and jettison Jean's entire staff. Segelstein at the same time insisted that Charles Rocket be fired; he wanted to be able to tell NBC's affiliates that Ebersol was in, Doumanian *and* Rocket were out. Ebersol, determined not to compromise his creative control before he had even taken the job, told Segelstein he'd have to make that judgment himself, once he took over. He also made it clear, however, that from what he'd seen he didn't care for Charles Rocket.

While the machinery of Jean's demise was in motion, Bill Murray was bringing a last spark of life to the 17th floor. He knew how grim things were on *Saturday Night*, and he came in seemingly determined to breathe some Gonzo fire into their tremulous souls. "It was," writer Pam Norris said, "like The Truth Teller had arrived." He jolted everyone awake with his energy, throwing barbs at the writers, uplifting every sketch he read, cracking people up with his imitations of Davey Wilson during blocking, even, at one point, wrestling Jean out of her chair. By *Saturday Night* he'd nearly lost his voice, but he'd invigorated everyone. His show would turn out to be the closest Jean ever came to reproducing the vitality of old.

The show opened with a backstage slice-of-life sketch. All the cast members sheepishly filed into Bill's dressing room to confess how disheartened they were about constantly being compared to the old cast. Clearly speaking to the audience as much as to the cast, Bill counseled patience. "Don't let it get you down," he said. "Because it doesn't matter. You started from scratch. It takes a while to put a show like this together. Look. The ratings are good. But even if they went even higher, people would still say the old show was better. And maybe it was. But it just doesn't matter! So maybe the show gets canceled. And you guys never get to do movies. Ever."

The cast sobbed.

"Listen to me," Billy went on. "Sure you need a lot—*a lot*—of help. But hey! I saved the old cast! I can do it for you!" By the end of the sketch he had them all chanting in unison: "It just doesn't matter! It just doesn't matter!"

Bill Murray did save the show that night, but only for that night. There was a bit of strangeness at the end, when during the goodnights Billy looked into the camera and solemnly said he wanted Danny, John, Gilda, Laraine, and Garrett to know, "I'm sorry for what I've done." Everyone around him laughed, but Billy didn't. Charles Rocket walked over to give him a hug, but Billy snubbed him. The only cast member he seemed at ease with was Eddie Murphy.

\* \* \*

Bill Murray explains to Jean's cast that the brutal criticism they're getting "just doesn't matter." Joe Piscopo, Gilbert Gottfried, Denny Dillon, Billy, Eddie Murphy, Gail Matthius, Ann Risley, Charles Rocket. © *NBC*

Dick Ebersol met again with Irwin Segelstein on Sunday at Segelstein's apartment. Fred Silverman called a couple of times from his apartment in the same building to see how things were going, but he didn't show up in person. After some more discussion about budgets and about firing Charles Rocket, they came to terms, and, on Monday, Ebersol formally accepted the job.

Despite Ebersol's attempts to keep his presence at NBC a secret, Jean had heard he was there, and she had a pretty good idea why. So she wasn't totally surprised when Brandon Tartikoff's secretary called around noon on Monday to say Brandon wanted to see her in his office. Jean said she was in the middle of something; could it wait? The answer was no, it couldn't. "I'm going down to talk to the network," she said to Alan Stern. "Wish me luck."

Tartikoff wasn't vindictive when he fired Jean. He told her he knew she'd worked hard and done her best, and that she would definitely be paid for the remaining shows in her contract. "It's an important franchise and we feel we have to make a change," he said. When Jean left his office, it was Tartikoff's impression that she was vastly relieved it was over.

By the time Jean got back to the 17th floor, many of those there already knew she'd been fired. Jean's secretaries, having set up innumerable appointments for Jean with the NBC brass over the past several months, had become friendly with the executives' secretaries, and, as Jean was meeting with Tartikoff, word was passed along to the 17th floor that the end was at hand.

Most of the writers and performers were by then milling around the office, waiting for the usual Monday meeting with Jean. Many of them had just come from an improv session with Del Close and that week's host, Robert Guillaume, star of the TV series *Benson*. The news that Jean was through spread among them quickly. Jean walked in about a half hour later. She looked, several people thought, years younger. She asked everyone to join her in her office.

Jean delivered a short, emotional speech, stopping a few times to choke back tears. The reactions of those listening varied between secret glee and overt sorrow, mixed with concern among allies and enemies alike about their own jobs. Mary Pat Kelly broke into tears a couple of times, and Jean turned to her and said, "I told you not to do that." Denny Dillon wept throughout. Mary Pat kept saying it wasn't fair, and even tried to rally the group to go to the network in support of Jean. But everyone, including Jean, knew that was useless.

Jean seemed more depressed than angry, but she remained defiant, blaming the network for making her a scapegoat. "They didn't help the show," she said. "They were out to get me and the show from the beginning." She said she believed in *Saturday Night*, and she believed in her team. They had needed time to develop, and NBC wouldn't give them that time. She thanked everyone for being "a great bunch" and told them they should "carry on in the *Saturday Night* tradition."

There was a pause, and Letty Aronson stood up and reminded the group that it was Del Close's birthday. "Right," Jean said, "enough of this. Let's all wish Del a happy birthday." The planned celebration commenced. A cake was brought in and everyone sang "Happy Birthday" to Del. Charles Rocket, when the word came down that Jean was fired, had ordered a case of champagne—if they were going out, he figured, they might as well go out in style—and when it came, there was a toast to Del. Del in turn toasted Jean, and everyone applauded. Then Rocket raised his glass to toast Jean's six years of service on *Saturday Night*, and again people clapped and drank. Joe Piscopo remembers looking over at Eddie Murphy and Gilbert Gottfried in utter disbelief. "It was," he said later, "the most bizarre thing I've seen in my life."

When the office cleared out, Jean slowly started packing her things as members of the staff came in to offer condolences. Charles Rocket took a moment alone with Jean to ask if her firing had been his fault. "No," she told him, "it was just politics. Let's just celebrate what we've accomplished." Behind her, on either side of her desk, sat two large black bookcases with glass doors in which Jean kept the videotapes of her shows. The sum of her accomplishments, twelve shows, barely filled the top shelf of one of them.

Bill Murray came up a little later to offer his sympathy and support. Late in the afternoon, everyone decided to go to a Japanese restaurant called Chin-Ya for one last blow out. It turned into a fairly large group, about thirty-five people, and they ended up drinking a lot of sake, among other libations. Al Franken and Tom Davis came by late in the evening, supposedly by coincidence. Jean asked Franken if he was working on anything in particular. Franken was vague, and Jean pressed.

"Come on, we're all in show business," she said.

"Well," Franken said, smiling, *"you're* not, Jean." They both laughed.

When the restaurant section closed, the party moved to the bar. Brandy flowed and the jukebox played. Everybody was drunk and dancing, including Bill Murray and, in a very rare moment of inebriated abandon, Jean. The disco song "Celebration" came on for what seemed like the hundredth time, and everyone was singing along. Suddenly Jean was snatched up from the floor and lifted high by a dozen pairs of upraised hands, and as they carried her around the room, laid flat across their shoulders, everybody shouted out the lyrics.

The next day, writer Billy Brown discovered he'd left his favorite hat behind at Chin-Ya. He called to see if they had it. "Oh, you leave hat?" an angry voice answered. "You never see hat again! No one pay bill! Five hundred dollar! You walk out! You never see hat!"

# CHAPTER 40

# Dick

For Dick Ebersol there was a deep sense of delayed justice that, after six long years, he'd finally won control of *Saturday Night*. He called a meeting of Jean's staff in studio 8H on Tuesday, March 10, one day after he'd come to terms with NBC and just hours after it was announced officially that he would be replacing Jean. Many of the *Saturday Night* veterans who were there knew him, but for the benefit of those who didn't, Ebersol introduced himself. "This show," he said, "or at least the general form, was borne out of me as much as anyone in the whole world."

Dick went on to say that, although he had nothing against Jean Doumanian personally, he'd been "saddened" by what had happened to *Saturday Night* during her tenure as producer, and that he was determined to bring it back to what it had been before her. NBC, he said, was still firmly behind the show, and had given him four weeks off the air in which to rebuild. During that time, he would talk to each member of the staff individually, but he wanted them to know from the outset that he intended to re-create the "family" atmosphere that had existed during the first years of *Saturday Night*.

Neil Levy, who was more familiar with Ebersol than most of those listening, remembers Dick using the word "family" so many times that Levy felt like throwing up. Dick also repeatedly mentioned the name of Lorne Michaels, which, another observer commented, seemed to those who had worked under Jean like invoking the name of Jehovah.

Reestablishing *Saturday Night*'s connection to the Lorne Michaels era, in fact, was the linchpin of Ebersol's strategy for rebuilding the show. He hoped to be able to demonstrate to the audience that, unlike Jean's show, this third incarnation of *Saturday Night* was no imposter, but had a direct and legitimate relationship to the show that viewers had known and loved. He planned to seek out as many of the original writers and performers as he could, inviting them to work with him. Either literally or figuratively, he wanted to convey a sense that the original cast members were standing onstage with their arms wrapped around the new cast members (whoever the new cast members might be), saying, "Hey, give the kids a chance, they're okay."

Underlying that strategy was Dick's conviction that public image would be fundamental to his success, or his failure. "The idea," he said later, "was merchandising: how the show was going to be perceived." With an audience as loyal as *Saturday Night*'s, it was essential that there be a perceptible transition that would serve to convince the old show's fans to accept the new. Having failed to accomplish such a passing of the torch had doomed Jean Doumanian, Dick believed, before she started.

So it was that Ebersol's first move upon accepting the job, before he allowed NBC to announce his hiring and before his speech to the staff that Tuesday, had been to pay a call to Lorne. Dick had talked with Lorne on the phone from Brandon Tartikoff's office on Monday afternoon, and the two of them met in Lorne's office at Broadway Video that evening. Their talk continued at a downtown restaurant named the Odeon, a hangout for many of the original *Saturday Night* regulars, and ended near dawn at Lorne's apartment on Central Park West. They talked a lot about the old days, discussing as they did their long-standing differences. Dick made it clear that he was asking for Lorne's benediction. Lorne, in turn, didn't hide the fact that in many respects he still wanted *Saturday Night* to die. But he agreed in the end that he wouldn't stand in Dick's way.

That was all Ebersol needed. In subsequent weeks he would mention Lorne's blessing over and over again to his staff, to the writers and performers from Lorne's show whom he pursued, and to the press. And, in accordance with his merchandising scheme, Dick gave as many interviews as he could in the weeks before his show went on.

Within two weeks of taking over, Dick fired no less than ten members of Jean's staff, including most of her inner circle, a handful of writers, and cast members Charles Rocket, Ann Risley, and Gilbert Gottfried. Ebersol said later that he would have fired Denny Dillon too had his budget allowed it. On the day Dick called the cast members into his office one by one to tell them their fates, Eddie Murphy and Joe Piscopo sat giggling gleefully as they watched the parade of performers file by. They found it especially funny when Charles Rocket, who hadn't expected to be fired, came out with a stunned look and embraced a tearful Gail Matthius in a corner. "We were hysterical," Piscopo said later, "like two little bastards."

In search of new performers, Dick made a quick trip to Chicago, where he hired Second City's Tim Kazurinsky, who had been strongly recommended by John Belushi. John, when he'd first heard the news of Dick's takeover, had called Dick, invited him to dinner at the Odeon, and promised to help in any way he could. But, as often happened with John, his attentions soon turned elsewhere (he was just starting work on the film *Neighbors* with Dan Aykroyd), and, besides recommending Kazurinsky, his actual contribution was limited mostly to an occasional phone call and an appearance or two on the 17th floor. His wife, Judy, however, joined the show as a writer. Dick also saw John's younger brother Jim at Second City, but told him he wasn't ready yet to follow in John's footsteps on *Saturday Night*.

Dick ran into his first major obstacle when he discovered that he wasn't going to be able, as he'd planned, to fill out his cast with members of the repertory troupe from *SCTV*, the syndicated comedy series from Canada that had gained a loyal following in the States. Before he took over *Saturday Night*, Dick had mentioned his intentions of pursuing some of SCTV's performers to both Brandon Tartikoff and Irv Wilson; what he didn't know was that Irv Wilson had gotten there first. Wilson, even as Ebersol was finalizing his deal, signed *SCTV* to replace the now-canceled *Midnight Special* on NBC's Friday night schedule. Originally, he'd had it in mind as a replacement for *Saturday Night*, thinking *Saturday Night* might be canceled.

When Wilson and his lieutenant, Nancy Geller, heard that Ebersol's people were talking with several members of the *SCTV* cast, they told him to keep his hands off their show. Dick was incensed, furious that the pool of talent he'd counted on raiding had instead been stolen in its entirety by his own network behind his back. He complained bitterly to his friend Brandon Tartikoff. Tartikoff, with Fred Silverman's friend Irwin Segelstein again behind him, told Geller and Wilson to back off.

Eventually Ebersol focused his efforts on two of SCTV's more popular performers, John Candy and Catherine O'Hara. Candy, who friends say was mortified at being caught in the middle of the tug of war between *Saturday Night* and *SCTV*, retreated to his farm, refusing to answer his telephone. In the end he stayed with *SCTV*. Dick did succeed in hiring Catherine O'Hara, as well as a lesser- known member of the *SCTV* cast, Tony Rosato.

* * *

Ebersol to that point had had only mixed success in enlisting the help of *Saturday Night*'s former luminaries. Besides John Belushi, he'd spoken to most of the other original cast members on the phone, but none of them made any commitments. He had only slightly better luck with the writers: Herb Sargent agreed to lend a hand, but only on an informal basis, Matt Neuman joined the staff full-time (though he wouldn't return the following fall), and Franken and Davis accepted Dick's offer to host his second show.

It looked as though the connection Dick so dearly wanted to make to the original show would be mostly illusory, until Lorne suggested he give Michael O'Donoghue a call. Dick was surprised at the suggestion—he thought Lorne and O'Donoghue weren't speaking anymore. It may not have occurred to either Lorne or Dick, especially Dick, that had Lorne wished to cause him as much grief as humanly possible, he hardly could have done better than to dump Michael O'Donoghue in his lap. In any event, unlike Jean Doumanian, Dick was well aware of his need for a creative supervisor who understood comedy better than he did. He'd actually offered such a job to Alan Zweibel, but after thinking it over a couple of weeks Zweibel decided against it. Dick was immediately intrigued at the thought of hiring O'Donoghue. None of the original writers, Dick knew, was as strongly identified with *Saturday Night*'s groundbreaking sense of adventure as the evil Mr. Mike. Getting O'Donoghue as his creative supervisor would mean instant credibility.

O'Donoghue, when Dick reached him, was intrigued too, but for reasons predictably different from what Dick had in mind. He hadn't changed his opinion that *Saturday Night* had been creatively comatose since he left. He had, he told Dick when they met, no illusions about resurrecting the show. All he would be interested in doing, he said, was to give it a "decent Viking funeral." He thought it would be fun to see the show go out in a blaze of glory, to make one last courageous charge into the banal maw of network TV.

There was, no doubt, some posturing in O'Donoghue's claim that the best the show could hope for was an honorable death. He thought there might be a possibility, he said later, to "cut out the cancer" and start over again from scratch. Convinced that Ebersol had no comedic sense whatsoever, and believing that Ebersol meant to turn creative control of the show over to him, O'Donoghue saw Dick's offer as a chance to make his mark, unhindered, on television. The money Dick was offering—in the area of $8,500 a show—also had something to do with O'Donoghue's accepting the job. "TV money," he said later, "is hard to turn down. It's the purest of motives."

Dick wasn't buying the "Viking funeral" approach, but he was so eager to have O'Donoghue's name on the credits he didn't withdraw his offer. O'Donoghue joined the show a few days later. He asked for one of two titles: "Reich Marshall" or "Godhead." NBC wasn't comfortable with either, and he was officially named Chief of Staff.

O'Donoghue insisted that Ebersol hire four of his friends as writers. Three of them would come and go within a month, but the fourth, Bob Tischler, would remain, and would quickly become one of the most, powerful people on the show. Tischler had been on the fringes of the *Saturday Night* circle from the *Lampoon* days, when he produced the *Lampoon Radio Hour*, all the way through his work on the Blues Brothers and Gilda Live albums. Although O'Donoghue described Tischler to Dick as essentially an audio engineer—"a good sound man"—he wanted him brought in as his head writer. Ebersol and Tischler met, liked each other, and Tischler was hired as O'Donoghue's "deputy."

O'Donoghue insisted that Ebersol hire four of his friends as writers. Three of them would come and go within a month, but the fourth, Bob Tischler, would remain, and would quickly become one of the most, powerful people on the show. Tischler had been on the fringes of the *Saturday Night* circle from the *Lampoon* days, when he produced the *Lampoon Radio Hour*, all the way through his work on the Blues Brothers and Gilda Live albums. Although O'Donoghue described Tischler to Dick as essentially an audio engineer—"a good sound man"—he wanted him brought in as his head writer. Ebersol and Tischler met, liked each other, and Tischler was hired as O'Donoghue's "deputy."

His first day on the job, O'Donoghue immediately recognized that the oppressive atmosphere that had prevailed under Jean still lingered on the 17th floor. He felt, he said, like a soldier walking into a concentration camp. He decided to do something about it. He sent a secretary out for a case of spray paint and a dozen or so Magic Markers. The staff was told to gather in the writers' wing. When they had, Ebersol and O'Donoghue marched in.

"There's somebody here you're all going to be working for," Dick said, "and I'd like to leave you alone with him for a little while. This is Reich Marshall Michael O'Donoghue."

Dick went back to his office, and O'Donoghue came straight to the point.

"Everybody on the show sucks, except for Murphy," he said. Turning

"Reich Marshall" Michael O'Donoghue, brought back by Dick Ebersol, wanted to give the show a "decent Viking funeral." © *NBC*

toward Eddie, he added, "You, you make me laugh sometimes. But everybody else, you do nothing for me." As he went on, his voice rose to a shout. People started cowering in their seats, which only heightened O'Donoghue's ferocity. Jean Doumanian's show, he said, "made me puke ... Did you think there were diamonds in that dog shit you were putting out? There weren't even zircons!" He repeated his contention that the only hope for *Saturday Night* now was that it would go down with a little class, with cannons blazing. Whether they could muster the guts necessary to pull that off was open to question. "Look at these walls," he said. "They're neat! Tidy! Sanitized! This is not the way to run a comedy show. You're a comedy show! You know what this show is missing?"

O'Donoghue took a can of red spray paint and, in huge, two-foot letters, wrote *Danger* on the wall. Some of the effect was lost because it takes a while to write with spray paint, and before O'Donoghue had finished, everyone knew the word he was spelling out. But the message came across.

"That's what's missing!" O'Donoghue said. Then he ordered everyone to grab a can of spray paint or a Magic Marker. "Make this place look like a comedy office!" he yelled. "Comedy writers work here!"

The startled group did as commanded, covering the walls with graffiti. As they did, O'Donoghue walked out, telling people to see him individually in his office.

Although some members of the staff found O'Donoghue's little demonstration liberating, not a few were appalled. Within minutes, "the wounded," as Dick Ebersol called them, were streaming into Dick's office to complain. Word of what had happened quickly spread, and soon Ebersol's phone was lighting up with calls from concerned managers, agents, and NBC executives who wanted to know what the hell was going on.

Catherine O'Hara, who had just arrived in town from Toronto, was one of those most shaken by her first encounter with Reich Marshall O'Donoghue. As she'd joined the others in painting the walls, she'd found herself thinking, "Why do I have a can of spray paint in my hand? This isn't me. Why should I be here?" Soon thereafter she told Dick she was leaving. She offered to call a good friend of hers, an *SCTV* co-star named Robin Duke, and three days later Duke came to New York as O'Hara's replacement.

Eddie Murphy, by contrast, hadn't been the least bit intimidated. The next time he saw O'Donoghue, he immediately launched into a perfect imitation of O'Donoghue in the midst of his "Danger" rant. This guy, O'Donoghue said to himself, has balls.

\* \* \*

With just a week and a half left before the show would return to the air. Dick didn't yet have a host. Then, the day after the "Danger" meeting, Chevy Chase, who Dick had tried unsuccessfully to reach, suddenly walked into Dick's office. He was tan and looked more fit than either Ebersol or O'Donoghue, who was there at the time, had seen him look for years. "Hey, Chev, how you doing?" O'Donoghue greeted him. "Let me look up your nose. You got Naugahyde up there?"

Chevy said he was on his way back to Hollywood to start work on a movie and had just stopped in to wish them well. But immediately Dick beseeched him to be his first host, saying that if his movie schedule was a problem, Chevy could fly back from Hollywood on the day of the show. Once again, public perception was uppermost in Dick's mind— having a host who was connected with the old *Saturday Night* was more important than having one who would actually be present during the week the show was being produced. Chevy accepted the offer.

On the 17th floor during the final week there was no time for politics or bickering, just the intense, almost round-the-clock work necessary to get a show together, and many felt a sense of commitment and even joy that had been nonexistent under Jean. Director Dave Wilson even laughed out loud during blocking, something he hadn't done for months. O'Donoghue's presence had been enough to bring back another respected writer from the original show, Marilyn Miller, and, in combination with Judy Belushi, Herb Sargent, and Matt Neuman, there was just enough of the old guard around to create the feeling that some of the former spirit had indeed returned.

Dick, plainly scared of falling very publicly on his face, contented himself, for the most part, with being a cheerleader. He called Lorne daily for advice, and acquiesced almost completely to O'Donoghue's creative decisions, giving him what one of the writers called "absolute power." Although O'Donoghue continued to berate people unmercifully— "It was," Audrey Dickman said, "like putting a demon in here"—he inspired them to produce their best work. Inspiration also came from the knowledge that it would be hard to look any worse than Jean's show had, and that therefore they had every chance of coming across as the saviors of *Saturday Night*.

A potentially serious complication developed late in the week when the Writers Guild, unable to settle its contract negotiations with the Alliance of Motion Pictures and Television Producers, declared that a threatened writers' strike would definitely begin on Friday night at midnight. There was a frantic last-minute push to get everything written before the deadline. Friday night, in the midst of that frenzy, Susan Forristal, Lorne's fiancée, stopped by the 17th floor to give Dick a present: Lorne's lucky duck lapel pin, which he'd worn on many a show night since the beginning. Later, Lorne himself showed up to offer his best wishes.

The cold opening of Dick's first show was about as overt an attempt to reconnect *Saturday Night* to its roots as it could have been. Chevy was seen rummaging through a cobweb-strewn storeroom filled with *Saturday Night* memorabilia, including some old Bee costumes, a stack of Conehead cones, and a samurai sword. There was also a carton of Bambu rolling papers and several cases of empty beer cans. Sifting through the rubble, Chevy came across Mr. Bill, who squeaked his gratitude at being rescued. They commiserated with each other that "the fans have forgotten about us old-timers." Then Chevy stumbled and fell, crushing Mr. Bill, and said, "Live from New York, it's *Saturday Night!*"

Later in the show, Al Franken appeared on Weekend Update. He too addressed the traditions of the past, but in considerably harsher terms. He began by saying that he had "suffered countless instances of personal embarrassment" when people stopped him on the street to ask if he was still involved with *Saturday Night Live*. He wanted everyone to know he had nothing to do with it, which prompted the audience to break into a hearty round of congratulatory applause. Then, resurrecting the style he'd used in his old Al Franken Decade commentaries, he went on to give his own version of what had happened to the show.

"You see," he said, "Lorne Michaels, the producer of *Saturday Night*, decided after last season that it was time to go on to different things. Now, he figured the first season had been great. Then Chevy left, and the show of course got even better. Then, after the fourth year, Danny and John left. Now them, them we missed. So after five golden years, Lorne decided to leave, and so did those close to him, including me, Al Franken. So NBC had to pick a new producer. Now most knowledgeable people, as you might imagine, hoped it would be me, Al Franken. But instead, without consulting the show's staff or cast, NBC picked Jean Doumanian, an associate producer on the show. Now I don't want to be cruel to Jean, because it might make you think less of me, Al Franken. Anyway, it took NBC twelve shows to figure out their horrendous mistake, and a month ago they fired Jean.

"Okay, now who do they pick to rectify the original error? Someone who knows what he's doing, someone like me, Al

Franken? No, they picked Dick Ebersol. Now I know Dick because he was a network executive in charge of late-night programming when *Saturday Night* started, and as such was the first person to steal credit for the success of *Saturday Night*. Credit which should rightfully go to Lorne Michaels, and me, Al Franken. Now let me give you some background on Dick 'Mr. Humor' Ebersol. His credits [as a network executive] include the *Waverly Wonders*, starring Joe Namath, *Roller Girls*, and a show called *Joe and Valerie*, about a kid from Brooklyn who dances every night at a disco. Now, to this day Dick claims that he never saw *Saturday Night Fever* and that it was all an amazing coincidence. Anyway, I know Dick, and I can tell you that he doesn't know dick.

"Okay. Now the show's going to be a little better. No English-speaking person could do a worse job than Jean. But it's clearly time to yank this tired old format off the air. So if you're wondering what you can do for me, Al Franken, please write a card or a letter to 'Put SNL to Sleep,' 30 Rockefeller Plaza, New York, New York, 10020. Let's put this show out of its misery. You'll be doing a great favor for yourselves, and for me, Al Franken. Thank you."

(Franken tacked on a plug for the next week's show, which he and his partner Tom Davis were set to host. "Watch next week," he said, "but not after that.")

Dick Ebersol didn't really care for F&D's humor, or for Al Franken personally, but again, he was willing to put up with a lot just to establish a link to the old *Saturday Night*. He also knew the public-relations value, within the show and without, of being big enough to allow himself to be the butt of a joke. At the same time, Franken's appearance served to promote F&D's show the following week by reminding viewers who Al Franken was.

The rest of the show was generally funny, reflecting the hard work and good feelings of the past week. Most of the reviews were positive. *The New York Times* said *Saturday Night* was "watchable" again, calling the show "a distinct improvement over others this year." Gary Deeb of the *Chicago Sun-Times* went further, calling it "an excellent program, crammed full of tough humor, the bizarre situations and the splendid acting that characterized the first four years of the program." Even the hard-to-please Marvin Kitman of *Newsday* found it "great ... better tasting and better written."

As it turned out, thanks to the Writers Guild strike, Dick was able to ride those reviews for the next five months. Part of the reason he'd asked F&D to host was that, as performers who wrote for themselves, they'd be able to produce enough material in advance to fill the show should the strike come off. F&D, prolific as always, had worked frantically to do just that, mailing their scripts to themselves so the postmark would prove that they hadn't violated the strike rules.

When Ebersol read F&D's scripts on Monday, he wasn't particularly enamored of what he saw, and he began thinking that maybe he ought to call off the show. Since all the material was already submitted, he moved the weekly read-through up a day, from Wednesday to Tuesday. After being just as unimpressed with the way the scripts sounded there, and already having had a nasty confrontation with Al Franken, Dick decided to quit while he was ahead. His friend Brandon Tartikoff had told him how much he liked the first show. More important, Tartikoff had also said that if the strike went on and the show was suspended, he intended to renew it for another season. Dick told Tartikoff he didn't want the second show to air. Tartikoff immediately approved the decision. *Saturday Night* was officially on hiatus until the strike ended. Dick consoled Franken and Davis by promising they could host the first show at the start of the 1981-82 season the following fall.

The writers' strike continued for the remainder of the season. The first week in May, NBC announced that it was renewing *Saturday Night* for another year. That gave Dick an entire summer to rebuild, a break that Bob Tischler later called "a miracle." On the strength of that miracle, Dick would decide he no longer needed Franken and Davis, and when they called a few months later to confirm they were to host, he didn't call them back.

# CHAPTER 41

# The Reich Marshall's Downfall

Like many members of the staff, including Dick, Michael O'Donoghue was paid for all the shows that were missed during the strike. He availed himself of the time off to take a long trip to Ireland, leaving Dick to do with the show as he pleased. Bob Tischler stayed around too, and together Tischler and Ebersol spent the summer restructuring the staff.

They finished their housecleaning of Jean's people: Gail Matthius and Denny Dillon were fired, as were several of Jean's remaining writers. Only Eddie Murphy, Joe Piscopo, and writers Barry Blaustein, David Sheffield, and Pam Norris kept their jobs. For the cast, Dick hired Christine Ebersole, a strawberry-blond singer-actress who'd recently starred opposite Richard Burton in a Broadway revival of *Camelot*, and Mary Gross, a gangly Second City veteran who, like Tim Kazurinsky, had been recommended by John Belushi. Among the new writers hired was another veteran of the old show, Rosie Shuster.

O'Donoghue realized as soon as he returned in early September that the situation had changed unfavorably for him. He wasn't happy with the cast— "the Angel of Talent," he said, "passed over these people." He also saw immediately that his power as Chief of Staff was no longer as secure as it had been. Dick, in contrast to his deference to O'Donoghue at first, had obviously regained his confidence and was now ready to run the show himself "He reverted," O'Donoghue said, "to his old arrogance." It was obvious as well that Tischler and Ebersol had grown closely aligned with one another, and O'Donoghue began to suspect he was becoming the odd man out. He was right. "A new attitude formed [over the summer]," Tischler said later, "and O'Donoghue really didn't have it. He kept looking at [the show] as a death ship."

Belatedly, O'Donoghue tried to reassert his creative control, or, more to the point, tried to upset the control that already existed. O'Donoghue was still convinced the only hope for *Saturday Night* was to somehow knock it out of the rut it had settled into, and he resolved to do anything he could to inject tension and risk into the production process. He hoped to re-create the feeling of imminent collapse that, he believed, had been responsible for the show's truly thrilling moments in the very beginning, when none of them was sure they could get through ninety minutes on the air without a major disaster.

Toward that end, O'Donoghue demanded that Dick fire director Dave Wilson. Like many of the show's original writers, O'Donoghue had always considered Wilson a reactionary influence on the show; he was fond of saying that everything Davey shot ended up looking like a police lineup. O'Donoghue had far more radical ideas in mind. One was to use only handheld cameras so the cameramen could roam the studio at will, giving the show the ragged immediacy of a sporting event— preferably a bullfight.

Dick refused to fire Wilson, but he did accede to O'Donoghue's suggestion that announcer Don Pardo be replaced. O'Donoghue felt that whatever camp value Pardo lent the show had long since disappeared, and he was tired of Pardo blowing jokes by misreading his lines on-air. A staff member who watched Pardo's firing says Pardo was so stunned at the news that "the look on his face was amazing." It's hard to imagine, then, what Pardo would have looked like if Dick had allowed O'Donoghue to carry through his original idea, which was to fire Pardo on-air, during the season premiere. "Don, you're finished," O'Donoghue planned to say. "Get your stuff and get outta here." Pardo had the last laugh, though, because Dick rehired him a year later, by which time O'Donoghue was long gone.

O'Donoghue also brought in as writers two more friends who shared his affection for anarchy. One was Nelson Lyon, a screenwriter, editor, and director, who, in terms of humor, philosophy, and style (he dressed entirely in black), struck many on the show as being a virtual O'Donoghue clone. He was also quite talented; Audrey Dickman called him "an artist, especially with film." The other was the legendary writer Terry Southern, who had co-written such classics as *Dr. Strangelove* and *Candy*. Southern was every bit as unconventional in person as he was in his writing. According to several staffers, he consumed large amounts of cognac and cocaine, although he was not the only one on Dick's show to be so inclined.

Drugs, less in evidence on the 17th floor during Jean Doumanian's reign, returned in force under Dick Ebersol. Dick himself didn't partake, but many of the performers, writers, and top production people used cocaine heavily. When asked about his experiences working on *Saturday Night*, Terry Southern preferred to answer in writing. Undoubtedly there was a certain amount of satiric hyperbole in the five pages he forwarded, but the primary topic he chose to write about was drugs. "Perhaps the most memorable aspect of working at SNL," he wrote, "was the quantity of dope or drugs on hand ... We were well nigh up to our proverbial A's in toot, hemp, speed, oil of hash, what have you. Talk about your ever-lovin' cornucopias of sense-derangement! Wow-ee! Boy-oh-boy! Brother! Holy Mack! I mean, I've been to some heavy-hitting Hollywood soirees, and on two Rolling Stone Tours, and I've seen nose-candy by the carload, toot by the truckful, but I've yet to see anything comparable to the sheer quantity of primo-primo heaped and stacked in the writer's wing of SNL!"

Cast member Tony Rosato, who was fired at the end of the season because of differences with Dick, later came to believe that firing saved his life: At the rate he was going, he says, cocaine would have destroyed him. Others apparently had similar thoughts, because after Dick's first full season, drug use on the show diminished dramatically.

O'Donoghue's determination to upset the stability of *Saturday Night* couldn't have been more diametrically opposed to the instincts of Dick Ebersol. Dick was a man who above all valued order and control. A heavy smoker, during meetings in his office he compulsively emptied his ashtray after almost every cigarette. He was also in the habit of making notes on a legal pad of the points he intended to make, crossing them off, wadding up the piece of paper, and throwing it in the wastebasket. He was, everyone who worked with him agreed, a superb "line" producer, a master at organizing technical detail, and as a result his shows always ran extremely smoothly. Dick liked it that way. He didn't pretend to be creative. "Hey, I'm no writer" was a phrase he said often, and, unlike Lorne and Jean, he didn't take a writing credit. Nor was he especially reflective, and even he admitted that a sense of humor was not among his strong points.

O'Donoghue knew that he and Ebersol were, as O'Donoghue put it, "on a collision course." He knew as well that ultimately he would be the one to lose. "Dick could fire me," O'Donoghue said later. "I couldn't fire him." He was determined to persevere nonetheless. "I kept my compass heading steady," he said, "even though I knew it would take me right into a reef."

The opening wedge between them developed over a long sketch called "The Last Ten Days of Silverman's Bunker," written for the season's first show by O'Donoghue and Nelson Lyon. Fred Silverman had finally been fired in June, ending what was undoubtedly the most tumultuous reign of any chief executive in the history of television. O'Donoghue and Lyon's sketch merged Silverman during his demise at NBC with Hitler during the final days of the Third Reich in Berlin. NBC was called the Nazional Broadcasting Company; its logo was a huge, golden Nazi eagle, a martial adaptation of the NBC peacock, with the NBC N logo gripped in its talons. Thirty Rock was to be depicted as the eerily deserted shell of a fallen corporate empire, the hallways strewn with attaché cases, press releases, videocassettes, toppled filing cabinets, and other debris.

As the camera passed over this tableau, a narrator introduced the piece saying, "Here, deep within a stone Deco fortress, one man manipulated the destinies of two hundred million people—a twisted genius whose strange experiments lobotomized his helpless victims, a power-mad tyrant who reduced a proud nation to a vast wasteland. This is his story." Silverman, to be played by John Belushi, was then seen in his office. Loyal aides entered with the latest devastating news from the front ("How many pilots have we lost?" Silverman asked at one point) and listened as Silverman desperately described his latest plans for turning the war around. He revealed his plan for a new game show called *Look Up Her Dress*, to be hosted by Marjoe Gortner, in which the contestants, all well endowed women, would stand on a large piece of Plexiglas. When they missed a question, the camera beneath the Plexiglas would go on. Another idea was *Hollywood Sex Clinic*, in which Jack Klugman would ask well- endowed young women humiliating questions about their love lives. Then there was NBC's answer to *Private Benjamin*, a sitcom called *The Lieutenant Wore Tampax*.

It was a powerful, funny, and very nasty sketch that Brandon Tartikoff, who'd been on the inside of the real Silverman's bunker, later described as "one of the most brilliant pieces of satire I've ever read." NBC, however, had predictable reservations about putting it on the air. Lampooning its former president in such a vicious fashion was not deemed to be in the best of corporate taste, and both Standards and Legal feared that comparing Silverman to Hitler was potentially libelous.

Dick, not among Fred Silverman's fans, was at first positively gleeful about "Silverman's Bunker," according to Nelson Lyon. "Let's give it to the son of a bitch," Lyon remembers Ebersol saying. The sketch, which would have combined both filmed and live segments and run for more than twenty minutes on-air, was launched into the production process, and eventually consumed something like $20,000 in sets and other costs. But, with the reservations of the brass, with all the production problems, and with John Belushi in the midst of one of his rough periods and unprepared to play Silverman, the piece was postponed, ostensibly until later in the season.

O'Donoghue later decided that Dick hadn't fought for it as vehemently as he should have. Instead of defying management, as Lorne always did, Dick *was* management, O'Donoghue thought. In the end he would conclude, probably unfairly, that Dick never had any intention of putting the sketch on the air.

\* \* \*

"Silverman's Bunker" would continue to be an object of contention between O'Donoghue and Ebersol as the season wore on, but it was just the beginning. Having now taken control of the show, Dick began imposing his comedic tastes on the material he chose. Those tastes were, by and large, pragmatically defined. Ratings statistics indicated that *Saturday Night*'s audience was skewing increasingly younger, and Dick consciously set out to cultivate those viewers. When a writer he fired complained in an interview that Dick was pandering to kids, he vehemently denied it. At the same time, however, he instructed NBC's Guest Relations department to lower the age limit for the studio audience. Previously only people eighteen and over were allowed in, but for Dick's show sixteen-year- olds were admitted.

Dick decided that younger viewers weren't interested in politics, and therefore he rejected most political sketches. Similarly, he believed that with the advent of rock videos, teenagers' attention spans had shortened, and thus he tended to reject any piece that lasted more than five minutes. Eventually he declared a flat rule that no sketch could exceed that length. He also frowned on material that wasn't immediately simple to grasp. He liked the jokes to come quickly and often—he told his troops they were "fighting sleep," and he seemed to believe that if there wasn't a laugh in the first ten seconds of a sketch, viewers would tune out.

None of those criteria fit the sorts of sketches O'Donoghue, or his friends Nelson Lyon and Terry Southern, were submitting. More and more all three of them found their pieces either buried in the final minutes of the show or cut entirely, often between dress and air, sometimes without even getting that far. Dick would later argue that Southern and O'Donoghue in particular were simply writing unusable material, but Southern and O'Donoghue believed Dick was just too timid and too lame to appreciate anything even slightly daring. Tony Rosato remembers the day Terry Southern walked into his office dejectedly, slumped into a chair, and told how he'd just taken an idea for a political satire in to Dick.

"Dick told me we did politics last week," he said. The man who'd co-written *Dr. Strangelove* sat there shaking his head, looking as if he'd fallen down a rabbit hole into one of his own stories.

O'Donoghue's last shot at having some control over *Saturday Night* came on the season's fourth show, which fell, fittingly enough, on Halloween. As it happened, Dick had fallen passionately in love with the host of the second show that year, Susan Saint James, and, during the week off preceding the Halloween show, he was in California wooing her. They would marry a month later. Dick wanted the staff to keep working in his absence, and he left the show in O'Donoghue's hands. O'Donoghue made the most of the opportunity.

The host was Donald Pleasence, who'd starred in the movie *Halloween*, among other horror films, and who fit quite comfortably into a number of ghoulish sketches that evolved over the week. In one, written by Lyon and Southern, he played an aging sophisticate dining with an attractive young woman. Near the end of the sketch, the camera was to pull back to reveal that the wine he'd been pouring throughout the meal came not from the bottle sitting on the table, but from an intravenous tube that was draining blood from her arm. In another sketch, written by O'Donoghue, Pleasence played the commander of a Nazi death camp who had a perfectly good excuse (which he whispered inaudibly to several people) for slaughtering thousands of Jews. The point, of course, was that there could never be an excuse. A third sketch, called "Grand Guignol White House," written by Lyon and Pam Norris, had Pleasence playing Ronald Reagan, who, along with his family and top aides, hacked Jane Fonda to pieces and ate her for dinner.

When Dick returned to the 17th floor on Monday, he was appalled at the material O'Donoghue had prepared. "Blood, blood, blood," is how Ebersol described it. He immediately killed the three Pleasence sketches, causing O'Donoghue to walk off the show temporarily, and set other writers to work on less gory ideas. He did, however, go along with the musical group that O'Donoghue, at the suggestion of John Belushi, had insisted be booked, a punk rock group from Los Angeles called Fear.

Fear was, even by punk's standards, a savage ensemble (their bass player was named Derf Scratch, the drummer, Spit Stix), which was why Belushi loved them. Belushi and O'Donoghue had arranged for thirty-five or so of Fear's rowdy fans to take a bus up from Washington so they could slam dance in 8H as the band played.

During dress rehearsal, some of the slam dancers got carried away, cursing and tumbling off the set, banging into one cameraman and nearly colliding with some of the others. The song was stopped in the middle to cool them down. When dress ended, members of the technical crew complained vehemently to Davey Wilson, and Wilson told Dick that the crew was threatening to walk off the show unless the slam dancers were dropped. Dick told him the dancers would go on, but he went up to see them in the greenroom to lay down some rules. O'Donoghue went with him, but only to watch.

Wearing a pair of gray flannel slacks and a sweater, Dick told the roomful of punks—"ridiculous-looking people," he later called them—that they had to keep themselves in check. He specifically warned that they shouldn't swear, since there were live microphones in the studio that would instantly broadcast any profanities to millions of viewers across the country. Dick didn't mention it, but for the air show, during Fear's song, he took the precaution of turning off all the mikes in the studio except the singer's.

On-air, the slam dancers showed no sign of thinking for a moment about what Dick had told them. They threw themselves at each other with what seemed to be complete abandon, jumping off the stage head-first and careening around the studio while the band blasted away deafeningly. All the running around kicked up a great deal of dust in the studio, so that everything looked hazy and distorted. It created a truly striking effect that resembled, as Nelson Lyon described it, "an after-hours Nuremberg rally." Michael O'Donoghue, watching backstage, had a look of pure ecstasy on his face, convinced that this was one of TV's greatest moments ever.

But to Dick Ebersol, crouched out of camera range near the stage, things seemed to be getting out of hand. He heard somebody yell "New York sucks!" and saw one of the dancers heading toward the singer's microphone. Frantically, Dick got up and ran as fast as he could into the control room and shouted at Dave Wilson, "Fade to black! Fade to black!" On-screen the image of Fear disappeared, abruptly replaced by a filmed bit from an earlier show, which Wilson kept cued up in case of just such an emergency. Order had been restored.

When the slam dancers, supposedly berserk, saw the stage lights go out and realized they were no longer on-air, they immediately stopped dancing and walked peacefully off the set. Dick, on the other hand, was so livid he kicked a trash can halfway across the control room. A few days later he was further incensed when the *New York Post* reported, completely inaccurately, that there had been a riot in the studio causing $200,000 worth of damage. In truth, a plastic camera-case lock worth something like $40 had been broken.

Dick immediately launched an all-out public-relations drive to counter the Post's story. Peter Hamilton, the NBC press representative assigned to *Saturday Night* at the time, said Dick couldn't bear the accusation that for a moment he'd lost control of his show.

\* \* \*

The relationship between O'Donoghue and Ebersol spiraled downward rapidly after that. Frequently their hostilities broke into what Bob Tischler called "huge screaming matches," about half of them in private and the rest in front of the staff. It got to the point where O'Donoghue was openly deriding Dick in meetings, making, in Tony Rosato's words, "smart cracks that totally cut Dick's balls off in front of the entire cast and crew." O'Donoghue couldn't even speak Ebersol's name without a contemptuous pause before and after it. "Go ask ... *Dick*," he'd say, or "See what ... *Dick* ... has to say."

O'Donoghue began to withdraw, spending most of his time shut away in his office with Lyon and Southern. His wardrobe grew steadily stranger as he became more alienated; for weeks he shuffled around in a pair of oversized Styrofoam "moon boots" from Switzerland. In the meantime, he continued to berate people, especially the actors. Tim Kazurinsky in particular bore the brunt of O'Donoghue's attacks, so much so that Kazurinsky at one point decided he'd had enough of what he called O'Donoghue's "vendetta" against him and decided to quit the show. His friends John Belushi and Judy Jacklin talked him out of it, and Belushi called Ebersol to tell him to keep O'Donoghue off Kazurinsky's back.

Dick felt that O'Donoghue's tantrums were having an increasingly detrimental effect on the spirit of the staff, and he began to suspect that O'Donoghue was intentionally trying to sabotage the show. O'Donoghue later agreed that that was exactly what he was doing.

One of his victories involved his hero, writer William Burroughs. After weeks of trying, O'Donoghue had finally convinced Dick to let Burroughs come on the show to read some excerpts from his novel *Naked Lunch*. Burroughs, then in his late sixties, had the demeanor of an undertaker, and Dick quickly decided he would go on as late as possible, after the A. C. Nielsen Company had stopped measuring ratings. In dress rehearsal, Dick found Burroughs so "boring and dreadful" that he ordered O'Donoghue to tell the author he would have to trim his reading down from six minutes to three and a half. O'Donoghue, of course, wouldn't dream of asking such a genius to change a syllable of his masterpiece, but all he said to Ebersol was, "Dick, no problem." O'Donoghue pretended to go off to give the news to Burroughs, then came back and told Dick everything had been taken care of. "I talked to

Bill," he lied, "and I said, 'This is coming out' and 'That's coming out.'"
Then he turned to Audrey Dickman, keeper of the stopwatch, and said
that, as best as he could estimate, the new timing should be about three
minutes and forty- five seconds. Burroughs, knowing nothing of all this,
went on for his full six minutes. There wasn't much Dick could do other
than fume, which he did.

O'Donoghue pulled a similar trick a few weeks later with a sketch
called "At Home with the Psychos," which he'd written with Southern,
Lyon, and Rosie Shuster. It depicted a family of mutants who lived much
too close to a nuclear power plant. The patriarch of the clan was obsessed
with the notion that after enough exposure to radiation, the entire human
race was sure to develop a new orifice, a "blow hole." He planned to
become fabulously rich making products to care for it, and he had a
sample case showing what the blow hole would look like. O'Donoghue
had instructed the props department that the blow hole should be a weird
combination of different organs. "Inevitably, though," he said later, "it
looked like a cunt. A cunt with ears, and it was deeply disturbing." Mary
Gross called it a "space vulva."

Dick, with Standards in full agreement, refused to allow it on the
air, and the sketch was postponed a week while a new blow hole was
designed. The props people took out some of the teeth and hair and
muted its purple color down to lavender, but it still looked like a vagina.
Nevertheless, O'Donoghue kept assuring Dick and Tischler that all was
well, and avoided showing them the new prop as long as possible. When
they finally saw it, they were enraged that so much of their time had been
wasted while O'Donoghue intentionally misled them. O'Donoghue continued to feign wide-eyed innocence. "A cunt?" he asked, incredulously.
"What—are you kidding? I don't see it, guys." The sketch finally went
on without the prop. (The blow-hole prop later became an ornament in
censor Bill Clotworthy's office.)

Soon after that, O'Donoghue's cherished "Silverman's Bunker"
sketch met its demise. After a meeting with O'Donoghue and Ebersol
on November 30, Standards and Legal chief Cory Dunham informed
them that the sketch would not go on. O'Donoghue had talked about
"Silverman's Bunker" and NBC's resistance to it in an interview with
New York magazine, and there was some concern ("legal mumbo jumbo,"
O'Donoghue called it) that by doing so he displayed malicious intent
toward Silverman, making it easier for Silverman to sue successfully for
libel. Cory Dunham later explained that his decision rested just as much
on the questionable taste of the piece as on the threat of a lawsuit. The
network clearly preferred to forget Fred Silverman rather than publicly
eviscerate him.

O'Donoghue decided not to accept his defeat meekly. Copies of the sketch were mailed out anonymously to thirty or so TV critics around the country with a cover letter characterizing the decision as "a gross act of corporate censorship." "Call us crazy," the letter read, "call us dreamers, there are some of us up here who still think that television can be something more than Dean Martin's Christmas at Sea World. Any help you can give us would be appreciated." The letter did generate several supportive columns, but not the uprising of indignation that might have resurrected the sketch.

Although Ebersol wasn't happy with O'Donoghue's public appeal, for him the final straw was a meeting that took place in his office just as the show was going on its four-week Christmas break. Dick had called all the cast members in to offer some "constructive" comments for them to think about during their time off. Several of the performers arrived thinking he was going to give them a Christmas bonus. O'Donoghue had purposely not been invited to the session because of his increasing propensity to abuse people, but he found out about it and showed up anyway, promising Dick he'd behave. Once again, he lied.

Soon after the meeting started, O'Donoghue unleashed yet another vicious tirade against the actors. He told Mary Gross she was so untalented she ought to be selling shoes. He even unloaded on Eddie Murphy, saying he needed acting lessons. Both Ebersol and Tischler kept trying to interrupt. "Mike … Mike, calm down," they kept saying. "I'm sure he doesn't mean that … We can talk about this later." Finally Dick shouted at him to shut up. It was the last time Dick ever talked to O'Donoghue.

Dick had been telling Bob Tischler for weeks that he wanted to get rid of O'Donoghue, but Tischler kept insisting that the show needed him, no matter how unsettling he was. After the Christmas meeting, Tischler gave up on O'Donoghue and agreed with Ebersol that he was damaging the show. Tischler was weary of defending O'Donoghue, and was convinced his actions had become indefensible. He let Dick know that if O'Donoghue was fired, he wouldn't feel compelled to go with him. Since Tischler had been taking more and more responsibility for working with the writers and actors, Dick no longer needed to worry that the show would be creatively adrift without O'Donoghue.

By the time the staff returned from the Christmas break, Dick had met with O'Donoghue's manager, Barry Secunda, and forced a settlement on O'Donoghue's contract, for about 50 cents on the dollar of what he was owed for the rest of the season. O'Donoghue would forever consider Bob Tischler a traitor for not resigning in his support. By the beginning of the next season both Terry Southern and Nelson Lyon would also be gone, although Lyon was invited to return.

O'Donoghue couldn't resist leaving one last missive for the *Saturday Night* staff. When they returned from vacation, they found a note on the bulletin board outside his empty office. "Just to set the matter straight," it read, "I was fired on Sunday, January 17th, by Dick Ebersol, with the cooperation of Robert Tischler. I did not leave the show by 'mutual consent' and if either claim otherwise, he is, to steal a phrase from Louisa May Alcott, a 'lying cunt.' I don't know why I was dismissed because Ebersol refused to meet with me and tell me.

"I am quite pleased by what we did together. We turned the show around and then some. There was more to be proud of than embarrassed by, and there were a few truly blazing moments. My thanks to you all.

"As for me, I plan to get out of show business and write my memoirs. Of course, there's always my work with the little deaf girls, so I'll be busy, busy, busy."

The note stayed posted for less than a day. A week or so later, Bob Tischler moved into O'Donoghue's office.

# CHAPTER 42

# Execu-stress Comedy Drone Units

Dick's second cast: Joe Piscopo, Robin Duke, Gary Kroeger, Tim Kazurinsky, Brad Hall, Julia Louis-Dreyfus, Mary Gross, and Eddie Murphy. © *NBC*

*Saturday Night* after O'Donoghue left became a far more disciplined and orderly place of business. Dick's power as executive producer was now unchallenged, and Bob Tischler, who the following season would be named producer, maintained a similarly inviolate control over the creative end.

Outwardly soft-spoken and easygoing, Tischler nonetheless applied a firm hand in his treatment of the writers and performers. There was, he said, a lot more "standing on people's backs" than there had been on *Saturday Night* previously. He was of the opinion that the writers had always had too much control over their work on the show; since they were by definition unable to view their material objectively, they were unable to edit it nearly as much it needed. He also felt that the show's current cast was not as able to cover weak writing as effectively as the original cast was, and that therefore strict editing was that much more necessary. In addition, Tischler and Dick tightened up the show's schedule, no longer allowing people to put off writing a cold opening or a monologue for the host until the last minute, and insisting on regular dialogue rehearsals for the cast.

Tischler worked closely with writers Barry Blaustein and David Sheffield, who were named head writers soon after O'Donoghue's departure and supervising producers the following season. Together, Blaustein, Sheffield, and Tischler wrote a good portion of the show, and every script passed through their hands. They edited so ruthlessly that the other writers started calling them "Blood, Sweat, and Tears."

In the studio, Dave Wilson's authority was seldom questioned. Last-minute changes in scripts were kept to a minimum, and late sketches were added with far less frequency than before. Wilson grew less tolerant of fooling around on the set; several hosts commented on how shocked they were at the rudeness with which Davey kept the actors in line. One *Saturday Night* veteran said that after seven years of battling the artistic types on the show, Wilson and his band of studio "techies" had finally won out.

Dick Ebersol, meanwhile, worked far more cordially with NBC than Lorne Michaels ever had. Dick took pride in the fact that every year he produced *Saturday Night*, it came in under budget. He earned unequivocal praise from the censors assigned to the show for his "professional" attitude toward Standards. When Dick first took over, he assured Standards boss Ralph Daniels that there would be no last-minute fights over material, as there had been so often with Lorne. Daniels says Dick kept that promise. At Dick's suggestion, Standards editor Bill Clotworthy started attending the Wednesday read-throughs, an excellent idea, Clotworthy felt, since it gave him an extra day to deal with any problematic material.

That cordiality tended to mask the fact that *Saturday Night*'s ratings during Dick's tenure were even lower than they had been under Jean Doumanian. In Dick's first full season, the show lost another million and a half viewers, and in his second full season, 1982–83, another million on top of that. Dick blamed those ratings mainly on the impact of cable TV. Cable had indeed eroded the audiences of network television in those years, but not that severely. Thirty-second commercial spots on *Saturday Night* consequently sold in the $28,000 range, about half what they'd gone for at Lorne's peak, and the show's profitability for NBC fell to what finance chief Don Carswell called the "marginal" range of between one million to two million dollars a year. That figure doesn't include the money the NBC-owned stations made on the show, nor the money NBC paid itself for the use of studio 8H. Even so, as comfortable as Dick's regime was to work with, each spring there was now some doubt on the 17th floor as to whether the show would be renewed for another season.

Many of those who worked with both Lorne and Dick appreciated some aspects of Dick's production style. They felt he was far more open and accessible than Lorne, and they preferred his efficiency in comparison to the chaos that prevailed in earlier years. One key production assistant noted that there weren't such rigid hierarchies on Dick's show, and that there was far less dead weight on the staff—everybody had a job to do. "The first show was saddled with cult status, drugs, and an elitist attitude," she said. "With Dick things run more smoothly, although it borders on dull."

Many others found that smoothness suffocating. "It's all clock-work," another production assistant said. "Meeting, meeting, meeting. The control is frightening." Rosie Shuster, who left after working one year for Dick, shared that view. Dick, she said, turned the staff into "Execu-Stress Comedy Drone Units." As a result, the atmosphere on 17, and even in the studio before the show, grew more subdued with the passage of time. Once people finished their work they generally went home. The legions of reporters and hangers-on disappeared; no longer did chaos prevail in the lobby of 30 Rock each *Saturday Night*.

Perhaps Dick's greatest failure was his inability to inspire the slightest loyalty among his staff. There was the nearly unanimous feeling that he treated people like pawns in his personal power game, reacting to them mainly for what they could do for him. "Dick," said one of his writers, "is too much of a manipulator and not enough of a human being." A cast member added that Dick's style was "straight out of a managerial handbook: Divide and conquer, say what people want to hear, throw people bones." There was a certain poignancy to that, several others thought, because Dick obviously wanted to be liked by those who worked for him. Unfortunately, they said, his ambition always seemed to get in the way.

Another tool Dick frequently employed in pursuit of what he wanted, many on the show believe, was outright deceit. "Dick," one staffer said, "juggles lies like some people juggle stocks." "You never knew," said another, "what was being sold and what was the truth. He always said one thing and ended up doing something else." A third, referring to Dick's pug nose, joked that "every time Dick lies, his nose gets shorter."

The cast members were among those who came away most disaffected. Many of them felt the only time Dick treated them well was just before the show was going on the air, and then only if they were in a sketch he wanted them to be up for. "We got no respect," one of the actors said, "until *Saturday Night*." Robin Duke said that Dick treated the performers "like sticks," mainly, she thought, because he didn't want them gaining the upper hand, as they had under Lorne. Christine Ebersole and Tony Rosato were both in the habit of challenging Dick, and both believe Dick fired them for that reason. Christine Ebersole described her one season on the show as "a constant struggle to maintain integrity and maintain principles and not to sacrifice them for this man."

The season after Ebersole and Rosato left, Dick brought three young performers aboard—Brad Hall, Julia Louis-Dreyfus and Gary Kroeger—who had comprised an improv group in Chicago called The Practical Theater Company. They were thrilled to be joining what they thought would be a band of outlaws, but disillusionment soon set in. "The show had become the Establishment by the time we arrived," says Brad Hall. "It was an institution, a giant ship that is difficult to turn without leaning on the rudder for many miles."

Jim Belushi, who Dick had decided was ready for the show, had the same reaction when he arrived a few weeks into the 1983–84 season. Being, like his brother, of an aggressive nature, he set out to take on the system. At his instigation, the cast members—except Piscopo and Murphy—started meeting after the read-through each Wednesday to discuss the sketches. Then they'd draft a note outlining what pieces they preferred, which was given to Ebersol and Tischler in hopes of influencing their decisions on the show's rundown. Those meetings faded away after several weeks when it became apparent they were having no impact whatsoever.

Belushi grew steadily more frustrated with Dick and the way he produced the show, and within two months of joining *Saturday Night* he was on the verge of quitting. Dick told him he'd be blowing a big opportunity if he did. What Dick didn't say was that he and Tischler were as fed up with Belushi's complaining as Belushi was with them, and that they were close to firing him anyway. Belushi also told Tim Kazurinsky about the way he was feeling, and this time it was Kazurinsky's turn to counsel patience. Kazurinsky advised Belushi to take his emotions off his sleeve and learn to play the backstage political game more subtly. "Get off the fucking cross," Kazurinsky told him. "This is a job."

Belushi took Kazurinsky's advice, and eventually ended up with a sort of perverse admiration for the Machiavellian skills of Dick Ebersol. "I really learned to respect Dick's business ways," Belushi said. "His handling of budgets, lawyers, schmoozing, the half-truths, the way he strokes, his corporate mind, his keeping you constantly insecure." Belushi may have gotten smarter, but not significantly happier, and on occasion his temper still flared.

\* \* \*

Not a little of the cast's anger at Dick derived from the overt manner in which he favored Eddie Murphy and Joe Piscopo. Dick had consciously set out in his first full season as producer to focus the show on Eddie and Joe—in effect discarding the repertory concept—and he made no attempt to conceal that fact from the other performers. Often on Tuesday nights he'd count the number of scripts featuring his two favorite stars and then tell the writers, including writer-performers such as Tim Kazurinsky and Tony Rosato, that there still wasn't enough for Joe and Eddie, even though Joe and Eddie already had far more to do than anyone else. The rest of the cast, Kazurinsky said, felt "emasculated." Bob Tischler confirms there was "a great deal of alienation and hard feelings" over the imbalance.

It didn't help that Joe and Eddie continued to set themselves apart from the rest of the cast, as they had under Jean. Jim Belushi had an angry confrontation with them his first week on the show. He was offended at the way they talked and joked with each other during read-through, blatantly disregarding, Belushi thought, the rest of the staff. Still in his aggressive stage, Belushi went to Joe's office when the read-through ended to set him straight.

"I don't like the way you and Eddie are acting," he said. "We're a team up here."

Piscopo, amazed at Belushi's effrontery, told him he didn't have any business criticizing the two people who'd been carrying the show for so long, especially when he'd been there less than a week.

That didn't satisfy Belushi. "I think you guys should straighten up," he said. Belushi later reconsidered and apologized, but his relationship with Joe and Eddie continued to be strained.

Being Dick's favorites didn't mean that Joe and Eddie were any fonder of him than the others. Both of them resented the fact that after Dick took over he never stopped saying how grateful they ought to be to him for picking them up off Jean's scrap heap and making them stars. "If I hadn't saved you," Dick would say, "where would you be? You're lucky to be here. You're lucky you weren't fired." Piscopo says that Dick always laughed as he made those comments, but they didn't doubt that beneath the laughter he meant it.

Eddie's ascent to superstardom over the 1982–83 and 1983–84 seasons changed that balance of power radically.

# CHAPTER 43

# The Elvis Phase

On the premiere show of Dick's first full season, Eddie appeared in the opening as a character named Little Richard Simmons, an unnatural merging of rock shouter Little Richard and TV exercise guru Richard Simmons. "Good Golly, Miss Molly," he sang, "you look like a hog." The audience roared its approval and Eddie was off and running on a remarkable string of characters, a streak that for sheer quantity outpaced any other performer ever on *Saturday Night*, with the possible exception of Dan Aykroyd.

Later in that first show there was Tyrone Green, the convict-poet whose ode to burglary was the highlight of *Prose and Cons*, a film written by Blaustein and Sheffield that satirized the relationship between Norman Mailer and his jailhouse literary protégé, murderer Jack Henry Abbott. "Dark and lonely on a summer night," he intoned, "Kill my landlord, kill my landlord/The watch dog barking/do he bite?/Kill my landlord, kill my landlord/Slip in his window/Break his neck/Then his house I start to wreck/Got no reason/What the heck?/Kill my landlord, kill my landlord/C-I-L-L my landlord."

Like so many of Eddie's bits, he'd improvised Tyrone Green's lines almost verbatim a few days earlier as he sat in Blaustein and Sheffield's office. Raheem Abdul Muhammed made another of his Update commentaries on that show, bemoaning the paucity of good film roles for blacks. "How," he demanded, "could they overlook a fine actor like J. J. Walker for *The Elephant Man*?"

A week later, Eddie introduced his loony impersonation of Buckwheat, the now-grown Little Rascal, and a week after that his processed-haired pimp, Velvet Jones. Buckwheat pitched his new record album, *Buh-wheet Sings*, which included his smash rendition of "New Nork, New Nork," while Velvet Jones offered his self-help booklet for female dropouts, "I Wanna Be a Ho." By the end of the season, Eddie brought an entirely different voice (modeled on a Jewish nightclub manager he'd once known) to his cantankerous characterization of the TV clay doll Gumby, who always waved his cigar, scowled, and shouted, "I'm Gumby, dammit!"

Gumby and Buckwheat revealed Eddie's credentials as a true second-generation child of television, even if his influences came via reruns. David Sheffield, who, along with Barry Blaustein, continued to write most of Eddie's sketches, remembers being in a room with Eddie once when the Little Rascals came on TV. Eddie sat and mouthed every word of the dialogue before it was spoken.

Perhaps Eddie's most popular character was Mr. Robinson, his ghetto-black version of the kindly kiddie-show host, Mr. Rogers. "Here's Mr. Landlord," Mr. Robinson would say when he heard the pounding on his door. "Can you say the word 'scumbucket' boys and girls?" Like Raheem and Velvet Jones, Mr. Robinson was actually born during Jean Doumanian's era, although a number of people on her staff argued against using a character they found racist. Eddie won that battle and Mr. Robinson went on, but he lost with Velvet Jones, and it wasn't until nearly a year later that Velvet finally appeared on-air. Another character of Eddie's who met with strong resistance on the 17th floor was his limp-wristed hairdresser, Dion, who was created by a new writer named Margaret Oberman. Dion was deemed homophobic, not only by many members of the staff but also by various gay groups, and, along with some of Eddie's stand-up routines about gays, helped earn him the passionate enmity of much of the homosexual community.

On the strength of his many characters, Eddie became without question the major attraction on *Saturday Night*, but his status as a superstar wasn't secured until he made his first movie, *48 Hours*. When *48 Hours* became a smash hit in the fall of 1982, Eddie Murphy was suddenly one of the hottest stars in show business, if not *the* hottest. He signed a deal with Paramount Pictures that paid him $1 million just to ensure he'd keep making movies for them. He kept an enlarged copy of the check in his office on 17.

At about the same time, his first record album came out. It quickly went gold, selling more than 500,000 copies. His fame catapulted to an even higher plateau in the summer of 1983 with the release of his second movie, *Trading Places*, which co-starred Dan Aykroyd. After *Trading Places* became a huge box-office hit, Eddie signed another, longer-term deal with Paramount, that one for a cool $15 million. He had just turned twenty-two.

Not surprisingly, Eddie's status within *Saturday Night* irrevocably changed. Indication of how much it had changed came soon after the release of *48 Hours*, when Eddie's co-star in the movie, Nick Nolte, backed out of his engagement to host the show. Nolte, who was partying at a torrid pace, called Dick from his hotel on Tuesday and rasped that he wasn't going to make it. "Uhh, Dick," he said. "I'm going to ruin your show. … I'm burned, man." Nolte explained that he'd gone directly from making *48 Hours* to the set of his next film, *Under Fire*, and directly from there to New York for the show. Dick wasn't ready to let Nolte off the hook that easily. He went to his hotel room to try to change his mind, but Nolte was out, probably celebrating his freedom. With four days left before the show, Dick was without a host.

It immediately occurred to Dick that he had the biggest new star in America—Eddie Murphy—right at his fingertips. Having a cast member be the host had never happened on *Saturday Night* before, and Dick casually walked around the offices feeling out some of the other performers, asking what they thought of the idea. No one objected, and Dick went ahead. In truth, making Eddie the host upset all the other performers. "It was a little hard to swallow," admitted Mary Gross. "We always knew he was a little more important, but this really said it."

The cast member who was most mortified by Eddie's hosting was Joe Piscopo. Joe hadn't been in the office when Dick polled the performers, and when Bob Tischler and Barry Blaustein told him about it the next day, he couldn't believe it. "Why didn't you ask Frank to host?" he asked. He meant Frank Sinatra. Blaustein and Tischler looked at him incredulously and said they doubted very seriously that Sinatra would agree. "No," Piscopo said, pointing at himself. "I mean Frank." Himself as Frank Sinatra, in other words.

Piscopo, whose impersonation of Sinatra was so brilliant, had been getting more and more in the habit of identifying himself as "Frank," a merging of performer and character that many on the 17th floor thought bordered on neurosis. He was fiercely protective of Frank's prerogatives. Often when a writer came up with an idea for a sketch featuring Sinatra, Joe would dismiss it by saying, "Frank wouldn't do that," Sometimes in doing so he used his own voice, others times he spoke as Frank. In one sketch, Joe as Sinatra was to sing the song "Ebony and Ivory" in a recording studio with Stevie Wonder, played with equal brilliance by Eddie Murphy. The script opened with Sinatra sitting in the studio waiting for Wonder to arrive, but Piscopo demanded it be changed. "Frank" he argued, "is too big to wait for Stevie Wonder." These sorts of debates came up so often that they eventually inspired a sketch, a game show parody called *What Would Frank Do?*

Dick consciously focused his show on Joe and Eddie, and they
delivered with a consistent stream of successful characters.
Two of the most popular:
Frank Sinatra and Stevie Wonder. © *NBC*

Having Frank host the show wasn't a bad idea, but by then the choice of
Eddie had already been made. It was a painful moment for Piscopo. He
and Eddie remained close, but there was no doubt in anyone's mind on
17 that Eddie's spectacular success was difficult for Joe to handle. One
writer said that being in Eddie's shadow caused "a terrible pain in Joe's
soul." Bob Tischler agreed. "It broke his heart," Tischler said, "to walk
down the street with Eddie and have everyone yell 'Eddie!' and pass
him by." Several on the show agree with the writer who believes Joe
"never recovered" from seeing Eddie named host, especially after Eddie
concluded his opening monologue that night by shouting, "Live, from
New York, it's the Eddie Murphy show!" For months afterward, Piscopo
complained to Blaustein and Sheffield, who'd written the monologue,
how wrong it had been for Eddie to say that.

Joe grew progressively more bitter at Dick. He was convinced that
Dick was using him to curry Eddie's favor, and he was angered by it.
At the same time, Joe says, Dick also put Eddie down behind Eddie's
back. Joe believed Dick was jealous of their friendship, and that he

intentionally tried to break it up by pitting them against each other. Those feelings provoked a violent and almost pitiful confrontation in the middle of the 1983-84 season.

Eddie and Joe had a scene together as Solomon and Pudge, two grizzled old men who sat around in a bar together, noodling on the piano and reminiscing. The Solomon and Pudge sketches were so loosely structured that they tended to ramble, which was part of their considerable charm. This particular week, however, Dick kept urging Joe to make sure the sketch was tight, asking him several times to keep Eddie focused. Just before they went on the air, Dick mentioned it again, telling Piscopo the show was running long. Joe did as Dick asked, and the sketch was brief but still funny.

When the sketch ended, the show broke for a commercial. As Joe and Eddie walked off the stage, Dick came up, put his arm around Eddie's shoulder, and began talking with him. Piscopo, who felt he was owed some thanks for keeping the sketch in line, was hurt and angry as he watched Ebersol fawn over his superstar. Piscopo was storming off to the makeup room when Dick caught him and told him he'd done a good job.

"Goddamn it," Piscopo yelled. "Why the hell did you put your arm around Eddie in front of the whole audience, and not me? I'm the one who drove the sketch through. You just like everyone to see you with your arm around Eddie Murphy!"

Dick explained that he'd just wanted to make sure Eddie didn't leave before the goodnights at the end of the show. (Eddie no longer felt it necessary to plant himself at center stage, or anywhere else onstage, for the goodnights.) That didn't mollify Piscopo, who walked off still fuming. When Joe arrived at the makeup room he found Eddie there, and continued his shouting about Dick.

"He's bribing me to get to you!" Joe told Eddie. "He treats me like crap—he always has."

"Well," Eddie said, a little coyly, "he just told me how good I was in Solomon and Pudge."

"Yeah?" Joe shot back. "You wanna know what he said about you last week? He told me your career wouldn't last three years."

"If you're telling me this to get me steamed," Eddie said, "it's working."

Eddie and Joe were soon shouting back and forth at each other. Somebody ran to tell Dick he'd better get into the makeup room, there was trouble. When Dick ran in, Piscopo turned to focus his anger on him.

"I give you my blood, Ebersol!" he screamed. "You always favored Eddie, but you don't really like him. And you never cared about me!"

Then he picked up a plastic bottle of makeup remover and hurled it at the mirror in front of him. The top to the bottle flew off and liquid sprayed all over the room.

Piscopo, who later described his emotional state at this moment as "crazed," kept shouting, and Dick wisely retreated.

\* \* \*

After the success of *48 Hours*, the question arose as to whether Eddie would be staying with *Saturday Night* for another season. On the interview circuit promoting the film, Eddie suggested a number of times that, no, he wouldn't be back, which prompted Dick to start figuring out a way to keep his biggest star.

Eddie called Dick from the set of *Trading Places* in January 1983 and said that, regardless of what Dick might have been reading in the papers, he would definitely be returning to the show in some capacity. Still, as of March there hadn't been any movement toward actually signing a new deal, and Dick was getting nervous.

At about that time a few stories started appearing in the press speculating that if Eddie Murphy didn't return, *Saturday Night* might not be renewed for another season. Brandon Tartikoff, still in charge of NBC programming, could easily have scotched those rumors, but instead he seemed to confirm them obliquely. "Our viewpoint," he told the widely syndicated *Chicago Sun-Times* columnist, Gary Deeb, "is that *Saturday Night* is quite likely to return next fall. We still have to button up Eddie Murphy's deal completely, but we expect to take care of that very soon. The prospects for the show look good."

Those statements left the door open for the appeal Ebersol planned to make to Eddie. On the night of April 7, Dick pulled Eddie aside on 17 and told him that for the good of the show, and everybody on it, they had to resolve the question of Eddie's return. Again the implication was that if Eddie didn't come back, the show might be doomed. Therefore, the jobs of the entire staff were resting on Eddie's shoulders.

Dick insisted later that he didn't specifically tell Eddie the show might be canceled without him; he'd merely raised it as a sort of hypothetical question. He did say, however, that at the very least Eddie could "save a lot of people a lot of grief" by agreeing to come back. NBC, in other words, would renew the show immediately if he did; if not, the staff would spend another six weeks wondering whether they still had their jobs. Both Eddie's good friend Clint Smith, who by then was working as an assistant to Dick, and his co- manager, Richie Tienken, say Eddie definitely got the impression during that conversation that the possibility of cancellation, and therefore the burden it imposed on him, were real. Eddie, to Dick's relief, said, "Okay. What kind of deal should we make?"

They talked for a few minutes about money. Dick said there was only so far he could go in terms of weekly salary, but he could get NBC to come up with almost anything Eddie wanted in a separate production deal. Eddie wasn't interested in being locked into any other TV commitments; in fact, his first suggestion was that he appear on *Saturday Night* in only half the shows the following season. That wasn't good enough for Ebersol; he needed Eddie's presence in every show. Eddie then proposed another alternative: What if he stockpiled some bits on videotape so that he could appear in half the season's shows live and the other half on tape? That would set a new precedent for *Saturday Night*, but Dick instantly agreed. "Absolutely," he said.

The deal was closed a week later. Eddie was to be paid in the area of $300,000, twice his previous season's salary for roughly half the work. A few hours after Eddie signed his contract, NBC announced that *Saturday Night* had been renewed for the 1983-84 season, and that Eddie Murphy would return as a member of the cast. It wasn't mentioned that he would be appearing on videotape half the time, and, after the season started, NBC and Dick did their best to sidestep the issue whenever possible. Thus, many viewers undoubtedly never realized they often weren't seeing Eddie live.

Eddie spent one long night in mid-September in 8H taping eleven sketches featuring his most popular characters. The taping dragged on twice as long as planned, but nonetheless Eddie seemed to be enjoying himself immensely. It was probably the last time he was really happy on *Saturday Night*. It hadn't taken Eddie very long to decide that Dick had conned him with the suggestion that the show's future depended on him. That, coupled with his phenomenal popularity following the release of *Trading Places* that summer and his new $15 million deal with Paramount, caused him very quickly to regret being obligated to Dick's show, even for half a season.

Eddie's attitude toward Dick had gone from disdain to disgust at approximately the same pace that Dick's attitude toward Eddie had moved from condescension to coddling. Instead of always reminding Eddie who was in charge, as he had done at the beginning, Dick now obsequiously curried Eddie's favor and bowed to almost any demand he made. And Eddie had grown considerably more demanding. Whereas in previous years he'd sometimes shown up a little late for a read-through or rehearsal, now he occasionally didn't show up for hours. Dick didn't say much about it. In the same fashion, Eddie had always backed off from performing parts he didn't like, but now he did so less diplomatically than before, loudly proclaiming of sketches he didn't care for: "This is shit; this isn't funny." Dick didn't argue.

Dick also went out of his way to associate himself with Eddie in the press, by implication taking credit for Eddie's success. One example Eddie found particularly galling was when Dick told anyone who'd listen, including some reporters, how he'd loaned Eddie his house in Los Angeles during the filming of *48 Hours*. Eddie found Dick's change of attitude toward him more than a little hypocritical.

"Eddie hated Dick," one of Ebersol's chief production assistants said. "He didn't like the way Dick got off on having his very own superstar. He felt used." Eddie himself once said to a friend, "Three years ago he wouldn't talk to me. Now he's kissing my ass." Another cast member embellished that description. "Dick had his nose so far up Eddie's ass," he said, "that if Eddie'd made a quick right turn, it would've broken off."

Dick firmly maintains that there was no animosity between him and Eddie, a contention others attribute to Dick's failure to recognize the depth of Eddie's feelings toward him. Nonetheless, Ebersol's arguments that Eddie had other things to be unhappy about in his final year were also true. His favorite writers, Blaustein and Sheffield, had left *Saturday Night* to write movies in Hollywood, and, with the exception of Margaret Oberman, Eddie didn't care for the writers who remained. As Ebersol points out, with all the attention now on him, Eddie felt he had more to lose by appearing in mediocre material than he had before. Thus, if he didn't simply refuse to perform a script he didn't like, sometimes in read-throughs he'd mumble or whisper his lines, effectively sabotaging the sketch. Once he slid beneath a table and read, inaudibly, from there. The writers reacted angrily, and, despite Eddie's fame, they progressively wrote less for him.

Eddie's melancholy that season, however, came as much from being where he'd always wanted and expected to be—rich and famous—than from being where he didn't. It was yet another case of the superstardom blues. Articles on Eddie during this period (and there were dozens) generally portrayed him, often in contrast to John Belushi, as drug-free, cocky, and happy, secure with his friends and family, unawed by stardom, and unafflicted by self-destructive drives. There was some truth to that characterization, but only so far as it went. Like everybody else whose fame reaches that level, Eddie felt the strain. A *TV Guide* profile in July 1982 was one of the few to penetrate the mask. "It scares me sometimes," he said of stardom. "I think, 'Hey, this is happening too fast. I'm getting old when I don't have to.'"

Tim Kazurinsky, who often played the role of den mother for the cast, says Eddie went through "Elvis phases." He was always surrounded by an entourage. By the 1983-84 season, he spent as little time as he could around the offices; if he didn't have to be there, he wasn't. He showed up late more often than ever, and sometimes not at all. Once he called Dick on a Thursday to say that he'd decided not to do the show that week. Dick managed to talk him out of it.

Eddie now always seemed to be angry about something; the funniest man in America, as the movie ads and fan magazines were describing him, hardly laughed anymore. During one staff meeting in Dick's office, Dick jokingly read a newspaper account of a promotional appearance Eddie had made the previous weekend at a Washington, D.C., record store. A huge crowd had gathered outside, and as it surged forward a policeman had been pushed through a plate-glass window. As Ebersol read the clip, the writers were making jokes, and Eddie didn't like it. "Any more Eddie Murphy wisecracks and I'll have you fired!" he shouted. The room went silent. When people showed up for read-through the next day, somebody had written Eddie's threat on the wall near the place where he usually sat. By then Eddie could chuckle about it, and the graffito stayed there for the rest of the season. The tension between Eddie and the writers also remained.

Dick Ebersol, ironically, was one of Eddie's chief defenders. His misbehavior, Dick felt, didn't come close to that of *Saturday Night*'s earlier stars. Many on the show, in fact, believe that Eddie's abuses were mainly his way of getting back at Dick. "Eddie thought he was doing an eye for an eye thing," one writer said. "You know—'he screwed me so I'll screw him.' But there were others involved." Again, though, it was more than that. Having achieved, at twenty- two, the dreams of a lifetime, friends say it was a little hard for Eddie to envision what to do next. "I'm bored and lonely," he told Tim Kazurinsky.

Eddie finished his ten-show obligation to *Saturday Night* on February 25, 1984. Like a convict scratching out the months of his sentence on the wall of his cell, Eddie had been counting down the weeks left before he could leave. "God, only four more," he'd say, then "only two more," and, finally, "last one." His last sketch was another two-character piece with his friend Joe Piscopo. During the goodnights, Eddie and Joe slipped off behind the rest of the other performers and, wrestling playfully, disappeared from view.

CHAPTER 44

# Living with Rebecca

By the middle of the 1983-84 season, Dick Ebersol told Brandon Tartikoff that he was thinking of quitting *Saturday Night*. He and Susan Saint James had just had a son and he wanted to spend more time at home. In addition, Dick was producing a new late-night series for NBC, an MTV-type music show called *Friday Night Videos*, which was easy to produce, since it consisted mainly of music videos supplied by record companies. Dick owned *Friday Night Videos*, and it helped make him a very wealthy man.

Bob Tischler, too, was growing restless, tired of playing second fiddle to Dick and tired of not getting credit for having helped save *Saturday Night*. When Dick told him his thoughts of quitting, Tischler suggested an alternate plan: that Dick become a true executive producer, coming in only on critical days and leaving the bulk of the production chores to him. Dick at first resisted that idea, mostly, Tischler believed, because it might give people the impression that *Saturday Night* could have survived without him all along. Dick, Tischler said, was "very reluctant to have the perception that it wasn't him in the same role as Lorne as father of the show."

The two of them argued about it, and for a brief time it even looked as though Tischler might be fired. But in the end they worked out a compromise. The show in the 1984–85 season would rely more heavily on prefilmed or pretaped segments, which Tischler would produce. That would reduce the burden on Dick, and gradually he would cede to Tischler more of the other day-to-day production responsibilities as well. Most on the show suspected that Dick, despite his claims of wanting rest, would probably continue to be as involved as he'd ever been. That's pretty much what happened, but, at least in theory, Tischler had gotten what he wanted.

One of Tischler's first initiatives was to embark on another house-cleaning of the cast. He was well aware that the show had been getting stale, and he hoped new faces would inject some fresh excitement into it. After a postseason trip to California and a lot of time on the phone, he and Ebersol recruited not a bunch of aspiring unknowns but a group of proven comedy veterans: Billy Crystal, who after missing his big break on *Saturday Night*'s first show ever had gone on to co-star in the TV series *Soap*; former *Saturday Night* cast member Harry Shearer and former *Lampoon* star Christopher Guest, who had both just been successful with the movie *This Is Spinal Tap*, a parody of rock documentaries and the rock scene, directed by Rob Reiner; Martin Short, a star of *SCTV*; Rich Hall, a cast member on the Home Box Office series *Not Necessarily the News* and before that a cast member on *Fridays*; and Pamela Stephenson, a star of the British series *Not the Nine O'Clock News*, which had inspired HBO's version.

Dick's third, and last, cast, with producer Bob Tischler (bearded, at left).
Back row: Harry Shearer, Julia Louis- Dreyfus, Rich Hall, Pamela Stephenson.
Middle row: Gary Kroeger, Jim Belushi, Martin Short. Seated: Mary Gross,
Billy Crystal, Christopher Guest, Dick. © *NBC*

To make room for the new ensemble, some of the current cast members had to go, and, in June, Tischler and Ebersol started trimming.

Joe Piscopo had spent the remainder of the 1983-84 season after Eddie's departure profoundly unhappy. His dislike for Dick Ebersol, already intense, grew more so, as did his certainty that he was not, and never had been, given the respect by Dick that he deserved. Like Eddie, Joe now clashed sharply with the writers. His dissatisfaction with the material they were producing for him was such that he often hissed or moaned when he read their scripts. A few on the show sided with Joe in his disputes with the writers, saying that he simply cared enough about his work to be demanding. But many considered him an insufferable prima donna, especially, they say, because he seemed to assume that with Eddie gone the show should revolve exclusively around him. Joe, several people said, preferred to think of *Saturday Night* as "The Joe Piscopo Show," or maybe "Joe Piscopo and the Seven Dwarfs."

Mindful of the friction between Joe and much of the staff, and tired of dealing with him themselves, Ebersol and Tischler decided not to renew his contract. At the time, Joe was making plans to do a film in the fall, and pondering whether he would return to the show for another year. Ebersol and Tischler made the decision for him. Dick, in announcing that Piscopo had decided to pursue his movie career, said he would be glad to have Joe back to host *Saturday Night*. Joe told reporters he would be too busy with other commitments.

Ebersol and Tischler also fired Tim Kazurinsky, feeling he was "burned out" and that he relied too much on the same characters. To that, Kazurinsky angrily replied that it was Dick and Bob who were constantly asking him to *do* the same characters. Robin Duke and Brad Hall, who had never had much impact on the show and who likewise blamed Ebersol for it, were let go as well. Hall had probably sealed his fate when he stood up in a crowded staff meeting and angrily called Dick a liar to his face. Duke, a very talented comedienne, felt so misused that by the time she left, another cast member said, "her spirit had been crushed."

The addition of all the new performers provoked an inevitable crowding for air time, and there was the inevitable bickering about it throughout the 1984–85 season. As he had done earlier with Joe and Eddie, Dick singled out first Billy Crystal and then Marty Short as his new stars, and they got the preponderance of exposure. As the season progressed, Christopher Guest would also begin to emerge. Harry Shearer's second stint on *Saturday Night* was as unhappy as his first. By the end of the first show, he was already outraged at Dick and at not getting the attention he thought he deserved; by mid- season he'd departed.

In the meantime, the production process grew more streamlined. Many of the cast members were happy about the growing reliance on films and tapes, because Dick had less influence over them than he had over live sketches. The prerecorded segments were, indeed, often quite successful; nonetheless they progressively watered down the live aspect of the show. As much as 40 percent of *Saturday Night Live* now wasn't live. Dick even put the song the band played leading in and out of commercials on tape. It was easier that way.

There were, besides the films, many funny and even brilliant moments on the new *Saturday Night*, and the new cast prompted articles in several major publications declaring that the show, in its tenth year on the air, had been rejuvenated. Some popular catchphrases even emerged: the "You look *mahvelous*" refrain of Billy Crystal's Fernando character; the "I *must* say" exclamation of Marty Short's hyperactive Ed Grimley; and the "*I* know that" defense of Short's sweating, chain-smoking corporate spokesman. But, despite its successful moments, a certain blandness remained. The fact was that Eddie Murphy had taken with him most of whatever fire the show had left. In spirit, *Saturday Night* now seemed by and large like just another comedy series, although its *form* continued, as it always had, to allow a more wide-ranging approach to humor than that seen on other TV shows.

Much of what was lacking was due to the sterility of the atmosphere under Dick. Michael O'Donoghue may have taken his quest for danger too far, but his instincts were correct: *Saturday Night*'s magic had always depended on its sense of risk, and without it the show came across as too safe, too predictable.

It was, however, by no means entirely Dick Ebersol's fault that this was so. The timing that had been so fortuitous for the first *Saturday Night* in 1975, when everything they did seemed original and new, had long since gone—just as the time when everything seemed original and new had gone for the generation that had given birth to the show. Even in Lorne's later years, the moment had passed. The show's popularity would almost certainly have declined even if Lorne had stayed, albeit more gradually than it did under his successors. *Saturday Night* would always be competing with itself, and would always come up short.

Writer Margaret Oberman compared working on Dick's show to the Alfred Hitchcock film *Rebecca*, in which Joan Fontaine, playing Laurence Olivier's second wife, found that she was always being unfavorably compared to her beloved predecessor. The memories of Rebecca, it turned out, weren't really true—as they weren't always true for *Saturday Night*. But the legend remained.

# Epilogue

Work commenced on this book in April, 1983. The manuscript was finished on April 1, 1985. What follows is the original epilogue, which tracks what happened in the lives of many of *Saturday Night*'s key figures up to September 1985. As everyone knows, the show has gone on to have a long and often distinguished history since that date. As of this writing, Lorne Michaels remains executive producer and *Saturday Night* continues to thrive as it embarks on its 40th season.

August 2014

* * *

The *Saturday Night* legend continued to hover over the lives of those from the show's early years as well. For most, there were lulls of varying periods after they left the show in 1980. Many of them— including Lorne, Al Franken, Alan Zweibel, Bill Murray, and Dan Aykroyd—got married. Billy, Jane Curtin, Franken, and Zweibel started families.

Chevy Chase most typified the image of the former wild young man grown up. After several difficult years in Hollywood, during which he starred in several forgettable movies (*Oh Heavenly Dog* and *Under the Rainbow*, to name two), Chevy began to turn his life around following the death in 1980 of his good friend Doug Kenney. Kenney was one of the founding members of the *National Lampoon*, the co-writer (with Harold Ramis and Chris Miller) of *Animal House*, and a much-respected, though little-known publicly, architect of the humor of the seventies. Anne Beatts described him as "like the white rabbit in *Alice in Wonderland*, always going 'Am I late? Am I late? Where are my gloves?'" Kenney and Chevy had been partners in cocaine as well as comedy, and Kenney's death from a fall in Hawaii came just a few days after Chevy had departed the islands, where they had been vacationing together.

By 1983, Chevy was cleaned up, happily married, and a devoted father. He spoke often to the press about how wrong it had been for *Saturday Night* to glorify the use of drugs. The show, he said, set a dangerous example for youngsters, and it clearly horrified him to think of someone joking about dope to his kids. His career, too, was on a healthy new tangent after the success of his movies *National Lampoon's Summer Vacation*, its sequel *European Vacation*, and *Fletch*. *People* magazine's headline caught the tone of many articles about him during this period: GOODBYE DRUGS; HELLO BABY.

Chevy remained wounded for many years by his estrangement from Lorne and his other former friends on *Saturday Night*. As late as 1983, he still didn't have copies of the shows on which he appeared; he said the only response he got when he called Lorne to ask for them was "a lot of exactlies and absolutelies." Chevy added that he was still "waiting to hear from somebody [from the show], when they're ready." He finally did: Not long after, he signed to co- star with Dan Aykroyd in a picture called *Spies Like Us*, which was directed by John Landis and co-written by Danny. Bernie Brillstein, Chevy's former manager, and still manager of Danny and Lorne, called Chevy when the deal was being negotiated and said, "I hear you're back in the fold." In the summer of 1985 Chevy agreed to co- star with Steve Martin and Marty Short in a musical comedy Lorne co-wrote with Martin and Randy Newman called *Three Amigos*.

The wild young man who didn't grow up, of course, was John Belushi, who died in March 1982, at the age of thirty-three, at the Chateau Marmont in Hollywood of an overdose of cocaine and heroin. By fulfilling his oft-claimed ambition to live fast and die young, John escaped the burden of having to maintain his success. He also escaped the necessity of growing old, and the possibility of growing tame.

John may have been one of the last in a long line of stars with roots in the sixties—rock stars, most of them—who became victims of the excesses of that particular era. Lorne told *The New York Times* that John had been "a person with difficulty controlling his appetites." The weekly regimen of *Saturday Night* had helped keep John focused, Lorne said, but after he left the show, "he was suddenly in an environment where there were no controls." Lorne confessed that he hadn't done as much as he might have to help John curb his appetite for drugs. "Part of the problem of my generation was a morality that said you don't tell people how to live," he said. "That was garbage. It was just a way to avoid taking responsibility."

Several of those from the show who attended John's funeral on Martha's Vineyard say it was a very strange and emotional reunion. Most hadn't seen much of each other since the show ended, and Anne Beatts was not the only one who spent the occasion "getting blasted on anything anyone handed me" just to get through it. Dan Aykroyd put on a remarkable display of Bully Boy machismo, leading the funeral procession to the gravesite on his Harley. Some of the mourners, drunk, urinated in full view of the gathered press. Danny's friends say it took him a long while to recover from John's death, if indeed he ever would completely recover. He has said in interviews that he sometimes talks to John in dreams.

Much more surprising was Andy Kaufman's death in 1984 of lung cancer. Kaufman had always been a health nut, and because in his last years he had been experimenting with what might be called Hostility humor—provoking mock fights, challenging women to wrestling matches to disprove their claims of equality with men—for months many who knew him believed, or hoped, he had faked his own death. Kaufman, one friend says, had actually talked about doing just that at one point, but decided against it because he hadn't wanted to frighten his mother.

Kaufman's last performance for *Saturday Night* was in November of 1982, when he had a nasty argument with Dick Ebersol in the hallway outside 8H after he was cut from the show. Word of the fight leaked to the press, and the following week Ebersol came on stage to announce that viewers would have the opportunity to call in to vote whether Andy Kaufman should be allowed to return to *Saturday Night* or be banned from it forever. The feud received extensive publicity, and during the next show more than 350,000 people called in to cast their votes. The fact that the entire episode was a hoax conceived by Kaufman was kept in the strictest secrecy, and has been a secret ever since. Even on the 17th floor only a handful of people were aware the fight had been carefully planned, and some on the staff complained vehemently at the time about how shabbily Andy was being treated. Producer Bob Tischler says Kaufman spent the week before the vote hiding out in his hotel room and worrying that the count would go against him, which it did. True to his word, and his joke, Andy Kaufman never appeared on *Saturday Night* again.

Dan Aykroyd and Bill Murray were the cast members who, along with Eddie Murphy, attained the most spectacular success in Hollywood. Billy achieved major box-office stardom with the movies *Caddyshack*, which co-starred Chevy; *Stripes*, which co- starred Harold Ramis; and *Tootsie*, in which he had a small but juicy role opposite Dustin Hoffman. Aykroyd, Murray, and Ramis hit the jackpot together in the summer of

1984 with *Ghostbusters*, which eventually grossed more than $300 mil-
lion, making it the most popular movie comedy of all time.

After *Ghostbusters*, Danny truly became the show business mogul
he had envisioned; one of the movies produced mostly because Danny
supported it was Franken and Davis's *Date Night*, which F&D appeared
in as well as wrote. Danny also became part owner and later "marketing
director" of the very successful Hard Rock Cafe nightclub in New York.
He married Donna Dixon, the statuesque co-star of one of his movie
failures, *Dr. Detroit*, and jealously guarded his private life.

Billy was married in 1981 to Mickey Kelly, a hometown girl from
Wilmette. The ceremony took place in a Las Vegas chapel on Super
Bowl Sunday. He traded his commitment to appear in *Ghostbusters*
into studio backing for a serious movie he wanted to make of Somerset
Maugham's *The Razor's Edge*. Released in the fall of 1984, it failed at
the box office. Billy, as he once said in an interview with *Rolling Stone*,
was still listed in the Hollywood phone book under "K" for comedy,
but he was one of the biggest box- office draws in Hollywood under
that listing. Billy took his profits from *Ghostbusters* and went to stay in
Paris, where he studied French, fathered a second boy, and, friends say,
enjoyed his life immensely.

Gilda Radner's first movie after leaving *Saturday Night* was Buck
Henry's political farce *First Family,* which was a disaster. She entered a
prolonged period of withdrawal from public exposure, spending a good
part of her time at her home in Connecticut. She divorced G. E. Smith and
married actor Gene Wilder. They made two unsuccessful movies together:
*Hanky Panky* and *The Woman in Red*. In late 1983, it appeared Gilda might
be ready for a re- emergence of sorts when she and Alan Zweibel collaborated on a paperback book called *Roseanne Roseannadanna's "Hey, Get
Back to Work!" Book*. But although she and Wilder kept making movies (the latest being *Haunted Honeymoon*), she continued to maintain her
low profile. Within the movie and TV industries, the quietness of Gilda's
post–*Saturday Night* career has been a curious mystery— "Where *is* Gilda
Radner?" many studio and network executives ask. Within *Saturday Night*
circles, Gilda is seen as the cast member who remains perhaps the most
gun-shy from the emotional toll of her years on the show.

Laraine Newman went home to Los Angeles after *Saturday Night*
and for a time disappeared even more completely than Gilda. When she
did reemerge, she sported a nose job and was involved in a long-term
relationship with a guitarist for the rock group Devo. She found it embarrassing and depressing during the years after leaving *Saturday Night* that
she had to audition for roles, and worse that she frequently didn't get
them; in 1983 she appeared in a summer-stock production in Mexico

City. "Seeing other people on the show push ahead really shook me," she told *People* magazine. "I thought it was over." Eventually, though, she won a few roles in TV movies and series, followed by an acclaimed supporting performance in the John Travolta-Jamie Lee Curtis movie, *Perfect*, and she seemed to be on the verge of establishing herself as a respected character actress.

Garrett Morris similarly disappeared and then reappeared as a supporting player in movies and a guest star on several TV shows, among them *Diff'rent* Strokes, *The Jeffersons*, *Hill Street Blues*, and *It's Your Move*. He sometimes became enraged when people asked him about *Saturday Night*. Like Laraine, he apparently has recovered from his drug problems of earlier years.

Of all "the girls," it was Jane Curtin who achieved the quickest post-*Saturday Night* success. She appeared sporadically on TV specials and movies and in commercials until 1984, when she became the co-star, with Susan Saint James, of the CBS prime-time series, *Kate and Allie*. A sophisticated sitcom about two divorced women living together with their children, *Kate and Allie* was produced in New York specifically so that both Curtin and Saint James could continue to enjoy relatively sane personal lives at home in Connecticut, where they lived in neighboring towns. *Kate and Allie* was a hit in the ratings and Jane won two Emmy awards for her work on it, but she continued to resist publicity and the other trappings of stardom as steadfastly as she had on *Saturday Night*.

Eddie Murphy became the biggest of all the *Saturday Night* alumni with the release, in the winter of 1984, of *Beverly Hills Cop*, which, after his earlier triumphs in *48 Hours* and *Trading Places*, established him as the preeminent star in show business. His $15 million contract with Paramount was renegotiated; it was now worth $25 million. The scale of Eddie's fame was such that inevitably it took on Sinatraesque proportions: Barbara Walters interviewed him at home, he made an all-music album with help from friends Rick James and Stevie Wonder, he played the Sands in Atlantic City, he rejected a movie script written by Neil Simon. His national concert tour in the spring of 1985 was hugely successful despite widespread criticism of his act for nastiness without redeeming social value. Like Chevy, Danny, and Billy, he seldom appeared on television anymore. In fact, one highly regrettable result of the *Saturday Night*-to-Hollywood career pattern was that television comedy regularly lost its greatest exponents to a form in which they were, by definition, unable to display anywhere near the range and adventure they had on the small screen.

Joe Piscopo, after his departure from *Saturday Night*, made an unsuccessful movie, *Johnny Dangerously*, in addition to a Home Box

Office comedy special and a record album. He is likely to remain at the very least a marketable performer on both television and film. In the spring of 1985, there was talk of his co-starring in a movie with Eddie, but Joe said he wouldn't hold his breath waiting for such a film to happen. "Eddie's a superstar now," Piscopo told Hollywood columnist Marilyn Beck, "and doing a buddy film would be a step back for him. I'm happy just to be his friend."

Many of *Saturday Night*'s other stars from later years—Billy Crystal, Mary Gross, Tim Kazurinsky, and Jim Belushi among them—went on to appear in movies as well, although they generally played smaller roles in smaller movies. Many, including Crystal, Belushi, Rich Hall, and Harry Shearer, also appeared in cable TV specials or movies. Even Charles Rocket showed signs of recovering from his post-"fuck" purgatory and appeared in several TV pilots and an occasional series. Charlie Barnett, the comedian who almost had a spot on *Saturday Night* until Eddie Murphy came along, spent a few more years in obscurity before becoming a supporting star in NBC's *Miami Vice*. Jean Doumanian started her own production company and remained very much out of the public eye.

Considering the impact *Saturday Night*'s performers have had on the entertainment business in the past decade, the pervasiveness of the show's influence has been equaled only by the likes of Steven Spielberg and George Lucas. The show not only was the most productive star-maker for a new generation of movie heroes, it was the most imitated and influential program in television comedy. *Saturday Night*'s attitude toward comedy, if not its style, infuses innumerable television shows (and comedy clubs, and publications, and records, and plays) today. Writer Jim Downey commented in an article in *New York* magazine that *Saturday Night* had single- handedly turned comedy writing into a viable profession, "one of the many career choices open to a bright young man or woman." "There are so many people in this business," Downey said, "that something only has about twenty minutes to exist as a cultural phenomenon before someone else does a comic version of it."

* * *

That Lorne Michaels did not become a Steven Spielberg or George Lucas of some variety seemed, inevitably, a disappointment after *Saturday Night*. Upon leaving the show he lay "fallow" (Lorne's word) for a couple of years, tending his garden in Amagansett and traveling in Europe and Africa. He would later say that he was surprised how much he missed *Saturday Night* and that he felt "useless" without it. One friend noticed that Lorne in those years seemed to lose some of his magical powers of persuasion. "His raps got rusty," this friend says. "Whereas they had been intricate and subtle, amazing things to hear, after the show he was much less spellbinding. People were saying, 'What happened to Lorne? He used to be so *devious*.'"

Lorne took care of business at Broadway Video and produced a few projects, including a Steve Martin special for NBC, a Simon and Garfunkel reunion concert in Central Park, and a Neil Young concert film for Home Box Office. People who worked with him say he was sometimes reluctant to put his name on Broadway Video's productions by taking a credit. His name did pop up in the gossip columns occasionally— Lorne and Paul Simon bought a radio station together in the Hamptons; Lorne's wife, Susan, opened an art gallery in SoHo; Lorne and Susan threw a party for Jack Nicholson and Anjelica Huston; Lorne angered his neighbors in Amagansett when he sought approval to build an observatory tower on his house; Lorne was seen at some affair with Steve Martin, Buck Henry, Penny Marshall, Randy Newman, or Mike Nichols. In May 1985 he produced a benefit in New York for AIDS research that featured a reunion performance by Mike Nichols and Elaine May.

None of the movie projects Lorne developed under his deals with Warner Brothers and subsequently MGM came off. One film he produced that did get made was a spacey science-fiction fantasy written and directed by Tom Schiller called *Nothing Lasts Forever*, which wasn't released. There were those close to Lorne who complained that the stars he made stars had turned their backs on him. Bernie Brillstein argues that if there was any sense in Hollywood, Lorne would be running a movie studio. "He could be the next Irving Thalberg," Brillstein says.

Tom Schiller was one of many former *Saturday Night* writers who continued to associate themselves in some fashion with Lorne. Franken and Davis, Tom Gammill, Max Pross, and Sarah Paley at one time or another either worked for Lorne or had offices in the Brill Building, as did former staff members Edie Baskin, John Head, Gary Weis, Cherie Fortis, and a half-dozen or so production assistants from the show. Former NBC facilities man Dan Sullivan and former unit manager Arthur White both went to work for Broadway Video. Michael O'Donoghue, Anne Beatts, and Marilyn Miller had offices in the suite maintained in the same building by their mutual manager, Barry Secunda, who also managed Jim Downey, Leo Yoshimura, and Karen Roston. Eugene Lee had an office next to Secunda's; Paul Simon's office was on the fifth floor.

Bernie Brillstein continued to manage Rosie Shuster and Alan Zweibel along with Lorne and Gilda and Danny.

Although all the writers kept projects going at the movie studios, the television networks, and elsewhere, none quite received the instant embrace of Hollywood they expected when they departed *Saturday Night*. "They came off a mammoth successful five-year run thinking they *were* the industry, and some pieces of the industry thinking they were the same thing," says Buck Henry. "They were pretty cocky: a lot of them walked into studios and said, 'We know what the secrets are.' And they didn't."

Anne Beatts produced a prime-time series for CBS, somewhat reminiscent of the Nerds, called *Square Pegs*. It was critically acclaimed but unsuccessful in the ratings; it was also the subject of a *TV Guide* exposé that claimed it was a series ruined by cocaine, a charge Beatts denied. Beatts's manager, Barry Secunda, says that when Beatts tried on *Square Pegs* to emulate the Lorne Michaels school of hardball production, it didn't work: Beatts would threaten to quit over some dispute and CBS would say, "Fine. Take a hike." Michael O'Donoghue made a comfortable income writing movie scripts that for various reasons didn't get produced. One was a post-nuclear sequel to *Easy Rider*; another, co-written with Marilyn Miller, was a parody of women-in-prison films, entitled *Kittens in a Can*. ABC based a TV movie on O'Donoghue's song "Single Women," which had been a hit record for Dolly Parton. For two years, Jim Downey was the head writer on *Late Night with David Letterman*, where Paul Shaffer appeared on air as Letterman's bandleader and second banana.

Among many of those who continued to work at Broadway Video, there was frequent discussion of the dangers of remaining within Lorne's purview, and the possibility of being trapped within the memory of *Saturday Night*. Some who broke away looked back contemptuously at those who stayed, calling them "Lornies." But even for those who left, *Saturday Night* remains an experience impossible to escape entirely. Alan Zweibel says that *Saturday Night*'s alumni watching the show in reruns now are like the former radicals in *The Big Chill* who grew misty dancing in the kitchen to old Motown songs. Gilda Radner has said that whenever she watches, she reverts to the mood she was in the week of that particular show, whether she was in love, or having her period, whatever she was going through at the time.

There is also, among most of those who worked on *Saturday Night*, a desire, for some a compulsion, to prove that their early success was more than just a fluke. Anne Beatts said that her recurring nightmare was to die in a plane crash and have the obits read EX-*SATURDAY NIGHT LIVE* WRITER … PEAKS EARLY, FAILS TO LIVE UP TO PROMISE.

Alan Zweibel, who has two babies to support (and who counts as his favorite ritual of the week the Sunday brunch he and his son have with Al Franken and his daughter), is one who is clearly determined not to become, at thirty-five, a has-been. He always seems to have at least a half-dozen projects in various stages of development—a children's book, a major piece of fiction for a major magazine, a movie, a TV pilot, a stage play. He talks a lot about *Your Show of Shows*. He points out that Woody Allen, Neil Simon, Mel Brooks, and Carl Reiner went on to brilliant, if not legendary, careers of their own after the show ended. But there were others—Sid Caesar, Imogene Coca, Howie Morris, and producer Max Liebman—who did not.

Zweibel remembers the time at the height of *Saturday Night*'s success when he received a package from his agent at William Morris. It was a copy of a program proposal from Max Liebman. He wanted to produce a new sitcom starring Sid Caesar and Imogene Coca, "who," the proposal reminded its readers, "entertained and delighted millions with their comedy in the 1950s." The cover note from the agent at William Morris read "Dear Alan: What do you think we can do with this?"

Another image that lingers in Zweibel's mind is that of Dick Van Dyke. It had been Van Dyke's role as comedy writer Rob Petrie on *The Dick Van Dyke Show* in the early sixties that inspired Zweibel to become a comedy writer in the first place. Since childhood he had wanted to joke around at the office with Morey Amsterdam, Rose Marie, and Carl Reiner and come home to Mary Tyler Moore in New Rochelle. A year after he left *Saturday Night*, Zweibel ran into Van Dyke in an elevator in Hollywood. He introduced himself, explaining how he'd achieved success on *Saturday Night*, married a beautiful and vivacious brunet (Robin Blankman, a former production assistant from the show), and was in the process of shopping for a home in the suburbs, quite possibly in New Rochelle. "And I just want to thank you," Zweibel said, "because my dream came true and you embodied it."

Van Dyke smiled and put his arm around Zweibel's shoulder. "That's very sweet of you to say this to me," he said, "but let me warn you, Alan. This is a word of caution. After five years, *The Dick Van Dyke Show* was canceled, and I became an alcoholic." Zweibel spent the rest of the elevator ride pounding the door and moaning "No! No! No!" while Van Dyke tried to comfort him.

\* \* \*

Lorne returned to weekly television in January of 1984 as the producer of a prime-time comedy-variety hour called *The New Show*. It aired on NBC Friday nights at 10:00, presumably on the theory that the same audience that in 1975 had watched *Saturday Night* had now grown more sedate, and might actually be sitting at home on Friday nights, perhaps minding the kids. Among the writers on *The New Show* were Franken and Davis, Jim Downey, Alan Zweibel, Buck Henry, and Gammill, Pross, and Paley. Tom Schiller and Neil Levy made films; Eugene Lee and Leo Yoshimura were the set designers; Karen Roston, the costume designer. Regulars on-air included Buck Henry, Dave Thomas of SCTV, and Valri Bromfield; guest stars included Gilda Radner, Laraine Newman, Steve Martin, John Candy, Catherine O'Hara, and Penny Marshall.

The onus of following *Saturday Night* was immediately apparent. In interviews before the show premiered, Lorne repeated some of the lines he had used to describe *Saturday Night* in the early days, saying that he knew what the ingredients of *The New Show* would be but not the recipe, and that he'd initially thought of calling it *Friday Night*, so that at least people would know when it was on. Over the bulletin board in the production office hung Lorne's sign: THE CAPTAIN'S WORD *IS LAW*.

Several of those who worked on *The New Show* say that uncertainty plagued it from the beginning and dissension soon followed. During pre-production there was, as one of the writers put it, "a lot of time spent trying to figure out 'What is the show?'" The definition seemed to change daily, but one thing remained constant: It had to be different somehow from *Saturday Night*. "I always thought on *Saturday Night* we were just trying to be funny," Lorne told *New York* magazine. "But quite often the subject matter we were trying to be funny about hadn't been dealt with on television. That gave us another dimension. This time, we aren't going to have the advantage of being new. You can't fake virginity."

Indeed, Tom Davis was sitting around *The New* Show's offices with some of the other writers one day and noticed that they were all talking about real-estate deals. "Funny how different it was from the other show," he thought. "The other show was filled with incredibly hungry people."

*The New Show* was produced along the lines of *Saturday Night*: It was taped in midweek before a studio audience as if it were a live show, in one take if possible, and then quickly edited for air. But the studio facilities the show used (in a CBS production facility on Manhattan's West Side) and the crew that manned them presented an unending series of nightmarish problems, problems that Lorne, this time, was unable to overcome. Sometimes the tapings dragged on until two o'clock in the morning, several hours overtime, at which point the studio audience, not to mention the performers, no longer felt much like laughing. Tickets for the first taping were some of the most prized in town, and the limousines lined up outside, but in subsequent weeks the studio pages couldn't give the seats away. Leo Yoshimura said that the chaos that prevailed on *The New Show* was even more horrifying than that during Jean Doumanian's reign in 8H.

Another unaccustomed problem was trying to figure out what would be a hit with the prime-time audience. Lorne had set out to do sophisticated comedy appealing to an adult sensibility, but the network kept coming up with research studies that showed viewers weren't responding to the more subtle material. They seemed, for example, to like it best when in *The New* Show's version of Weekend Update, Dave Thomas called co-anchorman Buck Henry "Bucko." The strangest thing of all, Tom Davis recalls, was that Lorne seemed to be listening to the network. "You *have* to in prime time!" Davis said.

After several weeks of struggling with the unfamiliar studio facilities, Lorne, desperate to get back to home ground, went to Dick Ebersol to ask him if *The New Show* could use studio 8H when Dick wasn't using it for *Saturday Night*. Dick had already been angered by Lorne's talent raids on the *Saturday Night* staff and had even threatened Leo Yoshimura with a lawsuit for defecting to *The New Show*. Dick did let Lorne in, but he didn't let him have everything he wanted, and some who know Dick say he enjoyed the opportunity to make Lorne squirm a little. Not a few executives at 30 Rock also relished the prospect of seeing Lorne squirm. As Buck Henry put it at the time, "There are an enormous number of people waiting for Lorne to fail."

He did. *The New Show* flopped both critically and in the ratings. NBC, giving it more time to improve than most series get, canceled *The New Show* after three months. In all the weeks it aired, it was one of the lowest-rated, if not *the* lowest-rated, show of all the programs in prime time. Lorne had expressed the hope that viewers would be patient and give *The New Show* time to evolve on-air, but from the evidence of the shows that were produced there was little reason to prolong the agony. Bob Tischler said that to those working on Dick Ebersol's *Saturday Night*, *The New* Show's failure was a vindication, proof that they no longer had to live with the assumption that Lorne and the original team were really better than they were. "Everybody here," he recalled, "took a big breath and said, 'We're legitimate.'"

At Broadway Video, there was a lot of finger pointing after *The New Show* ended. Lorne blamed NBC for giving him a bad time period and no support. He was convinced that some people at the network were out to get him and that they were, as Buck Henry suggested, gleeful that he failed. Many of the writers blamed Lorne for not preparing adequately—after he got the deal for the show, one noted, instead of getting right to work Lorne took a boat trip on the Nile with Paul Simon. Others complained that Lorne "walked through" *The New Show* without ever having a clear vision of what it would be. Some of the writers say Lorne blamed them and the performers for letting him down; during production, the writers and performers had blamed each other. One participant summed up the consensus on *The New Show*: "It was a death ship."

A year later, Lorne produced a situation comedy pilot for NBC called *Bigshots in America*. Written by Alan Zweibel and directed by Jim Burrows, one of the creators of *Cheers*, it concerned a pair of immigrants trying to make it in New York. When NBC gave *Bigshots* a trial broadcast, most reviews singled out the Robin Williams movie *Moscow on the Hudson* as the inspiration for the idea, but it also had distant similarities to the Czech Brothers sketches, the Olympia Restaurant sketches, and even to "The Wolverines" sketch on the first *Saturday Night*. NBC decided not to put *Bigshots* on its prime-time schedule, and Alan Zweibel left the project—as Franken and Davis had left *The New Show*—so angry at Lorne that he swore he'd never work with him again.

\* \* \*

At the end of its tenth season on the air, *Saturday Night* went through one more change of leadership, and came full circle.

Dick Ebersol had turned himself by the spring of 1985 into what Brandon Tartikoff described as the "George Steinbrenner of comedy"—he had gone out and spent a lot of money building an all- star team, but now he was faced with a restless batch of free agents. The stars around whom Dick had built his show in the 1984–85 season—Billy Crystal, Martin Short, and Christopher Guest—were all contractually free to do as they pleased, and all three made it clear that if they would be returning to *Saturday Night* at all it would be only on a limited basis.

Facing the task of assembling a new cast, and another nine months of *Saturday Night*'s brutal schedule, Dick decided to make good on his intentions of the previous year and, in March, told Tartikoff he would be leaving the show to spend time with his family. He planned to keep his hand in by producing a series of professional wrestling specials, which he co-owned. They were to air once a month in *Saturday Night*'s time period, starting in October 1985. Dick didn't pretend that the wrestling specials were something he expected to be especially proud of, but he considered them "a great lark."

Tartikoff, feeling that *Saturday Night* would have to be rebuilt entirely, decided against naming Bob Tischler to replace Ebersol. Again Tartikoff found himself looking for someone to produce the show, just as he had in 1980. But Tartikoff's own situation had changed considerably since then: He had become the hottest program executive in television.

Kept on as head of NBC Entertainment by Fred Silverman's successor, Grant Tinker, Tartikoff had more than justified Tinker's faith in him by gradually putting together a string of hits such as *Cheers*, *Hill Street Blues*, *Night Court*, *Miami Vice*, *The A Team*, *Family Ties*, and *The Cosby Show*, hits that finally took NBC out of third place in the ratings. That most of those shows were of an unusual originality and quality was not an insignificant footnote, for it could be said that by succeeding with them Tartikoff and Tinker contributed more than anyone to a movement in network television away from the crassness of the programs that dominated the medium during the Fred Silverman era. Ironically, it was in just such a direction that Fred Silverman himself had wanted to take NBC, but when high ratings for his more sophisticated efforts didn't immediately materialize, he gave up and in desperation returned to the lowest common denominator. Grant Tinker had more patience, and a more patient boss at RCA, Thornton Bradshaw.

Thus Tartikoff, confident and flush with money, was in a better position to do what he wanted with *Saturday Night* than he was in 1980. He started talking to Lorne Michaels about coming back to take over the show he had founded ten years before.

Lorne was spending much of his time just then in Hollywood, working on the script and score for *Three Amigos* with Steve Martin and Randy Newman. He told Tartikoff he was "intrigued" by the idea of producing *Saturday Night* again, and that he would at least be willing to come back as a consultant if not an executive producer. He insisted that the show would have to "graduate." There was no percentage, he felt, in trying to milk a style that was so dated and imitated already. He felt that whatever edge there was in network comedy in 1985 was being maintained by *Late Night with David Letterman*. It was Letterman, Lorne said, who had inherited the cult following and the image of being willing to try anything. *Saturday Night* would have to somehow "go beyond" what Letterman was doing. For that reason, Lorne wanted to do away with the name *Saturday Night Live* altogether.

Tartikoff didn't care for that idea—one of the things that interested him about bringing Lorne back was reaffirming the idea that NBC's *Saturday Night* was an ongoing, perpetual franchise, a comedy factory of talent on television just as Second City was on stage. Tartikoff was even more concerned that Lorne's primary devotion at the moment seemed to be to his movie. He suspected that Lorne would be too distracted to devote himself to *Saturday Night*, and the talks between them ended. Tartikoff would later say that the negotiations fell apart mainly "over the issue of getting Lorne's full attention." Lorne disagreed. He said in an interview with the *Daily News* that he had felt he could do both the movie and the show. "I told Tartikoff I'm at his service for whatever he wants me to do," Lorne said. "I'd be willing to help get the show started and headed in the right direction, if that's what he wanted."

But Tartikoff wasn't convinced, and, in late April, he went back to Dick Ebersol, whose resignation had not been announced. Under what conditions, Tartikoff wanted to know, might Dick be willing to return for another season? Dick, still mindful of his desire to take it easy, said he wanted to leave the show off the air until January and that when he did bring it back he wanted to produce it almost entirely on tape. That way, he could wrap up most of a season's worth of material in three months.

Tartikoff thought that surrendering the live aspect of the show to that degree wouldn't work. *Saturday Night Live* on tape, he said later, stood every chance of being received with all the enthusiasm of the new Coke. And a taped show was not worth waiting for till January. Dick said fine, and, in early May, announced his departure, saying he was "tired of the grind."

Tartikoff then began exploring other alternatives. As he did so, he kept in mind the alternative of canceling the show, an option he seriously considered. He wanted *Saturday Night* to continue, but not at the cost of enduring another Jean Doumanian-style debacle. The show was no longer one of NBC's biggest profit centers anyway, so the stakes weren't as high as they'd been before. "I'd rather go out gracefully than put on a pale imitation of what it used to be," he said.

The idea occurred to him that Lorne had been right: David Letterman was the hot comedian in television at the moment, So, Tartikoff thought, why not put Letterman on in the *Saturday Night* time slot? Tartikoff approached Letterman about doing a much more elaborate version of his show on *Saturday Night*s, with more guest stars, more variety, bigger sets—something along the lines of a hip *Ed Sullivan Show*. Letterman would continue his current show three nights a week. If Letterman had accepted, *Saturday Night* would have been off the air. Letterman expressed some interest before deciding that it would be too big a burden to do a show of that scale every week, and that trying to replace *Saturday Night* was only asking for trouble.

That prompted Tartikoff to start working on a "wheel" in which Letterman would alternate weeks in *Saturday Night*'s time period with two or three other hosts. Dick's wrestling specials would round out the cycle. One by one, Tartikoff asked Billy Crystal, Martin Short, and Joe Piscopo to be the other spokes of the wheel, but he was unable to work out the logistics and the idea crumbled.

A second round of talks with Lorne ensued. This time he and Tartikoff seemed to be close to reaching an agreement, but again the deal fell through. Lorne, according to some reports, was asking for a sizable hike in the production budget, more sizable than Tartikoff could accept.

Tartikoff denies this, saying that again the principal reason he had for withdrawing was a feeling that Lorne was so ambivalent about returning that he wasn't going to give the show the commitment it required. Lorne, Tartikoff felt, didn't have enough "passion" for the job. One of Lorne's friends laughingly said that NBC apparently hadn't been willing to go along with "Live from St. Barts."

Tartikoff approached other potential producers, among them David Steinberg, who is said to have turned down the job because he didn't want to be "the 11th man on the Moon." Eventually, Tartikoff focused on John Moffitt and Pat Tourk Lee, the producers of Home Box Office's *Not Necessarily the News*. (Pat Lee was the widow of *Fridays* co-producer Bill Lee. A former agent, she had represented Laraine Newman in 1975.) Moffitt and Lee had virtually agreed to take over the show when HBO got tough on the conditions of their contract there and they had to back out. By this point it was late June, a month beyond the date Tartikoff had been expected to announce his plans for *Saturday Night*. Again Tartikoff talked to Lorne.

Lorne had finished his script for *Three Amigos*, and it looked as though production on the movie was going to be delayed. Therefore, he had more time than he'd had before. According to Tartikoff, Lorne also seemed more eager to take over the show than he had been. Finally Tartikoff came to an agreement with Lorne and Bernie Brillstein. Lorne's return to *Saturday Night* was announced in late July. He would be keeping the name *Saturday Night Live*.

Lorne and Tartikoff compromised on the start date for the new season and the premiere was set for November 9. Lorne went to work in August. He hired Franken and Davis to be his producers (they were shocked to get his call, having heard only that Lorne's last negotiations had fallen through), and soon thereafter Jim Downey as head writer. Herb Sargent was still around on 17, occupying the same office he'd had since 1975, and there was talk of bringing back Michael O'Donoghue, Tom Schiller, and some of the other original writers as well. Dave Wilson remained as director and Audrey Dickman as supervising producer. A dozen or so other familiar names filled various production slots. Lorne had essentially implemented the plan for *Saturday Night* that he had submitted to Brandon Tartikoff five years before.

Besides the fact that the money was good, Franken and Davis changed their minds and agreed to work with Lorne again because, as had not been the case on *The New Show*, Lorne had promised them a significant say in the creative direction of *Saturday Night*. On *The New Show*, Lorne had specifically asked them to tone down the aggressive influence for which Franken in particular had been known. Franken and

Davis were also just coming off the accomplishment of getting (with Dan Aykroyd's help) their first movie produced, and thus felt more as if they were being asked to return instead of slinking back. They envisioned that in time they would be able to do with the show's comedy pretty much what they wanted, and that was appealing.

Franken and Davis also returned because with *Saturday Night* they had the certainty of knowing the format of the show, and of knowing that Lorne knew the format. Despite Lorne's insistence to Brandon Tartikoff that *Saturday Night* would have to "graduate," the decision was made early on that rather than trying to reinvent the show they would stay with its established style and simply try to produce the best *Saturday Night Live* they could. There would be none of the obsessing about coming up with something completely different that had consumed so much time and energy on *The New Show*. Tom Davis said that the fundamental goal on the new *Saturday Night* would be to "maintain the integrity of the engine." Some parts would have to be replaced, others restored; the main thing was to put some life back into a very workable body. "We're going to rebuild it with the genuine '62 Buick engine," Davis said.

Why Lorne agreed to come back to what had to be considered a momentous gamble with the past was a subject of much speculation among his friends. Few doubted that the money had something to do with it. While Lorne was not poverty stricken by any means (he has made, according to NBC sources, $2 million or thereabouts from his share of the profits from the syndicated version of *Saturday Night*), he had a rather lavish life-style, and he needed a cash flow to maintain it. Lorne himself complained that he had lost more than a million of his own money by going over budget on *The New Show*; since Broadway Video owned it, the overages came out of Lorne's pocket, not NBC's. Also mentioned was the fact that Lorne, when he accepted Tartikoff's offer to return, was facing a divorce suit and the possibility of an expensive settlement.

In any case, Lorne was single again, and it's likely that he was more ready than he had been in some time to throw himself into a project. The early word from the 17th floor indicated he was doing just that. Franken and Davis had themselves entered the job full of enthusiasm—checking out the New York comedy clubs, flying to see other performers in San Francisco, Toronto, Chicago, and Los Angeles, spending hours on the phone and in meetings—and both of them say Lorne has been every bit as involved. Tom Davis says there has been a "dramatic" change in Lorne's attitude between *The New Show* and *Saturday Night*. "He's fun again, and funny," Davis said. "I haven't seen him in this form in years."

It's possible that, after *The New Show*, Lorne felt he had something to prove. Certainly he made no secret of his feeling that *Saturday Night* needed his help. Even as he was still finalizing the specifics of his deal, Lorne told the *Daily News*, "What we're discussing now is the budget for the show. The ratings haven't been there and the show has been losing money for the past two years." (According to Brandon Tartikoff, *Saturday Night* continued to make a marginal profit.) In another *Daily News* article, Lorne added that the show would renew an emphasis on live rather than pretaped material. He told *The New York Times* that while it was "nice" that *Saturday Night* had lasted ten years, "it needs to be spruced up with fresh and energetic people. One of the things that got lost was the ensemble feeling." Lorne mentioned in the *Times* interview, "In my heart, I did miss it. It seemed like the right time to go back."

Lorne's criticisms of *Saturday Night* were evidence that the surface cordiality he and Dick Ebersol had maintained with one another for so long had more or less disintegrated after their exchanges during *The New Show*. Bob Tischler, who ever since the Gilda Live fiasco had felt no fondness for Lorne, says that he kept telling Dick over and over again during *The New Show* period that Lorne was running him down behind his back and that Dick was being "more of a sucker for Lorne's good word than was imaginable." "There was a fake friendliness, a fake interplay between them," Tischler said. "They do not like each other and it's all bullshit."

When Lorne started making unflattering remarks about *Saturday Night* in the press, Tischler says, Dick was finally convinced. Their relationship grew more strained. One day soon after he'd agreed to return to *Saturday Night*, Lorne came to the 17th floor to look things over. He walked over to his old office, assuming it was empty, and put his hand on the doorknob to go in. "Dick's in there," somebody told him. Lorne froze, gently pulled back his hand, and walked away. One of Dick's assistants ran in to tell Dick that Lorne was in the hall, did Dick want to see him? Dick did not.

Lorne found going to the 17th floor painful even when Dick Ebersol wasn't there. A writer who knows him well said that Lorne hadn't once set foot on 17 since he'd moved his things out at the end of the fifth season, and others say that over the years he had developed an aversion to going there—the memories and associations were that intense. When he first agreed to return, Lorne made it clear he didn't intend to spend his life at 30 Rock again. He told one associate that he would "godfather" *Saturday Night* from Broadway Video. "I'll do the show, but I won't give up the Brill," he said. One of the first things Lorne did, however, was to send his private decorator over to redo Dick's office, and there were indications as preproduction continued that Lorne was indeed settling in again on 17.

Nonetheless, Brandon Tartikoff's suspicions that Lorne had deeply ingrained ambivalences about coming back to *Saturday Night* were correct. Lorne had spent enough time inside the maelstrom, and had paid enough of a price for it, to know what he was facing, and risking, by coming back. Tom Davis described the challenge simply, if not poetically: "Our balls are on the chopping block again."

It took either courage, or foolhardiness, or pure pragmatism, for Lorne, Franken and Davis, Jim Downey, and the rest to put themselves back out on that line. As of September 1985, Tom Davis was promising that foolhardiness would carry the day.

# Afterword and Acknowledgments

We started our research on this book by systematically reading literally hundreds of newspaper and magazine articles that had been written about *Saturday Night* over the years, and we are indebted to all the reporters who wrote them for providing us with a firm foundation on which to begin, not to mention scores of leads. All along, *Saturday Night* benefited from the quality as well as the quantity of the coverage it received—a far-better-than-average share of it, anyway—thanks in large part to the Young Turks who were making their marks in journalism just as *Saturday Night* was making its mark in TV. In particular, *Rolling Stone*'s profiles of the cast members were excellent.

(Specifically we would like to credit *Rolling* Stone's interview with Lorne Michaels in the paperback book *Rolling Stone Visits Saturday Night Live* for providing the only existing outline of the show's formative stages; David Felton's profile of Bill Murray in the *Rolling Stone* of April 20, 1978, for his account of the "Shower Mike" sketch; *Rolling* Stone's John Belushi memorial issue of April 29, 1982, for the account of Lorne's dressing-room confrontation with John before the Kate Jackson show; the *SoHo Weekly News* for its account of the *Election Update* special canceled by Fred Silverman; and *TV Guide* for its quotation of the censor's memo on *The Smothers Brothers*.)

In all we interviewed some 250 people connected with the show. About 150 of them we spoke to more than once, and, of those, three dozen or so endured four or more lengthy sessions. We cannot express how grateful we are to everyone who took the time to talk; each added something to the book, and without them it would have been impossible. We are especially grateful to those for whom *Saturday Night* was a central and cherished part of their lives, and who therefore risked the most by confiding in us. We have been acutely conscious of their trust throughout. Inevitably some are going to feel misused by what we've written, and for that reason we would like to emphasize that, although we made our own judgments, most of the perspective as well as the facts in this book are derived directly from what we were told by the people involved.

Of the many people who helped us, first and foremost we would like to thank Lorne Michaels. Without his initial blessing, all of those who agreed to be interviewed only after checking with Lorne—and that included most of the original *Saturday Night* staff—would have been unavailable. The door was thus opened to countless memories that had never before been shared with outsiders. Lorne himself gave us seven key interviews. He began to have second thoughts about the project after the publication of *Wired*, Bob Woodward's biography of John Belushi, in June 1984. His cooperation (and the cooperation of quite a few other sources) diminished at that point, but he remained cordial throughout. He also generously opened the resources of Broadway Video, allowing us to screen every show he produced.

Dick Ebersol's support and assistance also contributed fundamentally to the book. He was more generous with his time than anyone, spending in all something like fifty hours being interviewed. Dick also permitted us completely unrestricted access to the 17th floor and studio 8H, which was invaluable. Bob Tischler went out of his way to help as well.

The writers from throughout the show's history were extremely cooperative, and again, without them the book would have been impossible. Many of the original cast members were unwilling to be interviewed. Laraine Newman and especially Chevy Chase spoke to us at length, however, and we thank them for it. We also thank Joe Piscopo, Tim Kazurinsky, Harry Shearer, Jim Belushi, Charles Rocket, Gail Matthius, Mary Gross, Christine Ebersole, Tony Rosato, Julia Louis-Dreyfus, Gary Kroeger, Brad Hall, and Robin Duke for their time, as well as the many hosts who agreed to be interviewed, especially Buck Henry, Lily Tomlin, and Steve Martin.

NBC, from the pages in 8H to the highest executives, extended truly exemplary cooperation throughout our research. We're especially grateful to Brandon Tartikoff, Don Carswell, Aaron Cohen, Jim Hicks, Barbara Gallagher, and Gerald Jaffe for extending far more than the usual time. Bud Rukeyser, Curt Block, and everyone in NBC's Press and Publicity department helped open many office doors and cheerfully answered far too many questions. Thanks as well to Joe Riccuiti, Anthony Paige, and Jay Kaplan in the Photo department. Special thanks to Helen Manasian, who helped most of all.

There is a core group of about two dozen people who provided us with penetrating insights into the spirit as well as the workings of *Saturday Night*. Since they had no control over how their confidences would be used, they would not want to be singled out by name, but they know who they are, and they will know from reading the book how important their contributions were. In addition we would like to express our appreciation to Dave Wilson, Leo Yoshimura, Joe Dicso, and all the others on the production end for their help, especially Audrey Peart Dickman, who knows where to find the details and found many of them for us. On the business end, thanks to Bernie Brillstein, Sandy Wernick, and Gigi Givertz in Los Angeles, and Barry Secunda and Linda Mitchell Kemp in New York. We are grateful, too, to Nils Nichols, Cynthia Rober, Joe Forristal, and everyone at Broadway Video, including Cristina McGinniss, who took at least a hundred calls. The same goes for Deborah Higgins, Evie Murray, Phil Morton, Clint Smith, Barry Nichols, and everyone else who helped us on the 17th floor. All were patient and friendly beyond the call of duty.

For tranquil shelter during the writing of the book, thanks to Carroll West in Thousand Islands, New York, and Elizabeth Whelan and the folks at Schlosser Real Estate in Lavallette, New Jersey. For endless patience and emotional support, thanks to our friends and families; for seemingly endless loans, thanks to the Robert Hills and the Ben Strausses.

*Doug Hill* and *Jeff Weingrad*

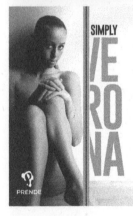
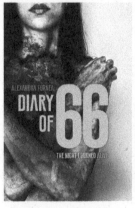